(ex·ploring)
SERIES

1. Investigating in a systematic way: examining. 2. Searching into or ranging over for the purpose of discovery.

Microsoft®

Access 2013

COMPREHENSIVE

Series Editor **Mary Anne Poatsy**

Krebs | Cameron | Williams

Series Created by Dr. Robert T. Grauer

Boston   Columbus   Indianapolis   New York   San Francisco   Upper Saddle River
Amsterdam   Cape Town   Dubai   London   Madrid   Milan   Munich   Paris   Montréal   Toronto
Delhi   Mexico City   São Paulo   Sydney   Hong Kong   Seoul   Singapore   Taipei   Tokyo

Editor in Chief: Michael Payne
Senior Editor: Samantha McAfee Lewis
Editorial Project Manager: Keri Rand
Product Development Manager: Laura Burgess
Development Editor: Lori Damanti
Editorial Assistant: Laura Karahalis
Director of Marketing: Maggie Moylan Leen
Marketing Manager: Brad Forrester
Marketing Coordinator: Susan Osterlitz
Marketing Assistant: Darshika Vyas
Managing Editor: Camille Trentacoste
Production Project Manager: Ilene Kahn
Senior Operations Specialist: Maura Zaldivar
Senior Art Director: Jonathan Boylan
Interior Design: Studio Montage
Cover Design: Studio Montage
Cover Photos: Supri Suharjoto/Shutterstock, wavebreakmedia/Shutterstock, Terry Chan/Shutterstock, Csaba Peterdi/Shutterstock
Associate Director of Design: Blair Brown
Digital Media Editor: Eric Hakanson
Director of Media Development: Taylor Ragan
Media Project Manager, Production: Renata Butera
Full Service Project Management: Andrea Stefanowicz/PreMediaGlobal
Composition: PreMediaGlobal

Credits and acknowledgments borrowed from other sources and reproduced, with permission, in this textbook appear on the appropriate page within text.

Microsoft and/or its respective suppliers make no representations about the suitability of the information contained in the documents and related graphics published as part of the services for any purpose. All such documents and related graphics are provided "as is" without warranty of any kind. Microsoft and/or its respective suppliers hereby disclaim all warranties and conditions with regard to this information, including all warranties and conditions of merchantability, whether express, implied or statutory, fitness for a particular purpose, title and non-infringement. In no event shall Microsoft and/or its respective suppliers be liable for any special, indirect or consequential damages or any damages whatsoever resulting from loss of use, data or profits, whether in an action of contract, negligence or other tortious action, arising out of or in connection with the use or performance of information available from the services.

The documents and related graphics contained herein could include technical inaccuracies or typographical errors. Changes are periodically added to the information herein. Microsoft and/or its respective suppliers may make improvements and/or changes in the product(s) and/or the program(s) described herein at any time. Partial screen shots may be viewed in full within the software version specified.

Microsoft® and Windows® are registered trademarks of the Microsoft Corporation in the U.S.A. and other countries. This book is not sponsored or endorsed by or affiliated with the Microsoft Corporation.

Many of the designations by manufacturers and sellers to distinguish their products are claimed as trademarks. Where those designations appear in this book, and the publisher was aware of a trademark claim, the designations have been printed in initial caps or all caps.

10 9 8 7 6 5 4 3

ISBN 10: 0-13-341220-2
ISBN 13: 978-0-13-341220-8

Dedications

For my husband, Ted, who unselfishly continues to take on more than his share to support me throughout the process; and for my children, Laura, Carolyn, and Teddy, whose encouragement and love have been inspiring.

Mary Anne Poatsy

To my students—you continue to inspire me. Thank you for all you have taught me and shared with me.

Cynthia Krebs

I dedicate this book to my fiancée, Anny, for encouraging me throughout the writing process and for being the person she is, to Sonny, to Drs. Hubey, Boyno, Bredlau, and Deremer at Montclair State University for educating and inspiring me, and to my students, who I hope will inspire others someday.

Eric Cameron

I offer thanks to my family and colleagues who have supported me on this journey. I would like to dedicate the work I have performed toward this undertaking to my little grandson, Yonason Meir (known for now as Mei-Mei), who as his name suggests, is the illumination in my life.

Jerri Williams

About the Authors

Mary Anne Poatsy, Series Editor

Mary Anne is a senior faculty member at Montgomery County Community College, teaching various computer application and concepts courses in face-to-face and online environments. She holds a B.A. in Psychology and Education from Mount Holyoke College and an M.B.A. in Finance from Northwestern University's Kellogg Graduate School of Management.

Mary Anne has more than 12 years of educational experience. She is currently adjunct faculty at Gwynedd-Mercy College and Montgomery County Community College. She has also taught at Bucks County Community College and Muhlenberg College, as well as conducted personal training. Before teaching, she was Vice President at Shearson Lehman in the Municipal Bond Investment Banking Department.

Cynthia Krebs, Access Author

Cynthia Krebs is the Director of Business and Marketing Education at Utah Valley University. She is a professor in the Information Systems and Technology Department at Utah Valley University (UVU). In 2008, she received the UVU College of Technology and Computing Scholar Award. She has also received the School of Business Faculty Excellence Award twice during her tenure at UVU. Cynthia teaches the Methods of Teaching Digital Media class to future teachers, as well as classes in basic computer proficiency, business proficiency applications, and business graphics.

Cynthia is active in the Utah Business and Computer Education Association, the Western Business Education Association, the National Business Education Association, and the Utah Association of Career and Technical Educators. She was awarded the WBEA Outstanding Educator at the University Level in 2009. Cynthia has written multiple texts on Microsoft Office software, consulted with government and business, and has presented extensively at the local, regional, and national levels to professional and business organizations.

Cynthia lives by a peaceful creek in Springville, Utah. When she isn't teaching or writing, she enjoys spending time with her children, spoiling her grandchildren Ava, Bode, Solee, and Morgan. She loves traveling and reading.

Eric Cameron, Access Author

Eric holds a M.S. in computer science and a B.S. degree in Computer Science with minors in Mathematics and Physics, both from Montclair State University. He is a tenured Assistant Professor at Passaic County Community College, where he has taught in the Computer and Information Sciences department since 2001. Eric is also the author of the *Your Office: Getting Started with Web 2.0* and *Your Office: Getting Started with Windows 8* textbooks. Eric maintains a professional blog at profcameron.blogspot.com.

Jerri Williams, Access Author

Jerri Williams is a Senior Adjunct Instructor at Montgomery County Community College in Pennsylvania. Jerri also works as an independent corporate trainer, technical editor, and author. She is interested in travel, cooking, and tending to her colonial farmhouse.

Jerri is married (to Gareth for 32 years!), the mother of two beautiful daughters (an Accounting graduate and a budding lawyer), a splendid son-in-law (also a soon-to-be lawyer), and grandmother to a handsome young grandson.

Rebecca Lawson, Office Fundamentals Author

Rebecca Lawson is a professor in the Computer Information Technologies program at Lansing Community College. She coordinates the curriculum, develops the instructional materials, and teaches for the E-Business curriculum. She also serves as the Online Faculty Coordinator at the Center for Teaching Excellence at LCC. In that role, she develops and facilitates online workshops for faculty learning to teach online. Her major areas of interest include online curriculum quality assurance, the review and development of printed and online instructional materials, the assessment of computer and Internet literacy skill levels to facilitate student retention, and the use of social networking tools to support learning in blended and online learning environments.

Dr. Robert T. Grauer, Creator of the Exploring Series

Bob Grauer is an Associate Professor in the Department of Computer Information Systems at the University of Miami, where he is a multiple winner of the Outstanding Teaching Award in the School of Business, most recently in 2009. He has written numerous COBOL texts and is the vision behind the Exploring Office series, with more than three million books in print. His work has been translated into three foreign languages and is used in all aspects of higher education at both national and international levels. Bob Grauer has consulted for several major corporations including IBM and American Express. He received his Ph.D. in Operations Research in 1972 from the Polytechnic Institute of Brooklyn.

Brief Contents

Contents

■ CHAPTER NINE Fine-Tuning the Database: Analyzing and Improving Database Performance **519**

■ CHAPTER TEN Using Macros and SQL in Access: Advanced Techniques **569**

■ Application Capstone Exercises

Acknowledgments

The Exploring team would like to acknowledge and thank all the reviewers who helped us throughout the years by providing us with their invaluable comments, suggestions, and constructive criticism.

We'd like to especially thank our Focus Group attendees and User Diary Reviewers for this edition:

Stephen Z. Jourdan
Auburn University at Montgomery

Ann Rovetto
Horry-Georgetown Technical College

Jacqueline D. Lawson
Henry Ford Community College

Diane L. Smith
Henry Ford Community College

Sven Aelterman
Troy University

Suzanne M. Jeska
County College of Morris

Susan N. Dozier
Tidewater Community College

Robert G. Phipps Jr.
West Virginia University

Mike Michaelson
Palomar College

Mary Beth Tarver
Northwestern State University

Alexandre C. Probst
Colorado Christian University

Phil Nielson
Salt Lake Community College

Carolyn Barren
Macomb Community College

Sue A. McCrory
Missouri State University

Lucy Parakhovnik
California State University, Northridge

Jakie Brown Jr.
Stevenson University

Craig J. Peterson
American InterContinental University

Terry Ray Rigsby
Hill College

Biswadip Ghosh
Metropolitan State University of Denver

Cheryl Sypniewski
Macomb Community College

Lynn Keane
University of South Carolina

Sheila Gionfriddo
Luzerne College

Dick Hewer
Ferris State College

Carolyn Borne
Louisiana State University

Sumathy Chandrashekar
Salisbury University

Laura Marcoulides
Fullerton College

Don Riggs
SUNY Schenectady County Community College

Gary McFall
Purdue University

James Powers
University of Southern Indiana

James Brown
Central Washington University

Brian Powell
West Virginia University

Sherry Lenhart
Terra Community College

Chen Zhang
Bryant University

Nikia Robinson
Indian River State University

Jill Young
Southeast Missouri State University

Debra Hoffman
Southeast Missouri State University

Tommy Lu
Delaware Technical Community College

Mimi Spain
Southern Maine Community College

We'd like to thank everyone who has been involved in reviewing and providing their feedback, including for our previous editions:

Adriana Lumpkin
Midland College

Alan S. Abrahams
Virginia Tech

Ali Berrached
University of Houston–Downtown

Allen Alexander
Delaware Technical & Community College

Andrea Marchese
Maritime College, State University of New York

Andrew Blitz
Broward College; Edison State College

Angel Norman
University of Tennessee, Knoxville

Angela Clark
University of South Alabama

Ann Rovetto
Horry-Georgetown Technical College

Astrid Todd
Guilford Technical Community College

Audrey Gillant
Maritime College, State University of New York

Barbara Stover
Marion Technical College

Barbara Tollinger
Sinclair Community College

Ben Brahim Taha
Auburn University

Beverly Amer
Northern Arizona University

Beverly Fite
Amarillo College

Bonita Volker
Tidewater Community College

Bonnie Homan
San Francisco State University

Brad West
Sinclair Community College

Brian Powell
West Virginia University

Carol Buser
Owens Community College

Carol Roberts
University of Maine

Carolyn Barren
Macomb Community College

Cathy Poyner
Truman State University

Charles Hodgson
Delgado Community College

Cheri Higgins
Illinois State University

Cheryl Hinds
Norfolk State University

Chris Robinson
Northwest State Community College

Cindy Herbert
Metropolitan Community College–Longview

Dana Hooper
University of Alabama

Dana Johnson
North Dakota State University

Daniela Marghitu
Auburn University

David Noel
University of Central Oklahoma

David Pulis
Maritime College, State University of New York

David Thornton
Jacksonville State University

Dawn Medlin
Appalachian State University

Debby Keen
University of Kentucky

Debra Chapman
University of South Alabama

Derrick Huang
Florida Atlantic University

Diana Baran
Henry Ford Community College

Diane Cassidy
The University of North Carolina at Charlotte

Diane Smith
Henry Ford Community College

Don Danner
San Francisco State University

Don Hoggan
Solano College

Doncho Petkov
Eastern Connecticut State University

Donna Ehrhart
State University of New York at Brockport

Elaine Crable
Xavier University

Elizabeth Duett
Delgado Community College

Erhan Uskup
Houston Community College–Northwest

Eric Martin
University of Tennessee

Erika Nadas
Wilbur Wright College

Floyd Winters
Manatee Community College

Frank Lucente
Westmoreland County Community College

G. Jan Wilms
Union University

Gail Cope
Sinclair Community College

Gary DeLorenzo
California University of Pennsylvania

Gary Garrison
Belmont University

George Cassidy
Sussex County Community College

Gerald Braun
Xavier University

Gerald Burgess
Western New Mexico University

Gladys Swindler
Fort Hays State University

Heith Hennel
Valencia Community College

Henry Rudzinski
Central Connecticut State University

Irene Joos
La Roche College

Iwona Rusin
Baker College; Davenport University

J. Roberto Guzman
San Diego Mesa College

Jan Wilms
Union University

Jane Stam
Onondaga Community College

Janet Bringhurst
Utah State University

Jeanette Dix
Ivy Tech Community College

Jennifer Day
Sinclair Community College

Jill Canine
Ivy Tech Community College

Jim Chaffee
The University of Iowa Tippie College of Business

Joanne Lazirko
University of Wisconsin–Milwaukee

Jodi Milliner
Kansas State University

John Hollenbeck
Blue Ridge Community College

John Seydel
Arkansas State University

Judith A. Scheeren
Westmoreland County Community College

Judith Brown
The University of Memphis

Juliana Cypert
Tarrant County College

Kamaljeet Sanghera
George Mason University

Karen Priestly
Northern Virginia Community College

Karen Ravan
Spartanburg Community College

Kathleen Brenan
Ashland University

Ken Busbee
Houston Community College

Kent Foster
Winthrop University

Kevin Anderson
Solano Community College

Kim Wright
The University of Alabama

Kristen Hockman
University of Missouri–Columbia

Kristi Smith
Allegany College of Maryland

Laura McManamon
University of Dayton

Leanne Chun
Leeward Community College

Lee McClain
Western Washington University

Linda D. Collins
Mesa Community College

Linda Johnsonius
Murray State University

Linda Lau
Longwood University

Linda Theus
Jackson State Community College

Linda Williams
Marion Technical College

Lisa Miller
University of Central Oklahoma

Lister Horn
Pensacola Junior College

Lixin Tao
Pace University

Loraine Miller
Cayuga Community College

Lori Kielty
Central Florida Community College

Lorna Wells
Salt Lake Community College

Lorraine Sauchin
Duquesne University

Lucy Parakhovnik (Parker)
California State University, Northridge

Lynn Mancini
Delaware Technical Community College

Mackinzee Escamilla
South Plains College

Marcia Welch
Highline Community College

Margaret McManus
Northwest Florida State College

Margaret Warrick
Allan Hancock College

Marilyn Hibbert
Salt Lake Community College

Mark Choman
Luzerne County Community College

Mary Duncan
University of Missouri–St. Louis

Melissa Nemeth
Indiana University-Purdue University
Indianapolis

Melody Alexander
Ball State University

Michael Douglas
University of Arkansas at Little Rock

Michael Dunklebarger
Alamance Community College

Michael G. Skaff
College of the Sequoias

Michele Budnovitch
Pennsylvania College of Technology

Mike Jochen
East Stroudsburg University

Mike Scroggins
Missouri State University

Muhammed Badamas
Morgan State University

NaLisa Brown
University of the Ozarks

Nancy Grant
Community College of Allegheny
County–South Campus

Nanette Lareau
University of Arkansas Community
College–Morrilton

Pam Brune
Chattanooga State Community College

Pam Uhlenkamp
Iowa Central Community College

Patrick Smith
Marshall Community and Technical College

Paul Addison
Ivy Tech Community College

Paula Ruby
Arkansas State University

Peggy Burrus
Red Rocks Community College

Peter Ross
SUNY Albany

Philip H. Nielson
Salt Lake Community College

Ralph Hooper
University of Alabama

Ranette Halverson
Midwestern State University

Richard Blamer
John Carroll University

Richard Cacace
Pensacola Junior College

Richard Hewer
Ferris State University

Rob Murray
Ivy Tech Community College

Robert Dušek
Northern Virginia Community College

Robert Sindt
Johnson County Community College

Robert Warren
Delgado Community College

Rocky Belcher
Sinclair Community College

Roger Pick
University of Missouri at Kansas City

Ronnie Creel
Troy University

Rosalie Westerberg
Clover Park Technical College

Ruth Neal
Navarro College

Sandra Thomas
Troy University

Sheila Gionfriddo
Luzerne County Community College

Sherrie Geitgey
Northwest State Community College

Sophia Wilberscheid
Indian River State College

Sophie Lee
California State University,
Long Beach

Stacy Johnson
Iowa Central Community College

Stephanie Kramer
Northwest State Community College

Stephen Jourdan
Auburn University Montgomery

Steven Schwarz
Raritan Valley Community College

Sue McCrory
Missouri State University

Susan Fuschetto
Cerritos College

Susan Medlin
UNC Charlotte

Suzan Spitzberg
Oakton Community College

Sven Aelterman
Troy University

Sylvia Brown
Midland College

Tanya Patrick
Clackamas Community College

Terri Holly
Indian River State College

Thomas Rienzo
Western Michigan University

Tina Johnson
Midwestern State University

Tommy Lu
Delaware Technical and Community College

Troy S. Cash
NorthWest Arkansas Community College

Vicki Robertson
Southwest Tennessee Community

Weifeng Chen
California University of Pennsylvania

Wes Anthony
Houston Community College

William Ayen
University of Colorado at Colorado Springs

Wilma Andrews
Virginia Commonwealth University

Yvonne Galusha
University of Iowa

Special thanks to our development and technical team:

Barbara Stover

Cheryl Slavick

Elizabeth Lockley

Heather Hetzler

Jennifer Lynn

Joyce Nielsen

Linda Pogue

Lisa Bucki

Lori Damanti

Mara Zebest

Susan Fry

Preface

The Exploring Series and You

Exploring is Pearson's Office Application series that requires students like you to think "beyond the point and click." In this edition, we have worked to restructure the Exploring experience around the way you, today's modern student, actually use your resources.

The goal of Exploring is, as it has always been, to go further than teaching just the steps to accomplish a task—the series provides the theoretical foundation for you to understand when and why to apply a skill.

As a result, you achieve a deeper understanding of each application and can apply this critical thinking beyond Office and the classroom.

You are practical students, focused on what you need to do to be successful in this course and beyond, and want to be as efficient as possible. Exploring has evolved to meet you where you are and help you achieve success efficiently. Pearson has paid attention to the habits of students today, how you get information, how you are motivated to do well in class, and what your future goals look like. We asked you and your peers for acceptance of new tools we designed to address these points, and you responded with a resounding "YES!"

Here Is What We Learned About You

You are goal-oriented. You want a good grade in this course—so we rethought how Exploring works so that you can learn the how and why behind the skills in this course to be successful now. You also want to be successful in your future career—so we used motivating case studies to show relevance of these skills to your future careers and incorporated Soft Skills, Collaboration, and Analysis Cases in this edition to set you up for success in the future.

You read, prepare, and study differently than students used to. You use textbooks like a tool—you want to easily identify what you need to know and learn it efficiently. We have added key features such as Step Icons, Hands-On Exercise Videos, and tracked everything via page numbers that allow you to navigate the content efficiently, making the concepts accessible and creating a map to success for you to follow.

You go to college now with a different set of skills than students did five years ago. The new edition of Exploring moves you beyond the basics of the software at a faster pace, without sacrificing coverage of the fundamental skills that you need to know. This ensures that you will be engaged from page 1 to the end of the book.

You and your peers have diverse learning styles. With this in mind, we broadened our definition of "student resources" to include Compass, an online skill database; movable Student Reference cards; Hands-On Exercise videos to provide a secondary lecture-like option of review; Soft Skills exercises to illustrate important non-technical skills; and the most powerful online homework and assessment tool around with a direct 1:1 content match with the Exploring Series, MyITLab. Exploring will be accessible to all students, regardless of learning style.

Providing You with a Map to Success to Move Beyond the Point and Click

All of these changes and additions will provide you with an easy and efficient path to follow to be successful in this course, regardless of your learning style or any existing knowledge you have at the outset. Our goal is to keep you more engaged in both the hands-on and conceptual sides, helping you to achieve a higher level of understanding that will guarantee you success in this course and in your future career. In addition to the vision and experience of the series creator, Robert T. Grauer, we have assembled a tremendously talented team of Office Applications authors who have devoted themselves to teaching you the ins and outs of Microsoft Word, Excel, Access, and PowerPoint. Led in this edition by series editor Mary Anne Poatsy, the whole team is equally dedicated to providing you with a **map to success** to support the Exploring mission of **moving you beyond the point and click**.

Key Features

- **White Pages/Yellow Pages** clearly distinguish the theory (white pages) from the skills covered in the Hands-On Exercises (yellow pages) so students always know what they are supposed to be doing.

- **Enhanced Objective Mapping** enables students to follow a directed path through each chapter, from the objectives list at the chapter opener through the exercises in the end of chapter.
  - **Objectives List:** This provides a simple list of key objectives covered in the chapter. This includes page numbers so students can skip between objectives where they feel they need the most help.
  - **Step Icons:** These icons appear in the white pages and reference the step numbers in the Hands-On Exercises, providing a correlation between the two so students can easily find conceptual help when they are working hands-on and need a refresher.
  - **Quick Concepts Check:** A series of questions that appear briefly at the end of each white page section. These questions cover the most essential concepts in the white pages required for students to be successful in working the Hands-On Exercises. Page numbers are included for easy reference to help students locate the answers.
  - **Chapter Objectives Review:** Appears toward the end of the chapter and reviews all important concepts throughout the chapter. Newly designed in an easy-to-read bulleted format.

- **Key Terms Matching:** A new exercise that requires students to match key terms to their definitions. This requires students to work actively with this important vocabulary and prove conceptual understanding.

- **Case Study** presents a scenario for the chapter, creating a story that ties the Hands-On Exercises together.

- **Hands-On Exercise Videos** are tied to each Hands-On Exercise and walk students through the steps of the exercise while weaving in conceptual information related to the Case Study and the objectives as a whole.

- **End-of-Chapter Exercises** offer instructors several options for assessment. Each chapter has approximately 12–15 exercises ranging from multiple choice questions to open-ended projects. Newly included in this is a Key Terms Matching exercise of approximately 20 questions, as well as a Collaboration Case and Soft Skills Case for every chapter.

- **Enhanced Mid-Level Exercises** include a **Creative Case** (for PowerPoint and Word), which allows students some flexibility and creativity, not being bound by a definitive solution, and an **Analysis Case** (for Excel and Access), which requires students to interpret the data they are using to answer an analytic question, as well as **Discover Steps**, which encourage students to use Help or to problem-solve to accomplish a task.

- **MyITLab** provides an auto-graded homework, tutorial, and assessment solution that is built to match the book content exactly. Every Hands-On Exercise is available as a simulation training. Every Capstone Exercise and most Mid-Level Exercises are available as live-in-the-application Grader projects. Icons are included throughout the text to denote which exercises are included.

Instructor Resources

The Instructor's Resource Center, available at **www.pearsonhighered.com**, includes the following:

- **Instructor Manual** provides an overview of all available resources as well as student data and solution files for every exercise.

- **Solution Files with Scorecards** assist with grading the Hands-On Exercises and end-of-chapter exercises.

- **Prepared Exams** allow instructors to assess all skills covered in a chapter with a single project.

- **Rubrics** for Mid-Level Creative Cases and Beyond the Classroom Cases in Microsoft® Word format enable instructors to customize the assignments for their classes.

- **PowerPoint® Presentations** with notes for each chapter are included for out-of-class study or review.

- **Lesson Plans** provide a detailed blueprint to achieve chapter learning objectives and outcomes.

- **Objectives Lists** map chapter objectives to Hands-On Exercises and end-of-chapter exercises.

- **Multiple Choice and Key Terms Matching Answer Keys**

- **Test Bank** provides objective-based questions for every chapter.

- **Grader Projects** textual versions of auto-graded assignments for Grader.

- **Additional Projects** provide more assignment options for instructors.

- **Syllabus Templates**

- **Scripted Lectures** offer an in-class lecture guide for instructors to mirror the Hands-On Exercises.

- **Assignment Sheet**

- **File Guide**

Student Resources

Companion Web Site

www.pearsonhighered.com/exploring offers expanded IT resources and self-student tools for students to use for each chapter, including:

- Online Chapter Review
- Glossary
- Chapter Objectives Review
- Web Resources
- Student Data Files

In addition, the Companion Web Site is now the site for Premium Media, including the videos for the Exploring Series:

- Hands-On Exercise Videos*
- Audio PPTs*

*Access code required for these premium resources.

Student Reference Cards

A two-sided card for each application provides students with a visual summary of information and tips specific to each application.

Office Fundamentals and File Management

Taking the First Step

Andresr/Shutterstock

OBJECTIVES — AFTER YOU READ THIS CHAPTER, YOU WILL BE ABLE TO:

1. Log in with your Microsoft account p. 2
2. Identify the Start screen components p. 3
3. Interact with the Start screen p. 4
4. Access the desktop p. 4
5. Use File Explorer p. 10
6. Work with folders and files p. 13
7. Select, copy, and move multiple files and folders p. 15
8. Identify common interface components p. 22
9. Get Office Help p. 28
10. Open a file p. 36
11. Print a file p. 38
12. Close a file and application p. 39
13. Select and edit text p. 45
14. Use the Clipboard group commands p. 49
15. Use the Editing group commands p. 52
16. Insert objects p. 60
17. Review a file p. 62
18. Use the Page Setup dialog box p. 66

CASE STUDY | Spotted Begonia Art Gallery

You are an administrative assistant for Spotted Begonia, a local art gallery. The gallery deals in local artists' work, including fiber art, oil paintings, watercolors, prints, pottery, and metal sculptures. The gallery holds four seasonal showings throughout the year. Much of the art is on consignment, but there are a few permanent collections. Occasionally, the gallery exchanges these collections with other galleries across the country. The gallery does a lot of community outreach and tries to help local artists develop a network of clients and supporters. Local schools are invited to bring students to the gallery for enrichment programs. Considered a major contributor to the local economy, the gallery has received both public and private funding through federal and private grants.

As the administrative assistant for Spotted Begonia, you are responsible for overseeing the production of documents, spreadsheets, newspaper articles, and presentations that will be used to increase public awareness of the gallery. Other clerical assistants who are familiar with Microsoft Office will prepare the promotional materials, and you will proofread, make necessary corrections, adjust page layouts, save and print documents, and identify appropriate templates to simplify tasks. Your experience with Microsoft Office 2013 is limited, but you know that certain fundamental tasks that are common to Word, Excel, and PowerPoint will help you accomplish your oversight task. You are excited to get started with your work!

Windows 8.1.1 Startup

You use computers for many activities for work, school, or pleasure. You probably have never thought too much about what makes a computer function and allows you to do so many things with it. But all of those activities would not be possible without an operating system running on the computer. An *operating system* is software that directs computer activities such as checking all components, managing system resources, and communicating with application software. *Windows 8.1.1* is a Microsoft operating system released in April 2014 and is available on laptops, desktops, and tablet computers.

The *Start screen* is what you see after starting your computer and entering your username and password. It is where you start all of your computing activities. See Figure 1.1 to see a typical Start screen.

FIGURE 1.1 Typical Start Screen Components and Charms

In this section, you will explore the Start screen and its components in more detail. You will also learn how to log in with your Microsoft account and access the desktop.

Logging In with Your Microsoft Account

Although you can log in to Windows 8.1.1 as a local network user, you can also log in using a Microsoft account. When you have a Microsoft account, you can sign in to any Windows 8.1.1 computer and you will be able to access the saved settings associated with your Microsoft account. That means the computer will have the same familiar look that you are used to seeing. Your Microsoft account will allow you to be automatically signed in to all of the apps and services that use a Microsoft account as the authentication. You can also save your sign-in credentials for other Web sites that you frequently visit.

Logging in with your Microsoft account not only provides all of the benefits just listed, but also provides additional benefits such as being connected to all of Microsoft's resources on the Internet. These resources include a free Outlook account and access to cloud storage at OneDrive. *Cloud storage* is a technology used to store files and to work with programs that are stored in a central location on the Internet. *OneDrive* is an app used to store, access, and share files and folders. It is accessible using an installed desktop app or as cloud storage using a Web address. Files and folders in either location can be synced. For Office 2013 applications, OneDrive is the default location for saving files. Documents saved in OneDrive are accessible from any computer that has an Internet connection. As long as the document has been saved in OneDrive, the most recent version of the document will be accessible from any computer connected to the Internet. OneDrive allows you to collaborate with others. You can easily share your documents with others or add Reply Comments next to the text that you are discussing together. You can work with others on the same document simultaneously.

STEP 1 » You can create a Microsoft account at any time by going to live.com. You simply work through the Sign-up form to set up your account by creating a username from your e-mail address and creating a password. After filling in the form, you will be automatically signed in to Outlook and sent to your Outlook Inbox. If you already have a Microsoft account, you can just go ahead and log in to Outlook. See Figure 1.2 to see the Sign-up page at live.com.

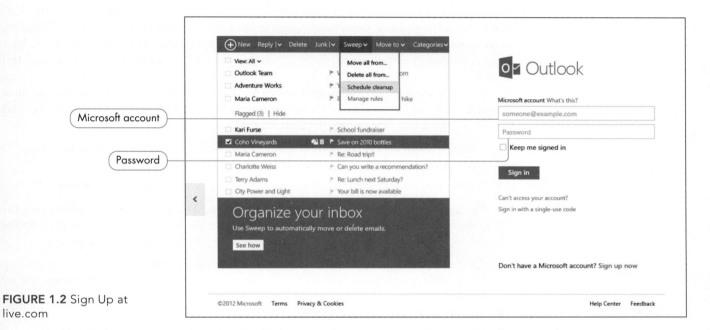

FIGURE 1.2 Sign Up at live.com

Identifying the Start Screen Components

The first thing you will notice when you turn on a computer running Windows 8.1.1 is that the Start screen has a new sleek, clean look and large readable type (refer to Figure 1.1). The user is identified in the top-right corner of the screen. You can click the user's name to access settings such as locking or signing out of the account. You can also change the picture associated with the account here.

You will notice that the Start screen is made up of several colorful block images called *tiles*. When you click a tile, you will be taken to a program, file, folder, or other *Windows 8.1.1 app*. Windows 8.1.1 apps are applications specifically designed to run in the Start screen interface of Windows 8.1.1. Some Windows 8.1.1 apps, such as desktop, Mail, and OneDrive, are already installed and ready to use. Others can be downloaded from the Windows Store. The default apps are brightly colored. Tiles for programs that run on the traditional Windows desktop are smaller and more transparent. The look of the tiles is customizable, but all tiles include the name of the app or program. Depending on the number of apps that you have installed, as you move your mouse to the bottom of the screen, you will see a horizontal scroll bar display. This can be used to access any app that does not display within the initial view of the Start screen.

STEP 2 » The traditional Start button is not present in Windows 8.1.1. Instead, the *Charms* are available (refer to Figure 1.1). The Charms are made up of five icons that provide similar functionality to the Start button found in previous versions of Windows. The icons are Search, Share, Start, Devices, and Settings. Using the Charms, you can search for files and applications, share information with others within an application that is running, or return to the Start screen. You can also control devices that are connected to your computer or modify various settings depending on which application is running when accessing the Setting icon. To display the Charms, point to the top-right or bottom-right corners of the screen. Refer to Figure 1.1 to view the Start screen components and the Charms.

Interacting with the Start Screen

To interact with any tile on the Start screen (refer to Figure 1.1), simply click it. If you have signed in with your Microsoft account, you will automatically be able to access any of the Internet-enabled programs. For example, if you click Mail, you will go straight to your Outlook Inbox. If you right-click a tile, you will see several contextual options displayed. For example, the option to unpin the tile from the Start screen displays. To return to the Start screen from the desktop, point your mouse in the bottom-left corner of the screen. Pointing your mouse to the top-left corner reveals the open applications or programs that you have been accessing during this session. You can also use Charms to navigate back to the Start screen.

You may want to set up the Start screen so that programs and apps that you use most frequently are readily available. It is very easy to add tiles to or remove tiles from the Start screen. To add a tile, first display the Start screen.

1. Locate a blank area of the Start screen and right-click to display the *All apps* icon.
2. Click *All apps* and locate the desired new app that you want to add.
3. Right-click the app and click *Pin to Start*. The app is added to the Start screen.

The new app's tile is added at the end of your apps. You can move tiles by dragging the tile to the desired location. You can remove a tile from the Start screen by right-clicking the tile and clicking *Unpin from Start*. You can also group the tiles and name the groups:

1. To create a new group of tiles, drag a tile to the space to the left or right of an existing tile group. A light gray vertical bar displays to indicate where the new group will be located.
2. Add more tiles to this new group as needed.
3. To name the group, right-click any blank area of the Start screen and click Name groups. Type in the space provided to name a group. If a name is not entered for a group, the horizontal Name group bar disappears.

Accessing the Desktop

Although the Start screen is easy to use, you may want to access the more familiar desktop that you used in previous versions of Windows. The Desktop tile is available on the Start screen. Click the tile to bring up the desktop. Alternatively, you can be pushed to the desktop when you click other tiles such as Word. In Windows 8.1.1, the desktop is simplified to accommodate use on mobile devices where screen space is limited. However, on a laptop or desktop computer, you may want to have more features readily available. The familiar Notification area is displayed in the bottom-right corner. You will see the Windows Start screen, File Explorer, and Internet Explorer icons. See Figure 1.3 to locate these desktop components.

Taskbar

File Explorer

Internet Explorer

FIGURE 1.3 Desktop Components

STEP 3 You can add more toolbars, such as the Address bar, to the taskbar by right-clicking the taskbar, pointing to Toolbars, and then selecting Address. The Address bar can be used to locate Web sites using the URL or to perform a keyword search to locate Web sites about a specific topic. You can also add programs such as the *Snipping Tool*. The Snipping Tool is a Windows 8.1.1 accessory program that allows you to capture, or *snip*, a screen display so that you can save, annotate, or share it. You can remove all of the icons displayed on the taskbar by right-clicking the icon you want to remove and selecting *Unpin this program from taskbar*.

TIP Using the Snipping Tool

The Snipping Tool can be used to take all sizes and shapes of snips of the displayed screen. Options include Free-form Snip, Rectangle Snip, Window Snip, and Full-screen Snip. You can save your snip in several formats, such as PNG, GIF, JPEG, or Single file HTML. In addition, you can use a pen or highlighter to mark up your snips. This option is available after taking a snip and is located under the Tools menu in the Snipping Tool dialog box.

You can return to the Start screen by clicking the Start screen icon on the taskbar.

Quick Concepts

1. Logging in to Windows 8.1.1 with your Microsoft account provides access to Internet resources. What are some benefits of logging in this way? *p. 2*

2. OneDrive allows you to collaborate with others. How might you use this service? *p. 3*

3. What is the Start screen, and how is it different from the desktop? *p. 3*

4. The desktop has been a feature of previous Windows operating systems. How is the Windows 8.1.1 desktop different from previous versions? *p. 4*

Hands-On Exercises

Watch the Video for this Hands-On Exercise!

MyITLab®
HOE1 Training

1 Windows 8.1.1 Startup

The Spotted Begonia Art Gallery has just hired several new clerical assistants to help you develop promotional materials for the various activities coming up throughout the year. It will be necessary to have a central storage space where you can save the documents and presentations for retrieval from any location. You will also need to be able to collaborate with others on the documents by sharing them and adding comments. To begin, you will get a Microsoft account. Then you will access the desktop and pin a toolbar and a Windows 8.1.1 accessory program to the taskbar.

Skills covered: Log In with Your Microsoft Account • Identify the Start Screen Components and Interact with the Start Screen • Access the Desktop

STEP 1 ➤➤ LOG IN WITH YOUR MICROSOFT ACCOUNT

You want to sign up for a Microsoft account so you can store documents and share them with others using the resources available with a Microsoft account, such as OneDrive. Refer to Figure 1.4 as you complete Step 1.

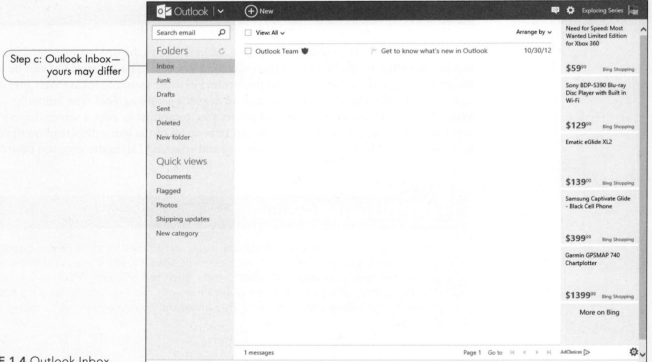

Step c: Outlook Inbox—yours may differ

FIGURE 1.4 Outlook Inbox

a. Start your computer and enter your local username and password. On the Start screen, click the **Internet Explorer tile**. Click in the **Address bar** at the bottom of the screen. Type **live.com** and press **Enter**.

Internet Explorer displays, and you are taken to the Sign-up page for Outlook. This is where you can create a username and password for your Microsoft account.

> **TROUBLESHOOTING:** If you already have a Microsoft account, you can skip Step 1 and continue with Step 2. If someone else was already signed in at your computer, you can locate your username and click it to begin to log in.

b. Click the **Sign up now** link at the bottom of the screen. Fill in all text boxes and make all menu selections on the screen. Scroll down as needed. Type the **CAPTCHA code** carefully.

CAPTCHA is a scrambled code used with online forms to prevent mass sign-ups. It helps to ensure that a real person is requesting the account. You can choose not to accept e-mail with promotional offers by clicking the check box near the bottom of the screen to remove the check.

> **TROUBLESHOOTING:** You may want to write down your username and password so that you do not forget it the next time you want to log in with your Microsoft account. Keep this information in a safe and confidential location.

c. Click **I accept**. Your screen should display similarly to Figure 1.4.

Your Microsoft account is created, and you are taken to your Outlook Inbox.

d. Keep Internet Explorer open if you plan to continue using Outlook. Otherwise, sign out of Outlook and close Internet Explorer.

STEP 2 ≫ IDENTIFY THE START SCREEN COMPONENTS AND INTERACT WITH THE START SCREEN

You decide to explore the Start screen components. Then you use the Desktop tile on the Start screen to access the desktop. Refer to Figure 1.5 as you complete Step 2.

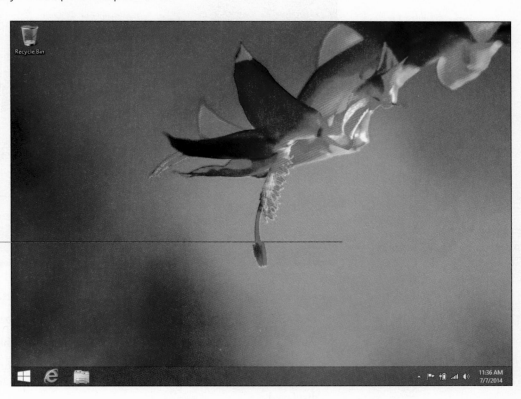

Step d: Display the Windows 8.1.1 desktop

FIGURE 1.5 Desktop

a. Point to the top-right corner to display the Charms. Click the **Start screen charm**.

Because you finished on the desktop after completing Step 1, clicking the Start screen charm takes you to the Start screen.

> **TROUBLESHOOTING:** If you skipped Step 1, log in to Windows with your username and password to display the Start screen.

b. Point to the bottom of the Start screen to display the horizontal scroll bar. Drag the scroll bar to the right to view all of the tiles available. Then drag the scrollbar back to the left to its original position.

Many components of the Start screen do not display until they are needed. This saves screen space on mobile devices. In this case, the horizontal scroll bar is hidden until needed.

c. Point to the bottom-right corner of the screen to display the Charms.

The Charms will display whenever you point to the top-right or bottom-right corners of the screen, regardless of the application you are using.

d. Locate and click the **Desktop tile**. See Figure 1.5.

STEP 3 ≫ ACCESS THE DESKTOP

You would like to add some components to make the desktop easier to use. You customize the desktop by adding the Address toolbar and the Snipping Tool to the taskbar. Refer to Figure 1.6 as you complete Step 3.

FIGURE 1.6 Taskbar with Address Bar and Snipping Tool

a. Locate and right-click the taskbar. Point to *Toolbars* and select **Address**.

The Address bar now displays on the right side of the taskbar.

b. Point to the top-right corner of the screen to display the Charms. Click the **Search charm**.

The Search pane displays on the right. The Search pane is organized into categories that you may want to search. For whatever category is selected, the relevant content is displayed.

In Windows 8.1.1, many dialog boxes have been changed to panes. This is in keeping with the sleek, clean look of Windows 8.1.1. Even though the look is different, the functionality remains the same.

c. Type **Sn** in the **Search box**. Below the search box, the results listed display everything that begins with Sn.

d. Click the **Snipping Tool app** in the results list.

The Snipping Tool app displays on the desktop and the Snipping Tool icon displays on the taskbar.

e. Right-click the **Snipping Tool icon** on the taskbar. Click **Pin this program to taskbar**. See Figure 1.6.

The Snipping Tool and the Address bar will now be part of your taskbar.

> **TROUBLESHOOTING:** If you are in a lab and cannot keep these changes, you can remove the Snipping Tool icon from the taskbar. Right-click the icon and click *Unpin this program from taskbar*. You can remove the Address bar by right-clicking the taskbar, pointing to Toolbars, and then clicking Address to remove the check mark.

f. Click the **Snipping Tool icon**. Click the **New arrow** in the Snipping Tool on the desktop. Click **Full-screen Snip**.

A snip of your desktop displays in the Snipping Tool program.

g. Click **File** and click **Save As**. Navigate to the location where you are saving your student files. Name your file **f01h1Desktop_LastFirst** using your own last name and first name. Check to see that *Portable Network Graphic file (PNG)* displays in the *Save as type* box. Click **Save**.

You have created your first snip. Snips can be used to show what is on your screen. Notice the Snipping Tool app does not display in your snip. When you save files, use your last and first names. For example, as the Office Fundamentals author, I would name my document *f01h1Desktop_LawsonRebecca*.

> **TROUBLESHOOTING:** If PNG does not display in the *Save as type* box, click the arrow on the right side of the box and select *Portable Network Graphic file (PNG)*.

h. Close the Snipping Tool. Submit the file based on your instructor's directions.

i. Shut down your computer if you are ready to stop working. Point to the top-right corner to display the Charms. Click the **Settings charm**, click the **Power icon**, and then click **Shut down**. Otherwise, leave your computer turned on for the next Hands-On Exercise.

Files and Folders

Most activities that you perform using a computer produce some type of output. That output could be games, music, or the display of digital photographs. Perhaps you use a computer at work to produce reports, financial worksheets, or schedules. All of those items are considered computer *files*. Files include electronic data such as documents, databases, slide shows, and worksheets. Even digital photographs, music, videos, and Web pages are saved as files.

You use software to create and save files. For example, when you type a document on a computer, you first open a word processor such as Microsoft Word. In order to access files later, you must save them to a computer storage medium such as a hard drive or flash drive, or in the cloud at OneDrive. And just as you would probably organize a filing cabinet into a system of folders, you can organize storage media by *folders* that you name and into which you place data files. That way, you can easily retrieve the files later. Windows 8.1.1 provides tools that enable you to create folders and to save files in ways that make locating them simple.

In this section, you will learn to use File Explorer to manage folders and files.

Using File Explorer

File Explorer is an app that you can use to create and manage folders and files. The sole purpose of a computer folder is to provide a labeled storage location for related files so that you can easily organize and retrieve items. A folder structure can occur across several levels, so you can create folders within other folders—called *subfolders*—arranged according to purpose. Windows 8.1.1 uses the concept of libraries, which are folders that gather files from different locations and display the files as if they were all saved in a single folder, regardless of where they are physically stored. Using File Explorer, you can manage folders, work with libraries, and view favorites (areas or folders that are frequently accessed).

Understand and Customize the Interface

You can access File Explorer in any of the following ways:

- Click the File Explorer icon from the taskbar on the desktop.
- Click File Explorer from the Start screen.
- Display the Charms (refer to Figure 1.1) and click the Search charm. Type F in the Search box and in the results list on the left, click File Explorer.

Figure 1.7 shows the File Explorer interface containing several areas. Some of those areas are described in Table 1.1.

FIGURE 1.7 File Explorer Interface

TABLE 1.1	File Explorer Interface
Navigation Pane	The Navigation Pane contains five areas: Favorites, Libraries, Homegroup, Computer, and Network. Click an item in the Navigation Pane to display contents and to manage files that are housed within a selected folder.
Back, Forward, and Up Buttons	Use these buttons to visit previously opened folders or libraries. Use the Up button to open the parent folder for the current location.
Ribbon	The Ribbon includes tabs and commands that are relevant to the currently selected item. If you are working with a music file, the Ribbon commands might include one for burning to a CD, whereas if you have selected a document, the Ribbon would enable you to open or share the file.
Address bar	The Address bar enables you to navigate to other folders or libraries.
Content pane	The Content pane shows the contents of the currently selected folder or library.
Search box	Find files and folders by typing descriptive text in the Search box. Windows immediately begins a search after you type the first character, further narrowing results as you type.
Details pane	The Details pane shows properties that are associated with a selected file. Common properties include information such as the author name and the date the file was last modified. This pane does not display by default but can display after clicking the View tab.
Preview pane	The Preview pane provides a snapshot of a selected file's contents. You can see file contents before actually opening the file. The Preview pane does not show the contents of a selected folder. This pane does not display by default but can display after clicking the View tab.

File Explorer has a Ribbon like all the Office applications. As you work with File Explorer, you might want to customize the view. The file and folder icons might be too small for ease of identification, or you might want additional details about displayed files and folders. Modifying the view is easy. To make icons larger or to provide additional detail, click the View tab (refer to Figure 1.7) and select from the views provided in the Layout group. If you want additional detail, such as file type and size, click Details. You can also change the size of icons by selecting Small, Medium, Large, or Extra Large icons. The List view shows the file names without added detail, whereas Tiles and Content views are useful to show file thumbnails (small pictures describing file contents) and varying levels of detail regarding file locations. To show or hide File Explorer panes, click the View tab and select the pane to hide or show in the Panes group. You can widen or narrow panes by dragging a border when the mouse changes to a double-headed arrow.

Work with Groups on the Navigation Pane

The *Navigation Pane* provides ready access to computer resources, folders, files, and networked peripherals such as printers. It is divided into five areas: Favorites, Libraries, Homegroup, Computer, and Network. Each of those components provides a unique way to organize contents. In Figure 1.8, the currently selected area is Computer.

Earlier, we used the analogy of computer folders to folders in a filing cabinet. Just as you would title folders in a filing cabinet according to their contents, computer folders are also titled according to content. Folders are physically located on storage media such as a hard drive or flash drive. You can also organize folders into *libraries*, which are collections of files from different locations that are displayed as a single virtual folder. For example, the Pictures library includes files from the My Pictures folder and from the Public Pictures folder, both of which are physically housed on the hard drive. Although the library content comes from two separate folders, the contents are displayed as a single virtual folder.

Windows 8.1.1 includes several libraries that contain default folders or devices. For example, the Documents library includes the My Documents and Public Documents folders, but you can add subfolders if you wish so that they are also housed within the Documents library. To add a folder to a library, right-click the library, point to New, and then select Folder. You can name the folder at this point by typing the folder name. To remove a folder from the Documents library, open File Explorer, right-click the folder, and then select Delete.

The Computer area provides access to specific storage locations, such as a hard drive, CD/DVD drives, and removable media drives, including a flash drive. Files and folders housed on those storage media are accessible when you click Computer. For example, click drive C, shown under Computer in the Navigation Pane, to view its contents in the Content pane on the right. If you simply want to see the subfolders of the hard drive, click the arrow to the left of drive C to expand the view, showing all subfolders. The arrow is filled in and pointing down. Click the arrow again to collapse the view, removing subfolder detail. The arrow is open and pointing right. It is important to understand that clicking the arrow—as opposed to clicking the folder or area name—does not actually select an area or folder. It merely displays additional levels contained within the area. Clicking the folder or area, however, does select the item. Figure 1.8 illustrates the difference between clicking the folder or area name in the Navigation Pane and clicking the arrow to the left.

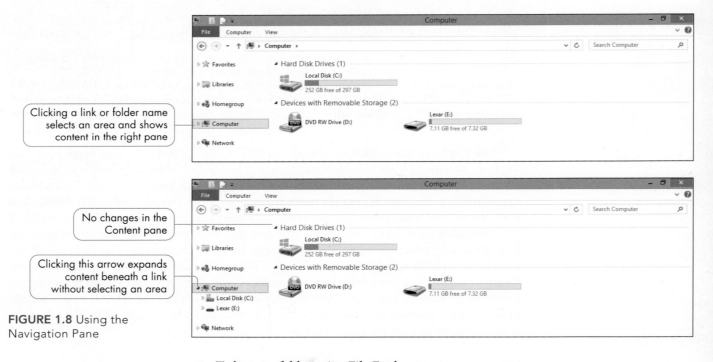

Clicking a link or folder name selects an area and shows content in the right pane

No changes in the Content pane

Clicking this arrow expands content beneath a link without selecting an area

FIGURE 1.8 Using the Navigation Pane

To locate a folder using File Explorer:

1. Click the correct drive in the Navigation Pane (or double-click the drive in the Content pane).
2. Continue navigating through the folder structure until you find the folder that you want.
3. Click the folder in the Navigation Pane (or double-click the folder in the Content pane) to view its contents.

The Favorites area contains frequently accessed folders and recent searches. You can drag a folder, saved search, library, or disk drive to the Favorites area. To remove a favorite, simply right-click the favorite and select Remove. You cannot add files or Web sites as favorites.

Homegroup is a Windows 8.1.1 feature that enables you to share resources on a home network. You can easily share music, pictures, videos, and libraries with other people in your home through a homegroup. It is password protected, so you do not have to worry about privacy.

Windows 8.1.1 makes creating a home network easy, sharing access to the Internet and peripheral devices such as printers and scanners. The Network area provides quick access to those devices, enabling you to see the contents of network computers.

Working with Folders and Files

As you work with software to create a file, such as when you type a report using Microsoft Word, your primary concern will be saving the file so that you can retrieve it later if necessary. If you have created an appropriate and well-named folder structure, you can save the file in a location that is easy to find later.

Create a Folder

You can create a folder a couple of different ways. You can use File Explorer to create a folder structure, providing appropriate names and placing the folders in a well-organized hierarchy. You can also create a folder from within a software application at the time that you need it. Although it would be wonderful to always plan ahead, most often you will find the need for a folder at the same time that you have created a file. The two methods of creating a folder are described next.

STEP 1 »   Suppose you are beginning a new college semester and are taking four classes. To organize your assignments, you plan to create four folders on a flash drive, one for each class. After connecting the flash drive and closing any subsequent dialog box (unless the dialog box is warning of a problem with the drive), open File Explorer. Click Computer in the Navigation Pane. Click the removable (flash) drive in the Navigation Pane or double-click it in the Content pane. You can also create a folder on the hard drive in the same manner, by clicking drive C instead of the removable drive. Click the Home tab on the Ribbon. Click *New folder* in the New group. Type the new folder name, such as Biology, and press Enter. Repeat the process to create additional folders.

Undoubtedly, you will occasionally find that you have just created a file but have no appropriate folder in which to save the file. You might have just finished the slide show for your speech class but have forgotten first to create a speech folder for your assignments. Now what do you do? As you save the file, a process that is discussed later in this chapter, you can click Browse to bring up the Save As dialog box. Navigate to the drive where you want to store your file. Click *New folder* (see Figure 1.9), type the new folder name, and then double-click to save the name and open the new folder. After indicating the file name, click Save.

FIGURE 1.9 Create a Folder

OneDrive makes it easy to access your folders and files from any Internet-connected computer or mobile device. You can create new folders and organize existing folders just as you would when you use File Explorer. Other tasks that can be performed at OneDrive include opening, renaming, and deleting folders and files. To create a new folder at OneDrive, you can simply click the OneDrive tile on the Start screen. By default, you will see three items: Documents, Pictures, and Public Shared. You can right-click any of these three items to access icons for creating a new folder or to upload files. Once files and folders are added or created here, you can access them from any computer with Internet access at onedrive.live. com. Similarly, you can create folders or upload files and folders at OneDrive and then access them using the OneDrive tile on your Start screen.

Open, Rename, and Delete Folders and Files

You have learned that folders can be created in File Explorer but files are more commonly created in other ways, such as within a software package. File Explorer can create a new file, and you can use it to open, rename, and delete files just as you use it for folders.

Using the Navigation Pane, you can locate and select a folder containing a file that you want to open. For example, you might want to open the speech slide show so that you can practice before giving a presentation to the class. Open File Explorer and navigate to the speech folder. In your storage location, the file will display in the Content pane. Double-click the file. The program that is associated with the file will open the file. For example, if you have the PowerPoint program associated with that file type on your computer, then PowerPoint will open the file. To open a folder and display the contents, just click the folder in the Navigation Pane or double-click it in the Content pane.

STEP 3>> At times, you may want to give a different name to a file or folder than the one that you originally gave it. Or perhaps you made a typographical mistake when you entered the name. In these situations, you should rename the file or folder. In File Explorer, move through the folder structure to find the folder or file. Right-click the name and select Rename. Type the new name and press Enter. You can also rename an item when you click the name twice— but much more slowly than a double-click. Type the new name and press Enter. Finally, you can click a file or folder once to select it, click the Home tab, and then select Rename in the Organize group. Type the new name and press Enter.

It is much easier to delete a folder or file than it is to recover it if you remove it by mistake. Therefore, be very careful when deleting items so that you are sure of your intentions before proceeding. When you delete a folder, all subfolders and all files within the folder are also removed. If you are certain you want to remove a folder or file, the process is simple. Right-click the item, click Delete, and then click Yes if asked to confirm removal to the Recycle Bin. Items are placed in the Recycle Bin only if you are deleting them from a hard drive. Files and folders deleted from a removable storage medium, such as a flash drive, are immediately and permanently deleted, with no easy method of retrieval. You can also delete an item (file or folder) when you click to select the item, click the Home tab, and then click Delete in the Organize group.

Save a File

STEP 2>> As you create or modify a project such as a document, presentation, or worksheet, you will most likely want to continue the project at another time or keep it for later reference. You need to save it to a storage medium such as a hard drive, CD, flash drive, or in the cloud with OneDrive. When you save a file, you will be working within a software package. Therefore, you must follow the procedure dictated by that software to save the file. Office 2013 allows you to save your project to OneDrive or to a location on your computer.

The first time that you save a file, you must indicate where the file should be saved, and you must assign a file name. Of course, you will want to save the file in an appropriately named folder so that you can find it easily later. Thereafter, you can quickly save the file with the same settings, or you can change one or more of those settings, perhaps saving the file to a different storage device as a backup copy. Figure 1.10 shows a typical Save As pane for Office 2013 that enables you to select a location before saving the file.

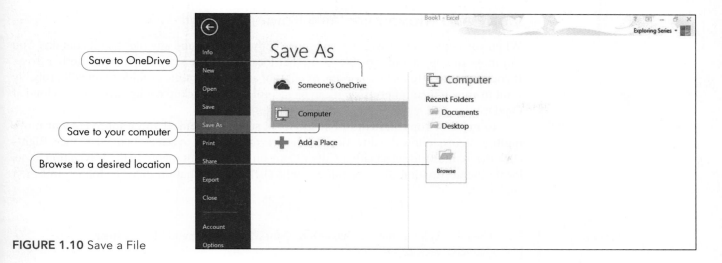

FIGURE 1.10 Save a File

Selecting, Copying, and Moving Multiple Files and Folders

You will want to select folders and files when you need to rename, delete, copy, or paste them, or open files and folders so that you can view the contents. Click a file or folder to *select* it; double-click a file or folder (in the Content pane) to *open* it. To apply an operation to several files at once, such as deleting or moving them, you will want to select all of them.

Select Multiple Files and Folders

You can select several files and folders, regardless of whether they are adjacent to each other in the file list. Suppose that your digital pictures are contained in the Pictures folder. You might want to delete some of the pictures because you want to clear up some hard drive space. To select pictures in the Pictures folder, open File Explorer and click the Pictures library. Locate the desired pictures in the Content pane. To select the adjacent pictures, select the first picture, press and hold Shift, and then click the last picture. All consecutive picture files will be highlighted, indicating that they are selected. At that point, you can delete, copy, or move the selected pictures at the same time.

If the files or folders to be selected are not adjacent, click the first item. Press and hold Ctrl while you click all desired files or folders, releasing Ctrl only when you have finished selecting the files or folders.

To select all items in a folder or disk drive, use File Explorer to navigate to the desired folder. Open the folder, press and hold Ctrl, and then press A on the keyboard. You can also click the Home tab, and in the Select group, click *Select all* to select all items.

Using a Check Box to Select Items

In Windows 8.1.1, it is easy to make multiple selections, even if the items are not adjacent. Open File Explorer and select your drive or folder. Click the View tab and select Item check boxes in the Show/Hide group. As you move the mouse pointer along the left side of files and folders, a check box displays. Click in the check box to select the file. If you want to quickly select all items in the folder, click the check box that displays in the Name column heading.

Copy and Move Files and Folders

When you copy or move a folder, you move both the folder and any files that it contains. You can move or copy a folder or file to another location on the same drive or to another drive. If your purpose is to make a *backup*, or copy, of an important file or folder, you will probably want to copy it to another drive. It can be helpful to have backup copies saved in the cloud at OneDrive as well.

STEP 4 ›››

To move or copy an item in File Explorer, select the item. If you want to copy or move multiple items, follow the directions in the previous section to select them all at once. Right-click the item(s) and select either Cut or Copy on the shortcut menu. In the Navigation Pane, locate the destination drive or folder, right-click the destination drive or folder, and then click Paste.

Quick Concepts

1. The File Explorer interface has several panes. Name them and identify their characteristics. *p. 11*

2. After creating a file, such as a PowerPoint presentation, you want to save it. However, as you begin to save the file, you realize that you have not yet created a folder in which to place the file. Is it possible to create a folder as you are saving the file? If so, how? *p. 13*

3. What should you consider when deleting files or folders from a removable storage medium such as a flash drive? *p. 14*

4. Office 2013 enables you to save files to OneDrive or your computer. Why might it be helpful to save a file in both locations? *p. 14*

5. You want to delete several files, but the files are not consecutively listed in File Explorer. How would you select and delete them? *p. 15*

Hands-On Exercises

2 Files and Folders

You will soon begin to collect files from volunteers who are preparing promotional and record-keeping material for the Spotted Begonia Art Gallery. It is important that you save the files in appropriately named folders so that you can easily access them later. You can create folders on a hard drive, flash drive, or at OneDrive. You will select the drive on which you plan to save the various files. As you create a short document, you will save it in one of the folders. You will then make a backup copy of the folder structure, including all files, so that you do not run the risk of losing the material if the drive is damaged or misplaced.

Skills covered: Create Folders and Subfolders • Create and Save a File • Rename and Delete a Folder • Open and Copy a File

STEP 1 ≫ CREATE FOLDERS AND SUBFOLDERS

You decide to create a folder titled *Artists* and then subdivide it into subfolders that will help categorize the artists' artwork promotional files as well as for general record keeping for the art gallery. Refer to Figure 1.11 as you complete Step 1.

Step c: Address bar showing folder and subfolder

Step e: Create subfolders

Step a: Navigate to your storage location—yours will differ

FIGURE 1.11 Artists' Folders

a. Navigate to the location where you are storing your files. If storing on your computer or a flash drive, navigate to the desktop. Click **File Explorer** on the taskbar and maximize the window. Click the **VIEW tab** and click to display the **Preview pane**, if necessary.

A removable drive is shown in Figure 1.11 and is titled *Lexar (E:)*, describing the drive manufacturer and the drive letter. Your storage area will be designated in a different manner, perhaps also identified by manufacturer (or perhaps you are saving your files on OneDrive). The storage area identification is likely to be different because the configuration of disk drives on your computer is unique.

> **TROUBLESHOOTING:** If you do not have a flash drive, you can use the hard drive. In the next step, simply click drive C in the Navigation Pane instead of the removable drive. You can also create and save folders and files at OneDrive.

b. Click the removable drive in the Navigation Pane (or click **drive C** if you are using the hard drive). Click the **HOME tab**, click **New folder** in the New group, type **Artists**, and then press **Enter**.

You create a folder where you can organize subfolders and files for the artists and their promotional materials and general record-keeping files.

> **TROUBLESHOOTING:** If the folder you create is called *New folder* instead of *Artists*, you probably clicked away from the folder before typing the name, so that it received the default name. To rename it, right-click the folder, click Rename, type the correct name, and then press Enter.

c. Double-click the **Artists folder** in the Content pane. The Address bar at the top of the File Explorer window should show that it is the currently selected folder. Click the **HOME tab**, click **New folder** in the New group, type **Promotional**, and then press **Enter**.

You decide to create subfolders of the *Artists* folder to contain promotional material, presentations, and office records.

d. Check the Address bar to make sure *Artists* is still the current folder. Using the same technique, create a new folder named **Presentations** and create a new folder named **Office Records**.

You create two more subfolders, appropriately named.

e. Double-click the **Promotional folder** in the Navigation Pane. Right-click in a blank area, point to *New*, and then click **Folder**. Type **Form Letters** and press **Enter**. Using the same technique, create a new folder named **Flyers** and press **Enter**.

To subdivide the promotional material further, you create two subfolders, one to hold form letters and one to contain flyers (see Figure 1.11).

f. Take a full-screen snip of your screen and name it **f01h2Folders_LastFirst**. Close the Snipping Tool.

g. Close File Explorer.

STEP 2 ≫ CREATE AND SAVE A FILE

To keep everything organized, you assign volunteers to take care of certain tasks. After creating an Excel worksheet listing those responsibilities, you will save it in the Office Records folder. Refer to Figure 1.12 as you complete Step 2.

FIGURE 1.12 Volunteers Worksheet

a. Navigate to the Start screen. Scroll across the tiles and click **Excel 2013**. If necessary, use the Search charm to locate Excel.

You use Excel 2013 to create the Volunteers worksheet.

b. Click **Blank workbook** in the Excel 2013 window that displays. Type **Volunteer Assignments** in **cell A1**. Press **Enter** twice.

Cell A3 is the active cell, as indicated by a green box that surrounds the cell.

c. Type **Category**. Press **Tab** to make the next cell to the right the active cell and type **Volunteer**. Press **Enter**. Complete the remaining cells of the worksheet as shown in Figure 1.12.

> **TROUBLESHOOTING:** If you make a mistake, click in the cell and retype the entry.

d. Click the **FILE tab** and click **Save**.

The Save As pane displays. The Save As pane is where you determine the location where your file will be saved, either your Computer or OneDrive.

e. Click **Browse** to display the Save As dialog box. Scroll down if necessary and click **Computer** or the location where you are saving your files in the Navigation Pane. In the Content pane, locate the Artists folder that you created in Step 1 and double-click to open the folder. Double-click **Office Records**. Click in the **File name box** and type **f01h2Volunteers_LastFirst**. Click **Save**. Refer to Figure 1.12.

The file is now saved as *f01h2Volunteers_LastFirst*. The workbook is saved in the Office Records subfolder of the Artists folder. You can check the title bar of the workbook to confirm the file has been saved with the correct name.

f. Click the **Close (X) button** in the top-right corner of the Excel window to close Excel.

STEP 3 ≫ RENAME AND DELETE A FOLDER

As often happens, you find that the folder structure you created is not exactly what you need. You will remove the Flyers folder and the Form Letters folder and will rename the Promotional folder to better describe the contents. Refer to Figure 1.13 as you complete Step 3.

Step d: Current folder structure

FIGURE 1.13 Artists Folder Structure

a. Navigate to the desktop, if necessary. Click **File Explorer** on the taskbar. Click the location where you are saving your files. Double-click the **Artists folder** in the Content pane.

b. Click the **Promotional folder** to select it.

> **TROUBLESHOOTING:** If you double-click the folder instead of using a single-click, the folder will open and you will see its title in the Address bar. To return to the correct view, click Artists in the Address bar.

c. Click the **HOME tab**. In the Organize group, click **Rename**, type **Promotional Print**, and then press **Enter**.

Because the folder will be used to organize all of the printed promotional material, you decide to rename the folder to better reflect the contents.

d. Double-click the **Promotional Print folder**. Click **Flyers**. Press and hold **Shift** and click **Form Letters**. Both folders should be selected (highlighted). Right-click either folder and click **Delete**. If asked to confirm the deletion, click **Yes**. Click **Artists** in the Address bar.

Your screen should appear as shown in Figure 1.13. You decide that dividing the promotional material into flyers and form letters is not necessary, so you deleted both folders.

e. Take a full-screen snip of your screen and name it **f01h2Artists_LastFirst**. Close the Snipping Tool.

f. Leave File Explorer open for the next step.

STEP 4 ›› OPEN AND COPY A FILE

You hope to recruit more volunteers to work with the Spotted Begonia Art Gallery. The Volunteers worksheet will be a handy way to keep up with people and assignments, and as the list grows, knowing exactly where the file is saved will be important for easy access. You will modify the Volunteers worksheet and make a backup copy of the folder hierarchy. Refer to Figure 1.14 as you complete Step 4.

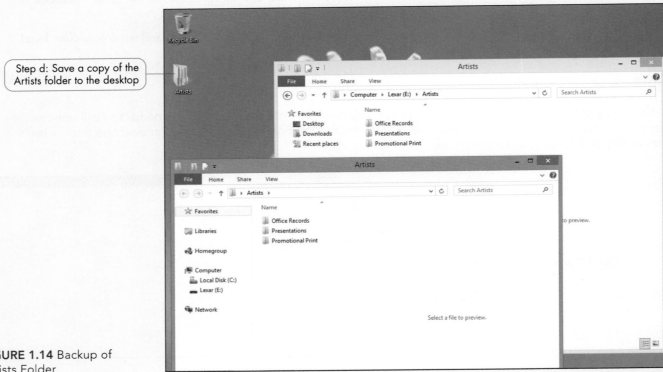

Step d: Save a copy of the Artists folder to the desktop

FIGURE 1.14 Backup of Artists Folder

a. Double-click the **Office Records folder**. Double-click *f01h2Volunteers_LastFirst*. Save the file with the new name **f01h2Stp4Volunteers_LastFirst** in the same location.

Because the file was created with Excel, that program opens, and the Volunteers worksheet is displayed.

b. Click **cell A11**, if necessary, and type **Office**. Press **Tab**, type **Adams**, and then press **Enter**. Click the **FILE tab** and click **Save**. The file is automatically saved in the same location with the same file name as before. Close Excel.

A neighbor, Sarah Adams, has volunteered to help in the office. You record that information on the worksheet and save the updated file in the Office Records folder.

c. Click the location where you save files in the Navigation pane in File Explorer so that the Artists folder displays in the Content pane. Right-click the **Artists folder** and click **Copy**.

d. Right-click **Desktop** in the Favorites group on the Navigation Pane and click **Paste**. Close File Explorer. If any other windows are open, close them also.

You made a copy of the Artists folder on the desktop.

e. Double-click the **Artists folder** on the desktop. Double-click the **Office Records folder**. Verify that the *f01h2Stp4Volunteers_LastFirst* worksheet displays in the folder. Take a full-screen snip of your screen and name it **f01h2Backup_LastFirst**. Close the Snipping Tool and close File Explorer.

f. Right-click the **Artists folder** on the desktop, select **Delete**, and then click **Yes** if asked to confirm the deletion.

You deleted the Artists folder from the desktop of the computer because you may be working in a computer lab and want to leave the computer as you found it. You may also want to empty the Recycle Bin.

g. Submit your files based on your instructor's directions.

Microsoft Office Software

Organizations around the world rely heavily on *Microsoft Office* software to produce documents, spreadsheets, presentations, and databases. Microsoft Office is a productivity software suite including a set of software applications, each one specializing in a particular type of output. You can use *Word* to produce all sorts of documents, including memos, newsletters, forms, tables, and brochures. *Excel* makes it easy to organize records, financial transactions, and business information in the form of worksheets. With *PowerPoint*, you can create dynamic presentations to inform groups and persuade audiences. *Access* is relational database software that enables you to record and link data, query databases, and create forms and reports.

You will sometimes find that you need to use two or more Office applications to produce your intended output. You might, for example, find that a Word document you are preparing for your investment club should also include a summary of stock performance. You can use Excel to prepare the summary and then incorporate the worksheet in the Word document. Similarly, you can integrate Word tables and Excel charts into a PowerPoint presentation. The choice of which software applications to use really depends on what type of output you are producing. Table 1.2 describes the major tasks of these four primary applications in Microsoft Office.

TABLE 1.2 Microsoft Office Software	
Office 2013 Product	**Application Characteristics**
Word 2013	Word processing software used with text to create, edit, and format documents such as letters, memos, reports, brochures, resumes, and flyers.
Excel 2013	Spreadsheet software used to store quantitative data and to perform accurate and rapid calculations with results ranging from simple budgets to financial analyses and statistical analyses.
PowerPoint 2013	Presentation graphics software used to create slide shows for presentation by a speaker, to be published as part of a Web site, or to run as a stand-alone application on a computer kiosk.
Access 2013	Relational database software used to store data and convert it into information. Database software is used primarily for decision making by businesses that compile data from multiple records stored in tables to produce informative reports.

As you become familiar with Microsoft Office, you will find that although each software application produces a specific type of output, all applications share common features. Such commonality gives a similar feel to each software application so that learning and working with Microsoft Office software products is easy. In this section, you will identify features common to Microsoft Office software, including such interface components as the Ribbon, the Backstage view, and the Quick Access Toolbar. You will also learn how to get help with an application.

Identifying Common Interface Components

As you work with Microsoft Office, you will find that each application shares a similar *user interface*. The user interface is the screen display through which you communicate with the software. Word, Excel, PowerPoint, and Access share common interface elements, as shown in Figure 1.15. One of the feature options includes the availability of templates as well as new and improved themes when each application is opened. A *template* is a predesigned file that incorporates formatting elements, such as a theme and layouts, and may include content that can be modified. A *theme* is a collection of design choices that includes colors, fonts, and special effects used to give a consistent look to a document, workbook, or presentation. As you can imagine, becoming familiar with one application's interface makes it that much easier to work with other Office software.

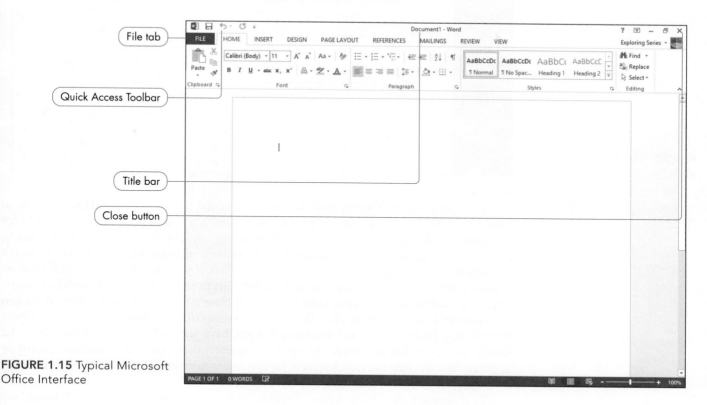

FIGURE 1.15 Typical Microsoft Office Interface

Use the Backstage View and the Quick Access Toolbar

The *Backstage view* is a component of Office 2013 that provides a concise collection of commands related to an open file. Using the Backstage view, you can find out information such as protection, permissions, versions, and properties. A file's properties include the author, file size, permissions, and date modified. You can create a new document or open, save, print, share, export, or close. The *Quick Access Toolbar*, located at the top-left corner of any Office application window, provides fast access to commonly executed tasks such as saving a file and undoing recent actions. The *title bar* identifies the current file name and the application in which you are working. It also includes control buttons that enable you to minimize, maximize, restore down, or close the application window (see Figure 1.15).

You access the Backstage view by clicking the File tab. When you click the File tab, you will see the Backstage view (see Figure 1.16). Primarily focusing on file activities such as opening, closing, saving, printing, and beginning new files, the Backstage view also includes options for customizing program settings, signing in to your Office account, and exiting the program. It displays a file's properties, providing important information on file permission and sharing options. When you click the File tab, the Backstage view will occupy the entire application window, hiding the file with which you might be working. For example, suppose that as you are typing a report you need to check the document's properties. Click the File tab to display a Backstage view similar to that shown in Figure 1.16. You can return to the application—in this case, Word—in a couple of ways. Either click the Back arrow in the top-left corner or press Esc on the keyboard.

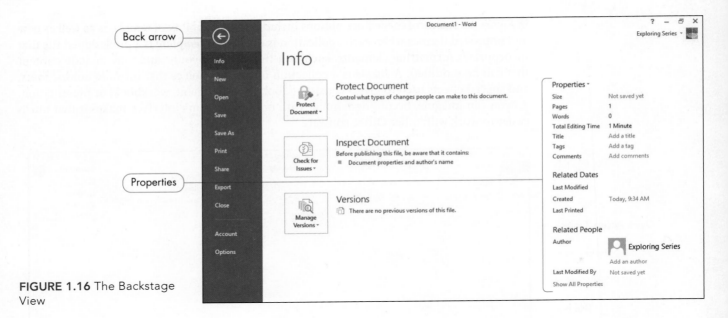

FIGURE 1.16 The Backstage View

STEP 4 »

The Quick Access Toolbar provides one-click access to common activities, as shown in Figure 1.17. By default, the Quick Access Toolbar includes buttons for saving a file and for undoing or redoing recent actions. You will probably perform an action countless times in an Office application and then realize that you made a mistake. You can recover from the mistake by clicking Undo on the Quick Access Toolbar. If you click the arrow beside Undo—known as the Undo arrow—you can select from a list of previous actions in order of occurrence. The Undo list is not maintained when you close a file or exit the application, so you can erase an action that took place during the current Office session only. Similar to Undo, you can also Redo (or Replace) an action that you have just undone. You can customize the Quick Access Toolbar to include buttons for frequently used commands such as printing or opening files. Because the Quick Access Toolbar is onscreen at all times, the most commonly accessed tasks are just a click away.

To customize the Quick Access Toolbar, click Customize Quick Access Toolbar (see Figure 1.17) and select from a list of commands. You can also click More Commands near the bottom of the menu options. If a command that you want to include on the toolbar is not on the list, you can right-click the command on the Ribbon and click *Add to Quick Access Toolbar*. Similarly, remove a command from the Quick Access Toolbar by right-clicking the icon on the Quick Access Toolbar and clicking *Remove from Quick Access Toolbar*. If you want to display the Quick Access Toolbar beneath the Ribbon, click Customize Quick Access Toolbar (see Figure 1.17) and click *Show Below the Ribbon*.

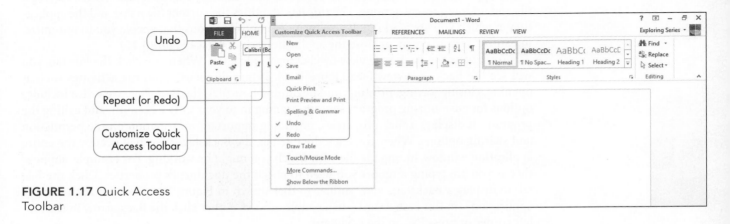

FIGURE 1.17 Quick Access Toolbar

Familiarize Yourself with the Ribbon

The **Ribbon** is the command center of Office applications. It is the long bar located just beneath the title bar, containing tabs, groups, and commands. Each **tab** is designed to appear much like a tab on a file folder, with the active tab highlighted. The File tab is always a darker shade than the other tabs and a different color depending on the application. Remember that clicking the File tab opens the Backstage view. Other tabs on the Ribbon enable you to modify a file. The active tab in Figure 1.18 is the Home tab.

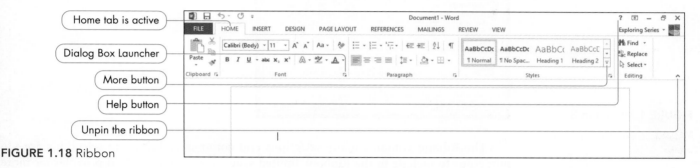

FIGURE 1.18 Ribbon

When you click a tab, the Ribbon displays several task-oriented **groups**, with each group containing related **commands**. A group is a subset of a tab that organizes similar tasks together. A command is a button or area within a group that you click to perform tasks. Microsoft Office is designed to provide the most functionality possible with the fewest clicks. For that reason, the Home tab, displayed when you first open an Office software application, contains groups and commands that are most commonly used. For example, because you will often want to change the way text is displayed, the Home tab in each Office application includes a Font group with activities related to modifying text. Similarly, other tabs contain groups of related actions, or commands, many of which are unique to the particular Office application.

Because Word, PowerPoint, Excel, and Access all share a similar Ribbon structure, you will be able to move at ease among those applications. Although the specific tabs, groups, and commands vary among the Office programs, the way in which you use the Ribbon and the descriptive nature of tab titles is the same regardless of which program you are working with. For example, if you want to insert a chart in Excel, a header in Word, or a shape in PowerPoint, you will click the Insert tab in any of those programs. The first thing that you should do as you begin to work with an Office application is to study the Ribbon. Take a look at all tabs and their contents. That way, you will have a good idea of where to find specific commands and how the Ribbon with which you are currently working differs from one that you might have used previously in another application.

If you are working with a large project, you might want to maximize your workspace by temporarily hiding the Ribbon. You can hide the Ribbon in several ways. Double-click the active tab to hide the Ribbon and double-click any tab to redisplay it. You can click *Unpin the ribbon* (see Figure 1.18), located at the right side of the Ribbon, and click any tab to redisplay the Ribbon.

The Ribbon provides quick access to common activities such as changing number or text formats or aligning data or text. Some actions, however, do not display on the Ribbon because they are not so common but are related to commands displayed on the Ribbon. For example, you might want to change the background of a PowerPoint slide to include a picture. In that case, you will need to work with a **dialog box** that provides access to more precise, but less frequently used, commands. Figure 1.19 shows the Font dialog box in Word, for example. Some commands display a dialog box when they are clicked. Other Ribbon groups include a **Dialog Box Launcher** that, when clicked, opens a corresponding dialog box (refer to Figure 1.18).

Dialog box Help button

FIGURE 1.19 Dialog Box

The Ribbon contains many selections and commands, but some selections are too numerous to include in the Ribbon's limited space. For example, Word provides far more text styles than it can easily display at once, so additional styles are available in a *gallery*. A gallery also provides a choice of Excel chart styles and PowerPoint transitions. Figure 1.20 shows an example of a PowerPoint Themes gallery. Most often, you can display a gallery of additional choices by clicking the More button (refer to Figure 1.18) that is found in some Ribbon selections.

Themes gallery

FIGURE 1.20 PowerPoint Themes Gallery

STEP 3》

When editing a document, worksheet, or presentation, it is helpful to see the results of formatting changes before you make final selections. The feature that displays a preview of the results of a selection is called *Live Preview*. You might, for example, be considering changing the font color of a selection in a document or worksheet. As you place the mouse pointer over a color selection in a Ribbon gallery or group, the selected text will temporarily display the color to which you are pointing. Similarly, you can get a preview of how color designs would display on PowerPoint slides by pointing to specific themes in the PowerPoint Themes group and noting the effect on a displayed slide. When you click the item, such as the font color, the selection is applied. Live Preview is available in various Ribbon selections among the Office applications.

Office applications also make it easy for you to work with objects such as pictures, *clip art*, shapes, charts, and tables. Clip art is an electronic illustration that can be inserted into an Office project. When you include such objects in a project, they are considered separate components that you can manage independently. To work with an object, you must click to select it. When you select an object, the Ribbon is modified to include one or more ***contextual tabs*** that contain groups of commands related to the selected object. Figure 1.21 shows a contextual tab related to a selected SmartArt object in a Word document. When you click outside the selected object, the contextual tab disappears.

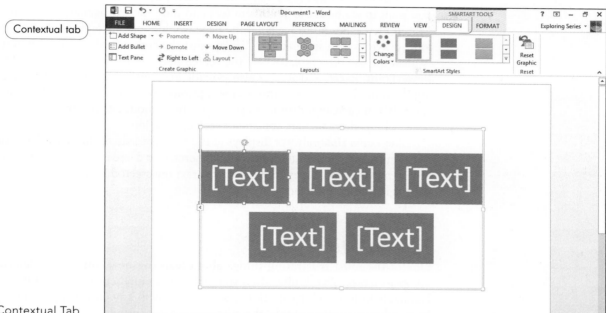

FIGURE 1.21 Contextual Tab

TIP   Using Keyboard Shortcuts

You might find that you prefer to use keyboard shortcuts, which are keyboard equivalents for software commands, when they are available. Universal keyboard shortcuts include Ctrl+C (copy), Ctrl+X (cut), Ctrl+V (paste), and Ctrl+Z (undo). To move to the beginning of a Word document, to cell A1 in Excel, or to the first PowerPoint slide, press Ctrl+Home. To move to the end of those items, press Ctrl+End. Press Alt to display keyboard shortcuts, called a ***Key Tip***, for items on the Ribbon and Quick Access Toolbar. You can press the letter or number corresponding to Ribbon items to invoke the action from the keyboard. Press Alt again to remove the Key Tips.

Use the Status Bar

The ***status bar*** is located at the bottom of the program window and contains information relative to the open file. It also includes tools for changing the view of the file and for changing the zoom size of onscreen file contents. Contents of the status bar are unique to each specific application. When you work with Word, the status bar informs you of the number of pages and words in an open document. The Excel status bar displays summary information, such as average and sum, of selected cells. The PowerPoint status bar shows the slide number, total slides in the presentation, and the applied theme. It also provides access to notes and comments.

STEP 3>>   Regardless of the application in which you are working, the status bar includes view buttons and a Zoom slider. You can also use the View tab on the Ribbon to change the current view or zoom level of an open file. The status bar's view buttons (see Figure 1.22) enable you to change the ***view*** of the open file. When creating a document, you might find it helpful to change the view. You might, for example, view a PowerPoint slide presentation with multiple slides displayed (Slide Sorter view) or with only one slide in large size (Normal view). In Word, you could view a document in Print Layout view (showing margins, headers, and footers), Web Layout view, or Read Mode.

FIGURE 1.22 Word Status Bar

Additional views are available in the View tab. Word's Print Layout view is useful when you want to see both the document text and such features as margins and page breaks. Web Layout view is useful to see what the page would look like on the Internet. The Read Mode view provides a clean look that displays just the content without the Ribbon or margins. It is ideal for use on a tablet where the screen may be smaller than on a laptop or computer. PowerPoint, Excel, and Access also provide view options, although they are unique to the application. The most common view options are accessible from *View shortcuts* on the status bar of each application. As you learn more about Office applications, you will become aware of the views that are specific to each application.

STEP 1 ▶

The *Zoom slider* always displays at the far right side of the status bar. You can drag the tab along the slider in either direction to increase or decrease the magnification of the file. Be aware, however, that changing the size of text onscreen does not change the font size when the file is printed or saved.

Getting Office Help

One of the most frustrating things about learning new software is determining how to complete a task. Thankfully, Microsoft includes comprehensive help in Office so that you are less likely to feel such frustration. As you work with any Office application, you can access help online as well as within the current software installation. Help is available through a short description that displays when you rest the mouse pointer on a command. Additionally, you can get help related to a currently open dialog box by clicking the question mark in the top-right corner of the dialog box, or when you click Help in the top-right corner of the application.

Use Office Help

STEP 2 ▶

To access the comprehensive library of Office Help, click the Help button, displayed as a question mark on the far right side of the Ribbon (refer to Figure 1.18). The Help window provides assistance with the current application as well as a direct link to online resources and technical support. Figure 1.23 shows the Help window that displays when you click the Help button while in Excel. For general information on broad topics, click a link in the window. However, if you are having difficulty with a specific task, it might be easier to simply type the request in the Search online help box. Suppose you are seeking help with using the Goal Seek feature in Excel. Simply type *Goal Seek* or a phrase such as *find specific result by changing variables* in the Search box and press Enter (or click the magnifying glass on the right). Then select from displayed results for more information on the topic.

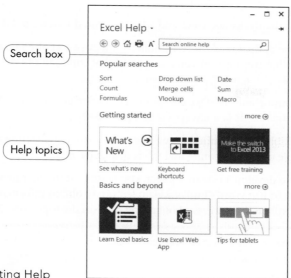

FIGURE 1.23 Getting Help

Use Enhanced ScreenTips

For quick summary information on the purpose of a command button, place the mouse pointer over the button. An *Enhanced ScreenTip* displays, giving the purpose of the command, short descriptive text, and a keyboard shortcut if applicable. Some ScreenTips include a suggestion for pressing F1 for additional help. The Enhanced ScreenTip in Figure 1.24 provides context-sensitive assistance.

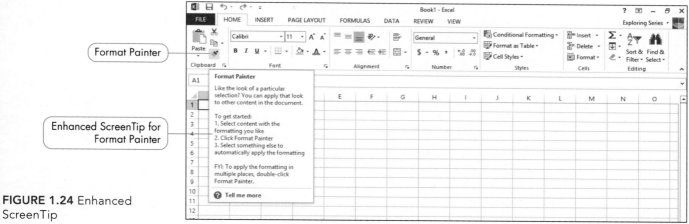

FIGURE 1.24 Enhanced ScreenTip

Get Help with Dialog Boxes

Getting help while you are working with a dialog box is easy. Simply click the Help button that displays as a question mark in the top-right corner of the dialog box (refer to Figure 1.19). The subsequent Help window will offer suggestions relevant to your task.

Quick
Concepts

1. How do you access the Backstage view, and what can you do there? **p. 23**

2. What is the purpose of the Quick Access Toolbar? Suppose you often engage in an activity such as printing. What steps would you take to add that command to the Quick Access Toolbar? **pp. 23–24**

3. The Ribbon is an important interface component of Office applications. What can you do with it? How is it organized? Is it always visible? **pp. 25–27**

4. Occasionally, the Ribbon is modified to include a contextual tab. Define a contextual tab and give an example of when a contextual tab is displayed. **p. 27**

5. After using Word to develop a research paper, you learn that the margins you used are incorrect. You plan to use Word's built-in Help feature to obtain information on how to change margins. Explain the process of obtaining help on the topic. **pp. 28–29**

Hands-On Exercises

3 Microsoft Office Software

As the administrative assistant for the Spotted Begonia Art Gallery, you need to get the staff started on a proposed schedule of gallery showings worksheet. Although you do not have access to information on all of the artists and their preferred media, you want to provide a suggested format for a worksheet to keep up with showings as they get booked. You will use Excel to begin design of the worksheet.

Skills covered: Open an Office Application, Get Enhanced ScreenTip Help, and Use the Zoom Slider • Get Help and Use the Backstage View • Change the View and Use Live Preview • Use the Quick Access Toolbar and Explore PowerPoint Views

STEP 1 ≫ OPEN AN OFFICE APPLICATION, GET ENHANCED SCREENTIP HELP, AND USE THE ZOOM SLIDER

Because you will use Excel to create the gallery showings worksheet, you will open the application. You will familiarize yourself with items on the Ribbon by getting Enhanced ScreenTip Help. For a better view of worksheet data, you will use the Zoom slider to magnify cell contents. Refer to Figure 1.25 as you complete Step 1.

FIGURE 1.25 Gallery Showings Worksheet

a. Navigate to the Start screen. Scroll across the tiles, if necessary, and click **Excel 2013**. Click **Blank workbook** in the Excel 2013 window that displays.

   You have opened Microsoft Excel because it is the program in which the gallery showings worksheet will be created.

b. Type **Date** in **cell A1**. As you type, the text appears in the current worksheet cell. Press **Tab** and type **Artist**. Press **Tab** and type **Media Used**. Press **Enter**. See Figure 1.25.

   The worksheet that you create is only a beginning. Your staff will later suggest additional columns of data that can better summarize the upcoming gallery showings.

c. Hover the mouse pointer over any command on the Ribbon and note the Enhanced ScreenTip that displays, informing you of the purpose of the command. Explore other commands and identify their purpose.

d. Click the **PAGE LAYOUT tab**, click **Orientation** in the Page Setup group, and then select **Landscape**.

   The PAGE LAYOUT tab is also found in Word, enabling you to change margins, orientation, and other page settings. Although you will not see much difference in the Excel screen display after you change the orientation to landscape, the worksheet will be oriented so that it is wider than it is tall when printed.

e. Drag the tab on the Zoom slider, located at the far right side of the status bar, to 190% to temporarily magnify the text. Take a full-screen snip of your screen and name it **f01h3Showings_LastFirst**.

f. Click the **VIEW tab** and click **100%** in the Zoom group to return the view to its original size.

When you change the zoom, you do not change the text size that will be printed or saved. The change merely magnifies or decreases the view while you work with the file.

g. Keep the workbook open for the next step in this exercise. Submit the file based on your instructor's directions.

STEP 2 ≫ GET HELP AND USE THE BACKSTAGE VIEW

Because you are not an Excel expert, you occasionally rely on the Help feature to provide information on tasks. You need assistance with saving a worksheet, previewing it before printing, and printing the worksheet. From what you learn, you will find that the Backstage view enables you to accomplish all of those tasks. Refer to Figure 1.26 as you complete Step 2.

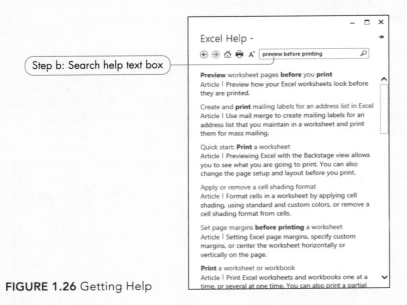

FIGURE 1.26 Getting Help

a. Click **Help**, which is the question mark in the top-right corner of the Ribbon.

The Help dialog box displays.

TIP | Using Shortcuts to Access Help

You can discover alternative ways to access Help. For example, the ScreenTip that displays as you point to the Help button suggests that you could press the F1 key.

b. Click in the **Search online help text box** at the top of the Help dialog box. Type **preview before printing** and press **Enter** (see Figure 1.26). In the Excel Help window, click **Preview worksheet pages before you print**. Read about how to preview a worksheet before printing. From what you read, can you identify a keyboard shortcut for previewing worksheets? Click the **Close (X) button**.

Before you print the worksheet, you would like to see how it will look when printed. You used Help to find information on previewing before printing.

c. Click the **FILE tab** and click **Print**.

Having used Office Help to learn how to preview before printing, you follow the directions to view the worksheet as it will look when printed. The preview of the worksheet displays on the right. To print the worksheet, you would click Print. However, you can first select any print options, such as the number of copies, from the Backstage view.

d. Click the **Back arrow** on the top left of the screen. Click **Help**. Excel Help presents several links related to the worksheet. Explore any that look interesting. Return to previous Help windows by clicking **Back** at the top-left side of the Help window. Close the Help dialog box.

e. Click the **HOME tab**. Point to *Bold* in the Font group.

You will find that, along with Excel, Word and PowerPoint also include formatting features in the Font group, such as Bold and Italic. When the Enhanced ScreenTip appears, identify the shortcut key combination that could be used to bold a selected text item. It is indicated as Ctrl plus the letter B.

f. Click the **Close (X) button** in the top-right corner of the Excel window to close both the workbook and the Excel program. When asked whether you want to save changes, click **Don't Save**.

You decide not to print or save the worksheet right now because you did not change anything during this step.

STEP 3 ≫ CHANGE THE VIEW AND USE LIVE PREVIEW

It is important that the documents you prepare or approve are error free and as attractive as possible. Before printing, you will change the view to get a better idea of how the document will look when printed. In addition, you will use Live Preview to experiment with font settings before actually applying them. Refer to Figure 1.27 as you complete Step 3.

FIGURE 1.27 Word Views

a. Navigate to the Start screen. Scroll across the tiles, if necessary, and click **Word 2013**. Click **Blank document**.

You have opened a blank Word document. You plan to familiarize yourself with the program for later reference.

b. Type your first and last names and press **Enter**. Drag to select your name.

Your name should be highlighted, indicating that it is selected. You have selected your name because you want to experiment with using Word to change the way text looks.

c. Click the **Font Size arrow** in the Font group. If you need help locating Font Size, check for an Enhanced ScreenTip. Place the mouse pointer over any number in the list, but do not click. As you move to different font sizes, notice the size of your name changes. The feature you are using is called Live Preview. Click **16** in the list to change the font size of your name.

d. Click any white space to deselect your name. Click **Read Mode** in the *View shortcuts* group on the status bar to change the view (see Figure 1.27). Click **Print Layout** to return to the original view.

e. Save the file as **f01h3Read_LastFirst** and click the **Close (X) button** to close the Word program. Submit the file based on your instructor's directions.

STEP 4 ≫ USE THE QUICK ACCESS TOOLBAR AND EXPLORE POWERPOINT VIEWS

In your position as administrative assistant, you will be asked to review documents, presentations, and worksheets. It is important that you explore each application to familiarize yourself with operations and commonalities. Specifically, you know that the Quick Access Toolbar is common to all applications and that you can place commonly used commands there to streamline processes. Also, learning to change views will enable you to see the project in different ways for various purposes. Refer to Figure 1.28 as you complete Step 4.

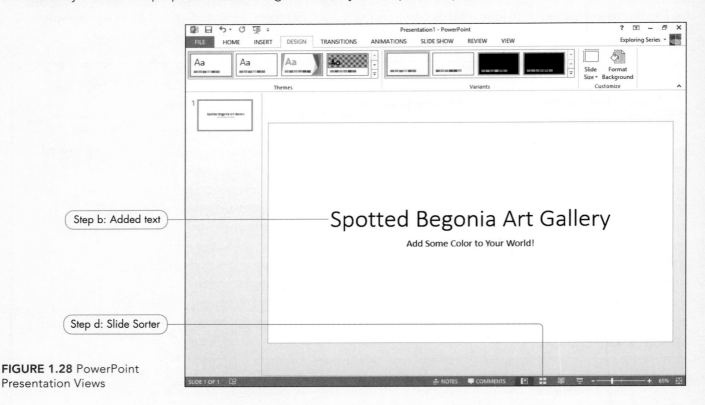

FIGURE 1.28 PowerPoint Presentation Views

a. Navigate to the Start screen. Scroll across the tiles, if necessary, and click **PowerPoint 2013**. Click **Blank Presentation**.

You have opened PowerPoint. A blank presentation displays.

b. Click **Click to add title** and type **Spotted Begonia Art Gallery**. Click in the bottom, subtitle box and type **Add Some Color to Your World!** Click the bottom-right corner of the slide to deselect the subtitle. Your PowerPoint presentation should look like that shown in Figure 1.28.

c. Click **Undo** two times on the Quick Access Toolbar.

The subtitle on the current slide is selected and removed because those are the most recent actions.

d. Click **Slide Sorter** in the *View shortcuts* group on the status bar.

The Slide Sorter view shows thumbnails of all slides in a presentation. Because this presentation has only one slide, you see a small version of one slide.

e. Move the mouse pointer to any button on the Quick Access Toolbar and hold it steady. See the tip giving the button name and the shortcut key combination, if any. Move to another button and see the description.

The Quick Access Toolbar has at least three buttons: Save, Undo, and Redo. In addition, a small arrow is included at the far-right side. If you hold the mouse pointer steady on the arrow, you will see the ScreenTip Customize Quick Access Toolbar.

f. Click **Customize Quick Access Toolbar** and select **New**. The New button is added to the toolbar. The New button enables you to quickly create a new presentation (also called a document).

g. Right-click **New** and click **Remove from Quick Access Toolbar**. The button is removed from the Quick Access Toolbar.

You can customize the Quick Access Toolbar by adding and removing items.

h. Click **Normal** in the *View shortcuts* group on the status bar.

The presentation returns to the original view in which the slide displays full size.

i. Click **Slide Show** in the *View shortcuts* group on the status bar.

The presentation is shown in Slide Show view, which is the way it will be presented to audiences.

j. Press **Esc** to end the presentation.

k. Save the presentation as **f01h3Views_LastFirst** and click the **Close (X) button** to close the PowerPoint program. Submit the presentation based on your instructor's directions.

The Backstage View Tasks

When you work with Microsoft Office files, you will often want to open previously saved files, create new ones, print items, and save and close files. You will also find it necessary to indicate options, or preferences, for settings. For example, you might want a spelling check to occur automatically, or you might prefer to initiate a spelling check only occasionally. Because those tasks are applicable to each software application within the Office 2013 suite, they are accomplished through a common area in the Office interface—the Backstage view. Open the Backstage view by clicking the File tab. Figure 1.29 shows the area that displays when you click the File tab in PowerPoint. The Backstage view also enables you to exit the application and to identify file information, such as the author or date created.

In this section, you will explore the Backstage view, learning to create, open, close, and print files.

FIGURE 1.29 The Backstage View

Opening a File

When working with an Office application, you can begin by opening an existing file that has already been saved to a storage medium, or you can begin work on a new file. Both actions are available when you click the File tab. When you first open an application within the Office 2013 suite, you will need to decide which template you want to work with before you can begin working on a new file. You can also open a project that you previously saved to a disk.

Create a New File

After opening an Office application, such as Word, Excel, or PowerPoint, you will be presented with template choices. Click *Blank document* to start a new blank document. The word *document* is sometimes used generically to refer to any Office file, including a Word document, an Excel worksheet, or a PowerPoint presentation. Perhaps you are already working with a document in an Office application but want to create a new file. Simply click the File tab and click New. Click *Blank document* (or *Blank presentation* or *Blank workbook*, depending on the specific application).

Open a File Using the Open Dialog Box

STEP 1 ⟩⟩ You may choose to open a previously saved file, such as when you work with the data files for this book or when you want to access any previously created file. You will work with the Open dialog box, as shown in Figure 1.30. The Open dialog box displays after you click Open from the File tab. You will click Computer and the folder or drive where your document is stored.

If it is not listed under Recent Folders, you can browse for it. Using the Navigation Pane, you will make your way to the file to be opened. Double-click the file or click the file name once and click Open. Most likely, the file will be located within a folder that is appropriately named to make it easy to find related files. Obviously, if you are not well acquainted with the file's location and file name, the process of opening a file could become quite cumbersome. However, if you have created a well-designed system of folders, as you learned to do in the "Files and Folders" section of this chapter, you will know exactly where to find the file.

FIGURE 1.30 Open Dialog Box

Open a File Using the Recent Documents List

STEP 3 ››› You will often work with a file, save it, and then continue the project at a later time. Office simplifies the task of reopening the file by providing a Recent Documents list with links to your most recently opened files (see Figure 1.31). To access the list, click the File tab, click Open, and then select Recent Documents. Click any file listed in the Recent Documents list to open that document. The list constantly changes to reflect only the most recently opened files, so if it has been quite some time since you worked with a particular file, you might have to work with the Open dialog box instead of the Recent Documents list.

FIGURE 1.31 Recent Documents List

TIP   Keeping Files on the Recent Documents List

The Recent Documents list displays a limited list of only the most recently opened files. You might, however, want to keep a particular file in the list regardless of how recently it was opened. In Figure 1.31, note the *Pin this item to the list* icon displays to the right of each file. Click the icon to pin the file to the list. At that point, you will always have access to the file by clicking the File tab and selecting the file from the Recent Documents list. The pushpin of the "permanent" file will change direction so that it appears to be inserted, indicating that it is a pinned item. If later you want to remove the file from the list, click the inserted pushpin, changing its direction and allowing the file to be bumped off the list when other, more recently opened, files take its place.

Open a File from the Templates List

You do not need to create a new file if you can access a predesigned file that meets your needs or one that you can modify fairly quickly to complete your project. Office provides templates, making them available when you click the File tab and New (see Figure 1.32). The Templates list is comprised of template groups available within the current Office installation on your computer. The Search box can be used to locate other templates that are available from Office.com. When you click one of the Suggested searches, you are presented with additional choices.

For example, you might want to prepare a home budget. After opening a blank worksheet in Excel, click the File tab and click New. From the template categories, you could click Budget from the *Suggested searches* list, scroll down until you find the right template, such as Family Budget, and then click Create to display the associated worksheet (or simply double-click Family Budget). If a Help window displays along with the worksheet template, click to close it or explore Help to learn more about the template. If you know only a little bit about Excel, you could then make a few changes so that the worksheet would accurately represent your family's financial situation. The budget would be prepared much more quickly than if you began the project with a blank workbook, designing it yourself.

FIGURE 1.32 Working with Templates

Templates available from Office.com

Templates available in a typical Office installation

Printing a File

There will be occasions when you will want to print an Office project. Before printing, you should preview the file to get an idea of how it will look when printed. That way, if there are obvious problems with the page setup, you can correct them before wasting paper on something that is not correct. When you are ready to print, you can select from various print options, including the number of copies and the specific pages to print. If you know that the page setup is correct and that there are no unique print settings to select, you can simply print the project without adjusting any print settings.

STEP 2 >>

It is a good idea to take a look at how your document will appear before you print it. The Print Preview feature of Office enables you to do just that. In the Print pane, you will see all items, including any headers, footers, graphics, and special formatting. To view a project before printing, click the File tab and click Print. The subsequent Backstage view shows the file preview on the right, with print settings located in the center of the Backstage screen. Figure 1.33 shows a typical Backstage Print view.

Print Preview
Print
Print Settings
Zoom to Page
Show Margins

FIGURE 1.33 Backstage Print View

To show the margins of the document, click Show Margins (see Figure 1.33). To increase the size of the file preview, click *Zoom to Page* (see Figure 1.33). Both are found on the bottom-right corner of the preview. Remember that increasing the font size by adjusting the zoom applies to the current display only; it does not actually increase the font size when the document is printed or saved. To return the preview to its original view, click *Zoom to Page* once more.

Other options in the Backstage Print view vary depending on the application in which you are working. Regardless of the Office application, you will be able to access Settings options from the Backstage view, including page orientation (landscape or portrait), margins, and paper size. You will find a more detailed explanation of those settings in the "Page Layout Tab Tasks" section later in this chapter. To print a file, click Print (see Figure 1.33).

The Backstage Print view shown in Figure 1.33 is very similar across all Office applications. However, you will find slight variations specific to each application. For example, PowerPoint's Backstage Print view includes options for printing slides and handouts in various configurations and colors, whereas Excel's focuses on worksheet selections and Word's includes document options. Regardless of software, the manner of working with the Backstage view print options remains consistent.

Closing a File and Application

Although you can have several documents open at one time, limiting the number of open files is a good idea. Office applications have no problem keeping up with multiple open files, but you can easily become overwhelmed with them. When you are done with an open project, you will need to close it.

You can easily close any files that you no longer need. With the desired file on the screen, click the FILE tab and click the Close (X) button. Respond to any prompt that might display suggesting that you save the file. The application remains open, but the selected file is closed. To close the application, click the Close (X) button in the top-right corner.

TIP Closing an Application

When you close an application, all open files within the application are also closed. You will be prompted to save any files before they are closed. A quick way to close an application is to click the X in the top-right corner of the application window.

Quick
Concepts

1. You want to continue to work with a PowerPoint presentation that you worked with yesterday, but cannot remember where you saved the presentation on your hard drive. How can you open a file that you recently worked with? *p. 37*

2. As part of your job search, you plan to develop a resume. However, you find it difficult to determine the right style for your resume, and wish you could begin with a predesigned document that you could modify. Is that possible with Word? If so, what steps would you take to locate a predesigned resume? *p. 38*

3. Closing a file is not the same as closing an application, such as closing Excel. What is the difference? *p. 39*

Hands-On Exercises

Watch the Video
for this Hands-
On Exercise!

MyITLab®
HOE4 Training

4 The Backstage View Tasks

Projects related to the Spotted Begonia Art Gallery's functions have begun to come in for your review and approval. You have received an informational flyer to be distributed to schools and supporting organizations around the city. It contains a new logo along with descriptive text. Another task on your agenda is to keep the project moving according to schedule. You will identify a calendar template to print and distribute. You will explore printing options, and you will save the flyer and the calendar as directed by your instructor.

Skills covered: Open and Save a File • Preview and Print a File • Open a File from the Recent Documents List and Open a Template

You have asked your staff to develop a flyer that can be used to promote the Spotted Begonia Art Gallery. You will open a Word document that may be used for the flyer, and you will save the document to a disk drive. Refer to Figure 1.34 as you complete Step 1.

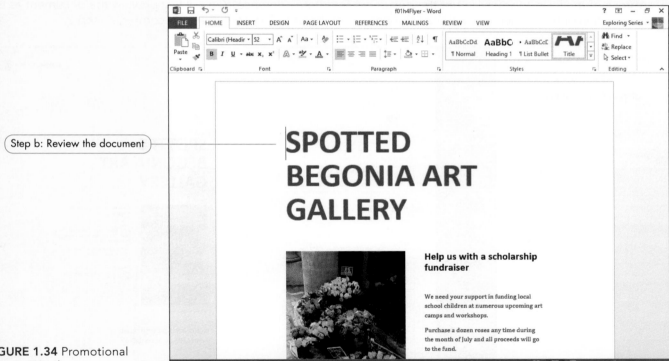

Step b: Review the document

FIGURE 1.34 Promotional Flyer in Word

a. Navigate to the Start screen. Scroll across the tiles, if necessary, and click **Word 2013**. Click **Open Other Documents** at the bottom-left corner of the Word 2013 window.

You have opened Microsoft Word because it is the program in which the promotional flyer is saved.

b. Click **Computer** and click **Browse**. Navigate to the location of your student files. Double-click *f01h4Flyer* to open the file shown in Figure 1.34. Familiarize yourself with the document. Then, if necessary, click **Read Mode** in the *View shortcuts* group on the Status bar to change to that view. Read through the document.

The graphic and the flyer are submitted for your approval. A paragraph next to the graphic will serve as the launching point for an information blitz and the beginning of the fundraising drive.

Read Mode displays the document. If the document is large enough, multiple screens may display. You can use the arrows found on the middle edges of the document to navigate and view the entire document.

c. Click **Print Layout** on the Status bar to change to that view. Click the **FILE tab** and click **Save As**.

You choose the Save As command because you know that it enables you to indicate the location to which the file should be saved, as well as the file name.

d. Click **Browse**, navigate to the drive where you save your files, and then double-click the **Artists folder** you created earlier. Double-click **Office Records**, click in the **File name box**, type **f01h4Flyer_LastFirst**, and then click **Save**.

STEP 2 ≫ PREVIEW AND PRINT A FILE

You approve of the flyer, so you will print the document for future reference. You will first preview the document as it will appear when printed. Then you will print the document. Refer to Figure 1.35 as you complete Step 2.

FIGURE 1.35 Backstage Print

Step e: Copies spin arrow

Step a: Print Preview

Step b: Zoom slider

a. Click the **FILE tab** and click **Print**.

Figure 1.35 shows the flyer preview. It is always a good idea to check the way a file will look when printed before actually printing it.

b. Drag the **Zoom slider** to increase the document view. Click **Zoom to Page** to return to the original size.

c. Click **Portrait Orientation** in the Print settings area in the center of the screen. Click **Landscape Orientation** to show the flyer in a wider and shorter view.

d. Click **Landscape Orientation** and click **Portrait Orientation** to return to the original view.

You decide that the flyer is more attractive in portrait orientation, so you return to that setting.

e. Click the **Copies spin arrow** repeatedly to increase the copies to **5**.

You will need to print five copies of the flyer to distribute to the office assistants for their review.

f. Click **Close** on the left side of the screen. When asked, click **Don't Save** so that changes to the file are not saved. Keep Word open for the next step.

STEP 3 ⟩⟩ OPEN A FILE FROM THE RECENT DOCUMENTS LIST AND OPEN A TEMPLATE

A large part of your responsibility is proofreading Spotted Begonia Art Gallery material. You will correct an error by adding a phone number in the promotional flyer. You must also keep the staff on task, so you will identify a calendar template on which to list tasks and deadlines. Refer to Figure 1.36 as you complete Step 3.

Step a: Recently opened flyer

Step b: Type phone number

FIGURE 1.36 Recent Documents List

a. Click the **FILE tab**, click **Recent Documents** if necessary, and then click **f01h4Flyer_LastFirst** in the **Recent Documents list**.

> **TROUBLESHOOTING:** If the file opens in Read Mode, use the status bar to change to the Print Layout view.

b. Press **Ctrl+End** to move the insertion point to the end of the document and press **Enter**. Type **1-335-555-5555**.

Figure 1.36 shows the phone number correction.

c. Click **Save** on the Quick Access Toolbar, click the **FILE tab**, and then click **Close**.

When you click Save on the Quick Access Toolbar, the document is saved in the same location with the same file name as was indicated in the previous save.

d. Click the **FILE tab** and click **New**. Click **Calendar** from the list of the *Suggested searches* category just beneath the *Search online templates* box.

Office.com provides a wide range of calendar choices. You will select one that is appealing and that will help you keep projects on track.

e. Click a calendar of your choice from the gallery and click **Create**. Respond to and close any windows that may open.

The calendar that you selected opens in Word.

TROUBLESHOOTING: It is possible to select a template that is not certified by Microsoft. In that case, you might have to confirm your acceptance of settings before you click Download.

---

f. Click **Save** on the Quick Access Toolbar. If necessary, navigate to your Office Records subfolder (a subfolder of Artists) on the drive where you are saving your student files. Save the document as **f01h4Calendar_LastFirst**. Because this is the first time to save the calendar file, the Save button on the Quick Access Toolbar opens a dialog box in which you must indicate the location of the file and the file name.

g. Click **Save** and exit Word. Submit your files based on your instructor's directions.

Home Tab Tasks

You will find that you will repeat some tasks often, whether in Word, Excel, or PowerPoint. You will frequently want to change the format of numbers or words, selecting a different *font* or changing font size or color. A font is a complete set of characters, both upper- and lowercase letters, numbers, punctuation marks, and special symbols, with the same design including size, spacing, and shape. You might also need to change the alignment of text or worksheet cells. Undoubtedly, you will find a reason to copy or cut items and paste them elsewhere in the document, presentation, or worksheet. And you might want to modify file contents by finding and replacing text. All of those tasks, and more, are found on the Home tab of the Ribbon in Word, Excel, and PowerPoint. The Access interface is unique, sharing little with other Office applications, so this section will not address Access.

In this section, you will explore the Home tab, learning to format text, copy and paste items, and find and replace words or phrases. Figure 1.37 shows Home tab groups and tasks in the various applications. Note the differences and similarities between the groups.

FIGURE 1.37 Home Tab in Word, PowerPoint, and Excel

Selecting and Editing Text

After creating a document, worksheet, or presentation, you will probably want to make some changes. You might prefer to center a title, or maybe you think that certain budget worksheet totals should be formatted as currency. You can change the font so that typed characters are larger or in a different style. You might even want to underline text to add emphasis. In all Office applications, the Home tab provides tools for selecting and editing text. You can also use the Mini toolbar for making quick changes to selected text.

Select Text to Edit

Before making any changes to existing text or numbers, you must first select the characters. A general rule that you should commit to memory is "Select, then do." A foolproof way to select text or numbers is to place the mouse pointer before the first character of the text you want to select, and then drag to highlight the intended selection. Before you drag, be sure that the mouse pointer takes on the shape of the letter I, called the *I-bar*. Although other methods for selecting exist, if you remember only one way, it should be the click-and-drag method. If your attempted selection falls short of highlighting the intended area, or perhaps highlights too much, simply click outside the selection and try again.

Sometimes it can be difficult to precisely select a small amount of text, such as a single character or a single word. Other times, the task can be overwhelming, such as when selecting an entire 550-page document. Shortcut methods for making selections in Word and PowerPoint are shown in Table 1.3. When working with Excel, you will more often need to select multiple cells. Simply drag the intended selection, usually when the mouse pointer displays as a large white plus sign. The shortcuts shown in Table 1.3 are primarily applicable to Word and PowerPoint.

TABLE 1.3 Shortcut Selection in Word and PowerPoint

Item Selected	Action
One word	Double-click the word.
One line of text	Place the mouse pointer at the left of the line, in the margin area. When the mouse changes to a right-pointing arrow, click to select the line.
One sentence	Press and hold Ctrl while you click in the sentence to select.
One paragraph	Triple-click in the paragraph.
One character to the left of the insertion point	Press and hold Shift while you press the left arrow on the keyboard.
One character to the right of the insertion point	Press and hold Shift while you press the right arrow on the keyboard.
Entire document	Press and hold Ctrl while you press A on the keyboard.

After having selected a string of characters, such as a number, word, sentence, or document, you can do more than simply format the selection. Suppose you have selected a word. If you begin to type another word, the newly typed word will immediately replace the selected word. With an item selected, you can press Delete to remove the selection. You will learn later in this chapter that you can also find, replace, copy, move, and paste selected text.

Use the Mini Toolbar

STEP 3 ❯❯

You have learned that you can always use commands on the Ribbon to change selected text within a document, worksheet, or presentation. All it takes is locating the desired command on the Home tab and clicking to select it. Although using the Home tab to perform commands is simple enough, an item called the *Mini toolbar* provides an even faster way to accomplish some of the same formatting changes. When you select any amount of text within a worksheet, document, or presentation, you can move the mouse pointer only slightly within the selection to display the Mini toolbar (see Figure 1.38). The Mini toolbar provides access to the most common formatting selections, such as adding bold or italic, or changing font type or color. Unlike the Quick Access Toolbar, the Mini toolbar is not customizable, which means that you cannot add or remove options from the toolbar.

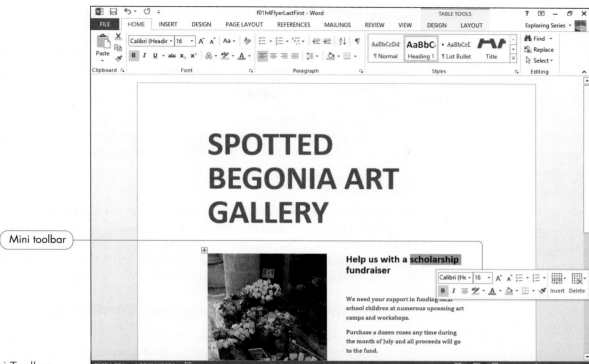

Mini toolbar

FIGURE 1.38 Mini Toolbar

The Mini toolbar will display only when text is selected. The closer the mouse pointer is to the Mini toolbar, the darker the toolbar becomes. As you move the mouse pointer away from the Mini toolbar, it becomes almost transparent. Make any selections from the Mini toolbar by clicking the corresponding button. To temporarily remove the Mini toolbar from view, press Esc.

If you want to permanently disable the Mini toolbar so that it does not display in any open file when text is selected, click the FILE tab and click Options. As shown in Figure 1.39, click General, if necessary. Deselect the *Show Mini Toolbar on selection* setting by clicking the check box to the left of the setting and clicking OK.

General

Click to disable the Mini toolbar

FIGURE 1.39 Disabling the Mini Toolbar

Apply Font Attributes

The way characters appear onscreen, including qualities such as size, spacing, and shape, is determined by the font. Each Office application has a default font, which is the font that will be in effect unless you change it. Other font attributes include boldfacing, italicizing, and font color, all of which can be applied to selected text. Some formatting changes, such as Bold and Italic, are called *toggle* commands. They act somewhat like light switches that you can turn on and off. For example, after having selected a word that you want to add bold to, click Bold in the Font group of the Home tab to turn the setting "on." If, at a later time, you want to remove bold from the word, select it again and click Bold. This time, the button turns "off" the bold formatting.

Change the Font

All applications within the Office suite provide a set of fonts from which you can choose. If you prefer a font other than the default, or if you want to apply a different font to a section of your project for added emphasis or interest, you can easily make the change by selecting a font from within the Font group on the Home tab. You can also change the font by selecting from the Mini toolbar, although that works only if you have first selected text.

Change the Font Size, Color, and Attributes

STEP 2 ▶▶

At times, you will want to make the font size larger or smaller, change the font color, underline selected text, or apply other font attributes. For example, if you are creating a handout for a special event, you may want to apply a different font to emphasize key information such as dates and times. Because such changes are commonplace, Office places those formatting commands in many convenient places within each Office application.

You can find the most common formatting commands in the Font group on the Home tab. As noted earlier, Word, Excel, and PowerPoint all share very similar Font groups that provide access to tasks related to changing the character font (refer to Figure 1.37). Remember that you can place the mouse pointer over any command icon to view a summary of the icon's purpose, so although the icons might at first appear cryptic, you can use the mouse pointer to quickly determine the purpose and applicability to your desired text change. You can also find a subset of those commands plus a few additional choices on the Mini toolbar.

If the font change that you plan to make is not included as a choice on either the Home tab or the Mini toolbar, you can probably find what you are looking for in the Font dialog box. Click the Dialog Box Launcher in the bottom-right corner of the Font group. Figure 1.40 shows a sample Font dialog box. Because the Font dialog box provides many formatting choices in one window, you can make several changes at once. Depending on the application, the contents of the Font dialog box vary slightly, but the purpose is consistent—providing access to choices related to modifying characters.

FIGURE 1.40 Font Dialog Box

Using the Clipboard Group Commands

On occasion, you will want to move or copy a selection from one area to another. Suppose that you have included text on a PowerPoint slide that you believe would be more appropriate on a different slide. Or perhaps an Excel formula should be copied from one cell to another because both cells should be totaled in the same manner. You can easily move the slide text or copy the Excel formula by using options found in the Clipboard group on the Home tab. The Office *Clipboard* is an area of memory reserved to temporarily hold selections that have been *cut* or *copied* and allows you to paste the selections. To cut means to remove a selection from the original location and place it in the Office Clipboard. To copy means to duplicate a selection from the original location and place a copy in the Office Clipboard. Although the Clipboard can hold up to 24 items at one time, the usual procedure is to *paste* the cut or copied selection to its final destination fairly quickly. To paste means to place a cut or copied selection into another location. When the computer is shut down or loses power, the contents of the Clipboard are erased, so it is important to finalize the paste procedure during the current session.

The Clipboard group enables you not only to copy and cut text and objects but also to copy formatting. Perhaps you have applied a font style to a major heading of a report and you realize that the same formatting should be applied to other headings. Especially if the heading includes multiple formatting features, you will save a great deal of time by copying the entire set of formatting options to the other headings. In so doing, you will ensure the consistency of formatting for all headings because they will appear exactly alike. Using the Clipboard group's *Format Painter*, you can quickly and easily copy all formatting from one area to another in Word, PowerPoint, and Excel.

In Office, you can usually accomplish the same task in several ways. Although the Ribbon provides ample access to formatting and Clipboard commands (such as Format Painter, Cut, Copy, and Paste), you might find it convenient to access the same commands on a *shortcut menu*. Right-click a selected item or text to open a shortcut menu such as the one shown in Figure 1.41. A shortcut menu is also called a *context menu* because the contents of the menu vary depending on the location at which you right-clicked.

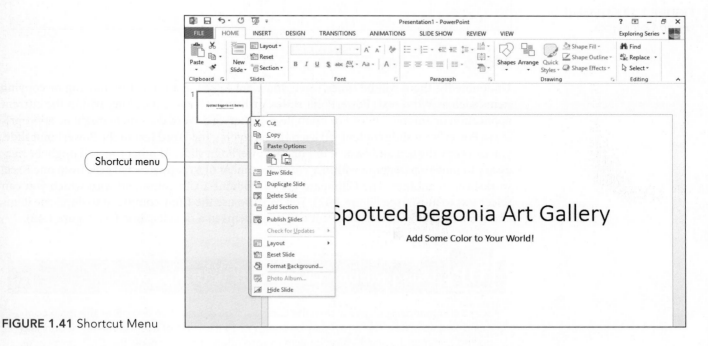

FIGURE 1.41 Shortcut Menu

Copy Formats with the Format Painter

STEP 3» As described earlier, the Format Painter makes it easy to copy formatting features from one selection to another. You will find the Format Painter command conveniently located in the Clipboard group of the Home tab (see Figure 1.42). To copy a format, you must first select the text containing the desired format. If you want to copy the format to only one other selection, *single-click* Format Painter. If, however, you plan to copy the same format to multiple areas, *double-click* Format Painter. As you move the mouse pointer, you will find that it has the appearance of a paintbrush with an attached I-bar. Select the area to which the copied format should be applied. If you single-clicked Format Painter to copy the format to one other selection, Format Painter turns off once the formatting has been applied. If you double-clicked Format Painter to copy the format to multiple locations, continue selecting text in various locations to apply the format. Then, to turn off Format Painter, click Format Painter again or press Esc.

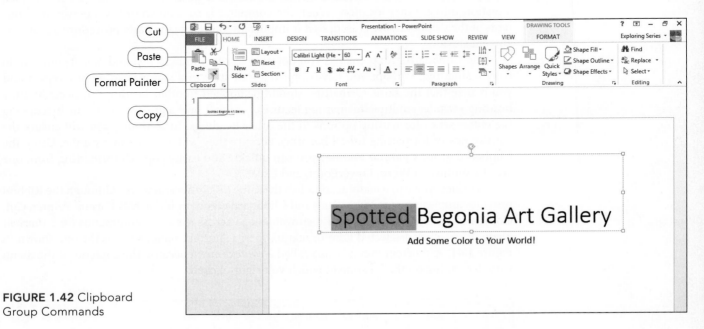

FIGURE 1.42 Clipboard Group Commands

Move and Copy Text

Undoubtedly, there will be times when you want to revise a project by moving or copying items such as Word text, PowerPoint slides, or Excel cell contents, either within the current application or among others. For example, a section of a Word document might be appropriate as PowerPoint slide content. To keep from retyping the Word text in the PowerPoint slide, you can copy the text and paste it in a blank PowerPoint slide. At other times, it might be necessary to move a paragraph within a Word document or to copy selected cells from one Excel worksheet to another. The Clipboard group contains a Cut command with which you can select text to move (see Figure 1.42). You can also use the Copy command to duplicate items and the Paste command to place cut or copied items in a final location (see Figure 1.42).

TIP | Using Ribbon Commands with Arrows

Some commands, such as Paste in the Clipboard group, contain two parts: the main command and an arrow. The arrow may be below or to the right of the command, depending on the command, window size, or screen resolution. Instructions in the *Exploring* series use the command name to instruct you to click the main command to perform the default action (e.g., Click Paste). Instructions include the word *arrow* when you need to select the arrow to access an additional option (e.g., Click the Paste arrow).

The first step in moving or copying text is to select the text. Then do the following:

1. Click the appropriate icon in the Clipboard group either to cut or copy the selection. Remember that cut or copied text is actually placed in the Clipboard, remaining there even after you paste it to another location. It is important to note that you can paste the same item multiple times, because it will remain in the Clipboard until you power down your computer or until the Clipboard exceeds 24 items.

2. Click the location where you want the cut or copied text to be placed. The location can be in the current file or in another open file within any Office application.

3. Click Paste in the Clipboard group on the HOME tab.

In addition to using the Clipboard group icons, you can also cut, copy, and paste in any of the ways listed in Table 1.4.

TABLE 1.4 Cut, Copy, and Paste Options

Command	Actions
Cut	• Click Cut in Clipboard group. • Right-click selection and select Cut. • Press Ctrl+X.
Copy	• Click Copy in Clipboard group. • Right-click selection and select Copy. • Press Ctrl+C.
Paste	• Click in destination location and select Paste in Clipboard group. • Right-click in destination location and select Paste. • Click in destination location and press Ctrl+V. • Click the Clipboard Dialog Box Launcher to open the Clipboard task pane. Click in destination location. With the Clipboard task pane open, click the arrow beside the intended selection and select Paste.

Use the Office Clipboard

When you cut or copy selections, they are placed in the Office Clipboard. Regardless of which Office application you are using, you can view the Clipboard by clicking the Clipboard Dialog Box Launcher, as shown in Figure 1.43.

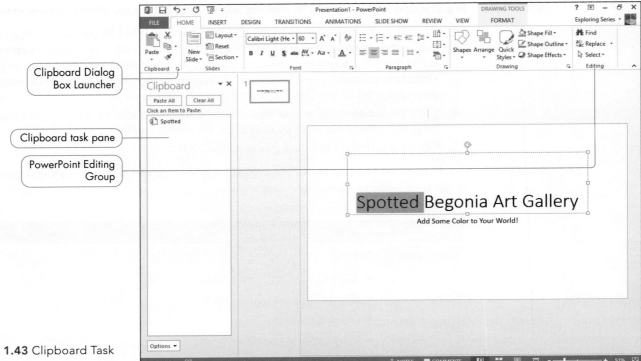

Clipboard Dialog Box Launcher

Clipboard task pane

PowerPoint Editing Group

FIGURE 1.43 Clipboard Task Pane

Unless you specify otherwise when beginning a paste operation, the most recently added Clipboard item is pasted. You can, however, select an item from the Clipboard task pane to paste. Similarly, you can delete items from the Clipboard by making a selection in the Clipboard task pane. You can remove all items from the Clipboard by clicking Clear All. The Options button in the Clipboard task pane enables you to control when and where the Clipboard is displayed. Close the Clipboard task pane by clicking the Close (X) button in the top-right corner of the task pane or by clicking the arrow in the title bar of the Clipboard task pane and selecting Close.

Using the Editing Group Commands

The process of finding and replacing text is easily accomplished through options in the Editing group of the Home tab. The Editing group also enables you to select all contents of a project document, all text with similar formatting, or specific objects, such as pictures or charts. The Editing group is found at the far-right side of the Home tab in Excel, Word, and PowerPoint.

The Excel Editing group is unique in that it also includes options for sorting, filtering, and clearing cell contents; filling cells; and summarizing numeric data. Because those commands are relevant only to Excel, this chapter will not address them specifically.

Find and Replace Text

STEP 4 ≫ Especially if you are working with a lengthy project, manually seeking a specific word or phrase can be time-consuming. Office enables you not only to *find* each occurrence of a series of characters, but also to *replace* what it finds with another series. You will at times find it necessary to locate each occurrence of a text item so that you can replace it with another or so that you can delete, move, or copy it. If you have consistently misspelled a person's name throughout a document, you can find the misspelling and replace it with the correct spelling in a matter of a few seconds, no matter how many times the misspelling occurs in the document. To begin the process of finding and replacing a specific item:

1. Click Replace in the Editing group on the HOME tab of Word or PowerPoint.
2. Or click Find & Select in the Editing group on the HOME tab of Excel. Then click Replace. The dialog box that displays enables you to indicate the word or phrase to find and replace.

The Advanced Find feature is one that you will use often as you work with documents in Word. It is beneficial to find each occurrence of a word you are searching for. But it is also very helpful to see all the occurrences of the word at once. Click Reading Highlight in the *Find and Replace* dialog box and select Highlight All to display each word highlighted, as shown in Figure 1.44. Click Reading Highlight again and select Clear Highlighting to remove the illumination.

FIGURE 1.44 Highlight All

TIP **Using a Shortcut to Find Items**

Ctrl+F is a shortcut used to find items in a Word, Excel, or PowerPoint file. When you press Ctrl+F, the *Find and Replace* dialog box displays in Excel and PowerPoint. Pressing Ctrl+F in Word displays a feature—the Navigation Pane—at the left side of a Word document. When you type a search term in the Search Document area, Word finds and highlights all occurrences of the search term. The Navigation Pane also makes it easy to move to sections of a document based on levels of headings.

To find and replace selected text, type the text to locate in the *Find what* box and the replacement text in the *Replace with* box. You can narrow the search to require matching case or find whole words only. If you want to replace all occurrences of the text, click Replace All. If you want to replace only some occurrences, click Find Next repeatedly until you reach the occurrence that you want to replace. At that point, click Replace. When you are finished, click the Close button (or click Cancel).

Use Advanced Find and Replace Features

The *Find and Replace* feature enables you not only to find and replace text, but also to restrict and alter the format of the text at the same time. To establish the format criteria associated with either the *Find or Replace* portion of the operation:

1. Click the More button to expand the dialog box options. Click Format in the bottom-left corner of the dialog box.
2. Add formatting characteristics from the Font dialog box or Paragraph dialog box (as well as many other formatting features).

In addition to applying special formatting parameters on a *Find and Replace* operation, you can specify that you want to find or replace special characters. Click Special at the bottom of the *Find and Replace* dialog box to view the punctuation characters from which you can choose. For example, you might want to look for all instances in a document where an exclamation point is being used and replace it with a period.

An Excel worksheet can include more than 1,000,000 rows of data. A Word document's length is unlimited. Moving to a specific point in large files created in either of those applications can be a challenge. That task is simplified by the Go To option, found in the Editing group as an option of the Find command in Word (or under Find & Select in Excel). Click Go To and enter the page number (or other item, such as section, comment, bookmark, or footnote) in Word or the specific Excel cell. Click Go To in Word (or OK in Excel).

Quick
Concepts

1. After selecting text in a presentation or document, you see a small transparent bar with formatting options displayed just above the selection. What is the bar called and what is its purpose? *p. 46*

2. What is the difference between using a single-click on the Format Painter and using a double-click? *p. 50*

3. What is the first step in cutting or copying text? How are cutting and copying related to the concept of the Clipboard? *p. 51*

4. What feature can you use to very quickly locate and replace text in a document? Provide an example of when you might want to find text but not replace it. *p. 52*

Hands-On Exercises

Watch the Video for this Hands-On Exercise!

MyITLab®
HOE5 Training

5 Home Tab Tasks

You have created a list of potential contributors to the Spotted Begonia Art Gallery. You have used Excel to record that list in worksheet format. Now you will review the worksheet and format its appearance to make it more attractive. You will also modify a promotional flyer. In working with those projects, you will put into practice the formatting, copying, moving, and editing information from the preceding section.

Skills covered: Move, Copy, and Paste Text • Select Text, Apply Font Attributes, and Use the Mini Toolbar • Use Format Painter and Work with the Mini Toolbar • Use the Font Dialog Box and Find and Replace Text

STEP 1 ≫ MOVE, COPY, AND PASTE TEXT

Each contributor to the Spotted Begonia Art Gallery is assigned a contact person. You manage the worksheet that keeps track of those assignments, but the assignments sometimes change. You will copy and paste some worksheet selections to keep from having to retype data. You will also reposition a clip art image to improve the worksheet's appearance. Refer to Figure 1.45 as you complete Step 1.

FIGURE 1.45 Contributor List (Excel)

a. Navigate to the Start screen. Scroll across the tiles, if necessary, and click **Excel 2013**. Click **Open Other Workbooks**.

You have opened Microsoft Excel because it is the program in which the contributors list is saved.

b. Open the student data file *f01h5Contributors*. Save the file as **f01h5Contributors_LastFirst** in the Office Records folder (a subfolder of Artists) you created.

The potential contributors list shown in Figure 1.45 is displayed.

c. Click **cell C7** to select the cell that contains *Nester, Ali*, and click **Copy** in the Clipboard group on the HOME tab. Click **cell C15** to select the cell that contains *Sammons, Roger*, click **Paste** in the Clipboard group, and then press **Esc** to remove the selection from *Nester, Ali*.

Ali Nester has been assigned as the Spotted Begonia Art Gallery contact for Harris Foster, replacing Roger Sammons. You make that replacement on the worksheet by copying and pasting Ali Nester's name in the appropriate worksheet cell.

d. Click the picture of the begonia. A box displays around the image, indicating that it is selected. Click **Cut** in the Clipboard group, click **cell D2**, and then click **Paste**. Drag the picture to resize and position it as needed (see Figure 1.45) so that it does not block any information in the list. Click anywhere outside the begonia picture to deselect it.

You decide that the picture of the begonia will look better if it is placed on the right side of the worksheet instead of the left. You move the picture by cutting and pasting the object.

> **TROUBLESHOOTING:** A Paste Options icon might display in the worksheet after you have moved the begonia picture. It offers additional options related to the paste procedure. You do not need to change any options, so ignore the button.

e. Click **Save** on the Quick Access Toolbar. Click **Minimize** to minimize the worksheet without closing it.

STEP 2 ▶ SELECT TEXT, APPLY FONT ATTRIBUTES, AND USE THE MINI TOOLBAR

As the opening of a new showing at the Spotted Begonia Art Gallery draws near, you are active in preparing promotional materials. You are currently working on an informational flyer that is almost set to go. You will make a few improvements before approving the flyer for release. Refer to Figure 1.46 as you complete Step 2.

Steps b–d: Enter and edit text

Step f: Set font size to 14

FIGURE 1.46 Promotional Flyer (Word)

a. Navigate to the Start screen. Scroll across the tiles, if necessary, and click **Word 2013**. Click **Open Other Documents**. Open *f01h5Event* and save the document as **f01h5Event_LastFirst** in the Promotional Print folder (a subfolder of Artists) you created.

You plan to modify the promotional flyer slightly to include additional information about the Spotted Begonia Art Gallery.

> **TROUBLESHOOTING:** If you make any major mistakes in this exercise, you can close the file without saving it, open *f01h5Event* again, and then start this exercise over.

b. Click after the exclamation mark after the word *more* at the end of the first paragraph. Press **Enter** and type the following text. As you type, do not press Enter at the end of each line. Word will automatically wrap the lines of text.

All items are for sale on the day of the event. Start your holiday shopping early! You'll find gifts for everyone on your list.

> **TROUBLESHOOTING:** If you make any mistakes while typing, press Backspace and correct them.

c. Select the sentence beginning with *You'll find gifts*. Press **Delete**.

When you press Delete, selected text (or characters to the right of the insertion point) is removed. Deleted text is not placed in the Clipboard.

d. Select the words *Start your holiday shopping early!* Click **Italic** in the Font group on the HOME tab and click anywhere outside the selection to see the result.

e. Select both paragraphs but not the final italicized line. While still within the selection, move the mouse pointer slightly to display the Mini toolbar, click the **Font arrow** on the Mini toolbar, and then scroll to select **Verdana**.

> **TROUBLESHOOTING:** If you do not see the Mini toolbar, you might have moved too far away from the selection. In that case, click outside the selection and drag to select it once more. Without leaving the selection, move the mouse pointer slightly to display the Mini toolbar.

You have changed the font of the two paragraphs.

f. Click after the period following the word *event* before the last sentence in the second paragraph. Press **Enter** and press **Delete** to remove the extra space before the first letter, if necessary. Drag to select the new line, click **Font Size arrow** in the Font group, and then select **14**. Click anywhere outside the selected area. Your document should appear as shown in Figure 1.46.

You have increased font size to draw attention to the text.

g. Save the document and keep open for Step 3.

STEP 3 ›› USE FORMAT PAINTER AND WORK WITH THE MINI TOOLBAR

You are on a short timeline for finalizing the promotional flyer, so you will use a few shortcuts to avoid retyping and reformatting more than is necessary. You know that you can easily copy formatting from one area to another using Format Painter. The Mini toolbar can also help you make changes quickly. Refer to Figure 1.47 as you complete Step 3.

Step b: Formatting applied

Step c: Increase font size to 16

FIGURE 1.47 Promotional Flyer (Word)

a. Select the words *Fall Gallery Event* in the first paragraph and click **Format Painter** in the Clipboard group.

b. Select the words *items are for sale* in the sixth line. Click anywhere outside the selection to deselect the phrase.

   The format of the area that you first selected (*Fall Gallery Event*) is applied to the line containing the phrase.

c. Select the text *Start your holiday shopping early!* in the Mini toolbar, click in the **Font Size box**, and then select **16** to increase the font size slightly. Click outside the selected area.

   Figure 1.47 shows the final document as it should now appear.

d. Save the document as **f01h5Stp3Event_LastFirst** in the Promotional Print folder you created and close Word. Submit your file based on your instructor's directions.

   The flyer will be saved with the same file name and in the same location as it was when you last saved the document in Step 2. As you close Word, the open document will also be closed.

STEP 4 ≫ USE THE FONT DIALOG BOX AND FIND AND REPLACE TEXT

The contributors worksheet is almost complete. However, you first want to make a few more formatting changes to improve the worksheet's appearance. You will also quickly change an incorrect area code by using Excel's *Find and Replace* feature. Refer to Figure 1.48 as you complete Step 4.

Step c: Open Fill Effects dialog box

Step c: Select a variant

FIGURE 1.48 Excel Format Cells Dialog Box

a. Click the **Excel icon** on the taskbar to redisplay the contributors worksheet that you minimized in Step 1.

The Excel potential contributors list displays.

> **TROUBLESHOOTING:** If you closed Excel, you can find the correct worksheet in your Recent Documents list.

b. Drag to select **cells A6** through **C6**.

> **TROUBLESHOOTING:** Make sure the mouse pointer looks like a large white plus sign before dragging. It is normal for the first cell in the selected area to be a different shade. If you click and drag when the mouse pointer does not resemble a white plus sign, text may be moved or duplicated. In that case, click Undo on the Quick Access Toolbar.

c. Click the **Dialog Box Launcher** in the Font group to display the Format Cells dialog box. Click the **Fill tab** and click **Fill Effects**, as shown in Figure 1.48. Click any style in the *Variants* section, click **OK**, and then click **OK** once more to close the Format Cells dialog box. Click outside the selected area to see the final result.

The headings of the worksheet are shaded more attractively.

d. Click **Find & Select** in the Editing group and click **Replace**. Type **410** in the **Find what box**. Type **411** in the **Replace with box**, click **Replace All**, and then click **OK** when notified that Excel has made seven replacements. Click **Close** in the *Find and Replace* dialog box.

You discovered that you consistently typed an incorrect area code. You used Find and Replace to make the corrections quickly.

e. Save the workbook as **f01h5Stp4Contributors_LastFirst** in the Office Records folder you created. Exit Excel, if necessary. Submit your files based on your instructor's directions.

Insert Tab Tasks

As its title implies, the Insert tab enables you to insert, or add, items into a file. Much of the Insert tab is specific to the particular application, with some commonalities to other Office applications. Word's Insert tab includes text-related commands, whereas Excel's is more focused on inserting such items as charts and tables. Word allows you to insert apps from the Microsoft app store, so you could add an application such as Merriam-Webster Dictionary. Both Word and Excel allow you to insert Apps for Office to build powerful Web-backed solutions. PowerPoint's Insert tab includes multimedia items and links. Despite their obvious differences in focus, all Office applications share a common group on the Insert tab—the Illustrations group. In addition, all Office applications enable you to insert headers, footers, text boxes, and symbols. Those options are also found on the Insert tab in various groups, depending on the particular application. In this section, you will work with common activities on the Insert tab, including inserting online pictures.

Inserting Objects

With few exceptions, all Office applications share common options in the Illustrations group of the Insert tab. PowerPoint places some of those common features in the Images group. You can insert pictures, shapes, and *SmartArt*. SmartArt is a diagram that presents information visually to effectively communicate a message. These items are considered objects, retaining their separate nature when they are inserted in files. That means that you can select them and manage them independently of the underlying document, worksheet, or presentation.

After an object has been inserted, you can click the object to select it or click anywhere outside the object to deselect it. When an object is selected, a border surrounds it with handles, or small dots, appearing at each corner and in the middle of each side. Figure 1.49 shows a selected object, surrounded by handles. Unless an object is selected, you cannot change or modify it. When an object is selected, the Ribbon expands to include one or more contextual tabs. Items on the contextual tabs relate to the selected object, enabling you to modify and manage it.

FIGURE 1.49 Selected Object

You can resize and move a selected object. Place the mouse pointer on any handle and drag (when the mouse pointer looks like a two-headed arrow) to resize the object. Be careful! If you drag a side handle, the object is likely to be skewed, possibly resulting in a poor image. Instead, drag a corner handle to proportionally resize the image. To move an object, drag the object when the mouse pointer looks like a four-headed arrow.

Insert Pictures

STEP 2 >>

Documents, worksheets, and presentations can include much more than just words and numbers. You can easily add energy and additional description to the project by including pictures and other graphic elements. Although a *picture* is usually just that—a digital photo—it is actually defined as a graphic element retrieved from storage media such as a hard drive or a CD. A picture could actually be a clip art item that you saved from the Internet onto your hard drive.

The process of inserting a picture is simple.

1. Click in the project where you want the picture to be placed. Make sure you know where the picture that you plan to use is stored.
2. Click the INSERT tab.
3. Click Pictures in the Illustrations group (or Images group in PowerPoint). The Insert Picture dialog box is shown in Figure 1.50. You can also use Online Pictures to search for and insert pictures.
4. Navigate to where your picture is saved and click Insert (or simply double-click the picture).

Insert Picture dialog box

FIGURE 1.50 Insert Picture Dialog Box

In addition, on some slide layouts, PowerPoint displays Pictures and Online Pictures buttons that you can click to search for and select a picture for the slide.

Insert and Modify SmartArt

The SmartArt feature enables you to create a diagram and to enter text to provide a visual representation of data. To create a SmartArt diagram, choose a diagram type that fits the purpose: List, Process, Cycle, Hierarchy, Relationships, Matrix, Pyramid, and Picture. You can get additional SmartArt diagrams at Office.com. To insert a SmartArt object, do the following:

1. Click the INSERT tab.
2. Click SmartArt in the Illustrations group to display the Choose a SmartArt Graphic dialog box.
3. Click the type of SmartArt diagram you want in the left pane of the dialog box.
4. Click the SmartArt subtype from the center pane.
5. Preview the selected SmartArt and subtype in the right pane and click OK.

Once you select the SmartArt diagram type and the subtype, a Text pane opens in which you can enter text. The text you enter displays within the selected object. If the SmartArt diagram contains more objects than you need, click the object and press Delete.

The SmartArt Tools Design tab enables you to customize the design of a SmartArt diagram. You can modify the diagram by changing its layout, colors, and style. The layout controls the construction of the diagram. The style controls the visual effects, such as embossing and rounded corners of the diagram. The SmartArt Tools Format tab controls the shape fill color, border, and size options.

Insert and Format Shapes

You can insert a shape to add a visual effect to a worksheet. You can insert various types of lines, rectangles, basic shapes (such as an oval, a pie shape, or a smiley face), block arrows, equation shapes, flowchart shapes, stars and banners, and callouts. You can insert shapes, such as a callout, to draw attention to particular worksheet data. To insert a shape, do the following:

1. Click the INSERT tab.
2. Click Shapes in the Illustrations group.
3. Select the shape you want to insert from the Shapes gallery.
4. Drag the cross-hair pointer to create the shape in the worksheet where you want it to appear.

After you insert the shape, the Drawing Tools Format tab displays so that you can change the shape, apply a shape style with fill color, and adjust the size.

Review Tab Tasks

As a final touch, you should always check a project for spelling, grammatical, and word usage errors. If the project is a collaborative effort, you and your colleagues might add comments and suggest changes. You can even use a thesaurus to find synonyms for words that are not quite right for your purpose. The Review tab in each Office application provides all these options and more. In this section, you will learn to review a file, checking for spelling and grammatical errors. You will also learn to use a thesaurus to identify synonyms.

Reviewing a File

As you create or edit a file, you will want to make sure no spelling or grammatical errors exist. You will also be concerned with wording, being sure to select words and phrases that best represent the purpose of the document, worksheet, or presentation. On occasion, you might even find yourself at a loss for an appropriate word. Not to worry. Word, Excel, and PowerPoint all provide standard tools for proofreading, including a spelling and grammar checker and a thesaurus.

Check Spelling and Grammar

STEP 1 > In general, all Office applications check your spelling and grammar as you type. If a word is unrecognized, it is flagged as misspelled or grammatically incorrect. Misspellings are identified with a red wavy underline, grammatical problems are underlined in green, and word usage errors (such as using *bear* instead of *bare*) have a blue underline. If the word or phrase is truly in error—that is, it is not a person's name or an unusual term that is not in the application's dictionary—you can correct it manually, or you can let the software correct it for you. If you right-click a word or phrase that is identified as a mistake, you will see a shortcut menu similar to that shown in Figure 1.51. If the application's dictionary can make a suggestion as to the correct spelling, you can click to accept the suggestion and make the change. If a grammatical rule is violated, you will have an opportunity to select a correction. However, if the text is actually correct, you can click Ignore or Ignore All (to bypass all occurrences of the flagged error in the current document). Click *Add to Dictionary* if you want the word to be considered correct whenever it appears in all documents. Similar selections on a shortcut menu enable you to ignore grammatical mistakes if they are not errors.

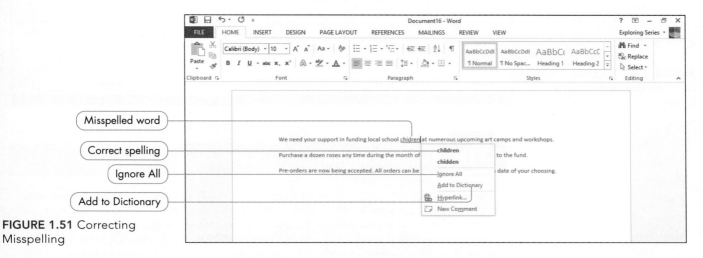

FIGURE 1.51 Correcting Misspelling

You might prefer the convenience of addressing possible misspellings and grammatical errors without having to examine each underlined word or phrase. To do so, click Spelling & Grammar in the Proofing group on the Review tab. Beginning at the top of the document, each identified error is highlighted in a pane similar to Figure 1.52. You can then choose how to address the problem by making a selection from the options in the pane.

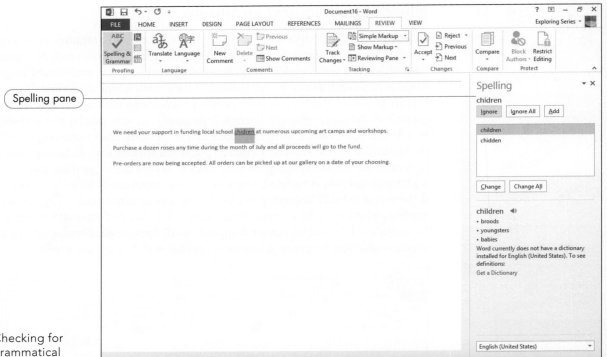

Spelling pane

FIGURE 1.52 Checking for Spelling and Grammatical Errors

Use the Thesaurus

As you write, there will be times when you are at a loss for an appropriate word. Perhaps you feel that you are overusing a word and want to find a suitable substitute. The Thesaurus is the Office tool to use in such a situation. Located in the Proofing group on the Review tab, Thesaurus enables you to search for synonyms, or words with similar meanings. Select a word and click Thesaurus in the Proofing group on the Review tab. A task pane displays on the right side of the screen, and synonyms are listed similar to those shown in Figure 1.53. You can also use the Thesaurus before typing a word to find substitutes. Simply click Thesaurus and type the word for which you are seeking a synonym in the Search box. Press Enter or click the magnifying glass to the right of the Search box for some suggestions. Finally, you can also identify synonyms when you right-click a word and point to Synonyms (if any are available). Click any word from the options offered to place it in the document.

Thesaurus pane

FIGURE 1.53 Thesaurus

Page Layout Tab Tasks

When you prepare a document or worksheet, you are concerned with the way the project appears onscreen and possibly in print. Unlike Word and Excel, a PowerPoint presentation is usually designed as a slide show, so it is not nearly as critical to concern yourself with page layout settings. The Page Layout tab in Word and Excel provides access to a full range of options such as margin settings and page orientation. In this section, you will identify page layout settings that are common to Office applications.

Because a document is most often designed to be printed, you will want to make sure it looks its best in printed form. That means that you will need to know how to adjust margins and how to change the page orientation. Perhaps the document or spreadsheet should be centered on the page vertically or the text should be aligned in columns. By adjusting page settings, you can do all these things and more. You will find the most common page settings, such as margins and page orientation, in the Page Setup group on the Page Layout tab. For less common settings, such as determining whether headers should print on odd or even pages, you can use the Page Setup dialog box.

Changing Margins

A **margin** is the area of blank space that displays to the left, right, top, and bottom of a document or worksheet. Margins are evident only if you are in Print Layout or Page Layout view or if you are in the Backstage view, previewing a document to print. To set or change margins, click the Page Layout tab. As shown in Figure 1.54, the Page Setup group enables you to change such items as margins and orientation. To change margins:

1. Click Margins in the Page Setup group on the PAGE LAYOUT tab.
2. If the margins that you intend to use are included in any of the preset margin options, click a selection. Otherwise, click Custom Margins to display the Page Setup dialog box in which you can create custom margin settings.
3. Click OK to accept the settings and close the dialog box.

You can also change margins when you click Print on the File tab.

FIGURE 1.54 Page Setup Group

Changing Page Orientation

STEP 3 Documents and worksheets can be displayed in *portrait* orientation or in *landscape*. A page displayed or printed in portrait orientation is taller than it is wide. A page in landscape orientation is wider than it is tall. Word documents are usually more attractive displayed in portrait orientation, whereas Excel worksheets are often more suitable in landscape. To select page orientation, click Orientation in the Page Setup group on the Page Layout tab (see Figure 1.55). Orientation is also an option in the Print area of the Backstage view.

Using the Page Setup Dialog Box

The Page Setup group contains the most commonly used page options in the particular Office application. Some are unique to Excel, and others are more applicable to Word. Other less common settings are available in the Page Setup dialog box only, displayed when you click the Page Setup Dialog Box Launcher. The subsequent dialog box includes options for customizing margins, selecting page orientation, centering vertically, printing gridlines, and creating headers and footers, although some of those options are available only when working with Word; others are unique to Excel. Figure 1.55 shows both the Excel and Word Page Setup dialog boxes.

FIGURE 1.55 Page Setup Dialog Boxes

1. Give two ways to resize an object, such as a picture, that has been inserted in a document. *p. 61*

2. Often, an Office application will identify a word as misspelled that is not actually misspelled. How can that happen? If a word is flagged as misspelled, how can you correct it (or ignore it if it is not actually an error)? *p. 63*

3. Give two ways to change a document from a portrait orientation to landscape. Identify at least one document type that you think would be better suited for landscape orientation rather than portrait. *p. 66*

4. What dialog box includes options for selecting margins, centering vertically, and changing page orientation? *p. 66*

Hands-On Exercises

6 Insert Tab Tasks, Page Layout Tab Tasks, and Review Tab Tasks

A series of enrichment programs at the Spotted Begonia Art Gallery is nearing kickoff. You are helping plan a ceremony to commemorate the occasion. To encourage interest and participation, you will edit a PowerPoint presentation that is to be shown to civic groups, the local retiree association, and to city and county leaders to solicit additional funding. You know that pictures add energy to a presentation when used appropriately, so you will check for those elements, adding whatever is necessary. A major concern is making sure the presentation is error free and that it is available in print so that meeting participants can review it later. As a reminder, you also plan to have available a handout giving the time and date of the dedication ceremony. You will use the Insert tab to work with illustrations and the Review tab to check for errors, and you will use Word to generate an attractive handout as a reminder of the date.

Skills covered: Check Spelling and Use the Thesaurus • Insert Pictures • Change Margins and Page Orientation

STEP 1 » CHECK SPELLING AND USE THE THESAURUS

As you check the PowerPoint presentation that will be shown to local groups, you make sure no misspellings or grammatical mistakes exist. You also use the Thesaurus to find a suitable substitution for a word you feel should be replaced. Refer to Figure 1.56 as you complete Step 1.

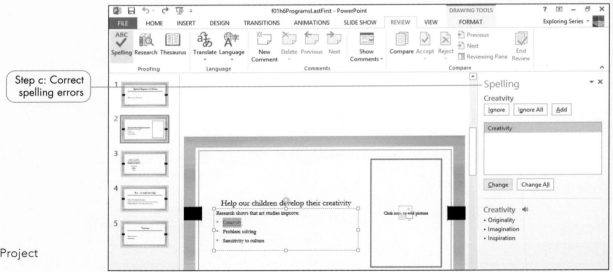

FIGURE 1.56 Project Presentation

a. Navigate to the Start screen. Scroll across the tiles, if necessary, and click **PowerPoint 2013**. Click **Open Other Presentations**. Open *f01h6Programs* and save the document as **f01h6Programs_LastFirst** in the Promotional Print folder (a subfolder of Artists) you created.

The PowerPoint presentation opens, with Slide 1 shown in Normal view.

b. Click the **SLIDE SHOW tab** and click **From Beginning** in the Start Slide Show group to view the presentation. Click to advance from one slide to another. After the last slide, click to return to Normal view.

c. Click the **REVIEW tab** and click **Spelling** in the Proofing group. Correct any words that are misspelled by clicking the correction and clicking Change or Ignore in the Spelling pane. Click **Change** to accept *Creativity* on Slide 2, click **workshops** and click **Change** on Slide 3, and click **Change** to accept *Thank* for Slide 5. Refer to Figure 1.56. Click **OK** when the spell check is complete and close the pane.

d. Click **Slide 2** in the Slides pane on the left. Double-click the bulleted word *Creativity*, click **Thesaurus** in the Proofing group, point to *Imagination* in the Thesaurus pane, click the arrow to the right of the word, and then select **Insert**.

The word *Creativity* is replaced with the word *Imagination*.

e. Click the **Close (X) button** in the top-right corner of the Thesaurus pane.

f. Save the presentation.

STEP 2 >> INSERT PICTURES

Although the presentation provides the necessary information and encourages viewers to become active participants in the enrichment programs, you believe that pictures might make it a little more exciting. Where appropriate, you will include a picture. Refer to Figure 1.57 as you complete Step 2.

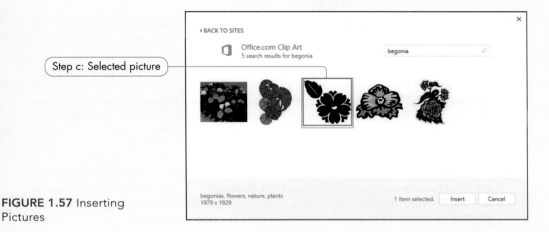

FIGURE 1.57 Inserting Pictures

a. Click **Slide 2** in the Slides pane on the left, if necessary. Click the **INSERT tab** and click **Online Pictures** in the Images group.

The Insert Pictures pane displays on the screen.

> **TROUBLESHOOTING:** You can add your own pictures to slides using the Pictures command. Or you can copy and paste images directly from a Web page.

b. Type **begonia** in the **Office.com Clip Art search box** and press **Enter**.

You will identify pictures that may be displayed on Slide 2.

c. Click to select the black flower shown in Figure 1.57 or use a similar image. Click **Insert**.

The picture may not be placed as you would like, but you will move and resize it in the next substep as necessary. Also, notice that the picture is selected, as indicated by the box and handles surrounding it.

> **TROUBLESHOOTING:** It is very easy to make the mistake of inserting duplicate pictures on a slide, perhaps because you clicked the image more than once in the task pane. If that should happen, you can remove any unwanted picture by clicking to select it and pressing Delete.

d. Click a corner handle—the small square on the border of the picture. Make sure the mouse pointer appears as a double-headed arrow. Drag to resize the image so that it fits well on the slide. Click in the center of the picture. The mouse pointer should appear as a four-headed arrow. Drag the picture slightly to the right corner of the slide. Make sure the picture is still selected (it should be surrounded by a box and handles). If it is not selected, click to select it.

> **TROUBLESHOOTING:** You may not need to perform this substep if the picture came in as desired. Proceed to the next substep if this occurs.

e. Click **Slide 5** in the Slides pane on the left. Click the **INSERT tab** and select **Online Pictures**. Type **happy art** in the **Office.com Clip Art search box** and press **Enter**. Click the **Three handprints picture** and click **Insert**.

A picture is placed on the final slide.

f. Click to select the picture, if necessary. Drag a corner handle to resize the picture. Click the center of the picture and drag the picture to reposition it in the bottom-right corner of the slide, as shown in Figure 1.57.

> **TROUBLESHOOTING:** You can only move the picture when the mouse pointer looks like a four-headed arrow. If instead you drag a handle, the picture will be resized instead of moved. Click Undo on the Quick Access Toolbar and begin again.

g. Click **Slide 3**. Click the **INSERT tab**, click **Online Pictures**, and then search for **school art**. Select and insert the picture named **Art Teacher working with student on a project in school**. Using the previously practiced technique, resize the image height to **3.9"** and position as necessary to add the picture to the right side of the slide.

h. Save the presentation and exit PowerPoint. Submit your file based on your instructor's directions.

STEP 3 ≫ CHANGE MARGINS AND PAGE ORIENTATION

You are ready to finalize the flyer promoting the workshops, but before printing it you want to see how it will look. You wonder if it would be better in landscape or portrait orientation, so you will try both. After adjusting the margins, you are ready to save the flyer for later printing and distribution. Refer to Figure 1.58 as you complete Step 3.

FIGURE 1.58 Page Setup Dialog Box

a. Navigate to the Start screen. Scroll across the tiles, if necessary, and click **Word 2013**. Click **Open Other Documents**. Open *f01h6Handout* and save the document as **f01h6Handout_ LastFirst** in the Promotional Print folder (a subfolder of Artists) you created.

b. Click the **PAGE LAYOUT tab**, click **Orientation** in the Page Setup group, and then select **Landscape** to view the flyer in landscape orientation.

You want to see how the handout will look in landscape orientation.

c. Click the **FILE tab**, click **Print**, and then click **Next Page** and click **Previous Page** (right- and left-pointing arrows at the bottom center of the preview page).

The second page of the handout shows only the last two bullets and the contact information. You can see that the two-page layout is not an attractive option.

d. Click the **Back arrow** in the top-left corner. Click **Undo** on the Quick Access Toolbar. Click the **FILE tab** and click **Print**.

The document fits on one page. Portrait orientation is a much better choice for the handout.

e. Click the **Back arrow** in the top-left corner. Click the **PAGE LAYOUT tab** if necessary, click **Margins** in the Page Setup group, and then select **Custom Margins**. Click the **spin arrow** beside the left margin box to increase the margin to **1.2**. Similarly, change the right margin to **1.2**. Refer to Figure 1.58. Click **OK**.

f. Save the document and exit Word. Submit your file based on your instructor's directions.

Chapter Objectives Review

After reading this chapter, you have accomplished the following objectives:

1. **Log in with your Microsoft account.**
   - Your Microsoft account connects you to all of Microsoft's Internet-based resources.

2. **Identify the Start screen components.**
   - The Start screen has a sleek, clean interface that is made up of tiles and Charms.

3. **Interact with the Start screen.**
   - Customize the Start screen to access programs and apps.

4. **Access the desktop.**
   - Simplified to accommodate mobile devices, laptops, and desktops.

5. **Use File Explorer.**
   - Understand and customize the interface: Change the view to provide as little or as much detail as you need.
   - Work with groups on the Navigation Pane: Provides access to all resources, folders, and files.

6. **Work with folders and files.**
   - Create a folder: A well-named folder structure can be created in File Explorer or within a program as you save a file.
   - Open, rename, and delete folders and files: File Explorer can be used to perform these tasks.
   - Save a file: When saving a file for the first time, you need to indicate the location and the name of the file.

7. **Select, copy, and move multiple files and folders.**
   - Select multiple files and folders: Folders and files can be selected as a group.
   - Copy and move files and folders: Folders and the files within them can be easily moved to the same or a different drive.

8. **Identify common interface components.**
   - Use the Backstage view and the Quick Access Toolbar: The Backstage view can perform several commands.
   - Familiarize yourself with the Ribbon: Provides access to common tasks.
   - Use the status bar: The status bar provides information relative to the open file and quick access to View and Zoom level options.

9. **Get Office Help.**
   - Use Office Help: The Help button links to online resources and technical support.
   - Use Enhanced ScreenTips: Provides the purpose of a command button as you point to it.
   - Get help with dialog boxes: Use the Help button in the top-right corner of a dialog box to get help relevant to the task.

10. **Open a file.**
    - Create a new file: A document can be created as a blank document or with a template.
    - Open a file using the Open dialog box: Previously saved files can be located and opened using a dialog box.
    - Open a file using the Recent Documents list: Documents that you have worked with recently display here.
    - Open a file from the Templates list: Templates are a convenient way to save time when designing a document.

11. **Print a file.**
    - Check and change orientation or perform other commands related to the look of your file before printing.

12. **Close a file and application.**
    - Close files you are not working on to avoid becoming overwhelmed.

13. **Select and edit text.**
    - Select text to edit: Commit to memory: "Select, then do."
    - Use the Mini toolbar: Provides instant access to common formatting commands after text is selected.
    - Apply font attributes: These can be applied to selected text with toggle commands.
    - Change the font: Choose from a set of fonts found within all Office applications.
    - Change the font size, color, and attributes: These commands are located in the Font group on the Ribbon.

14. **Use the Clipboard group commands.**
    - Copy formats with the Format Painter: Copy formatting features from one section of text to another.
    - Move and copy text: Text can be selected, copied, and moved between applications or within the same application.
    - Use the Office Clipboard: This pane stores up to 24 cut or copied selections for use later on in your computing session.

15. **Use the Editing group commands.**
    - Find and replace text: Finds each occurrence of a series of characters and replaces them with another series.
    - Use advanced find and replace feature: Change the format of every occurrence of a series of characters.

16. **Insert objects.**
    - Insert pictures: You can insert pictures from a CD or other media, or from an online resource such as Office.com.
    - Insert and modify SmartArt: Create a diagram and to enter text to provide a visual of data.
    - Insert and format shapes: You can insert various types of lines and basic shapes.

17. **Review a file.**
    - Check spelling and grammar: All Office applications check and mark these error types as you type for later correction.
    - Use the Thesaurus: Enables you to search for synonyms.

18. **Use the Page Setup dialog box.**
    - Change margins: You can control the amount of blank space that surrounds the text in your document.
    - Change margins and page orientations, and create headers and footers.

Key Terms Matching

Match the key terms with their definitions. Write the key term letter by the appropriate numbered definition.

a. Backstage view
b. Charms
c. Cloud storage
d. Find
e. Font
f. Format Painter
g. Group
h. Mini toolbar
i. Navigation Pane
j. Operating system
k. Quick Access Toolbar
l. Ribbon
m. OneDrive
n. Snip
o. Snipping Tool
p. Start screen
q. Subfolder
r. Tile
s. Windows 8.1.1
t. Windows 8.1.1 app

1. _____ A tool that copies all formatting from one area to another. **p. 49**

2. _____ Software that directs computer activities such as checking all components, managing system resources, and communicating with application software. **p. 2**

3. _____ A task-oriented section of the Ribbon that contains related commands. **p. 25**

4. _____ An app used to store, access, and share files and folders. **p. 2**

5. _____ Any of the several colorful block images found on the Start screen that when clicked takes you to a program, file, folder, or other Windows 8.1.1 app. **p. 3**

6. _____ A component of Office 2013 that provides a concise collection of commands related to an open file. **p. 23**

7. _____ A tool that displays near selected text that contains formatting commands. **p. 46**

8. _____ A level of folder structure indicated as a folder within another folder. **p. 10**

9. _____ An application specifically designed to run in the Start screen interface of Windows 8.1.1. **p. 3**

10. _____ A command used to locate each occurrence of a series of characters. **p. 52**

11. _____ A Windows 8.1.1 accessory program that allows you to capture a screen display so that you can save, annotate, or share it. **p. 5**

12. _____ What you see after starting your Windows 8.1.1 computer and entering your username and password. **p. 2**

13. _____ Provides handy access to commonly executed tasks such as saving a file and undoing recent actions. **p. 23**

14. _____ A Microsoft operating system released in 2012 that is available on laptops, desktops, and tablet computers. **p. 2**

15. _____ A component made up of five icons that provide similar functionality to the Start button found in previous versions of Windows. **p. 3**

16. _____ The captured screen display created by the Snipping Tool. **p. 5**

17. _____ The long bar located just beneath the title bar containing tabs, groups, and commands. **p. 25**

18. _____ Provides access to computer resources, folders, files, and networked peripherals. **p. 11**

19. _____ A technology used to store files and to work with programs that are stored in a central location on the Internet. **p. 2**

20. _____ A character design or the way characters display onscreen. **p. 45**

Multiple Choice

1. The Recent Documents list shows documents that have been previously:

   (a) Printed.

   (b) Opened.

   (c) Saved in an earlier software version.

   (d) Deleted.

2. Which of the following File Explorer features collects related data from folders and gives them a single name?

   (a) Network

   (b) Favorites

   (c) Libraries

   (d) Computer

3. When you want to copy the format of a selection but not the content, you should:

   (a) Double-click Copy in the Clipboard group.

   (b) Right-click the selection and click Copy.

   (c) Click Copy Format in the Clipboard group.

   (d) Click Format Painter in the Clipboard group.

4. Which of the following is *not* a benefit of using OneDrive?

   (a) Save your folders and files in the cloud.

   (b) Share your files and folders with others.

   (c) Hold video conferences with others.

   (d) Simultaneously work on the same document with others.

5. What does a red wavy underline in a document, spreadsheet, or presentation mean?

   (a) A word is misspelled or not recognized by the Office dictionary

   (b) A grammatical mistake exists

   (c) An apparent word usage mistake exists

   (d) A word has been replaced with a synonym

6. When you close a file:

   (a) You are prompted to save the file (unless you have made no changes since last saving it).

   (b) The application (Word, Excel, or PowerPoint) is also closed.

   (c) You must first save the file.

   (d) You must change the file name.

7. Live Preview:

   (a) Opens a predesigned document or spreadsheet that is relevant to your task.

   (b) Provides a preview of the results of a choice you are considering before you make a final selection.

   (c) Provides a preview of an upcoming Office version.

   (d) Enlarges the font onscreen.

8. You can get help when working with an Office application in which one of the following areas?

   (a) Help button

   (b) Status bar

   (c) The Backstage view

   (d) Quick Access Toolbar

9. The *Find and Replace* feature enables you to do which of the following?

   (a) Find all instances of misspelling and automatically correct (or replace) them

   (b) Find any grammatical errors and automatically correct (or replace) them

   (c) Find any specified font settings and replace them with another selection

   (d) Find any character string and replace it with another

10. A document or worksheet printed in landscape orientation is:

    (a) Taller than it is wide.

    (b) Wider than it is tall.

    (c) A document with 2" left and right margins.

    (d) A document with 2" top and bottom margins.

Practice Exercises

1 Designing Web Pages

You have been asked to make a presentation to the local business association. With the mayor's renewed emphasis on growing the local economy, many businesses are interested in establishing a Web presence. The business owners would like to know a little bit more about how Web pages are designed. In preparation for the presentation, you need to proofread and edit your PowerPoint file. This exercise follows the same set of skills as used in Hands-On Exercises 1–6 in the chapter. Refer to Figure 1.59 as you complete this exercise.

Replace dialog box

FIGURE 1.59 Designing Web Pages Presentation

a. Click **File Explorer** on the taskbar and select the location where you save your files. Click the **HOME tab** and click **New folder** in the New group. Type **Designing Web Pages** and press **Enter**.

Take a snip, name it **f01p1DesignSnip_LastFirst**, and then save it in the Designing Web Pages folder. Close File Explorer.

b. Point to the bottom-right corner of your screen to display the Charms and click the **Start charm**. Scroll if necessary and click **PowerPoint 2013** to start PowerPoint. Open *f01p1Design* and save it as **f01p1Design_LastFirst** in the Designing Web Pages folder. In Slide 1, drag to select the text *Firstname Lastname* and type your own first and last names. Click an empty area of the slide to cancel the selection.

c. Click the **REVIEW tab** and click **Spelling** in the Proofing group. In the Spelling pane, click **Change** or **Ignore** to make or not make a change as needed. Most identified misspellings should be changed. The words *KompoZer* and *Nvu* are not misspelled, so you should ignore them when they are flagged. Click **OK** to end the spell check.

d. Click the **SLIDE SHOW tab**. Click **From Beginning** in the Start Slide Show group. Click each slide to view the show and press **Esc** on the last slide.

e. Click **Slide 2** in the Slides pane on the left. Drag to select the *Other tools* text and press **Backspace** on the keyboard to delete the text.

f. Click **Slide 4** in the Slides pane. Click the **HOME tab** and click **Replace** in the Editing group. Type **HTML** in the **Find what box** and **HTML5** in the **Replace with box**. Click **Find Next**. Read the slide and click **Replace** to change the first instance of *HTML*. Refer to Figure 1.59. Click **Close**.

g. Click **Replace** in the Editing group. Type **CSS** in the **Find what box** and **CSS5** in the **Replace with box**. Click **Replace All** and click **OK**. Click **Close**.

h. Drag to select the *FrontPage, Nvu* text and press **Backspace** on the keyboard to delete the text.

i. Press **Ctrl+End** to place the insertion point at the end of *Templates* and press **Enter**. Type **Database Connectivity** to create a new bulleted item.

j. Click the **FILE tab** and click **Print**. Click the **Full Page Slides arrow** and click **6 Slides Horizontal** to see a preview of all of the slides as a handout. Click the **Back arrow** and click the **HOME tab**.

k. Click **Slide 1** in the Slides pane to move to the beginning of the presentation.

l. Drag the **Zoom slider** on the status bar to the right to **130%** to magnify the text. Then use the **Zoom Slider** to return to **60%**.

m. Save and close the file. Submit your files based on your instructor's directions.

2 | Upscale Bakery

You have always been interested in baking and have worked in the field for several years. You now have an opportunity to devote yourself full time to your career as the CEO of a company dedicated to baking cupcakes, pastries, and catering. One of the first steps in getting the business off the ground is developing a business plan so that you can request financial support. You will use Word to develop your business plan. This exercise follows the same set of skills as used in Hands-On Exercises 1, 3, 4, and 5 in the chapter. Refer to Figure 1.60 as you complete this exercise.

FIGURE 1.60 Business Plan Document

a. Click **File Explorer** on the taskbar and select the location where you save your files. Click the **HOME tab** and click **New folder** in the New group. Type **Business Plan** and press **Enter**.

Take a snip, name it **f01p2BusinessSnip_LastFirst**, and save it in the Business Plan folder. Close File Explorer.

b. Point to the bottom-right corner of your screen to display the Charms and click the **Start charm**. Scroll if necessary and click **Word 2013** to start Word. Open *f01p2Business* and save it as **f01p2Business_LastFirst** in the Business Plan folder.

c. Click the **REVIEW tab** and click **Spelling & Grammar** in the Proofing group. Click **Change** for all suggestions.

d. Drag the paragraphs beginning with *Our Staff* and ending with *(Nutritionist)*. Click the **HOME tab** and click **Cut** in the Clipboard group. Click to the left of *Our Products* and click **Paste**.

e. Select the text *Your name* in the first bullet and replace it with your first and last names. Select that entire bullet and use the Mini toolbar to use Live Preview to see some other Font sizes. Then click **11** to increase the size.

f. Double-click the **Format Painter** in the Clipboard group on the HOME tab. Drag the Format Painter to change the other *Our Staff* bullets to **11**. Drag all four *Our Products* bullets. Click the **Format Painter button** to toggle it off and click outside of the text to deselect it. Refer to Figure 1.60.

g. Select the last line in the document, which says *Insert and position picture here.*, and press **Delete**. Click the **INSERT tab** and click **Online Pictures** in the Illustrations group.

- Click in the **Office.com Clip Art search box**, type **Cupcakes**, and then press **Enter**.
- Select **Cupcake with a single birthday candle** or select any image and click **Insert**. Do not deselect the image.
- Click the **PICTURE TOOLS FORMAT tab**, if necessary, click the **More button** in the Picture Styles group, and then click the **Soft Edge Rectangle** (sixth from the left on the top row).
- Click outside the picture.

h. Click the **FILE tab** and click **Print**. Change *Normal Margins* to **Moderate Margins**. Click the **Back arrow**.

i. Click the picture and click **Center** in the Paragraph group on the HOME tab.

j. Save and close the file. Submit your files based on your instructor's directions.

3 Best Friends Pet Care

You and a friend are starting a pet sitting service and have a few clients already. Billing will be a large part of your record keeping, so you are planning ahead by developing a series of folders to maintain those records. This exercise follows the same set of skills as used in Hands-On Exercises 1, 2, and 5 in the chapter. Refer to Figure 1.61 as you complete this exercise.

FIGURE 1.61 Best Friends Pet Care

a. Click **File Explorer** on the taskbar and select the location where you save your files. Click the **Home tab** and click **New folder** in the New group. Type **Best Friends** and press **Enter**.

b. Double-click **Best Friends** in the Content pane to open the folder. Create new subfolders as follows:
- Click the **Home tab** and click **New folder** in the New group. Type **Business Letters** and press **Enter**.
- Click the **Home tab** and click **New folder** in the New group. Type **Billing Records** and press **Enter**. Compare your results to Figure 1.61. Take a snip and name it **f01p3FriendsSnip_LastFirst**. Save it in the Billing Records subfolder of the Best Friends folder. Close File Explorer.

c. Navigate to the Start screen and click on **Word 2013**. Click **Open Other Documents** and open *f01p3Friends*. Save it as **f01p3Friends_LastFirst** in the Business Letters subfolder of the Best Friends folder.

d. Use *Find and Replace* to replace the text *Your Name* with your name by doing the following:
- Click **Replace** in the Editing group on the HOME tab.
- Type **Your name** in the **Find what box**. Type your first and last names in the **Replace with box**.
- Click **Replace** and click **OK**. Close the *Find and Replace* dialog box. Close, save changes to the document, and exit Word.

e. Click **File Explorer** on the taskbar so that you can rename one of your folders:

- Click **Computer** in the Navigation Pane.
- In the Content pane, navigate to the drive where you earlier created the Best Friends folder. Double-click the **Best Friends folder**.
- Right-click **Billing Records**, click **Rename**, type **Accounting Records**, and then press **Enter**.

f. Take a snip and name it **f01p3FolderSnip_LastFirst**. Save it in the Business Letters subfolder of the Best Friends folder. Submit your files based on your instructor's directions.

Mid-Level Exercises

1 Reference Letter

You are an instructor at a local community college. A student has asked you to provide her with a letter of reference for a job application. You have used Word to prepare the letter, but now you need to make a few changes before it is finalized.

a. Open File Explorer. Create a new folder named **References** in the location where you are saving your student files. Take a snip, name it **f01m1ReferencesSnip_LastFirst**, and save it in the References folder. Close File Explorer.

b. Start Word. Open *f01m1Letter* and save it in the References folder as **f01m1Letter_LastFirst**.

c. Select the date and point to several font sizes in the Mini toolbar. Use the Live Preview to compare them. Click **11**.

d. Double-click the date and use the **Format Painter** to change the rest of the letter to font size 11.

e. Apply bold to the student's name, *Stacy VanPatten*, in the first sentence.

f. Correct all errors using Spelling & Grammar. Her last name is spelled correctly. Use the Thesaurus to find a synonym for *intelligent* and replace wih **gifted**. Change the *an* to *a* just before the new word. Replace each occurrence of *Stacy* with **Stacey**.

g. Move the last paragraph—beginning with *In my opinion*—to position it before the second paragraph—beginning with *Stacey is a gifted*.

h. Move the insertion point to the beginning of the document.

i. Change the margins to **Narrow**.

j. Preview the document as it will appear when printed.

k. Save and close the file. Submit your files based on your instructor's directions.

2 Medical Monitoring

You are enrolled in a Health Informatics program of study in which you learn to manage databases related to health fields. For a class project, your instructor requires that you monitor your blood pressure, recording your findings in an Excel worksheet. You have recorded the week's data and will now make a few changes before printing the worksheet for submission.

a. Open File Explorer. Create a new folder named **Medical** in the location where you are saving your student files. Take a snip, name it **f01m2MedicalSnip_LastFirst**, and save it in the Medical folder. Close File Explorer.

b. Start Excel. Open *f01m2Tracker* and save it as **f01m2Tracker_LastFirst** in the Medical folder.

c. Preview the worksheet as it will appear when printed. Change the orientation of the worksheet to **Landscape**. Preview the worksheet again.

d. Click in the cell to the right of *Name* and type your first and last names. Press **Enter**.

e. Change the font of the text in **cell C1** to **Verdana**. Use Live Preview to try some font sizes. Change the font size to **20**.

f. Check the spelling for the worksheet.

 g. Get help on showing decimal places. You want to increase the decimal places for the values in **cells E22, F22,** and **G22** so that each value shows two places to the right of the decimal. Use Excel Help to learn how to do that. You might use *Increase Decimals* as a Search term. When you find the answer, select the three cells and increase the decimal places to **2**.

h. Click **cell A1** and insert a picture of your choice related to blood pressure. Be sure the image includes content from Office.com. Resize and position the picture so that it displays in an attractive manner. Format the picture with **Soft Edges** set to **4 pt**. Change the margins to **Wide**.

i. Open the Backstage view and adjust print settings to print two copies. You will not actually print two copies unless directed by your instructor.

j. Save and close the file. Submit your files based on your instructor's directions.

3 Today's Musical Artists

COLLABORATION CASE

CREATIVE CASE ★

With a few of your classmates, you will use PowerPoint to create a single presentation on your favorite musical artists. Each student must create at least one slide and then all of the slides will be added to the presentation. Because everyone's schedule is varied, you should use either your Outlook account or OneDrive to pass the presentation file among the group.

a. Open File Explorer. Create a new folder named **Musical** in the location where you are saving your student files. Take a snip, name it **f01m3MusicalSnip_LastFirst**, and then save it in the Musical folder. Close File Explorer.

b. Start PowerPoint. Create a new presentation and save it as **f01m3Music_GroupName** in the Musical folder.

c. Add one slide that contains the name of the artist, the genre, and two or three interesting facts about the artist.

d. Insert a picture of the artist or clip art that represents the artist.

e. Put your name on the slide that you created. Save the presentation.

f. Pass the presentation to the next student so that he or she can perform the same tasks and save the presentation before passing it on to the next student. Continue until all group members have created a slide in the presentation.

g. Save and close the file. Submit your file based on your instructor's directions.

Beyond the Classroom

Fitness Planner

RESEARCH CASE

You will use Microsoft Excel to develop a fitness planner. Open *f01b2Exercise* and save it as **f01b2Exercise_LastFirst**. Because the fitness planner is a template, the exercise categories are listed, but without actual data. You will personalize the planner. Change the orientation to **Landscape**. Move the contents of **cell A2** (*Exercise Planner*) to **cell A1**. Click **cell A8** and use the Format Painter to copy the format of that selection to **cells A5** and **A6**. Increase the font size of **cell A1** to **26**. Use Excel Help to learn how to insert a header and put your name in the header. Begin the fitness planner, entering at least one activity in each category (warm-up, aerobics, strength, and cool-down). Submit as directed by your instructor.

Household Records

DISASTER RECOVERY

FROM SCRATCH

Use Microsoft Excel to create a detailed record of your household appliances and other items of value that are in your home. In case of burglary or disaster, an insurance claim is expedited if you are able to itemize what was lost along with identifying information such as serial numbers. You will then make a copy of the record on another storage device for safekeeping outside your home (in case your home is destroyed by a fire or weather-related catastrophe). Connect a flash drive to your computer and then use File Explorer to create a folder on the hard drive titled **Home Records**. Design a worksheet listing at least five fictional appliances and electronic equipment along with the serial number of each. Save the workbook as **f01b3Household_LastFirst** in the Home Records folder. Close the workbook and exit Excel. Use File Explorer to copy the Home Records folder from the hard drive to your flash drive. Use the Snipping Tool to create a full-screen snip of the screen display. Save it as **f01b3Disaster_LastFirst** in the Home Records folder. Close all open windows and submit as directed by your instructor.

Meetings

SOFT SKILLS CASE S

FROM SCRATCH

After watching the Meetings video, you will use File Explorer to create a series of folders and subfolders to organize meetings by date. Each folder should be named by month, day, and year. Three subfolders should be created for each meeting. The subfolders should be named **Agenda**, **Handouts**, and **Meeting Notes**. Use the Snipping Tool to create a full-screen snip of the screen display. Save it as **f01b4Meetings_LastFirst**. Submit as directed by your instructor.

You are a member of the Student Government Association (SGA) at your college. As a community project, the SGA is sponsoring a Stop Smoking drive designed to provide information on the health risks posed by smoking cigarettes and to offer solutions to those who want to quit. The SGA has partnered with the local branch of the American Cancer Society as well as the outreach program of the local hospital to sponsor free educational awareness seminars. As the secretary for the SGA, you will help prepare a PowerPoint presentation that will be displayed on plasma screens around campus and used in student seminars. You will use Microsoft Office to help with those tasks.

Manage Files and Folders

You will open, review, and save an Excel worksheet providing data on the personal monetary cost of smoking cigarettes over a period of years.

a. Create a folder called **SGA Drive**.

b. Start Excel. Open *f01c1Cost* from the student data files and save it in the SGA Drive folder as **f01c1Cost_LastFirst**.

c. Click **cell A10** and type your first and last names. Press **Enter**.

Modify the Font

To highlight some key figures on the worksheet, you will format those cells with additional font attributes.

a. Draw attention to the high cost of smoking for 10, 20, and 30 years by changing the font color in **cells G3 through I4** to **Red**.

b. Italicize the Annual Cost cells (**F3** and **F4**).

c. Click **Undo** on the Quick Access Toolbar to remove the italics. Click **Redo** to return the text to italics.

Insert a Picture

You will add a picture to the worksheet and then resize it and position it.

a. Click **cell G7** and insert an online picture appropriate for the topic of smoking.

b. Resize the picture and reposition it near cell B7.

c. Click outside the picture to deselect it.

Preview Print, Change Page Layout, and Print

To get an idea of how the worksheet will look when printed, you will preview the worksheet. Then you will change the orientation and margins before printing it.

a. Preview the document as it will appear when printed.

b. Change the page orientation to **Landscape**. Click the **PAGE LAYOUT tab** and change the margins to **Narrow**.

c. Preview the document as it will appear when printed.

d. Adjust the print settings to print two copies. You will not actually print two copies unless directed by your instructor.

e. Save and close the file.

Find and Replace

You have developed a PowerPoint presentation that you will use to present to student groups and for display on plasma screens across campus. The presentation is designed to increase awareness of the health problems associated with smoking. The PowerPoint presentation has come back from the reviewers with only one comment: A reviewer suggested that you spell out Centers for Disease Control and Prevention, instead of abbreviating it. You do not remember exactly which slide or slides the abbreviation might have been on, so you use *Find and Replace* to make the change quickly.

a. Start PowerPoint. Open *f01c1Quit* and save it in the SGA Drive folder as **f01c1Quit_LastFirst**.

b. Replace all occurrences of *CDC* with **Centers for Disease Control and Prevention**.

Cut and Paste and Insert a Text Box

The Mark Twain quote on Slide 1 might be more effective on the last slide in the presentation, so you will cut and paste it there in a text box.

a. On Slide 1, select the entire Mark Twain quote by clicking on the placeholder border. When the border is solid, the entire placeholder and its contents are selected.

b. On Slide 22, paste the quote, reposition it more attractively, and then format it in a larger font size.

Check Spelling and Change View

Before you call the presentation complete, you will spell check it and view it as a slide show.

a. Check spelling. The word *hairlike* is not misspelled, so it should not be corrected.

b. View the slide show and take the smoking quiz. Click after the last slide to return to the presentation.

c. Save and close the presentation. Exit PowerPoint. Submit both files included in this project as directed by your instructor.

Introduction to Access

Finding Your Way Through an Access Database

OBJECTIVES | AFTER YOU READ THIS CHAPTER, YOU WILL BE ABLE TO:

1. Understand database fundamentals p. 84

2. Use an existing database p. 91

3. Sort table data on one or multiple fields p. 102

4. Create, modify, and remove filters p. 103

5. Know when to use Access or Excel to manage data p. 111

6. Understand relational power p. 112

7. Create a database p. 119

CASE STUDY | Managing a Business in the Global Economy

Northwind Traders* is an international gourmet food distributor that imports and exports specialty foods from around the world. Northwind's products include meats, seafood, dairy products, beverages, and produce. Keeping track of customers, vendors, orders, and inventory is a critical task. The owners of Northwind have just purchased an order-processing database created with Microsoft Office Access 2013 to help manage their customers, suppliers, products, and orders.

You have been hired to learn, use, and manage the database. Northwind's owners are willing to provide training about their business and Access. They expect the learning process to take about three months. After three months, your job will be to support the order-processing team as well as to provide detail and summary reports to the sales force as needed. Your new job at Northwind Traders will be a challenge, but it is also a good opportunity to make a great contribution to a global company. Are you up to the task?

*Northwind Traders was created by the Microsoft Access Team as a sample database for Access 2003. Access 2013 does not include a sample database, so you will use a modified version of Northwind Traders. The names of companies, products, people, characters, and/or data are fictitious.

Databases Are Everywhere!

A *database* is a collection of data organized as meaningful information that can be accessed, managed, stored, queried, sorted, and reported. You probably participate in data collection and are exposed to databases on a regular basis. For example, your community college or university uses a database to store registration data. When you enrolled at your institution, you created a profile that was saved in a database. When you registered for this course, your data was entered into a database. If you have a bank account, have a Social Security card, have a medical history, or have booked a flight with an airline, your information is stored in a record in a database.

If you use the Internet, you probably use databases often because the Internet can provide you with easy access to databases. For example, when you shop online or check your bank statement online, you connect to a database. Even when you type a search phrase into Google and click Search, you are using Google's massive database with all of its stored Web page references and keywords. Look for something on Amazon, and you are searching Amazon's database to find a product that you might want to buy. Need a new driver for golfing? Log on to Amazon, search for "golf clubs driver" (see Figure 1.1), and find the right driver with your preferred loft, hand orientation, flex, shaft material, and price range. All of this information is stored in Amazon's products database.

FIGURE 1.1 Amazon Web Site

Photo: Copyright © 2013 Amazon.com, Inc.

Organizations rely on data to conduct daily operations, regardless of whether the organization exists as a profit or not-for-profit environment. Organizations maintain data about their customers, employees, orders, volunteers, activities, and facilities. Organizations maintain data about their customers, employees, orders, volunteers, activities, and facilities, and this data needs to be stored, organized, and made available for analysis. *Data* and *information* are two terms that are often used interchangeably. However, when it comes to databases, the two terms mean different things. *Data* is what is entered into a database. *Information* is the finished product that is produced by the database. Data is converted to information by selecting, calculating, sorting, or summarizing records. Decisions in an organization are usually based on information produced by a database, rather than raw data.

In this section, you will learn the fundamentals of organizing data in a database, explore what Access database objects are and what their purpose is, and examine the Access interface.

Understanding Database Fundamentals

People use databases to store collections of data. A *database management system (DBMS)* is a software system that provides the tools needed to create, maintain, and use a database. Database management systems make it possible to access and control data and display the information in a variety of formats such as lists, forms, and reports. *Access* is the database management system included in the Office 2013 Professional suite and the Office 2013 Professional Academic suite. Access is a valuable decision-making tool that many organizations are using. Advanced Access users and software developers can even use Microsoft Access to develop software applications for specific solutions to the needs of organizations. For example, a health organization uses Access to track and understand disease reports.

Organize Information in a Database and Recognize Access Objects

STEP 2 >> An Access database is a structured collection of *objects*, the main components that are created and used to make the database function. The main object types in an Access database are listed below and discussed in the following paragraphs.

- Tables
- Forms
- Queries
- Reports
- Macros
- Modules

The objects that make up an Access database are available from the **Navigation Pane**. The Navigation Pane is an Access interface element that organizes and lists the database objects in an Access database. You will learn about the object types and their benefits in the remainder of this section. Later you will learn to create and use these objects.

The foundation of every database is a *table*, the object in which data, such as a person's name or a product number, is stored. The other objects in a database are based on one or more underlying tables. To understand how an Access database works and how to use Access effectively, you should learn the structure of a table. Tables organize data into columns and rows. Columns display a *field*, the smallest data element of a table. For example, in the Northwind database, a table containing information about customers would include a Customer ID field. Another field would contain the Company Name. Fields may be required or optional—a contact name may be required, for example, but a contact title may be optional.

Each row in a table contains a *record*, a complete set of all the fields (data elements) about one person, place, event, or concept. A customer record, for example, would contain all of the fields about a single customer, including the Customer ID, the Company Name, Contact Name, Contact Title, Address, City, etc. Figure 1.2 shows the Northwind database with the Customers table selected in the Navigation Pane. The Customers table is open and shows the records of Northwind customers in the table rows. Each record contains multiple fields, with the field name displaying at the top of each column.

FIGURE 1.2 Customers Table

A *form* is an object that gives a user a way of entering and modifying data in databases. Forms enable you to enter, modify, or delete table data. They enable you to manipulate data in the same manner that you would in a table. The difference is that you can create a form that will limit the user to viewing only one record at a time. This helps the user to focus on the data being entered or modified and also provides for more reliable data entry. As an Access user, you will add, delete, and edit records in Form view. As the Access designer, you will create and edit the form structure.

A *query* is a question that you ask about the data in your database. For example, how many of our customers live in Boston? The answer is shown in the query results. A query can be used to display only records that meet certain conditions and only the fields that you require. In addition to helping you find and retrieve data that meets the conditions that you specify, you can use a query to update or delete records and to perform predefined or custom calculations with your data.

A *report* contains professional-looking formatted information from underlying tables or queries. Reports enable you to print the information in your database and are an effective way to present database information. You have control over the size and appearance of everything in a report. Access provides different views for designing, modifying, and running reports.

Two other object types, macros and modules, are used less frequently unless you are a power Access user. A *macro* object is a stored series of commands that carry out an action. You can create a macro to automate simple tasks by selecting an action from a list of macro actions. A *module* is similar to a macro, as it is an object that adds functionality to a database, but modules are written using the VBA (Visual Basic for Applications) programming language.

Figure 1.3 displays the different object types in Access with the foundation object—the table—in the center of the illustration. The purpose each object serves is explained underneath the object name. The flow of information between objects is indicated by single arrowhead arrows if the flow is one direction only. Two arrowhead arrows indicate that the flow goes both directions. For example, you can use forms to view, add, delete, or modify data from tables.

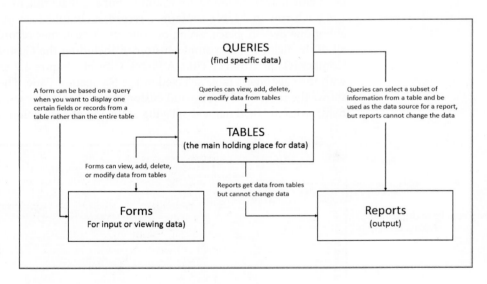

FIGURE 1.3 Object Types and Flow of Information

Examine the Access Interface

While Access includes the standard elements of the Microsoft Office applications interface such as the title bar, the Ribbon, the Home tab, the Backstage view, and scroll bars, it also includes elements unique to Access.

TIP   Access Title Bar

By default, the Access 2013 title bar displays the full path name and file name for the Access database. Displaying just the file name can give the application a cleaner or simpler look. To customize the title bar, click the File tab, click Options, and then click Current Database. Type the file name or the name you wish to display in the Application Title box. The title bars of the Access databases in this book have been modified to display only the file names of the databases.

The Access Ribbon has five tabs that will always display, as well as contextual tabs that appear only when particular objects are open. The File tab leads to the Backstage view, which gives you access to a variety of database tools such as Save, Save As, Compact and Repair, Backup Database, and Print. The Home tab, the default Access tab, contains basic editing functions, such as cut and paste, filtering, find and replace, and most formatting actions. This tab also contains the features that enable you to work with record creation and deletion, totals, and spelling.

The Create tab contains all the tools used to create new objects in a database whereas the External Data tab contains all of the operations used to facilitate data import and export. Finally, the Database Tools tab contains the feature that enables users to create relationships between tables and enables use of the more advanced features of Access, such as setting relationships between tables, analyzing a table or query, and migrating data to SharePoint.

On the left side of the screen, you will see the Navigation Pane. The Navigation Pane organizes and lists all of the objects that are needed to make the current database function. You can open any object by double-clicking the object's name in the list. You can also open an object by right-clicking the object name and selecting Open from the shortcut menu. Right-clicking provides other options, such as renaming the object, cutting the object, and copying the object.

Most databases contain multiple tables, queries, forms, and reports. By default, the objects display in groups by object type in the Navigation Pane. If you wish, you can collapse the contents of an object group by clicking the group heading or the double arrows to the right of the group heading. To expand the contents of an object group that has been hidden, click the heading again or click the double arrows to the right of the group heading again. If you wish to change the way objects are grouped in the Navigation Pane, click the list arrow on the Navigation Pane title bar and select your preferred configuration of the available options.

TIP   Navigation Pane Display

You may wish to expand the area available for an open object by changing the display of the Navigation Pane to a narrow vertical ribbon. You can toggle the display by clicking the Shutter Bar Open/Close button at the top-right corner of the Navigation Pane. The Shutter Bar Open/Close button looks like a double arrow. Click the button again to expand the Navigation Pane. F11 also toggles the display of the Navigation Pane.

By default, Access uses a Tabbed Documents interface. That means that each object that is open has its own tab beneath the Ribbon and to the right of the Navigation Pane. You can switch between open objects by clicking a tab to make that object active. Figure 1.4 shows the Access interface for the Northwind Traders database, which was introduced in the Case Study at the beginning of the chapter. The Navigation Pane is grouped by object type. The Tables and Reports groups in the Navigation Pane are expanded. The Table Tools contextual tab displays because the Employees table is open. The Employees table shows the records for nine employees. The employee records contain multiple fields about each employee, including the employee's Last Name, First Name, Hire Date, Region, and so on. Occasionally a field does not contain a value for a particular record. For example, one of the employees, Nancy Davolio, has not been assigned a title yet. The value of that field is missing. Access shows a blank cell when data is missing.

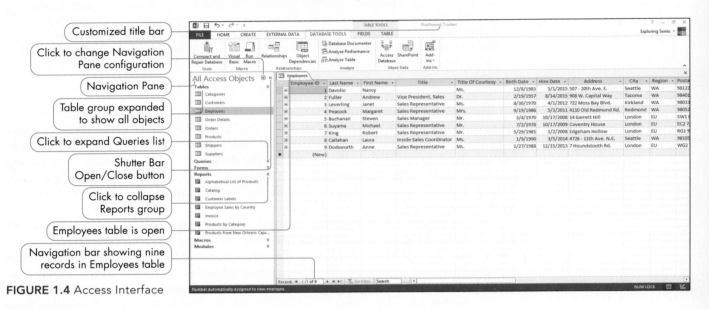

FIGURE 1.4 Access Interface

Explore Access Views

Access provides two different ways to view a table: the Datasheet view and the Design view. To switch between views:

- Click the HOME tab and click View in the Views group to toggle between the current view and the previous view.
- Click the HOME tab, click the View arrow in the Views group, and then select the view you want to use.
- Right-click the object tab and select the view you want to use.
- Right-click the object in the Navigation Pane and select the view you want to use.
- Click one of the view shortcuts in the lower-right corner of the Access window.

The **Datasheet view** is a grid containing fields (columns) and records (rows), similar to an Excel spreadsheet. You can view, add, edit, and delete records in the Datasheet view. Figure 1.5 shows the Datasheet view for the Northwind Customers table. Each row contains a record for a specific customer. Click the **record selector** at the beginning of a row to select the record. Each column represents a field or one attribute about a customer. Click the **field selector**, or column heading, to select a column.

Customers table is open

Pencil in record selector indicates the record is being edited

Navigation bar indicates record 9 of 91 customers in the table is selected

Datasheet view

FIGURE 1.5 Customers Table in Datasheet View

The navigation bar at the bottom of Figure 1.5 shows that the Customers table has 91 records and that record number 9 is the current record. The vertical scroll bar on the right side of the window displays only when the table contains more records than can appear in the window at one time. Similarly, the horizontal scroll bar at the bottom of the window displays only when the table contains more fields than can appear in the window at one time.

The pencil symbol to the left of Record 9 indicates that the data in that record is being edited and that changes have not yet been saved. The pencil symbol disappears when you move to another record. It is important to understand that Access saves data automatically as soon as you move from one record to another. This may seem counterintuitive at first because other Office applications, such as Word and Excel, do not save changes and additions automatically.

Figure 1.6 shows the navigation buttons on the *navigation bar* that you use to move through the records in a table, query, or form. The buttons enable you to go to the first record, the previous record, the next record, or the last record. The button with the yellow asterisk is used to add a new (blank) record. You can also type a number directly into the current record field, and Access will take you to that record. Finally, the navigation bar enables you to find a record based on a single word. Type the word in the search box, and Access will locate the first record that contains the word.

Type in a single search word

Create a new (blank) record

Go to the last record

Go to the next record

Type in the record you want to go to

Go to the previous record

Go to the first record

FIGURE 1.6 Navigation Buttons

You can also use the Find command in the Find group on the Home tab to locate specific records within a table, form, or query. You can search for a single field or the entire record, match all or part of the selected field(s), move forward or back in a table, or specify a case-sensitive search. The Replace command can be used to substitute one value for another. Select Replace All if you want Access to automatically search for and replace every instance of a value without first checking with you. Be careful when using the Replace All option for global replacement, however, because unintended replacements are possible.

The **Design view** gives you a detailed view of the table's structure and is used to create and modify a table's design by specifying the fields it will contain, the fields' data types, and their associated properties. Data types define the type of data that will be stored in a field, such as short text, long text, numeric, currency, etc. For example, if you need to store the hire date of an employee, you would enter the field name Hire Date and select the Date/Time data type. The **field properties** define the characteristics of the fields in more detail. For example, for the field Hire Date, you could set a field property that requires a Short Date format.

Figure 1.7 shows the Design view for the Customers table. In the top portion, each row contains the field names, the data type, and an optional description for each field in the table. In the bottom portion, the Field Properties pane contains the properties (details) for each field. Click on a field, and the properties for that field will be displayed in the bottom portion of the Design view window.

Figure 1.7 also shows the primary key. The **primary key** is the field (or combination of fields) that uniquely identifies each record in a table. The CustomerID field is the primary key in the Customers table; it ensures that each record in the table can be distinguished from every other record. It also helps prevent the occurrence of duplicate records. Primary key fields may be numbers, letters, or a combination of both. In Figure 1.7, the primary key has an **AutoNumber** data type (a number that is generated by Access and is automatically incremented each time a record is added). Another example of a primary key is an automatically generated Employee ID.

FIGURE 1.7 Customers Table in Design View

Open an Access File and Work with Content Security

STEP 1 ⟫ When Access is first launched, the Backstage view displays. The left side of the view provides a list of databases you have recently used. Beneath the list of recently used databases is the Open Other Files option. Click Open Other Files to access the Open options. You will see a list of the places your account allows you to open a file from: a recent location, your OneDrive account, your computer, or from any additional places you have added to your Places list. You can also add a new place by clicking the *Add a Place* option. If you select your OneDrive or another place and the desired database is not in the recent list, you will need to click Browse to open the Open dialog box. Then you can locate and select the database and click Open.

If you are currently using Access and wish to open another database, do the following:

1. Click the FILE tab.
2. Click Open in Backstage view to access Open options.
3. Select the place where the database is stored.

4. Click Browse to open the Open dialog box.
5. Locate and select the database and click Open.

If you open a database from a location you have not designated as a trusted location or open a database that does not have a digital signature from a publisher you can trust, Access will display a message bar immediately below the Ribbon. The message bar displays a security warning designed to prevent you from opening a database that may contain harmful code that can be hidden in macros or VBA modules. Click the Enable Content button if you trust the database's source—it becomes a trusted location. After you click Enable Content, Access closes the database and reopens the file to enable the content. Access also adds the database to its list of trusted documents so you will not see the security message again. All content from this publisher and associated with this book can be trusted.

Using an Existing Database

Databases must be carefully managed to keep information accurate. Records need to be edited when changes occur and when new records are added, and records may need to be deleted on occasion. All of these processes are easily accomplished using Access. Managing a database also requires that you understand when data is saved and when you need to use the Save commands.

Understand the Difference Between Working in Storage and Memory

STEP 3》 The way Access performs its save function is different from the other Microsoft Office applications. Word, Excel, and PowerPoint all work primarily from memory. In those applications, your work is not automatically saved to your storage location. You must save your work. This could be catastrophic if you are working with a PowerPoint presentation and you forget to save it. If the power is lost, you may lose your presentation. Access, on the other hand, works primarily from storage. As you enter and update the data in an Access database, the changes are automatically saved to the storage location you specified when you saved the database. If a power failure occurs, you will lose only the changes to the record that you are currently editing.

When you make a change to a record's content in an Access table (for example, changing a customer's cell phone number), Access saves your changes as soon as you move the insertion point to a different record. However, you are required to save after you modify the design of a table, a query, a form, or a report. When you modify an object's design, such as widening a field display on the Customers form, and then close it, Access will prompt you with the message "Do you want to save changes to the design of form 'Customers'?" Click Yes to save your changes.

Also in Access, you can click Undo to reverse the most recent change (the phone number you just modified) to a single record immediately after making changes to that record. However, unlike other Office programs that enable multiple Undo steps, you cannot use Undo to reverse multiple edits in Access.

With an Access database file, several users can work in the same file at the same time. Databases are often located on company servers, making it easy to have multiple users working in the same database at the same time. As long as multiple users do not attempt to change the same record at the same time, Access will let these users access the database simultaneously. So one person can be adding records to the Customers table while another can be creating a query based on the Products table. Two users can even work on the same table as long as they are not working on the same record.

Add, Edit, and Delete Records

STEP 4 To add a new record, click New in the Records group on the Home tab or click *New (blank)* *record* on the navigation bar. In a table, you can also click the first column of the blank row beneath the last record. As soon as you begin typing, the asterisk record indicator changes to a pencil icon to show that you are in editing mode. Press Tab to move to the next column so that you can enter the data for the next field. Pressing Tab in the last column in the record saves the record and moves the insertion point to the next record. You can also press Shift+Enter at any time in the record to save the record. The easiest way to save the record is to press the up or down arrow on your keyboard, which moves you to another record. As soon as you move to another record Access automatically saves the changes to the record you created or changed.

To edit a record, tab to the field you want to modify and type the new data. When you start typing, you erase all existing data in the field because the entire field is selected. You can switch to Edit mode by pressing F2. In Edit mode, you will not automatically delete all the data in the field. Instead, you can position your insertion point and make the changes you want.

REFERENCE Keyboard Shortcuts for Entering Data

Keystroke	Result
Up arrow (↑)	Moves insertion point up one row.
Down arrow (↓)	Moves insertion point down one row.
Left arrow (←)	Moves insertion point left one field in the same row.
Right arrow (→)	Moves insertion point right one field in the same row.
Tab or Enter	Moves insertion point right one field in the same row.
Shift+Tab	Moves insertion point left one field in the same row.
Home	Moves insertion point to the first field in the current row.
End	Moves insertion point to the last field in the current row.
Page Up	Moves insertion point up one screen.
Page Down	Moves insertion point down one screen.
Ctrl+Home	Moves insertion point to the first field in the first row.
Ctrl+End	Moves insertion point to the last field in the last row.
Esc	Cancels any changes made in the current field while in Edit mode.
Ctrl+Z	Reverses the last edit.
Ctrl+semicolon (;)	Enters the current date.
Ctrl+Alt+Spacebar	Enters the default value of a field.
Ctrl+single quote	Enters the value from the same field in the previous record.
Ctrl+plus sign (+)	Moves to a new record row.
Ctrl+minus sign (−)	Deletes the current record.

STEP 5 To delete a record, click the row selector for the record you want to delete and click Delete in the Records group on the Home tab. You can also delete a selected record by pressing Delete on the keyboard, or by right-clicking the row selector and selecting Delete Record from the shortcut menu.

Be careful about deleting records in a database. Deleting a record may result in the deletion of records in a related table. That information may be critical to the organization. For example, deleting an inactive customer may seem like a good idea, but if you delete the customer it could impact your order history.

Save As, Compact and Repair, and Back Up Access Files

STEP 6》

The Backstage view gives you access to the Save As command. When you click the Save As command, you can choose the file type you want to save: the database or the current object. Having the option of saving the entire database or just a component of it distinguishes Access from Word, Excel, and PowerPoint. Those applications have only one thing being saved—the primary document, workbook, or presentation. Save Database As enables you to select whether you want to save the database in the default database format (Access 2007–2013 file format), in one of the earlier Access formats, or as a template. Save Object As enables you to make a copy of the current Access object or publish a copy of the object as a PDF or XPS file. A PDF or XPS file looks the same on most computers because these file types preserve the object's formatting. PDF and XPS files also have a small file size. You can also click Save on the Quick Access Toolbar to save an active object—clicking Save on the Quick Access Toolbar does not save the database.

To help you manage your database so that it operates efficiently and securely, Access provides two utilities to help protect the data within a database: *Compact and Repair*, which reduces the size of the database, and *Back Up Database*, which creates a duplicate copy of the database.

Databases have a tendency to expand with everyday use and may become corrupt, so Access provides the *Compact and Repair Database* utility. Entering data, creating queries, running reports, and adding and deleting objects will all cause a database file to expand. This growth may increase storage requirements and may also impact database performance. When you run the Compact and Repair utility, it creates a new database file behind the scenes and copies all the objects from the original database into the new one. As it copies the objects into the new file, Access removes temporary objects and unclaimed space due to deleted objects, which results in a smaller database file. *Compact and Repair* will also defragment a fragmented database file if needed. When the utility is finished copying the data, it deletes the original file and renames the new one with the same name as the original. This utility can also be used to repair a corrupt database. In most cases, only a small amount of data—the last record modified—will be lost during the repair process. You should compact your database every day. To compact and repair an open database, do the following:

1. Close all open objects in the database.
2. Click the FILE tab.
3. Click *Compact and Repair Database* in the Info options.

As an alternative, you can click the Database Tools tab and click *Compact and Repair Database* in the Tools group.

You can have Access compact the open database each time you close it by using the *Compact and Close* option. To use this option, click File to open the Backstage view. Click Options and click Current Database. In the *Options for the current database* pane, click the *Compact on Close* check box under Application Options. Click OK.

The Back Up Database utility makes a copy of the entire database to protect your database from loss or damage. Imagine what would happen to a firm that loses the orders placed but not shipped, a charity that loses the list of donor contributions, or a hospital that loses the digital records of its patients. Making backups is especially important when you have multiple users working with the database. When you use the Back Up Database utility, Access provides a file name for the backup that uses the same file name as the database you are backing up, an underscore, and the current date. This makes it easy for you to keep track of databases by the date they were created. To back up a database, do the following:

1. Click the FILE tab and click Save As.
2. Click Save Database As under File Types, if necessary.
3. Click Back Up Database under the Advanced group.
4. Click Save As. Revise the location and file name if you want to change either and click Save.

In Hands-On Exercise 1, you will work with the Northwind Traders database discussed in the Case Study at the beginning of the chapter. You open the database and examine the interface and Access views, organize information, work with records, and save, compact, repair, and back up the database.

Quick Concepts

1. Name the six objects in an Access database and briefly describe the purpose of each. *p. 85*
2. What is the difference between Datasheet view and Design view in a table? *p. 88*
3. What is meant by the statement "Access works from storage"? *p. 91*
4. What is the purpose of the *Compact and Repair* utility? *p. 93*

Hands-On Exercises

Watch the Video
for this Hands-
On Exercise!

MyITLab®
HOE1 Training

1 Databases Are Everywhere!

Northwind purchases food items from suppliers around the world and sells them to restaurants and specialty food shops. Northwind depends on the data stored in its Access database to process orders and make daily decisions. In your new position with Northwind Traders, you need to spend time getting familiar with the Access database. You will open Northwind's database, examine the Access interface, review the existing objects in the database, and explore Access views. You will add, edit, and delete records using both tables and forms. Finally, you will compact and repair, and back up the database.

Skills covered: Open an Access File and Work with Content Security • Examine the Access Interface, Explore Access Views, Organize Information in a Database, and Recognize Access Objects and Edit a Record and Understand the Difference Between Working in Storage and Memory • Add a Record • Delete a Record • Save As, Compact and Repair, and Back Up the Database

---

STEP 1 ≫ OPEN AN ACCESS FILE AND WORK WITH CONTENT SECURITY

This exercise introduces you to the Northwind Traders database. You will use this database to learn the fundamentals of working with database files. Refer to Figure 1.8 as you complete Step 1.

FIGURE 1.8 Message Bar Displaying Security Warning

a. Open Access, click **Open Other Files**, click **Computer**, and then click **Browse**. Navigate to the folder location designated by your instructor. Click *a01h1Traders* and click **Open**.

b. Click the **FILE tab**, click **Save As**, click **Save Database As**, and then verify *Access Database* is selected under *Database File Types*. Click **Save As** and save the file as **a01h1Traders_LastFirst**.

When you save files, use your last and first names. For example, as the Access author, I would save my database as *a01h1traders_KrebsCynthia*. The Security Warning message bar appears below the Ribbon, indicating that some database content is disabled.

c. Click **Enable Content** on the Security Warning message bar.

When you open an Access file from the student files associated with this book, you will need to enable the content. You may be confident of the trustworthiness of the files for this book. Keep the database open for the rest of the exercise.

STEP 2 ≫ EXAMINE THE ACCESS INTERFACE, EXPLORE ACCESS VIEWS, ORGANIZE INFORMATION IN A DATABASE, AND RECOGNIZE ACCESS OBJECTS

Now that you have opened Northwind Traders, you examine the Navigation Pane, objects, and views to become familiar with these fundamental Access features. Refer to Figure 1.9 as you complete Step 2.

Step e: Tabs showing open table objects

Step a: Expanded Tables group

Step f: Shutter Bar Open/Close button

Step h: Collapsed Forms group

Step g: Expanded Reports group

FIGURE 1.9 Access Navigation Pane and Open Objects

a. Scroll through the Navigation Pane and note the Access objects listed under each expanded group.

The Tables group and the Forms group are expanded, displaying all of the tables and forms objects. The Queries, Reports, Macros, and Modules groups are collapsed so that the objects in those groups are not displayed.

b. Right-click the **Customers table** in the Navigation Pane and select **Open**.

The Customers table opens. The Customers tab displays below the Ribbon indicating the table object is open. The data contained in the table displays. Each customer's record displays on a table row. The columns of the table display the fields that comprise the records. You are viewing the table in Datasheet view.

c. Click **View** in the Views group on the HOME tab.

The view of the Customers table switches to Design view. The top portion of the view displays each field that comprises a customer record, the field's data type, and an optional description of what the field should contain. The bottom portion of the view displays the field properties (attributes) for the selected field.

d. Click **View** in the Views group on the HOME tab again.

Because View is a toggle button, your view returns to the Datasheet view, which resembles an Excel worksheet.

e. Double-click **Employees** in the Navigation Pane Tables group and double-click **Products** in the same location.

The tabs for three table objects display below the Ribbon: Customers, Employees, and Products.

f. Click the **Shutter Bar Open/Close button** on the title bar of the Navigation Pane to contract the Navigation Pane. Click the button again to expand the Navigation Pane.

The Shutter Bar Open/Close button toggles to allow you to view more in the open object window, or to enable you to view your database objects.

g. Scroll down in the Navigation Pane and click **Reports**.

The Reports group expands, and all report objects display.

h. Click the arrows to the right of Forms in the Navigation Pane.

The Forms group collapses and individual form objects no longer display.

You need to learn to edit the data in the Northwind database, because data can change. For example, employees will change their address and phone numbers when they move, and customers will change their order data from time to time. Refer to Figure 1.10 as you complete Step 3.

FIGURE 1.10 Edit the Employees Table

a. Click the **Employees tab** to activate the Employees table.

b. Click the **Last Name field** in the fourth row. Double-click **Peacock**; the entire name highlights. Type your last name to replace *Peacock*.

   Your last name replaces Peacock. For example, as the Access author, my last name, Krebs, replaces Peacock.

c. Press **Tab** to move to the next field in the fourth row. Replace *Margaret* with your first name and press **Tab**.

   Your first name replaces Margaret. For example, as the Access author, my first name, Cynthia, replaces Margaret. You have made changes to two fields in the same record. The pencil symbol in the row selector box indicates that the record has not yet been saved.

d. Click **Undo** on the Quick Access Toolbar.

   Your first and last names revert back to *Margaret Peacock* because you have not yet left the record.

e. Type your first and last names again to replace *Margaret Peacock*. Press **Tab**.

   You should now be in the title field and your title, *Sales Representative*, is selected. The record has not been saved, as indicated by the pencil symbol in the row selector box.

f. Click anywhere in the third row where Janet Leverling's data is stored.

   The pencil symbol disappears, indicating your changes have been saved.

g. Click the **Address field** in the first record, Nancy Davolio's record. Select the entire address and then type **4004 East Morningside Dr**. Click anywhere on the second record, Andrew Fuller's record.

h. Click **Undo**.

   Nancy Davolio's address reverts back to 507- 20th Ave. E. However, the Undo command is now faded. You can no longer undo the change that you made replacing Margaret Peacock's name with your own.

i. Click the **Close (X) button** at the top of the table to close the Employees table.

The Employees table closes. You are not prompted to save your changes; they have already been saved for you because Access works in storage, not memory. If you reopen the Employees table, you will see your name in place of Margaret Peacock's name.

> **TROUBLESHOOTING:** If you click the Close (X) button on the title bar at the top right of the window and accidentally close the database, locate the file and double-click it to reopen the file.

STEP 4 ≫ ADD A RECORD

You need to add new products to the Northwind database because the company is adding a new line of products. Refer to Figure 1.11 as you complete Step 4.

Step f: Click Find to locate a specific record

Step c: Forms group expanded

Step i: Type the new product information

Step h: Click New (blank) record to create a new record

Step e: Navigation (buttons)

FIGURE 1.11 Newly Created Record in the Products Form

a. Right-click the **Customers tab** and click **Close All**.

b. Click the **Tables group** in the Navigation Pane to collapse it and collapse the **Reports group**.

c. Click the **Forms group** in the Navigation Pane to expand the list of available forms.

d. Double-click the **Products form** to open it.

e. Locate the navigation buttons at the bottom of the Access window. Practice moving from one record to the next. Click **Next record** and click **Last record**; click **Previous record** and click **First record**.

f. Click **Find** in the Find group on the HOME tab, type **Grandma** in the **Find What box**, click the **Match arrow**, and then select **Any Part of Field**. Click **Find Next**.

You should see the data for Grandma's Boysenberry Spread. Selecting the Any Part of the Field option will return a match even if it is contained in the middle of a word.

g. Close the Find dialog box.

h. Click **New (blank) record** on the navigation bar.

i. Enter the following information for a new product.

Field Name	Value to Type
Product Name	*Your name*'s Pecan Pie
Supplier	Grandma Kelly's Homestead (click the arrow to select from the list of Suppliers)
Category	Confections (click the arrow to select from the list of Categories)
Quantity Per Unit	1
Unit Price	15.00
Units in Stock	18
Units on Order	50
Reorder Level	20
Discontinued	No (leave the check box unchecked)

As soon as you begin typing in the product name box, Access assigns a Product ID, in this case 78, to the record. The Product ID is used as the primary key in the Products table.

j. Click anywhere on the Pecan Pie record you just entered. Click the **FILE tab**, click **Print**, and then click **Print Preview**.

The first four records display in the Print Preview.

k. Click **Last Page** in the navigation bar and click **Previous Page** to show the new record you entered.

The beginning of the Pecan Pie record is now visible. The record continues on the next page.

l. Click **Close Print Preview** in the Close Preview group.

m. Close the Products form.

STEP 5 ≫ DELETE A RECORD

To help you understand how Access stores data, you verify that the new product is in the Products table. You also attempt to delete a record. Refer to Figure 1.12 as you complete Step 5.

FIGURE 1.12 Deleting a Record with Related Records

a. Click the **Forms group** in the Navigation Pane to collapse it and expand the **Tables group**.

b. Double-click the **Products table** to open it.

c. Click **Last record** in the navigation bar.

The Pecan Pie record you entered in the Products form is listed as the last record in the Products table. The Products form was created from the Products table. Your newly created record, Pecan Pie, is stored in the Products table even though you added it using the form.

d. Navigate to the fifth record in the table, *Chef Anton's Gumbo Mix*.

e. Use the horizontal scroll bar to scroll right until you see the Discontinued field.

The check mark in the Discontinued check box tells you that this product has been discontinued.

f. Click the **row selector** to the left of the fifth record.

The row highlights with a red-colored border to show that it is selected.

g. Click **Delete** in the Records group and read the error message.

The error message that displays tells you that you cannot delete this record because the table 'Order Details' has related records. (Customers ordered this product in the past.) Even though the product is now discontinued and no stock remains, it cannot be deleted from the Products table because related records exist in the Order Detail table.

h. Click **OK**.

i. Navigate to the last record and click the **row selector** to highlight the entire row.

j. Click **Delete** in the Records group. Read the warning.

The warning box that appears tells you that this action cannot be undone. Although this product can be deleted because it was just entered and no orders were created for it, you do not want to delete the record.

k. Click **No**. You do not want to delete this record. Close the Products table.

> **TROUBLESHOOTING:** If you clicked Yes and deleted the record, return to Step i. Reenter the information for this record. You will need it later in the lesson.

STEP 6 ≫ SAVE AS, COMPACT AND REPAIR, AND BACK UP THE DATABASE

You will protect the Northwind Traders database by using the two built-in Access utilities—Compact and Repair and Back Up Database. Refer to Figure 1.13 as you complete Step 6.

FIGURE 1.13 Back Up Database Utility

a. Click the **FILE tab** to open the Backstage view.

b. Click Compact & Repair Database.

Using the *Compact and Repair* utility helps improve the performance of your database.

c. Click the **FILE tab**, click **Save As**, and then click **Save Database As** under *File Types*, if necessary.

d. Double-click **Back Up Database** under the Advanced group to open the **Save As** dialog box.

The backup utility assigns the default name by adding a date to your file name.

e. Verify the *Save in* folder displays the location where you want your file saved and click **Save**.

You just created a backup of the database after completing Hands-On Exercise 1. The original database *a01h1traders_LastFirst* remains onscreen.

f. Keep the database open if you plan to continue with Hands-On Exercise 2. If not, close the database and exit Access.

Sorts and Filters

Access provides you with many tools that you can use to change the order of information and to identify and extract only the data needed at the moment. For example, you might need to display information by customer name in alphabetical order. Or you might need to know which suppliers are located in New Orleans or which customers have outstanding orders that were placed in the last seven days. You might use that information to identify possible disruptions to product deliveries or customers who may need a telephone call to let them know the status of their orders.

In this section, you will learn how to sort information and to isolate records in a table based on certain criteria.

Sorting Table Data on One or Multiple Fields

You can change the order of information by sorting one or more fields. A *sort* lists records in a specific sequence, such as alphabetically by last name or by ascending EmployeeID. To sort a table on one criteria, do the following:

STEP 4》

1. Click in the field that you want to use to sort the records.
2. Click Ascending or Descending in the Sort & Filter group on the HOME tab.

Ascending sorts a list of text data in alphabetical order or a numeric list in lowest to highest order. *Descending* sorts a list of text data in reverse alphabetical order or a numeric list in highest to lowest order. Figure 1.14 shows the Customers table for a bank sorted in ascending order by state.

Click Ascending to apply an A–Z sort

Click Remove Sort to undo the A–Z sort

Customers sorted in ascending order by State

FIGURE 1.14 Customers Table Sorted by State

Access can sort records by more than one field. Access sorts multiple criteria by first sorting the column on the left. The column immediately to the right of that column is sorted next. Because of this, you must arrange your columns in this order. To move a column, select the column and hold down the left mouse button. A heavy black bar appears to the left of the column. Drag the column to the position where you want it for the multiple sort.

Creating, Modifying, and Removing Filters

In Hands-On Exercise 1, you added Pecan Pie to the Products table with a category of Confections, but you also saw many other products. Suppose you wanted to see a list of just the products in the Confections category. To obtain this list, you would open the Products table in Datasheet view and create a filter. A *filter* displays a subset of records based on specified criteria. A *criterion* (or criteria, plural) is a number, a text phrase, or an expression used to select records from a table. Therefore, to view a list of all Confections, you would need to filter the Category field of the Products table using Confections as the criterion.

You can use filters to analyze data quickly. Applying a filter does not delete any records; filters only *hide* records that do not match the criteria. Two types of filters are discussed in this section: *Filter by Selection* and *Filter by Form*.

Use, Modify, and Remove a Filter

Filter by Selection displays only the records that match a criterion you select. To use *Filter by Selection*, do the following:

STEP 1 ≫

1. Click in any field that contains the criterion on which you want to filter.
2. Click Selection in the Sort & Filter group on the HOME tab.
3. Select *Equals "criterion"* from the list of options.

Figure 1.15 displays a Customers table with 10 records. The records in the table are displayed in sequence according to the CustomerID, which is also the primary key (the field or combination of fields that uniquely identifies a record). The navigation bar at the bottom indicates that the active record is the first row in the table. *Owner* in the Job Title field is selected.

Click Selection to use *Filter by Selection*

Criterion set to Equals "Owner"

All job titles are displayed

10 customers are showing

FIGURE 1.15 Unfiltered Customers Table

Figure 1.16 displays a filtered view of the Customers table, showing records with the job title *Owner*. The navigation bar shows that this is a filtered list containing 4 records matching the criteria. (The Customers table still contains the original 10 records, but only 4 records are visible with the filter applied.)

Click Toggle Filter to remove filter

Only records with the job title Owner are displayed

Filter icons

Only four customers are showing

FIGURE 1.16 Filtered Customers Table Shows Owners

Filter by Form is a more versatile method of selecting data because it enables you to display table records based on multiple criteria. When you use *Filter by Form*, all of the records are hidden and Access creates a blank form in a design grid. You see only field names with an arrow in the first field. Click on other fields and an arrow displays. Click an arrow and a list opens for you to use to specify your criterion. You can specify as many criteria as you need. When you apply the filter, Access displays the records that meet your criteria.

STEP 3≫

An advantage of using this filter method is that you can specify AND and OR logical operators. If you use the AND operator, a record is included in the results if all the criteria are true. If you use the OR operator, a record is included if at least one criterion is true. Another advantage of *Filter by Form* is that you can use a comparison operator. A **comparison operator** is used to evaluate the relationship between two quantities. For example, a comparison operator can determine if quantities are equal or not equal. If they are not equal, a comparison operator determines which one is greater than the other. Comparison operator symbols include: equal (=), not equal (<>), greater than (>), less than (<), greater than or equal to (>=), and less than or equal to (<=). To use *Filter by Form*, do the following:

1. Click Advanced in the Sort & Filter group on the HOME tab.
2. Click *Filter by Form*.
3. Click in the field you want to use as a criterion. Click the arrow to select the criterion from existing data.
4. Add additional criterion and comparison operators as needed.
5. Click Toggle Filter in the Sort & Filter group on the HOME tab to apply the filter.

In Figure 1.17, the Northwind Traders Products table is open. *Filter by Form* is set to select products with an inventory (Units in Stock) level greater than 30 (>30).

Click Advanced to access *Filter by Form*

Filter By Form

Filter set to display products with more than 30 units in stock

Add criteria by clicking the Or tab

FIGURE 1.17 Filter by Form Design Grid

The sort and filter operations can be done in any order; that is, you can sort a table first and apply a filter. Conversely, you can filter a table first to show only selected records and sort the filtered table to display the records in a certain order. It does not matter which operation is performed first.

STEP 2

You can also filter the table further by applying a second, third, or more criteria. For example, in the Products table shown in Figure 1.17, you can apply *Filter by Form* by clicking in the Supplier cell, selecting Exotic Liquids from the list, and then applying the filter. Then you could click Beverages and apply *Filter by Selection* to display all the beverages supplied by Exotic Liquids. You can also click Toggle Filter at any time to remove all filters and display all the records in the table. Filters are a temporary method for examining table data. If you close the filtered table and reopen it, the filter will be removed and all of the records will be restored.

TIP Use Undo After Applying a Filter by Selection

You can apply one *Filter by Selection* to a table, and then a second, and then a third to display certain records based on three criteria. If you click Toggle Filter, all three filters will be removed. What if you only want the last filter removed? Click Undo to remove only the last filter. Click Undo again and remove the second-to-last filter. This feature will help you apply and remove multiple filters, one at a time.

Quick Concepts

1. What are the benefits of sorting the records in a table? *p. 102*

2. What is the purpose of creating a filter? *p. 103*

3. What is the difference between *Filter by Selection* and *Filter by Form*? *pp. 103–104*

4. What is a comparison operator and how is it used in a filter? *p. 104*

Hands-On Exercises

2 Sorts and Filters

The sales manager at Northwind Traders needs quick answers to her questions about customer orders. You use the Access database to filter tables to answer these questions, then sort the records based on the manager's needs.

Skills covered: Use Filter by Selection with an Equal Condition • Use Filter by Selection with a Contains Condition • Use Filter by Form with a Comparison Operator • Sort a Table

---

STEP 1 ≫ USE FILTER BY SELECTION WITH AN EQUAL CONDITION

The sales manager asks for a list of customers who live in London. You use *Filter by Selection* with an equal condition to locate these customers. Refer to Figure 1.18 as you complete Step 1.

FIGURE 1.18 Customers Table Filtered for London Records

a. Open the *a01h1traders_LastFirst* database if you closed it after the last Hands-On Exercise and save it as **a01h2Traders_LastFirst**, changing *h1* to *h2*.

> **TROUBLESHOOTING:** If you make any major mistakes in this exercise, you can close the file, open *a01h1Traders_LastFirst* again, and then start this exercise over.

b. Double-click the **Customers table** in the Navigation Pane under *Tables*, navigate to record 4, and then replace *Thomas Hardy* with your name in the Contact Name field.

c. Scroll right until the City field is visible. The fourth record has a value of *London* in the City field. Click the field to select it.

d. Click **Selection** in the Sort & Filter group on the HOME tab.

e. Select **Equals "London"** from the menu. Note that six customers were located.

The navigation bar display shows that six records that meet the *London* criterion are available. The other records in the Customers table are hidden. The Filtered icon also displays on the navigation bar, indicating that the Customers table has been filtered.

f. Click **Toggle Filter** in the Sort & Filter group to remove the filter.

g. Click **Toggle Filter** again to reset the filter. Leave the Customers table open for the next step.

STEP 2 ›› USE FILTER BY SELECTION WITH A CONTAINS CONDITION

The sales manager asks you to narrow the list of London customers so that it displays only Sales Representatives. To accomplish this task, you add a second layer of filtering using the *Filter by Selection* feature. Refer to Figure 1.19 as you complete Step 2.

FIGURE 1.19 Customers in London with the Contact Title *Sales Representative*

a. Click in any field in the Contact Title column that contains the value *Sales Representative*.

b. Click **Selection** in the Sort & Filter group and click **Contains "Sales Representative"**. Locate your name in the filtered table. Compare your results to those shown in Figure 1.19.

Three records match the criteria you set. You have applied a second layer of filtering to the customers in London. The second layer further restricts the display to only those customers who have the words *Sales Representative* contained in their titles.

TROUBLESHOOTING: If you do not see the record for Victoria Ashworth, you selected *Equals "Sales Representative"* instead of *Contains "Sales Representative"*. Repeat steps a and b, making sure you select *Contains "Sales Representative"*.

---

c. Close the Customers table. Click **Yes** if a dialog box asks if you want to save the design changes to the Customers table.

STEP 3 ›› USE FILTER BY FORM WITH A COMPARISON OPERATOR

You are asked to provide a list of records that do not match just one set of criteria. You are asked to provide a list of all extended prices less than $50 for a specific sales representative. Use *Filter by Form* to provide the information when two or more criteria are needed. You also preview the results in Print Preview to see how the list would print. Refer to Figure 1.20 as you complete Step 3.

Step i: Enter <50 for the ExtendedPrice criteria

Step d: Click Advanced to select Filter by Form

Steps f–h: Select your first and last names

FIGURE 1.20 Filter by Form Selection Criteria

a. Click the **Tables group** in the Navigation Pane to collapse the listed tables.

b. Click the **Queries group** in the Navigation Pane to expand the list of available queries.

c. Locate and double-click the **Order Details Extended query** to open it.

This query contains information about orders. It has fields containing information about the sales person, the Order ID, the product name, the unit price, quantity ordered, the discount given, and an extended price. The extended price is a field used to total order information.

d. Click **Advanced** in the Sort & Filter group and select **Filter by Form** from the list.

All of the records are now hidden, and you see only field names and an arrow in the first field. Although you are applying *Filter by Form* to a query, you can use the same process as applying *Filter by Form* to a table. You are able to enter more than one criterion using *Filter by Form*.

e. Click in the first row under the First Name field, if necessary.

An arrow appears at the right of the box.

f. Click the **First Name arrow**.

A list of all available first names appears. Your name should be on the list. Figure 1.20 shows *Cynthia Krebs*, which replaced Margaret Peacock in Hands-On Exercise 1.

> **TROUBLESHOOTING:** If you do not see your name and you do see Margaret on the list, you probably skipped steps in Hands-On Exercise 1. Close the query without saving changes, return to the first Hands-On Exercise, and then rework it, making sure not to omit any steps. Then you can return to this location and work the remainder of this Hands-On Exercise.

g. Select your first name from the list.

h. Click in the first row under the Last Name field to reveal the arrow. Locate and select your last name by clicking it.

i. Scroll right until you see the Extended Price field. Click in the first row under the Extended Price field and type **<50**.

This will select all of the items that you ordered where the total was under $50. You ignore the arrow and type the expression needed.

j. Click **Toggle Filter** in the Sort & Filter group.

You have specified which records to include and have executed the filtering by clicking Toggle Filter. You should have 31 records that match the criteria you specified.

k. Click the **FILE tab**, click **Print**, and then click **Print Preview**.

You instructed Access to preview the filtered query results. The preview displays the query title as a heading. The current filter is applied, as well as page numbers.

l. Click **Close Print Preview** in the Close Preview group.

m. Close the Order Details Extended query. Click **Yes** if a dialog box asks if you want to save your changes.

Deleting Filter by Form Criterion

While working with *Filter by Selection* or *Filter by Form*, you may inadvertently save a filter. To view a saved filter, open the table or query that you suspect may have a saved filter. Click Advanced in the Sort & Filter group and click *Filter by Form*. If criteria appear in the form, then a filter has been saved. To delete a saved filter, toggle the filter, click Advanced, and then click Close All Filters. Close and save the table or query.

STEP 4 ≫ SORT A TABLE

The Sales Manager is pleased with your work; however, she would like some of the information to appear in a different order. You will now sort the records in the Customers table using the manager's new criteria. Refer to Figure 1.21 as you complete Step 4.

Step i and j: Records are sorted by Country, then City

Step c: Shutter Bar Open/Close button

Steps i and j: Click Ascending to sort by Country, then City

FIGURE 1.21 Customers Table Sorted by Country, Then City

a. Click the **Queries group** in the Navigation Pane to collapse the listed queries.

b. Click the **Tables group** in the Navigation Pane to expand the list of available tables and double-click the **Customers table** to open it.

  This table contains information about customers. The table is sorted in alphabetical order by Company Name.

c. Click the **Shutter Bar Open/Close button** in the Navigation Pane to close the Navigation Pane.

  It will be easier to locate fields in the Customer table if the Navigation Pane is closed.

d. Click any field in the Customer ID column, the first field in the table. Click **Descending** in the Sort & Filter group on the HOME tab.

  Sorting in descending order on a character field produces a reverse alphabetical order.

e. Scroll right until you can see both the Country and City fields.

f. Click the **Country column heading**.

  The entire column is selected.

g. Click the **Country column heading** again and hold down the **left mouse button**.

  A thick dark blue line displays on the left edge of the Country field.

h. Check to make sure that you see the thick blue line. Drag the **Country field** to the left until the thick black line moves between the City and Region fields. Release the mouse and the Country field position moves to the right of the City field.

You moved the Country field next to the City field so that you can easily sort the table based on both fields. In order to sort by two or more fields, they need to be placed adjacent to each other.

i. Click any city name in the City field and click **Ascending** in the Sort & Filter group.

The City field displays the cities in alphabetical order.

j. Click any country name in the Country field and click **Ascending**.

The countries are sorted in alphabetical order. The cities within each country also are sorted alphabetically. For example, the customer in Graz, Austria, is listed before the customer in Salzburg, Austria.

k. Close the Customers table. Click **Yes** to save the changes to the design of the table.

l. Click the **Shutter Bar Open/Close button** in the Navigation Pane to open the Navigation Pane.

m. Click the **FILE tab** to open the Backstage view and click **Compact & Repair Database**.

n. Click the **FILE tab**, click **Save As**, and then click **Save Database As** in File Types, if necessary.

o. Double-click **Back Up Database** under the Advanced group to open the Save As dialog box.

p. Verify the *Save in* folder displays the location where you want your file saved and click **Save**.

q. Close the database and submit based on your instructor's directions. Leave Access open if you plan to continue with Hands-On Exercise 3. If not, exit Access.

Access Versus Excel, and Relational Databases

Both Access and Excel contain powerful tools that enable you to extract the information you need and arrange it in a way that makes it easy to analyze. An important part of becoming a proficient Office user is learning which of these applications to use to accomplish a task.

In this section, you will learn how to decide whether to use Access or Excel by examining the distinct advantages of each application. Ideally, the type of data and the type of functionality you require should determine which program will work best.

Knowing When to Use Access or Excel to Manage Data

You are probably familiar with working in an Excel spreadsheet. You type the column headings, enter the data, perhaps add a formula or two, and then add totals to the bottom. Once the data has been entered, you can apply a filter, sort the data, or start all over—similar to what you learned to do in Access with filters. It is true that you can accomplish many of the same tasks using either Excel or Access. Although the two programs have much in common, they each have distinct advantages. How do you choose whether to use Access or Excel? The choice you make may ultimately depend on how well you know Access. Users who know Excel only are more likely to use a spreadsheet even if a database would be better. When database features are used in Excel, they are generally used on data that is in one table. When the data is better suited to be on two or more tables, then using Access is preferable. Learning how to use Access will be beneficial to you because it will enable you to work more efficiently with large groups of data.

Select the Software to Use

A contact list (for example, name, address, phone number) created in Excel may serve your needs just fine in the beginning. Each time you enter a new contact, you can add another row to the bottom of your worksheet. You can sort the list by last name for easier look-up of names. In Excel, you can easily move an entire column, insert a new column, or copy and paste data from one cell to another. This is the "ease of use" characteristic of Excel.

If you need to expand the information in Excel to keep track of each time you contacted someone on your contact list, you may need an additional worksheet. This additional sheet would only list the contacts whom you have contacted and some information about the nature of the contact. Which contact was it? When was the contact made? Was it a phone contact or a face-to-face meeting? As you track these entries, your worksheet will contain a reference to the first worksheet using the contact name.

If a contact is deleted on the first worksheet, that contact's information will still remain on the second worksheet, unless someone remembers to remove it. Similarly, information could be added about a contact on the second worksheet without the contact being officially entered into the first worksheet. As the quantity and complexity of the data increase, the need to organize your data logically also increases.

Access provides built-in tools to help organize data better than Excel. One tool that helps Access organize data is the ability to create relationships between tables. A *relationship* is a connection between two tables using a field that is common to the two tables. The benefit of a relationship is the ability to efficiently combine data from related tables for the purpose of creating queries, forms, and reports. Relationships are the reason Access is referred to as a relational database.

Use Access

STEP 1 » Use Access to manage data when you:

- Require multiple related tables to store your data.
- Have a large amount of data.
- Need to connect to and retrieve data from external databases, such as Microsoft SQL Server.
- Need to group, sort, and total data based on various parameters.
- Have an application that requires multiple users to connect to one data source at the same time.

Use Excel

Use Excel to manage data when you:

- Need only one worksheet to handle all of your data.
- Have mostly numeric data—for example, you need to maintain an expense statement.
- Require subtotals and totals in your worksheet.
- Want to primarily run a series of "what if" scenarios on your data.
- Need to create complex charts and/or graphs.

Understanding Relational Power

In the previous section, we compared Excel worksheets to Access relational databases. Access has the ability to create relationships between two tables, whereas Excel does not. Access is known as a *relational database management system* (RDBMS); using an RDBMS, you can manage groups of data (tables) and set rules (relationships) between tables. When relational databases are designed properly, users can easily combine data from multiple tables to create queries, forms, and reports.

Good database design begins with grouping data into the correct tables. This practice, known as *normalization*, will take time to learn, but over time you will begin to understand the fundamentals. The design of a relational database management system is illustrated in Figure 1.22, which shows the table design of the Northwind Traders database. The tables have been created, the field names have been added, and the data types have been set. The diagram shows the relationships that were created between tables using *join lines*. Join lines enable you to create a relationship between two tables using a common field. Figure 1.22 also shows the join lines between related tables as a series of lines connecting common fields. For example, the Suppliers table is joined to the Products table using the common field SupplierID. If you examine some of the connections, you will see that the EmployeeID is linked to the Orders table by a join line. This means that you can produce a report displaying all orders for a customer and the employee who entered the order. The Orders table is joined to the Order Details table where the OrderID is the common field. The Products table is joined to the Order Details table where the ProductID is the common field. These table connections enable you to query the database for information stored in multiple tables. This feature gives the manager the ability to ask questions like "How many different beverages were shipped last week?" or "What was the total revenue generated from seafood orders last year?"

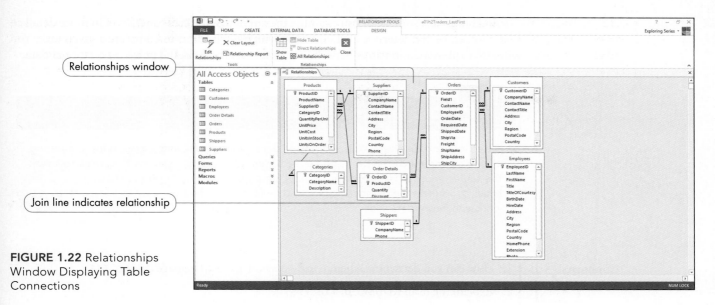

Relationships window

Join line indicates relationship

FIGURE 1.22 Relationships Window Displaying Table Connections

Use the Relationships Window

Relationships are set in the Relationships window by the database developer after the tables have been created but before any sample data is entered. The most common method of connecting two tables is to connect the primary key from one table to the foreign key of another. A *foreign key* is a field in one table that is also the primary key of another table. In the previous figure, Figure 1.22, the SupplierID (primary key) in the Suppliers table is joined to the SupplierID (foreign key) in the Products table. Remember, a primary key is a field that uniquely identifies each record in a table.

To create a relationship between two tables, follow these guidelines:

1. Click Relationships in the Relationships group on the DATABASE TOOLS tab.
2. Add the two tables that you want to join together to the Relationships window.
3. Drag the common field (e.g., SupplierID) from the primary table (e.g., Suppliers) onto the common field (e.g., SupplierID) of the related table (e.g., Products). The data types of the common fields must be the same.
4. Check the Enforce Referential Integrity check box.
5. Close the Relationships window.

STEP 2 ▷▷

 View Join Lines

Databases with many tables with relationships may make it difficult to see the join lines between tables. Tables may be repositioned to make it easier to see the join lines. To reposition a table, drag the table by its table name to the new position.

Enforce Referential Integrity

STEP 3 ▷▷ Enforce referential integrity is one of three options you can select when setting a table relationship. When *enforce referential integrity* is checked, Access ensures that data cannot be entered into a related table unless it first exists in the primary table. For example, in Figure 1.22 you cannot enter a product into the Products table using a SupplierID that does not exist in the Suppliers table. This rule ensures the integrity of the data in the database and improves overall data accuracy. Referential integrity also prohibits users from deleting a record in one table if it has records in related tables.

In Hands-on Exercise 3, you examine the strengths of Access and Excel in more detail so that you can better determine when to use which application to complete a given task. You will also explore relationships between tables and learn about the power of relational data.

Create Sample Data

When learning database skills, starting with a smaller set of sample data prior to entering all company records can be helpful. A small amount of data gives you the ability to check the tables and quickly see if your results are correct. Even though the data amounts are small, as you test the database tables and relationships, the results will prove useful as you work with larger data sets.

Quick Concepts

1. How can you determine when to use Access or Excel to manage data? *p. 111*

2. Explain the term RDBMS. *p. 112*

3. What is the purpose of a join line? *p. 112*

Hands-On Exercises

Watch the Video for this Hands-On Exercise!
MyITLab® HOE3 Training

3 Access Versus Excel, and Relational Databases

In this exercise, you review the relationships set in the Northwind Traders database. This will help you learn more about the overall design of the database. Examining the relationships will also help you understand why Access rather than Excel is used by Northwind Traders for data management.

Skills covered: Know When to Use Access or Excel to Manage Data • Use the Relationships Window, Use Filter by Form with a Comparison Operator, and Reapply a Saved Filter • Enforce Referential Integrity

STEP 1 ≫ KNOW WHEN TO USE ACCESS OR EXCEL TO MANAGE DATA

In this exercise, you examine the connections between the tables in the Northwind Traders database and review the reasons that Access was selected as the application for this data. Refer to Figure 1.23 as you complete Step 1.

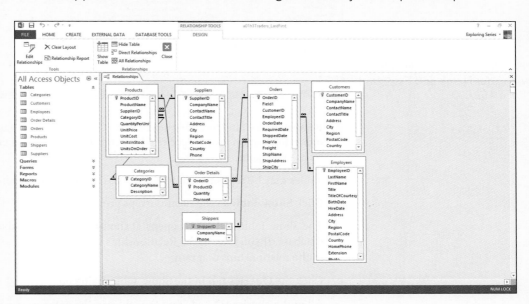

FIGURE 1.23 Relationships Window for the Northwind Database

a. Open the *a01h2Traders_LastFirst* database if you closed it after the last Hands-On Exercise and save it as **a01h3Traders_LastFirst**, changing *h2* to *h3*.

b. Click the **DATABASE TOOLS tab** and click **Relationships** in the Relationships group.

c. Examine the join lines showing the relationships that connect the various tables. For example, the Orders table is connected to the Order Details table.

Examining the number of tables in a database and their relationships is a good way to determine whether you need to use Excel or Access for your data. Because this data needs more than one table, involves a large amount of connected data, needs to group, sort, and total data based on various parameters, and needs to allow multiple users to connect to one data source at the same time, it is better to manipulate this data using Access rather than using Excel.

Use the Relationships window to move tables to make the join lines easier to view. To reinforce your filter skills, use *Filter by Form* to solve more complex questions about the Northwind data. After you retrieve the records, save the *Filter by Form* specifications so that you can reapply the filter later. Refer to Figure 1.24 as you complete Step 2.

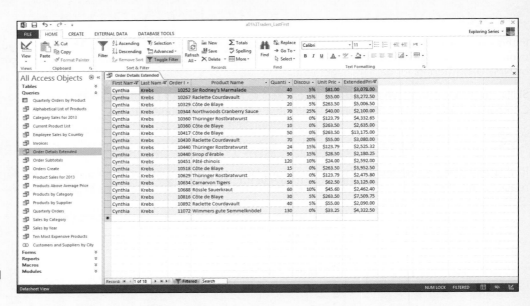

FIGURE 1.24 Query Results with Your Name and Extended Price >$2,000

a. Reposition the Shippers table beneath the Orders table by dragging it to the right by its table name. Reposition the Categories table beneath the Order Details table by dragging it to the right by its table name.

Tables may be repositioned to make it easier to see the join lines creating the relationships.

b. Click **Show Table** in the Relationships group on the RELATIONSHIPS TOOLS DESIGN tab.

The Show Table dialog box opens. It shows you the eight tables that are available in the database. If you look in the Relationships window, you will see that all eight tables are open in the relationships diagram.

c. Click the **Queries tab** in the Show Table dialog box.

All of the queries created from the tables in the database are listed in the Show Table dialog box. You could add all of the queries to the Relationships window. Things might become cluttered, but you could tell at a glance from where the queries get their information.

d. Close the Show Table dialog box.

e. Click the **Shutter Bar Open/Close button** in the Navigation Pane to open the Navigation Pane, if necessary.

f. Click **All Access Objects** on the Navigation Pane and click **Tables and Related Views**.

You now see each table and all the queries, forms, and reports that are based on each table. If a query is created using more than one table, it appears multiple times in the Navigation Pane.

g. Close the Relationships window. Save the changes to the design. Click **All Tables** on the Navigation Pane and click **Object Type**.

h. Collapse the Tables group in the Navigation Pane, expand the **Queries** group, and then double-click the **Order Details Extended query**.

i. Click **Advanced** in the Sort & Filter group, select **Filter by Form**, click in the first row under the Last Name field, and then select your last name.

j. Scroll right (or press **Tab**) until the Extended Price field is visible. Click in the first row in the Extended Price field and type **>2000**.

The Extended Price field shows the purchased amount for each item ordered. If an item sold for $15 and a customer ordered 10, the Extended Price would display $150.

k. Click **Toggle Filter** in the Sort & Filter group. Examine the filtered results.

Your comparison operator, >2000, identified 18 items ordered where the extended price exceeded $2,000.

l. Close the Order Details Extended query by clicking the **Close (X) button**. Click **Yes** to save changes.

m. Open the Order Details Extended query again.

The filter disengages when you close and reopen the object. However, because you opted to save the changes before closing, the filter has been stored with the query. You may reapply the filter at any time by clicking the Toggle Filter command (until the next filter replaces the current one).

n. Click **Toggle Filter** in the Sort & Filter group. Compare your results to Figure 1.24.

o. Save and close the query.

STEP 3 ≫ ENFORCE REFERENTIAL INTEGRITY

You need an additional relationship created between the Orders table and the Customers table. You create the relationship and enforce referential integrity. Refer to Figure 1.25 as you complete Step 3.

FIGURE 1.25 Relationship Created Between Orders Table and Customers Table

a. Click the **DATABASE TOOLS tab** and click **Relationships** in the Relationships group.

b. Locate the CustomerID field in the Orders table and drag it to the CustomerID field (primary key) in the Customers table.

The Edit Relationships dialog box opens. It shows that the Table/Query is from the Customers table and the related Table/Query comes from the Orders table. The relationship type is displayed at the bottom of the dialog box and indicates that this will be a One-To-Many relationship.

c. Click **Enforce Referential Integrity**.

Access will now ensure that data cannot be entered into the related table (Orders) unless it first exists in the primary table (Customers).

d. Click **Create**.

A join line displays between the Orders and Customers tables.

e. Click the **FILE tab** and click **Compact & Repair Database**. Click **Yes** if asked if you want to save changes to the layout of Relationships.

f. Click the **FILE tab**, click **Save As**, and then click **Save Database As** under *File Types* if necessary. Double-click **Back Up Database** in the Advanced group to open the Save As dialog box.

g. Verify the *Save in* folder displays the location where you want your backup file saved and click **Save**.

A duplicate copy of the database is saved with the default file name that is the original file name followed by the current date.

h. Exit Access.

Access Database Creation

Now that you have examined the fundamentals of an Access database and explored the power of relational databases, it is time to create one! In this section, you explore the benefits of creating a database using each of the methods discussed in the next section.

Creating a Database

When you first start Access, the Backstage view opens and provides you with three methods for creating a new database. These methods are:

- Creating a custom Web app
- Creating a blank desktop database
- Creating a database from a template

Creating a *custom Web app* enables you to create a database that you can build and then use and share with others through the Web. Creating a blank desktop database lets you create a database specific to your needs. Rather than starting from scratch by creating a blank desktop database, you may want to use a template to create a new database. An Access *template* is a predefined database that includes professionally designed tables, forms, reports, and other objects that you can use to jumpstart the creation of your database.

Figure 1.26 shows the options for creating a custom Web app, a blank desktop database, and multiple templates from which you can select the method for which you want to create a database.

FIGURE 1.26 Backstage View with Database Creation Options

Create a Web Application Using a Template

Creating a Web app (application) is new in Access 2013. An Access Web app is a new type of database that lets you build a browser-based database application— you can create a database in the cloud that you and others can access and use simultaneously. This requires that you use a host server such as SharePoint (a Web application platform developed by Microsoft) or Office 365 (a cloud service edition of SharePoint).

To create a Web app, click *Custom web app* in the Backstage view, give your app a name, and then choose a location. Once you click Create, a blank database opens. You then create the tables that will serve as the foundation of your database. The easiest way to add a table is to use the Access library of Table Templates. Each of the templates in the library includes tables, fields, and views that you will need to create an app. Some templates also include related tables.

As an alternative to creating a Web app from scratch, you can select a Web app template from the Backstage view. These templates are fully functional Web databases. Click one of the Web app template tiles and an introduction screen appears that previews the datasheet, provides a description of the purpose of the datasheet, lets you know the download size of the database, and even displays how users like you have rated the database. You give the app a name and select the Web location where the app is to be saved. Finally, you create the app. When you have completed the database, click Launch App in the View group on the Home tab. You can then use it and share it on the Web. Figure 1.27 shows the introduction screen for the Asset tracking template. This template requires SharePoint so that you can share content with others.

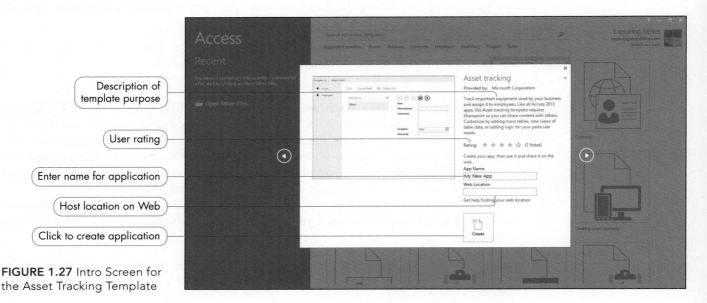

Description of template purpose

User rating

Enter name for application

Host location on Web

Click to create application

FIGURE 1.27 Intro Screen for the Asset Tracking Template

Create a Blank Desktop Database

To create a blank desktop database specific to your needs, click *Blank desktop database* in the Backstage view. Access opens to a blank table in Datasheet view where you can add data. You can refine the table in Design view. You would then create additional tables and objects as necessary. To create a blank desktop database, do the following:

1. Open Access or click the FILE tab to open the Backstage view and click New.
2. Click the *Blank desktop* database tile.
3. Enter the file name for the file in the text box, click the Browse button to navigate to the folder where you want to store the database file, and then click OK.
4. Click Create.
5. Enter data in the empty table that displays.

Create a Desktop Database Using a Template

Using a template to start a database saves you a great deal of creation time. Working with a template can also help a new Access user become familiar with database design. Templates are available from the Backstage view, where you can select from a variety of templates or search online for more templates.

Access also provides templates for desktop use. To create a desktop database from a template, do the following:

STEP 1▶

1. Open Access or click the FILE tab to open the Backstage view and click New.
2. Click the database template you want to use.
3. Enter the file name for the file in the text box, click the Browse button to navigate to the folder where you want to store the database file, and then click OK.

4. Click Create to download the template.

5. Open the database and click Enable Content in the Security Warning message bar if you trust the source of the database.

Once the database is open, you may see a Getting Started page that includes links you can use to learn more about the database. A new Access user can gain valuable information by watching any associated videos and clicking provided hyperlinks. When finished reviewing the learning materials, close the Getting Started page to view the database. Figure 1.28 displays the Getting Started page included with the *Desktop task management* template. Two videos are provided to aid you in using and modifying the database. Because this database contains a Contacts table, there is a hyperlink to a wizard that will import contacts from Microsoft Outlook (if you use Microsoft Outlook). Links are available that will connect you with experts, enable you to get free advice from a forum, and get more help from Microsoft .com. The Getting Started page also includes a button you can click to open a survey that provides feedback to Microsoft. Close the Getting Started page to return to the database.

FIGURE 1.28 Getting Started Page for Desktop Task Management Template

STEP 2 Because you downloaded a template, some objects will have already been created. You can work with these objects just as you did in the first three sections of this chapter. For example, you can enter data directly into any existing table in the database by opening the table, clicking in the first empty field, typing the data, tabbing to the next empty field, and then typing the data for the next field. You can also open any form that is part of the downloaded template and enter the data directly in the forms. Some templates will include queries and reports. Edit any object to meet your requirements.

STEP 3 Once the database is opened, review the objects listed in the Navigation Pane. Change the Navigation Pane category from Object Type to *Tables and Related Views* to become familiar with the relationships between the tables and other database objects. Note the tables and the objects that are based on them.

After noting the objects in the database, open the Relationships window to see the connections between them. Once you are familiar with the database design, you can enter your data.

Figure 1.29 displays the open Task Management database with the Navigation Pane set to display *Tables and Related Views*. The Tasks table displays with its related queries, forms, and reports. The Relationships window shows the relationship between the Contacts table and the Tasks table.

Relationships window

Navigation Pane displaying tables and related views

Tasks table

Queries, forms, and reports based on Task table

Join line indicates relationship

FIGURE 1.29 Relationships Window for the Task Management Database

Quick **Concepts**

1. Name the three methods for creating a new database. ***p. 119***

2. What is a custom Web app, and what is required to build a custom Web app? ***p. 119***

3. What are two benefits of using a template to create a database? ***p. 120***

Hands-On Exercises

4 Access Database Creation

After working with the Northwind Traders database on the job, you decide to use Access to create a personal contact database. Rather than start from scratch, you use an Access Contact Manager desktop template to jumpstart your database creation. A Web app is not necessary because you do not want to share your contacts with others.

Skills covered: Create a Desktop Database Using a Template • Add Records to a Downloaded Desktop Database Template • Explore the Database Objects in a Downloaded Desktop Database Template

---

STEP 1 >> CREATE A DESKTOP DATABASE USING A TEMPLATE

You locate an Access desktop template that you can use to create your personal contact database. This template not only allows you to store names, addresses, telephone numbers, and other information, but also lets you categorize your contacts, send e-mail messages, and create maps of addresses. You download and save the template. Refer to Figure 1.30 as you complete Step 1.

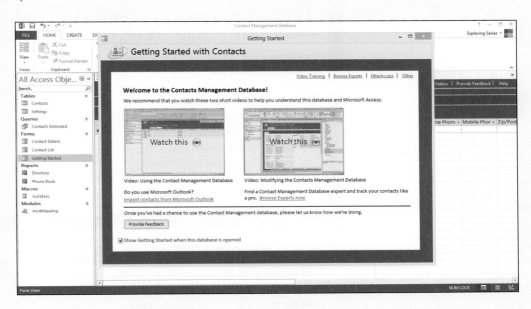

FIGURE 1.30 Desktop Contacts Intro Screen

a. Open Access. Click the Contacts link in the Suggested searches list. Click *Desktop contacts* from the available contacts.

   The Create Intro Screen page for the Desktop contacts database opens.

b. Click the **Browse icon** to navigate to the folder where you are saving your files, enter **a01h4Contacts_LastFirst** as the file name, and then click **OK**.

c. Click **Create** to download the template.

d. Click **Enable Content** on the Security Warning message bar.

> **TROUBLESHOOTING:** If the Getting Started page does not display, click Getting Started in the Forms category on the Navigation Pane.

> **TROUBLESHOOTING:** The Getting Started page opens every time you open the Contacts Management database. To close this page until you want to view it again, clear the *Show Getting Started when this database is opened* check box at the bottom-left corner of the dialog box before closing the Getting Started page.

    e. Close the Getting Started page.

       The database displays with the Contact List table open.

STEP 2 » ADD RECORDS TO A DOWNLOADED DESKTOP DATABASE TEMPLATE

Because the database opens in the Contact List form, you decide to begin by entering a contact—your dentist—in the form. Refer to Figure 1.31 as you complete Step 2.

FIGURE 1.31 Contact Details Form

    a. Click in the empty first field of the first row. Enter the following information, pressing **Tab** between each entry. Do not press Tab after entering the ZIP/Postal Code.

Field Name	Value to Type
First Name	Tanya
Last Name	Machuca
Company	Hobblecreek Mountain Dentistry
Job Title	D.D.S.
Category	Business (select from list)
E-mail Address	HMDentistry@email.com
Business Phone	801-555-8102
Home Phone	(leave blank)
Mobile Phone	801-555-8921
ZIP/Postal Code	84664

    b. Click **Save and Close**.

    c. Double-click **Contact List** in the Forms group on the Navigation Pane.

d. Click **Open** in the first field of Dr. Machuca's record.

Open is a hyperlink to a different form in the database. The Contact Details form opens, displaying Dr. Machuca's information. More fields are available for you to use to store information.

e. Enter the following additional information to the record:

Field Name	Value to Type
Street	56 West 200 North
City	Mapleton
State/Province	UT
Country/Region	USA
Notes	Available Tuesday - Friday 7 a.m. to 4 p.m.

f. Click the **Click to Map hyperlink** to view a map to Dr. Machuca's office. Close the map.

Bing displays a map to the address in the record. You can get directions, locate nearby businesses, and use many other options.

g. Click **Save and Close** in the top center of the form to close the Contact Details form.

The record is saved.

h. Click **New Contact** beneath the Contact List title bar.

The Contact Details form opens to a blank record.

i. Enter the following information for a new record, pressing **Tab** to move between fields. Some fields will be blank.

Field Name	Value to Type
First Name	Rowan
Last Name	Westmoreland
Company	Phoenix Aesthetics
Job Title	Aesthetician
Mobile Phone	801-555-2221
Street	425 North Main Street
City	Springville
State/Province	UT
ZIP/Postal Code	84663
Category	Personal
E-mail Address	Rowan55W5@email.com
Notes	Recommended by Michelle

j. Click **Save and Close**.

STEP 3 ›› EXPLORE THE DATABASE OBJECTS IN A DOWNLOADED DESKTOP DATABASE TEMPLATE

You explore the objects created by the template so that you understand the organization of the database. Refer to Figure 1.32 as you complete Step 3.

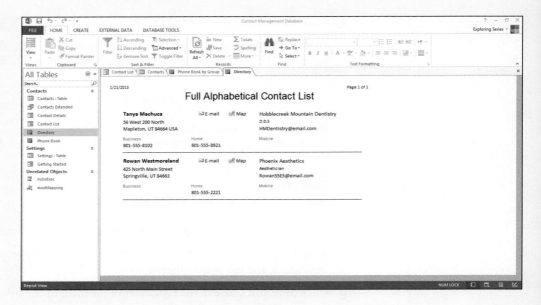

FIGURE 1.32 Directory Form

a. Double-click the **Contacts table** in the Navigation Pane to open it.

The information you entered using the Contact List form and the Contact Details form displays in the Contacts table.

b. Click the **Reports group** in the Navigation Pane to expand the list of reports, if necessary.

The list of reports contained in the database file opens.

c. Double-click **Phone Book** in the Navigation Pane to open it.

The Phone Book report opens displaying the contact name and phone information organized by category.

d. Double-click the **Directory report** in the Navigation Pane to open it.

The Directory report opens, displaying a full alphabetical contact list. The Directory report was designed to display more fields than the Phone Book, but it is not organized by category.

e. Click **All Access Objects** on the Navigation Pane and select **Tables and Related Views**.

You can now see the objects that are based on the Contacts table.

f. Right-click the **Directory report tab** and click **Close All**.

g. Exit Access and submit your work based on your instructor's directions.

Chapter Objectives Review

After reading this chapter, you have accomplished the following objectives:

1. **Understand database fundamentals.**
   - A database is a collection of data organized as meaningful information that can be accessed, managed, stored, queried, sorted, and reported.
   - Organize information in a database and recognize Access objects: An Access database is a structured collection of six types of objects—tables, forms, queries, reports, macros, and modules.
   - The foundation of a database is its tables, the objects in which data is stored. Each table in the database is composed of records, and each record is in turn comprised of fields.
   - The primary key in a table is the field (or combination of fields) that makes every record in a table unique.
   - Examine the Access interface: Objects are organized and listed in the Navigation Pane. Access also uses a Tabbed Documents interface in which each object that is open has its own tab.
   - Explore Access views: The Datasheet view enables the user to view, add, edit, and delete records, whereas the Design view is used to create and modify a table's design by specifying the fields it will contain, the fields' data types, and their associated properties.
   - Open an Access file and work with Content Security: When a database is opened from a location that has not been designated as a trusted location or that does not have a digital signature from a publisher you can trust, Access displays a message bar with a security warning. Click the Enable Content button if you trust the database's source.

2. **Use an existing database.**
   - Understand the difference between working in storage and memory: Access works primarily from storage. Records can be added, modified, or deleted in the database, and as the information is entered it is automatically saved.
   - Add, edit, and delete records: A pencil icon displays in the row selector box to indicate when you are in editing mode. Moving to another record or clicking Save on the Quick Access Toolbar saves the changes.
   - To add a new record, click *New (blank) record* on the navigation bar. To delete a record, click the row selector and click Delete in the Records group on the Home tab.
   - Save As, Compact and Repair, and Back Up Access files: *Compact and Repair* reduces the size of the database, and Back Up creates a duplicate copy of the database.

3. **Sort table data on one or multiple fields.**
   - Sorting changes the order of information, and information may be sorted by one or more fields.

4. **Create, modify, and remove filters.**
   - A filter is a set of criteria that is applied to a table to display a subset of records in that table.
   - *Filter by Selection* displays only the records that match the selected criteria.
   - *Filter by Form* displays records based on multiple criteria and enables the user to apply logical operators and use comparison operators.

5. **Know when to use Access or Excel to manage data.**
   - Use Access to manage data when you require multiple related tables to store your data; have a large amount of data; need to connect to and retrieve data from external databases; need to group, sort, and total data based on various parameters; and/or have an application that requires multiple users to connect to one data source.
   - Use Excel to manage data when you need one worksheet to handle all of your data; have mostly numeric data; require subtotals and totals in your worksheet; want to primarily run a series of "what if" scenarios on your data; and/or need to create complex charts and/or graphs.

6. **Understand relational power.**
   - Use the Relationships window: A relationship is a connection between two tables using a common field. The benefit of a relationship is to efficiently combine data from related tables for the purpose of creating queries, forms, and reports.
   - Enforce referential integrity: Enforcing referential integrity when setting a table relationship ensures that data cannot be entered into a related table unless it first exists in the primary table.

7. **Create a database.**
   - Create a Web application using a template: Creating a custom Web app enables you to create a database that you can build and use and share with others through the Web.
   - Creating a blank desktop database: Creating a blank desktop database lets you create a database specific to your needs.
   - Create a desktop database using a template: A template is a predefined database that includes professionally designed tables, forms, reports, and other objects that you can use to jumpstart the creation of your database.

Key Terms Matching

Match the key terms with their definitions. Write the key term letter by the appropriate numbered definition.

a. Back Up Database
b. Compact and Repair
c. Custom Web app
d. Datasheet view
e. Design view
f. Field
g. Filter by Form
h. Filter by Selection
i. Form
j. Navigation Pane
k. Object

l. Primary key
m. Query
n. Record
o. Relational database management system (RDBMS)
p. Relationship
q. Report
r. Sort
s. Table
t. Template

1. _____ View that enables you to add, edit, and delete the records of a table. **p. 88**

2. _____ An Access object that enables you to enter, modify, or delete table data. **p. 86**

3. _____ An Access utility that reduces the size of the database and can repair a corrupt database. **p. 93**

4. _____ A main component that is created and used to make a database function. **p. 85**

5. _____ A filtering method that displays records based on multiple criteria **p. 104**

6. _____ A system that uses the relational model to manage groups of data (tables) and rules (relationships) between tables. **p. 112**

7. _____ A database that can be built, used, and shared with others through the use of a host server. **p. 119**

8. _____ An object that contains professional-looking formatted information from underlying tables or queries. **p. 86**

9. _____ An object used to store data, and the foundation of every database. **p. 85**

10. _____ An Access utility that creates a duplicate copy of the database. **p. 93**

11. _____ A predefined database that includes professionally designed tables, forms, reports, and other objects. **p. 119**

12. _____ A filtering method that displays only records that match selected criteria. **p. 103**

13. _____ A connection between two tables using a common field. **p. 111**

14. _____ A method of listing records in a specific sequence. **p. 102**

15. _____ View that enables you to create tables, add and delete fields, and modify field properties. **p. 90**

16. _____ An Access interface element that organizes and lists the database objects in a database. **p. 85**

17. _____ A question you ask that can help you find and retrieve table data meeting conditions you specify. **p. 86**

18. _____ The smallest data element in a table, such as first name, last name, address, or phone number. **p. 85**

19. _____ Complete set of all the fields (data elements) about one person, place, event, or concept. **p. 85**

20. _____ The field (or combination of fields) that uniquely identifies each record in a table. **p. 90**

Multiple Choice

1. Which sequence represents the hierarchy of terms, from smallest to largest?

   (a) Database, table, record, field

   (b) Field, record, table, database

   (c) Record, field, table, database

   (d) Field, record, database, table

2. You edit several records in an Access table. When should you execute the Save command?

   (a) Immediately after you edit a record

   (b) When you close the table

   (c) Once at the end of the session

   (d) Records are saved automatically; the save command is not required.

3. Which of the following is *not* true of an Access database?

   (a) Short Text, Number, AutoNumber, and Currency are valid data types.

   (b) Every record in a table has the same fields as every other record.

   (c) Every table in a database contains the same number of records as every other table.

   (d) Each table should contain a primary key; however, a primary key is not required.

4. Which of the following is *true* regarding the record selector box?

   (a) An orange border surrounds the record selector box and the active record.

   (b) A pencil symbol indicates that the current record already has been saved.

   (c) An asterisk indicates the first record in the table.

   (d) An empty square indicates that the current record is selected.

5. Which of the following will be accepted as valid during data entry?

   (a) Adding a record with a duplicate primary key

   (b) Entering text into a numeric field

   (c) Entering numbers into a text field

   (d) Omitting an entry in a required field

6. You have finished an Access assignment and wish to turn it in to your instructor for evaluation. As you prepare to transfer the file, you discover that it has more than doubled in size. You should:

   (a) Delete extra tables or reports or fields to make the file smaller.

   (b) Zip the database file prior to sending it to your instructor.

   (c) Compact and repair the database before sending it to your instructor.

   (d) Turn it in; the size does not matter.

7. Which of the following conditions is available through *Filter by Selection*?

   (a) Equals condition

   (b) Delete condition

   (c) AND condition

   (d) OR condition

8. An Employees table is open in Datasheet view. You want to sort the names alphabetically by last name and then by first name (e.g., Smith, Andrew). To do this, you must:

   (a) First sort ascending on first name and then on last name.

   (b) First sort descending on first name and then on last name.

   (c) First sort ascending on last name and then on first name.

   (d) First sort descending on last name and then on first name.

9. Which of the following is *not* true when creating relationships between tables?

   (a) Join lines create a relationship between two tables.

   (b) The common fields used to create a relationship must both be primary keys.

   (c) The data types of common fields must be the same.

   (d) Enforcing referential integrity ensures that data cannot be entered into a related table unless it first exists in the primary table.

10. All of the following statements are *true* about creating a database *except*:

    (a) Creating a custom Web app requires that you use a host server.

    (b) When creating a blank desktop database, Access opens to a blank table in Datasheet view.

    (c) Using a template to create a database saves time because it includes predefined objects.

    (d) The objects provided in a template cannot be modified.

Practice Exercises

1 Hotel Rewards

The Lakes Hotel and Conference Center caters to upscale business travelers and provides stylish hotel suites, sophisticated meeting and reception facilities, and state-of-the-art media equipment. The hotel is launching a rewards club to help the marketing department track the purchasing patterns of its most loyal customers. All of the hotel transactions will be stored in an Access database. Your task is to create a member table and enter sample customers. You will practice filtering on the table data. This exercise follows the same set of skills as used in Hands-On Exercises 1 and 2 in the chapter. Refer to Figure 1.33 as you complete this exercise.

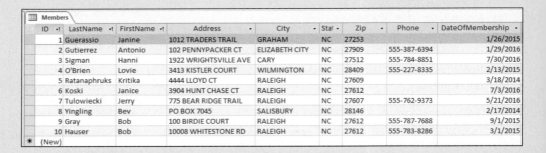

FIGURE 1.33 Enter Data into the Members Table

a. Open Access and click **Blank desktop database**.

b. Type **a01p1Rewards_LastFirst** in the **File Name box**. Click the **Browse icon**. Navigate to the location where you are saving your files in the File New Database dialog box, click **OK** to close the dialog box, and then click **Create** to create the new database.

c. Click **View** in the Views group on the TABLE TOOLS FIELDS tab to switch to Design view. Type **Members** in the **Save As dialog box** and click **OK**.

d. Type **LastName** under the ID field and press **Tab**. Accept **Short Text** as the Data Type. Type **FirstName** in the third row and press **Tab**. Accept **Short Text** as the Data Type.

e. Type the next five fields into the Field Name column: **Address**, **City**, **State**, **Zip**, and **Phone**. Accept **Short Text** as the Data Type for each of these fields.

f. Type **DateOfMembership** as the last Field Name and select **Date/Time** as the Data Type.

g. Click **View** in the Views group to switch to Datasheet view. Click **Yes** to save the table. Type the data as shown in Figure 1.33. Increase the column widths to fit the data as necessary. Press **Tab** to move to the next field.

h. Find a record that displays *Raleigh* as the value in the City field. Click **Raleigh** to select that data value.

i. Click **Selection** in the Sort & Filter group on the HOME tab. Select **Equals "Raleigh"**.

j. Find a record that displays *27612* as the value in the Zip field. Click **27612** to select that data value.

k. Click **Selection** in the Sort & Filter group on the HOME tab. Select **Equals "27612"**.

l. Click any value in the FirstName field. Click **Ascending** in the Sort & Filter group on the HOME tab. Click any value in the LastName field. Click **Ascending** in the Sort & Filter group on the HOME tab.

m. Click the **FILE tab**, click **Print**, and then click **Print Preview** to preview the sorted and filtered table.

n. Click **Close Print Preview** in the Close Preview group.

o. Close the table and save the changes.

p. Click the **FILE tab** and click **Compact and Repair Database** under *Advanced*.

q. Click the **FILE tab**, click **Save As**, and then double-click **Back Up Database**.

r. Click **Save** to accept the default backup file name with today's date.

s. Click the **FILE tab** and click **Exit** (to exit Access). Submit the database based on your instructor's directions.

The Custom Coffee Company provides coffee, tea, and snacks to offices in Miami. Custom Coffee also provides and maintains the equipment for brewing the beverages. The firm has a reputation for providing outstanding customer service. To improve customer service even further, the owner recently purchased an Access database to keep track of customers, orders, and products. This database will replace the Excel spreadsheets currently maintained by the office manager. The Excel spreadsheets are out of date, and they do not allow for data validation while data is being entered. The company hired you to verify and enter all the Excel data into the Access database. This exercise follows the same set of skills as used in Hands-On Exercises 1–3 in the chapter. Refer to Figure 1.34 as you complete this exercise.

FIGURE 1.34 Order Details Report Filtered for *YourName* and *Miami*

a. Open the *a01p2Coffee* file and save the database as **a01p2Coffee_LastFirst**.

b. Click the **DATABASE TOOLS tab** and click **Relationships** in the Relationships group. Review the table relationships. Take note of the join line between the Customers and Orders tables.

c. Click **Close** in the Relationships group.

d. Double-click the **Sales Reps table** in the Navigation Pane to open it. Replace *YourName* with your name in both the LastName and FirstName fields. For example, as the Access author, I used the name Cynthia Krebs in place of FirstName LastName. Close the table by clicking the **Close (X) button** on the right side of the Sales Reps window.

e. Double-click the **Customers Form** to open it. Click **New (blank) record** in the navigation bar at the bottom of the window. Add a new record by typing the following information; press **Tab** after each field.

Customer Name:	*your name* Company
Contact:	*your name*
Email:	*yourname*@email.com
Address1:	123 Main St
Address2:	(leave blank)
City:	Miami
State:	FL
Zip Code:	33133
Phone:	(305) 555-1234

Fax:	(leave blank)
Service Start Date:	01/17/2016
Credit Rating:	A
Sales Rep ID:	2

Note the pencil in the top-left margin of the form window. This symbol indicates the new record has not been saved. Press **Tab**. The pencil symbol disappears, and the new customer is automatically saved to the table.

f. Close the Customers Form.

g. Double-click the **Orders Form** to open it. Click **New (blank) record** in the navigation bar at the bottom of the window. Add a new record by typing the following information:

Customer ID:	15 (Access will convert it to C0015)
Payment Type:	Cash (select using the arrow)
Comments:	Ship this order in 2 days
Product ID:	4 (Access will convert it to P0004)
Quantity:	2

h. Add a second product using the following information:

| Product ID: | 6 (Access will convert it to P0006) |
| Quantity: | 1 |

i. Close the form.

j. Double-click the **Order Details Report** to open it in Report view. Click your name in the Last Name field, click **Selection** in the Sort & Filter group, and then click **Equals "Your Name"**.

k. Right-click **Miami** in the City field and select **Equals "Miami"** from the shortcut menu.

l. Click the **FILE tab**, click **Print**, and then click **Print Preview**.

m. Click **Close Print Preview** in the Close Preview group. Close the report.

n. Click the **FILE tab** and click **Compact & Repair Database**.

o. Click the **FILE tab**, click **Save As**, and then double-click **Back Up Database**. Use the default backup file name.

p. Close Access. Submit based on your instructor's directions.

3 Camping Trip

FROM SCRATCH

You and your friends have decided to spend your annual reunion camping at the Wawona Campground in Yosemite National Park. Wawona Campground is an extremely popular campground. Campground reservations are available in blocks of one month at a time, up to five months in advance, on the 15th of each month at 7 AM Pacific time. Nearly all reservations are filled the first day they become available, usually within seconds or minutes after 7 AM. Realizing that making reservations is a high-priority, critical task, and that there are many other tasks that must be completed before you can have a successful trip, your group decides to use the Access Task Management Database to begin getting organized for their trip on September 15, 2015. Other tasks can be entered at a later time. This exercise follows the same set of skills as used in Hands-On Exercises 3 and 4 in the chapter. Refer to Figures 1.35–1.38 as you complete this exercise.

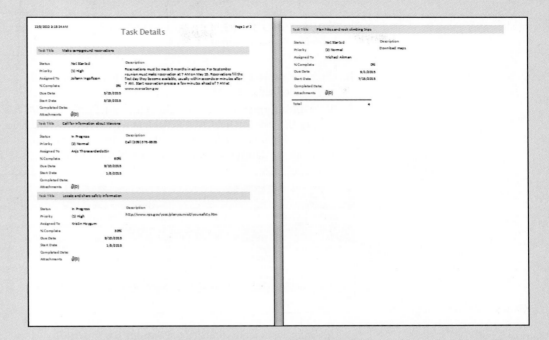

FIGURE 1.35 Task Details Report

a. Open Access and click the **Desktop task management template** in the Access Backstage view.

b. Type **a01p3Camping_LastFirst** in the **File name box**. Click the **Browse icon**. Navigate to the location where you are saving your files in the File New Database dialog box, click **OK** to close the dialog box, and then click **Create** to create the new database.

c. Click the **Watch this arrow** for the *Using the Tasks Database* template video on the left side of the Getting Started page. If the Getting Started page does not open, open the Getting Started form in the Forms group in the Navigation Pane. Click **Watch this>>** and watch the video. Close the video when you have finished watching it. Click **Close** again to return to the *Getting Started with Tasks* page.

d. Remove the check in the *Show Getting Started when this database is opened* check box so that the page does not automatically display in the future. If you want to view Getting Started again, you can click **Getting Started** in the Forms category on the Navigation Pane. Click the **Close (X) button**.

e. Click **Relationships** in the Relationships group on the DATABASE TOOLS tab and note the relationship between the Contacts table and the Tasks table. Close the Relationships window.

f. Double-click **Contact List** in the Forms category on the Navigation Pane. Type the information for each field in the Contact list form using the information displayed in Figure 1.36, pressing **Tab** between each field.

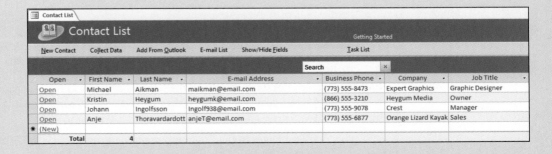

FIGURE 1.36 Contact List

g. Close the Contact List form. The Task List form displays because it was the form open when you downloaded the database.

> **TROUBLESHOOTING:** If the Task List form does not display, double-click the Task List form in the Navigation Pane to open it.

h. Click the **Shutter Bar Open/Close button** to close the Navigation Pane, which enables you to see more table fields.

i. Enter the information for each field in the Task List form using the information displayed in Figure 1.37. In the Priority field, Status field, and Assigned To field, click the arrow and select the list of options. When typing the Start Date and Due Date, type the date and add **7 AM** after the date. Although the date does not show in the table, it is required.

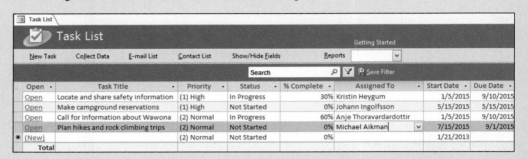

FIGURE 1.37 Task List Form

j. Close the Tasks table and click the **Shutter Bar Open/Close button** to open the Navigation Pane.

k. Double-click **Task Details** in the Forms category in the Navigation Pane.

l. Refer to Figure 1.38 to enter the information in the **Description box** and close the Task Details form.

FIGURE 1.38 Description in Task Details Form

m. Refer to Figure 1.35 and continue entering the descriptions for each of the records.

n. Double-click **Task Details** in the Reports category in the Navigation Pane to view the report displaying the details about the tasks you have created. Scroll down to see all tasks.

o. Click the **FILE tab**, click **Print**, and then click **Print Preview**.

p. Click **Two Pages** in the Zoom group on the Print Preview tab. Note the report format groups the information by Task Title.

q. Click **Close Print Preview** in the Close Preview group. Close the report.

r. Click the **FILE tab** and click **Compact & Repair Database**.

s. Click the **FILE tab**, click **Save As**, and then double-click **Back Up Database**. Use the default backup file name.

t. Close Access. Submit based on your instructor's directions.

1 Home Sales

FROM SCRATCH

You are the senior partner in a large, independent real estate firm that specializes in home sales. Most of your time is spent supervising the agents who work for your firm. The firm needs to create a database to hold all of the information on the properties it has listed. You will use the database to help find properties that match the goals of your customers. You will create the database, create two tables, add data to both tables, and create a relationship. Refer to Figure 1.39 as you complete this exercise.

ID	DateListed	DateSold	ListPrice	SalesPrice	SqFeet	Beds	Baths	Address	SubDivision	Agent	Style	Construction	Garage	YearBuilt
1	5/28/2015		$246,000.00		1928	2	2	1166 Avondale	3	1	Ranch	Brick	1 Car Attached	2010
2	7/22/2015		$263,600.00		1896	2	2	1684 Riverdale	3	2	2 Story	Frame	1 Car Attached	2009
3	6/7/2015		$270,000.00		2026	2	1	1166 So;verdate	3	4	Split Level	Stone	2 Car Attached	2007
4	6/7/2015		$298,000.00		1672	1	1	4520 Oakdale	3	3	Ranch	Brick	1 Car Attached	1997
5	6/22/2015		$312,000.00		2056	2	2	1838 Hillendale	3	4	Split Level	Frame	2 Car Attached	2003
6	7/24/2015		$339,600.00		2456	3	3	1255 Copperdale	3	5	Ranch	Brick	2 Car Attached	2008
7	6/22/2015		$339,600.00		2539	3	3	1842 Gardendale	3	3	2 Story	Stone	1 Car Detached	1983
8	8/12/2015		$239,600.00		2032	2	2	1605 Lakedale	3	2	Split Foyer	Frame	Carport	2002
9	6/22/2015		$379,000.00		2540	3	2	1775 Jerrydale	3	1	Ranch	Brick	3 Car Attached	2014
10	6/23/2015	9/14/2015	$172,500.00	$168,000.00	2030	3	2	213 Merrydale	3	3	Ranch	Stone	1 Car Attached	2010
* (New)			$0.00	$0.00	0	0	0			0	0			0

FIGURE 1.39 Properties Table

a. Open Access and click **Blank desktop database**. Type **a01m1Homes_LastFirst** in the **File Name box**. Click **Browse** and navigate to the location where you are saving your files. Click **OK** to close the dialog box and click **Create** to create the new database.

b. Switch to Design view. Type **Properties** in the **Save As dialog box** and click **OK**.

c. Type **DateListed** under the ID field and press **Tab**. Select **Date/Time** as the Data Type.

d. Type the remainder of the fields and Data Types as shown:

Field Name	Data Type
DateSold	Date/Time
ListPrice	Currency
SalesPrice	Currency
SqFeet	Number
Beds	Number
Baths	Number
Address	Short Text
SubDivision	Number
AgentID	Number
Style	Short Text
Construction	Short Text
Garage	Short Text
YearBuilt	Number

e. Switch to Datasheet view. Type the first 10 records as shown in Figure 1.39.

f. Open the *a01m1Properties.xlsx* workbook file in Excel. Click **row 2**, press and hold the **left mouse button**, and then drag through **row 70** so that all the data rows are selected. Click **Copy** in the Clipboard group on the HOME tab. Click **Yes** to save the data to the Clipboard when prompted. Close the Excel file.

g. Return to Access and click on the **asterisk (*)** on the first new row of the Properties table. Click **Paste** in the Clipboard group to paste all 69 rows into the Properties table. Save and close the table.

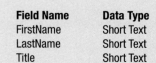
DISCOVER

h. Click **Table** in the Tables group on the CREATE tab. Click **View** in the Views group on the TABLE TOOLS FIELDS tab to switch to Design view. Save the table as **Agents**. Change the primary key from ID to **AgentID**. Add the following fields and switch to Datasheet view. Save changes to the table design when prompted.

Field Name	Data Type
FirstName	Short Text
LastName	Short Text
Title	Short Text

i. Enter the following data in the Agents table and close the table.

AgentID	FirstName	LastName	Title
1	Kia	Hart	Broker
2	Keith	Martin	Agent
3	Kim	Yang	Agent
4	Steven	Dougherty	Agent in Training
5	Angela	Scott	Agent in Training
6	Juan	Resario	President

j. Click the **DATABASE TOOLS tab** and click **Relationships** in the Relationships group. Add both tables to the Relationships window and close the Show Table dialog box.

k. Drag the bottom border of the Properties table downward until all fields display. Drag the **AgentID field** from the Agents table and drop it onto the **AgentID field** in the Properties table. Click the **Enforce Referential Integrity check box** in the Edit Relationships dialog box to activate it. Click **Create** and close the Relationships window. Click **Yes** to save your changes.

l. Open the **Properties** table. Click **Advanced** in the Sort & Filter group and click **Filter By Form**. Set the criteria to identify properties with a list price less than $300,000 and with two bedrooms. (You will use the expression <300000 for the criteria of the list price.) Display the results and sort by ascending list price. Save and close the table.

m. Compact, repair, and back up the database.

n. Exit Access. Submit the database based on your instructor's directions.

2   National Conference

The Association of Higher Education will host its National Conference on your campus next year. To facilitate the conference, the information technology department has replaced last year's Excel spreadsheets with an Access database containing information on the rooms, speakers, and sessions. Your assignment is to create a room itinerary that will list all of the sessions, dates, and times for each room. The list will be posted on the door of each room for the duration of the conference. Refer to Figure 1.40 as you complete this exercise.

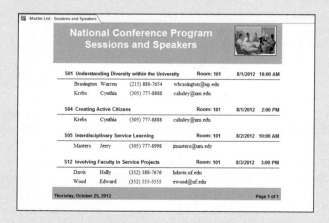

FIGURE 1.40 Sessions and Speakers Report—Room 101

a. Open the *a01m2NatConf* file and save the database as **a01m2NatConf_LastFirst**.

b. Open the Relationships window.

c. Review the objects in the database to see if any of the existing objects will provide the room itinerary information displayed in Figure 1.40.

DISCOVER

d. Open the SessionSpeaker table. Scroll to the first blank record at the bottom of the table and enter a new record using SpeakerID **99** and SessionID **09**. (Note: Speaker 99 does not exist.) How does Access respond? Close the dialog box, recognizing that you are not saving this record. Close the SessionSpeaker table. In the Relationships window, right-click the join line between the Speakers table and SessionSpeaker table and click **Delete**. Click **Yes** to permanently delete the selected relationship from the database. Close the Relationships window. Open the SessionSpeaker table and enter the same record again. How does Access respond this time? Close the SessionSpeaker table.

e. Open the Speakers table. Find and replace *YourName* with your name. Close the Speakers table.

f. Open the Speaker–Session Query and apply a filter to identify the sessions where you or Holly Davis are the speakers. Use *Filter by Form* and the Or tab. (Nine records should display.)

g. Sort the filtered results in ascending order by the RoomID field and save and close the query.

h. Open the Master List–Sessions and Speakers report. Right-click the **Master List–Sessions and Speakers tab** and select **Report View**.

i. Apply a filter that limits the report to sessions in Room 101 only.

j. Click the **FILE tab**, click **Print**, and then click **Print Preview**. Compare the report to Figure 1.40 and make any corrections necessary. Close Print Preview and close the report.

k. Compact and repair the database.

l. Back up the database. Use the default backup file name.

m. Exit Access. Submit based on your instructor's directions.

---

3 | **Used Cell Phones for Sale**

COLLABORATION CASE

You and a few of your classmates decide to start a new business selling used cell phones, MP3 players, and accessories. You will use an Access database to track your inventory. To begin, one person in your group will locate the Access database for this exercise, complete steps b through f, and then post the database to a OneDrive folder. The next person in your group will retrieve the revised database and also complete steps b through f (and so on until everyone has completed steps b through f). After everyone has completed steps b through f, you will retrieve the database again and complete step g. At the completion of this exercise, each person will submit his or her own Word document containing the answers to the questions below.

a. Open the *a01m3Phones* database and save it as **a01m3PhonesGroupX_LastFirst**. (Replace *X* with the number assigned to your group by your instructor.)

b. Open the Inventory table and review the records in the table. Take note of the data in the TypeOfDevice column. Close the table and open the DeviceOptions table. Review the data and close the table.

c. Open the Relationships window. What is the benefit of the relationship between the Inventory table and the DeviceOptions table? Create a Word document with both the question and your answer. After you complete this exercise, you will submit this Word document to your instructor using the file name **a01m3PhonesAnswers_LastFirst**. Close the Relationships window.

d. Open the Inventory Form and add the information about your cell phone to the table (or search the Internet for any model if you do not have a cell phone) in the first new blank record. Enter your name in the SellerName field. With your information showing in the form, take a screenshot of the form using the Snipping Tool. Paste the image into the Word document you created in step c. Close the form.

e. Open the Inventory Report by Manufacturer in Report view. Filter the records for only items that have not been sold. Take a screenshot using the Snipping Tool and paste the image into the Word document. Close the report, close the database, and then exit Access.

f. Create a folder on your OneDrive account named **Exploring Access** and share the folder with other members in your group and the instructor. Upload the database to this new folder and notify another person in your group. The next person will complete steps b through f, and then the next person, until all group members have added their information.

g. After all the new phone records have been added, each person in the group should download the **a01m3PhonesGroupX** database again and use filters to answer the following questions. Add the questions and your answers to the Word document you created.

1. How many phones are still for sale? _____

2. How many phones are made by Apple or Samsung? _____

3. How many phones were sold in the first half of 2013? _____ List the ID numbers _____

4. Sort the phones from lowest to highest asking price. Which phone is the least expensive? _____ Most expensive? _____

5. How many items are not phones? _____

h. Use e-mail or text messaging to communicate with the other members in your group if you have any questions.

i. Submit the Word document based on your instructor's directions.

Beyond the Classroom

Northwind Revenue Report

RESEARCH CASE

Open the *a01b2NWind* file and save the database as **a01b2NWind_LastFirst**. Open the Employees table and replace *YourName* with your first and last names. Before you can filter the Revenue report, you need to update the criterion in the underlying query to match the dates in the database. Right-click the **Revenue query** in the Navigation Pane and click **Design view** in the shortcut menu. Scroll to the right until you see *OrderDate*. Right-click in the **Criteria row** under *OrderDate* and click **Zoom**. Change the criterion to **Between#1/1/2015#And#3/31/2015#** and click **OK**. Click **Run** in the Results group on the Query Tools Design tab and save the query. Open the Revenue report. Use the tools that you have learned in this chapter to filter the report for only your sales of Confections. Close the report. Compact, repair, and back up your database and exit Access.

Lugo Computer Sales

DISASTER RECOVERY

You are having trouble with an Access 2013 database. One of the employees accidentally changed the CustomerID of Lugo Computer Sales. This change caused a problem in one of the relationships. Open the *a01b3Recover* file and save the database as **a01b3Recover_LastFirst**. Open the Customers and Orders tables and examine the data. Change the Lugo Computer Sales CustomerID in the Customers table back to the original number of 6. Reset the relationship between the Customers table and the Orders table and enforce referential integrity. Compact, repair, and back up your database and exit Access. Submit the database based on your instructor's directions.

Financial Literacy

SOFT SKILLS CASE [S]

The Cambridge Resources Group stated that surveyed executives ranked the "toll on productivity caused by financial stress" as one of the "most critical unaddressed issues in the workplace today." Dr. E. Thomas Garman*, the president of Personal Finance Employee Education Foundation, stated that "60% of employees live paycheck to paycheck" and that research shows that "those with more financial distress report poor health; financially distressed workers (40–50%) report that their financial problems cause their health woes; and that positive changes in financial behaviors are related to improved health."

Tracking your income and your expenses enables you to see where your money is going. With this information you can create a budget that will help you reach your goals. To aid you with this process, Microsoft created a downloadable Personal Account Ledger template. This database includes a form that enables you to record transactions; reports to display transactions, expenses by category, and income by category; and a tax report. Open *a01b4Ledger*, a database based on the Microsoft Personal Account Ledger, and save it as **a01b4Ledger_LastFirst**. Use the Account Transaction List to enter your income and expenses for the previous month. Then view the Income by Category report and the Expenses by Category report. Compact, repair, and back up your database and exit Access. Submit the database based on your instructor's directions.

---

* Employee Financial Wellness slideshare presentation, http://www.slideshare.net/irwink/Employee-Financial-Wellness, by Dr. E. Thomas Garman, President, Personal Finance Employee Education Foundation.

Capstone Exercise

Your boss expressed concern about the accuracy of the inventory reports in the bookstore. He needs you to open the inventory database, make modifications to some records, and determine if the changes you make carry through to the other objects in the database. You will make changes to a form and verify those changes in a table, a query, and a report. When you have verified that the changes update automatically, you will compact and repair the database and make a backup of it.

Database File Setup

You will open an original database file and save the database with a new name, replace an existing author's name with your name, create a table, create table relationships, sort, and apply a filter by selection.

a. Open the *a01c1Books* file and save the database as **a01c1Books_LastFirst**.

b. Create a new table in Design view. Save the table as **Publishers**. Change the primary key from ID to **PubID** with a Data Type of **Short Text**. Add the following fields and switch to Datasheet view. Save changes to the table design when prompted.

Field Name	Data Type
PubName	Short Text
PubAddress	Short Text
PubCity	Short Text
PubState	Short Text
PubZIP	Short Text

c. Enter the following data in the Publishers table and close the table.

PubID	PubName	PubAddress	PubCity	PubState	PubZIP
BB	Bantam Books	1540 Broadway	New York	NY	10036
FS	Farrar, Straus and Giroux	12 Union Square West	New York	NY	10003
KN	Knopf	299 Park Avenue	New York	NY	10171
LB	Little, Brown and Company	1271 Avenue of the Americas	New York	NY	10020
PH	Pearson/Prentice Hall	1 Lake Street	Upper Saddle	NJ	07458
SS	Simon & Schuster	100 Front Street	Riverside	NY	08075

d. Open the Maintain Authors form.

e. Navigate to Record 7 and replace *YourName* with your name.

f. Add a new Title: **Technology in Action**. The ISBN is **0-13-148905-4**, the PubID is **PH**, the PublDate is **2015**, the Price is $89.95 (just type **89.95**, no $), and StockAmt is **95** units. Move to any other record to save the new record. Close the form.

g. Open the Maintain Authors form again and navigate to Record 7. The changes are there because Access works from storage, not memory. Close the form again.

Sort a Query and Apply a Filter by Selection

You need to reorder a detail query so that the results are sorted alphabetically by the publisher name.

a. Open the Publishers, Books, and Authors Query.

b. Click in any record in the PubName column and sort the field in ascending order.

c. Check to make sure that four books list you as the author.

d. Click your name in the Author's Last Name field and filter the records to show only your books.

e. Close the query and save the changes.

View a Report

You need to examine the Publishers, Books, and Authors Report to determine if the changes you made in the Maintain Authors form appear in the report.

a. Open the Publishers, Books, and Authors Report.

b. Check to make sure that the report shows four books listing you as the author.

c. View the layout of the report in Print Preview.

d. Close the report.

Filter a Table

You need to examine the Books table to determine if the changes you made in the Maintain Authors form carried through to the related table. You also will filter the table to display books published after 2010 with fewer than 100 copies in inventory.

a. Open the Books table.

b. Use *Filter by Form* to create a filter that will identify all books published after 2010 with fewer than 100 items in stock.

c. Apply the filter and preview the filtered table.

d. Close the table and save the changes.

Compact and Repair a Database and Back Up a Database

Now that you are satisfied that any changes made to a form or query carry through to the table, you are ready to compact, repair, and back up your file.

a. Compact and repair your database.

b. Create a backup copy of your database, accept the default file name, and save it.

c. Exit Access. Submit based on your instructor's directions.

Tables and Queries in Relational Databases

CHAPTER 2

Designing Databases and Extracting Data

Yuri Arcurs/Shutterstock

CHAPTER 5

OBJECTIVES AFTER YOU READ THIS CHAPTER, YOU WILL BE ABLE TO:

1. Design a table p. 142

2. Create and modify tables p. 146

3. Share data p. 157

4. Establish table relationships p. 160

5. Create a single-table query p. 171

6. Specify query criteria for different data types p. 173

7. Understand query sort order p. 177

8. Run, copy, and modify a query p. 177

9. Use the Query Wizard p. 178

10. Create a multitable query p. 184

11. Modify a multitable query p. 185

CASE STUDY | Bank Audit

During a year-end review, a bank auditor uncovers mishandled funds at Commonwealth Federal Bank in Wilmington, Delaware. In order to analyze the data in more detail, the auditor asks you to create an Access database so he can enter the compromised accounts, the associated customers, and the involved employees. Once the new database is created and all the data are entered, you will help the auditor answer questions by creating and running queries.

As you begin, you realize that some of the data are contained in Excel spreadsheets. After discussing this with the auditor, you decide importing these data directly into the new database would be best. Importing from Excel into Access is commonplace and should work well. Importing will also help avoid errors that are associated with data entry. Once the Excel data have been imported, you will use queries to determine which data do not belong in the database. Unaffected records will be deleted.

This chapter introduces the Bank database case study to present the basic principles of table and query design. You will use tables and forms to input data, and you will create queries and reports to extract information from the database in a useful and organized way. The value of that information depends entirely on the quality of the underlying data—the tables.

Table Design, Creation, and Modification

Good database design begins with the tables. Tables provide the framework for all of the activities you perform in a database. If the framework is poorly designed, the rest of the database will be poorly designed as well. Whether you are experienced in designing tables or just learning how, the process should not be done haphazardly. You should follow a systematic approach when creating tables for a database. This process will take practice; however, over time, you will begin to see the patterns and eventually see the similarities among all databases.

In this section, you will learn the principles of good table design. You will review essential guidelines used when creating tables. After developing and testing the table design on paper, you will implement that design in Access. The first step is to list all the tables you need for the database and list all the fields in each table. While you learned to create tables in the previous chapter, in this chapter, you will learn to refine them by changing the properties of various fields. You will also be introduced to the concept of data validation. You want to make sure the data entered into the database are valid for the field and valid for the organization. Allowing invalid data into the tables will only cause problems later.

Designing a Table

Recall that a table is a collection of records, with each record made up of a number of fields. During the table design process, think of the specific fields you need in each table; list the fields under the correct table and assign each field a data type (such as short text, number, or date) as well as its size (length) or format. The order of the fields within the table and the specific field names are not significant because they can be changed later. What is important is that the tables contain all necessary fields so that the system can produce the required information.

For example, consider the design process necessary to create a database for a bank. Most likely you have a bank account and know that the bank maintains data about you. Your bank has your name, address, phone number, and Social Security number. It also knows what accounts you have (checking, savings, money market), if you have a credit card with that bank, and what its balance is. Additionally, your bank keeps information about its branches around the city or state. If you think about the data your bank maintains, you could make a list of the categories of data needed to store that information. These categories for the bank—customers, accounts, branches—become the tables in the bank's database. A bank's customer list is an example of a table: It contains a record for each bank customer.

After the tables have been identified, add the necessary fields using these six guidelines. (These guidelines are discussed in detail in the following paragraphs.)

- Include the necessary data.
- Design for now and for the future.
- Store data in their smallest parts.
- Add calculated fields to a table.
- Design to accommodate date arithmetic.
- Link tables using common fields.

Figure 2.1 shows a customer table and two other tables found in a sample bank database. It also lists fields that would be needed in each table record.

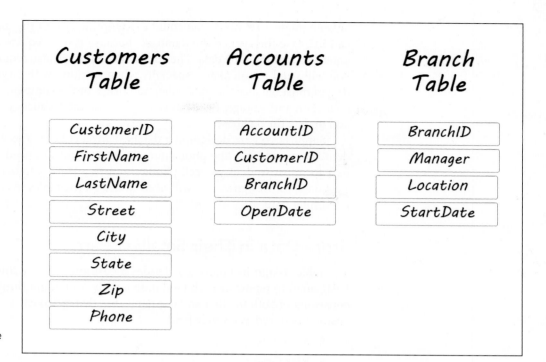

FIGURE 2.1 Rough Draft of Tables and Fields in a Sample Database

Include Necessary Data

A good way to determine what data are necessary in tables is to consider the output you need. It will probably be necessary for you to create professional-looking reports for others, so begin by creating a rough draft of the reports you will need. Then design tables that contain the fields necessary to create those reports. In other words, ask yourself what information will be expected from the system and determine the data required to produce that information. Consider, for example, the tables and fields in Figure 2.1. Is there required information that could not be generated from those tables?

- You can determine which branch a customer uses because the Accounts table includes the CustomerID and the BranchID.

- You can determine who manages a particular branch and which accounts are located there because the Branch table contains the Manager and Location fields.

- You can determine how long a customer has banked with the branch because the date he or she opened the account is stored in the Accounts table.

- You cannot generate the monthly bank statement. In order to generate a customer bank statement (showing all deposits and withdrawals for the month), you would need to add an additional table—an Account Activity table.

- You cannot e-mail a customer because the Customers table does not contain an E-mail field.

If you discover a missing field, such as the E-mail field, you can insert a row anywhere in the appropriate table and add the missing field. The databases found in a real bank are more complex, with more tables and more fields; however, the concepts illustrated here apply both to our sample bank database and to real bank databases.

Design for Now and for the Future

As the data requirements of an organization evolve over time, the information systems that hold the data must change as well. When designing a database, try to anticipate the future needs of the system and build in the flexibility to satisfy those demands. For example, when you add a text field, make sure that the number of characters allocated is sufficient to accommodate future expansion. On the other hand, if you include all the possible fields that anyone might ever need, you could drive up the cost of the database. Each additional field can increase the cost of the database, because it will require additional employee time to enter and maintain the data. The additional fields will also require more storage space, which you will need to calculate, especially when working with larger databases. Good database design must balance the data collection needs of the company with the cost associated with collection and storage. Plans must also include the frequency and cost necessary to modify and update the database.

Suppose you are designing a database for a college. You would need to store each student's name, address, and phone number. You would also need to store multiple phone numbers for most students—a cell phone number, a work number, and an emergency number. As a database designer, you will need to design the tables to accommodate multiple entries for similar data.

Store Data in Their Smallest Parts

The table design in Figure 2.1 divides a customer's name into two fields (FirstName and LastName) to reference each field individually. You might think it easier to use a single field consisting of both the first and last name, but that approach is too limiting. Consider a list of customers stored as a single field:

- Sue Grater
- Rick Grater
- Nancy Gallagher
- Harry Weigner
- Barb Shank
- Pete Shank

The first problem in this approach is the lack of flexibility: You could not easily create a salutation for a letter of the form *Dear Sue* or *Dear Ms. Gallagher* because the first and last names are not accessible individually.

A second difficulty is that the list of customers cannot be easily displayed in alphabetical order by last name because the last name begins in the middle of the field. The names could easily be alphabetized by first name because the first name is at the beginning of the field. However, the most common way to sort names is by the last name, which can be done more efficiently if the last name is stored as a separate field.

Think of how an address might be used. The city, state, and postal code should always be stored as separate fields. Any type of mass mailing requires you to sort on ZIP codes to take advantage of bulk mail. Other applications may require you to select records from a particular state or postal code, which can be done more efficiently if you store the data as separate fields. Often database users enter the postal code, and the database automatically retrieves the city and state information. You may need to direct a mailing only to a neighborhood or to a single street. The guideline is simple: Store data in their smallest parts.

Add Calculated Fields to a Table

A ***calculated field*** produces a value from an expression or function that references one or more existing fields. Access enables you to store calculated fields in a table using the calculated data type. An example of a calculated field can be found in the bank database. Suppose the bank pays its customers 1.0% interest on the principal each month. A calculated field, such as Monthly Interest, could store the expression Principal × 0.01. The interest amount would then appear on the customer's monthly bank statement.

Storing calculated data in a table enables you to add the data easily to queries, forms, and reports without the trouble of an additional calculation. Storing calculated data in a table may increase the size of the database slightly, but the benefits may outweigh this drawback. In the chapters ahead, you will examine calculations and calculated fields in greater detail. You will learn when to add calculated fields to a table and when to avoid them.

Design to Accommodate Date Arithmetic

Calculated fields are frequently created with numeric data, as the preceding Monthly Interest field example illustrates. You can also create calculated fields using date/time data. If you want to store the length of time a customer has been a customer, you would first create a field to hold the start date for each customer. Next, you would create a calculated field that contains an expression that subtracts the start date from today's date. The resulting calculation would store the number of days each customer has been a customer. Divide the results by 365 to convert days to years. If you want to calculate days to years and account for leap year, you could divide the results by 365.25.

This same concept applies to bank accounts; a bank is likely to store the OpenDate for each account in the Accounts table, as shown in Figure 2.1. Using this date, you can subtract the open date from today's date and calculate the number of days the account has been open. (Again, divide the results by 365 to convert to years.) If you open the Accounts table at least one day later, the results of the calculated field will be different.

A person's age is another example of a calculated field using date arithmetic—the date of birth is subtracted from today's date and the result is divided by 365. It might seem easier to store a person's age rather than the birth date to avoid the calculation. But that would be a mistake because age changes over time and would need to be updated each time age changes. Storing the date of birth is much better because the data remains *constant*. You can use *date arithmetic* to subtract one date from another to find out the number of days, months, or years that have lapsed between them. You can also add or subtract a constant from a date.

Plan for Common Fields Between Tables

As you create the tables and fields for the database, keep in mind that the tables will be joined in relationships using common fields. Draw a line between common fields to indicate the joins, as shown in Figure 2.2. These join lines will be created in Access when you learn to create table relationships later in the chapter. For now, you should name the common fields the same and make sure they have the same data type. For example, CustomerID in the Customers table will join to the CustomerID field in the Accounts table. CustomerID must have the same data type (in this case number/long integer) in both tables; otherwise, the join line will not be allowed.

FIGURE 2.2 Create Relationships Using Common Fields

Avoid *data redundancy*, which is the unnecessary storing of duplicate data in two or more tables. You should avoid duplicate information in multiple tables in a database, because errors may result. Suppose the customer address data were stored in both the Customers and Accounts tables. If a customer moved to a new address, it is possible that the address would be updated in only one of the two tables. The result would be inconsistent and unreliable data. Depending on which table served as the source for the output, either the new or the old address might be given to someone requesting the information. Storing the address in only one table is more reliable.

Creating and Modifying Tables

Tables can be created in a new blank database or in an existing database. You can create a table by:

STEP 1 »

- Typing a field name in a row in Design view.
- Entering table data into a new row in Datasheet view.
- Importing data from another database or application such as Excel.

Regardless of how a table is first created, you can always modify it later to include a new field or change an existing field. Figure 2.3 shows a table created by entering fields in Design view.

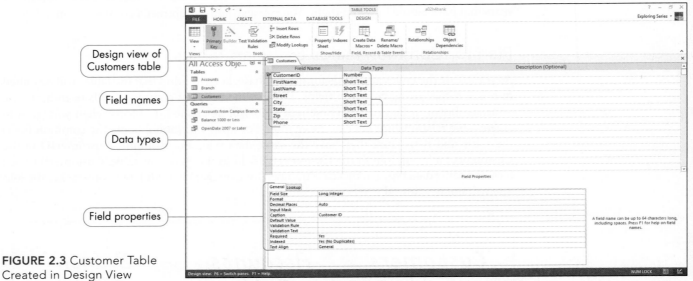

FIGURE 2.3 Customer Table Created in Design View

STEP 4 »

When you add a new field in Design view, the field must be given a field name to identify the data it holds. The field name should be descriptive of the data and can be up to 64 characters in length, including letters, numbers, and spaces. Database developers use *CamelCase notation* for field names. Instead of spaces in multiword field names, use uppercase letters to distinguish the first letter of each new word, for example, ProductCost or LastName. It is best to avoid spaces in field names, because spaces can cause problems when creating the other objects—such as queries, forms, and reports—based on tables.

Fields may be renamed either in Design view or in Datasheet view. In Design view, double-click the field name you want to change, type the new field name, and then click Save on the Quick Access Toolbar. To rename a field in Datasheet view, double-click the field selector of the field that you want to rename, type the new field name, and then press Enter.

Fields can be also be deleted in Design view or Datasheet view. To delete a field in Datasheet view, select the field or fields you want to delete and press Delete. To delete fields in Design view, do the following:

1. Click the Record Selector of the field you want to delete to select it.
2. Click Delete Rows in the Tools group.

3. Click Yes in the message box that appears if you want to permanently delete the field(s). Click No if you do not want to delete the field(s).

4. Click Yes in the second message box that will appear if the selected field you are deleting is a primary key. Click No if you do not want to delete the primary key.

 TIP **Freeze Fields in an Access Database**

To keep a field viewable while you are scrolling through a table, select the field or fields you want to freeze, right-click, and then click Freeze Fields. If you want the field(s) to remain frozen when you are finished working, save the changes when you close the table. To unfreeze all fields, right-click the field(s) and select Unfreeze All Fields.

Determine Data Type

Every field also has a ***data type*** property that determines the type of data that can be entered and the operations that can be performed on that data. Access recognizes 12 data types. Table 2.1 lists these data types, their uses, and examples of the data type.

TABLE 2.1	Data Types and Uses	
Data Type	**Description**	**Example**
Short Text	Stores alphanumeric data, such as a customer's name or address. It can contain alphabetic characters, numbers, and/or special characters (e.g., an apostrophe in O'Malley). Social Security numbers, telephone numbers, and postal codes should be designated as text fields since they are not used in calculations and often contain special characters such as hyphens and parentheses. A short text field can hold up to 255 characters. Formerly Text data type.	2184 Walnut Street
Long Text	Lengthy text or combinations of text and numbers, such as several sentences or paragraphs; used to hold descriptive data. Formerly Memo data type.	A description of product packaging
Number	Contains a value that can be used in a calculation, such as the number of credits a course is worth. The contents are restricted to numbers, a decimal point, and a plus or minus sign.	12
Date/Time	Holds dates or times and enables the values to be used in date or time arithmetic.	10/31/2016 1:30:00 AM
Currency	Used for fields that contain monetary values.	$1,200
AutoNumber	A special data type used to assign the next consecutive number each time you add a record. The value of an AutoNumber field is unique for each record in the file.	1, 2, 3
Yes/No	Assumes one of two values, such as Yes or No, True or False, or On or Off (also known as a Boolean). For example, is a student on the Dean's list: Yes or No.	Yes
OLE Object	Contains an object created by another application. OLE objects include spreadsheets, pictures, sounds, and graphics.	JPG image
Hyperlink	Stores a Web address (URL) or the path to a folder or file. Hyperlink fields can be clicked to retrieve a Web page or to launch a file stored locally.	http://www.keithmast.com
Attachment	Used to store multiple images, spreadsheet files, Word documents, and other types of supported files.	An Excel workbook
Calculated	The results of an expression that references one or more existing fields.	[IntRate] + 0.25
Lookup Wizard	Creates a field that enables you to choose a value from another table or from a list of values by using a list box or a combo box.	Customers table with an AccountID field that looks up the Account ID from an Accounts table

Establish a Primary Key

STEP 2 » As you learned earlier, the primary key is the field (or combination of fields) that uniquely identifies each record in a table. Access does not require that each table have a primary key. However, good database design usually includes a primary key in each table. You should select unique and infrequently changing data for the primary key. For example, a complete address (street, city, state, and postal code) may be unique but would not make a good primary key because it is subject to change when someone moves.

You probably would not use a person's name as the primary key, because several people could have the same name. A customer's account number, on the other hand, is unique and is a frequent choice for the primary key, as in the Customers table in this chapter. The primary key can be easily identified in many tables—for example, a PartNumber in a parts table, the ISBN in the book database of a bookstore, or a StudentID that uniquely identifies a student. When no primary key occurs naturally, you can create a primary key field with the AutoNumber data type. The *AutoNumber* data type is a number that automatically increments each time a record is added.

In Figure 2.4, the book's ISBN is the natural primary key for the book table because no two book titles can have the same ISBN. This field uniquely identifies the records in the table. Figure 2.5 depicts the Speakers table, where no unique field can be identified from the data. Because of this, you can add the SpeakerID field with an AutoNumber data type. Access automatically numbers each speaker record sequentially with a unique ID as each record is added.

FIGURE 2.4 Books Table with a Natural Primary Key

FIGURE 2.5 Speakers Table with an AutoNumber Primary Key

Explore a Foreign Key

A *foreign key* is a field in one table that is also the primary key of another table. The CustomerID is the primary key in the Customers table. It serves to uniquely identify each customer. It also appears as a foreign key in a related table. For example, the Accounts table contains the CustomerID field to establish which customer owns the account. A CustomerID can appear only once in the Customers table, but it may appear multiple times in the Accounts table (when viewed in Datasheet view) because one customer may own multiple accounts (checking, money market, home equity). Therefore, the CustomerID is the primary key in the Customers table and a foreign key in the Accounts table.

If you were asked to create an Access database for the speakers at a national conference, you would create a database with the tables Speakers and SessionSpeaker. You would add a primary key field to the Speakers table (SpeakerID) along with a speaker's FirstName and LastName fields; you would also add two fields to the SessionSpeaker table (SpeakerID and SessionID). The SpeakerID field in the Speakers table is a primary key and would not allow duplicates; the SpeakerID field in the SessionSpeaker table is a foreign key and would allow duplicates so that a speaker may speak more than once at the conference. The SpeakerID in the SessionSpeaker table enables you to join the two tables in a relationship. Figure 2.6 shows portions of the Speakers and SessionSpeaker tables.

SpeakerID is the primary key of the Speakers table (no duplicates)

SpeakerID is a foreign key in the Session Speaker table so speakers can be assigned multiple sessions

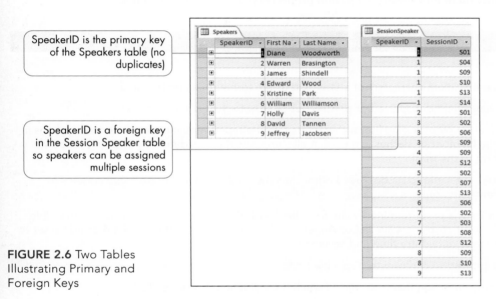

FIGURE 2.6 Two Tables Illustrating Primary and Foreign Keys

Work with Field Properties

STEP 3 ❯❯ While a field's data type determines the type of data that can be entered and the operations that can be performed on that data, it is its *field properties* that determine how the field looks and behaves.

Field Size is a commonly changed field property. A field with a *short text data type* can hold up to 255 characters; however, you can limit the characters by reducing the field size property. For example, you would limit the State field to only two characters because all state abbreviations are two letters. A field with a *number data type* can be set to Integer to display the field contents as integers from –32,768 to 32,768 or to Long Integer for larger values.

You can set a *caption property* to create a label more readable than a field. The caption displays at the top of a table or query column in Datasheet view and when the field is used in a report or form. For example, a field named ProductCostPerUnit could have the caption *Per Unit Product Cost*. Even if a caption is used, however, you must use the actual field name, ProductCostPerUnit, in any calculation.

Set the validation rule property to restrict data entry in a field to ensure the correct type of data are entered or that the data do not violate other enforced properties. The *validation rule* checks the data entered when the user exits the field. If the data entered violate the validation rule, an error message displays and prevents the invalid data from being entered into the field. For example, if you have set the data type for a field as Number and then try to enter text in the field, you will receive an error message telling you that the value you entered does not match the Number data type in the column.

The field properties are set to default values according to the data type, but you can modify them if necessary. Common property types are defined in Table 2.2.

TABLE 2.2 Common Access Table Property Types and Descriptions

Property Type	Description
Field Size	Determines the maximum characters of a text field or the format of a number field.
Format	Changes the way a field is displayed or printed but does not affect the stored value.
Input Mask	Simplifies data entry by providing literal characters that are typed for every entry, such as hyphens in a Social Security Number or slashes in a date. It also imposes data validation by ensuring that data entered conform to the mask.
Caption	Enables an alternate name to be displayed other than the field name; alternate name appears in datasheets, forms, and reports.
Default Value	Enters automatically a predetermined value for a field each time a new record is added to the table. For example, if most customers live in Los Angeles, the default value for the City field could be set to Los Angeles to save data entry time and accuracy.
Validation Rule	Requires data entered to conform to a specified rule.
Validation Text	Specifies the error message that is displayed when the validation rule is violated.
Required	Indicates that a value for this field must be entered.
Allow Zero Length	Allows entry of zero length text strings ("") in a Hyperlink, or Short or Long Text fields.
Indexed	Increases the efficiency of a search on the designated field.
Expression	Used for calculated fields only. Enters the expression you want Access to evaluate and store.
Result Type	Used for calculated fields only. Enters the format for the calculated field results.

Enter Table Records in Datasheet View

STEP 5 » While Design view is used to create and modify the table structure by enabling you to add and edit fields and set field properties, Datasheet view is used to add, edit, and delete records. As you have learned, the Datasheet view of an Access table resembles an Excel spreadsheet and displays data in a grid format—rows represent records and columns represent fields. Datasheet view indicates the current record using a gold border; you can select a record by clicking the record selector on the left side of each record. Use the new blank record (marked with an asterisk) at the end of the table to add a new record.

In Hands-On Exercise 1, you will create a new database and enter fields into a table. Then you will switch to the table's Design view to add additional fields and modify selected field properties of various fields within the table. Finally, you will enter data in the table in Datasheet view.

Quick Concepts

1. What is meant by "Design for now and the future" when designing database fields? *p. 143*

2. What is the difference between a primary key and a foreign key? *p. 149*

3. What is a field property? Which field property creates a more readable label that displays in the top row in Datasheet view and in forms and reports? *p. 149*

Hands-On Exercises

Watch the Video for this Hands-On Exercise!

MyITLab®
HOE1 Training

1 Table Design, Creation, and Modification

Assisting the bank auditor at Commonwealth Federal Bank as he investigates the mishandled funds will be a great opportunity for you to showcase your Access skills. Be sure to check your work each step of the way, because your work will come under substantial scrutiny. Do a good job with this Access project and more opportunities might come your way.

Skills covered: Create a Table in Datasheet View • Delete a Field and Set a Table's Primary Key • Work with Field Properties • Create a New Field in Design View • Modify the Table in Datasheet View

STEP 1 ≫ CREATE A TABLE IN DATASHEET VIEW

You create a new desktop database to store information about the mishandled funds database. You enter the data for the first record (BranchID, Manager, and Location). Refer to Figure 2.7 as you complete Step 1.

Step h: Type the data directly into the datasheet

Step i: Save the table as Branch

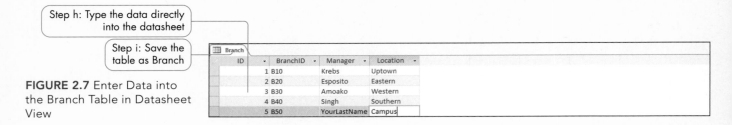

FIGURE 2.7 Enter Data into the Branch Table in Datasheet View

a. Start Microsoft Office Access 2013 and click **Blank desktop database**.

b. Type **a02h1Bank_LastFirst** into the **File Name box**.

c. Click **Browse** to find the folder location designated by your instructor and click **OK**. Click **Create** to create the new database.

Access will create the new database named *a02h1Bank_LastFirst* and a new table will automatically open in Datasheet view.

d. Click **Click to Add** and select **Short Text** as the Data type.

Click to Add changes to *Field1*. *Field1* is selected to make it easier to change the field name.

e. Type **BranchID** and press **Tab**.

A list of Data types for the third column opens so that you can select the data type for the third column.

f. Select **Short Text**, type **Manager**, and then press **Tab**.

g. Select **Short Text**, type **Location**, and then click in the first column next to the New Record asterisk.

h. Enter the data for the new table as shown in Figure 2.7, letting Access assign the ID field for each new record. Replace *YourLastName* with your own last name.

Entering data in Datasheet view provides an easy way to create the table initially. You can now modify the table in Design view as described in the next several steps.

i. Click **Save** on the Quick Access Toolbar. Type **Branch** in the **Save As dialog box** and click **OK**.

STEP 2 >> DELETE A FIELD AND SET A TABLE'S PRIMARY KEY

It is possible to modify tables even after data have been entered; however, pay attention to the messages from Access after you make a design change. In this step, you will be modifying the Branch table. You examine the design of the table and realize that the BranchID field is a unique identifier, making the ID field redundant. You delete the ID field and make the BranchID field the primary key field. Refer to Figure 2.8 as you complete Step 2.

Step d: Click to establish primary key

Step a: Branch table in Design view

Step c: Selected field with orange border

FIGURE 2.8 Branch Table in Design View

a. Click **View** in the Views group to switch to the Design view of the Branch table.

The Field Name for each of the four fields displays along with the Data Type.

b. Click the **ID field** to select it, if necessary. Click **Delete Rows** in the Tools group. Click **Yes** to both warning messages.

Access responds with a warning that you are about to permanently delete a field and a second warning that the field is the primary key. You delete the field because you will set the BranchID field as the primary key.

c. Click the **BranchID field,** if necessary.

The cell field name now has a orange border, as shown in Figure 2.8.

d. Click **Primary Key** in the Tools group on the DESIGN tab.

You set the BranchID as the primary key. The Indexed property in the *Field Properties* section at the bottom of the design window displays *Yes (No Duplicates)*.

e. Click **Save** on the Quick Access Toolbar to save the table.

TIP Shortcut Menu

You can right-click a row selector to display a shortcut menu to copy a field, set the primary key, insert or delete rows, or to access field properties. Use the shortcut menu to make these specific changes to the design of a table.

You need to modify the table design further to comply with the bank auditor's specifications. Be aware of messages from Access that indicate you may lose data. Refer to Figure 2.9 as you complete Step 3.

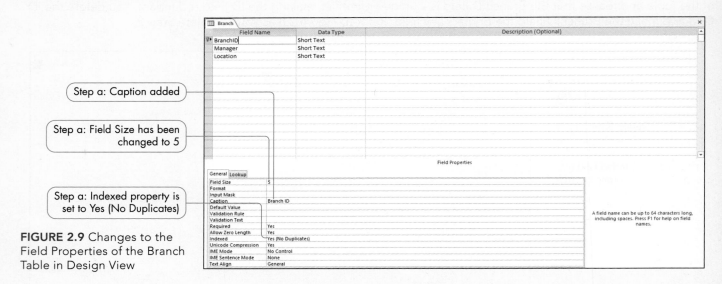

FIGURE 2.9 Changes to the Field Properties of the Branch Table in Design View

a. Click the **BranchID field name** in the top section of the design window; modify the BranchID field properties in the bottom of the design window.

- Click in the **Field Size property** and change *255* to **5**.
- Click in the **Caption property** and type **Branch ID**. Make sure *Branch* and *ID* have a space between them.
  A caption provides a more descriptive field name. It will appear as the column heading in Datasheet view.
- Check the Indexed property; confirm it is *Yes (No Duplicates)*.

b. Click the **Manager field name** at the top of the window; modify the following field properties:

- Click in the **Field Size property** and change *255* to **30**.
- Click in the **Caption property** and type **Manager's Name**.

c. Click the **Location field name** and modify the following field properties:

- Click in the **Field Size property** and change *255* to **30**.
- Click in the **Caption property** and type **Branch Location**.

You notify the auditor that a date field is missing in your new table. Modify the table to add the new field. The data can be entered at a later time. Refer to Figure 2.10 as you complete Step 4.

Step a: New field added

Step b: Date/Time data type added

Step f: Message indicating the field size was reduced

Step c: Description added

FIGURE 2.10 Adding a New Field to the Branch Table

a. Click in the first blank row below the Location field name and type **StartDate**.

You added a new field to the table.

b. Press **Tab** to move to the Data Type column. Click the **Data Type arrow** and select **Date/Time**.

TIP Keyboard Shortcut for Data Types

You also can type the first letter of the data type, such as d for Date/Time, s for Short Text, or n for Number. To use the keyboard shortcut, click on the field name and press Tab to advance to the Data Type column. Next, type the first letter of the data type.

c. Press **Tab** to move to the Description column and type **This is the date the manager started working at this location.**

d. Click the **Format property**, click the arrow, and then select **Short Date** from the list of date formats.

e. Click in the **Caption property** and type **Manager's Start Date**.

f. Click **Save** on the Quick Access Toolbar.

A warning dialog box opens to indicate that "Some data may be lost" because the size of the BranchID, Manager, and Location field properties were shortened. It asks if you want to continue anyway. Always read the Access warning! In this case, you can click Yes to continue because you know that the existing data are no longer than the new field sizes.

g. Click **Yes** in the warning box.

STEP 5 ≫ MODIFY THE TABLE IN DATASHEET VIEW

As you work with the auditor, you will modify tables in the bank database from time to time. To modify the table, you will need to switch between Design view and Datasheet view. Refer to Figure 2.11 as you complete Step 5.

FIGURE 2.11 Start Dates
Added to the Branch Table

Branch ID	Manager's Name	Branch Location	Manager's Start Date	Click to Add
B10	Krebs	Uptown	12/3/2014	
B20	Esposito	Eastern	6/18/2013	
B30	Amoako	Western	3/13/2011	
B40	Singh	Southern	9/15/2014	
B50	YourLastName	Campus	10/11/2016	

a. Right-click the **Branch tab** and select **Datasheet View** from the shortcut menu. (To return to Design view, right-click the tab again and select Design view.)

The table displays in Datasheet view. The field captions display at the top of the columns, but they are cut off.

b. Double-click the border between *Branch ID* and *Manager's Name*, the border between *Manager's Name* and *Branch Location*, the border between *Branch Location* and *Manager's Start Date*, and the border after *Manager's Start Date*.

The columns shrink or expand to display the best fit for the field name.

c. Click inside the **Manager's Start Date** in the first record and click the **Calendar** next to the date field. Use the navigation arrows to find and select **December 3, 2014** from the calendar.

You can also enter the dates by typing them directly into the StartDate field.

d. Type the start date directly in each field for the rest of the managers, as shown in Figure 2.11.

e. Click the **Close (X) button** at the top-right corner of the datasheet, below the Ribbon.

> **TROUBLESHOOTING:** If you accidentally click the Close (X) button on top of the Ribbon, you will exit Access completely. To start again, launch Access and click the first file in the Recent list.

f. Double-click the **Branch table** in the Navigation Pane to open the table. Check the start dates.

The start dates are still there even though you did not save your work in the previous step. Access saves the data to your storage location as soon as you move off the current record or close an object.

g. Click the **FILE tab**, click **Print**, and then click **Print Preview**.

Occasionally, users will print an Access table. However, database developers usually create reports to print table data.

h. Click **Close Print Preview** and close the Branch table.

i. Keep the database open if you plan to continue with Hands-On Exercise 2. If not, close the database and exit Access.

Multiple-Table Databases

In Figure 2.1, the sample bank database contains three tables—Customers, Accounts, and Branch. You created one table, the Branch table, in the previous section using the Datasheet view and modified the table fields in Design view. You will create the two remaining tables using a different method—importing data from Excel. In this section, you will learn how to import data from Excel, modify tables, create indexes, create relationships between tables, and enforce referential integrity.

Sharing Data

Most companies store some type of data in Excel spreadsheets. Often, the data stored in those spreadsheets can be more efficiently managed in an Access database. Fortunately, Access provides you with a wizard that guides you through the process of importing data from Excel. The wizard can also guide you as you import data from other Access databases. You can import tables, queries, forms, reports, pages, macros, and modules from another database.

Import an Excel Spreadsheet

STEP 1»
STEP 2»

Figures 2.12 through 2.17 show the steps of the Get External Data – Excel Spreadsheet feature. Launch the feature by clicking the External Data tab and clicking Excel in the Import & Link group. Figure 2.12 shows the first screen of the Get External Data – Excel Spreadsheet feature. In this step, you specify the source of the data. Locate the Excel file you want to import by clicking Browse. Then choose between three options for the incoming data: *Import the source data into a new table in the current database*; *Append a copy of the records to the table*, which adds the data to an existing table; or *Link to the data source by creating a linked table*, which creates a link to the Excel source. Importing or appending data stores a copy of the data in Access, whereas linking the data keeps the data in the original file and Access retrieves the data each time the database is opened.

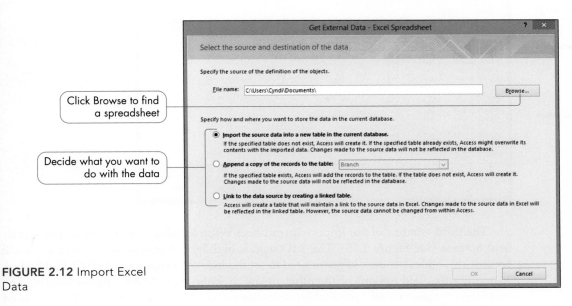

Click Browse to find a spreadsheet

Decide what you want to do with the data

FIGURE 2.12 Import Excel Data

After you locate and select an Excel workbook, accept the default option (*Import the source data into a new table in the current database*) and click OK. The Import Spreadsheet Wizard dialog box launches and displays a list of the worksheets in the specified workbook. Select the worksheet you want to import and click Next. Figure 2.13 shows the Accounts worksheet selected. The bottom of the Import Spreadsheet Wizard dialog box displays a preview of the data stored in the specified worksheet.

FIGURE 2.13 Show Available Worksheets and Preview Data

- Choose the worksheet to import
- Preview of the worksheet data
- Click Next to continue

Although a well-designed spreadsheet may include descriptive column headings that can be used as field names, not all spreadsheets are ready to import. You may have to revise the spreadsheet before importing it. The second window of the Import Spreadsheet Wizard dialog box contains a check box that enables you to convert the first row of column headings to field names in Access (see Figure 2.14). If a column heading row exists in the spreadsheet, check the box. If no column headings exist, leave the check box unchecked, and the data will import using Field1, Field2, Field3, and so forth as the field names.

FIGURE 2.14 Column Headings Become Field Names

- Check if spreadsheet contains column headings
- Column headings
- Click Next to continue

The third window of the Import Spreadsheet Wizard dialog box enables you to specify field options (see Figure 2.15). The AID field is highlighted in this figure. Because it will become this table's primary key, you need to set the Indexed Property to *Yes (No Duplicates)*. To modify the field options of the other fields, click the Field Name column heading and make the changes. Not all Access table properties are supported by the wizard. You may need to open the table in Design view after importing it to make any additional field property changes.

When you set the primary key in Access, the *indexed property* is automatically set to *Yes (No Duplicates)*. The indexed property setting enables quick sorting in primary key order and quick retrieval based on the primary key. For non–primary key fields, it may be beneficial to set the Indexed property to *Yes (Duplicates OK)*. Again, Access uses indexing to sort and retrieve data quickly based on the indexed field. As a general rule, indexed fields are usually foreign keys and are numeric.

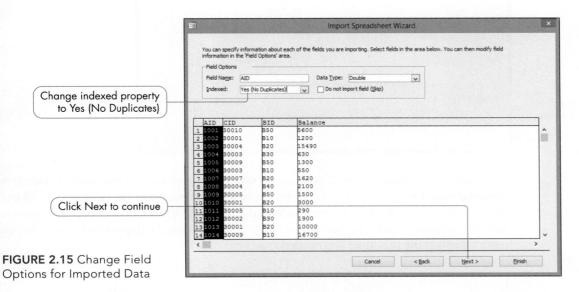

FIGURE 2.15 Change Field Options for Imported Data

The fourth window of the Import Spreadsheet Wizard dialog box enables you to choose a primary key before the import takes place (see Figure 2.16). If the option *Let Access add primary key* is selected, Access will generate an AutoNumber field and designate it as the primary key. Otherwise, you can designate a field to be the primary key or choose to have no primary key. In the import depicted in the Figure 2.16, the Excel data have a unique identifier (AID) that will become the table's primary key.

FIGURE 2.16 Set the Primary Key

Use the final window of the Import Spreadsheet Wizard to name the Access table. If the worksheet in the Excel workbook was named, Access uses the worksheet name as the table name (see Figure 2.17).

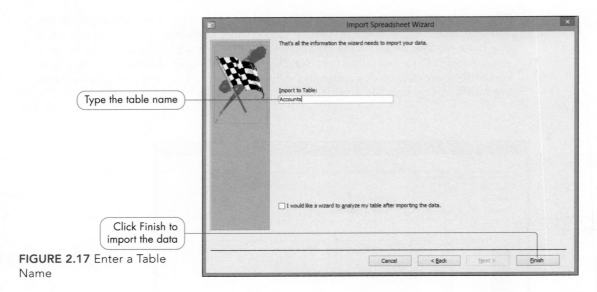

Type the table name

Click Finish to import the data

FIGURE 2.17 Enter a Table Name

Finally, the Wizard will ask if you wish to save the import steps. If the same worksheet is imported from Excel to Access on a recurring basis, you could save the parameters and use them again. To save the import steps, such as the indexing option and any new field names, click Save Import Steps in the Save Import Steps group. Saving the import steps will help you import the data the next time it is needed.

Modify an Imported Table's Design and Add Data

STEP 3 ❯❯ Importing data saves typing and prevents errors that may occur while entering data, but modifications will usually be required. After you have imported a table, open the table and examine the design to see if changes need to be made. You may need to modify the table by renaming fields so that they are more meaningful. To rename a field in Datasheet view, right-click the arrow next to the field name and click Rename Field. Type the new field name. To rename a field in Design view, select the field name and type the new name. In the bank example, you would change the name of the AID field to AccountID. Switch to Design view to modify the data type and field size.

STEP 4 ❯❯ You may need to add new fields or delete unnecessary fields. To add a new field in Datasheet view, right-click the field name to the right of where you want the new field to be added. Click Insert Field. To delete a field in Datasheet view, right-click the name of the field you want to delete and click Delete Field. To create a new field in Design view, click in the row below where you want the new field to be added and click Insert Rows in the Tools group on the Design tab. To delete a row in Design view, click in the row you want to delete and click Delete Rows in the Tools group on the Design tab. After making the modifications, you can add any data needed to the table.

Establishing Table Relationships

As previously discussed, the benefit of a relationship is to efficiently combine data from related tables for the purpose of creating queries, forms, and reports. Because this is such an important concept in designing and creating relational databases, this chapter reviews creating relationships and enforcing referential integrity. To ensure you are creating redundancy, you should store like data items together in the same table. In the example we are using, the customer data are stored in the Customers table. The Branch table stores data about the bank's branches, management, and locations. The Accounts table stores data about account ownership and balances.

STEP 5 » Once you have created the tables by storing like data items together, you will be able to recognize that some tables have common fields with others. Our Accounts table shares a common field with the Customers table—the CustomerID. It also shares a common field with the Branch table—BranchID. These common fields can be used to establish relationships between two tables.

Once you determine the common fields, you drag the field name from one table to the field name on the table you want to be joined.

Figure 2.18 shows the Bank database with relationships created by joining common fields.

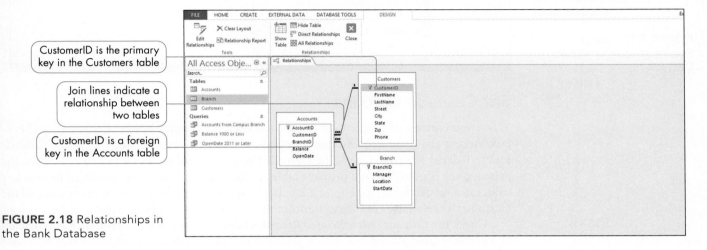

CustomerID is the primary key in the Customers table

Join lines indicate a relationship between two tables

CustomerID is a foreign key in the Accounts table

FIGURE 2.18 Relationships in the Bank Database

The primary key of a table plays a significant role when setting relationships. You cannot join two tables unless a primary key has been set in the primary table. In our Bank database, the CustomerID has been set as the primary key in the Customers table. Therefore, a relationship can be set between the Customers table and the Accounts table. Similarly, the Branch table can be joined to the Accounts table because BranchID has been set as the primary key in the Branch table.

The other side of the relationship join line is most often a foreign key of the related table. A foreign key is a field in one table that is also the primary key of another table. In the previous example, CustomerID in the Accounts table is a foreign key; BranchID in the Accounts table is a foreign key. Relationships between tables will almost always be set using primary and foreign keys.

Establish Referential Integrity

When you create a relationship in Access, the Edit Relationships dialog box displays. The first check box, Enforce Referential Integrity, should be checked in most cases. Remember, *referential integrity* enforces rules in a database that are used to preserve relationships between tables when records are changed.

STEP 6 » When referential integrity is enforced, you cannot enter a foreign key value in a related table unless the primary key value exists in the primary table. In the case of the Bank database, a customer's account information (which includes CustomerID) cannot be entered into the Accounts table unless the customer information is first entered into the Customers table. If you attempt to enter an account prior to entering the customer information, an error will appear, as shown in Figure 2.19. When referential integrity is enforced, you cannot delete a record in one table if it has related records.

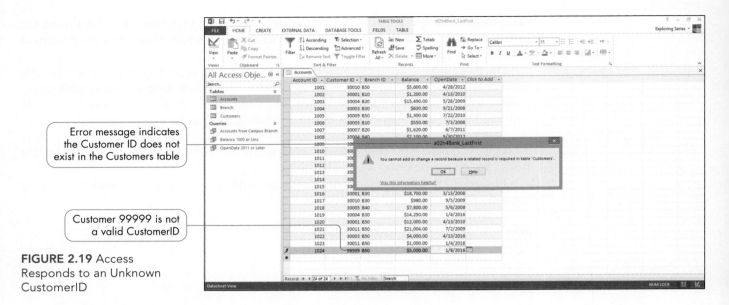

Error message indicates the Customer ID does not exist in the Customers table

Customer 99999 is not a valid CustomerID

FIGURE 2.19 Access Responds to an Unknown CustomerID

Set Cascade Options

When you create a relationship in Access and click the Enforce Referential Integrity checkbox, Access gives you two additional options: Cascade Update Related Fields and Cascade Delete Related Records. Check the *Cascade Update Related Fields* option so that when the primary key is modified in a primary table, Access will automatically update all foreign key values in a related table (see Figure 2.20). If a CustomerID is updated for some reason, all the CustomerID references in the Accounts table will automatically be updated.

Check the *Cascade Delete Related Records* option so that when the primary key is deleted in a primary table, Access will automatically delete all records in related tables that reference the primary key (see Figure 2.20). If one branch of a bank closes and its record is deleted from the Branch table, any account that still remains with this branch would be deleted. Access will give a warning first and enable you to avoid the action. This may be a desired business rule, but it should be set with caution.

One-To-Many relationship

Click to Enforce Referential Integrity

Click Cascade Update in case the primary key changes

Click Cascade Delete with caution

FIGURE 2.20 Cascade Options

Establish a One-to-Many Relationship

Figure 2.20 also shows that the relationship that will be created will be a one-to-many relationship. Access provides three different relationships for joining your data: one-to-one, one-to-many, and many-to-many. The most common type by far is the one-to-many relationship. A *one-to-many relationship* is established when the primary key value in the primary table can match many of the foreign key values in the related table.

For example, a bank customer will be entered into the Customers table once and only once. The primary key value, which is also the customer's CustomerID number, might be 1585. That same customer could set up a checking, savings, and money market account.

With each account, the CustomerID (1585) is required and therefore will occur three times in the Accounts table. The value appears once in the Customers table and three times in the Accounts table. Therefore, the relationship between Customers and Accounts would be described as one to many.

Table 2.3 lists and describes all three types of relationships you can create between Access tables.

TABLE 2.3   Relationship Types

Relationship Type	Description
One-to-Many	The primary key table must have only one occurrence of each value. For example, each customer must have a unique identification number in the Customers table, or each employee must have a unique EmployeeID in the Employee table. The foreign key field in the second table may have repeating values. For example, one customer may have many different account numbers, or one employee can perform many services.
One-to-One	Two different tables use the same primary key. Exactly one record exists in the second table for each record in the first table. Sometimes security reasons require a table be split into two related tables. For example, anyone in the company can look in the Employee table and find the employee's office number, department assignment, or telephone extension. However, only a few people need to have access to the employee's network login password, salary, Social Security number, performance review, or marital status. Tables containing this information would use the same unique identifier to identify each employee.
Many-to-Many	This is an artificially constructed relationship giving many matching records in each direction between tables. It requires construction of a third table called a junction table. For example, a database might have a table for employees and one for projects. Several employees might be assigned to one project, but one employee might also be assigned to many different projects. When Access connects to databases using Oracle or other software, you find this relationship type.

Figure 2.21 shows the Relationships window for the Bank database and all the relationships created using referential integrity. The join line between the CustomerID field in the Customers table and the CustomerID field in the Accounts table indicates that a one-to-many relationship has been set. You can rearrange the tables by dragging the tables by the title bar. You can switch the positions of the Branch and Accounts tables in the Relationships window without changing the relationship itself.

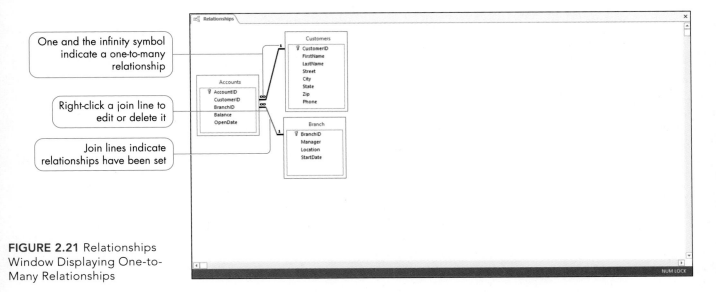

FIGURE 2.21 Relationships Window Displaying One-to-Many Relationships

TIP Navigating Between the Relationships Window and a Table's Design

When you right-click on a table's title bar in the Relationships window, the shortcut menu offers you a chance to open the table in Design view. This is a convenient feature because if you want to link one table to another table, the joined fields must have the same data type. This shortcut enables you to check the fields and revise them if necessary if a table contains a field with the wrong data type.

In the following Hands-On Exercise, you will create two additional tables in the Bank database by importing data from an Excel spreadsheet and from an Access database. You will establish and modify field properties. Then you will connect the newly imported data to the Branch table by establishing relationships between the tables.

Quick Concepts

1. Describe a scenario that may require you to import Excel data into Access. **p. 157**

2. What is the purpose of setting a relationship between two tables? **p. 160**

3. Why would you enforce referential integrity when setting a relationship? **p. 161**

4. Give an example of two database tables that would contain a one-to-many relationship. Describe the relationship. **pp. 162–163**

Hands-On Exercises

2 Multiple-Table Databases

You created a new Bank database, and you created a new Branch table. Now you are ready to import additional tables—one from an Excel spreadsheet and one from an Access database. Assume that the data are formatted correctly and are structured properly so that you can begin the import process.

Skills covered: Import Excel Data • Import Data from an Access Database • Modify an Imported Table's Design and Add Data • Add Data to an Imported Table • Establish Table Relationships • Test Referential Integrity

---

STEP 1 >> IMPORT EXCEL DATA

You and the auditor have discovered several of Commonwealth's files that contain customer data. These files need to be analyzed, so you decide to import the data into Access. In this exercise, you import an Excel spreadsheet into the Bank database. Refer to Figure 2.22 as you complete Step 1.

FIGURE 2.22 Imported Customers Table

a. Open *a02h1Bank_LastFirst* if you closed it at the end of Hands-On Exercise 1. Click the **FILE tab**, click **Save As**, and then click **Save As** in the *Save Database As* section. Type **a02h2Bank_LastFirst**, changing *h1 to h2*. Click **Save**.

b. If necessary, click **Enable Content** below the Ribbon to indicate you trust the contents of the database

> **TROUBLESHOOTING:** If you make any major mistakes in this exercise, you can close the file, open *a02h1Bank_LastFirst* again, and then start this exercise over.

c. Click the **EXTERNAL DATA tab** and click **Excel** in the Import & Link group to launch the Get External Data – Excel Spreadsheet feature. Select the **Import the source data into a new table in the current database option**, if necessary.

d. Click **Browse** and go to the student data folder. Select the *a02h2Customers* workbook. Click **Open** and click **OK** to open the Import Spreadsheet Wizard.

e. Ensure that the *First Row Contains Column Headings* check box is checked to tell Access that column headings exist in the Excel file.

The field names CID, FirstName, LastName, Street, City, State, ZIP, and Phone will import from Excel along with the data stored in the rows in the worksheet. The field names will be modified later in Access.

f. Click **Next**.

g. Ensure that *CID* is displayed in the Field Name box in Field Options. Click the **Indexed arrow** and select **Yes (No Duplicates)**. Click **Next**.

The CID (CustomerID) will become the primary key in this table. It needs to be a unique identifier, so we must change the properties to no duplicates.

h. Click the **Choose my own primary key option**. Make sure that the CID field is selected. Click **Next**.

The final screen of the Import Spreadsheet Wizard asks you to name your table. The name of the Excel worksheet was Customers, and Access defaults to the worksheet name. It is an acceptable name.

i. Click **Finish** to accept the Customers table name.

A dialog box opens asking if you wish to save the steps of this import to use again. If this were sales data that was collected in Excel and updated to the database on a weekly basis, saving the import steps would save time. You do not need to save this example.

j. Click the **Close (X) button**.

The new table displays in the Navigation Pane and resides in the Bank database.

k. Open the imported Customers table in Datasheet view and double-click the border between each of the field names to adjust the columns to Best fit. Compare your table to Figure 2.22.

l. Close the table.

STEP 2 ≫ IMPORT DATA FROM AN ACCESS DATABASE

The Customers spreadsheet that you imported contains customer information. The auditor asks you to import an Access database table that contains account information related to the mishandled funds. You use the Import Wizard to import the database table. Refer to Figure 2.23 as you complete Step 2.

FIGURE 2.23 Imported Accounts Table

a. Click the **EXTERNAL DATA tab** and click **Access** in the Import & Link group to launch the Get External Data – Access Database feature. Select the **Import tables, queries, forms, reports, macros, and modules into the current database option**, if necessary.

b. Click **Browse** and go to the student data folder. Select the *a02h2Accounts* database. Click **Open** and click **OK** to open the Import Objects dialog box.

The Accounts table is active; you will import this table.

c. Ensure that the Accounts table is selected and click **OK**.

d. Click **Close** on the Save Import Steps dialog box.

The Navigation Pane contains three tables: Accounts, Branch, and Customers.

e. Open the imported Accounts table in Datasheet view and compare it to Figure 2.23.

STEP 3 ⟫ MODIFY AN IMPORTED TABLE'S DESIGN AND ADD DATA

When importing tables from either Excel or Access, the fields may have different data types and property settings than required to create table relationships. You need to modify the tables so that each field has the correct data type and field size. Refer to Figure 2.24 as you complete Step 3.

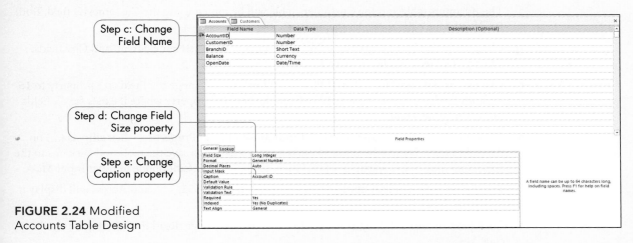

FIGURE 2.24 Modified Accounts Table Design

a. Right-click the **Accounts table** in the Navigation Pane.

b. Click **Design View** to open the table in Design view.

The Accounts table displays with the primary key AID selected.

c. Change the AID field name to **AccountID**.

d. Change the Field Size property to **Long Integer** in the Field Properties at the bottom of the Design window.

Long Integer ensures that there will be enough numbers as the number of customers grows over time and may exceed 32,768 (the upper limit for Integer values).

e. Type **Account ID** in the **Caption property box** for the AccountID field. The caption contains a space between *Account* and *ID*.

f. Change the CID field name to **CustomerID**.

g. Change the Field Size property to **Long Integer** in the Field Properties at the bottom of the Design window.

You can select the Field Size option using the arrow, or you can type the first letter of the option you want. For example, type l for Long Integer or s for Single. Make sure the current option is completely selected before you type the letter.

h. Type **Customer ID** in the **Caption property box** for the CustomerID field. The caption contains a space between *Customer* and *ID*.

i. Click the **BID field**. Change the BID field name to **BranchID**.

j. Type **5** in the **Field Size property box** in the Field Properties.

k. Type **Branch ID** in the **Caption property box** for the Branch ID field.

l. Change the Data Type of the Balance field to **Currency**.

The Currency data type is used for fields that contain monetary values.

m. Change the Data Type of the OpenDate field to **Date/Time** and add **Short Date** in the Format field property. Type **Open Date** in the **Caption property box**.

The OpenDate field stores the date that each account was opened.

n. Click **View** in the Views group to switch to Datasheet view. Read the messages and click **Yes** twice.

In this case, it is OK to click Yes because the shortened fields will not cut off any data. Leave the table open.

o. Right-click the **Customers table** in the Navigation Pane and select **Design View** from the shortcut menu.

p. Change the CID field name to **CustomerID**. Change the Field Size property of the CustomerID field to **Long Integer** and add a caption, **Customer ID**. Take note of the intentional space between *Customer* and *ID*.

The Accounts table and the Customers table will be joined using the CustomerID field. Both fields must have the same data type.

q. Change the Field Size property to **20** for the FirstName, LastName, Street, and City fields. Change the Field Size for State to **2**.

r. Change the data type for ZIP and Phone to **Short Text**. Change the Field size property to **15** for both fields. Remove the @ symbol from the Format property where it exists for all fields in the Customers table.

s. Click the **Phone field name** and click **Input Mask** in Field Properties. Click **ellipsis (...)** on the right side to launch the Input Mask Wizard. Click **Yes** to save the table and click **Yes** to the *Some data may be lost* warning. Click **Finish** to apply the default phone number Input Mask.

The phone number input mask enables users to enter 6105551212, and Access will display it as (610)555-1212.

t. Click **Save** to save the design changes to the Customers table. Read the warning box and click **Yes**.

STEP 4 ≫ ADD DATA TO AN IMPORTED TABLE

Now that you have created the Access tables, you add records. You may also need to update and delete records if you and the auditor decide the information is no longer needed. Refer to Figure 2.25 as you complete Step 4.

Step b: Enter yourself as a new customer

FIGURE 2.25 Customers Table Displaying Your Information

a. Click **View** in the Views group to display the Customers table in Datasheet view.

The asterisk at the bottom of the table data in the row selector area is the indicator of a place to enter a new record.

b. Click the **Customer ID field** in the record after *30010*. Type **30011**. Fill in the rest of the data using your information as the customer. You may use a fictitious address and phone number.

Note the phone number format. The input mask you set formats the phone number.

c. Close the Customers table. The Accounts table tab is open.

> **TROUBLESHOOTING:** If the Accounts table is not open, double-click Accounts in the Navigation Pane.

d. Locate the new record indicator—the * in the row selector—and click in the **Account ID column**. Type **1024**. Type **30011** as the Customer ID and **B50** as the Branch ID. Type **14005** for the Balance field value. Type **8/7/2015** for the OpenDate.

e. Add the following records to the Accounts table:

Account ID	Customer ID	Branch ID	Balance	Open Date
1025	30006	B40	$11,010	3/13/2013
1026	30007	B20	$7,400	5/1/2014

f. Close the Accounts table; keep the database open.

STEP 5 >> ESTABLISH TABLE RELATIONSHIPS

The tables for the bank investigation have been designed. Now you will need to establish connections between the tables. Look at the primary and foreign keys as a guide. Refer to Figure 2.26 as you complete Step 5.

FIGURE 2.26 Relationships Between Tables

a. Click the **DATABASE TOOLS tab** and click **Relationships** in the Relationships group.

The Relationships window opens and the Show Table dialog box appears.

> **TROUBLESHOOTING:** If the Show Table dialog box does not open, click Show Table in the Relationships group on the Relationships Tools Design tab.

b. Double-click each of the three tables displayed in the Show Table dialog box to add them to the Relationships window. (Alternatively, click a table and click **Add**.) Click **Close** in the Show Table dialog box.

> **TROUBLESHOOTING:** If you have a duplicate table, click the title bar of the duplicated table and press Delete.

c. Resize the Customers table box so all of the fields are visible. Arrange the tables as shown in Figure 2.26.

d. Drag the **BranchID field** in the Branch table onto the BranchID field in the Accounts table. The Edit Relationships dialog box opens. Click the **Enforce Referential Integrity** and **Cascade Update Related Fields check boxes**. Click **Create**.

A black line displays, joining the two tables. It has a 1 at the end near the Branch table and an infinity symbol on the end next to the Accounts table. You have established a one-to-many relationship between the Branch and Accounts tables.

e. Drag the **CustomerID field** in the Customers table onto the CustomerID field in the Accounts table. The Edit Relationships dialog box opens. Click the **Enforce Referential Integrity** and **Cascade Update Related Fields check boxes**. Click **Create**.

You have established a one-to-many relationship between the Customers and Accounts tables. A customer will have only a single CustomerID number. The same customer may have many different accounts: Savings, Checking, CDs, and so forth.

> **TROUBLESHOOTING:** If you get an error message when you click Create, verify that the data types of the joined fields are the same. To check the data types from the Relationships window, right-click the title bar of a table and select Table Design from the shortcut menu. Modify the data type and field size of the join fields if necessary.

f. Click **Save** on the Quick Access Toolbar to save the changes to the relationships. Close the Relationships window.

STEP 6 ≫ TEST REFERENTIAL INTEGRITY

The design of the Bank database must be 100% correct; otherwise, data entry may be compromised. Even though you are confident that the table relationships are correct, you decide to test them by entering some invalid data. If the relationships are not working, the invalid data will be rejected by Access. Refer to Figure 2.27 as you complete Step 6.

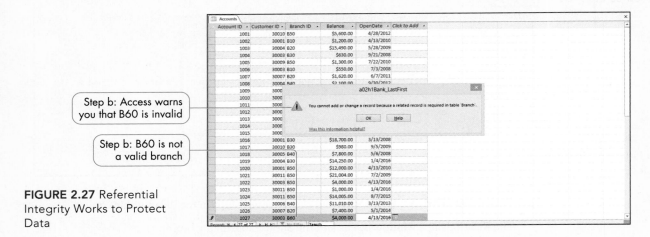

Step b: Access warns you that B60 is invalid

Step b: B60 is not a valid branch

FIGURE 2.27 Referential Integrity Works to Protect Data

a. Double-click the **Accounts table** to open it in Datasheet view.

b. Add a new record, pressing **Tab** after each field: Account ID: **1027**, Customer ID: **30003**, Branch: **B60**, Balance: **4000**, OpenDate: **4/13/2016**.

You attempted to enter a nonexistent BranchID and were not allowed to make that error. A warning message is telling you that a related record in the Branch table is required because the Accounts table and the Branch table are connected by a relationship with Enforce Referential Integrity checked.

c. Click **OK**. Double-click the **Branch table** in the Navigation Pane and examine the data in the BranchID field. Notice the Branch table has no B60 record. Close the Branch table.

d. Replace *B60* with **B50** in the new Accounts record and press **Tab** three times. As soon as the focus moves to the next record, the pencil symbol disappears and your data are saved.

You successfully identified a BranchID that Access recognizes. Because referential integrity between the Accounts and Branch tables has been enforced, Access looks at each data entry item in a foreign key and matches it to a corresponding value in the table where it is the primary key. In step b, you attempted to enter a nonexistent BranchID and were not allowed to make that error. In step d, you entered a valid BranchID. Access examined the index for the BranchID in the Branch table and found a corresponding value for B50.

e. Close the Accounts table. Reopen the Accounts table; you will find that the record you just entered for 1027 has been saved. Close the table.

You have established a one-to-many relationship between the Customers and Accounts tables. A customer will have only a single CustomerID number. The same customer may have many different accounts: Savings, Checking, CDs, and so forth.

f. Close all open tables, if necessary.

g. Keep the database open if you plan to continue with Hands-On Exercise 3. If not, close the database and exit Access.

Single-Table Queries

If you wanted to see which customers currently have an account with a balance over $5,000, you could find the answer by creating an Access query. A *query* enables you to ask questions about the data stored in a database and then provides the answers to the questions by providing subsets or summaries of data. Because data are stored in tables in a database, you always begin a query by asking, "Which table holds the data I want?" For the question about account balances over $5,000, you would reference the Accounts table. If you want to invite customers in a certain ZIP code to the Grand Opening of a new branch, you could create a query based on the Customers table.

You use the *Query Design view* to create queries. The Query Design view is divided into two parts: The top portion displays the tables, and the bottom portion (known as the query design grid) displays the fields and the criteria. You select only the fields you want arranged in the order that you want the resulting data displayed. The design grid also enables you to sort the records based on one or more fields. You can also create calculated fields to display data based on expressions that use the fields in the underlying table. For example, you could calculate the monthly interest earned on each bank account.

In this section, you will use the Query Design view and the Query Wizard to create queries that display only data that you select. Multitable queries will be covered in the next section.

Creating a Single-Table Query

You can create a single-table query in two ways—by using the Simple Query Wizard or the Query Design tool in the Queries group on the Create tab. The Query Design tool is the most flexible way to create a query. You can add criteria to a query while in the Query Design view. After you design a query, you can display the results of the query by switching to Datasheet view. A query's datasheet looks and acts like a table's datasheet, except that it is usually a subset of the records found in the entire table. The subset shows only the records that match the criteria that were added in the query design. The subset may contain different sorting of the records than the sorting in the underlying table. Datasheet view allows you to enter a new record, modify an existing record, or delete a record. Any changes made in Datasheet view are reflected in the underlying table that the query is based upon.

STEP 3 »   Be aware that query results display the actual records that are stored in the underlying table(s). Being able to correct an error immediately while it is displayed in query results is an advantage. You save time by not having to close the query, open the table, find the error, fix it, and then run the query again. However, you should use caution when editing records in query results since you will be changing the table data.

Create a Single-Table Select Query

The Query Design tool is used to create *select queries*, a type of query that displays only the records that match criteria entered in Query Design view. To create a select query using the Query Design tool, do the following:

STEP 2 »
1. Click the CREATE tab.
2. Click Query Design in the Queries group.
3. Select the table you need in your query from the Show Table dialog box.
4. Click Add to add the table to the top section of the query design and close the Show Table dialog box.
5. Drag the fields needed from the table to the query design grid (or alternatively, double-click the field names); then add criteria and sorting options.
6. Click Run in the Results group to show the results in Datasheet view.

Use Query Design View

The Query Design view consists of two parts. The top portion contains tables with their respective field names. If a query contains more than one table, the join lines between tables will be displayed as they were created in the Relationships window.

The bottom portion (known as the query design grid) contains columns and rows. Each field in the query has its own column and contains multiple rows. The rows permit you to control the query results.

- The *Field row* displays the field name.
- The *Table row* displays the data source.
- The *Sort row* enables you to sort in ascending or descending order.
- The *Show row* controls whether the field will be displayed in the query results.
- The *Criteria row* is used to set the rules that determine which records will be selected, such as customers with account balances greater than $5,000.

Figure 2.28 displays the query design grid with the Show Table dialog box open. The Accounts table has been added from the Show Table dialog box. Figure 2.29 shows the Design view of a sample query with four fields, with a criterion set for one field and sorting set on another. The results of the query are shown in Datasheet view, as shown in Figure 2.30.

TIP Examine the Records

An experienced Access user always examines the records returned in the query results. Verify that the records in the query results match the criteria that you specified in Design view. As you add additional criteria, the number of records returned will usually decrease.

Click Show Table to display the Show Table dialog box if it has been closed

Show Table dialog box appears automatically

Select a table and click Add

FIGURE 2.28 Query Design View with Open Show Table Dialog Box

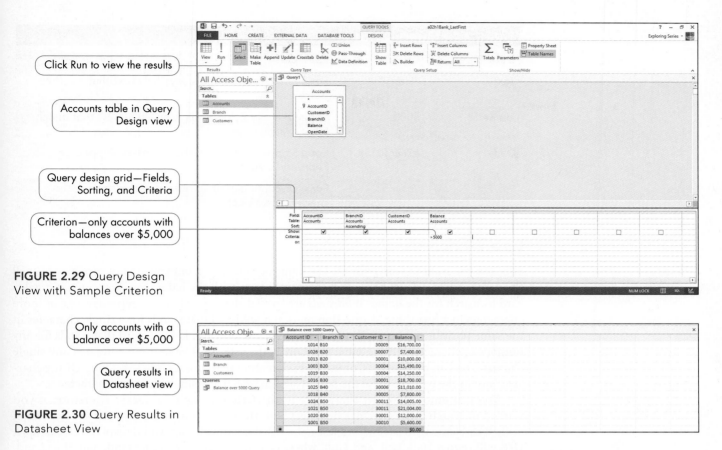

Click Run to view the results

Accounts table in Query Design view

Query design grid—Fields, Sorting, and Criteria

Criterion—only accounts with balances over $5,000

FIGURE 2.29 Query Design View with Sample Criterion

Only accounts with a balance over $5,000

Query results in Datasheet view

FIGURE 2.30 Query Results in Datasheet View

When you developed the tables, you toggled between the Design view and Datasheet view. Similarly, you will toggle between Design view and Datasheet view when you create queries. Use Design view to specify the criteria; you can use the results that display in Datasheet view to answer a question or to make a decision about the organization. Use Datasheet view to see the results of your query. Each time you need to fine-tune the query, switch back to Design view, make a change, and then test the results in Datasheet view. After you are satisfied with the query results, you may want to save the query so it can become a permanent part of the database and can be used later.

Specifying Query Criteria for Different Data Types

When specifying the criteria for a query, you may need to include a *delimiter*—a special character that surrounds a criterion's value. The delimiter needed is determined by the field data type, and Access will automatically enter the delimiter for you for some data types. Text fields require quotation marks before and after the text. Access automatically adds the quotation marks around text, but to ensure that the correct delimiter is used, you may want to include the delimiters yourself.

Use plain digits (no delimiter) for the criteria of a numeric field, currency, or AutoNumber. You can enter numeric criteria with or without a decimal point and with or without a minus sign. Commas and dollar signs are not allowed.

When the criterion is in a date field, you enclose the criterion in pound signs, such as #10/14/2016#. Access accepts a date with or without the pound signs, but if you enter 1/1/2016 without the pound signs, Access will automatically add the pound signs when you move to another column in the design grid. The date value can be entered using any allowed format, such as February 2, 2016, 2/2/2016, or 2-Feb-16. You enter criteria for a Yes/No field as Yes or No. See Table 2.4 for query criteria and examples.

TABLE 2.4 Query Criteria

Data Type	Criteria	Example
Text	"Harry"	For a FirstName field, displays only text that matches Harry exactly.
Numeric	5000	For a Quantity field, displays only numbers that match 5000 exactly.
Date	#2/2/2015#	For a ShippedDate field, shows orders shipped on February 2, 2015.
Yes/No	Yes	For a Discontinued field, returns records where the check box is selected.

Use Wildcards

Suppose you want to search for the last name of a customer, but you are not sure how to spell the name; however, you know that the name starts with the letters Sm. You can use a wildcard to search for the name. *Wildcards* are special characters that can represent one or more characters in a text value. A question mark is a wildcard that stands for a single character in the same position as the question mark, whereas an asterisk is a wildcard that stands for any number of characters in the same position as the asterisk. Use brackets to match any single character within the brackets, or use an exclamation mark inside brackets to match any character not in the brackets. Use the pound sign to match any single numeric character.

You can enter wildcard characters in the Criteria row of a query. Therefore, if you wanted to search for just names that start with the letters Sm, you can specify the criterion in the LastName field as Sm*. All last names that begin with Sm would display. For example, H?ll will return Hall, Hill, and Hull, whereas S*nd will return Sand, Stand, and StoryLand. Table 2.5 shows more query examples that use wildcards.

TABLE 2.5 Query Criteria Using Wildcards

Character	Description	Example	Result
*	Matches for any number of characters in the same position as the asterisk	Sm*	Small, Smiley, Smith, Smithson
?	Matches for a single character in the same position as the question mark	H?ll	Hall, Hill, Hull
[ ]	Matches any single character within the brackets	F[ae]ll	Fall and Fell, but not Fill or Full
[!]	Matches any character not in the brackets	F[!ae]ll	Fill and Full, but not Fall or Fell

Use Comparison Operators in Queries

A comparison operator, such as equal (=), not equal (<>), greater than (>), less than (<), greater than or equal to (>=), and less than or equal to (<=), can be used in the criteria of a query. Comparison operators enable you to limit the query results to only those records that meet the criteria. For example, if you only want to see accounts that have a balance greater than $5,000, you would type >5000 in the Criteria row. Table 2.6 shows more comparison operator examples as well as other sample expressions.

TABLE 2.6 Comparison Operators in Queries

Expression	Example
=10	Equals 10
<>10	Not equal to 10
>10	Greater than 10
>=10	Greater than or equal to 10
<10	Less than 10
<=10	Less than or equal to 10

Work with Null

Sometimes finding what is missing is an important part of making a decision. For example, if you need to know which orders have been completed but not shipped, you would create a query to find the orders with a missing ShipDate. Are there missing phone numbers or addresses for some of your customers? Create a query to find customers with a missing PhoneNumber. The term that Access uses for a blank field is *null*. Table 2.7 gives two illustrations of when to use the null criterion in a query.

TABLE 2.7 Establishing Null Criteria Expressions

Expression	Description	Example
Is Null	Use to find blank fields	For an Employee field in the Customers table when the customer has not been assigned a sales representative.
Is Not Null	Used to find fields with data	For a ShipDate field; a value inserted indicated the order was shipped to the customer.

Establish AND, OR, and NOT Criteria

Remember the earlier question, "Which customers currently have an account with a balance over $5,000?" This question was answered by creating a query with a single criterion, as shown in Figure 2.29. At times, questions are more specific and require queries with multiple criteria. For example, you may need to know "Which customers from the Eastern branch currently have an account with a balance over $5,000?" To answer this question, you need to specify criteria in multiple fields using the *AND logical operator*. When the criteria are in the same row of the query design grid, Access interprets the instructions using the AND operator. This means that the query results will display only records that match *all* criteria.

When you have multiple sets of criteria and you need to satisfy one set only, use the *OR logical operator*. The query results will display records that match any of the specified criteria. To use the OR operator, type your expression into the Criteria row, separating the criteria with the OR operator. Table 2.8 shows an example of an OR operator created using this method. You can also type the first expression into the Criteria row and then type the subsequent expression by using the Or row in the design grid. Figure 2.31b displays an example of an OR operator using this method.

The *NOT logical operator* returns all records except the specified criteria. For example, "Not Eastern" would return all accounts except those opened at the Eastern branch.

TABLE 2.8 AND, OR, and NOT Queries

Logical Operator	Example	Result
AND	"Eastern" AND "Campus"	For a Branch field, returns all records for the Eastern and Campus branches.
AND	>5000 AND <10000	For a Balance field, returns all accounts with a balance greater than $5,000 and less than $10,000.
OR	5000 OR 10000	For a Balance field, returns all accounts with a balance of exactly $5,000 or $10,000.
NOT	Not "Campus"	For a Branch field, returns all records except those in the Campus branch.

The first example in Figure 2.31 shows a query with an AND logical operator (criteria on the same row are implicitly joined by AND). It will return all of the B20 branch accounts with balances over $5,000. (Both conditions must be met for the record to be included.) The second example in Figure 2.31 shows a query with an OR logical operator. It will return all of the B20 branch accounts regardless of balance plus all accounts at any branch with a balance over $5,000. (One condition must be met for a record to be included.) The third example in Figure 2.31 shows a query that uses the NOT logical operator. It will return all of the accounts—excluding the B20 branch—with a balance over $5,000. The last example in Figure 2.31 shows a query that combines AND and OR logical operators. The top row will return B20 branch accounts with a balance over $5,000, and the second row will return B30 branch accounts with a balance over $15,000.

AND condition—criteria are in the same row

OR condition—criteria are in different rows

Use NOT to exclude specific records

Combination of AND and OR in the same query

FIGURE 2.31 Query Design Views Showing the AND, OR, and NOT Conditions

---

TIP **Finding Values in a Date Range**

To find the values contained within a data range, use the > (greater than) and < (less than) operators. For example, to find the values of a date after January 1, 2015, and before December 31, 2015, use the criterion >1/1/2015 and <12/31/2015. You can also use the BETWEEN operator. For example BETWEEN 1/1/2015 and 12/31/2015.

Understanding Query Sort Order

The **query sort order** determines the order of records in a query's Datasheet view. You can change the order of records by specifying the sort order in the Design view. When you want to sort using more than one field, the sort order is determined from left to right. The order of columns should be considered when first creating the query. For example, a query sorted by LastName and then by FirstName must have those two fields in the correct order in the design grid. You can change the order of the query fields in the design grid to change the sort order of the query results.

STEP 2 »

To change the order of fields, select the column you want to move by clicking the column selector. Release the mouse, then click again and drag the selected field to its new location. To insert additional columns in the design grid, select a column and click Insert Columns in the Query Setup group. The inserted column will insert to the left of the selected column. To delete a column, click the column selector to select the column and click the Delete Columns button on the Design tab or press Delete on the keyboard.

Running, Copying, and Modifying a Query

Several ways exist to run a query. One method is to click Run in the Results group when you are in Design view. Another method is to locate the query in the Navigation Pane and double-click it. A similar method is to select the query and press Enter.

After you create a query, you may want to create a duplicate copy to use as the basis for creating a similar query. Duplicating a query saves time when you need the same tables and fields but with slightly different criteria.

Run a Query

After you create a query and save it, you can run it directly from the Design view. You run a query by clicking the Run command (the red exclamation point) in the Results group on the Query Tools Design tab. You can also run a query from the Navigation Pane. Locate the query you want to run and double-click the query. The results will display as a tab in the main window.

Copy a Query

Sometimes you have a one-of-a-kind question about your data. You would create a query to answer this question and then delete the query. However, sometimes you need a series of queries in which each query is similar to the first. For example, you need a list of accounts in each branch. In a case like this, you create a query for one branch and then save a copy of the query and give it a new name. Finally, you would change the criteria to match the second branch. To accomplish this, do the following:

1. Open the query you want to copy.
2. Click the FILE tab and click Save As.
3. Click Save Object As in the *File Types* section.
4. Ensure Save Object As is selected in the *Database File Types* section and click Save As.
5. Type the name you want to use for the new query in the Save As dialog box and click OK (see Figure 2.32).
6. Switch to Design view and modify the query criteria.

FIGURE 2.32 Using Save Object As to Copy a Query

You can also right-click the original query in the Navigation Pane and click Copy. Click in the Navigation Pane again and click Paste. Type a name for the new query in the Paste As dialog box.

Using the Query Wizard

STEP 1 You may also create a query using the Query Wizard. Like all of the Microsoft wizards, the ***Simple Query Wizard*** guides you through the query design process. The wizard is helpful for creating basic queries that do not require criteria. After the query is created using the Wizard, you can switch to Design view and add criteria manually. Even if you initiate the query with a wizard, you will need to learn how to modify it in Design view. Often, copying an existing query and making slight modifications to its design is much faster than starting at the beginning with the wizard. You also will need to know how to add additional tables and fields to an existing query when conditions change. To launch the Query Wizard, click the Create tab and click Query Wizard in the Queries group (see Figure 2.33).

FIGURE 2.33 Launching the Query Wizard

Select the Simple Query Wizard in the Query Wizard dialog box, as shown in Figure 2.34.

FIGURE 2.34 Simple Query Wizard

In the first step of the Simple Query Wizard dialog box, you specify the tables or queries and fields needed in your query. When you select a table from the Tables/Queries arrow (queries can also be based on other queries), a list of the table's fields displays in the Available Fields list box. See Figures 2.35 and 2.36.

FIGURE 2.35 Specify Which Tables or Queries to Use

Fields already moved to the Selected Fields list

Move a single field to the Selected Fields list

Move all fields to the Selected Fields list

Remove a single field from the Selected Fields list

Remove all fields from the Selected Fields list

FIGURE 2.36 Specify the Fields for the Query

Select the necessary fields and add them to the Selected Fields list box using the directional arrows shown in Figure 2.36.

In the next screen (shown in Figure 2.37), you choose between a detail and a summary query. The detail query shows every field of every record in the result. The summary query enables you to group data and view only summary records. For example, if you were interested in the total funds deposited at each of the bank branches, you would set the query to Summary, click Summary Options, and then click Sum on the Balance field. Access would then sum the balances of all accounts for each branch.

Select detail or summary data

FIGURE 2.37 Choose Detail or Summary Data

The final dialog box of the Simple Query Wizard asks for the name of the query. Assign a descriptive name to your queries so that you know what each does by looking at the query name. See Figure 2.38.

Type the Query name

FIGURE 2.38 Name the Query

The next Hands-On Exercise enables you to create and run queries in order to find answers to questions you have about your data. You will use the Query Wizard to create a basic query and modify the query in Query Design view by adding an additional field and by adding query criteria.

Quick
Concepts

1. Define a query. Give an example. *p. 171*
2. Give an example of how to use the criteria row to find certain records in a table. *p. 172*
3. When would you need to use the "is null" and "is not null" criteria? *p. 175*
4. When would you want to copy a query? *p. 177*

Hands-On Exercises

 Watch the Video for this Hands-On Exercise!

 MyITLab® HOE3 Training

3 Single-Table Queries

The tables and table relationships have been created, and some data have been entered. Now, you need to begin the process of analyzing the bank data for the auditor. You will do so using queries. You decide to begin with the Accounts table.

Skills covered: Create a Query Using a Wizard • Specify Query Criteria and Query Sort Order • Change Query Data

---

STEP 1 ›› CREATE A QUERY USING A WIZARD

You decide to start with the Query Wizard, knowing you can always alter the design of the query later in Query Design view. You will show the results to the auditor using Datasheet view. Refer to Figure 2.39 as you complete Step 1.

FIGURE 2.39 Query Results Before Criteria Are Applied

a. Open *a02h2Bank_LastFirst* if you closed it at the end of Hands-On Exercise 2. Save the database as **a02h3Bank_LastFirst**, changing *h2* to *h3*.

b. Click the **CREATE tab** and click **Query Wizard** in the Queries group to launch the New Query wizard.

   The New Query Wizard dialog box opens. Simple Query Wizard is selected by default.

c. Click **OK**.

d. Verify that *Table: Accounts* is selected in the Tables/Query box.

e. Select **AccountID** from the **Available Fields list** and click >. Repeat the process with CustomerID, BranchID, and Balance.

   The four fields should now display in the Selected Fields list box.

f. Click **Next**.

g. Confirm *Detail* is selected and click **Next**.

h. Name the query **Accounts from Campus Branch**. Click **Finish**.

   This query name describes the data in the query results. Your query should have four fields: AccountID, CustomerID, BranchID, and Balance. The Navigation bar indicates 27 records meet the query criteria.

The auditor indicated that the problem seems to be confined to the Campus branch. You use this knowledge to revise the query to display only Campus accounts. Refer to Figure 2.40 as you complete Step 2.

Step c: Sort by Ascending AccountID

Step b: "B50" criterion added

FIGURE 2.40 Enter Criteria and Add Sort Order

a. Click the **HOME tab** and click **View** in the Views group to view the Accounts from Campus Branch query in Design view.

You have created the Campus Branch Customers query to view only those accounts at the Campus branch. However, other branches' accounts also display. You need to limit the query results to only the records of interest.

b. Click in the **Criteria row** (fifth row) in the BranchID column and type **B50**.

B50 is the BranchID for the Campus branch. Access queries are not case sensitive; therefore, b50 and B50 will produce the same results. Access adds quotation marks around text criteria.

c. Click in the **Sort row** (third row) in the AccountID column and select **Ascending**.

d. Click **Run** in the Results group.

You should see nine records, all from Branch B50, in the query results.

When the query results are on the screen, the auditor notices that some of the data are incorrect, and one of the accounts is missing. From your experience with Access, you explain to the auditor that the data can be changed directly in a query rather than switching back to the table. Refer to Figure 2.41 as you complete Step 3.

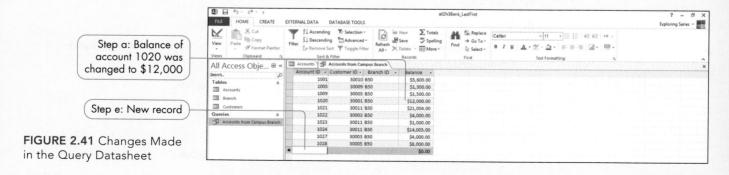

Step a: Balance of account 1020 was changed to $12,000

Step e: New record

FIGURE 2.41 Changes Made in the Query Datasheet

a. Click on the **Balance field** in the record for account 1020. Change *$1,200* to **$12,000**. Press **Enter**. Save and close the query.

You are modifying the record directly in the query results.

b. Double-click the **Accounts table** in the Navigation Pane to open it.

Only one account shows a $12,000 balance. The Account ID is 1020 and the Customer ID is 30001. The change you made in the Accounts table from the Campus Branch query datasheet automatically changed the data stored in the underlying table.

c. Open the Customers table. Find the name of the customer whose CustomerID is 30001. Note that the account belongs to Allison Millward. Close the Customers table.

d. Add a new record to the Accounts table with the following data: **1028** (Account ID), **30005** (Customer ID), **B50** (Branch ID), **8/4/2016** (Open Date) , and $8,000 (Balance). Press **Tab**.

> **TROUBLESHOOTING:** If the Accounts table is not open, double-click Accounts in the Navigation Pane.

The new record is added to the Accounts table.

e. Double-click the **Accounts from Campus Branch query** in the Navigation Pane.

Customer 30005 now shows two accounts: one with a balance of $1,500 and one with a balance of $8,000.

f. Close the Accounts from Campus Branch query and close the Accounts table.

g. Keep the database open if you plan to continue with Hands-On Exercise 4. If not, close the database and exit Access.

Multitable Queries

Multitable queries contain two or more tables. They enable you to take advantage of the relationships that have been set in your database. When you need to extract information from a database with a query, most times you will need to pull the data from multiple tables to provide the answers you need. One table may contain the core information that you need, while another table may contain the related data that makes the query relevant to the users.

For example, the sample bank database contains three tables: Customers, Accounts, and Branch. You connected the tables through relationships in order to store data efficiently and enforce consistent data entry. The Accounts table lists the balances of each account at the bank—the key financial information. However, the Accounts table does not list the contact information of the owner of the account. Therefore, the Customers table is needed to provide the additional information.

Creating a Multitable Query

STEP 2 » Creating a multitable query is similar to creating a single-table query; however, choosing the right tables and managing the table relationships will require some additional skills. First, you should only include related tables in a multitable query. *Related tables* are tables that are joined in a relationship using a common field. As a rule, related tables should already be established when you create a multitable query. Using Figure 2.42 as a guide, creating a query with the Accounts and Branch tables would be acceptable, as would using Accounts and Customers tables, or Accounts, Branch, and Customers tables. All three scenarios include related tables. Creating a query with the Branch and Customers tables would not be acceptable because these tables are *not* directly related. To create a multitable query, do the following:

1. Click the CREATE tab.
2. Click Query Design in the Queries group.
3. Select the table you need in your query from the Show Table dialog box.
4. Click Add to add the table to the top section of the query design.
5. Select the next table you want to add to the query and click Add. Continue selecting and adding tables to the top section of the query design until all the tables you need display.
6. Drag the fields needed from the tables to the query design grid (or alternatively, double-click the field names); then add criteria and sorting options.
7. Click Run in the Results group to show the results in Datasheet view.

 TIP **Print the Relationship Report to Help Create a Multitable Query**

When creating a multitable query, you should only include related tables. As a guide, you can print the Relationship Report in the Tools group on the Relationship Tools Design tab when the Relationships window is open. This report will help you determine which tables are related in your database.

Refer to Figure 2.31 (the top image) showing the results of the query "Which customers from the Campus branch have an account with a balance over $5,000?" To make this report more understandable to others, we can modify the query by adding the Branch Location (in place of the BranchID) and the Customer LastName (in place of the CustomerID). To make these changes, we would need to add the Branch table (which contains the Location field) and the Customers table (which contains the LastName field) to the query design.

Add Additional Tables to a Query

STEP 1 >> To modify a saved query, open the query in Design view. If you wanted to change the Balance Over $5000 query as discussed earlier, first open the query in Design view. To add additional tables to a query, open the Navigation Pane (if necessary) and drag tables directly into the top portion of the query design grid. For example, the Branch and Customers tables were added to the query, as shown in Figure 2.42. The join lines between tables indicate that relationships were previously set in the Relationships window.

Join lines indicate new tables are related to the Accounts table

FIGURE 2.42 Two Additional Tables Added to a Query

Modifying a Multitable Query

STEP 3 >> After creating a multitable query, you may find that you did not include all of the fields you needed, or you may find that you included fields that are unnecessary and complicate the results. You may find that other fields could be included that would make the results more understandable to others. To modify multitable queries, you use the same techniques you learned for single-table queries. Add tables using the Show Table dialog box; remove tables by clicking the unwanted table and pressing Delete. Add fields by double-clicking the field you want; remove fields by clicking the column selector and pressing Delete. Join lines between related tables should display automatically in a query if the relationships were previously established, as shown in Figure 2.42.

>
> ### TIP Changes in Multitable Queries Do Not Affect Relationships
>
> When you add two or more tables to a query, join lines appear automatically. You can delete the join lines in a query with no impact on the relationships themselves. Deleting a join line only affects the relationships in the individual query. The next time you create a query with the same tables, the join lines will be restored. And, if you open the Relationships window, you will find the join lines intact.

Add and Delete Fields in a Multitable Query

In Figure 2.43, three tables, as well as the join lines between the tables, display in the top pane of the Query Design view. All the fields from each of the tables are now available to be used in the query design grid. Figure 2.43 shows that Location (from the Branch table) replaced BranchID and LastName (from the Customers table) replaced CustomerID to make the results more useful. The BranchID was deleted from the query; therefore, the "B50" criterion was removed as well. "Campus" was added to the Location field's criteria row in order to extract the same results. Because criteria values are not case sensitive, typing "campus" is the same as typing "Campus," and both will return the same results. The results of the revised query are shown in Figure 2.44.

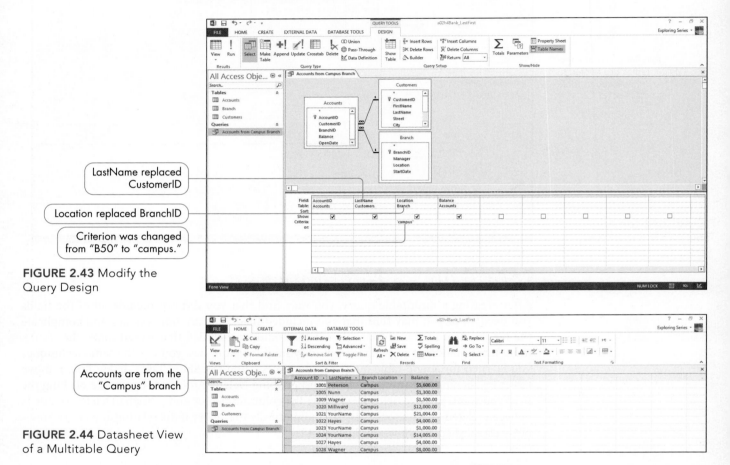

LastName replaced CustomerID

Location replaced BranchID

Criterion was changed from "B50" to "campus."

FIGURE 2.43 Modify the Query Design

Accounts are from the "Campus" branch

FIGURE 2.44 Datasheet View of a Multitable Query

Add Join Lines in a Multitable Query

In Figure 2.45, two tables are added to the query design, but no join line connects them. The results of the query will be unpredictable and will display more records than expected. The Customers table contains 11 records, and the Branch table contains 5 records. Because Access does not know how to interpret the unrelated tables, the results will show 55 records—every possible combination of customer and branch (11 × 5). See Figure 2.46.

FIGURE 2.45 Avoid Unrelated Tables in a Multitable Query

Tables are not joined (and not related)

Access shows one record for every Branch for each Customer

Result shows 55 records

FIGURE 2.46 Query Result with Unrelated Tables

To fix this problem, you can create join lines using the existing tables if the tables facilitate this by having common fields. In a situation like this, in which there are no common fields, you must add an additional table that will provide a join between all three tables. In the Branch query, you can add the Accounts table, which will facilitate a join between the two existing tables, Customers and Branch. As soon as the third table is added to the query design, the join lines appear automatically, as shown in Figure 2.43.

Over time, your database will grow, and additional tables will be added. Occasionally, new tables are added to the database but not added to the Relationships window. When queries are created with the new tables, join lines will not be established. When this happens, add join lines to the new tables. Or you can create temporary join lines in the query design. These join lines will provide a temporary relationship between two tables and enable Access to interpret the query properly.

Get Answers Using a Multitable Query

STEP 4 ▶▶ You can get key information from your database using a multitable query. For example, if you want to know how many orders each customer placed since the database was created, you would create a new query and add the Customers and Orders tables to the Query Design view. After you verify that the join lines are correct, you add the CustomerID field from the Customers table and the OrderID field from the Order table to the query design grid.

When you run the query, the results show duplicates in the CustomerID column because customers place multiple orders. Then return to the Query Design view and click Totals in the Show/Hide group. Both columns show the Group By option in the Total row. Change the total row of the OrderID field to Count and run the query again. This time the results show one row for each customer and the number of orders each customer placed since the database was created.

Quick Concepts

1. Define a multitable query. *p. 184*

2. What are the benefits of creating multitable queries? *p. 184*

3. What is the result of creating a query with two unrelated tables? *p. 186*

4. Describe the purpose adding a join line in a multitable query. *p. 187*

Hands-On Exercises

4 Multitable Queries

Based on the auditor's request, you will need to evaluate the data further. This requires creating queries that are based on multiple tables rather than on a single table. You decide to open an existing query, add additional tables, and then save the query with a new name.

Skills covered: Add Additional Tables to a Query • Create a Multitable Query • Modify a Multitable Query • Get Answers Using a Multitable Query

STEP 1 ≫ ADD ADDITIONAL TABLES TO A QUERY

The previous query was based on the Accounts table, but now you need to add information to the query that is in the Branch and Customers tables. You will need to add the Branch and Customers tables to the query. Refer to Figure 2.47 as you complete Step 1.

Steps c and l: Customers and Branch tables added

FIGURE 2.47 Add Tables to Query Design View

a. Open *a02h3Bank_LastFirst* if you closed it at the end of Hands-On Exercise 3. Save the database as **a02h4Bank_LastFirst**, changing *h3* to *h4*.

b. Right-click the **Accounts from Campus Branch query** in the Navigation Pane and select **Design View** from the shortcut menu.

c. Drag the **Branch table** from the Navigation Pane to the top pane of the query design grid next to the Accounts table.

    A join line connects the Branch table to the Accounts table. The query inherits the join lines from the relationships created in the Relationships window.

d. Drag the **Location field** from the Branch table to the first empty column in the design grid.

    The Location field should be positioned to the right of the Balance column.

e. Click the **Show check box** under the BranchID field to clear the check box and hide this field in the results.

    The BranchID field is no longer needed because the Location field provides the same information. Because you unchecked the BranchID show check box, the BranchID field will not display the next time the query is opened.

f. Delete the B50 criterion in the BranchID field.

g. Type **Campus** as a criterion in the Location field and press **Enter**.

    Access adds quotation marks around *Campus* for you; quotes are required for text criteria. You are substituting the Location criterion *(Campus)* in place of the BranchID criterion (B50).

h. Remove Ascending from the AccountID sort row. Click in the **Sort row** of the Balance field. Click the arrow and select **Descending**.

i. Click **Run** in the Results group.

The BranchID field does not display in the Datasheet view because you hid the field in step e. Only Campus accounts should display in the datasheet (10 records). Next, you will add the Customer LastName and delete the CustomerID from the query.

j. Save the changes to the query design.

k. Click **View** in the Views group to return to the Design view.

The BranchID field no longer displays on the field as it has been hidden.

l. Drag the **Customers table** from the Navigation Pane to the top section of the query design grid and reposition the tables so that the join lines are not blocked (see Figure 2.47).

The one-to-many relationship lines automatically connect the Customers table to the Accounts table (similar to step c on the previous page).

m. Drag the **LastName field** in the Customers table to the second column in the design grid.

The LastName field should be positioned to the right of the AccountID field.

n. Click the column selector in the CustomerID field to select it. Press **Delete**.

The CustomerID field is no longer needed in the results because we added the LastName field.

o. Click **Run** in the Results group.

The last names of the customers now display in the results.

p. Save and close the query.

STEP 2 ≫ CREATE A MULTITABLE QUERY

After discussing the query results with the auditor, you realize that another query is needed to show those customers with account balances of $1,000 or less. You create the query and view the results in Datasheet view. Refer to Figure 2.48 as you complete Step 2.

Step d: Add the balance criterion

FIGURE 2.48 Create a Multitable Query

a. Click the **CREATE tab** and click **Query Design** in the Queries group.

b. Double-click the **Branch table name** in the Show Table dialog box and double-click **Accounts** and **Customers** to add all three to the Query Design view. Click **Close** in the Show Table dialog box.

Three tables were added to the query.

c. Double-click the following fields to add them to the design grid: **LastName**, **FirstName**, **Balance**, and **Location**.

d. Type **<=1000** in the **Criteria row** of the Balance column.

e. Click **Run** in the Results group to see the query results.

Six records that have a balance of $1,000 or less display.

f. Click **Save** on the Quick Access Toolbar and type **Balance 1000 or Less** as the Query Name in the **Save As dialog box**. Click **OK**.

STEP 3 >> MODIFY A MULTITABLE QUERY

The auditor requests additional changes to the Balance 1000 or Less query you just created. You will modify the criteria to display the accounts that were opened after January 1, 2011, with balances of $2,000 or less. Refer to Figure 2.49 as you complete Step 3.

FIGURE 2.49 Query Using the AND Condition

a. Click **View** in the Views group to switch the *Balance 1000 or Less* query to Design view.

b. Type **<=2000** in place of *<=1000* in the **Criteria row** of the Balance field.

c. Double-click the **OpenDate field** in the Accounts table in the top section of the Query Design view to add it to the first blank column in the design grid.

d. Type **>=1/1/2011** in the **Criteria row** of the OpenDate field to extract only accounts that have been opened since January 2011.

After you type the expression and then move to a different column, Access will add the # symbols around the date automatically.

e. Click **Run** in the Results group to display the results of the query.

Five records display in the query results.

f. Click the **FILE tab**, click **Save As**, click **Save Object As**, and then click **Save As**. Type **OpenDate 2011 or Later** as the query name. Click **OK**.

g. Click **View** in the Views group to return to the Design view of the query.

h. Click in the **Sort row** of the OpenDate field and select **Ascending**.

i. Click **Run** in the Results group.

The records are sorted from the earliest open date after January 1, 2011, to the most recent open date.

j. Save and close the query.

The auditor wants to know the number of accounts each customer has opened. You create a query using a Totals row to obtain these data. Refer to Figure 2.50 as you complete Step 4.

Step f: Click Totals

Step g: Change to Count

FIGURE 2.50 Number of Accounts Opened by a Customer

a. Click the **CREATE tab** and click **Query Design** in the Queries group.

b. Add the Accounts table and the Customers table to the top section of the Query Design view. Click **Close** in the Show Table dialog box.

c. Double-click the **CustomerID** in the Customers table in the top section of the Query Design view to add it to the first blank column in the design grid and double-click the **AccountID** in the Accounts table to add it to the second column.

d. Click **Run** in the Results group.

The results show there are 28 records. Every account a customer has opened is displayed. The auditor only wants the total number of accounts a customer has, so you need to modify the query.

e. Click **View** in the Views group to return to the Design view of the query.

f. Click **Totals** in the Show/Hide group.

Both columns show the Group By option in the Total row.

g. Click **Group By** in the Total row of the AccountID field and select **Count**.

h. Click **Run** in the Results group.

The results show one row for each customer and the number of accounts each customer has opened since the database was created.

i. Click **Save** on the Quick Access Toolbar and type **Number of Customer Accounts** as the query name. Close the query.

j. Submit based on your instructor's directions and close Access.

Chapter Objectives Review

After reading this chapter, you have accomplished the following objectives:

1. Design a table.
- Include necessary data: Consider the output requirements when creating table structure. Determine the data required to produce the expected information.
- Design for now and for the future: When designing a database, try to anticipate the future needs of the system and build in the flexibility to satisfy those demands.
- Store data in its smallest parts: Store data in its smallest parts to make it more flexible. Storing a full name in a Name field is more limiting than storing a first name in a separate FirstName field and a last name in a separate LastName field.
- Add calculated fields to a table: A calculated field produces a value from an expression or function that references one or more existing fields. Storing calculated data in a table enables you to add the data easily to queries, forms, and reports without the trouble of an additional calculation.
- Design to accommodate date arithmetic: Calculated fields are frequently created with numeric data. You can use date arithmetic to subtract one date from another to find out the number of days, months, or years that have lapsed between them. You can also add or subtract a constant from a date.
- Plan for common fields between tables: Tables are joined in relationships using common fields. Name the common fields with the same name and make sure they have the same data type.

2. Create and modify tables.
- Create tables: Create tables in Datasheet view or Design view. You can also import data from another database or an application such as Excel.
- Determine data type: Data type properties determine the type of data that can be entered and the operations that can be performed on that data. Access recognizes 12 data types.
- Establish a primary key: The primary key is the field that uniquely identifies each record in a table.
- Explore a foreign key: A foreign key is a field in one table that is also the primary key of another table.
- Work with field properties: Field properties determine how the field looks and behaves. Examples of field properties are the field size property and the caption property.
- Enter table records in Datasheet view: Datasheet view is used to add, edit, and delete records. Design view is used to create and modify the table structure by enabling you to add and edit fields and set field properties.

3. Share data.
- Import data: You can import data from other applications such as an Excel spreadsheet or import data from another database by using the Import Wizard.
- Modify an imported table's design and add data: After importing a table, examine the design and make necessary modifications. Modifications may include changing a field name, adding new fields, or deleting unnecessary fields.

4. Establish table relationships.
- Set relationships in the Relationships window: Use Show Table to add tables to the Relationships window. Drag a field name from one table to the corresponding field name in another table to join the tables.
- Establish referential integrity: Referential integrity enforces rules in a database that are used to preserve relationships between tables when records are changed.
- Set cascade options: The Cascade Update Related Fields option ensures that when the primary key is modified in a primary table, Access will automatically update all foreign key values in a related table. The Cascade Delete Related Records option ensures that when the primary key is deleted in a primary table, Access will automatically delete all records in related tables that reference the primary key.
- Establish a one-to-many relationship: A one-to-many relationship is established when the primary key value in the primary table can match many of the foreign key values in the related table. One-to-one and many-to-many are also relationship possibilities, but one-to-many relationships are the most common.

5. Create a single-table query.
- Create a single-table select query: A single-table select query uses fields from one table to display only those records that match certain criteria.
- Use Query Design view: Use Query Design view to create and modify a query. The top portion of the view contains tables with their respective field names and displays the join lines between tables. The bottom portion, known as the query design grid, contains columns and rows that you use to control the query results.

6. Specify query criteria for different data types.
- Different data types require different syntax: Date fields are enclosed in pound signs (#) and text fields in quotations (""). Numeric and currency fields require no delimiters.
- Use wildcards: Wildcards are special characters that can represent one or more characters in a text value. A question mark is a wildcard that stands for a single character in the same position as the question mark, while an asterisk is a wildcard that stands for any number of characters in the same position as the asterisk.
- Use comparison operators in queries: Comparison operators such as equal (=), not equal (<>), greater than (>), less than (<), greater than or equal to (>=), and less than or equal to (<=) signs can be used in the criteria of a query to limit the query results to only those records that meet the criteria.

- Work with null: Access uses the term *null* for a blank field. Null criteria can be used to find missing information.
- Establish AND, OR, and NOT criteria: The AND, OR, and NOT logical operators are used when queries require multiple criteria. The AND logical operator returns only records that meet all criteria. The OR logical operator returns records meeting any of the specified criteria. The NOT logical operator returns all records except the specified criteria.

7. Understand query sort order.

- Query sort order: The query sort order determines the order of records in a query's Datasheet view. You can change the order of records by specifying the sort order in Design view.
- Determining sort order: The sort order is determined from the order of the fields from left to right. Move the field columns to position them in left to right sort order.

8. Run, copy, and modify a Query.

- Run a query: To obtain the results for a query, you must run the query. To run the query, click Run in the Results group when you are in Design view. Another method is to locate the query in the Navigation Pane and double-click it. A similar method is to select the query and press Enter.
- Copy a query: To save time, after specifying tables, fields, and conditions for one query, copy the query, rename it, and then modify the fields and criteria in the second query.

9. Use the Query Wizard.

- Create a query using the Query Wizard: The Query Wizard is an alternative method for creating queries. It enables you to select tables and fields from lists. The last step of the wizard prompts you to save the query.

10. Create a multitable query.

- Creating a multitable query: Multitable queries contain two or more tables enabling you to take advantage of the relationships that have been set in your database.
- Add additional tables to a query: Open the Navigation Pane and drag the tables from the Navigation Pane directly into the top section of the Query Design view.

11. Modify a multitable query.

- Add and delete fields in a multitable query: Multitable queries may need to be modified. Add fields by double-clicking the field name in the table you want; remove fields by clicking the column selector and pressing Delete.
- Add join lines in a multitable query: If the tables have a common field, create join lines by dragging the field name of one common field onto the field name of the other table. Or you can add an additional table that will provide a join between all three tables.
- Get answers using a multitable query: Use the total row options of a field such as Count to get answers.

Key Terms Matching

Match the key terms with their definitions. Write the key term letter by the appropriate numbered definition.

a. AND logical operator
b. AutoNumber
c. CamelCase notation
d. Caption property
e. Cascade Update Related Fields
f. Criteria row
g. Data redundancy
h. Data type
i. Field property
j. Foreign key

k. Multitable query
l. Number data type
m. Null
n. One-to-many relationship
o. OR logical operator
p. Query
q. Referential Integrity
r. Simple Query Wizard
s. Sort row
t. Wildcard

1. _____ A special character that can represent one or more characters in the criterion of a query. **p. 174**

2. _____ A characteristic of a field that determines how a field looks and behaves. **p. 149**

3. _____ Returns only records that meet all criteria. **p. 175**

4. _____ A row in the Query Design view that determines which records will be selected. **p. 172**

5. _____ Determines the type of data that can be entered and the operations that can be performed on that data. **p. 147**

6. _____ Used to create a more readable label that displays in the top row in Datasheet view and in forms and reports. **p. 149**

7. _____ Enables you to ask questions about the data stored in a database. **p. 171**

8. _____ The term *Access* uses to describe a blank field. **p. 175**

9. _____ A data type that is a number that automatically increments each time a record is added. **p. 148**

10. _____ The unnecessary storing of duplicate data in two or more tables. **p. 146**

11. _____ A data type that can store only numerical data. **p. 149**

12. _____ A relationship established when the primary key value in the primary table can match many of the foreign key values in the related table. **p. 162**

13. _____ A field in one table that is also the primary key of another table. **p. 149**

14. _____ An option that directs Access to automatically update all foreign key values in a related table when the primary key value is modified in a primary table. **p. 162**

15. _____ Rules in a database that are used to preserve relationships between tables when records are changed. **p. 161**

16. _____ Uses no spaces in multiword field names, but uses uppercase letters to distinguish the first letter of each new word. **p. 146**

17. _____ A row in the Query Design view that enables you to reorder data in ascending or descending order. **p. 172**

18. _____ Contains two or more tables, enabling you to take advantage of the relationships that have been set in your database. **p. 184**

19. _____ Returns records meeting any of the specified criteria. **p. 175**

20. _____ Provides dialog boxes to guide you through the query design process. **p. 171**

Multiple Choice

1. All of the following are suggested guidelines for table design *except*:
   - (a) Include all necessary data.
   - (b) Store data in its smallest parts.
   - (c) Avoid date arithmetic.
   - (d) Link tables using common fields.

2. Which of the following determines the type of data that can be entered and the operations that can be performed on that data?
   - (a) Field properties
   - (b) Data type
   - (c) Caption property
   - (d) Normalization

3. When entering, deleting, or editing table data:
   - (a) The table must be in Design view.
   - (b) The table must be in Datasheet view.
   - (c) The table may be in either Datasheet or Design view.
   - (d) Data may only be entered in a form.

4. When importing data into Access, which of the following statements is *true*?
   - (a) The Import Wizard only works for Excel files.
   - (b) The Import Wizard is found on the Create tab.
   - (c) You can assign a primary key while you are importing Excel data.
   - (d) The wizard will import the data in one step after you select the file.

5. The main reason to enforce referential integrity in Access is to:
   - (a) Limit the number of records in a table.
   - (b) Make it possible to delete records.
   - (c) Keep your database safe from unauthorized users.
   - (d) Keep invalid data from being entered into a table.

6. An illustration of a one-to-many relationship would be a:
   - (a) Person changes his/her primary address.
   - (b) Customer may have multiple orders.
   - (c) Bank branch location has an internal BranchID code.
   - (d) Balance field is totaled for all accounts for each person.

7. A query's specifications providing instructions about which records to include must be entered on the:
   - (a) Table row of the query design grid.
   - (b) Show row of the query design grid.
   - (c) Sort row of the query design grid.
   - (d) Criteria row of the query design grid.

8. When adding Value criteria to the Query Design view, the value you enter must be delimited by:
   - (a) Nothing ().
   - (b) Pound signs (#).
   - (c) Quotes (" ").
   - (d) At signs (@).

9. It is more efficient to make a copy of an existing query rather than create a new query when which of the following is *true*?
   - (a) The existing query contains only one table.
   - (b) The existing query and the new query use the same tables and fields.
   - (c) The existing query and the new query have the exact same criteria.
   - (d) The original query is no longer being used.

10. Which of the following is *true* for the Query Wizard?
    - (a) You can only select tables as a source.
    - (b) No criteria can be added.
    - (c) Fields from multiple tables are not allowed.
    - (d) You do not need a summary.

Practice Exercises

1 Our Corner Bookstore

Tom and Erin Mullaney own and operate a bookstore in Philadelphia, Pennsylvania. Erin asked you to help her create an Access database because of your experience in this class. You believe that you can help her by creating a database and importing the Excel spreadsheets they use to store the publishers and the books that they sell. You determine that a third table—for authors—is also required. Your task is to design and populate the three tables, set the table relationships, and enforce referential integrity. If you have problems, reread the detailed directions presented in the chapter. This exercise follows the same set of skills as used in Hands-On Exercises 1 and 2 in the chapter. Refer to Figure 2.51 as you complete this exercise.

FIGURE 2.51 Books Relationships Window

a. Open Access and click **Blank desktop database**. Type **a02p1Books_LastFirst** in the **File Name box**. Click **Browse** to locate your student data files folder in the File New Database dialog box, click **OK** to close the dialog box, and then click **Create** to create the new database.

b. Type **11** in the **Click to Add column** and click **Click to Add**. The field name becomes *Field1*, and *Click to Add* now appears as the third column. Click in the third column, type **Benchloss**, and then press **Tab**. The process repeats for the fourth column; type **Michael R.** and press **Tab** twice.

c. The cursor returns to the first column where *(New)* is selected. Press **Tab**. Type the rest of the data using the following table. These data will become the records of the Author table.

ID	Field1	Field2	Field3
1	11	Brenchloss	Michael R.
(New)	12	Turow	Scott
	13	Rice	Anne
	14	King	Stephen
	15	Connelly	Michael
	16	Rice	Luanne
	17	*your last name*	*your first name*

d. Click **Save** on the Quick Access Toolbar. Type **Author** in the **Save As dialog box** and click **OK**.

e. Click **View** in the Views group to switch to the Design view of the Author table.

f. Select **Field1**—in the second row—in the top portion of the table design and type **AuthorID** to rename the field. In the *Field Properties* section in the lower portion of the table design, type **Author ID** in the **Caption property box** and verify that *Long Integer* displays for the Field Size property.

g. Select **Field2** and type **LastName** to rename the field. In the *Field Properties* section in the bottom portion of the Design view, type **Author's Last Name** in the **Caption property box** and type **20** as the field size.

h. Select **Field3** and type **FirstName** to rename the field. In the *Field Properties* section in the bottom portion of the table design, type **Author's First Name** as the caption and type **15** as the field size.

i. Click the **ID field row selector** (which shows the primary key) to select the row and click **Delete Rows** in the Tools group. Click **Yes** twice to confirm both messages.

j. Click the **AuthorID row selector** and click **Primary Key** in the Tools group to reset the primary key.

k. Click **Save** on the Quick Access Toolbar to save the design changes. Click **Yes** to the *Some data may be lost* message. Close the table.

l. Click the **EXTERNAL DATA tab** and click **Excel** in the Import & Link group to launch the Get External Data – Excel Spreadsheet feature. Verify the *Import the source data into a new table in the current database* option is selected, click **Browse**, and then go to the student data folder. Select the *a02p1Books* workbook, click **Open**, and then click **OK**. This workbook contains two worksheets. Follow these steps:

- Select the **Publishers worksheet** and click **Next**.
- Click the **First Row Contains Column Headings check box** and click **Next**.
- Select the **PubID field**, click the **Indexed arrow**, select **Yes (No Duplicates)**, and then click **Next**.
- Click the **Choose my own primary key arrow**, select **PubID**, if necessary, and then click **Next**.
- Accept the name *Publishers* for the table name, click **Finish**, and then click **Close** without saving the import steps.

m. Repeat the Import Wizard to import the Books worksheet from the *a02p1Books* workbook into the Access database. Follow these steps:

- Select the **Books worksheet** and click **Next**.
- Ensure the *First Row Contains Column Headings* check box is checked and click **Next**.
- Click on the **ISBN column**, set the Indexed property box to **Yes (No Duplicates)**, and then click **Next**.
- Click the **Choose my own primary key arrow**, select **ISBN** as the primary key field, and then click **Next**.
- Accept the name *Books* as the table name. Click **Finish** and click **Close** without saving the import steps.

n. Right-click the **Books table** in the Navigation Pane and select **Design View**. Make the following changes:

- Change the PubID field name to **PublisherID**.
- Change the Caption property to **Publisher ID.**
- Change the PublisherID Field Size property to **2**.
- Click the **ISBN field** and change the Field Size property to **13**.
- Change the AuthorCode field name to **AuthorID**.
- Change the AuthorID Field Size property to **Long Integer**.
- Click the **ISBN field row selector** (which shows the primary key) to select the row. Drag the row up to the first position.
- Click **Save** on the Quick Access Toolbar to save the design changes to the Books table. Click **Yes** to the *Some data may be lost* warning.
- Close the table.

o. Right-click the **Publishers table** in the Navigation Pane and select **Design View**. Make the following changes:

- Change the PubID field name to **PublisherID**.
- Change the PublisherID Field Size property to **2**.
- Change the Caption property to **Publisher's ID.**
- Change the Field Size property to **50** for the PubName and PubAddress fields.
- Change the Pub Address field name to **PubAddress** (remove the space).
- Change the PubCity Field Size property to **30**.
- Change the PubState Field Size property to **2**.
- Change the Pub ZIP field name to **PubZIP** (remove the space).
- Click **Save** on the Quick Access Toolbar to save the design changes to the Publishers table. Click **Yes** to the *Some data may be lost* warning. Close all open tables.

p. Click the **DATABASE TOOLS tab** and click **Relationships** in the Relationships group. Click **Show Table** if necessary. Follow these steps:

- Double-click each table name in the Show Table dialog box to add it to the Relationships window and close the Show Table dialog box.
- Drag the **AuthorID field** from the Author table onto the AuthorID field in the Books table.

- Click the **Enforce Referential Integrity** and **Cascade Update Related Fields check boxes** in the Edit Relationships dialog box. Click **Create** to create a one-to-many relationship between the Author and Books tables.
- Drag the **PublisherID field** from the Publishers table onto the PublisherID field in the Books table.
- Click the **Enforce Referential Integrity** and **Cascade Update Related Fields check boxes** in the Edit Relationships dialog box. Click **Create** to create a one-to-many relationship between the Publishers and Books tables.
- Click **Save** on the Quick Access Toolbar to save the changes to the Relationships window and click **Close**.

q. Click the **FILE tab** and click **Close** to exit Access.

r. Submit based on your instructor's directions.

2 Morgan Insurance Company

The Morgan Insurance Company offers a full range of insurance services in four locations: Miami, Boston, Chicago, and Philadelphia. They store all of the firm's employee data in an Excel spreadsheet. This file contains employee name and address, job performance, salary, and title. The firm is converting from Excel to Access. A database file containing two of the tables already exists; your job is to import the employee data from Excel for the third table. Once imported, you need to modify field properties and set new relationships. The owner of the company, Victor Reed, is concerned that some of the Atlanta and Boston salaries may be below the guidelines published by the national office. He asks that you investigate the salaries of the two offices and create a separate query for each city. If you have problems, reread the detailed directions presented in the chapter. This exercise follows the same set of skills as used in Hands-On Exercises 2–4 in the chapter. Refer to Figure 2.52 as you complete this exercise.

FIGURE 2.52 Boston Salaries Query Design

a. Open *a02p2Insurance*. Click the **FILE tab**, click **Save As**, and then click **Save As** again to save the database as **a02p2Insurance_LastFirst**. Double-click the **Location table** and look at the contents to become familiar with the field names and the type of information stored in the table. Repeat with the Titles table.

b. Click the **EXTERNAL DATA tab**, click **Excel** in the Import & Link group, and then do the following:
- Click **Browse** and locate the *a02p2Employees* workbook in your student data files location. Select the file, click **Open**, and then click **OK**.
- Select the **Employees worksheet**, if necessary, and click **Next**.
- Click the **First Row Contains Column Headings check box** and click **Next**.
- Click the **Indexed arrow** for the EmployeeID field, select **Yes (No Duplicates)**, and then click **Next**.

- Click **Choose my own primary key arrow**, select the **EmployeeID** as the primary key, and then click **Next**.
- Accept the name *Employees* for the table name, click **Finish**, and then click **Close** without saving the import steps.

c. Double-click the **Employees table** in the Navigation Pane, click the **HOME tab**, and then click **View** in the Views group to switch to the Design view of the Employees table. Make the following changes:
  - Click the **LastName field** and change the Field Size property to **20**.
  - Change the Caption property to **Last Name**.
  - Click the **FirstName field** and change the Field Size property to **20**.
  - Change the Caption property to **First Name**.
  - Click the **LocationID field** and change the Field Size property to **3**.
  - Change the Caption property to **Location ID**.
  - Click the **TitleID field** and change the Field Size property to **3**.
  - Change the Caption property to **Title ID**.
  - Change the Salary field data type to **Currency** and change *General Number* in the Format property in field properties to **Currency**.
  - Save the design changes. Click **Yes** to the *Some data may be lost* warning.

d. Click **View** in the Views group to view the Employees table in Datasheet view and examine the data. Click any record in the Title ID and click **Ascending** in the Sort & Filter group on the HOME tab. Multiple employees are associated with the T01, T02, T03, and T04 titles.

e. Double-click the **Titles table** in the Navigation Pane to open it in Datasheet view. Notice the T04 title is not in the list.

f. Add a new record in the first blank record at the bottom of the Titles table. Use the following data:
  - Type **T04** in the **TitleID field**.
  - Type **Senior Account Rep** in the **Title field**.
  - Type **A marketing position requiring a technical background and at least three years of experience** in the **Description field**.
  - Type **Four-year degree** in the **Education Requirements field**.
  - Type **45000** in the **Minimum Salary field**.
  - Type **75000** in the **Maximum Salary field**.

g. Close all tables. Click **Yes** if you are asked to save changes to the Employees table.

h. Click the **DATABASE TOOLS tab** and click **Relationships** in the Relationships group. Click **Show Table** if necessary. Follow these steps:
  - Double-click each table name in the Show Table dialog box to add them to the Relationships window and close the Show Table dialog box.
  - Adjust the height of the tables so that all fields display.
  - Drag the **LocationID field** in the Location table onto the LocationID field in the Employees table.
  - Click the **Enforce Referential Integrity** and **Cascade Update Related Fields check boxes** in the Edit Relationships dialog box. Click **Create** to create a one-to-many relationship between the Location and Employees tables.
  - Drag the **TitleID field** in the Titles table onto the TitleID field in the Employees table.
  - Click the **Enforce Referential Integrity** and **Cascade Update Related Fields check boxes** in the Edit Relationships dialog box. Click **Create** to create a one-to-many relationship between the Titles and Employees tables.
  - Click **Save** on the Quick Access Toolbar to save the changes to the Relationships window and close the Relationships window.

i. Click the **CREATE tab** and click the **Query Wizard** in the Queries group. Follow these steps:
  - Select **Simple Query Wizard** and click **OK**.
  - Select **Table: Employees** in the Tables/Queries box, if necessary.
  - Double-click **LastName** in the **Available Fields list** to move it to the Selected Fields list.
  - Double-click **FirstName** in the **Available Fields list** to move it to the Selected Fields list.

- Double-click **LocationID** in the **Available Fields list** to move it to the Selected Fields list.
- Click **Next**.
- Select the **Detail (shows every field of every record) option**, if necessary, and click **Next**.
- Type **Employees Location** as the query title and click **Finish**.

j. Click the **CREATE tab** and click the **Query Wizard** in the Queries group. Follow these steps:
  - Select **Simple Query Wizard** and click **OK**.
  - Select **Table: Location** in the Tables/Queries box.
  - Double-click **Location** in the **Available Fields list** to move it to the Selected Fields list.
  - Select **Table: Employees** in the Tables/Queries box.
  - Double-click **LastName**, **FirstName**, and **Salary**.
  - Select **Table: Titles** in the Tables/Queries box.
  - Double-click **MinimumSalary** and **MaximumSalary**. Click **Next**.
  - Select the **Detail (shows every field of every record) option**, if necessary, and click **Next**.
  - Type **Atlanta Salaries** as the query title and click **Finish**.

k. Click the **HOME tab** and click **View** to switch to the Design view of the Atlanta Salaries Query. In the Criteria row of the Location field, type **Atlanta**. Click in the **Sort row** in the Salary field and select **Ascending**. Click **Run** in the Results group on the DESIGN tab. Visually inspect the data to see if any of the Atlanta employees have a salary less than the minimum or greater than the maximum when compared to the published salary range. These salaries will need to be updated later. Save and close the query.

l. Right-click on the **Atlanta Salaries query** in the Navigation Pane and select **Copy**. Right-click a blank area in the Navigation Pane and select **Paste**. In the Paste As dialog box, type **Boston Salaries** for the query name. Click **OK**.

m. Right-click on the **Boston Salaries query** in the Navigation Pane and select **Design View**. In the Criteria row of the Location field, replace *Atlanta* with **Boston**. Click **Run** in the Results group on the DESIGN tab. Visually inspect the data to see if any of the Boston employees have a salary less than the minimum or greater than the maximum when compared to the published salary range. Save and close the query.

n. Click the **FILE tab** and click **Close** to exit Access.

o. Submit based on your instructor's directions.

1 My Game Collection

ANALYSIS CASE

Over the years, you have collected quite a few video games, so you cataloged them in an Access database. After opening the database, you create two tables—one to identify the game system that plays your game and the other to identify the category or genre of the game. Then, you will join each table in a relationship so that you can query the database. Refer to Figure 2.53 as you complete this exercise.

FIGURE 2.53 Game List Query

a. Open *a02m1Games* and save the database as **a02m1Games_LastFirst**. Open the *Games* table and review the fields containing the game information.

b. Click the **CREATE tab** and click **Table Design** in the Tables group. To save time, you opened Table Design to create the fields for a new table rather than creating a table and switching to Design View.

c. Type **SystemID** for the first Field Name and select **Number** as the Data Type.

d. Type **SystemName** for the second Field Name and accept **Short Text** as the Data Type.

e. Change to Design view. Delete the ID row. Make **SystemID** the primary key and change the Data Type to **AutoNumber**. Add the caption **System ID**.

f. Change the SystemName Field Size property to **15**. Add the caption **System Name**, making sure there is a space between System and Name. Save the table as **System**, saving the changes to the table design. Switch to Datasheet view.

g. Add the system names to the System table as shown below, letting Access use AutoNumber to create the SystemID field. Close the table.

System ID	System Name
1	XBOX 360
2	PS3
3	Wii
4	NES
5	PC Game
6	Nintendo 3DS

h. Click the **CREATE tab** and click **Table Design** in the Tables group. Delete the existing ID row. Type **CategoryID** for the first Field Name and select **AutoNumber** as the Data Type. Set the CategoryID as the **Primary Key**.

i. Type **CategoryDescription** for the second Field Name and accept **Short Text** as the Data Type. Change the Field Size property to **25**. Add the caption **Category Description**, making sure there

j. Add the category descriptions to the Category table as shown below, letting Access use AutoNumber to create the CategoryID field. Close the table.

CategoryID	Category Description
1	Action
2	Adventure
3	Arcade
4	Racing
5	Rhythm
6	Role-playing
7	Simulation
8	Sports

k. Click the **DATABASE TOOLS tab** and click **Relationships** in the Relationships group. Add all three tables to the Relationships window and close the Show Table dialog box. Create a one-to-many relationship between CategoryID in the Category table and CategoryID in the Games table. Enforce referential integrity and cascade update related fields.

l. Create a one-to-many relationship between SystemID in the System table and SystemID in the Games table. Enforce referential integrity and cascade update related fields. Close the Relationships window, saving changes.

m. Use the Query Wizard to create a simple query using the Games table. Use the following fields in the query: GameName, Rating. Save the query using the title **Ratings Query**.

n. Switch to Query Design view. Sort the rating field in ascending order and run the query. Close the query, saving the changes to the design of the Ratings Query.

o. Create a multitable query in Design view using all three tables. Use the following fields: GameName, CategoryDescription, Rating, SystemName, and DateAcquired.

p. Sort the query in Ascending order by GameName and run the query. Save the query as **Game List Query** and close the query.

q. Copy the **Game List Query** and paste it in the Navigation Pane using the name **PS3 Games**. Modify the query in Design view by using **PS3** as the criteria for SystemName. Remove the sort by GameName and sort in ascending order by CategoryDescription. The query results should include 7 records.

r. Close the PS3 Games query, saving the changes to the design.

 s. Assume you are going home for Thanksgiving and you want to take your Wii gaming system and games home with you—but you only want to take home games with a rating of Everyone. Create a query named **Thanksgiving Games** that shows the name of the game, its rating, the category description of the games, and the system name. The results of the query will tell you which games to pack.

t. Submit based on your instructor's directions.

2 **The Prestige Hotel**

The Prestige Hotel chain caters to upscale business travelers and provides state-of-the-art conference, meeting, and reception facilities. It prides itself on its international, four-star cuisine. Last year, it began a member reward club to help the marketing department track the purchasing patterns of its most loyal customers. All of the hotel transactions are stored in the database. Your task is to help the managers of the Prestige Hotel in Denver and Chicago identify their customers who stayed in a room last year and who had three persons in their party. Refer to Figure 2.54 as you complete this exercise.

FIGURE 2.54 Denver Rooms 3 Guests Query

a. Open *a02m2Hotel* and save the file as **a02m2Hotel_LastFirst**. Review the data contained in the three tables. Specifically, look for the tables and fields containing the information you need: dates of stays in Denver suites, the members' names, and the numbers in the parties.

b. Import the location data from the Excel file *a02m2Location* into your database as a new table. The first row does contain column headings. Set the LocationID Indexed property to **Yes (No Duplicates)** and set the Data Type to **Long Integer**. Select the **LocationID field** as the primary key. Name the table **Location**. Do not save the import steps.

c. Open the Relationships window and create a relationship between the Location table and the Orders table using the LocationID field. Enforce referential integrity and select **Cascade Update Related Fields**. Create a relationship between the Orders and Members tables using the MemNumber field, ensuring that you enforce referential integrity and cascade update related fields. Create a relationship between the Orders and Service tables using the ServiceID field, ensuring that you enforce referential integrity and cascade update related fields. Save and close the Relationships window.

d. Open the Members table and find Bryan Gray's name. Replace his name with your own first and last names. Use Find to locate Nicole Lee's name and replace it with your name. Close the table.

 DISCOVER

e. Create a query using the following fields: ServiceDate (Orders table), City (Location table), NoInParty (Orders table), ServiceName (Service table), FirstName (Members table), and LastName (Members table). Set the criteria to limit the output to **Denver**. Use the Between command to only show services from **7/1/2012** to **6/30/2013**. Set the Number in Party criterion to **3**. Sort the results in ascending order by the Service Date. Compare your query to Figure 2.54.

f. Run the query and examine the number of records in the status bar at the bottom of the query. It should display *154*. If your number of records is different, examine the criteria.

g. Change the order of the query fields so that they display as FirstName, LastName, ServiceDate, City, NoInParty, and ServiceName.

h. Save the query as **Denver Rooms 3 Guests**. Close the query and copy and paste it, renaming the new query **Chicago Rooms 3 Guests**; one of your colleagues in Chicago asked for your help in analyzing the guest data.

i. Open the Chicago Rooms 3 Guests query in Design view and change the criterion for Denver to **Chicago**. Run and save the changes. You should have 179 results.

 DISCOVER

j. Combine the two previous queries into a third query named **Denver and Chicago Rooms 3 Guests**. Use the criteria from the two individual queries to create a combination AND–OR condition. The records in the combined query should equal the sum of the records in the two individual queries (333 records).

k. Submit based on your instructor's directions.

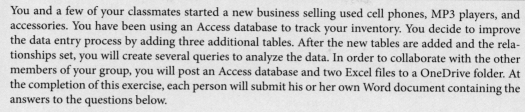

Used Cell Phones for Sale

You and a few of your classmates started a new business selling used cell phones, MP3 players, and accessories. You have been using an Access database to track your inventory. You decide to improve the data entry process by adding three additional tables. After the new tables are added and the relationships set, you will create several queries to analyze the data. In order to collaborate with the other members of your group, you will post an Access database and two Excel files to a OneDrive folder. At the completion of this exercise, each person will submit his or her own Word document containing the answers to the questions below.

a. Open the *a02m3Phones* database and save the file as **a02m3Phones_GroupX**. Close the database. (This step will be completed by only one person in your group. Replace *X* with the number assigned to your group by your instructor.) Create a folder on your OneDrive account named **Exploring Access** and share the folder with the other members in your group and the instructor. Upload the database to this new folder and notify the other members in your group.

b. Download the database from the Exploring Access OneDrive folder created in step a and save it locally as **a02m3Phones_GroupX_LastFirst**. (Everyone in the group will complete this step.) Open the database, open the Inventory table, and than review the records in the table. Take note of the data in the TypeOfDevice column; this field is joined to the DeviceOptions table, and the *enforce referential integrity* option has been set. Only the options in the DeviceOptions table are allowed to be entered. What other fields in this table could be joined to a table in the same way? Type your answer into a Word document named **a02m3Phones_Answers_LastFirst**.

c. Import the data in the *a02m3Carriers* Excel spreadsheet into a new table named **Carriers**. Let Access add a primary key field (ID). Open the table and verify that the data imported correctly. Change the ID field to **CarrierID**. Save and close the Carriers table.

d. Open the Inventory table in Design view and add a new field under the Carrier field named **CarrierID**. Set the Data Type to **Number**. Save and close the table. Open the Relationships window and the Carriers table. Create a relationship between the Carriers table and the Inventory table using the CarrierID field. Enforce referential integrity. Take a screen shot of the Relationships window using the Snipping Tool and paste the image into the Word document you created in step b. Close the Relationships window.

e. Open the Inventory table and the Carriers table. Using the CarrierID field in the Carriers table, enter the correct CarrierID into each record in the Inventory table.

f. Repeat steps c, d, and e for the fields Manufacturer and Color. To do this, one member of the group must create an Excel spreadsheet named **a02m3Manufacturers**, which contains all the manufacturers found in the Inventory table. Another member of the group must create an Excel spreadsheet named **a02m3Colors**, which contains all the colors found in the Inventory table. Both of these Excel spreadsheets must be saved to the Exploring Access folder created in step a so all members can access the data.

g. Create relationships between the tables based on common fields. Take a screen shot of the Relationships window using the Snipping Tool and paste the image into the Word document. Close the Relationships window.

h. After all the new tables have been added, each person in the group should create all of the following queries. Make sure the text fields from the supporting tables appear in the queries (not the ID fields). Save each query as noted below. Take a screen shot of the datasheet of each query using the Snipping Tool and paste the image into the Word document.

　1. Display all the phones that are still for sale (SellDate is Null). Save as **qry1 Phones For Sale**.

　2. Display all the phones that are not made by Apple. Save as **qry2 Not Apple Phones**.

　3. List the Manufacturer and Model and asking price of sold phones; also include phones that are less than $50. Sort by asking price; only include tables that are required. Save as **qry3 Phones Sold or less than $50**.

　4. Display the phones that were purchased before 4/1/2012. Exclude the sold phones. Sort by purchase date. Save as **qry4 Obsolete Phones**.

i. Use e-mail or text messaging to communicate with other members in your group if you have any questions.

j. Exit all applications. Submit both the Word document and the database based on your instructor's directions.

Beyond the Classroom

Database Administrator Position

You arrive at Secure Systems, Inc., for a database administrator position interview. After meeting the human resources coordinator, you are given a test to demonstrate your skills in Access. You are asked to create a database from scratch to keep track of all the candidates for the positions currently open at Secure Systems. Use the Internet to search for information about database management. One useful site is published by the federal government's Bureau of Labor Statistics. It compiles an Occupational Outlook Handbook describing various positions, the type of working environment, the education necessary, salary information, and the projected growth. The Web site is http://www.bls.gov/ooh. After researching the database administrator position requirement, create a database using these requirements:

a. Name the database **a02b2Admin_LastFirst**.

b. Create three tables including these fields: Candidates (CandidateID, FirstName, LastName, Phone, Email), JobOpenings (Job OpeningID, JobName, Required Skill, HourlyPayRate, DataPosted, Supervisor), and Interviews (InterviewSequenceID, CandidateID, JobOpeningID, InterviewedBy, DateOfInterview, Rank).

c. Set the table relationships.

d. Add 10 candidates—yourself and 9 other students in your class.

e. Add the Database Administrator job and four other sample jobs.

f. Add eight sample interviews—four for the Database Administrator position and four others. Rank each candidate on a scale of 1 to 5 (5 is highest).

g. Create a query that lists the LastName, FirstName, JobOpeningID, InterviewedBy, DateofInterview, and Rank fields. Display only Database Administrator interviews with a ranking of 4 or 5. Sort by last name and first name. Run the query.

h. Compact and repair the database. Close Access. Submit based on your instructor's directions.

May Beverage Sales

A coworker called you into his office, explained that he was having difficulty with Microsoft Access 2013, and asked you to look at his work. Open *a02b3Traders* and save it as **a02b3Traders_LastFirst**. It contains two queries, *May 2015 Orders of Beverages and Confections* and *2015 Beverage Sales by Ship Country*. The May 2015 Orders of Beverages and Confections query is supposed to have only information from May 2015. You find other dates included in the results. Change the criteria to exclude the other dates. The 2015 Beverage Sales by Ship Country query returns no results. Check the criteria in all fields and modify so that the correct results are returned. After you find and correct the error(s), compact and repair the database. Close Access. Submit based on your instructor's directions.

Conflict Database

After watching the Conflict: Sexual Harassment video, search the Web for the Equal Employment Opportunities Commission (EEOC) government site. Open the EEOC site and read the *About EEOC: Overview* information. Open a Word document and save it as **a02b4Harrassment_Answers_LastFirst**. Type a paragraph about the responsibilities of the EEOC.

Locate the *EEOC Laws, Regulations, Guidance & MOUs* page. The *Discrimination by Type* section includes a list of hyperlinks to discrimination type pages—pages that include laws, regulations and policy guidance, and also fact sheets, Q&As, best practices, and other information organized by basis of discrimination. Select a discrimination link and review the material on the page. Type two to three additional paragraphs in the Word document to summarize what you have read. Be sure to use good grammar, punctuation, and spelling in your document. Save the Word document and submit based on your instructor's directions.

Capstone Exercise

The Morris Arboretum in Chestnut Hill, Pennsylvania, tracks donors in Excel. They also use Excel to store a list of plants in stock. As donors contribute funds to the Arboretum, they can elect to receive a plant gift from the Arboretum. These plants are both rare plants and hard-to-find old favorites, and they are part of the annual appeal and membership drive to benefit the Arboretum's programs. The organization has grown, and the files are too large and inefficient to handle in Excel. Your task will be to begin the conversion of the files from Excel to Access.

Create a New Database

You need to examine the data in the Excel worksheets to determine which fields will become the primary keys in each table and which fields will become the foreign keys. Primary and foreign keys are used to form the relationships between tables.

a. Open the *a02c1Donors* Excel workbook.

b. Open the *a02c1Plants* Excel workbook.

c. Examine the data in each worksheet and identify the column that will become the primary key in an Access table. Identify the foreign keys in each table.

d. Create a new, blank database named **a02c1Arbor_LastFirst**.

Create a New Table

Use the new blank table created automatically by Access to hold the donations as they are received from the donors.

a. Switch to Design view and save the table as **Donations**.

b. Add the remaining field names in Design view. Note: The data for this table will be added later in this exercise.

- Change *ID* to **DonationID** with the **AutoNumber Data Type**.

- Add **DonorID** (a foreign key) with the **Number Data Type** and a field size of **Long Integer**.

- Add **PlantID** (a foreign key) as **Number Data** and a field size of **Long Integer**.

- Enter two additional fields with an appropriate data type and field properties. Hint: You need the date of donation and the amount of donation.

c. Verify the primary key is *DonationID*.

d. Save the table. Close the table.

Import Data from Excel

You need to use the Import Spreadsheet Data Wizard twice to import a worksheet from each Excel workbook into Access. You need to select the worksheets, specify the primary keys, set the indexing option, and name the newly imported tables (see Figures 2.12 through 2.17).

a. Click the **EXTERNAL DATA tab** and click **Excel** in the Import & Link group.

b. Locate and select the *a02c1Donors* workbook.

c. Set the DonorID field Indexed option to **Yes (No Duplicates)**.

d. Select **DonorID** as the primary key when prompted.

e. Accept the table name *Donors*.

f. Import the *a02c1Plants* file, set the **ID field** as the primary key, and then change the indexing option to **Yes (No Duplicates)**.

g. Accept the table name *Plants*.

h. Open each table in Datasheet view to examine the data.

i. Change the ID field name in the Plants table to **PlantID**.

Create Relationships

You need to create the relationships between the tables using the Relationships window. Identify the primary key fields in each table and connect them with their foreign key counterparts in related tables. Enforce referential integrity and cascade and update related fields.

a. Open the Donors table in Design view and change the Field Size property for DonorID to **Long Integer** so it matches the Field Size property of DonorID in the Donations table.

b. Open the Plants table in Design view and change the Field Size property for PlantID to **Long Integer** so it matches the Field Size property for PlantID in the Donations table.

c. Close the open tables and open the Relationships window.

d. Add the three tables to the Relationships window using the Show Table dialog box. Close the Show Tables dialog box.

e. Drag the **DonorID field** in the Donors table onto the DonorID field in the Donations table. Enforce referential integrity and cascade and update related fields. Drag the **PlantID field** from the Plants table onto the PlantID field of the Donations table. Enforce referential integrity and check the **Cascade Update Related Fields option**.

f. Close the Relationships window and save your changes.

Add Sample Data to the Donations Table

Add 10 records to the Donations table.

a. Add the following records to the Donations table.

Donation ID	Donor ID	Plant ID	Date Of Donation	Amount Of Donation
10	8228	611	3/1/2015	$150
18	5448	190	3/1/2015	$15
6	4091	457	3/12/2015	$125
7	11976	205	3/14/2015	$100
1	1000	25	3/17/2015	$120
12	1444	38	3/19/2015	$50
2	1444	38	4/3/2015	$50
4	10520	49	4/12/2015	$460
5	3072	102	4/19/2015	$450
21	1204	25	4/22/2015	$120

b. Sort the Donations table by the AmountOfDonation field in descending order.

Use the Query Wizard

Use the Query Wizard to create a query of all donations greater than $100 in the Donations table. Use the following guidelines:

a. Include the DonorID and AmountOfDonation fields.

b. Name the query **Donations Over 100**.

c. Add criteria to include only donations of more than $100.

d. Sort by ascending AmountOfDonation.

e. Save and close the query.

Create a Query in Design View

You need to create a query that identifies the people who made a donation after April 1, 2015. The query should list the date of the donation, donor's full name (LastName, FirstName), phone number, the amount of the donation, and name of the plant they want. Sort the query by date of donation, then by donor last name. This list will be given to the Arboretum staff so they can notify the donors that a plant is ready for pickup.

a. Click the **CREATE tab** and click **Query Design** in the Queries group.

b. Add the tables and fields necessary to produce the query as stated previously. Name the query **Plant Pickup List**.

c. Run and print the query from Datasheet view.

Modify a Query in Design View

a. Copy the Plant Pickup List query on the Navigation Pane and paste it using **ENewsletter** as the query name.

b. Open the ENewsletter query in Design view and delete the DateofDonation column.

c. Add the ENewsletter field to the design and set it to sort in Ascending order. Position the ENewsletter field on the grid so that the query sorts first by ENewsletter and then by LastName.

d. Compact and repair the database. Close Access.

e. Submit based on your instructor's directions.

Customize, Analyze, and Summarize Query Data

Creating and Using Queries to Make Decisions

OBJECTIVES | AFTER YOU READ THIS CHAPTER, YOU WILL BE ABLE TO:

1. Create a calculated field in a query p. 212

2. Format and save calculated results p. 215

3. Create expressions with the Expression Builder p. 223

4. Use built-in functions in Access p. 225

5. Add aggregate functions to datasheets p. 233

6. Create queries with aggregate functions p. 234

CASE STUDY | Housing Slump Means Opportunity for College Students

Two students from Passaic County Community College (PCCC) decided they would take advantage of the declining housing market. After taking several business courses at PCCC and a weekend seminar in real estate investing, Donald Carter and Matthew Nevoso were ready to test their skills in the marketplace. Don and Matt had a simple strategy—buy distressed properties at a significant discount, then resell the properties for a profit one year later when the market rebounds.

As they drove through the surrounding neighborhoods, if they noticed a For Sale sign in a yard, they would call the listing agent and ask for the key information such as the asking price, the number of bedrooms, square feet, and days on the market. Because they were just starting out, they decided to target houses that were priced at $150,000 or below and only houses that had been on the market at least six months.

For the first two months, they gathered lots of information and began to get a feel for the houses and prices in the area. Some neighborhoods were definitely more distressed than others! But they still had not made any offers. The two PCCC investors realized they needed a more scientific approach to finding an investment property. Based on a tip from the real estate seminar, they decide to create a database using Access 2013, using data from free lists of homes for sale. They would then like to use Access to help them find houses that meet their criteria. Once the data is in Access, you can help Don and Matt easily identify the qualifying properties. This new database approach should help them become more successful and hopefully help them acquire their first investment property.

Calculations and Expressions

One reason you might choose Excel over a program like Word is for the ability to perform calculations. At first glance, you may not see an obvious location for you to enter a calculation in Access. However, Access includes many of the same built-in calculations and functions that Excel does.

So, why do you need to create calculated fields? Similar to Excel, there are going to be times when you have to process data into information. For example, it could be as simple as needing to calculate a paycheck amount. If you have one field storing the number of hours worked and another field storing the hourly pay rate, you would be able to multiply them together to get the total amount the person is owed. Basic calculations such as these can be done using a query, so you do not have to rely on doing calculations by hand, which can lead to mistakes.

Unfortunately, calculations may not always be that easy. We did not consider some of the common deductions, such as Social Security, Medicare/FICA, federal and state income taxes, unemployment insurance, and possibly union dues. Some of these may be a flat rate, and others may be calculated based on your paycheck amount.

Expressions go beyond simple mathematical functions. Access includes extremely powerful logical functions as well. For example, your employees will claim a certain number of allowances. Based on the number of allowances an employee claims, the amount deducted from the paycheck will be different. This advanced topic will not be covered in this chapter.

When working with Access, there will be times when you need to create arithmetic calculations—using expressions and functions—in your database. In Access 2013, you can add calculations to tables, queries, forms, and reports. Often, rather than storing a calculated value, you would instead store the components of it and calculate the field when necessary. For example, if you have a list price and amount ordered, you would not need to also store the total amount due, because this is the list price multiplied by the amount ordered. Calculating fields rather than storing them will reduce the likelihood of errors and inconsistencies and also save space, as you are storing less information.

In this section, you will learn about the order of operations and how to create a calculated field in a query.

Creating a Calculated Field in a Query

When creating a query, in addition to using fields from tables, you may also need to create a calculation based on the fields from one or more tables. For example, a table might contain the times when employees clock in and out of work. You could create a calculated field (as defined in an earlier chapter) to determine, or calculate, how many hours each employee worked by subtracting the ClockIn field from the ClockOut field. You create calculated fields in the Design view of a query. A formula used to calculate new fields from the values in existing fields is known as an *expression*. An expression can consist of a number of different elements to produce the desired output. The elements used in an expression may include the following:

- Identifiers (the names of fields, controls, or properties)
- Arithmetic operators (for example, *, /, +, or –)
- Functions (built-in functions like Date or Pmt)
- Values that do not change, known as *constants* (numbers such as 30 or 0.5)

You can use calculations to create a new value based on an existing field, verify data entered, set grouping levels in reports, or help set query criteria.

Understand the Order of Operations

The *order of operations* determines the sequence by which operations are calculated in an expression. You may remember PEMDAS from a math class, or the mnemonic device "Please Excuse My Dear Aunt Sally." Evaluate expressions in parentheses first, then exponents, then multiplication and division, and, finally, addition and subtraction. Table 3.1 shows some examples of the order of operations. You must have a solid understanding of these rules in order to create calculated fields in Access. Access, like Excel, uses the following symbols:

- Parentheses   ( )
- Exponentiation   ^
- Multiplication   *
- Division   /
- Addition   +
- Subtraction   –

TABLE 3.1 Examples of Order of Operations

Expression	Order to Perform Calculations	Output
=2+3*3	Multiply first and then add.	11
=(2+3)*3	Add the values inside the parentheses first and then multiply.	15
=2+2^3	Evaluate the exponent first, $2^3=2*2*2$ (or 8). Then add.	10
=10/2+3	Divide first and then add.	8
=10/(2+3)	Add first to simplify the parenthetical expression and then divide.	2
=10*2–3*2	Multiply first and then subtract.	14

Build Expressions with Correct Syntax

Expressions are entered in the first row of the query design grid. You must follow the correct *syntax*, which dictates the structure and components required to perform the necessary calculations in an equation or evaluate expressions. You can create expressions to perform calculations using field names, constants, and functions. If you use a field name, such as Balance, in an expression, you must spell the field name correctly; otherwise, Access displays an error. Access ignores spaces in calculations.

For example, if you worked at a company that was planning on allowing customers to pay off their balance in 12 monthly payments, you would divide the balance by 12. However, let's say you wanted to add a 3.5% surcharge. In this case, you would multiply the balance by 0.035 (3.5%) and then divide that total by 12. An example of an expression with correct syntax is:

STEP 1 »

Balance*0.035/12

If you type the preceding function into a line in a query and save the query, you may be surprised to see Access add a few things to the line (see Figure 3.1):

Expr1: [Balance]*0.035/12

Access made a few changes to your entry. First, it removed extra spaces. Secondly, Access added brackets [ ] around the Balance field, which Access uses to indicate a field name. In addition, you see that Access added *Expr1:* to the start of the line. This is how Access assigns a column heading to this field. If you were to run the query, the column heading would be *Expr1*. As this is not a descriptive name, it would probably be better to include your own title. If you wanted to name this column MonthlySurcharge, you would start the expression with the name, followed by a colon, followed by the expression:

MonthlySurcharge: Balance*0.035/12

Field calculates monthly surcharge

FIGURE 3.1 Calculated Field in a Query Design

TIP Avoid Spaces in Calculated Field Names

Although you can use spaces in calculated field names, it is a good habit not to use spaces. For example, use NewPrice: [Price]*1.1 rather than New Price: [Price]*1.1. If you avoid spaces in calculated field names, it will be easier to reference these fields in other queries, related forms, and related reports. If you want a column heading to have spaces in it, you should set the Caption property, which will be discussed later in this section.

Again, if you saved the query, Access would add brackets around the Balance field.

In calculated fields, the parts of the formula are usually a constant (for example, 0.035 and 12 in the preceding example), a field name (for example, Balance), or another calculated field. Figure 3.1 shows the MonthlySurcharge field, calculated by multiplying the Balance field by 0.035 (or 3.5%) and dividing by 12. This calculation shows what a customer would pay as a monthly surcharge if you offered him or her the monthly payments and added a 3.5% fee.

The arithmetic operators, the * symbol (multiply) and the / symbol (divide), first multiply [Balance] by 0.035 and then divide the result by 12. There is no real issue in this example with order of operations because the order of operations states that multiplication and division are at the same level of precedence. In other words, if you state 12*3/3, whether you do the multiplication or division first, the result will be exactly the same (12).

The query results, as shown in Figure 3.2, display a decimal number in the MonthlySurcharge column. Notice the results are not formatted well. This will be addressed later in this section.

CustomerName	Balance	MonthlySurcharge
Terri Mccoy	$24,286.00	70.8341666666667
Willie Mann	$47,041.00	137.202916666667
Michael Warren	$26,888.00	78.4233333333333
Tammy Mason	$28,255.00	82.4104166666667
Ashley Smith	$38,108.00	111.148333333333
Paul Johnson	$38,664.00	112.77
Leroy Morrison	$8,070.00	23.5375
Phyllis Daniel	$19,166.00	55.9008333333333
Ryan Weaver	$34,000.00	99.1666666666667
Aaron Jordan	$39,889.00	116.342916666667
Howard Hernandez	$2,296.00	6.69666666666667
Francisco Byrd	$17,146.00	50.0091666666667
Jacob Santos	$49,218.00	143.5525
Willie Anderson	$40,940.00	119.408333333333
Oscar Porter	$12,064.00	35.1866666666667
Evelyn Moore	$42,199.00	123.080416666667
Cheryl Carr	$40,620.00	118.475
Ana Keller	$49,509.00	144.40125
Glenn Brewer	$24,820.00	72.3916666666667
Peter Dean	$48,987.00	142.87875
Sheila Turner	$32,572.00	95.0016666666667
Jason Rodgers	$28,864.00	84.1866666666667
Joel Gonzales	$31,350.00	91.4375
Dolores Hayes	$13,745.00	40.0895833333333
Nancy Daniels	$4,639.00	13.5304166666667
Vivian Cannon	$24,358.00	71.0441666666667

MonthlySurcharge shows many digits

FIGURE 3.2 Results of a Calculated Field in a Query

Another example of when to use a calculated field is calculating a price increase for a product or service. Suppose you need to calculate a 10% price increase on certain products you sell. You could name the calculated field NewPrice and use the expression (CurrentPrice) + (CurrentPrice × 0.10). The first segment represents the current price, and the second segment adds an additional 10%. (Recall that to get 10% of a number, you would multiply by 0.10.) The expression would be entered into the query design grid as follows:

NewPrice: [CurrentPrice] + [CurrentPrice]*0.10

Note that if you are adept at math, you may find other ways to calculate this increase.

TIP Use Zoom (Shift+F2) to View Long Expressions

To see the entire calculated field expression, click the field in Query Design view and press Shift+F2. A new window will appear to enable you to easily see and edit the entire contents of the cell. Access refers to this window as the Zoom dialog box, as shown in Figure 3.3.

Zoom can also be used in a number of other contexts. If you are ever having trouble viewing the entirety of a text box, try using Shift+F2 to expand it. Once you are done modifying a field, click the X in the top-right corner of the Zoom dialog box.

MonthlySurcharge field zoomed in

FIGURE 3.3 Using Zoom to See an Entire Field

Formatting and Saving Calculated Results

In the previous example, we saw inconsistent results in the formatting, with some results showing only two decimal places and others showing many decimal places. In Figure 3.2, the MonthlySurcharge field was extremely difficult to read. Part of the purpose of queries is to perform calculations, but an overlooked portion of that is the formatting. You can create a clever calculation, but if it is not labeled and formatted correctly, it may leave your users confused. Spending a few moments formatting your output will make your query more usable.

There is a way to give Access instructions as to how to format the field. You can use the *Property Sheet* to do so. The Property Sheet enables you to change settings such as number format, number of decimal places, and caption, among many others. You can select a predefined format (for example, currency), change the number of decimal places, and also change the caption, as you did in the earlier chapter on tables. To format the calculated results:

STEP 2 »

1. Open the query in Design view.
2. Click in the calculated field cell (the cell you just created).
3. On the QUERY TOOLS DESIGN tab, click Property Sheet in the Show/Hide group.
4. To change the format, click the *Format property* arrow and select your desired format. For numeric fields, the Decimal Places property will allow you to choose exactly how many decimal places display.

5. To change the caption, click in the text box next to the caption and type your desired column heading. This will override the column name, much like the caption property does for a field name in a table, as shown in a previous chapter.

Formats vary based on the data type. A currency field will have options related to number format, whereas a date/time field will have options related to changing the display of the date and/or time. Figure 3.4 shows the Property Sheet options related to a numeric field.

FIGURE 3.4 Property Sheet

Recover from Common Errors

A number of common errors can occur while creating calculated fields. Access may not provide as much assistance as you may be used to in cases like this. The following are three common errors that occur when you begin creating formulas.

STEP 3

- Forgetting the colon between the column title and the formula
  - A correct formula would look like this:

    Expr1: [Balance]*0.035/12

    If you forget the colon, the formula looks like this instead:

    Expr1 [Balance]*0.035/12

    and you will get an error about invalid syntax.
- Typing a field name incorrectly
  - If your field name is Balance and you mistype it, you will not get an error until you attempt to run the query. You may end up with a formula that looks like this:

    Expr1: [Baalnce]*0.035/12
  - When you run the query, you will be prompted by Access to give a value for Baalnce.
- Forgetting the order of operations
  - If you do not check your formulas, you may get bad values. For example, the following would not produce the expected output:

    Expr2: [NumberOfDays] + 7/365
  - If you need addition to be done before division, you must remember the parentheses:

    Expr2: ([NumberOfDays] + 7)/365

Verify Calculated Results

STEP 4 » After your query runs, look at the field values in the Datasheet view and look at the calculated values. Ask yourself, "Does the data make sense?" Assume you are calculating a mortgage payment for a $300,000 house, with monthly payments for 20 years. If your formula is incorrect, you may end up calculating a monthly payment such as $30,000. If you look at your data, you should say to yourself, "Does it make sense for me to pay $30,000 a month for a mortgage?" or perhaps "Does it make sense that, on a $300,000 loan, my total repayment is $7,200,000 ($30,000 a month times 12 months a year times 20 years)?" In a real-world scenario, you will not be given step-by-step directions, and you will need to apply critical thinking skills to your work. Access will calculate exactly what you tell it to calculate, even if you make logical errors in the calculation. Although it will catch some errors, it will not catch or note logic errors.

Use a calculator to manually calculate some of the results in the calculated fields and compare the answers to the datasheet results. Another method to verify the results is to copy and paste all or part of the datasheet into Excel. Recreate the calculations in Excel and compare the answers to the query results in Access. The Access calculated field, the calculator, and the Excel calculations should all return identical results.

In the first Hands-On Exercise, you will create a query with a calculated field, format the results, learn how to recover from common errors, and verify your results.

Quick Concepts

1. Briefly describe the order of operations. Give an example of how order of operations makes a difference in a calculation. **p. 213**

2. When might you need a calculated field in a query? Give an example. **p. 213**

3. Define syntax. How does Access respond to incorrect syntax? **p. 213**

4. Why is it important to verify calculated results? **p. 217**

Hands-On Exercises

Watch the Video for this Hands-On Exercise!

MyITLab®
HOE1 Training

1 Calculations and Expressions

Using the data from the homes for sale lists that Don and Matt acquired, you are able to help them target properties that meet their criteria. As you examine the data, you discover other ways to analyze the properties. You create several queries and present your results to the two investors for their comments.

Skills covered: Create a Query with a Calculated Field • Format and Save Calculated Results • Recover from Common Errors • Verify the Calculated Results

STEP 1 ≫ CREATE A QUERY WITH A CALCULATED FIELD

You begin your analysis by creating a query using the Properties and Agents tables. The Properties table contains all the properties the investors will evaluate; the Agents table contains a list of real estate agents who represent the properties' sellers. In this exercise, add the fields you need and only show properties that have not been sold. Refer to Figure 3.5 as you complete Step 1.

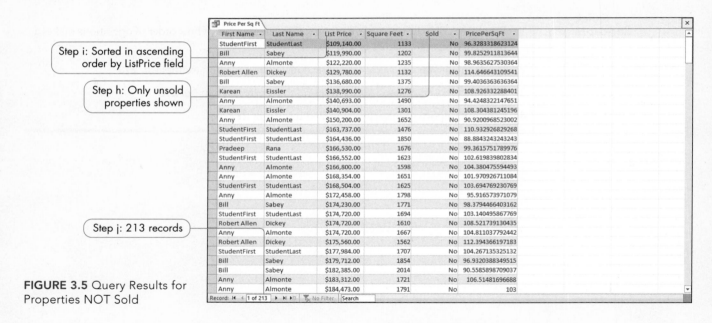

FIGURE 3.5 Query Results for Properties NOT Sold

a. Open *a03h1Property*. Save the database as **a03h1Property_LastFirst**.

> **TROUBLESHOOTING:** Throughout the remainder of this chapter and textbook, click Enable Content whenever you are working with student files.

> **TROUBLESHOOTING:** If you make any major mistakes in this exercise, you can delete the *a03h1Property_LastFirst* file, repeat step a above, and then start this exercise over.

b. Open the Agents table and replace *Angela Scott* with your name. Close the table.

c. Click the **CREATE tab** and click **Query Design** in the Queries group to create a new query.

The Show Table dialog box opens so you can specify the table(s) and/or queries to include in the query design.

d. Select the **Agents table** and click **Add**. Select the **Properties table** and click **Add**. Close the Show Table dialog box.

e. Double-click the **FirstName** and **LastName fields** in the Agents table to add them to the design grid.

f. Double-click the **ListPrice, SqFeet**, and **Sold fields** in the Properties table to add them to the query design grid.

g. Click **Run** in the Results group to display the results in Datasheet view.

You should see 303 properties in the results.

h. Switch to Design view. Type **No** in the Criteria row of the Sold field.

i. Select **Ascending** from the Sort row of the ListPrice field.

j. Click **Run** to see the results.

You only want to see properties that were not sold. There should now be 213 properties in the datasheet.

k. Click **Save** on the Quick Access Toolbar and type **Price Per Sq Ft** as the Query Name in the Save As dialog box. Click **OK.**

l. Switch to Design view. Click in the top row of the first blank column of the query design grid and use **Shift+F2** to show the Zoom dialog box. Type **PricePerSqFt: ListPrice/SqFeet** and click **OK.**

Access inserts square brackets around the fields for you. The new field divides the values in the ListPrice field by the values in the SqFeet field. The : after *PricePerSqFt* is required.

m. Click **Run** in the Results group to view the results.

The new calculated field, PricePerSqFt, is displayed. Compare your results to those shown in Figure 3.5.

TROUBLESHOOTING: If you see pound signs (#####) in an Access column, use the vertical lines between column indicators to increase the width.

TROUBLESHOOTING: If, when you run the query, you are prompted for PricePerSqFt, cancel and return to Design view. Ensure you have entered the formula from step l to the field line of the query, not the criteria line.

---

n. Save the changes to the query and close the query.

STEP 2 >> FORMAT AND SAVE CALCULATED RESULTS

Don and Matt would like the field formatted differently. You will change the format to Currency and add a caption to the calculated field. Refer to Figure 3.6 as you complete Step 2.

Steps d–e: PricePerSqFt field formatted as Currency with added caption

First Name	Last Name	List Price	Square Feet	Sold	Price Per Sq Ft
StudentFirst	StudentLast	$109,140.00	1133	No	$96.33
Bill	Sabey	$119,990.00	1202	No	$99.83
Anny	Almonte	$122,220.00	1235	No	$98.96
Robert Allen	Dickey	$129,780.00	1132	No	$114.65
Bill	Sabey	$136,680.00	1375	No	$99.40
Karean	Eissler	$138,990.00	1276	No	$108.93
Anny	Almonte	$140,693.00	1490	No	$94.42
Karean	Eissler	$140,904.00	1301	No	$108.30
Anny	Almonte	$150,200.00	1652	No	$90.92
StudentFirst	StudentLast	$163,737.00	1476	No	$110.93
StudentFirst	StudentLast	$164,436.00	1850	No	$88.88
Pradeep	Rana	$166,530.00	1676	No	$99.36
StudentFirst	StudentLast	$166,552.00	1623	No	$102.62
Anny	Almonte	$166,800.00	1598	No	$104.38
Anny	Almonte	$168,354.00	1651	No	$101.97
StudentFirst	StudentLast	$168,504.00	1625	No	$103.69
Anny	Almonte	$172,458.00	1798	No	$95.92
Bill	Sabey	$174,230.00	1771	No	$98.38
StudentFirst	StudentLast	$174,720.00	1694	No	$103.14
Robert Allen	Dickey	$174,720.00	1610	No	$108.52
Anny	Almonte	$174,720.00	1667	No	$104.81
Robert Allen	Dickey	$175,560.00	1562	No	$112.39
StudentFirst	StudentLast	$177,984.00	1707	No	$104.27
Bill	Sabey	$179,712.00	1854	No	$96.93
Bill	Sabey	$182,385.00	2014	No	$90.56
Anny	Almonte	$183,312.00	1721	No	$106.51
Anny	Almonte	$184,473.00	1791	No	$103.00

FIGURE 3.6 Results of Calculated Field Creation

a. Make a copy of the Price Per Sq Ft query. Name the copy **Price Per Sq Ft Formatted**.

b. Open the Price Per Sq Ft Formatted query in Design view.

c. Click in the **PricePerSqFt calculated field cell**. Click **Property Sheet** in the Show/Hide group on the DESIGN tab.

   The Property Sheet displays on the right side of your screen.

d. Click the **Format box**. Click the **Format property arrow** and select **Currency**.

e. Click in the **Caption box** and type **Price Per Sq Ft**. Press **Enter**. Close the Property Sheet.

f. Click **Run** to view your changes.

   The calculated field values are formatted as Currency, and the column heading displays *Price Per Sq Ft* instead of *PricePerSqFt*.

g. Save the changes to the query.

STEP 3 >> RECOVER FROM COMMON ERRORS

A few errors arise as you test the new calculated fields. You check the spelling of the field names in the calculated fields because that is a common mistake. Refer to Figure 3.7 as you complete Step 3.

FIGURE 3.7 Results of a Misspelled Field Name

Step g: Same results ($100.00) for every record

a. Switch to Design view of the Price Per Sq Ft Formatted query. Scroll to the first blank column of the query design grid and click in the top row.

b. Use **Shift+F2** to display the Zoom dialog box. Type **WrongPricePerSqFt: xListPrice/ xSqFeet**. Click the **OK button** in the Zoom dialog box.

Be sure that you added the extra *x*'s to the field names. You are intentionally misspelling the field names to see how Access will respond. Access inserts square brackets around the field names for you.

c. Click **Property Sheet** in the Show/Hide group of the DESIGN tab. Click the **Format box**. From the menu, select **Currency**. Click in the **Caption box** and type **Wrong Price Per Sq Ft**. Close the Property Sheet.

d. Click **Run** in the Results group.

You should see the Enter Parameter Value dialog box. The dialog box indicates that Access does not recognize xListPrice in the tables defined for this query in the first record. When Access does not recognize a field name, it will ask you to supply a value.

e. Type **100000** in the first parameter box. Press **Enter** or click **OK**.

Another Enter Parameter Value dialog box displays, asking that you supply a value for xSqFeet. Again, this error occurs because the tables defined for this query do not contain an xSqFeet field.

f. Type **1000** in the second parameter box and press **Enter**.

The query has the necessary information to run and returns the results in Datasheet view.

g. Examine the results of the calculation for *Wrong Price Per Sq Ft*. You may have to scroll right to see the results.

All of the records show 100 because you entered the values 100000 and 1000, respectively, into the parameter boxes. The two values are treated as constants and give the same results for all the records.

h. Return to Design view. Press **Shift+F2** to zoom. Correct the errors in the WrongPricePerSqFt field by changing the formula to **WrongPricePerSqFt: [ListPrice]/ [SqFeet]**. Click the **Close (X) button** in the top-right corner of the Zoom dialog box to close it.

i. Run and save the query. Close the query.

The calculated values in the last two columns should be the same.

STEP 4 >> VERIFY THE CALCULATED RESULTS

Because you are in charge of the Access database, you decide to verify your data prior to showing it to the investors. You use two methods to check your calculations: estimation and checking your results using Excel. Refer to Figure 3.8 as you complete Step 4.

Step e: Column G results should match first 10 results in column F

	First Name	Last Name	List Price	Square Feet	Sold	PricePerSqFt	
2	StudentFirst	StudentLast	$109,140.00	1133	FALSE	96.32833186	$96.33
3	Bill	Sabey	$119,990.00	1202	FALSE	99.82529118	$99.83
4	Anny	Almonte	$122,220.00	1235	FALSE	98.96356275	$98.96
5	Robert Allen	Dickey	$129,780.00	1132	FALSE	114.6466431	$114.65
6	Bill	Sabey	$136,680.00	1375	FALSE	99.40363636	$99.40
7	Karean	Eissler	$138,990.00	1276	FALSE	108.9263323	$108.93
8	Anny	Almonte	$140,693.00	1490	FALSE	94.42483221	$94.42
9	Karean	Eissler	$140,904.00	1301	FALSE	108.3043812	$108.30
10	Anny	Almonte	$150,200.00	1652	FALSE	90.92009685	$90.92
11	StudentFirst	StudentLast	$163,737.00	1476	FALSE	110.9329268	$110.93

FIGURE 3.8 Results Validated in Excel

a. Open the Price Per Sq Ft query in Datasheet view. Examine the PricePerSqFt field.

   One of the ways to verify the accuracy of the calculated data is to ask yourself if the numbers make sense.

b. Locate the second record with *Bill Sabey* as the listing agent, an asking price of *$119,990*, and square footage of *1202*. Ask yourself if the calculated value of *$99.83* makes sense.

   The sale price is $119,990, and the square footage is 1202. You can verify the calculated field easily by rounding the two numbers (to 120,000 and 1,200) and dividing the values in your head (120,000 divided by 1,200 = 100) to verify that the calculated value, $99.83 per square foot, makes sense.

> **TROUBLESHOOTING:** If the second record is not the one listed above, ensure you have sorted the query by the List Price in ascending order, as specified in Step 1i.

c. Open a new, blank workbook in Excel and switch to Access. Drag over the record selector for the first 10 records (the tenth record has a list price of $163,737). Click **Copy** in the Clipboard group on the HOME tab.

   You will verify the calculation in the first 10 records by pasting the results in Excel.

d. Switch to Excel and, click **Paste** in the Clipboard group on the HOME tab.

   The field names display in the first row, and the 10 records display in the next 10 rows. The fields are located in columns A–F. The calculated field results are pasted in column F as values rather than as a formula.

> **TROUBLESHOOTING:** If you see pound signs (#####) in an Excel column, use the vertical lines between column indicators to increase the width.

e. Type =C2/D2 in **cell G2** and press **Enter**. Copy the formula from **cell G2** and paste it into **cells G3 to G11**.

   The formula divides the list price by the square feet. Compare the results in columns F and G. The numbers should be the same, except for a slight difference due to rounding.

> **TROUBLESHOOTING:** If the values differ, look at both the Excel and Access formulas. Determine which is correct, and then find and fix the error in the incorrect formula.

f. Save the Excel workbook as **a03Property_LastFirst**. Exit Excel.

g. Keep the database open if you plan to continue with the next Hands-On Exercise. If not, close the database and exit Access.

The Expression Builder and Functions

In the last Hands-On Exercise, you calculated the price per square foot for real estate properties. That simple calculation helped you to evaluate all the properties on the investment list. You were able to type the expression manually.

When you encounter more complex expressions, you can use the ***Expression Builder*** tool to help you create more complicated expressions. When you create an expression in the field cell, you must increase the column width to see the entire expression. The Expression Builder's size enables you to easily see complex formulas and functions in their entirety. In addition, it provides easy access to objects, operators, functions, and explanations for functions.

In this section, you will learn how to create expressions using the Expression Builder. You also will learn how to use built-in functions.

Creating Expressions with the Expression Builder

Launch the Expression Builder while in the query design grid to assist with creating a calculated field (or other expression). (See "Launch the Expression Builder" later in this section for directions.) The Expression Builder helps you create expressions by supplying you with the fields, operators, and functions you need to create them. When you use the Expression Builder to help you create expressions, you can eliminate spelling errors in field names. Another advantage is when you are inserting functions; functions require specific arguments in a specific order. When you insert a function using the Expression Builder, the builder gives you placeholders that tell you which values belong where.

You may not always need the Expression Builder. As you become familiar with programs like Access, some of the more common tasks may become second nature to you. Rather than clicking to find what you need, you may be able to do your day-to-day work without the aid of the Expression Builder. However, when working with a less familiar calculation, having this tool gives you extra support.

Though you will learn about the Expression Builder in queries in this chapter, this tool can be used in many other areas. You can also use the Expression Builder when working with forms and reports. For example, if you need to perform a calculation in a form or report, you can launch the Expression Builder to assist you with this task. The same skills you learn here can be applied there as well.

 TIP | **Missing Field Names**

If you have not yet saved your query, you may not see the names of the fields you are working with. This is especially true of any calculated fields you want to use as part of another expression. If you cannot see a field you need to use, exit the Expression Builder, save the query, and close and reopen the query. Once you reenter the Expression Builder, you should see the missing fields.

Create an Expression

The left column of the Expression Builder dialog box contains Expression Elements (see Figure 3.9), which include the built-in functions, the tables and other objects from the current database, and common expressions. Select an item in this column.

The middle column displays the Expression Categories based on the item selected in the Expression Elements box (see Figure 3.9). For example, when the Built-In Functions item is selected in the Expression Elements box, the available built-in function categories, such as the Math category, are displayed in the Expression Categories box.

The right column displays the Expression Values, if any, for the categories that you selected in the Expression Categories box (see Figure 3.9). For example, if you click Built-In Functions in the Expression Elements box and click Date/Time in the Expression Categories box, the Expression Values box lists all of the built-in functions in the Date/Time category.

You can create an expression by manually typing text in the expression box or by double-clicking the elements from the bottom section in the Expression Builder dialog box. For example, to create a calculated field using the fields in the tables, type the calculated field name and type a colon. Next, click the desired table listed in the Expression Elements section and double-click the field you want. Click the Operators item in the Expression Elements section and choose an operator (such as + or *) from the Expression Categories section (or just type the operator). The Expression Builder is flexible and will enable you to find what you need while still enabling you to modify the expression manually.

Calculated fields are relatively simple to create, and most Access developers can create them without the Expression Builder. The main reason to use the builder for a calculated field is to eliminate spelling errors in field names. Using functions in Access almost always requires the Expression Builder because the syntax of functions can be difficult to remember. When you double-click the Functions command in the Expression Elements box and click Built-In Functions, the Expression Categories box lists all the available functions in Access. The Expression Values box lists the functions in each of the categories. When you find the function you need, double-click it and the function displays in the expression box. You can see the «placeholder text» where the arguments belong; replace each placeholder text with the argument values, either numbers or fields from a table.

Launch the Expression Builder

STEP 1 ▶ To launch the Expression Builder:

1. Open a query in Design view (or create a new query).
2. Verify the QUERY TOOLS DESIGN tab is selected on the Ribbon.
3. Click the top cell of a blank column (also known as the Field cell, because it appears in the row labeled Field) where you would like your expression to appear.
4. Click Builder in the Query Setup group, and the Expression Builder launches (see Figure 3.9). (You can also launch the Expression Builder by right-clicking the cell where you want the expression and selecting Build from the shortcut menu.)

FIGURE 3.9 Expression Builder

5. The top section of the Expression Builder dialog box contains a rectangular area (known as the *expression box*) where you create an expression. You can type your expression in the expression box manually, or you can use the Expression Elements, Expression Categories, and Expression Values in the bottom portion of the Expression Builder. The bottom area allows you to browse for functions, tables, queries, and more. Refer to Figure 3.9.

6. Double-click an item in the *Expression Categories* or *Expression Values* section to add it automatically to the expression box, thus allowing you to use this interface to avoid typographical errors.

7. After you create the expression, click OK to close the Expression Builder window. The expression is then entered into the current cell in the query design grid. From the query design, click Run in the Results group to view the results (in Datasheet view). If the results are incorrect, you can return to Design view and use the Expression Builder again to correct the expression.

Using Built-In Functions in Access

STEP 2 ≫ Similar to Excel, a number of functions are built into Access. A *function* is a predefined computation that performs a complex calculation. It produces a result based on inputs known as arguments. An *argument* is any data that is needed to produce the output for a function. The term *argument*, outside of computers, can mean a fact. For example, in court, you may have a judge ask a lawyer to present his argument. Similarly, Access will need arguments, or facts, to execute a function. Arguments can be a variable (such as a field name) or a constant (such as a number). Some functions require no arguments, but many require at least one. Some functions have optional arguments, which are not required but may be necessary for your task.

Many of the tasks that are built in are tasks that would otherwise be difficult to perform. If you had to figure out the payment of a loan or determine the year portion of a date without functions, it would not be an easy task.

Once you identify what you need a function to do, you can check the Built-In Functions in the Expression Builder to see if the function exists. If it does, add the function to the expression box and replace the «placeholder text» with the argument values. Functions work the same in Access and Excel and other programming languages (such as Visual Basic). There are nearly 150 built-in functions in Access, and many of them will not apply to the task you are performing. Be aware that if you want to perform complex operations, there may be a function that can do it for you. In cases like this, search engines or Microsoft Help are extremely useful. This chapter will demonstrate one function.

Calculate Payments with the Pmt Function

Figure 3.10 shows the *Pmt function*, which calculates the periodic loan payment given the interest rate per period (for example, monthly), term of the loan (in months), and the original value of the loan (the principal). To use this function, you will need to supply at least three arguments as field names from underlying tables or as constants:

- The first argument is the interest rate per period. Interest rates are usually stated as annual rates, so you will need to convert the annual interest rate to the rate per period. For example, if a loan is paid monthly, you can calculate the rate by dividing the yearly rate by 12.

- The second argument is the number of periods. Because loan terms are usually stated in years, you will need to multiply the number of years by the number of payments per year. For example, a monthly payment would be calculated as the number of years multiplied by 12.

- The third argument is the present value—or principal—of the loan. It is the amount a customer is borrowing.

- The last two arguments—future value and type—are both optional, so they are usually 0 or blank. The future value shows the amount the borrower will owe after the final payment has been made. The type tells Access whether the payment is made at the beginning or the end of the period.

Pmt function arguments

Pmt function is under the Financial expression category

FIGURE 3.10 Pmt Function in the Expression Builder

The following example shows how to use the Pmt function to calculate the monthly payment on a $12,500 loan, at a 5.0% interest rate, with a four-year loan term.

Function: Pmt(*rate, num_periods, present_value, future_value, type*)

Example: Pmt(0.06/12, 5*12, 12500)

The Pmt function will return a negative value (as a loan payment is considered a debit). If you would like to display this as a positive number, you will need to negate it.

Table 3.2 describes the arguments for the Pmt function in more detail.

TABLE 3.2 Arguments of the Pmt Function

Part	Description
( )	Items inside the parentheses are arguments for the function. The arguments are separated by commas. Some arguments are optional; some arguments have a default value. In the Pmt function, the first three arguments are required and the last two are optional.
rate	Required. Expression or value specifying interest rate per period, usually monthly. A mortgage with an annual percentage rate of **6.0%** with monthly payments would have a rate entered as **0.06/12**, since the rate of 6% would be entered as .06, and because there are 12 months in a year. A loan with a 4% interest rate paid quarterly would be expressed as .04/4 for the same reason. A common cause of issues with this function is that people forget to divide the annual percentage rate by the number of periods in a year.
num_periods	Required. Expression or integer value specifying total number of payment periods in the loan. For example, monthly payments on a five-year car loan give a total of 5 * 12 (or 60) payment periods. Quarterly payments on a six-year loan would give a total of 6 * 4 (or 24) payment periods.
present_value	Required. Expression or value specifying the present value of the money you borrow. If you borrow $12,500 for a car, the value would be 12500.
future_value	*Optional* (can be left blank). Expression or value specifying the future value after you've made the final payment. Most consumer loans have a future value of $0 after the final payment. However, if you want to save $50,000 over 18 years for your child's education, then 50000 is the future value. Zero is assumed if left blank.
type	*Optional* (can be left blank). Value (0 or 1) identifying when payments are due. Use 0 if payments are due at the end of the payment period (the default), or 1 if payments are due at the beginning of the period. Zero is assumed if left blank.

In the second Hands-On Exercise, you will practice using the Expression Builder to add and modify a field, and use a built-in function.

Quick Concepts

1. List two benefits of creating expressions with the Expression Builder. *p. 223*

2. Give an example of a built-in function. *p. 224*

3. What is an argument in a function? Give an example. *p. 225*

4. Describe a scenario where you might use the Pmt function. *p. 225*

Hands-On Exercises

Watch the Video for this Hands-On Exercise!

MyITLab®
HOE2 Training

2 The Expression Builder and Functions

When Don and Matt ask you to calculate the price per bedroom and the price per room for each property, you use the Expression Builder to make the task easier. You also add two additional fields that calculate the days on market and the estimated commission for each property.

Skills covered: Use the Expression Builder to Add and Modify a Field • Use Built-In Functions

---

STEP 1 » USE THE EXPRESSION BUILDER TO ADD AND MODIFY A FIELD

You create a copy of the Price Per Sq Ft Formatted query from the previous Hands-On Exercise and paste it using a new name. You will add a few more calculated fields to the new query. You will create one calculation to determine the price per bedroom for each house. You will create a second field to calculate the price per room. For this calculation, you will assume that each property has a kitchen, a living room, a dining room, and the listed bedrooms and bathrooms. The calculations you will create are shown in Figure 3.11. Your expected output is shown in Figure 3.12.

FIGURE 3.11 Design View of Query

a. Open *a03h1Property_LastFirst* if you closed it at the end of Hands-On Exercise 1 and save it as **a03h2Property_LastFirst**, changing *h1* to *h2*.

b. Create a copy of the Price Per Sq Ft Formatted query with the name **List Price Calculations**.

   The new query is displayed in the Navigation Pane. The name of the query suggests it should contain calculations based on each property's list price.

c. Open the List Price Calculations query in Design view. Click the **WrongPricePerSqFt field**. Click **Delete Columns** in the Query Setup group on the QUERY TOOLS DESIGN tab.

> **TROUBLESHOOTING:** If instead of the column being deleted, a new row named *Delete* appears on the bottom half of the screen, close the query without saving, open in Design view once more, and ensure you are clicking Delete Columns in the Query Setup group. If you click Delete under Query Type, you will get very different results.

d. Click in the top cell in the PricePerSqFt column and click **Builder** in the Query Setup group.

   The Expression Builder dialog box opens, displaying the current formula.

> **TROUBLESHOOTING:** If the Builder is gray and cannot be clicked, ensure you have clicked in the top cell of the column.

e. Change the PricePerSqFt field name to **PricePerBR**.

f. Double-click the **[SqFeet] field** in the expression and press **Delete**.

g. Click the **plus sign (+)** under Expression Elements, next to the *a03h2Property_LastFirst* database in the Expression Elements box, to expand the list. Click + next to *Tables* and click the table named **Properties**.

The fields from the Properties table are now listed in the middle column (Expression Categories).

h. Double-click the **Beds field** to add it to the expression box.

The expression now reads *PricePerBR: [ListPrice]/[Properties]![Beds]*.

i. Highlight the **[Properties]! prefix** in front of *Beds* and press **Delete**.

The expression now reads *PricePerBR: [ListPrice]/[Beds]*. As the Beds field name is unique within our query, the table name is not necessary. Removing this makes the query easier to read. If a field named Beds appeared in more than one table in our query, removing the table name would cause problems.

j. Click **OK** and click **Run** to view the query results.

Notice the column heading still reads Price Per Sq Ft. Also notice the column's contents are formatted as Currency. These settings were copied when we copied the query.

k. Switch to Design view and ensure the **PricePerBR field** is selected. Click **Property Sheet** in the Show/Hide group and change the **Caption** to **Price Per Bedroom**. Close the Property Sheet. Run the query and examine the changes.

The PricePerBR column now has an appropriate caption.

l. Switch to Design view. Select the entire **PricePerBR expression**, right-click the selected expression, and then select **Copy**. Right-click in the top cell of the next blank column and select **Paste**.

You will edit the copy so that it reflects the price per room. As stated already, you assume the kitchen, living room, dining room, and the bedrooms and bathrooms will make up the number of rooms. Your final formula would be the list price divided by the total number of rooms, which is the number of bedrooms (in the Beds field), plus the number of bathrooms (found in the Baths field), plus 3 (a constant representing the kitchen, living room, and dining room).

m. Click **Builder** in the Query Setup group.

n. Change the PricePerBR field name to **PricePerRoom**.

o. Add **parentheses** before the [Beds] portion of the formula. Type a **plus sign (+)** after *[Beds]*.

As you want the addition to be done first, the order of operations states we must enclose the addition in parentheses. The expression box should read *PricePerRoom: [ListPrice]/([Beds]+*

p. Click the **plus sign (+)** next to the *a03h2Property_LastFirst* database in the Expression Elements box to expand the list. Click the **plus sign (+)** next to *Tables* and click the **Properties table**.

The fields from the Properties table are now listed in the Expression Categories box.

q. Double-click the **Baths field** to add it to the expression box.

The expression now reads *PricePerRoom: [ListPrice]/([Beds]+[Properties]![Baths]*.

r. Type another plus sign after *[Baths]* and type **3)**.

The expression now reads *PricePerRoom: [ListPrice]/([Beds]+[Properties]![Baths]+3)*.

s. Delete the [Properties]! portion of the expression and click **OK** to close the Expression Builder.

The expression now reads *PricePerRoom: [ListPrice]/([Beds]+[Baths]+3)*.

t. Click **Property Sheet**. Type **Price Per Room** in the **Caption box**. Close the Property Sheet.

u. Run the query. Widen the PricePerRoom column if necessary in order to see all the values.

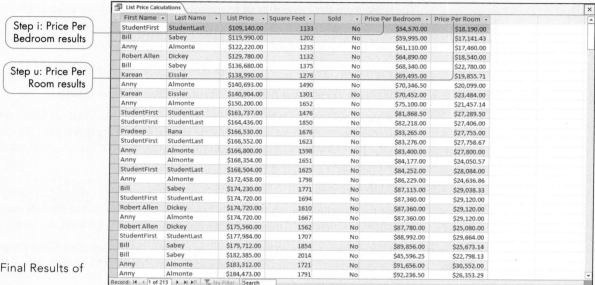

Step i: Price Per Bedroom results

Step u: Price Per Room results

FIGURE 3.12 Final Results of Query

v. Save and close the query.

TIP Switching Between Object Views

You can switch between object views quickly by clicking View, or you can click the View arrow and select the desired view from the list. Another way to switch between views is to right-click the object tab and select the view from the shortcut menu.

TIP Expression Builder and Property Sheet

You can launch the Expression Builder by either clicking Builder in the Query Setup group on the Design tab or by right-clicking in the top row of the query design grid and selecting Build. Similarly, you can display the Property Sheet by clicking Property Sheet in the Show/Hide group on the Design tab or by right-clicking the top row of the query design grid and selecting Properties from the shortcut menu.

STEP 2 ›› USE BUILT-IN FUNCTIONS

Don and Matt feel like they are close to making an offer on a house. They would like to restrict the query to houses that cost $150,000 or less. They would also like to calculate the estimated mortgage payment for each house. You create this calculation using the Pmt function. You will use the Pmt function to calculate an estimated house payment for each of the sold properties. You make the following assumptions: 100% of the sale price will be financed, a 30-year term, monthly payments, and a fixed 6.0% annual interest rate. Refer to Figures 3.13 and 3.14 as you complete Step 2.

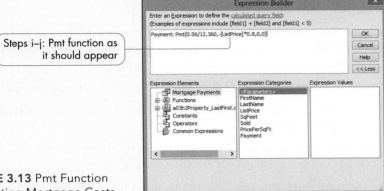

FIGURE 3.13 Pmt Function Calculating Mortgage Costs

a. Create a copy of the Price Per Sq Ft Formatted query named **Mortgage Payments**.

The new query is displayed in the Navigation Pane.

b. Right-click **Mortgage Payments** and select **Design View**.

c. Delete the WrongPricePerSqFt field.

The WrongPricePerSqFt field is not needed for this query.

> **TROUBLESHOOTING:** If you do not see the WrongPricePerSqFt field, ensure you copied the correct query.

d. Type **<=150000** in the Criteria row of the ListPrice column. Press **Enter**.

The query, when it is run, will show only the houses that cost $150,000 or less.

e. Click in the top cell of the first blank column. Click **Builder** in the Query Setup group to open the Expression Builder dialog box.

f. Double-click **Functions** in the Expression Elements box and click **Built-In Functions**.

g. Click **Financial** in the Expression Categories box.

h. Double-click **Pmt** in the Expression Values box.

The expression box displays:

Pmt(«rate», «num_periods», «present_value», «future_value», «type»)

i. Position the insertion point before the Pmt function. Type **Payment:** to the left of the Pmt function.

The expression box now displays:

Payment:Pmt(«rate», «num_periods», «present_value», «future_value», «type»)

> **TROUBLESHOOTING:** If you forget to add the calculated field name to the left of the expression, Access will add *Expr1* to the front of your expression for you. You can edit the Expr1 name later, after the Expression Builder is closed.

j. Click each argument to select it and substitute the appropriate information. Make sure there is a comma between each argument.

Argument	Replacement Value
«rate»	0.06/12
«num_periods»	360
«present_value»	[ListPrice]*0.8
«future_value»	0
«type»	0

Note the loan is a 30-year loan with 12 payments per year, hence the 360 value for the number of payments. Also note, Don and Matt plan on financing 80% of the cost, putting 20% down. Therefore, you need to multiply the list price times 0.8 (80%).

k. Examine Figure 3.13 to make sure that you have entered the correct arguments. Click **OK**.

l. Click **OK**. Open the **Property Sheet** for *Payment* and change the format to **Currency**. Close the Property Sheet. **Run** the query.

Notice the payment amounts are negative numbers (displayed in parentheses). You will edit the formula to change the negative payment values to positive.

m. Right-click the **Mortgage Payments tab** and select **Design View**. Click **Builder**. Add a **minus sign** (–) to the left of *[ListPrice]* and click **OK**.

By adding the negative sign in front of the ListPrice field, you ensure the value is displayed as a positive number. The expression now reads *Payment: Pmt(0.06/12,360, –[ListPrice]*0.8,0,0)*.

The calculated field values should now appear as positive values formatted as currency, as shown in Figure 3.14.

Steps l–n: Payment field displayed as a positive number, formatted as Currency

Mortgage Payments

First Name	Last Name	List Price	Square Feet	Sold	Price Per Sq Ft	Payment
StudentFirst	StudentLast	$109,140.00	1133	No	$96.33	$523.48
Bill	Sabey	$119,990.00	1202	No	$99.83	$575.52
Anny	Almonte	$122,220.00	1235	No	$98.96	$586.22
Robert Allen	Dickey	$129,780.00	1132	No	$114.65	$622.48
Bill	Sabey	$136,680.00	1375	No	$99.40	$655.57
Karean	Eissler	$138,990.00	1276	No	$108.93	$666.65
Anny	Almonte	$140,693.00	1490	No	$94.42	$674.82
Karean	Eissler	$140,904.00	1301	No	$108.30	$675.83

FIGURE 3.14 Results of Mortgage Payments Query

n. Click **OK**. Run the query and examine the results.

The query displays a column containing the calculated monthly mortgage payment, formatted as currency.

o. Save and close the query. Keep the database open if you plan to continue with the next Hands-On Exercise. If not, close the database and exit Access.

Aggregate Functions

Aggregate functions perform calculations on an entire column of data and return a single value. Aggregate functions—such as Sum, Avg, and Count—are used when you need to evaluate a group of record values rather than the individual records in a table or query.

Access refers to aggregate functions as Totals. Totals can be added to the Datasheet view of a query, or they can be added to a query's Design view. Based on the data type, different aggregate functions will be available. Numeric fields are eligible for all of the functions, whereas Short Text fields are not. A list of common aggregate functions is shown in Table 3.4.

A car dealer's monthly inventory report is a good example of a report that might contain aggregate information. The cars would be grouped by model, then by options package and color. At the end of the report, a summary page would list the count of cars in each model for quick reference by the sales reps. In the property database, aggregate information could be grouped by county or by subdivision. For example, the average home price per county could be presented in a query or a report. This would give prospective buyers a good idea of home prices in their target counties. Almost every company or organization that uses a database will require some type of aggregate data.

TABLE 3.4	Common Aggregate Functions	
Function	**Description**	**Use with Data Type(s)**
AVG	Calculates the average value for a column. The function ignores null values.	Number, Currency, Date/Time
COUNT	Counts the number of items in a column. The function ignores null values.	All data types except a column of multivalued lists.
MAXIMUM	Returns the item with the highest value. For text data, the highest value is "Z." The function ignores null values.	Number, Currency, Date/Time, Short Text
MINIMUM	Returns the item with the lowest value. For text data, the lowest value is "a." The function ignores null values.	Number, Currency, Date/Time, Short Text
SUM	Adds the items in a column. Works only on numeric and currency data.	Number, Currency

In this section, you will learn how to create and work with aggregate functions. Specifically, you will learn how to use the Total row and create a totals query.

Adding Aggregate Functions to Datasheets

Aggregate functions are most commonly used in tables, queries, and reports. Occasionally, aggregate functions are also added to the *form footer* section of forms. Aggregate data helps users evaluate the values in a single record as compared to the aggregate of all the records. If you are considering buying a property in Bergen County, New Jersey, for $150,000, and the average price of a property in that county is $450,000, you know you are getting a good deal (or buying a bad property).

Access provides two methods of adding aggregate functions to a query—a *Total row*, which displays the results of the aggregate function as the last row in the Datasheet view of a table or query, and a totals query created in Query Design view.

The first method enables you to add a Total row to the Datasheet view. This method is quick and easy and has the advantage of showing the total information while still showing the individual records. Adding a Total row to a query or table can be accomplished by most users, even those who are not familiar with designing a query. Note the Total row values cannot be modified; you can change the aggregate function displayed there, but you cannot overwrite the numbers.

Add a Total Row in a Query or Table

STEP 1 » Figure 3.15 shows the Total row added to the Datasheet view of a query. You can choose any of the aggregate functions that apply to numeric fields. Follow these steps to add a Total row to a query or table:

1. Ensure you are viewing the query in Datasheet view.
2. Click Totals in the Records group on the HOME tab. The Total row is added at the bottom of the datasheet, below the new record row of the query or table.
3. In the new Total row, you can select one of the aggregate functions by clicking in the cell and clicking the arrow. The list of aggregate functions includes Sum, Avg, Count, and others.

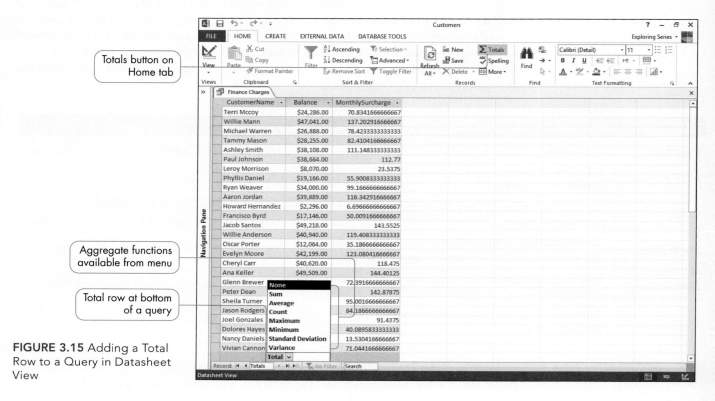

FIGURE 3.15 Adding a Total Row to a Query in Datasheet View

Creating Queries with Aggregate Functions

The second method to display aggregate functions requires you to alter the design of a query and add a Total row in the Query Design view. Once the totals data is assembled, you can use it to make decisions. For example, you can use the Count function to show the number of houses sold. You could also use the Avg function to show the average sale price for houses. This method has the advantage of enabling you to group your data by categories.

Many times, you will need to find some sort of averages for fields, and you may need to do more in-depth statistics than just an overall set as we did in the previous few pages. Instead of wanting to see the average sale price for houses, you may want to see the average sale price by city. Using the total row in the previous example, this is not feasible. Another limitation of the previous example is that I might want to see the average sale price, minimum sale price, and maximum sale price. Using the previous method, we would have to put the sale price field into our query three times, leading to repeated columns.

Instead of showing detail, we can quickly see the overall statistics for the entire table or query. For example, if you want to see the number of listings, average value, and the average size in square feet for all properties in your table, you can run a totals query to get that data and not see details. Instead of doing that, we can create a different type of query to summarize our data.

Create a Basic Totals Query

A *totals query* contains an additional row in the query design grid and is used to display aggregate data when the query is run. Figure 3.16 shows a totals query in Design view, and Figure 3.17 shows the results.

To create a Totals query:

1. Create a query in Design view and add the fields for which you want to get statistics. For example, in the preceding example, we would add the Listing, List Price, and Square Feet fields.

2. Click Totals in the Show/Hide group on the QUERY TOOLS DESIGN tab to display the total row. A new row should display in your query between the Table and Sort options. You will notice it defaults to Group By.

3. For each field, select the menu next to Group By and select the aggregate function you want applied to that field. For example, we want to count the number of listings and average both the list price and square feet values.

4. If you would like to apply specific formats, display the Property Sheet (as we did earlier in this chapter) and adjust the settings for each field.

5. Run the query to see your results.

FIGURE 3.16 Totals Query in Design View

FIGURE 3.17 Totals Query Results

Create a Totals Query with Grouping

Grouping a query allows you to summarize your data by the values of a field. For example, you want to see the results not for the entire table, but instead by state. You can add the State field as a grouping level, and Access will show you the statistics you request for each state.

To group an existing query, add the field you wish to group by to the query in Design view. You would then verify the Total row displays Group By (see Figure 3.18). So if you want to see the results by state, add the State field to the query and leave the Total with the default of Group By. You may want to move this column to the beginning, as it will make your query easier to read.

Figure 3.18 shows the Design view of a totals query with five columns, one of which is the grouping field. Figure 3.19 shows the results of this query.

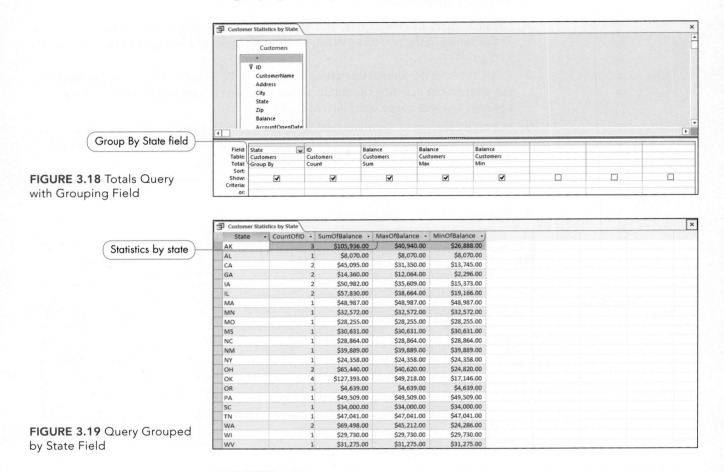

Group By State field

FIGURE 3.18 Totals Query with Grouping Field

Statistics by state

FIGURE 3.19 Query Grouped by State Field

TIP Too Much Grouping

Beware that the more grouping levels you add, the less valuable the data is probably going to be; a typical totals query will group by only a few columns. As the purpose of grouping is to get some sort of aggregate data (such as a sum) for related data, grouping by more fields leads to less data being summarized.

Create a Totals Query with a Condition

Totals queries can provide even better information if you add criteria. For example, if you wanted to see the number of houses, average price, and average square feet for only the unsold properties, grouped by state, you can add the Sold field to the query. You would set the criteria to No to indicate that the Sold field is no. You should select Where from the menu in the Total row for any field you add to which you wish to apply criteria. Figure 3.20 shows a query with a condition added, and Figure 3.21 shows the results. You can compare this to Figure 3.19 to see the change in results.

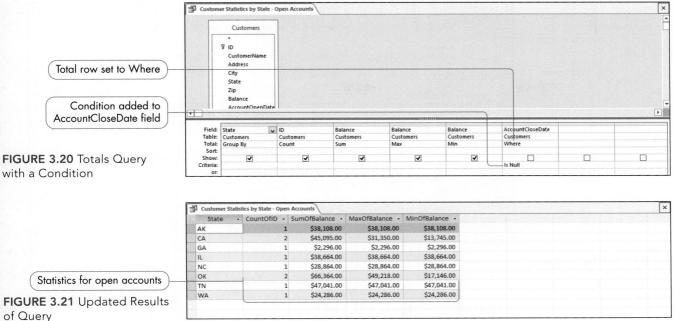

Total row set to Where

Condition added to AccountCloseDate field

FIGURE 3.20 Totals Query with a Condition

Statistics for open accounts

FIGURE 3.21 Updated Results of Query

Create a Totals Query with Multiple Grouping Levels

At times, you may want to add multiple grouping fields. For example, instead of grouping by State, you might want to group by City. However, if you group by city, customers with the same city name in different states would be grouped together. For example, all 50 states have a location named Greenville. If you grouped by city, all customers with a city of Greenville, regardless of state, would appear as a group. This is probably not your intention. Instead, you probably would want to see results by City and State, and thus would want to add multiple grouping levels. Figure 3.22 shows a second grouping level, and Figure 3.23 shows the results of the query if we group by State and then by City. Notice the multiple Greenville results.

Second Group By field added

FIGURE 3.22 Query with Two Group By Fields

Each state may have
multiple entries

City field added
to query

State	City	CountOfID	SumOfBalance	MaxOfBalance	MinOfBalance
AK	Greenville	2	$67,828.00	$40,940.00	$26,888.00
AK	Kaktovik	1	$38,108.00	$38,108.00	$38,108.00
AL	Greenville	1	$8,070.00	$8,070.00	$8,070.00
CA	Los Angeles	1	$13,745.00	$13,745.00	$13,745.00
CA	San Diego	1	$31,350.00	$31,350.00	$31,350.00
GA	Austell	1	$2,296.00	$2,296.00	$2,296.00
GA	Leary	1	$12,064.00	$12,064.00	$12,064.00
IA	Albert City	1	$15,373.00	$15,373.00	$15,373.00
IA	Iowa City	1	$35,609.00	$35,609.00	$35,609.00
IL	Champaign	2	$57,830.00	$38,664.00	$19,166.00
MA	Southampton	1	$48,987.00	$48,987.00	$48,987.00
MN	Beltrami	1	$32,572.00	$32,572.00	$32,572.00
MO	De Kalb	1	$28,255.00	$28,255.00	$28,255.00
MS	Meridian	1	$30,631.00	$30,631.00	$30,631.00
NC	Raleigh	1	$28,864.00	$28,864.00	$28,864.00
NM	Bard	1	$39,889.00	$39,889.00	$39,889.00
NY	Saint Bonavent	1	$24,358.00	$24,358.00	$24,358.00
OH	Canton	1	$40,620.00	$40,620.00	$40,620.00
OH	Cincinnati	1	$24,820.00	$24,820.00	$24,820.00
OK	Albany	1	$17,146.00	$17,146.00	$17,146.00
OK	Canadian	1	$42,199.00	$42,199.00	$42,199.00
OK	Lahoma	1	$18,830.00	$18,830.00	$18,830.00
OK	Rufe	1	$49,218.00	$49,218.00	$49,218.00
OR	Fall Creek	1	$4,639.00	$4,639.00	$4,639.00
PA	Pine Bank	1	$49,509.00	$49,509.00	$49,509.00
SC	Clemson	1	$34,000.00	$34,000.00	$34,000.00
TN	Auburntown	1	$47,041.00	$47,041.00	$47,041.00

FIGURE 3.23 Results of Query with Two Group By Fields

Add a Calculated Field to a Totals Query

STEP 3 Once you have created a totals query, you can create calculated fields as you did earlier in the chapter. Often, you will want to apply an aggregate function to an existing field, such as summing up the values in a field. However, there may be times when you would prefer to apply an aggregate function to a calculation rather than a field.

We will use a customer purchases database to demonstrate this. When working with a customer order database, you may have a field for each order containing the total order cost and another field for each order containing the shipping cost. If you use the Sum aggregate function and group by the customer ID, you would have the total amount of their orders, and then as a separate column the total cost of the shipping they have paid. Instead of doing that, you may prefer to first create a calculated field that adds the total order cost and shipping cost for each order, and then group by a CustomerName. You will notice in Figure 3.24 we need to change the total row to Expression. After making that change, your results will resemble Figure 3.25.

Calculation added
to query

Total row set
to Expression

FIGURE 3.24 Grouping Query Using a Calculation in a Purchases Database

Total Bills	
CustomerName	TotalBill
Alice Ray	$688.99
Alicia Byrd	$810.50
Amber Ingram	$506.50
Annette Gibson	$720.99
Arthur Powell	$477.99
Beth Vaughn	$203.99
Carla Black	$478.50
Crystal Delgado	$166.99
Esther Bennett	$198.50
Eva Turner	$673.99
Florence Douglas	$633.99
Frances Foster	$317.50
Gina West	$629.99
Gloria Medina	$615.99
Harold Wolfe	$432.50
Heather Davidson	$343.50
Jamie Wheeler	$243.99
Jeanette Griffin	$436.50
Keith Strickland	$349.50
Lawrence Payne	$390.50
Leonard Delgado	$161.50
Lynn Brooks	$363.50
Marvin Santiago	$757.98
Megan Wheeler	$720.99
Phillip Medina	$676.50
Steve Mills	$674.50
Thelma Burgess	$529.99

FIGURE 3.25 Results of Grouping Query with a Calculation in a Purchases Database

In the third Hands-On Exercise, you will add aggregate functions to datasheets, create a totals query, and add grouping, conditions, and calculated fields to totals queries.

Quick **Concepts**

1. What are the benefits of aggregate functions? Give an example. *p. 233*

2. How do you add a Total row to a datasheet? *p. 234*

3. What is a totals query? *p. 235*

4. What is the difference between a query with a Total row and a totals query? *p. 235*

3 Aggregate Functions

The investors decide it would be helpful to analyze the property lists they purchased. Some of the lists do not have homes that match their target criteria. The investors will either need to purchase new lists or alter their criteria. You create several totals queries to evaluate the property lists.

Skills covered: Add Aggregate Functions to Datasheets • Create a Totals Query with Grouping and Conditions • Add a Calculated Field to a Totals Query

STEP 1 >> ADD AGGREGATE FUNCTIONS TO DATASHEETS

You begin your property list analysis by creating a total row in the Datasheet view of the Mortgage Payments query. This will give you a variety of aggregate information for each column. Refer to Figure 3.26 as you complete Step 1.

Step g: Average of PricePerSqFt
Step f: Count of Listing
Step e: Average of ListPrice
Step c: Total row

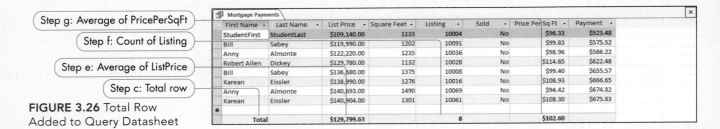

FIGURE 3.26 Total Row Added to Query Datasheet

a. Open *a03h2Property_LastFirst* if you closed it at the end of Hands-On Exercise 2 and save it as **a03h3Property_LastFirst**, changing *h2* to *h3*.

b. Right-click the **Mortgage Payments query** in the Navigation Pane and select **Design View**. Drag the **Listing field** from the Properties table to the fifth column.

The Listing field is now in the fifth column, between the SqFeet and Sold fields. The other columns shift to the right.

> **TROUBLESHOOTING:** If you drag the Listing field to the wrong position, you can drag it again to the correct location.

c. Switch to Datasheet view. Click **Totals**, in the Records group on the HOME tab to display the Total row.

The Total row displays as the last row of the query results.

d. Click in the cell that intersects the Total row and the List Price column.

e. Click the arrow and select **Average** to display the average value of all the properties that have not sold. Widen the List Price column if you can't see the entire total value.

The average list price of all properties is $129,799.63.

f. Click the arrow in the Total row in the Listing column and select **Count** from the list.

The count of properties in this datasheet is 8.

g. Click in the **Total row** in the Price Per Sq Ft column. Click the arrow and select **Average** to display the average price per square foot.

The average price per square foot is $102.60.

h. Save and close the query.

STEP 2 ≫ CREATE A TOTALS QUERY WITH GROUPING AND CONDITIONS

You create a totals query to help Don and Matt evaluate the properties in groups. Refer to Figure 3.27 and Figure 3.28 as you complete Step 2.

FIGURE 3.27 Overall Results Query

a. Click **Query Design** in the Queries group of the CREATE tab.

You create a new query in Query Design; the Show Table dialog box opens.

b. Add the Properties table from the Show Table dialog box. Close the Show Table dialog box.

c. Add the SalePrice and Sold fields from the Properties table to the query design grid.

d. Click **Totals** in the Show/Hide group of the QUERY TOOLS DESIGN tab to show the Total row.

A new row labeled Totals displays at the bottom of the screen in the design grid, between the Table and Sort rows. Each field will have Group By listed in the new row by default.

e. Click the **Group By arrow** in the SalePrice column Total row and select **Avg.**

f. Click the **Group By arrow** in the Sold column Total row and select **Where**. Type **Yes** in the Criteria row.

This criterion will limit the results to sold houses only.

g. Click in the **SalePrice field** and click **Property Sheet** in the Show/Hide group. Change the SalePrice format to **Currency**. Close the Property Sheet. Run the query and compare your results to Figure 3.27.

The results show an overall average of $273,588.34 for the sold properties in the database.

h. Click **Save** on the Quick Access Toolbar and type **Overall Results** as the Query Name in the Save As dialog box. Click **OK**. Close the query.

i. Click **Query Design** in the Query group of the HOME tab to create a new query.

j. Add the Properties table and the Lists table from the Show Table dialog box. Close the Show Table dialog box.

k. Add the NameOfList field from the Lists table and the SalePrice, Listing, and Sold fields from the Properties table to the query design grid.

l. Click **Totals** on the QUERY TOOLS DESIGN tab in the Show/Hide group to show the Total row.

A new row labeled Total appears at the bottom of the screen in the design grid between the Table and Sort rows.

m. Change the Total row for *SalePrice* to **Avg.**

n. Change the Total row for *Listing* to **Count.**

o. Change the Total row for *Sold* to **Where**. Type **Yes** in the Criteria row.

This criterion will limit the results to sold houses only.

p. Click in the **SalePrice field** and click **Property Sheet** in the Show/Hide group. Change the SalePrice format to **Currency**.

q. Change the caption of the Listing column to **Number Sold**. Run the query and widen the columns as shown in Figure 3.28.

Notice Major Houses has the only average sale price under $200,000. As Don and Matt are hoping to focus on inexpensive properties, they will focus on properties offered by this source. Notice the query results show the number of properties sold in each source, in addition to the average sale price. This will help determine which sources have been more effective.

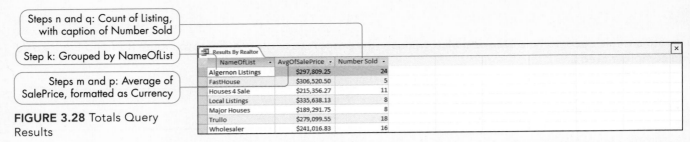

Steps n and q: Count of Listing, with caption of Number Sold

Step k: Grouped by NameOfList

Steps m and p: Average of SalePrice, formatted as Currency

FIGURE 3.28 Totals Query Results

NameOfList	AvgOfSalePrice	Number Sold
Algernon Listings	$297,809.25	24
FastHouse	$306,520.50	5
Houses 4 Sale	$215,356.27	11
Local Listings	$335,638.13	8
Major Houses	$189,291.75	8
Trullo	$279,099.55	18
Wholesaler	$241,016.83	16

r. Click **Save** on the Quick Access Toolbar and type **Results By Realtor** as the Query Name in the Save As dialog box. Click **OK**. Keep the query open for the next step.

STEP 3 ≫ ADD A CALCULATED FIELD TO A TOTALS QUERY

The previous query shows the average value of the properties by realtor. However, Don and Matt learned at the seminar they attended that the longer a property has been on the market, the better your chances of negotiating a better price. You will revise the query to include the average number of days on the market for each realtor. Refer to Figure 3.29 as you complete Step 3.

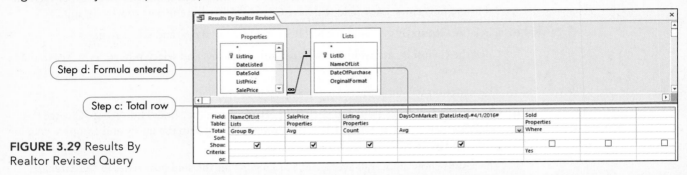

Step d: Formula entered

Step c: Total row

FIGURE 3.29 Results By Realtor Revised Query

a. Click the **FILE tab**, click **Save As**, and then click **Save Object As**. Click **Save As**, and in the *Save 'Results By Realtor' to:* box, type **Results By Realtor Revised**.

b. Switch to the Datasheet view for the new Results By Realtor Revised query, if necessary.

c. Click **Totals** in the Records group of the HOME tab. Change the Total to **Sum** in the Number Sold column.

The total number of houses sold (90) now displays at the bottom of the Number Sold column.

d. Switch to Design view. In the first blank column, type **DaysOnMarket: [DateListed] – #4/1/2016#** to create a new calculated field. Change the Total row to **Avg**.

The DaysOnMarket field will show the average number of days on the market for each realtor's listings.

e. Display the Property Sheet for the DaysOnMarket field and change the Format property to **Fixed**. Change the Decimal Places property to **0**. Close the Property Sheet.

> **TROUBLESHOOTING:** If you do not see a Decimal Places property immediately beneath the Format property, change the format to Fixed, save and close the query, and then reopen the query. Refer to Figure 3.4 for the location of Decimal Places.

f. Run the query and examine the DaysOnMarket field.

Major Houses listings have an average of 117 days on the market. The combination of inexpensive prices and properties that do not sell quickly may help Don and Matt negotiate with the realtor.

g. Save and close the query.

h. Exit Access. Submit based on your instructor's directions.

Chapter Objectives Review

After reading this chapter, you have accomplished the following objectives:

1. **Create a calculated field in a query.**
   - Calculations can be based on fields, constants, and/or functions.
   - Understand the order of operations: Calculated fields follow the same order of operations as mathematical equations—parentheses, then exponentiation, then multiplication and division, and finally addition and subtraction.
   - Build expressions with correct syntax: Expressions must be written using proper syntax—the rules governing the way you give instructions to Access.

2. **Format and save calculated results.**
   - Calculated results may not have the format you want; change the properties of a calculated field using the Property Sheet.
   - Recover from common errors: Common errors include forgetting the colon in the appropriate location, spelling errors, and misuse of the order of operations.
   - Verify calculated results: Always check the results of your equation; Access will check for syntax errors, but not logic errors.

3. **Create expressions with the Expression Builder.**
   - Expression Builder helps create complex expressions.
   - Create an expression: Expression Builder allows you to choose fields and built-in functions easily, and gives you a larger screen to view your expression.
   - Launch the Expression Builder: Clicking the Builder button will open the tool.

4. **Use built-in functions in Access.**
   - Access includes functions, or predefined computations that perform complex calculations.
   - There are almost 150 built-in functions in Access.

   - Some require arguments: inputs (often fields or constants) given to a function.
   - Calculate payments with the Pmt Function: The Pmt function accepts the rate per term, number of payments, and loan amount and calculates a loan payment.

5. **Add aggregate functions to datasheets.**
   - Aggregate functions perform calculations on an entire column of data and return a single value.
   - Include functions such as Sum, Avg, and Count.
   - Add a total row in a query or table: The total row displays at the bottom of a query or table; it can perform any aggregate function on each column.

6. **Create queries with aggregate functions.**
   - This gives you more control over application of your aggregate functions.
   - Create a basic totals query: Create a query as usual and click the Totals button in Design view.
   - Create a totals query with grouping: Grouping allows you to summarize your data by the values of a field; instead of showing overall averages, add state as a grouping field and see averages for each state.
   - Create a totals query with a condition: Conditions can be added to totals queries, such as only showing listings with the Sold field equal to No.
   - Create a totals query with multiple grouping levels: You can add multiple grouping levels; for example, you could group by State and then by City to get more detailed results.
   - Add a calculated field to a totals query: You can apply an aggregate function to the results of a calculation; for example, subtract a date from today's date to get the number of days a listing is active and calculate the overall average of days listings are active.

Key Terms Matching

Match the key terms with their definitions. Write the key term letter by the appropriate numbered definition.

a. Aggregate Function
b. Argument
c. Constant
d. Expression
e. Expression Builder
f. Function
g. Grouping

h. Order of Operations
i. Pmt Function
j. Property Sheet
k. Syntax
l. Total Row
m. Totals Query

1. _____ A value that does not change. **p. 212**

2. _____ A formula used to calculate new fields from the values in existing fields. **p. 212**

3. _____ Determines the sequence by which operations are calculated in an expression. **p. 213**

4. _____ Dictates the structure and components required to perform the necessary calculations in an equation or evaluate expressions. **p. 213**

5. _____ Enables you to change settings such as number format, number of decimal places, and caption. **p. 215**

6. _____ An Access tool that helps you create more complicated expressions. **p. 223**

7. _____ A predefined computation that performs a complex calculation. Almost 150 are built into Access. **p. 225**

8. _____ Any data needed to produce output for a function. **p. 225**

9. _____ Calculates the periodic loan payment given the interest rate per period, term of the loan in months, and the original value of the loan. **p. 225**

10. _____ Performs calculations on an entire column of data and returns a single value. Includes functions such as Sum, Avg, and Count. **p. 233**

11. _____ Displays aggregate function results as the last row in the Datasheet view of a table or query. **p. 233**

12. _____ Makes an additional row available in the query design grid. Used to display aggregate data when the query is run. **p. 235**

13. _____ Allows you to summarize your data by the values of a field. **p. 235**

Multiple Choice

1. Which of the following correctly identifies the rules for the order of operations?

   (a) Parentheses, exponentiation, addition, subtraction, multiplication, division
   (b) Exponentiation, parentheses, addition, subtraction, multiplication, division
   (c) Addition, subtraction, multiplication, division, exponentiation, parentheses
   (d) Parentheses, exponentiation, multiplication, division, addition, subtraction

2. What is the result of the following expression?
   $(3 * 5) + 7 - 2 - 6 / 2$

   (a) 17
   (b) 7
   (c) 14.5
   (d) 13

3. Which of the following *cannot* be adjusted in the Property Sheet?

   (a) Number of decimal places
   (b) Mathematical expression
   (c) Caption
   (d) Number format (for example, Currency)

4. Which of the following is *not* an aggregate function?

   (a) Pmt
   (b) Avg
   (c) Count
   (d) Min

5. Which of the following can be added to a totals query?

   (a) Conditions
   (b) Grouping fields
   (c) Aggregate functions
   (d) All of the above can be added to a totals query

6. Which statement about a totals query is *true*?

   (a) A totals query is created in Datasheet view.
   (b) A totals query may contain several grouping fields but only one aggregate field.
   (c) A totals query is limited to only two fields, one grouping field and one aggregate field.
   (d) A totals query may contain several grouping fields and several aggregate fields.

7. Which of the following statements is *true*?

   (a) A total order cost would be a common field to group by.
   (b) A last name would be a common field to group by.
   (c) For best results, add as many group by fields as possible.
   (d) None of the above statements is true.

8. After creating a calculated field, you run the query and a Parameter dialog box appears on your screen. How do you respond to the Parameter dialog box?

   (a) Click OK to make the parameter box go away.
   (b) Look for a possible typing error in the calculated expression.
   (c) Type numbers in the Parameter box and click OK.
   (d) Close the query without saving changes. Reopen it and try running the query again.

9. A query contains student names. You run the query and while in Datasheet view, you notice a spelling error on one of the student's names. You correct the error in Datasheet view. Which statement is *true*?

   (a) The name is correctly spelled in this query but will be misspelled in the table and all other queries based on the table.
   (b) The name is correctly spelled in this query and any other queries, but will remain misspelled in the table.
   (c) You cannot edit data in a query.
   (d) The name is correctly spelled in the table and in all queries based on the table.

10. Which of the following about the Total row in the query design grid is *false*?

    (a) The Total row enables you to apply aggregate functions to the fields.
    (b) The Total row does not display by default in all new queries.
    (c) The Total row is located between the Table and Sort rows.
    (d) The Total row cannot be applied to numeric fields.

Practice Exercises

1 Comfort Insurance

The Comfort Insurance Agency is a mid-sized company with offices located across the country. Each employee receives a performance review annually. The review determines employee eligibility for salary increases and the annual performance bonus. The employee data is stored in an Access database, which is used by the human resources department to monitor and maintain employee records. Your task is to calculate the salary increase for each employee; you will also calculate the average salary for each position. This exercise follows the same set of skills as used in Hands-On Exercises 1 and 2 in the chapter. Refer to Figure 3.30 as you complete this exercise.

Last Name	First Name	Performance	Salary	2016 Increase	New Salary
Lacher	Tom	Good	$31,200.00	3.00%	$32,136.00
Fantis	Laurie	Good	$28,000.00	3.00%	$28,840.00
Fleming	Karen	Average	$41,100.00	3.00%	$42,333.00
Mc Key	Boo	Good	$39,600.00	3.00%	$40,788.00
Daniels	Phil	Good	$42,600.00	3.00%	$43,878.00
Park	Johnny	Excellent	$48,400.00	3.00%	$49,852.00
Johnson	Debbie	Excellent	$39,700.00	3.00%	$40,891.00
Drubin	Lolly	Good	$37,000.00	3.00%	$38,110.00
Titley	David	Good	$40,200.00	3.00%	$41,406.00
Grippando	Joan	Average	$26,100.00	3.00%	$26,883.00
Block	Leonard	Excellent	$26,200.00	3.00%	$26,986.00
Mills	Jack	Average	$44,600.00	3.00%	$45,938.00
Nagel	Mimi	Average	$46,200.00	3.00%	$47,586.00
Rammos	Mitzi	Excellent	$32,500.00	3.00%	$33,475.00
Vieth	Paula	Good	$40,400.00	3.00%	$41,612.00
Novicheck	Deborah	Good	$46,800.00	3.00%	$48,204.00
Brumbaugh	Paige	Average	$49,300.00	3.00%	$50,779.00
Abrams	Wendy	Good	$47,500.00	3.00%	$48,925.00
Harrison	Jenifer	Excellent	$44,800.00	3.00%	$46,144.00
Gander	John	Average	$38,400.00	3.00%	$39,552.00
Sell	Mike	Excellent	$43,500.00	3.00%	$44,805.00
Smith	Denise	Average	$45,200.00	3.00%	$46,556.00
Pawley	Eleanor	Excellent	$42,700.00	3.00%	$43,981.00
Harris	Jennifer	Average	$34,900.00	3.00%	$35,947.00
North	Randy	Excellent	$31,700.00	3.00%	$32,651.00
Shuffield	Jan	Good	$33,700.00	3.00%	$34,711.00
Barnes	Jeb	Excellent	$46,900.00	3.00%	$48,307.00

Record: 1 of 311 — No Filter — Search

FIGURE 3.30 Raises and Bonuses Query

a. Open *a03p1Insurance*. Save the database as **a03p1Insurance_LastFirst**.

b. Examine the Relationships for the database. Notice the table structure, relationships, and fields. Once you are familiar with the database, close the Relationships window.

c. Create a new query in Design view. Add the Employees and Titles tables.

d. Add the LastName, FirstName, Performance, and Salary fields from the Employees table to the query. Add the 2016Increase field from the Titles table to the query.

e. Click the top row of the first blank column in the query design grid and type **NewSalary:[Salary]+[Salary]*[2016Increase]** to create a calculated field that adds the existing salary to the increase. You may opt to use the Expression Builder if you prefer.

f. Click **Run** in the Results group to run the query. Look at the output in the Datasheet view. Verify that your answers are correct. Notice that the fourth column heading displays *2016 Increase*.

This is the caption for the 2016Increase field in the Titles table that was carried over to the query. When a caption exists for a field in the table Design view, the caption also displays in the Query Datasheet view instead of the field name in the query.

g. Switch back to Design view. Click in the **NewSalary calculated field**, display the Property Sheet, and then change the format to **Currency**. Type **New Salary** in the **Caption box**. Close the Property Sheet.

h. Save the query as **Raises and Bonuses**. Close the query.

i. Create a new query in Design view. Add the Employees and Titles tables.

You will create a query to show the average salary by position.

j. Add the TitleName field from the Titles table. From the Employees table, add the Salary field.

k. Display the Total row. Change the Total row for Salary to **Avg**. Leave the TitleName field set to **Group By**.

l. Click the **Salary field** and display the Property Sheet. Change the format for the field to **Currency**.

m. Run the query. Save the query as **Average Salary By Position** and close the query.

n. Exit Access and submit based on your instructor's directions.

2 Analyze Orders

You are the marketing manager of your company, and you must use the order information from an Access database to analyze sales trends. You need to determine the order revenue for all orders, grouped by Ship Country. The company would also like to check to see if there are order delays related to a specific employee. You must analyze shipping performance based on the number of days it takes to ship each order. This exercise follows the same set of skills as used in Hands-On Exercises 2 and 3 in the chapter. Refer to Figure 3.31 as you complete this exercise.

Shipping Issues		✕
EmployeeID ▾	**TimeToShip** ▾	
1	26	
2	47	
3	44	
4	50	
4	29	
5	50	
6	29	
9	80	

FIGURE 3.31 Shipping Issues Query

a. Create a new blank desktop database named **a03p2Orders_LastFirst**.

   You will be shown a blank table in Datasheet view.

b. Click **View** in the Views group to switch to Design view. Save the table as **Orders**.

c. Change the first Field Name to **OrderID** and change the Data Type to **Number**. Type **CustomerID** in the second row and press **Tab**. Accept **Short Text** as the Data Type. Type **EmployeeID** in the third row and press **Tab**. Select **Number** for the Data Type.

d. Type and format the remainder of the fields as follows:

OrderDate	Date/Time
ShippedDate	Date/Time
ShipVia	Number
Revenue	Currency
ShipCountry	Short Text

e. Click **View** in the Views group to switch to Datasheet view. Click **Yes** to save the table. Add the three records as shown in the following table. Press **Tab** to move to the next field.

Order ID	Customer ID	Employee ID	Order Date	Shipped Date	Ship Via	Revenue	Ship Country
10248	WILMK	5	1/6/2017	1/19/2017	1	$142.86	Belgium
10249	TRADH	6	1/7/2017	1/10/2017	2	$205.38	Germany
10250	HANAR	4	1/10/2017	1/30/2017	2	$58.60	Venezuela

f. Open the *a03p2Orders* Excel file and click **Enable Editing**, if necessary. Click and hold **row 2** and drag through **row 828** so that all of the data rows are selected. Click **Copy** in the Clipboard group.

g. Return to Access and click on the **asterisk (*)** on the fourth row of the Orders table. Click **Paste** in the Clipboard group and click **Yes** to confirm that you want to paste all 827 rows into the Orders table. Save and close the table, and then close the spreadsheet and Excel. If prompted to save the data in the clipboard, click **No**.

h. Click the **CREATE tab** and click **Query Design** in the Queries group to start a new query. The Show Table dialog box opens. Add the Orders table and close the Show Table dialog box.

i. Add EmployeeID to the query and sort the table by EmployeeID in ascending order.

j. Use the Expression Builder to create a new calculated field. Type the following: **TimeToShip: [ShippedDate]-[OrderDate]**

Run the query and verify that TimeToShip is displaying valid values.

k. Switch back to Design view. Add the criteria **>21** to the TimeToShip field. Run the query and compare your results with Figure 3.31.

The results do not show a pattern of one employee's orders being delayed.

l. Save the query as **Shipping Issues**. Close the query.

m. Click the **CREATE tab** and click **Query Design** in the Queries group to start a new query. The Show Table dialog box opens. Add the Orders table and close the Show Table dialog box. Click **Totals** in the Show/Hide group.

n. Insert the ShipCountry and Revenue fields from the Orders table.

o. Verify the value for ShipCountry is set to **Group By** in the Totals row in Design view and verify that the value for the Revenue field is set to **Sum**.

p. Click in the **Revenue field**. Display the Property Sheet and change the caption to **Total Revenue**.

q. Click **Run** to see the results and save the query as **Revenue by Ship Country**. Close the query.

r. Exit Access and submit based on your instructor's directions.

1 Small Business Loans

You are the manager of the small business loan department for the U.S. government. You need to calculate the payments for the loans that are currently on the books. To do this, you will need to create a query and add the Pmt function to calculate the loan payments for each loan. You will also summarize each loan by loan type (M=Mortgage, C=Car, and O=Other). Refer to Figure 3.32 as you complete this exercise.

Company	LoanID	Amount	InterestRate	Term	LoanClass	Payment
Jones and Co	1	29,000.00	5.90%	15	M	$243.15
Elements, Inc.	2	23,000.00	5.25%	5	C	$436.68
Godshall Meats, LLC	3	24,000.00	4.50%	3	C	$713.93
Godshall Meats, LLC	4	12,000.00	3.99%	10	O	$121.44
Godshall Meats, LLC	5	60,000.00	5.50%	30	M	$340.67
Elements, Inc.	6	4,000.00	6.50%	5	O	$78.26
Jones and Co	7	43,000.00	5.50%	5	O	$821.35
Jones and Co	8	37,000.00	5.80%	30	M	$217.10
Jones and Co	9	15,000.00	4.75%	3	O	$447.88
Jones and Co	10	8,000.00	5.50%	15	M	$65.37
Godshall Meats, LLC	11	34,000.00	5.00%	3	C	$1,019.01
Godshall Meats, LLC	12	13,000.00	7.99%	5	O	$263.53
Jones and Co	13	46,000.00	6.50%	5	C	$900.04
Godshall Meats, LLC	14	56,000.00	5.99%	15	M	$472.26
Godshall Meats, LLC	15	54,000.00	6.25%	15	M	$463.01
Jones and Co	16	39,000.00	6.50%	15	M	$339.73
Jones and Co	17	21,000.00	6.00%	30	M	$125.91
Godshall Meats, LLC	18	27,000.00	5.50%	3	O	$815.29
Elements, Inc.	19	44,000.00	5.50%	5	C	$840.45
Godshall Meats, LLC	20	22,000.00	6.25%	4	C	$519.20
Godshall Meats, LLC	21	6,000.00	6.75%	4	C	$142.98
Godshall Meats, LLC	22	46,000.00	6.50%	15	M	$400.71
Jones and Co	23	25,000.00	5.00%	15	M	$197.70
Jones and Co	24	11,000.00	5.55%	30	M	$62.80
Jones and Co	25	52,000.00	4.99%	15	M	$410.94
Total		751,000.00	5.74%	12		

FIGURE 3.32 Loan Payments Query Results

a. Open Access and create a new blank desktop database named **a03m1Loans_LastFirst**. Access will display a table named Table1 with one field, ID.

b. Switch to Design view. Type **Customers** in the **Save As dialog box** and click **OK**.

c. Change the first Field Name to **CustomerID** and accept **AutoNumber** as the Data Type. Type **Company** in the second row and press **Tab**. Accept **Short Text** as the Data Type. Type **FirstName** in the third row and press **Tab**. Accept **Short Text** as the Data Type.

d. Type the remainder of the fields:

LastName	Short Text
City	Short Text
State	Short Text
Zip	Short Text

e. Verify the first field is set as the primary key.

f. Switch to Datasheet view. Click **Yes** to save the table. Add the records as shown in the following table. Note you will allow Access to assign an ID. Once you have entered the records, close the Customers table.

Company	FirstName	LastName	City	State	Zip
Jones and Co	Robert	Paterson	Greensboro	NC	27401
Elements, Inc.	Merve	Kana	Paterson	NJ	07505
Godshall Meats, LLC	Francisco	De La Cruz	Beverly Hills	CA	90210

g. Click the **External Data tab** and click **Excel** in the Import & Link group. Click **Browse** to locate the *a03m1Loans* spreadsheet. Select the database and click **Open** at the bottom of the dialog box.

h. Ensure the *Import the source data into a new table in the current database option* is selected and click **OK**. Click **Next** three times, until you are asked to add a primary key. From the *Choose my own Primary Key* menu, select **LoanID** (this should be the default option). Click **Next** once more and click **Finish**. Click **Close** in the Save Import Steps dialog box.

i. Open the Loans table in Design view. Select the **InterestRate field** and change the format to **Percent**. Change the field size for the CustomerID field to **Long Integer**. Click **Yes** when prompted that some data may be lost. Save and close the table.

j. Click the **Database Tools tab** and click **Relationships** in the Relationships group. Add both tables to the Relationships window and close the Show Table dialog box.

k. Drag the **CustomerID field** from the Customers table and drop it onto the CustomerID field in the Loans table. Check the **Enforce Referential Integrity check box** in the Edit Relationships dialog box and click **Create**. Save and close the Relationships window.

l. Create a query using the two tables that will calculate the payment amount for each loan. Add the following fields: **Company**, **LoanID**, **Amount**, **InterestRate**, **Term**, and **LoanClass**. Sort the query by LoanID in ascending order. Save the query as **Loan Payments**.

⭐ **m.** Add a calculated field named **Payment** in the first blank column to calculate the loan payment for each loan, using the Expression Builder. Use the Pmt function. Insert the appropriate field names in place of the placeholder arguments. Assume the loans have monthly payments (12 payments per year). Ensure the payment displays as a positive number. Run the query.

The first loan should have a value of approximately $243.15 (the extra decimal places will be removed shortly). Refer to Figure 3.32. If your number does not match up, reexamine your formula.

> **TROUBLESHOOTING:** If you cannot see the fields from your current query, ensure you have saved the query. Try closing and reopening the query.

n. Switch to Design view and change the display to **Currency format**. Run the query again to verify your changes. Compare your results to Figure 3.32.

o. Switch to Datasheet view and add a **Totals row**. Use it to calculate the sum of the amount column, the average interest rate, and the average term. Save and close the query.

p. Create a copy of Loan Payments. Save the new query as **Loan Payments Summary**.

q. Open the Loan Payments Summary query in Design view and rearrange the columns as follows: LoanClass, LoanID, Amount, and InterestRate. Delete columns CompanyName, Term, and Payment. Click **Totals** in the Show/Hide group. Change the Total row from left to right as follows: Group By, Count, Sum, and Avg. Run the query.

As we sorted the previous query by LoanID in Ascending order, this query will have the same sort by default.

r. Switch to Design view and display the Property Sheet. For the LoanID field, change the caption to **Loans**. For the Amount field, change the caption to **Total Amount** and change the format to **Currency**. For the InterestRate field, change the caption to **Avg Interest Rate** and change the format to **Percent**. Run the query. Save and close the query.

s. Exit Access, and submit based on your instructor's directions.

2 Investment Properties

You are in charge of LGS Investment's database, which contains all of the information on the properties your firm has listed and sold. Your task is to determine the length of time each property was on the market before it sold. You also need to calculate the sales commission from each property sold. Two agents will receive commission on each transaction: the listing agent and the selling agent. You also need to summarize the sales data by employee and calculate the average number of days each employee's sales were on the market prior to selling and the total commission earned by the employees. Refer to Figure 3.33 as you complete this exercise.

FIGURE 3.33 Sales Summary Query

Sales Summary by Subdivision				
Subdivision	Total Sales	Days on Market	Listing Commission	Selling Commission
The Orchards	$1,288,000.00	22.75	$45,080.00	$32,200.00
Fair Brook	$1,053,900.00	24.75	$36,886.50	$26,347.50
Eagle Valley	$4,012,000.00	39.00	$140,420.00	$100,300.00
Wood	$1,428,650.00	47.91	$50,002.75	$35,716.25
Red Canyon	$3,790,000.00	52.00	$132,650.00	$94,750.00
Total	$11,572,550.00		$405,039.25	$289,313.75

a. Open *a03m2Homes*. Save the database as **a03m2Homes_LastFirst**.

b. Create a new query, add the necessary tables, and then add the following fields: from the Agents table, add the LastName field; from the Properties table, the DateListed, DateSold, SalePrice, SellingAgent, and ListingAgent fields; and from the SubDivision table, the Subdivision field.

c. Add criteria to the table to ensure the DateSold field is not empty (in other words, properties that have not been sold). Format the SalePrice field as **Currency**. Save the query as **Sales Report**.

d. Create a calculated field using the Expression Builder named **DaysOnMarket** by subtracting DateListed from DateSold. This will calculate the number of days each sold property was on the market when it sold. Add a caption of **Days on Market**.

e. Calculate the commissions for the selling and listing agents using two calculated fields. The listing commission rate is **3.5%** of the sale price, and the selling commission rate is **2.5%** of the sale price. You can type these in directly or use the Expression Builder. Name the newly created fields **ListComm** and **SellComm**. These fields contain similar expressions. They need to be named differently so that the proper agent—the listing agent or the selling agent—gets paid. Add captions and format the fields as **Currency**.

f. Save the query after you verify that your calculations are correct. In Datasheet view, add the Total row. Calculate the average number of days on the market and the sum for the SalePrice and the two commission fields. Save and close the query.

g. Create a copy of the Sales Report query named **Sales Summary by Last Name**. Remove the DateListed, SellingAgent, ListingAgent, and Subdivision fields.

h. Display the Total row. Group by LastName and change the DateSold field Total row to **Where**, so the condition carries over. Show the sum of SalePrice, the average of DaysOnMarket, and the sum for both ListComm and SellComm. Change the caption for the SalePrice field to **Total Sales** and format the DaysOnMarket field as **Fixed**. Run the query. Adjust column widths as necessary.

i. Adjust the Total row in the Datasheet view so it shows the sum of TotalSales. Save the query.

DISCOVER

j. Create a copy of the Sales Summary by Last Name query named **Sales Summary by Subdivision**. Modify the query so the grouping is based on the Subdivision field, not LastName. Sort the query results so the fewest Days on Market is first and the most Days on Market is last. Limit the results to the top five rows.

k. Exit Access and submit based on your instructor's directions.

---

3 | Political Pollsters

COLLABORATION CASE

You are working with a group that would like to analyze survey results. You are specifically looking for trends in the data based on gender, political affiliation, and income level. To demonstrate the power of Access, you and your group will perform a small survey, add the results to a database, and create some queries to demonstrate how grouping can help get results.

a. Individually, open the *a03t1Survey.docx* file. Collect 10 responses each (unless directed to do otherwise by your instructor). You should try to survey a diverse group of people. You can do this survey via e-mail, Facebook, or another appropriate method. Bring the collected data to your group.

b. Open the *a03t1Survey* database and save the database as **a03t1Survey_GroupName**. Use the Enter New Survey Result form to enter all of your information into the existing database. There are four records to start your database.

c. Open the Questions By Gender query. Notice your average for question 1 is a number between 1 and 3. As your survey document listed Agree as a 3, Neutral as 2, and Disagree as 1, the higher the value, the more strongly people agree with the question. Modify the query so that you display the average of Question2, Question3, Question4, and Question5. Change the format for the new fields to **Fixed**.

d. Create a query named **Questions By Party**, using the Questions By Gender query as a guide, grouping by the PoliticalAffiliation field rather than the Gender field.

e. Create a query named **Questions By Income Level**, using the Questions By Gender query as a guide, grouping by the IncomeLevel field rather than the Gender field.

f. Examine your results. Discuss the results with your group and type up your conclusions in a new Word document named **a03t1SurveyResults_GroupName**. You should be able to make around five conclusions. An example of a conclusion might be that people of lower income levels are less interested in being taxed to support free Internet than people of higher income.

g. Exit Access and Word and submit based on your instructor's directions.

Beyond the Classroom

Too Many Digits
RESEARCH CASE

This chapter introduced you to calculated fields. Open the database *a03b2Interest* and save the database as **a03b2Interest_LastFirst**. Open the Monthly Interest query in Datasheet view. Notice the multiple digits to the right of the decimal in the Monthly Interest column; there should only be two digits. Search the Internet to find a function that will resolve this rounding problem. You only want to display two digits to the right of the decimal (even when you click on a Monthly Interest value). Apply your changes to the Monthly Interest field, change the format to **Currency**, and then run the query to test your changes. Save the query as **Monthly Interest Revised**. If you manage to find a solution, add a second column named **MonthlyInterestRounded** that rounds to the nearest dollar. Close the query, close the database, and then exit Access. Submit your work based on your instructor's directions.

Payroll Summary Needed
DISASTER RECOVERY

You were given an Excel spreadsheet that contains paycheck information for your company. Your task is to summarize this data by employee Social Security Number (SSN) and report your results to your supervisor. Open the spreadsheet *a03b3Paychecks* and examine the data. Select all the data and copy the data. You will use Access to summarize the data in this spreadsheet. Open the Access database named *a03b3Payroll* and save it as **a03b3Payroll_LastFirst**. Open the Payroll table, select the first row, and then paste the records. Create a new totals query that summarizes the data by SSN; include the count of pay periods (using the ID field) and the sum of each currency field. Do not include the PayDate field in this query. Create a calculated field named **Total Compensation**, which totals all assets the employees have, including pay, 401(k) retirement, and health benefits. Add appropriate captions to shorten the default captions. Run the query and save it as **Payroll Summary**. Close the query, close the database, and then exit Access. Submit the database based on your instructor's directions.

Customer Service Dialog
SOFT SKILLS CASE

Passaic County Technology Services (PCTS) provides technical support for a number of local companies. Part of their customer service evaluation involves logging how calls are closed and a quick, one-question survey given to customers at the end of a call, asking them to rate their experience from 1 (poor) to 5 (excellent). To evaluate the effectiveness of their operation, they have asked you to create some queries to help evaluate the performance of the company. Open the database *a03b4PCTS* and save the database as **a03b4PCTS_LastFirst**.

1. Create a query to show each technician and his or her effectiveness.
   - List each technician's first and last names, the number of calls, and the average of the customer's satisfaction for all calls assigned to the rep.
   - Format the average in Standard format and sort by the average so the highest average customer satisfaction appears first.
   - Save the query as **Tech Effectiveness**.

2. Create a query to show how effective the company is by call type.
   - List the call type's description (for example, Hardware Support) and the number of calls and average customer satisfaction for all calls of that type.
   - Format the average in Standard format and sort by the average so the highest average customer satisfaction appears first.
   - Save the query as **Call Type Effectiveness**.

3. Create a query to show how satisfied each customer is.

- List the company name and the number of calls and average customer satisfaction for all calls.
- Format the average in Standard format and sort by the average so the highest average customer satisfaction appears first.
- Save the query as **Customer Happiness**.

Now that you have created these queries, your supervisor should be able to quickly determine which technicians have the happiest customers, which call types the company is most effective on, and which customers are less happy than others. Close the queries, close the database, and then exit Access. Submit the database based on your instructor's directions.

Northwind Traders, an international gourmet food distributor, is concerned about shipping delays over the past six months. Review the orders over the past six months and identify any order that was not shipped within 30 days. Each customer that falls within that time frame will be called to inquire about any problems the delay may have caused. In addition, you will create an order summary and an order summary by country.

Database File Setup

Open the food database, use Save As to make a copy of the database, and then use the new database to complete this capstone exercise. You will add yourself to the employee database.

a. Locate and open *a03c1Food* and save the database as **a03c1Food_LastFirst**.

b. Open the Employees table. Add yourself as an employee. Fill in all information, with the hire date as today. Set your *Title* to **Technical Aide**, extension to **1144**, and the Reports To field to **Buchanan, Steven**. Leave the EmployeePicture field blank.

c. Close the Employees table.

Shipping Efficiency Query

You need to create a query to calculate the number of days between the date an order was placed and the date the order was shipped for each order. As you create the query, run the query at several intervals so you can verify that the data look correct. The result of your work will be a list of orders that took more than three weeks to ship. The salespeople will be calling each customer to see if there was any problem with their order.

a. Create a query using Query Design. From the Customers table, include the fields CompanyName, ContactName, ContactTitle, and Phone. From the Orders table, include the fields OrderID, OrderDate, and ShippedDate.

b. Run the query and examine the records. Save the query as **Shipping Efficiency**.

c. Add a calculated field named **DaysToShip** to calculate the number of days taken to fill each order. (*Hint:* The expression will include the OrderDate and the ShippedDate; the results will not contain negative numbers.)

d. Run the query and examine the results. Does the data in the DaysToShip field look accurate? Save the query.

e. Add criteria to limit the query results to include any order that took more than 30 days to ship.

f. Add the Quantity field from the Order Details table and the ProductName field from the Products table to the query. Sort the query by ascending OrderID. When the sales reps contact these customers, these two fields will provide useful information about the orders.

g. Switch to Datasheet view to view the final results. This list will be distributed to the sales reps so they can contact the customers. In Design view, add the caption **Days to Ship** to the DaysToShip field.

h. Save and close the query.

Order Summary Query

You need to create an Order Summary that will show the total amount of each order in one column and the total discount amount in another column. This query will require four tables: Orders, Order Details, Products, and Customers. Query to determine if employees are following the employee discount policy. You will group the data by employee name, count the orders, show the total dollars, and show the total discount amount. You will then determine which employees are following the company guidelines.

a. Create a query using Query Design and add the four tables above. Add the fields OrderID and OrderDate. Set both fields' Total row to **Group By**.

b. Add a calculated field in the third column. Name the field **ExtendedAmount**. This field should multiply the number of items ordered by the price per item. This will calculate the total amount for each order. Format the calculated field as **Currency** and change the caption to **Total Dollars**. Change the Total row to **Sum**.

c. Add a calculated field in the fourth column. Name the field **DiscountAmount**. The field should multiply the number of items ordered, the price per item, and the discount field. This will calculate the total discount for each order. Format the calculated field as **Currency** and add a caption of **Discount Amt**. Change the Total row to **Sum**.

d. Run the query. Save the query as **Order Summary**. Return to Design view.

e. Add criteria to the OrderDate field so only orders made between 1/1/2016 and 12/31/2016 are displayed. Change the Total row to **Where**. This expression will display only orders that were created in 2016.

f. Run the query and view the results. Save and close the query.

Order Financing Query

Northwind is considering offering financing options to their customers with 5% interest, to be paid over 12 months.

a. Create a copy of the Order Summary query named **Order Financing**.

b. Switch to Design view of the new query and remove the DiscountAmount field.

c. Add a new field using the Expression Builder named **SamplePayment**. Insert the Pmt function with the following parameters:

- Use **.05/12** for the rate argument (5% interest, paid monthly)

- Use the number **12** for the num_periods argument (12 months)

- Use the calculated field **ExtendedAmount** for the present_value

d. Change the Total row to **Expression** for the SamplePayment field.

e. Change the Format for the SamplePayment field to **Currency**.

f. Save and close the query.

Order Summary by Country Query

You need to create one additional query based on the Order Summary query you created in a previous step. This new query will enable you to analyze the orders by country.

a. Create a copy of the Order Summary query named **Order Summary by Country**.

b. Replace the OrderID field with the Country field in Design view of the new query.

c. Run the query and examine the summary records; there should be 21 countries listed.

d. Switch to Design view and change the sort order so that the country with the highest ExtendedAmount is first and the country with the lowest ExtendedAmount is last.

e. Run the query and verify the results.

f. Save and close the query.

g. Exit Access and submit based on your instructor's directions.

Creating and Using Professional Forms and Reports

CHAPTER 4

Moving Beyond Tables and Queries

OBJECTIVES   AFTER YOU READ THIS CHAPTER, YOU WILL BE ABLE TO:

1. Create forms using form tools p. 258

2. Use form views p. 265

3. Work with a form layout control p. 268

4. Sort records in a form p. 270

5. Create reports using report tools p. 278

6. Use report views p. 285

7. Modify a report p. 287

8. Sort records in a report p. 290

CASE STUDY | Coffee Shop Starts New Business

The La Vida Mocha coffee shop in Paterson, New Jersey, once was an ordinary coffee shop selling retail coffee, tea, and pastries to its loyal customers in northern New Jersey. Then, in 2012, owner Ryung Park decided to use her knowledge of the coffee industry to sell coffee products to businesses in her area. This new venture grew quickly and soon became 25% of her annual revenue. Realizing that this new business would need more of her time each day, she decided to create an Access database to help track her customer, product, and order information.

With the help of a student from Passaic County Community College, she created a database with tables to hold data for customers, products, sales reps, and orders. She is currently using these tables to enter and retrieve information.

Ryung wants to have one of her employees, Nabil, manage the database. However, she does not want him to work in the tables; she wants him to work with forms. Ryung heard that forms have an advantage over tables because they can be designed to show one record at a time—this will reduce data-entry errors. Ryung would also like to create several reports for her own benefit so she can stay on top of the business by reviewing the reports each week.

You have been hired to help Ryung create the new forms and reports that she needs for the business. She will describe the forms and reports to you in detail and also provide written instructions. You will be expected to work independently to create the forms and reports.

Form Basics

A *form* is a database object that is used to add data into or edit data in a table. Most Access database applications use forms rather than tables for data entry and for looking up information. Three main reasons exist for using forms rather than tables for adding, updating, and deleting data. They are:

- You are less likely to edit the wrong record by mistake.
- You can create a form that shows data from more than one table simultaneously.
- You can create Access forms to match paper forms.

If you are adding data using a table with many columns, you could jump to the wrong record in the middle of a column accidentally. For example, you could enter the data for one record correctly for the first 10 fields but then jump to the row above and overwrite existing data for the remaining field values unintentionally. In this case, two records would have incorrect or incomplete data. A form will not allow this type of error because most forms restrict entry to one record at a time.

Many forms require two tables as their record source. For example, you may want to view a customer's details (name, address, e-mail, phone, etc.) as well as all of the orders he or she has placed. This would require using data from both the Customers and the Orders tables in one form. Similarly, you may want to view the header information for an order while also viewing the detail line items for the order. This would require data from both the Orders and Order Details tables. Both of these examples enable a user to view two record sources at the same time and make changes—additions, edits, or deletions—to one or both sources of data.

Finally, when paper forms are used to collect information, it is a good idea to design the electronic forms to match the paper forms. This will make data entry more efficient and reliable and ease the transition from paper form to computer form. Access forms can be designed to emulate the paper documents already in use in an organization. This facilitates the simultaneous use of both paper forms and electronic data. Databases do not necessarily eliminate paper forms; they supplement and coexist with them.

In this section, you will learn the basics of form design. You will discover multiple methods to create and modify Access forms.

Creating Forms Using Form Tools

Access provides a variety of options for creating forms. There are a number of built-in layouts that you can choose from. Database designers may eventually develop a preference for one or two types of form layouts, but keep in mind you have a lot of options if needed. You will want to find a balance between creating a form that is simple while still powerful enough to be of use.

Access provides 14 different tools for creating forms. You can find these options in the Forms group on the Create tab. The Forms group contains four of the most common form tools (Form, Form Design, Blank Form, and Form Wizard), a list of Navigation forms, and More Forms, as shown in Figure 4.1. Navigation forms provides a list of six templates to create a user interface for a database; the More Forms command lists four additional form tools (Multiple Items, Datasheet, Split Form, and Modal Dialog). Select a table or query, click one of the tools, and Access will create a form using the selected table or query. The most common of these tools, the *Form tool*, is used to create data-entry forms for customers, employees, products, and other primary tables.

Forms group

FIGURE 4.1 Forms Group on Create Tab

A complete list of all the Form tools available in Access is found in the Form Tools Reference at the end of this section. Many of the tools will be covered in this chapter. Some tools will not be covered, however, because they are not commonly used or because they are beyond the scope of this chapter (e.g., Form Design, Blank Form, Navigation forms, and Modal Dialog form). Use Microsoft Access Help to find more information about Form tools not covered in this chapter.

 Usability Testing

After a database object (such as a form) is finalized, it should be tested by both the database designer and the end users. The designer should be certain the report meets any criteria the users have given him or her. The designer should also browse through the records to make sure the values in all records (and not just the first record) display correctly. Likewise, the end users should have the opportunity to test the form and provide feedback. After all, they will be the ones using it, so the database designer has a responsibility to ensure the end users are comfortable with the object.

Ideally, a form should simplify data entry. Creating a form is a collaborative process between the form designer and the form users. This process continues throughout the life of the form, because the data needs of an organization may change. Forms designed long ago to collect information for a new customer account may not have an e-mail field; the form would have to be modified to include an e-mail field. The form designer needs to strike a balance between collecting the information users need to do their jobs and cluttering the form with extraneous fields. The users of the data know what they need and usually offer good feedback about which fields should be on a form. If you listen to their suggestions, your forms will function more effectively, the users' work will be easier, and your data will contain fewer data-entry errors.

After discussing the form with the users, it will help you to create the form in Access if you sketch the form first. After sketching the form, you will have a better idea of which form tool to use to create the form. After the form is created, use the sketch to determine which fields are required and in what the order of fields should be.

Identify a Record Source

Before you create a form, you must identify the record source. A **record source** is the table or query that supplies the records for a form or report. You may also see the record source referred to as a data source in certain help files and instructions. Use a table if you want to include all the records from a single table. Use a query if you need to filter the records in a table, if you need to combine records from two or more related tables, or if you do not want to display all fields.

For example, if a sales rep wants to create a form that displays customers from a single state only—where his customers reside—he should base the form on a query. Or, if a parts manager needs to review only parts with a zero on-hand quantity, he could create a form based on a query that includes only records with on-hand equal to zero.

Use the Form Tool

 As noted earlier, the Form tool is the most common tool for creating forms. To use the Form tool:

1. Select a table or query from the Navigation Pane
2. On the CREATE tab, in the Forms group, click Form.

Based on that table or query, Access automatically creates a new form. You may need to modify the form slightly, but you can create a stacked layout form in a just one click. A *stacked layout* displays fields in a vertical column. Because this is a form, it will display one record at a time, as shown in Figure 4.2. The other type of layout you may use is a *tabular layout*, which displays data horizontally across the page.

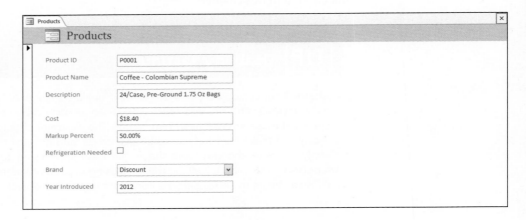

FIGURE 4.2 Form with a Stacked Layout

Understand Controls

Notice in Figure 4.3 that each field has a label on the left and a text box on the right. These are referred to as controls. *Controls* are the text boxes, buttons, boxes, and other tools you use to add, edit, and display the data in a form or report. In Figure 4.3, Product ID, Product Name, Description, and the rest of the field labels are controls. In addition, the boxes containing the values for each field (P0001, Coffee–Colombian Supreme, etc.) are all controls. More specifically, the form locations that hold data are generally text box controls, and the text in front of those, marking what the field means, are label controls.

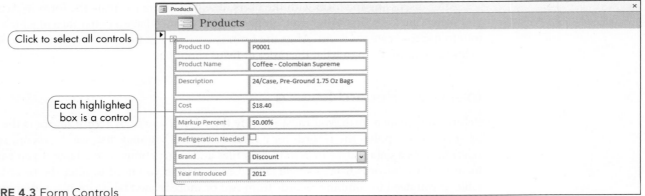

FIGURE 4.3 Form Controls

A *layout control* provides guides to help keep controls aligned horizontally and vertically and give your form a uniform appearance. The fields are all aligned in Figure 4.3 because a layout control keeps them that way. Picture the layout control as a bookcase, with each field being a shelf on the bookcase.

Work with Form Views

There are three different views of a form available. The first, *Form view*, is a simplified interface primarily used for data entry. This view does not enable you to make changes to the layout. As such, the Form view is an excellent way for users to interact with the form. This ensures they do not accidentally change the form layout. Figure 4.4 shows a form in Form view. Notice forms can include features such as drop-down lists.

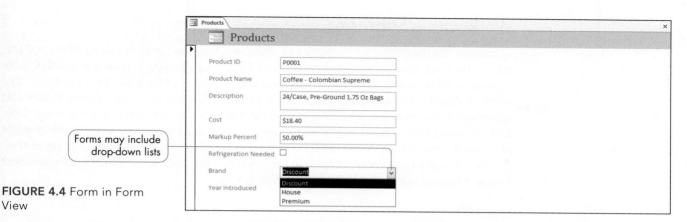

FIGURE 4.4 Form in Form View

Forms may include drop-down lists

The second view, *Layout view,* enables users to make changes to the layout while viewing the data on the form. Reports have a similar view with the same name. This will be discussed later in the chapter. Layout view is useful for testing the functionality of the form and adjusting sizes of fields as needed. In the previous section, you were shown how to create a form using the Form Tool. When you do this, Access opens the form in Layout view ready for customizing. Figure 4.5 shows a form in Layout view.

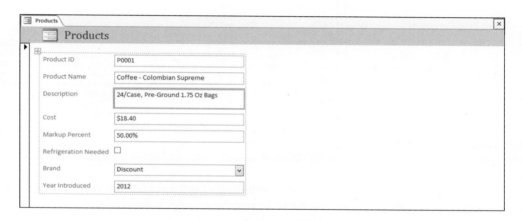

FIGURE 4.5 Form in Layout View

The third view, *Design view,* allows you to change advanced design settings you cannot see in the Layout view, such as a background image. Reports also have a Design view, which will also be discussed later in this chapter. Design view is a much more powerful way of changing the form layout. It is more complex than Layout view, so you would likely use Design view only when you need to perform advanced form layout adjustments. Figure 4.6 shows a form in Design view.

FIGURE 4.6 Form in Design View

These three views will be described in more detail later in this chapter.

Work with a Subform

When you use the Form tool to create a form, Access analyzes the table relationships you created in the database. If the table that the main form is based upon is related to another table through a relationship, then Access automatically adds a subform to the main form. The subform displays records in the related table, generally laid out in a table, similar to an Excel spreadsheet. For example, assume you have sales representatives stored in a SalesReps table and customer information stored in a Customers table. Also assume a relationship exists between the two tables. If you create a new form based on SalesReps using the Form tool, Access will add a Customers subform to the bottom of the main form, showing all customers assigned to each sales representative (see Figure 4.7).

Subform displays related records

FIGURE 4.7 Form with a Subform

At times, you may want the subform as part of your form; at other times, you may want to remove it. To remove a subform from a form:

1. Switch to Design view.
2. Click anywhere inside the subform.
3. Press Delete.

Create a Split Form

A *split form* combines two views of the same record source—one section is displayed in a stacked layout (form view) and the other section is displayed in a tabular layout (datasheet view). By default, the form view is positioned on the top and the datasheet view is displayed on the bottom; however, the form's page orientation can be changed from horizontal to vertical in Layout view. If you select a record in the top half of the form, the same record will be selected in the bottom half of the form and vice versa. For example, if you create a split form based on an Orders table, you can select an Order in the datasheet section and then see the order's information in the *Form view* section (see Figure 4.8). This gives you the option to enter data in the Form view while being able to navigate between orders more quickly. The top and bottom halves are synchronized at all times.

FIGURE 4.8 Split Form

Splitter bar

Bottom half allows quick switching between records

To create a split form, do the following:

1. Select a table or query in the Navigation Pane.
2. Click the CREATE tab.
3. Click More Forms in the Forms group.
4. Select Split Form.

Once you have completed those steps, a new split form displays. You can add, edit, or delete records in either section. The *splitter bar* divides the form into two halves. Users can adjust the splitter bar up or down unless the form designer disables this option.

Create a Multiple Items Form

A *Multiple Items form* displays multiple records in a tabular layout similar to a table's Datasheet view. However, a Multiple Items form gives you more customization options than a datasheet, such as the ability to add graphical elements, buttons, and other controls. Figure 4.9 shows a Multiple Items form created from the Employees table.

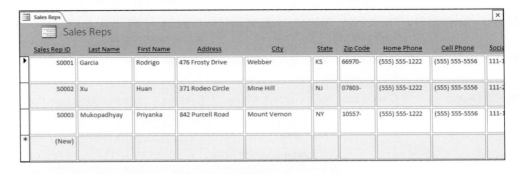

FIGURE 4.9 Multiple Items Form

To create a Multiple Items form, do the following:

1. Select a table or query from the Navigation Pane.
2. Click the CREATE tab.
3. Click More Forms in the Forms group.
4. Select Multiple Items from the list of options.

Create Forms Using the Other Form Tools

A Datasheet form is a replica of a table or query's Datasheet view except that it still retains some of the form properties. Database designers can also use the Datasheet form to display data in a table-like format but change the form properties to not allow a record to be deleted. This would protect the data from accidental damage while still providing the users with the familiar Datasheet view.

The Form Design tool and the Blank Form tools can be used to create a form manually. Click one of these tools and Access will open a completely blank form. Click Add Existing Fields in the Tools group on the Design tab and add the necessary fields.

The Navigation option in the Forms group enables you to create user interface forms that have the look and feel of a Web-based form and enable users to open and close the objects of a database. In other words, you could set up a form that allows users to click on the forms you want them to view. This is an excellent option to simplify the database for data-entry personnel who may not understand the program. These forms are also useful for setting up an Access database on the Internet.

The Modal Dialog Form tool can be used to create a dialog box. This feature is useful when you need to gather information from the user before working with another object. Dialog boxes are common in all Microsoft Office applications.

REFERENCE | Form Tools

Form Tool	Location	Use
Form	Create tab, Forms group	Creates a form with a stacked layout displaying all of the fields in the record source.
Form Design	Create tab, Forms group	Create a new blank form in Design view.
Blank Form	Create tab, Forms group	Create a new blank form in Layout view.
Form Wizard	Create tab, Forms group	Answer a series of questions and Access will create a custom form for you.
Navigation	Create tab, Forms group, Navigation button	Create user-interface forms that can also be used on the Internet. Six different Navigation form layouts are available from the drop-down list.
Split Form	Create tab, Forms group, More Forms button	Creates a two-part form with a stacked layout in one section and a tabular layout in the other.
Multiple Items	Create tab, Forms group, More Forms button	Creates a tabular layout form that includes all of the fields from the record source.
Datasheet	Create tab, Forms group, More Forms button	Creates a form that resembles the datasheet of a table or query.
Modal Dialog	Create tab, Forms group, More Forms button	Creates a custom dialog box that forces the user to respond before working with another object.

 TIP | Print with Caution!

Users can print a form by clicking the File tab and selecting the Print option. However, printing from a form should be done with caution. Forms are not generally designed for printing, so you may end up with hundreds of pages of printouts. A form with a stacked layout of 1,000 records could print thousands of pages unless you choose the Selected Record(s) option in the Print dialog box. The Selected Record(s) option, as shown in Figure 4.10, will only print the current record (or selected records).

Selected Record(s) option

FIGURE 4.10 Printing Selected Records

Using Form Views

Access provides different views for a form, similar to the different views in tables and queries. Tables and queries have Design view and Datasheet view. Most forms have Layout view, Form view, and Design view.

As you work with the form tools to create and modify forms, you will often need to switch between the three form views in Access: Layout view, Form view, and Design view. Most of your design work will be done in Layout view; occasionally, you will switch to Design view to add a more advanced feature, such as a background, or to use a layout option that is otherwise unavailable. Users of the form will only work in Form view. There should be no reason for a user to switch to Layout or Design view. Modifications to the form should be done by the designated form designer.

After a form is generated by a Form tool, you may need to modify it. Commonly, you may add a field, remove a field, change the order of fields, change the width of a field, modify the theme, or modify label text. These changes can be made in a form's Layout view. Advanced changes, such as changing headers or footers or adding a background image, can be made in a form's Design view.

Edit Data in Form View

STEP 2 Use Form view to add, edit, and delete data in a form; the layout and design of the form cannot be changed in this view. Recall from a previous chapter that you can move from one field to another field by pressing Tab on your keyboard or clicking the desired field with your mouse.

Alter a Form in Layout View

Use Layout view to alter the form design while still viewing the data. You use Layout view to add or delete fields in a form, modify field properties, change the column widths, and enhance a form by adding a color scheme or styling. While you are working in Layout view, you can see the data as it would appear in Form view, but you cannot edit the data in Layout view. Seeing the data in Layout view makes it easier to size controls, for example, to ensure the data is visible. It is good practice to test a form in Form view after making changes in Layout view.

Use the Form Layout Tools Tabs

Forms have a number of options you can use to format. Once you are in Layout or Design view, you will have access to the report layout tools. You have three tabs available:

- Design: Use this tab to make changes to the design of the form, such as adding sorting, changing themes, and inserting additional controls.
- Arrange: Use this tab to change the layout of a form, to move fields, or to insert space.
- Format: Use this tab to change the font; add or remove bolding, italics, or underlining; change font size; change font color or background; adjust text alignment; or add a background image.

Add a Field to a Form

STEP 3 » To add a field to a form, do the following:

1. Open the form in Layout view.
2. Click Add Existing Fields in the Tools group on the DESIGN tab to reveal the available fields from the form's record source. A Field List pane appears at the right of your screen.
3. For a single-table form, you will be presented with a list of fields. For a multiple-table form, you will first need to click the + (plus) next to the appropriate table to locate the desired field.
4. Drag the new field to the precise location on the form, using the shaded line (the color may vary, based on your Office configuration) as a guide for the position of the new field. The other fields will automatically adjust to make room for the new field.

Depending on the layout of the form, the shaded line will appear vertically (tabular layouts) or horizontally (stacked).

Delete a Field from a Form

To delete a field, do the following:

1. Switch to Layout view.
2. Click the text box control of the field to be deleted (note the shaded border around the control).
3. Click the Select Row option on the Layout tab in the Rows & Columns group.
4. Press Delete. The other fields will automatically adjust to close the gap around the deleted field.

Adjust Column Widths in a Form

When column widths are adjusted in a form with a stacked layout, all columns will increase and decrease together. Therefore, it is best to make sure that field columns are wide enough to accommodate the widest value in the table. For example, if a form contains information such as a customer's first name, last name, address, city, state, ZIP, phone, and e-mail address, you will need to make sure the longest address and the longest e-mail address are completely visible (because those fields are likely to contain the longest data values).

To decrease column widths in a form with a stacked layout, do the following:

1. Open the form in Layout view.
2. Click the text box control of the first field to select it.
3. Move the mouse over the right border of the field until the mouse pointer turns into a double arrow.
4. Drag the right edge to the left or right until you arrive at the desired width.

You will notice that all the fields change as you change the width of the first field. All fields that are part of the layout will have a standard width. If you wanted to resize one specific field, you would need to remove that field from the layout control. Note that "removing a field from the layout control" does not mean "removing a field from the form." Recall that the layout control keeps each field in place. If you remove a field from the layout control, it stays on the form but can be moved more freely.

Modify Form Controls using the Format Tab

When you view a form in Layout view, the Form Layout Tools tab displays the Design tab, Arrange tab, and Format tab. The Format tab, shown in Figure 4.11, contains a series of commands that enable you change the font, display, and alignment of the controls on a form. This is useful if you need to quickly change the look of one cell. For example, if you have a form that shows the information about the sale of a vehicle, you might want to emphasize the net profit of each transaction.

Background Color arrow

Font Color arrow

FIGURE 4.11 Format Tab

From this tab, you can change a number of properties. For example, you can perform these tasks, and more:

- Change the font size: Click the Font Size arrow in the Font group.
- Change emphasis: In the Font group, add bold, italics, or underlining.
- Change alignment: In the Font group, choose left, center, or right align.
- Change a control's background color: Click the Background Color arrow (refer to Figure 4.11) and select a color for the background.
- Change a control's font color: Click the Font Color arrow (refer to Figure 4.11) and select a color for the cell's font.
- Change number format: In the Number group, change to currency, percentage, or add commas; increase or decrease decimal places.

Selecting Controls

Controls, as mentioned, include both the labels identifying a field and the text box displaying field values. There may be times you want to select multiple controls. You will notice when you click on one control and click on another that the original control is deselected. If you need to select multiple controls, click on the first control you wish to select, hold down CTRL on your keyboard, and then click on the other controls you wish to select. Once they are selected, you can perform many tasks, such as formatting or deletion.

Add a Theme to a Form

You can apply a theme to a form in order to give the form a more professional finish. A *theme* is a defined set of colors, fonts, and graphics that can be applied to a form (or report). Click Themes in the Themes group on the Design tab, select a theme from the Themes Gallery, and Access will apply the theme to the form. Each theme has a name; you can determine the name of a theme by pointing the mouse to a theme and waiting for the tip to pop up, showing the name.

You can apply a theme to a single form or to all the forms in your database that share a common theme. Applying the same theme to all forms will provide a consistent look to your database; most users prefer a consistent theme when using Access forms. The same themes found in Access are also available in Excel, Word, and PowerPoint. Therefore, you can achieve a uniform look across all Office applications. Themes can be customized and saved so that the theme you create can be used again. Click the Save Current Theme command as shown in Figure 4.12 to do so.

Save Current Theme

FIGURE 4.12 Themes

Add Styling to a Form

Modifying the font size of labels, changing the font color of labels, and adding a background color can enhance a form and also make it more usable. It is best to choose a familiar font family, such as Arial or Calibri, for both the form label controls and the text box controls. Apply bold to the labels in order to help the user distinguish labels from the text boxes. You should also consider right-aligning the labels and left-aligning the text box controls to reduce distance between the label and field, as illustrated in Figure 4.13. You may also want to separate the primary key field from the rest of the form by providing a sufficient visual boundary.

One note of caution: Try to avoid what graphic artists refer to as the "ransom note effect." Using too many font families, font sizes, colors, and other effects can take away from your design.

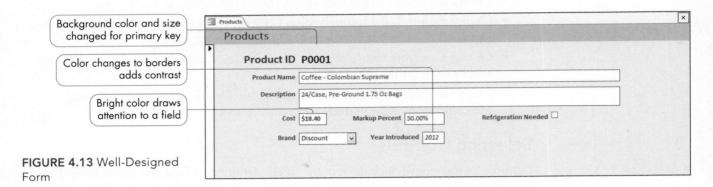

FIGURE 4.13 Well-Designed Form

Working with a Form Layout Control

Whenever you use one of the form tools to create a new form, Access will add a layout control to help align the fields. Recall that the layout control helps keep controls aligned in order to give your form a uniform appearance. The layout control provides structure for the fields but is restrictive. If you wish to have more control over the location of your fields, you can remove the layout control and position the controls manually on the grid.

Modify a Form Using the Arrange Tab

The Arrange tab appears in both Layout view and Design view. Use this tab to change the layout of a form, to move fields up and down, to insert a space above or below your current position, or to insert a space to the left or the right of the current field. To use these commands, first open a form in Layout view or Design view and click the Arrange tab. Next, select a field or fields and click the appropriate command.

The Table group contains commands that enable you to add gridlines to a form's layout, to change a form's layout from stacked to tabular (and vice versa), or to remove a form's layout. The Remove Layout command is only available in Design view.

STEP 4》 To change the arrangement of a form, do the following:

1. Open the form in Layout view.
2. Click any of the field text boxes.
3. Click the ARRANGE tab.
4. Click Select Layout in the Rows & Columns group.
5. Click Tabular or Stacked in the Table group.

To remove a form layout control, do the following:

1. Switch to Design view (if you are not in Design view, you will not see the Remove Layout option).
2. Click on one of the fields that is currently part of the layout.
3. On the ARRANGE tab, click Select Layout in the Rows & Columns group.
4. Click Remove Layout in the Table group.
5. Switch to Layout view to arrange fields.

If you have removed the layout control or have a form that never had one, you can add one if you do the following:

1. Switch to Layout view or Design view (you can switch in either view).
2. Select all the controls you would like added back to the layout control, such as the field labels and text boxes. Hold down CTRL on your keyboard and click on each control, or click the FORMAT tab and in the Selection group, click Select All if you want to add everything to a layout.
3. On the ARRANGE tab, in the Table group, click Tabular or Stacked

The Rows & Columns group contains commands that enable you to insert rows and columns inside a form's layout. For example, in a form with a stacked layout, you may want to separate some fields from the rest of the fields. To do this, you could select a text box and click Insert Below. This will create a space after the selected field. This group also contains the Select Layout, Select Column, and Select Row commands. In Figure 4.14, three rows have been inserted above the Cost field.

FIGURE 4.14 Rows Inserted Using the Arrange Tab

The Move group contains two commands that enable you to move a field up or down in a stacked layout. For example, if you want to move the second field in a stacked layout to the first position, select the second field's text box and label and click Move Up in the Move group. Moving fields up or down in a form may cause unexpected results; you can always use the Undo command if you need to revert back to a previous layout.

The Position group contains commands that enable you to modify the margins and the padding of controls in a form. This group also contains the Anchoring command, which enables you to change where the form's controls appear on the screen. By default, forms are anchored at the top left; however, you can change this to any of the nine options using the anchoring command.

TIP Apply a Background Image to a Form

To apply a Background Image to a form, open the form in Design view, click the Format tab, and then click Background Image in the Background group. Next, click Browse to locate the image you want to apply to the form. Once the image has been applied to the form, you can change the properties of the image so that the image is anchored and sized correctly.

Sorting Records in a Form

When a form is created using a Form tool, the sort order of the records in the form is dependent on the sort order of the record source—a table or a query. Tables are usually sorted by the primary key, whereas queries can be sorted in a variety of ways. Adding and removing sorts are shown in Figure 4.15.

FIGURE 4.15 Home Tab Sort & Filter Group

Sorting by a Single Field

You can easily sort on a single field, in ascending or descending order.

To sort by a single field, do the following:

1. Open the form in Form view.
2. Select the field you want to use for sorting.
3. On the HOME tab, in the Sort & Filter group, click Ascending or Descending.

If the form is based on a query, you can instead modify the underlying query's sort order. This method enables you to create a more advanced sort order based on multiple fields. Open the query in Design view, add the sorting you want, and then save and close the query.

Remove Sorting in a Form

To remove the sort order in a form, do the following:

1. Switch to Form view.
2. On the HOME tab, in the Sort & Filter group, click Remove Sort.

 Inconsistent Sorting Due to Spaces

Including extra spaces when you enter values into fields can cause issues with sorting. To Access, the following values are not the same:

Little Falls, NJ 07424

Little Falls, NJ 07424

Notice the extra space after the word *Little*. If you attempt to sort, these cities will end up in different places in the sort. The first Little Falls (without the extra space) would appear between Little Egg Harbor Township and Little Ferry. However, the second version would end up above Little Egg Harbor Township, because Access treats the space as a different character.

Inconsistent spacing can cause inconsistent sorting. Try to remember that when performing data entry. If you inherit a database with this issue, you might consider performing a Replace, replacing two spaces with one.

Quick
Concepts ✓

1. How does a form simplify data entry (when compared to entering data into a table)? *p. 258*
2. What is the record source of a form? *p. 259*
3. What is the difference between Layout view and Design view? *pp. 260–261*
4. What is the difference between a form with a subform and a split form? *p. 262*
5. What is a layout control? What are the pros and cons of a layout control? *p. 268*

Hands-On Exercises

Watch the Video
for this Hands-
On Exercise!

MyITLab®
HOE1 Training

1 Form Basics

It is your first day on the job at La Vida Mocha. After talking with Ryung about her data-entry needs, you decide to create several sample forms with different formats. You will show each form to Ryung and Nabil to get feedback and see if they have a preference.

Skills covered: Create Forms Using Form Tools • Use Form Views • Work with a Form Layout Control • Sort Records in a Form

STEP 1 ▶▶ CREATE FORMS USING FORM TOOLS

You will create some forms to help Ryung and Nabil with their data entry process. After discussing their needs, you created some sketches that you will implement. Refer to Figure 4.16 as you complete Step 1.

FIGURE 4.16 Customer Information Form After Step f

a. Open *a04h1Coffee*. Click the **FILE tab**, select **Save As**, and click **Save As**. Type **a04h1Coffee_LastFirst** as the file name. Click **Save**.

> **TROUBLESHOOTING:** Throughout the remainder of this chapter and textbook, click Enable Content whenever you are working with student files.

> **TROUBLESHOOTING:** If you make any major mistakes in this exercise, you can close the file, repeat step a above, and then start over.

b. Click the **Customers table** in the Navigation Pane. Click the **CREATE tab** and click **Form** in the Forms group.

Access creates a new form with two record sources—Customers (with stacked layout, on top) and Orders (with datasheet layout, below). Access found a one-to-many relationship between the Customers and Orders tables. The form opens in Layout view.

c. Click the top text box containing *C0001* if it is not already selected. The text box is outlined with a shaded border. Move the mouse to the right edge of the shaded border until the mouse pointer changes to a double-headed arrow. Drag the right edge to the left until the text box is approximately half of its original size.

All the text boxes and the subform at the bottom adjust in size when you adjust the top text box. This is a characteristic of Layout view—enabling you to easily modify all controls at once.

> **TROUBLESHOOTING:** You may need to maximize the Access window or close the Navigation Pane if the right edge of the text box is not visible.

d. Ensure the labels at the left all appear without being cut off. If they are cut off, adjust the size of the labels like you did in step c.

e. Click **Save** in the Quick Access Toolbar, and then type **Customer Information** as the form name in the **Save As dialog box**. Click **OK**.

f. Click the **Customers title** at the top of the form to select it, click again, and then change the title to **Customer Information**. Press **Enter** to accept the change. Your form should now look like Figure 4.16. Close the form.

> **TROUBLESHOOTING:** If you make a mistake that you cannot easily recover from, consider deleting the form and starting over. The Form tool makes it easy to start over again.

g. Verify the Customers table is selected in the Navigation Pane. Click the **CREATE tab** and click **More Forms** in the Forms group. Select **Split Form**.

Access creates a new form with a split view, one view in stacked layout and one view laid out like a datasheet.

h. Click anywhere on the Coulter Office Supplies customer record in the bottom portion of the form (record 14). Note: You may need to scroll down to see this record.

The top portion shows all the information for this customer.

i. Click the **Customers title** at the top of the form to select it, click **Customers** again, and then change the title to **Customers - Split View**. Press **Enter** to accept the change.

j. Click **Save** on the Quick Access Toolbar and type **Customers - Split View** in the **Form Name box**. Click **OK**. Close the form.

k. Click the **Products table** in the Navigation Pane. Click the **CREATE tab**, click **More Forms** in the Forms group, and then select **Multiple Items**.

Access creates a new multiple-item form based on the Products table. The form resembles a table's Datasheet view.

l. Click the **Products title** at the top of the form to select it, click again on **Products**, and then change the title to **Products - Multiple Items**. Press **Enter** to save the title.

m. Save the form as **Products - Multiple Items** and close the form.

n. Click the **Orders table** in the Navigation Pane. Click **Form** in the Forms group on the CREATE tab.

A form with a subform showing each line of the order is created.

o. Switch to Design view. Click anywhere inside the subform and press **Delete** on your keyboard.

The subform is removed.

p. Save the form as **Order Information**. Close all open objects.

STEP 2 >> USE FORM VIEW TO CHANGE DATA

Now that you have created three forms, you will show Nabil how to use the forms to perform data entry.

a. Right-click the **Customer Information** form in the Navigation Pane and click **Open**. Advance to the sixth customer, *Lugo Computer Sales*, using the **Next Record button** on the Navigation Bar at the bottom of the form.

> **TROUBLESHOOTING:** Two Navigation bars exist, one for the main form and one for the subform. Make sure you use the bottom-most one that shows 14 records.

b. Double-click the **Customers table** in the Navigation Pane.

Two tabs now display in the main window. You will compare the table data and the form data while you make changes to both.

c. Verify the sixth record of the Customers table is *Lugo Computer Sales*, which corresponds to the sixth record in the Customer Information form. Click the tabs to switch between the table and the form.

d. Click the **Customer Information tab** and replace *Adam Sanchez*, the contact for Lugo Computer Sales, with your name. Advance to the next record to save the changes. Click the **Customers tab** to see that the contact name changed in the table as well.

The contact field and the other fields on the Customer Information form automatically change the data in the underlying table.

> **TROUBLESHOOTING:** If the change to Adam Sanchez does not display in the Customers table, check the Customer Information form to see if the pencil displays in the left margin. If it does, save the record by advancing to the next customer and recheck to see if the name has changed.

e. Close the Customer Information form and the Customers table.

f. Open the Customers – Split View form. In the bottom portion of the split form, click **Lugo Computer Sales**, the sixth record. Notice the top portion now displays the information for Lugo Computer Sales. Notice there is an error in the e-mail address—*service* is misspelled. In the top portion of the form, change the e-mail address to **service@lugocomputer.net**.

g. Click another record in the bottom pane and click back on **Lugo Computer Sales**.

The pencil disappears from the record selector box and the changes are saved to the table.

STEP 3 >> USE LAYOUT VIEW TO MODIFY A FORM LAYOUT

You will make some changes to the layouts based on recommendations Nabil gave you after seeing the forms in action. You will also add a missing field to the main table and add it to the form. Refer to Figure 4.17 as you complete Step 3.

Step d: Refrig? column resized

FIGURE 4.17 Final Version of Products—Multiple Items Report

a. Switch the Customers – Split View form to Layout view. Move your mouse over the splitter bar, the border between the top and bottom portions of the window. When the pointer shape changes to a double-headed arrow, drag the **splitter bar** up until it almost touches the Sales Rep ID field. Save and close the form.

b. Open the Products – Multiple Items form in Layout view. Move the mouse over the bottom edge of cell P0001 until the pointer shape changes to a two-headed arrow. Drag the bottom edge up to reduce the height of the rows so they are as tall as they need to be to accommodate the information.

Changing the height of one row affects the height of all the rows.

c. Click anywhere on the Cost column and click **Select Column** in the Rows & Columns group on the ARRANGE tab. Press **Delete** to remove the column. Repeat the process to delete *MarkupPercent*.

d. Click the **Refrigeration Needed label** to select it. Change the label to the abbreviation **Refrig?**. Shrink the field so it is as wide as necessary. Save and close the form.

You removed fields from the Products – Multiple Items form and the other fields adjust to maintain an even distribution (after you remove the blank space).

e. Open the Customer Information form in Layout view.

f. Click **Themes** in the Themes group on the DESIGN tab. Right-click the **Slice theme** and click **Apply Theme to This Object Only**.

The font and color scheme adjust to match this theme.

TROUBLESHOOTING: Recall that you can determine which theme is named Slice by pointing the mouse to a theme and waiting for a tip to display. Themes are displayed in alphabetical order.

---

g. Click **Shape Fill** in the Control Formatting group on the FORMAT tab. Click **Light Turquoise, Background 2**.

The background color of the CustomerID field changes to light turquoise.

TROUBLESHOOTING: If you do not see a Light Turquoise, Background 2 in the first row, ensure you have selected the Slice theme.

> **TROUBLESHOOTING:** If the entire background changes to blue, undo and ensure you have selected the control containing *C0001*.

h. Select the **Customer Name field** (which should be *McAfee, Rand, & Karahalis*). Change the font size to **16**.

   The customer name appears in a larger font, setting it apart from the other fields.

i. Save and close the form.

j. Right-click the **Customers table** in the Navigation Pane and click **Design View**.

   You will add the HomePage field to the Customers table.

k. Click the **Address1 field** and click **Insert Rows** in the Tools group.

   A new row is inserted above the Address1 field.

l. Type **HomePage** in the blank **Field Name box** and choose **Hyperlink** as the Data Type.

m. Save and close the Customers table.

n. Right-click the **Customer Information form** in the Navigation Pane and click **Layout View**.

   You will add the HomePage field to the Customer Information form.

o. Click **Add Existing Fields** in the Tools group on the DESIGN tab to display the Field List pane (if necessary).

p. Click the **HomePage field**. Drag the field from the Field List pane to the form, below the E-mail Address field, until a shaded line displays between *E-mail Address* and *Address1*, and release the mouse. Close the Field List pane.

   Access shows a shaded line to help you place the field in the correct location.

> **TROUBLESHOOTING:** If the placement of this field does not look correct, you can use the Undo button and try again.

q. Switch to Form view. Press **Tab** until you reach the HomePage field and type www.mrk.com into the field. Save and close the form.

r. Click the **Revenue query** in the Navigation Pane. Click **Form** in the Forms group on the CREATE tab to create a new form based on this query.

s. Display the form in Design view. Select all text box field controls (from *Last Name* down to *Revenue*) by clicking on the first field (Last Name), holding down **CTRL** on your keyboard, and clicking on each of the other controls. Click **Remove Layout** in the Table group on the ARRANGE tab. Switch to Layout view.

> **TROUBLESHOOTING:** Recall the Remove Layout option only appears in Design view, so if you do not see the option, ensure you are in Design view.

t. Resize the controls individually so they are approximately the same size as shown in Figure 4.18.

u. Click the **Price control**. Hold down **CTRL** and click the **Revenue control**, the **Price label**, and the **Revenue label**. Drag the fields to the locations shown in Figure 4.18. Switch to Form view.

Step t: Fields resized

Step u: Price and Revenue fields moved

FIGURE 4.18 Final Version of Revenue by Order Item Form

v. Save the form as **Revenue by Order Item**. Close the form.

STEP 4 ≫ USE A CONTROL LAYOUT AND SORT RECORDS IN A FORM

Ryung tested the Customer Information form and likes the way it is working. She asks you to change the sorting to make it easier to find customers with a similar customer name. She also has an old form that she hopes you can make easier to read but keep in the vertical format.

a. Open the Sales Reps form in Layout view. Notice the form is not laid out well.

b. Click **Select All** in the Selection group on the FORMAT tab.

All 14 controls are outlined.

c. Click **Tabular** in the Table group on the ARRANGE tab.

The controls are lined up horizontally.

d. Click **Stacked** in the Table group on the ARRANGE tab. Switch to Form view.

Ryung wanted the form laid out vertically. The controls are lined up vertically and are much easier to read.

e. Save and close the form.

f. Open the Customer Information form in Form view. Click **Next record** in the Navigation bar at the bottom several times to advance through the records.

Take note that the customers are in Customer ID order.

g. Click **First record** in the Navigation bar to return to customer *McAfee, Rand, & Karahalis*.

h. Click the **Customer Name field** and click **Ascending** in the Sort & Filter group on the HOME tab.

Advantage Sales displays, as they are the first customer name in alphabetical order.

i. Click **Next record** in the Navigation bar at the bottom to advance through the records.

The records are in Customer Name order.

j. Save and close the Customer Information form.

k. Keep the database open if you plan to continue with the next Hands-On Exercise. If not, close the database and exit Access.

Report Basics

By now, you know how to plan a database, create a table, establish relationships between tables, enter data into tables, and extract data using queries. You generated output by printing table and query datasheets. You also learned how to create several types of data-entry forms. These forms can also be used for inquiries about the data in a database. In this section, you will learn how to create professional reports using the report-writing tools in Access.

A *report* is a document that displays information from a database in a format that outputs meaningful information to its readers. Access reports can be printed, viewed on screen, or even saved as a file. Much like a report you might do for a class, Access does research (gets information from the tables or queries) and organizes and presents it in a meaningful way (the final report, formatted for on-screen viewing or for printing). Reports are unable to change data in your database; a report is designed for output of information only, whether to the screen, to the printer, or to a file.

The following are all examples of reports that might be created in Access:

1. A telephone directory sorted by last name
2. A customer list grouped by sales rep
3. An employee list sorted by most years of service
4. A financial statement
5. A bill or invoice
6. A bar chart showing sales over the past 12 months
7. A shipping label
8. A letter to customers reminding them about a past due payment

Although you can print information from forms, information printed may not be easily understood or economical in terms of paper use. Most of the printed documents generated by Access will come from reports. Reports can be enhanced to help the reader understand and analyze the data. For example, if you print the Datasheet view from the Customers table, you will be able to locate the key information about each customer. However, using report tools, you can group the customers by sales rep and highlight the customers who have not placed an order in six months. This is an example of converting a list of customers into an effective business tool. To increase business, the sales reps could contact their customers who have not ordered in six months and review the findings with the sales manager. A sales report could be run each month to see if the strategy has helped produce any new business.

In this section, you will create reports in Access by first identifying a record source, then sketching the report, and finally choosing a Report tool. You will learn how to modify a report by adding and deleting fields, resizing columns, and adding a color scheme. You will also learn about the report sections, the report views, and controls on reports. After having worked through forms in the earlier section on forms, you will discover that there are many similarities between forms and reports.

Creating Reports Using Report Tools

Access provides five different report tools for creating reports. The report tools are found on the Create tab, in the Reports group, as shown in Figure 4.19. Click one of these tools and Access will base the report using the table or query that is currently selected. The most common of the tools, the *Report tool*, is used to instantly create a tabular report based on the table or query currently selected. The Report Design tool is used to create a new blank report in Design view. This tool is used by advanced users who want to create a blank report with no help from Access. The Blank Report tool is used to create a new blank report so that you can insert fields and controls manually and design the report. The Report Wizard tool will ask a series of questions and help you create a report based on your answers. The Labels tool is used to create a page of labels using one of the preformatted templates provided by Access. Table 4.1 provides a summary of the five report tools and their usage.

Report Wizard
Labels tool
Report group

FIGURE 4.19 Create Tab
Reports Group

After you create a report using one of the report tools, you can perform modifications in Layout view or Design view.

TABLE 4.1 Report Tools and Their Usage	
Report Tool	**Usage**
Report	Create a tabular report showing all of the fields in the record source.
Report Design	Create a new blank report in Design view. Add fields and controls manually.
Blank Report	Create a new blank report in Layout view. Add fields and controls manually.
Report Wizard	Answer a series of questions and Access will design a custom report for you.
Labels	Choose a preformatted label template and create a sheet of labels.

Before you create a report in Access, you should ask these questions:

- What is the purpose of the report?
- Who will use the report?
- Which tables are needed for the report?
- What information needs to be included?
- How will the report be distributed? Will users pull the information directly from Access, or will they receive it through e-mail, fax, or the Internet?
- Will the results be converted to Word, Excel, HTML, or another format?

In the *Forms* section of this chapter, you learned that it is helpful to talk to users and sketch an Access form before you launch Access. The same holds true for creating an Access report. Users can give you solid feedback, and creating a sketch will help you determine which report tool to use to create the report.

The first step in planning your report is to identify the record source. You may use one or more tables, queries, or a combination of tables and queries as the report's record source. Sometimes, a single table contains all of the records you need for the report. Other times, you will need to incorporate several tables. When multiple tables are needed to create a report, you can add all the necessary tables into a single query and then base the report on that query. (As stated earlier, multiple tables in a query must be related, as indicated with join lines. Tables with no join lines usually indicate an incorrect record source.)

Reports can also contain graphics as well as text and numeric data. For example, you can add a company logo. After you identify the record source, you also need to specify which graphic images are needed (and the location of the images).

Use the Report Tool

STEP 1 ❯❯ After you sketch the report, you can decide which report tool is appropriate to produce the desired report. Access provides several tools that you can use to create a report (refer to Figure 4.20). Which one you select depends on the layout of the report, the record source, and the complexity of the report design.

The easiest way to create a report is with the Report tool. The Report tool is used to instantly create a tabular report based on the table or query currently selected. To create a report using the Report tool, do the following:

1. Select a table or query in the Navigation Pane.
2. Click the CREATE tab and click Report in the Reports group. Access creates a tabular layout report instantly. Notice, this type of report displays data horizontally across the page in a landscape view, as shown in Figure 4.20.

FIGURE 4.20 Tabular Report

If you prefer, you can display a report using a stacked layout, which displays fields in a vertical column. This type of report is less common, as it would result in longer printouts. The number of records on one page depends on the number of records in the record source. You can also force a new page at the start of each record.

Use the Report Wizard to Create a Basic Report

You can also create a professional report with the Report Wizard. The **Report Wizard** asks you questions and then uses your answers to generate a customized report. The wizard uses six dialog boxes to collect information about your report. After thinking through the structure, the layout, and the record source, you are ready to launch the Report Wizard.

1. Select the report's record source in the Navigation Pane and click Report Wizard in the Reports group on the CREATE tab.

   The wizard opens with the table or query (the record source) displayed in the first dialog box. Although you chose the record source before you started, the first dialog box enables you to select fields from additional tables or queries.

2. Choose the fields you want to include in the report. Click the Tables/Queries drop-down list to display a list of available tables or queries. As with the query wizard you used in a previous chapter, you can click > to choose a single field, >> to choose all fields, < to remove a field, and << to remove all fields from the report. See Figure 4.21. Set the desired fields and click Next.

FIGURE 4.21 Selecting Fields for a Report

3. The next dialog box, shown in Figure 4.22, asks, "Do you want to add any grouping levels?" As you learned in a previous chapter, grouping lets you organize and summarize your data, based on values in a field. For a basic report, you will not select any grouping fields and instead just click Next.

FIGURE 4.22 Grouping Options

4. The next dialog box, shown in Figure 4.23, asks "What sort order do you want for your records?" For the sort options, specify which field you want to sort by first and optionally add a second, third, and fourth sort. For each field, choose ascending order and/or descending order. Click on the word Ascending and it will toggle to Descending; clicking again will switch back to Ascending. Set the desired sort options and click Next.

FIGURE 4.23 Sort Options for a Basic Report

5. The next dialog box will determine the report's appearance. You will be given the option to select Columnar, Tabular, or Justified as the layout.

- Columnar will display the information in a column. This leads to reports that are easier to read, but long printouts.
- Tabular will display the data in a table format. This is good for saving space, but it may be difficult to fit all fields on one printed page.
- Justified will display the information in a column as well. If you have Long Text fields, this is a good option to ensure all your data fits.

Tabular is the option you choose to fit the report on as few pages as possible. Clicking an option will give you a general preview in the preview area. You can also select the orientation for the report, either Portrait or Landscape (see Figure 4.24). Select an appropriate format for the report. Set the desired options and click Next.

FIGURE 4.24 Layout Options for a Basic Report

6. Decide on an appropriate name for the report. Type a descriptive report name so you can easily determine what information is in the report based on the title. This step, shown in Figure 4.25, is the last step in the Report Wizard. Name the report and click Finish.

Type name for report

FIGURE 4.25 Final Step of the Report Wizard

Now that you have stepped through the wizard, you will get a report incorporating all the options you chose, as shown in Figure 4.26. You may need to adjust the size of fields, as some may not be fully displayed.

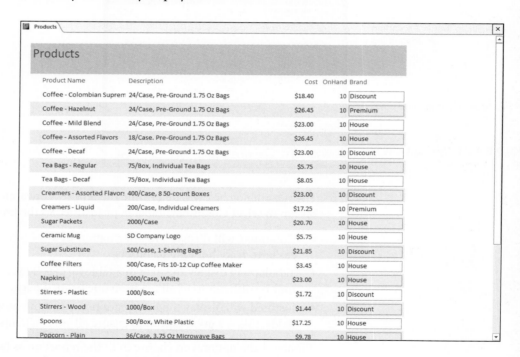

FIGURE 4.26 Results of Report Wizard

Use the Report Wizard with Grouping

In the previous example, we created a basic report using the Report Wizard. However, we can use grouping if we want to summarize our report by a certain field. We can also display overall totals and percentages based on a predefined format. The Report Wizard still has six dialog boxes when you add grouping, but two dialog boxes will change.

1. Select the report's record source in the Navigation Pane and click Report Wizard in the Reports group on the CREATE tab.
2. Choose the fields you want to appear in the report and click Next.
3. The next dialog box asks, "Do you want to add any grouping levels?" In the previous example, we just clicked Next. Here is where you add grouping. As we learned in a previous chapter, grouping lets you organize and summarize your data based on values in a field. Select the field you want to group by and click the > button to add the new

group. If you need a second or third grouping level, add those field names in order. The order in which you select the groups dictates the order of display in the report. Figure 4.27 shows the sort options for a grouped report. In this specific example, records are being grouped by the Brand. Once you have selected the appropriate options, click Next.

4. Because we have specified grouping, the next dialog box asks, "What sort order and summary information do you want for detail records?" Here, you can click Summary Options if you want to add aggregate functions (e.g., sum, average, minimum, and maximum) and to specify whether you want to see detail records on the report or only the aggregate results (see Figure 4.28). You can also choose to calculate percentages, so if you had one group that made up half your sales, you would see 50%. Click OK to return to the Report Wizard. The sort options are the same as before. Set the appropriate options and click Next.

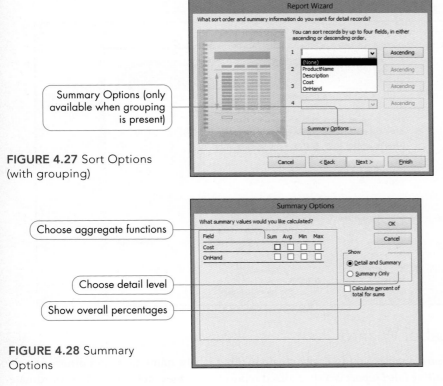

FIGURE 4.27 Sort Options (with grouping)

FIGURE 4.28 Summary Options

5. The next dialog box, shown in Figure 4.29, will determine the report's appearance. If you have selected grouping, you will be prompted to select the layout from three options:

- Stepped Layout will display column headings at the top of the page and keep the grouping field(s) in their own row.
- Block Layout will include the grouping field(s) inline with the data, saving some space when printing. It has one set of column headings at the top of each page.
- Outline Layout will display the grouping field(s) on their own separate rows and has column headings inside each group. This leads to a longer report when printing but may help make the report easier to read.

Clicking any of these layouts will give you a general preview in the preview area. The option to choose Portrait or Landscape is still available. Click Next.

FIGURE 4.29 Layout Options (with grouping)

Layout (options)

6. Decide on an appropriate name for the report. Type a descriptive report name. Click Finish. Your grouped report will resemble Figure 4.30.

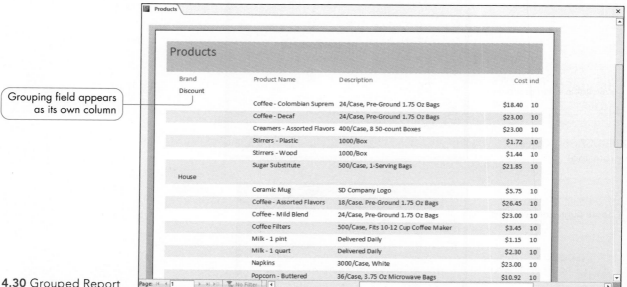

FIGURE 4.30 Grouped Report

Grouping field appears as its own column

Use the Label Wizard

The *Label Wizard* enables you to easily create mailing labels, name tags, and other specialized tags. A *mailing label report* is a specialized report that comes preformatted to coordinate with name-brand labels, such as Avery. Access includes most common labels built into the program. Even if you purchase a store brand from an office supply store, they will generally state the comparable Avery label number.

To use the Label Wizard, do the following:

1. Select the table or query that will serve as the record source for the report.
2. Click Labels in the Reports group on the CREATE tab.
3. Select the manufacturer, the product number, and the label type and click Next.
4. Choose the font type and size and click Next.
5. Add the fields to the label template, as shown in Figure 4.31. You will need to place the fields exactly as you wish them to appear, including adding a comma between City and State and pressing Enter after the CustomerName.
6. Add any sort fields and click Next.
7. Name the report and click Finish to generate your labels. The results are shown in Figure 4.32.

Select from Available fields

Label fields should be exactly as you want them to appear

FIGURE 4.31 Setting up Labels

FIGURE 4.32 Output of Label Wizard

Using Report Views

As you work with the report tools to create and modify reports, you will find the need to frequently switch between the four report views in Access—Layout view, Print Preview, Design view, and Report view. Most of your design work will be done in Layout view, but occasionally, you will need to switch to Design view to apply a more advanced feature, such as a calculated field. Users of the report will use Print Preview or Report view. There should be no reason for a user to switch to Layout view or Design view. Modifications to the report should be done by the designated report designer. To switch between the four views, click the View arrow in the Views group and select the desired view.

View a Report in Report View

Report view enables you to view a report onscreen in a continuous page layout. Report view is similar to Form view for forms. However, because the data shown in a report cannot be changed, it is simply a way of viewing the information without having to worry about accidentally moving a control. In addition, using report view allows quick access to filtering options.

Alter a Report in Layout View

Use Layout view to alter the report design while still viewing the data. You should use Layout view to add or delete fields in the report, modify field properties, change the column widths, sort, and filter data by excluding certain records. Although Layout view appears similar to Print

Preview, you will find sufficient variations between the two views, so that you will still always need to verify the report in Print Preview to evaluate all the changes made in Layout view.

Print or Save a Report in Print Preview

STEP 2 » *Print Preview* enables you to see exactly what the report will look like when it is printed. Most users prefer to use Print Preview prior to printing the report. This enables you to intercept errors in reports before you send the report to the printer. You cannot modify the design in this view; switch to Layout view or Design view to modify the design. To switch to Print Preview, you can click View and select Print Preview. By default, Print Preview will display all the pages in the report. Figure 4.33 shows an Access report in Print Preview.

Once you are in Print Preview, you have the option to save the report to a file as well. This is a useful option if you plan on distributing some of your information electronically but do not want to distribute the entire database. On the Print Preview tab in the Data group, you will find a number of different data types. See Figure 4.33. Simply choose the type of file you wish to create, and choose the directory and file name.

FIGURE 4.33 Data Group on Print Preview Tab

Commonly used formats include Excel, Word, or Portable Document Format (PDF). *Portable Document Format (PDF)* is a file type that was created for exchanging documents independent of software applications and operating system environment. In other words, you can e-mail files in this format to users running Mac operating system or a Linux operating system, and they can open it, even if they do not have Microsoft Office. Acrobat files often open in a program called Adobe Reader, a free tool that displays PDF files.

Because databases contain a great deal of information, Access reports may become very long, requiring many pages to print. Experienced Access users always use Print Preview prior to printing their reports. Some reports may require hundreds of pages to print. Other reports may be formatted incorrectly, and a blank page may print after each page of information. It would be better to correct this problem prior to sending it to the printer.

Modifying a Report

After a report is generated by one of the report tools, you may need to modify it. Similar to forms, the common changes to a report are add a field, remove a field, change the order of fields, change the width of a field, and modify the title. Much like a form, the Report has many options you can use to format a report. Once you are in Layout or Design view, you will have access to the report layout tools. You have four tabs available:

- Design: Use this tab to make changes to the design of the report, such as adding sorting, changing themes, and inserting additional controls.
- Arrange: Use this tab to change the layout of a report, to move fields up and down, to insert a space above or below your current position, or to insert a space to the left or the right of the current field.
- Format: Use this tab to change the font; add or remove bolding, italics, or underlining; change font size; change font color or background; adjust text alignment; or add a background image.
- Page Setup: Use this tab to change paper size, margins, page orientation, or to add columns.

Modify a Report Using the Arrange Tab

The Arrange tab displays in both Layout view and Design view. To use these commands, first open a report in Layout view or Design view and click the Format tab. Next, select a field or fields and click the appropriate command. Some key commands are highlighted in Figure 4.34.

FIGURE 4.34 Arrange Tab

The Table group contains commands that enable you to add gridlines to a report's layout, to change a report's layout from stacked to tabular (and vice versa), or to remove a report's layout. The Remove Layout command is available in Design view only. For example, if a report was created with a tabular layout, you could change it to a stacked layout by doing the following:

STEP 3
1. Open the report in Layout view.
2. Click the ARRANGE tab.
3. Click on any text box in the *Detail* section.
4. Click Select Layout in the Rows & Columns group.
5. Click Stacked in the Table group.

The Rows & Columns group contains commands that enable you to insert rows and columns inside a report's layout. For example, in a report with a stacked layout, you may want to separate the first three fields from the rest of the fields. To do this, you could select the third text box and click Insert Below. This will create a space after the third field. This group also contains the Select Layout, Select Column, and Select Row commands.

The Merge/Split group contains commands that enable you to merge and split the cells on a report. There are times when you may want to deviate from the basic row and column formats that the Access Report Wizards create. In this case, you can change the layout of the report using the merge cells and split cell commands. These commands do not change the actual controls, only the layout of the controls.

The Move group contains two commands that enable you to move a field up or down in a stacked layout. For example, if you want to move the second field in a stacked layout to the first position, select the second field's text box and label, and then click Move Up in the Move group. Moving fields up or down in a report may cause unexpected results; you can always use the undo command if you need to revert back to the beginning.

The Position group contains commands that enable you to modify the margins and the padding of controls in a report. This group also contains the Anchoring command, which enables you to change where the report's controls appear on the screen. By default, reports are anchored at the top left; however, you can change this to any of the nine options using the anchoring command.

Modify Report Controls using the Format Tab

The Format tab contains a series of commands that enable you change the font, display, and alignment of the controls on a report, as shown in Figure 4.35. This is useful if you need to quickly change the look of one cell. For example, you may have an important field you want to emphasize. To do so, do the following:

1. Switch to Layout view (or Design view).
2. Select the field you wish to format.
3. Click the FORMAT tab.
4. Change the format as desired. You can format the text as you would in Microsoft Word.

FIGURE 4.35 Format Tab

TIP **Apply a Background Image to a Report**

To apply a Background Image to a report, open the report in Layout view (or Design view), click the Format tab, and then click Background Image in the Background group. Next, click Browse to locate the image you want to apply to the report. Once the image has been applied to the report, you can change the properties of the image so that the image is anchored and sized correctly.

Add a Field to a Report

Adding a field to a report with a tabular layout is similar to adding a field to a form with a tabular layout. To add a field to a report, do the following:

1. Switch to Layout view.
2. On the DESIGN tab, in the Tools group, click Add Existing Fields to reveal the available fields in the report's record source. The Field List pane will display on the right-hand side of your screen.
3. For a single-table report, you will be presented with a list of fields. For a multiple-table report, you will first need to click the + (plus) next to the appropriate table to locate the desired field.
4. Drag the new field to a precise location on the report, using the vertical shaded line as a guide for the position of the new field, and release the mouse. The other fields will automatically adjust to make room for the new field.

The process of adding a field to a report with a stacked layout is the same as a tabular layout. The only difference is the shaded line will appear horizontally.

Delete a Field from a Report

To delete a field from the *Detail* section of a tabular report, do the following:

1. Switch to the Layout view (or Design view) of the report.
2. Click the text box of the field to be deleted. Click Select Column in the Rows & Columns group on the ARRANGE tab. Note the shaded border appears around the field and the label for the field.
3. With the shaded border visible, press Delete on your keyboard. The field disappears and the other fields fill in the gap.

Adjust Column Widths in a Report

You can adjust the width of each column in a tabular report individually so that each column is wide enough to accommodate the widest value. For example, if a report contains first name, last name, address and city, and email address, you will need to make sure the longest value in each field is completely visible. Scroll through the records to make sure this is the case.

To modify column widths in a tabular report, do the following:

1. Switch to the Layout view (or Design view) of the report.
2. Click the text box of the field you want to adjust. The field will have a shaded border around it, indicating it is selected.
3. Move the mouse to the right border of the selected field; when the mouse pointer turns to a double arrow, drag the edge to the right (to increase) or the left (to decrease) until you arrive at the desired width.

Changing Margins and Orientation

Sometimes, you may wish to print a page in Landscape or adjust the margins rather than adjusting widths. You will notice the Page Setup tab has these options. In the Page Size group, you can change the margins, and in the Page Layout group, you can choose Portrait or Landscape. See Figure 4.36 for locations of commonly used tools on this tab.

FIGURE 4.36 Report Layout Tools Page Setup Tab

Add a Theme to the Report

You can enhance the report's appearance by applying one of the themes provided by Access. To apply a theme, do the following:

1. Switch to Layout view (or Design view).
2. Click Themes in the Themes group on the DESIGN tab. Scroll through the themes until you find a theme you like; hover over one of the options to see a quick preview of the current report using the current theme. (This is easier to preview in Layout view.)
3. Right-click a theme and select *Apply Theme to This Object Only*. You can also apply the theme to all objects.

Work with a Report Layout Control

Whenever you use one of the report tools to create a new report, Access will add a layout control to help align the fields. Layout controls in reports work the same as layout controls in forms. As discussed earlier in this chapter, the layout control provides guides to help keep controls aligned horizontally and vertically and give your report a uniform appearance.

There are times when you may want to remove the layout control from a report in order to position the fields without aligning them to each other. If you want to remove the layout control from a report, do the following:

1. Switch to Design view (this is not available in Layout view).
2. Click anywhere inside the layout control you want to remove.
3. Click Select Layout in the Rows & Columns group on the ARRANGE tab.
4. In the Table group, click Remove Layout and the layout control is gone. All of the controls are still on the report, but the rectangle binding them together is gone.

You can add a layout control to a report by first selecting all the controls you want to keep together. Then, click Stacked or Tabular in the Table group and the layout control appears.

Sorting Records in a Report

When a report is created using the Report tool, the sort order of the records in the report is initially dependent on the sort order of the record source—similar to the way records are sorted in a form. The primary key of the record source usually dictates the sort order. However, a report has an additional feature for sorting. While in Layout view or Design view, click Group & Sort in the Grouping & Totals group on the Design tab. The Group, Sort, and Total pane displays at the bottom of the report. This section enables you to set the sort order for the report and override the sorting in the report's record source. Note that if you did not use the Report Wizard, this is how you would add grouping and totals to a report.

Sorting is important because sorting by a primary key may not be intuitive. For example, sorting by a field like LastName might be a better choice than a primary key so users see the records are in alphabetical order by LastName.

Change the Sorting in a Report

STEP 4 ≫ If you want to change the sorting in the report, do the following:

1. Switch to Layout view.
2. On the DESIGN tab, in the Grouping & Totals group, click Group & Sort to display the *Group, Sort, and Total* section, as shown in Figure 4.37. This will appear at the bottom of the report.

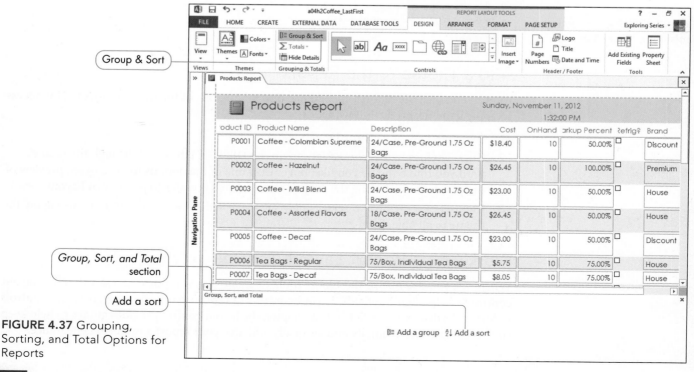

FIGURE 4.37 Grouping, Sorting, and Total Options for Reports

3. Click *Add a sort* and select the field you wish to sort by, which you can change as shown in Figure 4.38. The default sort order is ascending.

Select sort field

FIGURE 4.38 Adding a Sort to a Report

4. If you wish to add a second sort, click *Add a Sort* again. For example, you could sort first by Brand and then by ProductName, as shown in Figure 4.39.

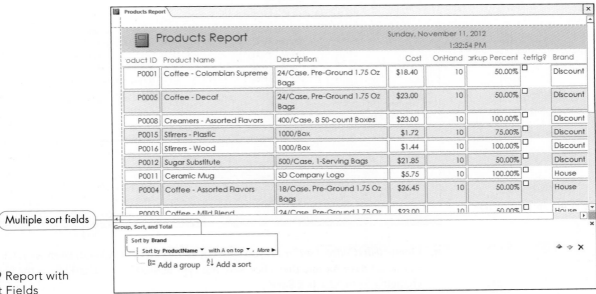

Multiple sort fields

FIGURE 4.39 Report with Multiple Sort Fields

Quick **Concepts**

1. Compare controls in forms and controls in reports. **pp. 266, 288**

2. What are the benefits of using the report wizard? **p. 280**

3. What is the difference between Print Preview and Report view? **pp. 285–286**

4. What are the benefits of a report layout control when modifying a report? **pp. 289–290**

5. Why is sorting the records in a report important? **p. 290**

Watch the Video for this Hands-On Exercise!

MyITLab®
HOE2 Training

2 Report Basics

You create a Products report using the Access Report tool to help Ryung stay on top of the key data for her business. After Access creates the report, you modify the column widths so the entire report fits on one page (portrait or landscape, depending on the report). You also use the Report Wizard tool to create other reports for Ryung.

Skills covered: Create Reports Using Report Tools • Use Report Views • Modify a Report • Sort Records in a Report

STEP 1 ≫ CREATING REPORTS USING REPORT TOOLS

You use the Report tool to create an Access report to help Ryung manage her product information. This report is especially useful for determining which products she needs to order to fill upcoming orders. Refer to Figure 4.40 as you complete Step 1.

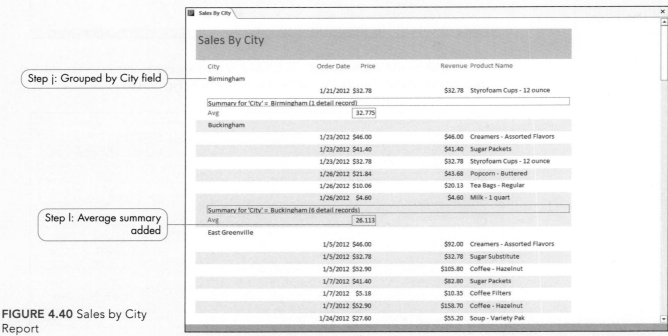

FIGURE 4.40 Sales by City Report

a. Open *a04h1Coffee_LastFirst* if you closed it at the end of Hands-On Exercise 1. Click the **FILE tab**, select **Save As**, and then click **Save As**. Type **a04h2Coffee_LastFirst** as the file name, changing *h1* to *h2*. Click **Save**.

b. Select the **Products table** in the Navigation Pane. Click the **CREATE tab** and click **Report** in the Reports group.

Access creates a new tabular layout report based on the Products table. The report opens in Layout view ready to edit.

c. Click the **Products title** at the top of the report to select it, click again on **Products**, and then change the title to **Products Report**. Press **Enter** to accept the change.

d. Right-click the **Products report tab** and select **Print Preview**.

The report is too wide for the page; you will exit Print Preview and change the orientation to Landscape.

e. Click **Close Print Preview**.

   f. Click the **PAGE SETUP tab** and click **Landscape** in the Page Layout group.

   The report changes to Landscape orientation. Most of the columns now fit onto one page. You will make further revisions to the report later on so that it fits on one page.

   g. Save the report as **Products Report**. Close the report.

   h. Select the **Revenue query** in the Navigation Pane. Click the **CREATE tab** and click **Report Wizard** in the Reports group.

   The Report Wizard launches.

   i. Click the **City field** and click the **> button** to add the City field to the report. Repeat the same process for the **OrderDate, Price, Revenue,** and **ProductName fields**. Click **Next**.

   j. Select **City** and click the **> button** to add grouping by city. Click **Next**.

   k. Select **OrderDate** for the sort order and leave the order as **Ascending**. Click **Summary Options**.

   l. Click the **Avg check box** on the Price row to summarize the Price field. Click **OK**.

   m. Click **Next**. Click **Next** again to accept the default layout.

   n. Type **Sales by City** for the title of the report. Click **Finish**.

   The report is displayed in Print Preview mode. Some of the data values and labels cannot be seen. Next, you will adjust the controls.

   o. Click **Close Print Preview**.

   p. Switch to Layout view if necessary and adjust the controls so all the field values are visible as shown in Figure 4.40.

   q. Display the report in Print Preview to verify your changes.

   r. Save and close the report.

STEP 2 ≫ USING REPORT VIEWS

The Products report you created for La Vida Mocha looks very good, according to Ryung. However, she does not have Access at home and would like to have a copy of the report saved so she can bring it home. You will save a copy of the report for her.

   a. Open the **Products Report** and switch to **Print Preview**. Click **PDF or XPS** in the Data group on the PRINT PREVIEW tab. Enter the file name **a04h2Products_LastFirst** and click **Publish**.

   Windows will open the report in your system's default PDF viewer, which may be Adobe Reader or the Windows 8.1.1 Reader app.

   b. Switch back to Access, if necessary. Click **Close** when asked if you want to save the export steps.

   c. Click **Close Print Preview** and close the report.

STEP 3 ≫ MODIFYING A REPORT

Ryung realized the Products table is missing a field. She would like you to add this to the table and update the report to reflect the new field. She would also like to make sure the report fits nicely onto one landscape page. She has also asked you to show her some sample color schemes.

   a. Right-click the **Products table** and select **Design view**.

   You need to add the OnHand field to the Products table.

   b. Click the **MarkupPercent field** and click **Insert Rows** in the Tools group on the DESIGN tab.

   A new blank row displays above the MarkupPercent field.

   c. Type **OnHand** in the **Field Name box** and select **Number** as the Data Type.

d. Save the table. Click **View** to change to Datasheet view.

The new OnHand column appears empty in each row. Next, you will add sample data to the new field.

e. Fill in the number **10** for each item's OnHand field.

f. Close the Products table.

g. Right-click the **Products Report** and select **Layout view**.

h. Click **Add Existing Fields** in the Tools group on the DESIGN tab unless the Field List already appears on the right of your screen.

i. Drag the **OnHand field** from the Field List pane between the Cost and MarkupPercent fields. Close the Field List pane.

Because of the tabular layout control, Access adjusts all the columns to make room for the new OnHand field.

j. Display the report in Print Preview.

The report is still too wide for a single page.

k. Click **Close Print Preview**. Switch to Layout view if necessary.

l. Click anywhere on the **Year Introduced column**. Click the **ARRANGE tab** and click **Select Column** in the Rows & Columns group. Press **Delete** to remove the column.

The Year Introduced column is removed from the report and the other fields fill the empty space.

> **TROUBLESHOOTING:** If you cannot see the Year Introduced column, try scrolling to the right.

m. Click the **ProductID column heading** and drag the right border to the left until the Product ID heading still fits, but any extra white space is removed.

n. Click the **Refrigeration Needed column heading** and rename the column **Refrig?**. Adjust the column width of the Refrig? column so any extra white space is removed.

o. Click **Themes** in the Themes group on the DESIGN tab.

The available predefined themes display.

p. Right-click the **Organic theme** and choose **Apply Theme to This Object Only**. Display the report in Print Preview.

Access reformats the report using the Organic theme.

> **TROUBLESHOOTING:** If you cannot figure out which theme is which, you can hover the mouse over each theme and a ScreenTip will display the theme name.

q. Click **Close Print Preview**. Click the **FILE tab**, select **Save As**, select **Save Object As**, and then click **Save As**. Type **Products Organic** as the report name and click **OK**.

You saved the report with one theme. Now, you will apply a second theme to the report and save it with a different name.

r. Switch to Layout view and click **Themes** in the Themes group to apply a different theme.

s. Right-click the **Retrospect theme** and choose **Apply Theme to This Object Only**. Display the report in Print Preview.

If we do not tell Access to apply the theme to this object only, all objects will change.

t. Click **Close Print Preview**. Click the **FILE tab**, select **Save As**, select **Save Object As**, and then click **Save As**. Type **Products Retrospect** as the report name and click **OK**. Close the report.

You will be able to show Ryung two different themes.

STEP 4 ≫ SORTING RECORDS IN A REPORT

Ryung would like the Products Report report to be sorted by Product Name order (rather than ProductID order). You change the sort order and preview again to see the results.

a. Open **Products Report** in Layout view.

> **TROUBLESHOOTING:** If you cannot see the Products Report, click the Shutter Bar to maximize the Navigation Pane.

b. Click **Group & Sort** in the Grouping & Totals group on the DESIGN tab.

The *Add a group* and *Add a sort* options appear at the bottom of the report.

> **TROUBLESHOOTING:** If the options do not appear, they may have been showing. Try clicking Group & Sort again.

c. Click **Add a sort**.

A new Sort bar displays at the bottom of the report.

d. Select **Brand** from the list.

The report is now sorted by Brand in Ascending order (with Discount on top).

e. Click **Add a group**.

f. Select **Brand** from the list.

The report is now grouped by Brand.

g. Display the report in Print Preview.

h. Close Print Preview and save and close the report.

i. Close the database. Submit the database and the PDF file *a04h2Products_LastFirst* based on your instructor's directions.

Chapter Objectives Review

After reading this chapter, you have accomplished the following objectives:

1. **Create forms using form tools.**
   - A form is used to add data to or edit data in a table.
   - Access provides 14 different tools for creating forms.
   - If you use a form, you are less likely to edit the wrong record.
   - Forms can show data from multiple tables at once.
   - Forms can be customized to match a paper form.
   - Identify a record source: A record source is the table or query that supplies the records.
   - Use the Form tool: The Form tool creates a basic form.
   - Understand controls: Controls are the text boxes, buttons, boxes, and other tools you use to add, edit, and display data in a form or report.
   - Work with form views: Form view is a simplified interface used for data entry, but it allows no changes. Layout view allows users to make changes to the layout while viewing the data on the form. Design view allows you to change advanced design settings you cannot see in the Layout view.
   - Work with a subform: A subform displays data from a related table for each record in the main table.

2. **Create a split form: A split form combines two views of the same record source—one section is displayed in a stacked layout and the other section is displayed in a tabular layout.**
   - Create a multiple-item form: This form displays multiple records in a tabular layout similar to a table's Datasheet view, with more customization options.
   - Create forms using the other form tools: A Datasheet form is a replica of a table or query's Datasheet view except that it still retains some of the form properties. The Form Design tool and the Blank Form tools can be used to create a form manually. The Navigation option in the Forms group enables you to create user interface forms that have the look and feel of a Web-based form and enable users to open and close the objects of a database. The Modal Dialog Form tool can be used to create a dialog box.

3. **Use form views.**
   - Edit data in Form view: Most users will work in Form view. This allows changes to data but not to design elements.
   - Alter a form in Layout view: Layout view allows you to change the design of a form while viewing data.
   - Add a field to a form: Fields can be added to an existing form using the Field List.
   - Delete a field from a form: Fields can be removed, but you may need to select the entire control to avoid leaving empty space in the form.
   - Adjust column widths in a form: Column widths often need to be adjusted. Numeric fields may show up as #### if the value cannot be displayed in the box.
   - Use the Form Layout tools tabs: There are three Form Layout tabs that allow you to manipulate the design of a form.

   - Modify form controls using the Format tab: The Format tab allows changes to the font, including bold, italic, underlining, font size, font color, font background, and alignment.
   - Select controls: Controls can be selected manually or by using the Arrange tab.
   - Add a theme to a form: Themes can be applied to a single form or to all objects in the database.
   - Add styling to a form: Forms can have many types of styles applied. Take care to avoid too many styles on a single form, as it can distract from the form.

4. **Work with a form layout control.**
   - Modify a form using the Arrange tab: The Arrange tab appears in both Layout view and Design view and allows you to change form layout, field order, and spacing options.
   - The Table group lets you add gridlines, change from stacked to tabular layout (and vice versa), or remove a form's layout.
   - The Move group contains lets you move fields.
   - The Position group lets you modify the margins and the padding of controls in a form.

5. **Sort records in form.**
   - Default sort order is the sort order of the data source (table, query, etc.).
   - Sort by a single field: Forms can be sorted by a single field in either ascending or descending order.
   - Remove sorting in a form: Sorts can be removed from a form at any point.

6. **Create reports using report tools.**
   - A report is a document that displays information from a database in a format that outputs meaningful information to its readers.
   - Access reports can be printed, viewed on screen, or saved as files.
   - Reports cannot change data in your database.
   - Use the Report tool: Access has five report tools: The Report tool instantly creates a tabular report based on the table or query currently selected. The Report Design tool creates a new blank report in Design view. The Blank Report tool creates a new blank report so that you can insert fields and controls manually and design the report. The Report Wizard tool helps you create a report. The Labels tool creates a page of mailing labels using a template.
   - Use the Report Wizard to create a report: The Report Wizard will guide you step by step through creating a report, asking questions and generating output.
   - Use the Report Wizard with grouping: The Report Wizard options will change when you add grouping. It will also allow summary options such as creating a sum of a field for each grouping level.
   - Use the Label Wizard: The Label Wizard can produce printable labels. Access includes predefined standard formats for common labels.

7. **Use report views.**
   - View a report in Report view: Report view is ideal for viewing data onscreen. Neither data nor design can be changed.
   - Alter a report in Layout view: Layout view allows you to change the design of a report while viewing data.
   - Print or save a report in Print Preview: Print Preview shows the way the report will display when printed. It also allows you to save the report as a file in a number of formats.

8. **Modify a report.**
   - Modify a report using the Design tab: The Design tab allows you to add or change sorting, change report theme, and insert additional controls.
   - Modify a report using the Arrange tab: The Arrange tab allows you to change the report layout, move fields, and insert spaces.
   - Modify report controls using the Format tab: The Format tab allows changes to the font, including bold, italic, underlining, font size, font color, font background, and alignment.
   - Add a field to a report: Fields can be added to an existing report using the Field List.

- Delete a field from a report: Fields can be removed, but you may need to select the entire control to avoid leaving empty space in the report.
- Adjust column widths in a report: Column widths often need to be adjusted. Numeric fields may show up as #### if the value cannot be displayed in the box.
- Change margins and orientation: You can display the report in portrait or landscape format and increase or decrease margin size.
- Add a theme to the report: Themes can be applied to a single report or to all objects in the database.
- Work with a Report Layout control: The Layout control keeps the fields neatly spaced, making it harder to place fields in an exact location but keeping a standard format.

9. **Sort records in a report.**
   - Default sort order for reports is the sort order of the record source.
   - Change the sorting in a report: Sorting can be done by a single or by multiple fields.

Match the key terms with their definitions. Write the key term letter by the appropriate numbered definition.

a. Controls
b. Design view
c. Form
d. Form tool
e. Form view
f. Label Wizard
g. Layout control
h. Layout view
i. Multiple Items form
j. Portable Document Format (PDF)

k. Print Preview
l. Record source
m. Report
n. Report tool
o. Report view
p. Report Wizard
q. Split form
r. Stacked layout
s. Tabular layout
t. Theme

1. _____ A database object that is used to add data into or edit data in a table. **p. 258**

2. _____ Used to create data entry forms for customers, employees, products, and other primary tables. **p. 258**

3. _____ The table or query that supplies the records for a form or report. **p. 259**

4. _____ Displays fields in a vertical column. **p. 260**

5. _____ Displays data horizontally. **p. 260**

6. _____ The text boxes, buttons, boxes, and other tools you use to add, edit, and display the data in a form or report. **p. 260**

7. _____ Provides guides to help keep controls aligned horizontally and vertically and give your form a uniform appearance. **p. 260**

8. _____ A simplified interface primarily used for data entry; does not allow you to make changes to the layout. **p. 260**

9. _____ Enables users to make changes to a layout while viewing the data on the form or report. **p. 261**

10. _____ Enables you to change advanced design settings you cannot see in the Layout view, such as a background image. **p. 261**

11. _____ Combines two views of the same record source—one section is displayed in a stacked layout and the other section is displayed in a tabular layout. **p. 262**

12. _____ Displays multiple records in a tabular layout similar to a table's Datasheet view, with more customization options. **p. 263**

13. _____ A defined set of colors, fonts, and graphics that can be applied to a form or report. **p. 267**

14. _____ A document that displays information from a database in a format that outputs meaningful information to its readers. **p. 278**

15. _____ Used to instantly create a tabular report based on the table or query currently selected. **p. 278**

16. _____ Asks you questions and then uses your answers to generate a customized report. **p. 280**

17. _____ Enables you to easily create mailing labels, name tags, and other specialized tags. **p. 284**

18. _____ Enables you to see what a printed report will look like in a continuous page layout. **p. 285**

19. _____ Enables you to see exactly what the report will look like when it is printed. **p. 286**

20. _____ A file type that was created for exchanging documents independent of software applications and operating system environment. **p. 286**

Multiple Choice

1. The table or query that supplies the records for a form or report is also known as the:

   (a) Control.
   (b) Record Source.
   (c) Theme.
   (d) Tabular Layout.

2. Which of the following statements is *false*?

   (a) Both forms and reports can use tabular and stacked layouts.
   (b) A stacked layout displays data in a vertical column.
   (c) A tabular layout displays data horizontally.
   (d) Stacked layouts are more common for reports because they will use less paper when printed.

3. Which of the following is *not* an example of a control?

   (a) A text box on a form
   (b) Buttons on a report
   (c) A report
   (d) A box on a report

4. The simplest interface you can use to modify control widths in a form is in:

   (a) Layout view.
   (b) Form view.
   (c) Design view.
   (d) Report view.

5. Which of the following views is the most powerful, but also the most complicated?

   (a) Design view.
   (b) Layout view.
   (c) Form view/Report view.
   (d) Print Preview.

6. Which of the following statements about reports are *false*?

   (a) Reports can be saved to a file on your computer.
   (b) Reports are primarily used to modify data.

   (c) Reports can produce output in a number of ways, including mailing labels.
   (d) Reports can be created simply using the Report tool.

7. Use the _____ to see exactly what the printed report will look like before printing.

   (a) Report tool
   (b) Report Wizard
   (c) Report view
   (d) Print Preview

8. If you have a client working on a Mac system, which of the following file formats would be the best choice to use to ensure the client can open it?

   (a) Microsoft Word
   (b) Microsoft Excel
   (c) Microsoft Access
   (d) Portable Document Format (PDF)

9. Which of the following statements is *false*?

   (a) Reports are generally used for printing, emailing, or viewing data on the screen.
   (b) Layout controls for forms and reports are the defined sets of colors, fonts, and graphics.
   (c) Forms are often used for inputting data.
   (d) Forms and reports both include controls, such as text boxes, that can be resized.

10. Which of the following statements is *false*?

    (a) You can use grouping to show a list of properties by state.
    (b) Sorting can be done on both forms and reports.
    (c) Sorting can be done in ascending or descending order.
    (d) You can either group or sort (but not both).

Practice Exercises

1 Financial Management

You are working as a customer service representative for a financial management firm. Your task is to contact a list of prospective customers and introduce yourself and the services of your company. You will create a form to help you view one customer at a time while also helping add and update the data. After creating the form, you will customize it and add sorting. You will also create a report to show you all the data on one screen, for viewing purposes. This exercise follows the same set of skills as used in Hands-On Exercises 1 and 2 in the chapter. Refer to Figure 4.41 as you complete this exercise.

Step d: Title changed to New Leads

Step g: NetWorth field moved above FirstName

Step f: Font size changed to 14 for NetWorth

Step j: Sort added; Farrah Aaron is the first record

FIGURE 4.41 Form After Moving Net Worth Control

a. Start Access and open **a04p1Prospects**. Save the database as **a04p1Prospects_LastFirst**.

b. Click the **Leads table**. Click the **CREATE tab** and click **Form** in the Forms group.

   A new form based on the Leads table displays in Layout view.

c. Click the **ID text box** and drag the right border of the first field to the left to shrink the column by approximately half of its original size.

   The other columns will shrink as well.

d. Change the title of the form to **New Leads**.

e. Click **Themes** in the Themes group of the DESIGN tab. Select the **Integral theme** (first row, third column).

f. Change the font size to **14** for the NetWorth text box control.

g. Click **Select Row** in the Rows & Columns group on the ARRANGE tab. Click **Move Up** in the Move group on the ARRANGE tab until *NetWorth* appears above *First*.

> **TROUBLESHOOTING:** If both items do not move together, undo, ensure both are selected, and then follow the instructions in step g.

   NetWorth should now appear above the FirstName. See Figure 4.41.

h. Save the form as **Leads Form**. Switch to Form view.

i. Navigate to record 63. Enter your first and last names in the appropriate fields. Leave the e-mail address blank.

j. Click in the **Last field** (if necessary) and click **Ascending** in the Sort & Filter group of the HOME tab Farrah Aaron should be the first record displayed unless your last name appears before hers alphabetically.

k. Save and close the form.

l. Click the **Leads table**. Click **Report** in the Reports group on the CREATE tab.

   A new report is created based on the Leads table.

m. Make fields as small as possible to remove extra white space. Do not try to fit the entire report all on one page, as you will be using this for on-screen viewing only.

n. Save the report as **Leads Report**. Close the report.

o. Exit Access. Submit the database based on your instructor's directions.

2 Comfort Insurance

The Human Resources department of the Comfort Insurance Agency has initiated its annual employee performance reviews. You will create a form for them to help organize input and a report showing employee salary increases and bonuses. The employee data, along with forms and reports, are stored in an Access database. You need to prepare a report showing employee raises and bonuses by city. This exercise follows the same set of skills as used in Hands-On Exercises 1 and 2 in this chapter. Refer to Figure 4.42 as you complete this exercise.

FIGURE 4.42 Final Employee Compensation Report

a. Open *a04p2Insurance*. Save the database as **a04p2Insurance_LastFirst**.

b. Select the **Locations table**. Click the **CREATE tab** and click **Form** in the Forms group.

   A new form based on the Locations table opens in Layout view.

c. Click the **LocationID text box** containing *L01*. Move the mouse to the right edge of the shaded border until the mouse pointer changes to a double-headed arrow. Drag the right edge to the left to reduce the size of the text box to approximately half of its original size.

The LocationID field and all the other fields should become smaller.

d. Click the subform at the bottom of the form. Press **Delete** to delete the subform.

e. Click **Themes** in the Themes group on the DESIGN tab. Right-click the **Wisp theme** (third row, first column) and select **Apply Theme to This Object Only**.

f. Save the form as **Locations**. Close the form.

g. Select the **Locations table**. Click the **CREATE tab** and click **Report** in the Reports group.

A new tabular layout report based on the Locations table opens in Layout view.

h. Click the **LocationID label** and drag the right border of the label to the left to reduce the size of the control to approximately half of its original size.

i. Repeat the sizing process with the **Zipcode label** and the **OfficePhone label**. Adjust the other columns if necessary until there are no controls on the right side of the vertical dashed line.

j. Display the report in Print Preview. Verify that the report is only one page wide. Save the report as **Locations** and close the report.

k. Select the **Employees Query**. Click the **CREATE tab** and click **Report Wizard** in the Reports group to launch the Report Wizard. Respond to the questions as follows:

- Click (≫) to add all the fields to the Selected Fields box. Click **Next**.
- Accept grouping by Location. Click **Next**.
- Select **LastName** for the first sort order and **FirstName** for the second. Click **Summary Options**.

TROUBLESHOOTING: If you do not see summary options, click Back and click Summary Options at the bottom of the dialog box.

- Click **Sum** for Salary, **Avg** for 2012Increase, and **Avg** for YearsWorked. Accept all other defaults. Click **OK**. Click **Next**.
- Accept the Stepped layout. Change Orientation to **Landscape**. Click **Next**.
- Type **Employee Compensation** for the title of the report. Click **Finish**.

The report is displayed in Print Preview mode. Some of the columns are too narrow. Next, you will adjust the columns.

l. Click **Close Print Preview**. Switch to Layout view.

m. Adjust the column widths so that all the data values are showing and the report appears on one page. Some of the columns will need to be reduced, and some will need to be widened.

n. Click **Themes** in the Themes group on the DESIGN tab. Right-click the **Slice theme** and choose **Apply Theme to This Object Only**.

o. Display the report in Print Preview. Close the Navigation Pane and verify that the report is still one page wide. Compare your report to Figure 4.42. Adjust column widths to display all values.

p. Save and close the Employee Compensation report. Close the database.

q. Exit Access. Submit based on your instructor's directions.

Mid-Level Exercises

1 Hotel Chain

ANALYSIS CASE

You are the general manager of a large hotel chain. You track revenue by categories, such as conference room rentals and weddings. You need to create a report that shows which locations are earning the most revenue in each category. You will also create a report to show you details of your three newest areas: St. Paul, St. Louis, and Seattle.

a. Open *a04m1Rewards*. Save the database as **a04m1Rewards_LastFirst**.

b. Select the **Members table** and create a Multiple Items form. Save the form as **Maintain Members**.

c. Modify the form in Layout view as follows:
   - Change the MemNumber label to **MemID** and reduce the MemNumber column width.
   - Adjust the column widths to eliminate extra white space.
   - Delete the form icon (the picture next to the title of the form) in the Form Header.

d. Change the sorting on the MemberSince control so that the members who joined most recently are displayed first.

DISCOVER

e. Click on the **LastName field**. Change the Control Padding to **Wide**. Hint: Search **Control Padding Wide** in Access Help.

   The controls have some extra space between them.

f. Save and close the form.

g. Select the **Revenue query** and create a report using the Report Wizard. Answer the wizard prompts as follows:
   - Include all fields.
   - Add grouping by City and by ServiceName.
   - Add a Sum to the Revenue field and check the **Summary Only option**.
   - Choose **Outline Layout**.
   - Name the report **Revenue by City and Service**.

h. Scroll through all the pages to check the layout of the report while in Print Preview mode.

i. Exit Print Preview. Switch to Layout view and delete the NumInParty and PerPersonCharge controls.

j. Change the font size, font color, and/or background color of the Sum control (not the Revenue control) so the control stands out from the other controls.

k. Change the font size, font color, and/or background color of the Grand Total control (found at the end of the report) so the control stands out as well.

l. Change the sort on the report, so that it sorts by city in descending order—that is, so that the last city alphabetically (St. Paul) is displayed first.

 m. Examine the data in the report to determine which city of St. Paul, St. Louis, and Seattle has the highest Sum of event revenue. You will use this information to modify a query.

 n. Modify the Totals by Service query so the criteria for the City field is the city you determined had the highest sum from St. Paul, St. Louis, or Seattle. Save and close the query.

o. Create a report using the Report tool based on the Totals by Service query. Name the report **Targeted City**.

p. Close the report. Close the database.

q. Exit Access. Submit based on your instructor's directions.

2 Benefit Auction

FROM SCRATCH

You are helping to organize a benefit auction to raise money for families who lost their homes in a natural disaster. The information for the auction is currently stored in an Excel spreadsheet, but you have volunteered to migrate this to Access. You will create a database that will store the data from Excel in an Access database. You will create a form to manage the data-entry process. You also need to create two reports: one that lists the items collected in each category and one for labels so you can send the donors a thank-you letter after the auction.

a. Open Access and create a new database named **a04m2Auction_LastFirst**. A new table appears with an ID column.

b. Switch to Design view. Type **Items** in the **Save As dialog box** and click **OK**.

c. Change the ID Field Name to **ItemID**. Type **Description** in the second row and press **Tab**. Accept **Short Text** as the Data Type. Type **50** in the **Field Size property** in Field Properties.

d. Type the remainder of the fields and adjust the data types as shown:

Field Name	Data Type
DateOfDonation	Date/Time
Category	Short Text
Price	Currency
DonorName	Short Text
DonorAddress1	Short Text
DonorAddress2	Short Text

e. Open Excel. Open the **a04m2_Items** file. Examine the length of the Category, DonorName, DonorAddress1, and DonorAddress2 columns. Determine how many characters are needed for each field, and round to the nearest 5. For example, if a field needs 23 characters, you would round up to 25. You will use this to change field sizes in the table.

f. Change the field size for the Category, DonorName, DonorAddress1, and DonorAddress2 to the sizes you chose in step e. Save the table.

g. Copy and paste the rows from the Excel file into the table. Resize the columns so all data is visible. Close the table.

> **TROUBLESHOOTING:** Recall that you must click the Record Selector (pencil icon, to the left of a blank row) to paste data.

> **TROUBLESHOOTING:** Once you have pasted the data, ensure your chosen field sizes did not cause you to lose data. If so, update the field size, delete the records you pasted in, and then repeat step g.

h. Verify that the Items table is selected. Create a new form using the Form tool.

i. Change the layout of the form to a **Tabular Layout**. Resize field widths to reduce extra space. It is acceptable for field values to appear on two lines.

j. Change the title of the form to **Items for Auction**.

DISCOVER

k. Add conditional formatting so that each Price that is greater than 90 has a text color of **Green**. Use the Green color in the first row of the options.

l. Save the form as **Auction Items Form**.

m. Switch to Form view. Create a new record with the following information. Note it will automatically assign an ItemID of 27 for you.

Description	DateOfDonation	Category	Price	DonorName	DonorAddress1	DonorAddress2
iPad	12/31/2016	House	$400	Staples	500 Market St	Brick, NJ 08723

n. Add a sort to the form, so the lowest priced items appear first. Close the form.

o. Select the **Items table** in the Navigation Pane and create a report using the Report Wizard. Include all fields except the donor address fields, group by Category, include the Sum of Price as a Summary Option, accept the default layout, and then save the report **Auction Items by Category**.

p. Switch to Layout view and adjust the controls so all data is visible. Preview the report to verify the column widths are correct.

q. Sort the report so the least expensive items are shown first. Save and close the report.

r. Create mailing labels based on the Avery 5660 template. Place the donor name on the first line, address on the second, and city, state, and ZIP on the third line. Sort the labels by DonorName. Name the report **Donor Labels**. After you create the labels, display them in Print Preview mode verify everything will fit onto the label template. Close the label report.

s. Exit Access. Submit the database based on your instructor's directions.

3 | Used Cell Phones for Sale

 COLLABORATION CASE

You and a few of your classmates started a new business selling used cell phones, MP3 players, and accessories. You have been using an Access database to track your inventory. You need to create several forms and reports to increase database efficiency and analysis. You have used Access forms and reports as part of your classwork, but you would like to experiment with them as they apply to you in a real-world scenario.

a. Choose one unique type of form and one unique type of report each. Based on your experience in class, you saw there were a number of different types of forms and reports that can be created. Choose one each from the following:

Forms: Form tool, Form Wizard, Multiple Items Form, Split Form

Reports: Report Tool, Report Wizard, Label Wizard

b. Open Access and open the *a04t1Phones* database individually. Save the file as **a04t1Phones_LastFirst**. Each of you will create your forms and reports in an individual database.

c. Create a form and a report based on the Inventory table, using the type of form and report you chose in step a, unless you chose Label Wizard. If you chose Label Wizard, you should create a report based on the Mailing List table, using Avery 8660 as your destination label.

d. Save the form and report as **LastFirst**, replacing Last and First with your last and first names.

e. Make the report as attractive and useful as possible. You may want to change sorting, add grouping (to reports), remove or add a layout control, change formatting options, and/or change the background color. Modify the form and report, save the changes, and exit Access.

f. Meet as a group. Open the *a04t1Phones* database and save the file as **a04t1Phones_GroupName**.

g. Import the form and report from each of your databases.

Your *a04t1Phones_GroupName* file will now have one form and one report for each student.

h. Examine the forms and reports each of you created.

i. Examine your results. Determine which forms and reports you would keep, if this were the real world. Rename the forms and reports you would keep as **Keep_LastFirst** and rename the ones you would discard as **Discard_LastFirst**. Do not delete the forms and reports you will not use.

j. Modify the forms and reports you plan to keep as a group, if necessary. Save the changes and close all forms and reports. Ensure each student has a copy of the final *a04t1Phones_GroupName* database.

k. Exit Access and submit both the *a04t1Phones_GroupName* and *a04t1Phones_LastFirst* databases based on your instructor's directions.

Beyond the Classroom

Create a Split Form

RESEARCH CASE

FROM SCRATCH

This chapter introduced you to Access forms, including the split form. It is possible to turn an existing form into a split form if you modify a few form properties. Perform an Internet search to find the steps to convert a form to a split form. First, create a new database and name the file **a04b2Split_LastFirst**. Next, import *only* the Books table and Books form from the *a04b2BooksImport* database. To import the objects, click the **External Data tab** and click **Access** in the Import & Link group. After the new objects have been imported, use the information from the Internet to convert the Books form into a split form. Make sure the datasheet is on the bottom half. Change the form so it sorts by Title in ascending order. Save the form as **Split Form Books**. Close Access. Submit the database based on your instructor's directions.

Properties by City

DISASTER RECOVERY

Munesh, a co-worker, is having difficulty with an Access report and asked you for your assistance. He was trying to fix the report and seems to have made things worse. Open the *a04b3Sales* database and save the file as **a04b3Sales_LastFirst**. In the new database, open Properties Report in Report View. Notice Munesh moved fields around and the report does not fit on one page. In addition, there is a big gap between two fields and he moved the Bed and Bath fields so they are basically on top of one another. Add all of the fields to a Tabular Layout. Add grouping by City. Sort the report by Year Built in descending order. Change the report to Landscape orientation and adjust the column widths so they all fit onto one page. Save the new report as **Properties by City**. Close Access. Submit the database based on your instructor's directions.

Performance Reviews

SOFT SKILLS CASE **S**

Passaic County Medical Monitoring provides visiting nurse care for patients in and around Passaic County, New Jersey. They have recently moved their records into an Access database. The director of Human Resources, Farrah Hassan, brings the nurses in yearly for a performance review. Employees are rated by a survey given to patients, asking them to rate the nurses on a scale of 1 (poor) to 5 (superb). You have been asked to create a one-page summary report to show the average of each employee's ratings. You will open her *a04b4Perform* database and save it as **a04b4Perform_LastFirst**. Use the Report Wizard to create a report based on the Performance and Nurses tables, group by the nurse, and add summary options to average the results for Promptness, Attitude, Knowledge, and Gentleness. The final report should display the NurseID, NurseFirst, and NurseLast fields and the averages for each of the four columns. You will also want to format each of the columns in the final report so they show two decimal places. You calculated the results by hand for nurse 1, Lan Wang, and her averages were 3.00 for Promptness, 3.11 for Attitude, 3.67 for Knowledge, and 3.67 for Gentleness, so when you create your report, you can check that it shows the correct data. Save the report as **Overall Ratings**, close Access, and submit the database based on your instructor's directions.

Capstone Exercise

Your boss asked you to prepare a schedule for each speaker for the national conference being hosted next year on your campus. She wants to mail the schedules to the speakers so that they can provide feedback on the schedule prior to its publication. You assure her that you can accomplish this task with Access.

Database File Setup

You need to copy an original database file, rename the copied file, and then open the copied database to complete this capstone exercise. After you open the copied database, you replace an existing employee's name with your name.

a. Open *a04c1_NatConf*.

b. Save the database as **a04c1NatConf_LastFirst**.

c. Open the Speakers table.

d. Find and replace *YourName* with your name. Close the table.

Create and Customize a Form

You need to create a form to add and update Speakers. Use the Form tool to create the form and modify the form as explained. You will also add a layout to an existing form.

a. Select the **Speakers table** as the record source for the form.

b. Use the Form tool to create a new stacked form.

c. Change the title to **Enter/Edit Speakers**.

d. Reduce the width of the text box controls to approximately half of their original size.

e. Delete the Sessions subform.

f. View the form and data in Form view. Sort the records by LastName in ascending order.

g. Save the form as **Edit Speakers**. Close the form.

h. Open the Room Information form in Layout view. The form does not have a Form Layout. Select all controls and apply the **Stacked Layout**.

i. Save and close the form.

Create a Report

You need to create a report based on the Speaker and Room Schedule query. You decide to use the Report Wizard to accomplish this task. You will also need to email the schedule to the presenters, so you will save the report as a PDF.

a. Select the **Speaker and Room Schedule query** as the record source for the report.

b. Activate the **Report Wizard** and use the following options as you go through the Wizard:

- Select all of the available fields for the report.
- View the data by Speakers.
- Accept LastName and FirstName as grouping levels.
- Use **Date** as the primary sort field in ascending order.
- Accept the Stepped and Portrait options.
- Save the report as **Speaker Schedule**.
- Switch to Layout view and apply the **Organic theme** to only this report.

c. Preview the report. Switch to Layout view. Adjust the column widths if necessary.

d. Switch to Print Preview and save the report as a PDF named **a04c1Speaker_LastFirst**.

e. When the PDF displays, close the program that displays it and return to Access. Exit Print Preview. Close the report.

Add an Additional Field

You realize the session times were not included in the query. You add the field to the query and then start over with the Report Wizard.

a. Open the Speaker and Room Schedule query in Design view.

b. Add the **StartingTime field** in the Sessions table to the design grid, after the Date field. Run the query.

c. Save and close the query.

d. Click the **Speaker and Room Schedule query**. Start the Report Wizard again and use the following options:

- Select all of the available fields for the report.
- View the data by Speakers.
- Use the LastName, FirstName fields as the primary grouping level.
- Use Date as the primary sort field in ascending order.
- Use StartingTime as the secondary sort field in Ascending order.
- Select the **Stepped** and **Portrait options**.
- Name the report **Speaker Schedule Revised**.
- Switch to Layout view and apply the **Facet theme** (first row, second column) to only this report.

e. Adjust the column widths in Layout view so that all the data is visible.

f. Add a space to the column heading labels as needed. For example, the column LastName should read Last Name.

g. Save and close the report. Close the database.

h. Exit Access. Submit the database and PDF based on your instructor's directions.

Data Validation and Data Analysis

Reducing Errors and Extracting Better Information

OBJECTIVES | AFTER YOU READ THIS CHAPTER, YOU WILL BE ABLE TO:

1. Establish data validation p. 310

2. Create an input mask p. 313

3. Create and modify a lookup field p. 315

4. Create a parameter query p. 325

5. Use advanced functions in the Expression Builder p. 329

6. Perform date arithmetic p. 335

CASE STUDY | Implementing a New Database at Tommy's Shelter

Tommy Mariano operates a small animal shelter. He has been keeping records by hand, but due to a large turnover in volunteers, record-keeping has become a problem. He has decided to move to a database solution, and his hope is that this will help reduce errors. Though volunteers may still make mistakes, he believes that a well-designed database will prevent some common errors.

As a volunteer, you have offered to create a database to assist him in this process. You have created the tables and done some data entry, and you will now work to make sure data validation takes place.

In addition to the problem of data entry, Tommy has been examining a lot of the data from his shelter by hand. As someone with some database experience, you know that advanced queries are the answer here. You will use advanced queries to help streamline his data gathering and reporting so Tommy can focus on what is important—finding homes for the animals in his shelter.

Data Validation in Tables

When filling out forms online, you may notice certain pieces of information are required. You may also notice that information you enter is checked for validity and that some fields are menus rather than text fields. For example, you cannot complete a checkout if you leave the credit card information blank. Likewise, on most sites, you cannot enter an e-mail address without the @ sign. Instead of entering Male or Female for a gender box, you may be given a menu offering only those two options. Having a list of options for the user to choose from helps narrow the possible answers as well as eliminates spelling errors.

Access also contains most of the validation features that are found in Web forms. Many of these features are found in the table settings; some are available in forms as well. In this section, you will explore setting data validation in tables in order to create more reliable data in your database. By setting up data validation, you reduce user errors, which is a key reason to use a database.

Establishing Data Validation

Data validation is a set of constraints or rules that help control how data is entered into a field. Access provides some data validation automatically. For example, you cannot enter text into a field with a number data type or add a new record to a table with the same primary key value as another record. Access provides the following data validation methods to help minimize the number of data entry errors:

- **Required**—Sets the Required property of a field to force data entry, such as a last name.

- **Default Value**—Specifies a value that is automatically entered into a field. For example, if most of your customers live in New Jersey, you can set the default value of the State field to NJ. The user can overwrite the default value with a different state abbreviation when needed.

- **Validation Rule**—Limits the type or range of data a user can enter into a field. For example, you could establish a rule for salary to ensure it is greater than zero.

- **Validation Text**—Provides the error message telling users what they did wrong and giving them instructions on what they need to do to fix it. For example, the validation text for the rule violation above might be, "You cannot enter a negative salary amount."

- **Input Mask**—Forces users to conform to a specific data-entry format for a given field. For example, a Social Security number must be entered in the format 123-45-6789. The hyphens would not need to be typed; they can be optionally stored or not stored with the entered data.

- **Lookup List**—Field values are limited to a predefined list of values. For example, a company might have temporary and full-time employees and enable users to choose either *temporary* or *full time* from a menu.

- **Multiple-Value Field**—Accepts multiple values in a single field. For example, an employee might have a status of both full time and temporary.

- **Data Macro**—Enables you to execute programming tasks whenever data in a table is changed. This is similar to a Validation Rule except the logic is more complex and the actions taken are more powerful when table data is changed.

The location of some of these properties is shown in Figure 5.1.

FIGURE 5.1 Short Text Field Data Validation Properties

Establish Required Fields

A required field is one that cannot be left blank when you create a new record. You have already learned about setting the Required property of a field. Primary keys are required fields by definition. The default Required setting is No for all the remaining fields, which enables you to create a record with no data in those fields. To ensure the integrity of the records in a table, you should set the Required property to Yes for critical fields. To change a field to Required, do the following:

1. Open the table in Design view.
2. Click the field you want to set to Required in the table design grid.
3. Click the Required property in the Field Properties pane. When you click in the box, an arrow appears with the options Yes and No.
4. Select Yes. For all new records, Access will require you to enter data into the required field. However, Access enables existing records to have blanks. Save the table.
5. Click No when asked if you want to test existing data with the new rules.

> **TIP** **Existing Blank Fields**
>
> If you set the Required property to Yes after data has already been entered in a table, you will see the message, "Data integrity rules have been changed; existing data may not be valid for the new rules. This process may take a long time. Do you want the existing data to be tested with the new rules?" If you click Yes and if blank fields exist, you are prompted to keep the new required setting, to revert to the old optional setting, or to stop testing the existing data for the requirement. Keeping the required setting (option 1) does not indicate which records have a blank field. To find existing records that contain empty values for a particular field, create a query and set the field's criterion to null (which means blank).

Set Default Field Values

When a majority of new records contain a common value, such as the same city or state, you can set a default value for that field to reduce data entry time. To change a default value, do the following:

1. Open the table in Design view.
2. Click the field you want to add a default value to in the table design grid.
3. Click the Default Value property in the Field Properties pane.
4. Type the default value you wish to add.

For example, suppose the majority of the animals the shelter handles are cats. If you set the default to Cat, all new records will display Cat. You can enter a different piece of information if necessary.

Set a Validation Rule and Generate Validation Text

A **validation rule** is designed to restrict the data values that can be entered into a field. Data values that do not conform are rejected, and the user is prompted to change the value. As mentioned earlier, you could add *Salary > 0* to a salary field to make sure a pay rate is greater than zero. For most data types, you can enter a validation rule by specifying an expression in the Validation Rule property.

If you violate a validation rule, Access does not let you continue until the data value conforms to the rule. Validation rules can cause frustration when filling out a form, especially if you cannot continue to the next step and you do not know why. Access helps you notify the user by entering an error message in the Validation Text property. Validation text provides feedback to users when a validation rule has been broken. For the salary example, when a user enters a negative value, the validation text displays. The validation text might state, "You have entered a negative value." Though not required, a database designer can be more specific to provide users guidance and tell them how to correct the validation-rule violation. Stating "You entered a negative salary. Salary must be greater than zero." provides the users with better feedback. The validation rule and validation text can be entered in the Field Properties pane, as shown in Figure 5.1. If a field violates a validation rule, the validation text displays as shown in Figure 5.2.

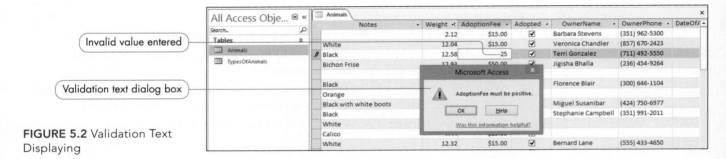

Invalid value entered

Validation text dialog box

FIGURE 5.2 Validation Text Displaying

To set up a validation rule, do the following:

STEP 2

1. Open the table in Design view.
2. Click the field you want to add a default value to in the table design grid.
3. Click the Validation Rule property in the Field Properties pane.
4. Enter the validation you wish to add.
5. (Optional, but recommended) Enter a meaningful error message in the Validation Text property in the Field Properties pane.

TIP Existing Data Violates New Validation Rule

If you add a validation rule to a table with existing records, some data in those records may violate the rule. When Access warns you that existing data may violate the new validation rule, you can click Yes to test the data. If existing data is in violation, you will be prompted to do one of three things: to keep the new setting and continue testing (Yes), revert to the old setting and continue testing (No), or stop testing (Cancel). To correct this situation, you can click No to remove the rule, switch to Datasheet view, find and correct the data that violates the new rule, and then return to Design view and add the rule again. Alternately, you can use a query to find and update nonconforming data.

Validation rules only check values entered for a field. They do not prevent users from skipping the field. Unless you set the Required property to Yes, having a validation rule does not force data entry for the field. Therefore, if you add a validation rule to a field, you should also consider setting the Required property to Yes.

Creating an Input Mask

In addition to controlling what users enter into a data table, database designers must also control how users enter data into tables. The first method for controlling data input is by selecting the appropriate data type when adding fields to a table. For that reason, database developers usually design tables with fields that have the most constraining data type. The Date/Time data type restricts input to dates and/or times; the Number data type restricts input to numeric data. Short Text is the most forgiving data type, but it is also the type that can collect the most invalid data. For example, a phone number might be stored in a Short Text field with a size of 14. The database designer might expect users to enter (973) 555-1212. However, users could enter 973.555.1212, 9735551212, 973-555-1212, or even 9999999999999 just as easily. If they are performing data entry through a form, they will not see how other users have entered the numbers and may accidentally create inconsistencies. Sorting, as well as some filters and queries, would not work correctly with such data.

By creating an *input mask* you can further restrict the data being input into a field by specifying the exact format of the data entry. Social Security number and phone number are two common text fields that often use input masks. Figure 5.3 shows a field with a phone number input mask applied.

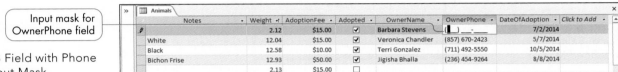

Input mask for OwnerPhone field

FIGURE 5.3 Field with Phone Number Input Mask

Use the Input Mask Wizard

The *Input Mask Wizard* is frequently used to generate data restrictions (an input mask) for a field based on responses to a few questions. You launch the Input Mask Wizard by opening the table in Design view, and then selecting the field for which you want to create a mask. In the Field Properties pane, in the lower part of the table Design view, click the input mask property. The Build button appears to the right of the field as shown in Figure 5.4; click Build to start the Input Mask Wizard. Figure 5.5 shows the first screen in the Input Mask Wizard dialog box. In this step, you select the type of input mask.

For example, select Social Security number to create the 123-45-6789 input mask format. This type creates an input mask with three digits, then a dash, then two digits, then another dash, and then four more digits. The input mask property for the field would appear as 000\-00\-0000;0; in the table Design view. Users doing data entry will see ###-##-#### to let them know the expected format of the Social Security number.

For phone numbers, the input mask also helps ensure consistency in data entry. As stated earlier, users may enter phone numbers in different ways. Good database design promotes consistent data input, and consistent data input leads to reliable data output. For example, if you query the database and ask for a count of customers who reside in the 973 area code, consistent data entry produces the correct results. If the data were entered in a variety of formats—some in the format (973), some in the format 973-, and some in the format 973.—the results would be unreliable because each of these entries would be perceived as being different by Access, even though users may recognize them to be the same.

To create an input mask, do the following:

STEP 3>>

1. Ensure you are in Design view for the table and click the field to which you want to add an input mask.

2. Click the Input Mask Wizard, designated by the ellipsis (…) at the end of the Input Mask row, as shown in Figure 5.4.

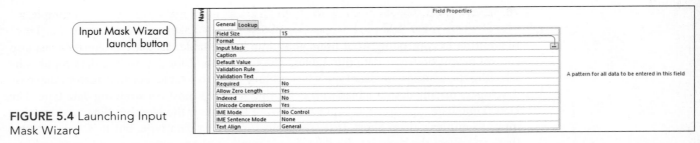

Input Mask Wizard
launch button

FIGURE 5.4 Launching Input
Mask Wizard

3. Choose one of the built-in input masks from the menu. A number of common formats exist, including Phone Number, Social Security Number, and Zip Code, as shown in Figure 5.5. Click Next.

Built-in input masks

FIGURE 5.5 Input Mask
Wizard: Selecting a
Predefined Mask

4. The next step in the Input Mask Wizard enables you to select a placeholder character, such as an underscore (_) or the pound sign (#), to display in the field in Datasheet view until you type the data. This tells the user what format is required when entering the information, as shown in Figure 5.6. Click Next.

Choosing Placeholder character

FIGURE 5.6 Input Mask
Wizard: Selecting Placeholder

5. The next step enables you to tell Access if you want the symbols, such as the parentheses and hyphens, to be stored with the data. Although a small amount of additional disk space is required, it is a good idea to store the symbols with the data. This helps avoid confusion later when you create queries and enter criteria for that field, as shown in Figure 5.7. Click Next.

Storing data with symbols

Storing data without symbols

FIGURE 5.7 Input Mask
Wizard: Choose How to Store
the Data

CHAPTER 5 • Data Validation and Data Analysis

6. Click Finish. The input mask now appears in the input mask property. For example, a phone number field might appear as !\(999") "000\-0000;0; or something similar. This mask forces you to enter the phone number in a consistent manner in the database table or form (as shown earlier in Figure 5.3). The underscore placeholder appears for each digit as you type the phone number, and the symbols are stored with the data.

 TIP Custom Input Masks

Access enables the creation of custom input masks. For example, to have a code start with *PC*, followed by a dash, followed by two required letters, followed by five required numbers, the mask would be:

"PC-"LL00000

As you can imagine, custom input masks can be complex, but they also enable you to control user input. For more information, search Microsoft Help or the Internet for custom input masks.

Creating and Modifying a Lookup Field

Input masks provide good validation for data, but at times you may want even more control. When looking at a datasheet, you may notice repetitive data. A field with a number of repeated values may be better suited as a *lookup field*, which provides the user with a finite list of values to choose from in a menu. For example, the shelter houses three types of animals: cats, dogs, and birds. Data entry would be faster and more accurate if the options for this field were limited to the three values in a list format. Changing the field to a lookup field would present users with the three options and ensure uniformity and consistency of the data.

 TIP State as a Lookup Field

State may make sense as a lookup field, as a limited number of options exist. However, if you are using a State field for shipping, do not forget about Washington, D.C. Though it is not a state, DC is as valid an abbreviation as NY or CA.

In addition to DC, the U.S. Postal Service recognizes a number of other abbreviations (such as U.S. territories and countries with free associations with the United States): American Samoa (AS), Guam (GU), the Marshall Islands (MH), Micronesia (FM), the Northern Marianas (MP), Palau (PW), Puerto Rico (PR), and the Virgin Islands (VI).

In addition, three abbreviations are used for the U.S. military. AA represents Armed Forces Central and South Americas, AE represents Armed Forces Europe, and AP represents Armed Forces Pacific.

Each of these areas has its own ZIP code, so these should be considered when creating a lookup field for State. This means that though 50 states exist, 62 different locations have ZIP codes.

Search the Internet for ZIP code 96960 to see an example of this.

Usually, the options in a lookup field are stored in a separate table. For example, if an AnimalType field has the three options listed above, you may want to create a table to store the values. In this case, a *Types of Animals* table would contain three records, one for each option. Storing the options in a separate table makes it easier for users to update the list. To add another option, for example Snakes, the user opens the *Types of Animals* table and adds a new record to the table. The new option automatically appears the next time the list is activated. The other method for lookup field options is to store the lookup values with the lookup field. This method is not recommended because modifications to the list are difficult for end users. Figure 5.8 shows an example of a lookup field.

Lookup field arrow

Options for AnimalType field

FIGURE 5.8 Lookup Field

Access provides a Lookup Wizard to help you create a lookup field. Before you launch the wizard, it is best to create the new table that will hold the lookup field options (for example, the *Types of Animals* table previously mentioned). The ***Lookup Wizard*** creates the menu of finite values (lookup field) by asking you six questions and using your answers to create the options list.

TIP | A Lookup Field Creates a Hidden Relationship

When you use the Lookup Wizard to create a lookup field, Access creates a hidden relationship between two tables—the table that contains the lookup field and the table that holds the options. Access needs this relationship to populate the options list for the lookup field. After you create the lookup field and save the table, click Relationships in the Relationships group on the Database Tools tab. When the Relationships window displays, the new relationship does not appear. Click All Relationships in the Relationships group and the new hidden relationship appears.

Create a Lookup Field

The first step in creating a lookup field is often to create a new table that will hold the options. As mentioned, it is usually best to look up the values in a table because end users can update the list easily. For the AnimalType field in the Animals table, shown in Figure 5.8, the new table is named *Types of Animals* and contains three records, as shown in Figure 5.9. To start the Lookup Wizard, open the Animals table in Design view, select the AnimalType field that will be converted to a lookup field, and then select Lookup Wizard as the data type (see Figure 5.10).

Types of Animals table stores values

FIGURE 5.9 Types of Animals Table

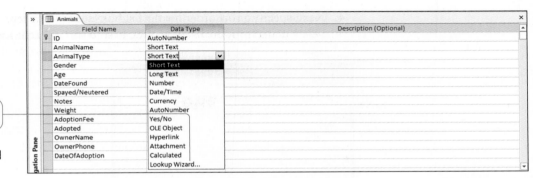

FIGURE 5.10 Lookup Wizard Data Type

Select Lookup Wizard… to set up lookup field

To create a field using the Lookup Wizard, do the following:

STEP 4

1. First, you are asked if you want to look up the values in a table or type in the values (shown in Figure 5.11). Select the appropriate option (likely to look up values in a table). Click Next.

FIGURE 5.11 Lookup Wizard: Choosing Source for Field

2. Next, identify the table that holds the values for the lookup column. Figure 5.12 shows the *Types of Animals* table selected. Click Next.

FIGURE 5.12 Lookup Wizard: Select Table

3. Next, select the field or fields from the *Types of Animals* table for the lookup field (see Figure 5.13). These fields help the user determine which option to choose. Click Next.

FIGURE 5.13 Lookup Wizard: Select Fields

4. Next, specify a sort order for the list box (see Figure 5.14). Because you will add to and delete items from the list, it is often best to sort alphabetically. Click Next.

FIGURE 5.14 Lookup Wizard: Choose Sort Order

5. Next, adjust the column width for the lookup column. Columns should be wide enough to display the longest value (see Figure 5.15). Use the mouse to resize the column; drag the right column edge to the right or left to the appropriate width. As an aside, there may also be times you are given the option Hide Key Field. In this case, because AnimalType does not have a primary key, you do not see that message, but if your lookup table does have a primary key, this option appears. Click Next.

FIGURE 5.15 Lookup Wizard: Adjust Column Width

6. Finally, label the lookup field; usually, the original field name is listed and accepted. See Figure 5.16. Click the check box to Enable Data Integrity and only allow options from the lookup table. In other words, if a user tries to enter a value not found in the table, it is rejected. The Restrict Delete option is the default, which does not enable you to delete a record in the lookup table (e.g., Dog) if related records (Dogs) exist in the table that is doing the lookup.

7. Click Finish.

FIGURE 5.16 Lookup Wizard: Choose a Field Label and Finish

Modify a Lookup Field by Adding and Deleting Values

 STEP 5 You can add, delete, or edit values in the lookup field to accommodate changing data needs. For example, if the shelter expands the types of animals it cares for to include rabbits, you open the *Types of Animals* table and add the new record to the bottom of the table. You also decide to delete Snakes because the shelter cannot properly care for them. When you click the category field the next time, the new option is listed. When making a change to a lookup table, you may need to go through the table data first and reclassify the records prior to changing the lookup values. For example, any animals that are snakes need to be reclassified or removed.

TIP | Using a Multivalued Lookup Field

A multivalued field is one that accepts multiple choices in a lookup field. If a local charity received golf lessons as an auction item, you could classify the donation as either *service* or *gift certificate*. The user would have to choose only one. A multivalued field enables you to choose two or more options—the golf lessons could be classified as both a service and a gift certificate. The last step in the Lookup Wizard contains the option Allow Multiple Values, as shown in Figure 5.14. Be cautious using this feature if you plan to migrate your Access database to another database product. The multivalued field is not supported in all database management tools.

In Hands-On Exercise 1, you will practice using the Access features that help validate data entry. You will use the field data type and field properties to restrict the users from entering invalid data. You will use the Lookup Wizard to create an option list to help ensure data consistency.

Quick
Concepts

1. Why would you set a default value for a field? *p. 310*

2. What sort of validation rule would you add to a Number field named CustomerAge? Why? *p. 312*

3. What is the purpose of adding an input mask to a field? *p. 313*

4. What would make a field a good candidate to be switched to a lookup field? *p. 315*

Hands-On Exercises

Watch the Video for this Hands-On Exercise!

1 Data Validation in Tables

The purpose of the shelter database is to cut down on errors, so you will add some data validation rules to the tables. You will set default field values, set validation rules, create input masks, and establish a lookup field.

Skills covered: Establish Required Fields and Set Default Field Values • Set a Validation Rule and Generate Validation Text • Use the Input Mask Wizard • Create a Lookup Field • Modify a Lookup Field

---

STEP 1 ≫ ESTABLISH REQUIRED FIELDS AND SET DEFAULT FIELD VALUES

It is important that the most critical fields in a table do not contain blanks. You decide to review the Animals table and set the required value to Yes for important fields. You also establish default values for fields that usually repeat. Refer to Figure 5.17 as you complete Step 1.

Step h: Default value of Cat appears for New record

ID	AnimalName	AnimalType	Gender	Age	DateFound	Spayed/Neutered	Notes	Weight	Adop
109	Evelyn	Cat	Female	2 years	12/26/2014	☑	Calico	12.48	
110	Taquito	Cat	Male	3 year	9/25/2014	☐	Orange	12.68	
111	Christopher	Cat	Male	7 weeks	6/9/2014	☐	Orange	12.58	
112	Jessica	Cat	Female	8 months	1/22/2014	☐	Black	12.02	
113	Connie	Dog	Female	2 years	2/12/2014	☑	Bichon Frise	10.53	
114	Evelyn	Dog	Female	1 year	9/3/2014	☐	Shih Tzu	12.61	
115	Donna	Dog	Female	1 year	4/4/2014	☐	Bichon Frise	9.10	
116	Simba	Cat	Male	2 years	7/30/2014	☑	Orange striped. Short hair	12.88	
117	Gerald	Cat	Male	2 years	12/1/2014	☐	White	12.03	
* (New)		Cat				☐		0.00	

FIGURE 5.17 Default Value for AnimalType Field

a. Open *a05h1Tommys*. Click the **FILE tab**, click **Save As**, click **Save Database As**, and then verify Access Database is selected under *Database File Types*. Click **Save As** and save the file as **a05h1Tommys_LastFirst**.

When you save files, use your last and first names. For example, as the Access author, I would name my document *a05h1Tommys_CameronEric*.

> **TROUBLESHOOTING:** Throughout the remainder of this chapter and textbook, click Enable Content whenever you are working with student files.

b. Open the Animals table in Design view.

c. Click the **AnimalName field** in the design grid.

d. Click in the **Required field** in the Field Properties pane. Click the arrow on the right side of the Required property box and select **Yes** from the list.

An entry in the AnimalName field is now required for each animal.

e. Click the **AnimalType field** in the table design grid.

f. Click **Default Value** in the Field Properties pane and type **Cat**.

Because most of the animals in the shelter are cats, you set the default value to Cat. You now need to test the changes you made to the table design.

g. Click **Save** on the Quick Access Toolbar. If you get a warning about testing the data integrity rules, click **Yes**.

h. Switch to the Datasheet view of the Animals table. Look at the new record row to ensure that the AnimalType is displayed as Cat by default. See Figure 5.17.

i. Click in the **Gender field** of the New record row and type **Female**. Type **2 months** in the **Age field**, **8/11/2014** in the **DateFound field**, **Very shy. Black and White** in the **Notes field**, **3** in the **Weight field**, and **$25** in the **AdoptionFee field**. The AnimalName, Spayed/Neutered, Adopted, OwnerName, OwnerPhone, and DateOfAdoption fields should be left blank.

To test data validation rules, you have left a required field blank.

j. Press **Tab** until you get an error message.

An error message appears indicating that you must enter a value in the AnimalName field. This is because you made the AnimalName field a required field, so every record must contain a value in that field.

k. Click **OK**, click in the **AnimalName field** for the new record you just typed, and then type **Pepper** in the **AnimalName field**. Click the next record to save the new record. Notice you no longer see an error.

STEP 2 ≫ SET A VALIDATION RULE AND GENERATE VALIDATION TEXT

One issue Tommy reported was that people accidentally entered incorrect adoption fees. You add a validation rule and validation text to enforce this rule. Refer to Figure 5.18 as you complete Step 2.

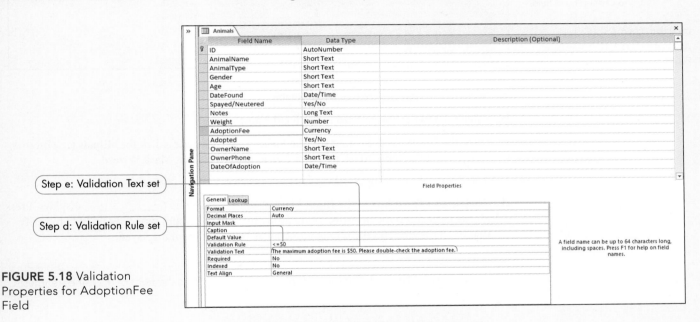

FIGURE 5.18 Validation Properties for AdoptionFee Field

a. Switch to Design view of the Animals table.

b. Click the **AdoptionFee field** in the table design grid.

c. Click the **Validation Rule property** in the Field Properties pane.

The maximum adoption fee is $50. You will establish a rule that notifies the user if a value greater than $50 is entered in the AdoptionFee field.

d. Type **<=50** in the **Validation Rule property box**.

e. Click the **Validation Text property** and type **The maximum adoption fee is $50. Please double-check the adoption fee.**

When a user enters an adoption fee that is too high, a message appears telling the user to modify the entry.

f. Compare your settings to Figure 5.18 and save the changes. Click **Yes** in response to the message about changed data integrity rules.

Access tests the data in the table to make sure that none of the adoption fees are too high.

g. Switch to the Datasheet view of the Animals table.

h. Click in the **AdoptionFee field** of the first record. Replace the current value with **51** and press **Tab**.

You receive an error message stating the maximum adoption fee is $50.

i. Click **OK** in the error message box. Change the first record to **20** for the AdoptionFee field. Press **Tab**.

As $20 is an acceptable value, you do not receive an error message.

STEP 3 ≫ USE THE INPUT MASK WIZARD

You decide to add an input mask to the phone number field so that all users follow a consistent data entry format. Refer to Figure 5.19 as you complete Step 3.

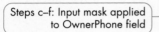 Steps c–f: Input mask applied to OwnerPhone field

FIGURE 5.19 Input Mask Applied to Phone Number Field

AdoptionFee ▾	Adopted ▾	OwnerName ▾	OwnerPhone ▾	DateOfAdoption ▾	Click to Add ▾
$20.00	☑	Barbara Stevens	(__) __-__	7/2/2014	
$15.00	☑	Veronica Chandler	(857) 670-2423	5/7/2014	
$10.00	☑	Terri Gonzalez	(711) 492-5550	10/5/2014	
$50.00	☑	Jigisha Bhalla	(236) 454-9264	8/8/2014	
$15.00	☐				
$15.00	☑	Florence Blair	(300) 646-1104	8/11/2014	

a. Switch to Design view of the Animals table.

b. Click the **OwnerPhone field** in the Field Name column.

c. Click the **Input Mask property** in the Field Properties pane. Click the **ellipsis (…)** on the right side of the Input Mask property box to open the Input Mask Wizard.

The Phone Number input mask is already selected.

d. Click in the **Try It box** of the Input Mask Wizard dialog box. (___) ___-____ displays. Press **Home** to position the insertion point at the first character and type **5556667777** to verify that the mask displays the phone numbers as you want them displayed.

> **TROUBLESHOOTING:** Make sure you place the cursor just to the right of the left parenthesis.

The sample data entry works fine.

e. Click **Next** twice.

You accept the mask with the default placeholder character.

f. Click the **With the symbols in the mask option**. Click **Next** and click **Finish**.

g. Save the table. Switch to the Datasheet view of the Animals table.

The phone numbers display in the preset format with parentheses and hyphens.

h. Type your phone number into the first record to test the input mask. Your entry should resemble Figure 5.19. Press **ESC** to return the record to its original state.

Rather than typing in the name of an option (from a list of options) and risk the possibility of a misspelled or invalid animal type, you decide to create a lookup field that enables the volunteers to choose from a list.

a. Switch to Design view of the Animals table.

b. Click the **AnimalType field**.

c. Click the **Data Type arrow** and choose **Lookup Wizard** from the list.

The Lookup Wizard launches.

d. Verify that the *I want the lookup field to get the values from another table or query* option is selected. Click **Next**.

e. Click **Table: Types of Animals** and click **Next**.

This table was prefilled with animal types.

f. Double-click **AnimalType** to move it to the Selected Fields box. Click **Next**.

g. Click the arrow in the first sort box and select **AnimalType**. Click **Next**.

h. Adjust the column width so AnimalType is visible, if necessary. Click **Next**.

i. Verify that *AnimalType* is the label for the lookup column. Click **Finish**. Click **Yes** to save the table.

The Lookup Field has now been established.

j. Switch to the Datasheet view of the Animals table. Add a new animal using the following data, pressing **Tab** between each entry. Note that once you enter an AnimalName, you are given an ID automatically:

AnimalName	Marco
Gender	Male
Age	2 months
DateFound	8/14/2014
Spayed/Neutered	Yes
Notes	Parakeet. Yellow and blue
Weight	0.2
AdoptionFee	$50

The AnimalType, Adopted, OwnerName, OwnerPhone, and DateOfAdoption fields should be left blank.

> **TROUBLESHOOTING:** If you make a mistake in the middle of entering and start again, the ID automatically skips a number. Do not try to fix the ID; just add the record again using the next sequential number.

k. Click the **AnimalType field** for Marco. Select **Bird** from the menu.

The lookup field gives you a menu of animal types. The default is Cat from Step 1.

l. Close the Animals table.

After a few days of testing, you decide to modify the table containing the lookup values for the lookup field. Volunteers have pointed out they do not accept snakes, but they do accept rabbits, which are not listed as an option. Refer to Figure 5.20 as you complete Step 5.

Steps g–h: New record added

FIGURE 5.20 Updated Lookup

a. Open the Types of Animals table in Datasheet view.

b. Delete the Snake record.

c. Add a new row with **Rabbit** as the AnimalType.

d. Close the *Types of Animals* table.

e. Open the Animals table in Datasheet view.

f. Add a new record to the table. Accept the default ID and enter **Thumper** as the value for the **AnimalName field**.

g. Select the menu for AnimalType. Notice that Snake is no longer an option, but Rabbit is. Select **Rabbit** for the AnimalType.

h. Enter the rest of the data below, leaving any fields not mentioned blank:

Gender	Female
Age	3 months
DateFound	8/18/2014
Spayed/Neutered	No
Notes	Extremely friendly. White.
Weight	1
AdoptionFee	$25

i. Save and close all open tables.

j. Keep the database open if you plan to continue with Hands-On Exercise 2. If not, close the database and exit Access.

Data Analysis Using Advanced Select Queries

In a previous chapter, you used some basic query techniques to extract data from your database. Extracting and manipulating data is the center of the database experience, one of the major reasons to use a database rather than a spreadsheet.

Aside from extracting information more effectively, you may also want to be more efficient. Creating a group of queries to extract information from one table is not a bad thing, but imagine for a moment a database with dozens of tables. If you have many queries for each of the tables, it becomes more difficult to manage. You may spend time recreating queries you have already created, for example. You can apply special conditions that enable you to make a query more versatile. This may remove the need for you to create multiple similar queries with minor differences in the criteria.

One of the reasons people choose Excel over Access is a perceived lack of built-in functions. However, Access does include a number of functions through the Expression Builder (as discussed in a previous chapter). You have the ability to create advanced functions, similar to Excel, while being able to enjoy the benefits of a database software package.

In this section, you will learn advanced select queries including parameter queries and advanced functions in the Expression Builder.

Creating a Parameter Query

Access provides a variety of query types to help business owners make decisions. To determine how many pets of a certain animal type were adopted at Tommy's this year, you could construct a query with the relevant fields, and then enter Cat into the Criteria row of the AnimalType field. You could save the query as Cat Adoptions. If you wanted to see the same information for dogs, you could copy the first query, rename the copy as Dog Adoptions, and then enter Dog into the Criteria row of the AnimalType field. This process could be repeated for other animal types as needed. However, you might ask yourself if there is a better way to handle this situation. The answer is yes—using a parameter query.

A *parameter query* is a select query where the user provides the criterion at run time. A parameter query provides flexibility that other queries do not. It enables you to create a query for one situation and then expand it into a query for unlimited situations.

Create a Parameter Query to Provide Flexibility

A parameter query reduces your development time because you can use the query repeatedly without modifying the design as only the criterion changes. The parameter query is not different from the queries you have used before—it is still a select query. However, it is unique in the way it asks the user to respond before completing its execution.

Suppose the alumni relations office at Passaic County Community College, in Paterson, New Jersey, contacts alumni to keep them connected to the college after graduation. For example, when college events—sporting events, theater events, musical presentations, and so forth—are in a certain geographical area, the college contacts the alumni in the area. Akira Yamamoto, professor of communication, might need a list of the alumni in the same city as her next off-campus production. Each time a new event is scheduled, the query criterion would have to be changed—unless a parameter query is created. A parameter query would prompt the user to Enter City, and after Akira enters a city, the list of alumni would appear. The alumni office can then mail an announcement (or send an e-mail) to inform the Passaic alumni about the event. Parameter queries enable you to create a more versatile select query.

Creating a parameter query is similar to creating most other query types. The major difference is in the criteria. To create a parameter query, do the following:

1. Click Query Design in the Queries group on the CREATE tab.
2. Choose a table that contains the records that you want included in the query.

3. Drag the relevant fields from the table to the query design grid.
4. Click inside the Criteria row of the field that you need to filter, but instead of entering the criteria, type a text phrase enclosed in brackets [ ] that you want to appear in a dialog box. The text should instruct the user what to do, such as [Enter the City] or [Enter State Abbreviation] or [Enter Type of Animal], as shown in Figure 5.21. When a user runs the query, this text appears as a prompt in the Enter Parameter Value dialog box (see Figure 5.22).

Criteria enclosed in brackets

FIGURE 5.21 Criteria for a Parameter Query

5. If you need additional parameters for other fields, move to the Criteria row for the next field and type the user instructions in brackets in that field.
6. Save the query as you normally would.

In the Passaic County Community College example, you could create a query based on the Alumni table. Then you would add all the fields relevant to the mailing address (name, address, city, state, ZIP) to the design grid. If you want to find all the alumni from a specific city, type [Enter the City] in the Criteria of the City field. You will be prompted as shown in Figure 5.22. Figure 5.23 shows the results after *Paterson* is typed into the Enter Parameter Value dialog box.

FIGURE 5.22 Parameter Query Prompt

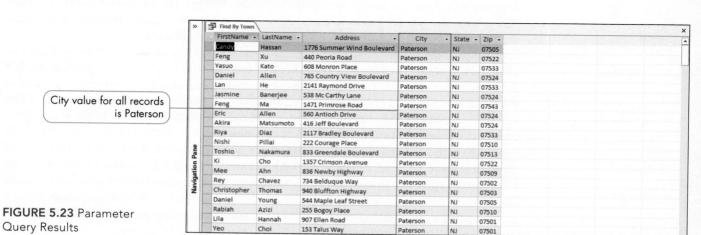

City value for all records is Paterson

FIGURE 5.23 Parameter Query Results

In an earlier chapter, you learned about advanced operators such as Between and Like. These can be added to a parameter query to extend the capabilities even more.

When multiple parameters are involved, Access asks for the information starting from the left and moving to the right. You can also use multiple parameters within a single criteria selection. For example, if you want to see events with certain date ranges, you could use the Between operator. Type *Between [Enter Start Date] And [Enter End Date]* into the criteria of the EventDate column. This expression generates two dialog boxes, one for the starting date and one for the ending date. After the user supplies the date criteria by typing them in the Enter Parameter Value dialog box, Access uses the responses to create a criteria expression as if it were typed into the Criteria row of the query. For example, if you enter 6/1/2014 when prompted for the starting date and 6/30/2014 as the ending date, Access interprets that as *Between #6/1/2014# And #6/30/2014#*. Recall that Access encloses date fields with the # character. Also recall that the Between operator is inclusive; that is, saying *between 6/1/2014 and 6/30/2014* includes any events on 6/1/2014 and 6/30/2014.

You can also use the Like operator to create a parameter query. The Like operator enables you to significantly expand your match criteria. Instead of searching for an exact match, you can use the Like operator as you did in an earlier chapter. For example, if you were to set the parameter to [Enter City] for a City field, you could revise the criterion to allow users to enter the partial name of a city. The new criterion would be *Like [Enter Partial City] & '*'* (use single quotation marks around the *), as shown in Figure 5.24. This new expression enables you to enter P at the prompt, and Access finds all cities that begin with P. The results, shown in Figure 5.25, include Paterson, Pompton Lakes, and Passaic.

FIGURE 5.24 Combining Like and a Parameter

FIGURE 5.25 Results of Parameter Query

When a parameter query contains multiple parameter questions, Access provides a Query Parameters window to organize and keep track of these multiple parameters. To display the Query Parameters window, do the following:

1. Switch to Layout or Design view.
2. Display the DESIGN tab.
3. Click Parameters in the Show/Hide group.
4. In the first Parameter row, type the name of the parameter excluding the brackets [ ]. Use the Data Type column to specify what data type is stored in the parameter's field. When you run the query, the Parameter dialog boxes appear in the order they are listed in the Query Parameters window.

Create a Parameter Report

The effectiveness of parameter queries can be extended to reports. By creating a report based on a parameter query, you automatically receive the benefits of a parameter query—adding flexibility that enables a user to control the content of the report. A report based on a parameter query becomes an effective management tool for any organization. The creation of a parameter report is simple once the parameter query has been created. To create a parameter report from an existing parameter query, do the following:

1. Select a parameter query in the Navigation Pane.
2. Click the CREATE tab.
3. Click Report in the Reports group. As the new report is being created, the familiar Enter Parameter Value dialog box appears asking you to enter the criterion.
4. Enter a value, click OK, and then the report opens in Layout view.
5. Save the report. Note each time the report is opened, it prompts you for new criteria.

Any other type of report can be created as well using the same process as you used in previous chapters. This can work well with labels reports.

For example, at Passaic County Community College, Akira wants to run a label report so she can notify alumni who are close to a college theatrical event. To create this report, first create a parameter query that gives the prompt [Enter City] so Akira can choose a city. Next, select the parameter query in the Navigation Pane and click Labels in the Reports group. Choose the appropriate label and layout. At this point, the dialog box appears and the user can enter Paterson (or whatever city). The query results then become the record source for the label report, and Access displays the labels. Parameter queries work well in this situation because the criterion (the city) changes for each event. Figure 5.26 shows the City query with the city value of Paterson.

City value for all records is Paterson

FIGURE 5.26 Parameter Report Based on City Query

TIP **Add a Parameter to an Existing Report**

Often, database design evolves over time. Even after careful planning and implementation, a database may have incomplete requirements or may be designed by a less experienced database designer. If you have a report that is perfectly formatted and laid out but you want to add parameters, it can be done even if the original design did not call for it.

To do so, create a parameter query as demonstrated earlier. Open the report in Layout or Design view and open the Property Sheet. Locate and click the Record Source property. Type the new query name that you created in place of the table name currently shown. Save the report changes and the next time you run the report, the Enter Parameter Value dialog box will appear.

Using Advanced Functions in the Expression Builder

As shown in an earlier chapter, the Expression Builder is a powerful tool enabling you to create mathematical functions. You used the Pmt function to calculate a periodic payment for a loan. However, over 125 built-in functions exist in Access. Although most users are just familiar with the ones they use on a daily basis, searching the Web or using Microsoft Help may be useful to find assistance with unfamiliar functions. As you gain experience with Access functions, you may remember functions and their parameters and just type them in. To start, you will likely use the Expression Builder.

TIP **Renaming Columns**

From a previous chapter, recall that the default titles for calculated columns are names like Expr1. To fix this, you can add any name you like (without spaces) before the expression, followed by a colon (:).

Use the Date Function

You performed date arithmetic in an earlier chapter. However, you started with a fixed date for the arithmetic. This is not always realistic. You may want to run the same query over and over and, based on the current date, perform some sort of calculation. To do so, you can use the *Date function*, which calculates the current date. The Date function takes no parameters. For example, you could calculate days since a student's last payment using the Date function and subtracting the last PaymentDate from it. The Date function also is commonly used as a default value for date fields.

Date()

The Date function can be typed in manually or entered through the Expression Builder. In the Expression Builder, it can be found by double-clicking Functions. Then click Built-In Functions, followed by Date/Time, in the Expression Categories section of the Expression Builder. Date appears in the Expression Values portion of the Expression Builder, as shown in Figure 5.27.

Function in Expression Builder

FIGURE 5.27 Date Function

TIP | **Default a Date Field to Today**

You can type Date() in the Default Value property to insert the current date when a new record is added. This type of default value is useful for fields like Date of Entry, Date Record Added, and Order Date.

Use the Round Function

The **Round function** returns a number rounded to a specific number of decimal places. You may not want to round to the nearest number necessarily. You can round to a different number of decimal places by changing the precision parameter. If you leave the precision parameter blank, Access assumes the nearest whole number.

In the Expression Builder, the Round function is in the Math category of Built-In Functions. It has the following syntax:

Round(expression, precision)

Going back to our previous example, Akira Yamamoto, the communication professor, has her final grades in an Access database. She generally rounds her grades before she submits them to the registrar's office.

Akira has set up a query to do this for her. She used the Expression Builder to do so. See Figure 5.28. Notice the main function is written as Round([Grade]). As you saw in an earlier chapter, the parameters appear between the brackets. In this case, the Round function requires one parameter. Rounding to a whole number, a student with an 89.25 would receive an 89, but a student with an 83.95 would end up with an 84 for the class. See Figure 5.29 to see results.

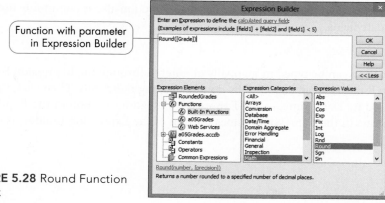

Function with parameter in Expression Builder

FIGURE 5.28 Round Function Syntax

89.25 rounds down to 89

83.95 rounds up to 84

FIGURE 5.29 Round Function Results

The precision element is important in determining how to round. If you choose a precision of zero (or leave it blank), the value of the field is rounded to a whole number. If you choose a precision of 1, it is rounded to the first decimal place, and so on. Precision cannot be a negative number. Here are some examples of the Round function in practice:

- Round(500.554) would return 501. Because no parameter exists, Access assumes nearest integer, which is 501.
- Round(500.554,0) would return 501. We have given a parameter of zero decimal places, so it returns 501.
- Round(500.554,1) would return 500.6. A parameter of 1 rounds to the first decimal place.
- Round(500.554,2) would return 500.55. A parameter of 2 rounds to two decimal places.

Use the IsNull Function

The *IsNull function* checks whether a field has no value. You learned in an earlier chapter that null essentially means an absence of value. IsNull checks if a field has no value assigned. For example, you may have a Date/Time field. Instead of trying to determine what an absence of a value is for a Date/Time field, you can simply use IsNull. This can be useful in comparisons (to be discussed shortly) or as part of a query. In the Expression Builder, the IsNull function can be found in the Math category of Built-In Functions.

STEP 3 » IsNull(expression)

For example, Akira is preparing to send a mailing to a list of students. However, some of the students in the database, as you may have noticed in an earlier example, do not have street addresses listed. This may happen when a student moves and does not inform the college. If no address exists, a label is unnecessary. In this case, Akira can use an IsNull function to determine if each person has a street address. In this case, the function would be IsNull([Address]).

When the IsNull function is added to a query, it displays one of two values. Access determines "is this value null"? If the value is null, it displays –1. If the value is not null—that is, it has a value—the function displays 0. Figure 5.30 shows the syntax of the function in the Expression Builder, and Figure 5.31 shows the results.

IsNull is frequently paired with some sort of condition. For example, you could display only null values by typing –1 in the condition row. You could display non-null values by setting a condition of 0.

Function in Expression Builder

FIGURE 5.30 IsNull Function Syntax

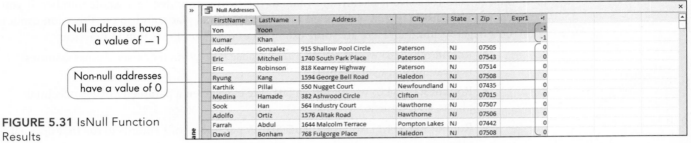

Null addresses have a value of −1

Non-null addresses have a value of 0

FIGURE 5.31 IsNull Function Results

Create Conditional Output with the IIf Function

Another common function used in Access is the ***IIf function***, which evaluates an expression and displays one value when the expression is true and another value when the expression is false. When creating an IIf statement, you will find three options that need to be filled in: the expression (the question you are asking Access to check), the true part (what to do if the expression is yes), and the false part (what to do if the expression is false). The expression in this case is a statement that can be evaluated to true or false. You can find the function through the Expression Builder in the Program Flow category of Built-In Functions.

IIf (expression, truepart, falsepart)

The important piece of the IIf function is the expression, which involves some sort of comparison. In your day-to-day life, you are constantly performing IIf statements. Based on the weather, you make a decision on whether to carry an umbrella. In that case, you check the weather. If the weather is rainy, you bring the umbrella. If the weather is not rainy, you leave the umbrella at home.

Another example in your daily life might have to do with traffic. If too much traffic exists on Route 3, take Route 21. If it is 7:00 AM, get up; otherwise, do not. If you are thirsty, get a glass of water; otherwise, do not. The commonality here is that some sort of condition determines the action. In the case of any condition, it is something that can be evaluated as yes or no.

You can perform six types of comparisons, as you saw in an earlier chapter. The six comparison operators are equal (=), not equal (<>), greater than (>), less than (<), greater than or equal to (>=), and less than or equal to (<=). As you do with queries, you can use these comparison operators in an IIf statement.

The expression must evaluate as yes (or true) or no (or false) only. For example, *Balance >= 10000* or *City = "Sarasota"* are valid expressions because they can be evaluated as true or false. Either the balance is greater than or equal to 10000 or it is not; either the city is Sarasota or it is not. *DateListed + 90* is not a valid criterion for the IIf function because this expression is a calculation, not a comparison. Access evaluates the expression, determines whether it is true or false, then performs one action if the expression is true and another if the expression is false. For example, if accounts with balances of $10,000 or more earn

3.5% interest, whereas accounts with balances below $10,000 earn only 1.5% interest, the following IIf function could be created: IIf (Balance>=10000, .035, .015).

The IIf function can also evaluate text values. For example, to classify a list of students based on whether they are in or out of the state of New Jersey, you could create the following IIf function: IIf([State]="NJ", "In State", "Out of State"). Figure 5.32 shows the expression syntax in the Expression Builder, and Figure 5.33 shows the results.

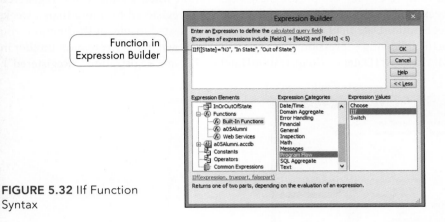

Function in Expression Builder

FIGURE 5.32 IIf Function Syntax

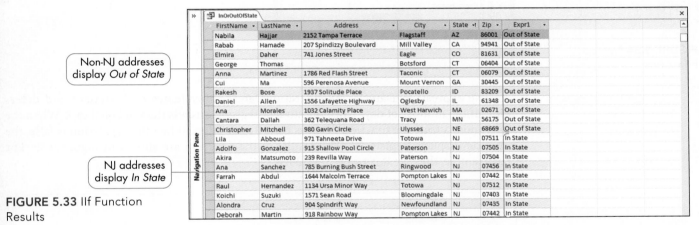

Non-NJ addresses display *Out of State*

NJ addresses display *In State*

FIGURE 5.33 IIf Function Results

TIP **Using Comparison Operators**

To create an expression with a *greater than or equal to* comparison operator, type the two operators >=. To create an expression with a *less than or equal to* comparison operator, type the two operators <=. Both of these comparison operators require two operators, and they must be typed in the correct order with the equal sign in the second position.

Notice that when you say one number is not equal to another, you are effectively saying it is either less than or greater than that number. Hence, you type <> to represent *not equal to*.

It would be easier to read if you could use ≥, ≤, or ≠, but you do not have those keys on your keyboard.

Nesting Functions

As with Excel, you may wish to combine functions. For example, if you had to find the square root of a number, you might want to first make sure the number is positive by using the absolute value function. If you were trying to perform this on a field named Hypotenuse, you would end up with the following formula: Sqr(Abs([Hypotenuse])). Using one function within another function is known as **nesting functions**. The combination of parentheses and brackets may be hard to read, but sometimes combining functions is the only way to accomplish a task. IIf functions are one function often used in as a nested function.

Combine IIf with Other Expressions

Suppose you want to display the phrase New Registration when a student has registered in the last week, and Registered when a student has been registered for more than a week. Using the RegistrationDate field and the Date() function nested inside an IIf function, you would create the following expression. The expression is shown in the Expression Builder in Figure 5.34. It reads: IIf (Date() – [RegistrationDate] <=7, "New Registration", "Registered").

FIGURE 5.34 Nested Functions

The expression Date() – [RegistrationDate]<=7 evaluates each student and determines if the number of days since the student registered is less than or equal to 7. When the expression is true, the function displays New Registration. When the expression is false, the function displays Registered. The results of the function are shown in Figure 5.35. For that example, the date it is run is 8/31/2016.

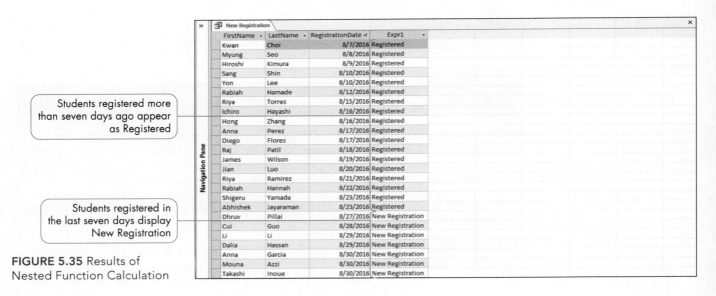

FIGURE 5.35 Results of Nested Function Calculation

This IIf statement includes one function, math, and a comparison inside of it. This may be a little difficult to read, but to get the full benefit of Access it is often necessary to nest functions.

Use Nested IIf Functions

Experienced Access users sometimes need to create nested IIf functions. This happens when two conditions are not sufficient to evaluate an expression. For example, the function IIf (Date() − [RegistrationDate] <=7, "New Registration", "Registered") was used based on two conditions existing.

Let us say a third status is needed, with the following conditions:

- If a student has registered in the past 2 days, mark as Brand New Registration.
- If a student has registered in the past 2 to 7 days, mark as New Registration.
- If a student has been registered for more than 7 days, mark as Registered.

The IIf statement to accomplish this would read as follows:

IIf (Date() − [RegistrationDate] <=2, "Brand New Registration", IIf (Date() − [RegistrationDate] <=7, "New Registration", "Registered"))

Access would process this as follows:

1. Subtract the RegistrationDate from today's date. If it is less than or equal to 2, display *Brand New Registration*.
2. If that is not the case, subtract the RegistrationDate from today's date. If it is less than or equal to 7, display *New Registration*. Note that Access has already determined it is not less than or equal to 2 with the first condition, so only registrations between 2 and 7 days old display *New Registration*.
3. If neither of those things are true, the student has been registered for more than 7 days, so display *Registered*.

Performing Date Arithmetic

Working with dates in Access can be challenging, especially when performing date arithmetic. This can be even more problematic if your output will contain multiple formats for the United States, Europe, and Asia. Each has its own method of formatting dates. Fortunately, Access has some built-in functions to help work with dates and date arithmetic.

Date formatting affects the date's display without changing the actual underlying value in the table. All dates and times in Access are stored as the number of days that have elapsed since December 31, 1899. For example, January 1, 1900, is stored as 1, indicating one day after December 31, 1899. If the time were 9:00 PM on November 20, 2010, no matter how the date or time is formatted, Access stores it as 40502.875. The 40502 represents the number of days elapsed since December 31, 1899, and the .875 reflects the fraction of the 24-hour day that has passed at 9:00 PM. Because dates are stored by Access as sequential numbers, you can calculate the total numbers of hours worked in a week if you record the starting and ending times for each day. Using *date arithmetic*, you can create expressions to calculate lapsed time, such as a person's age based on birth date or the number of years since a person's start at a college.

Identify Partial Dates with the DatePart Function

Using a date function, you can isolate a portion of the date that is of interest to you. The date math you have worked with thus far included basic subtraction of one date from another. However, you may not always just want to get the number of days between two dates. Assume you are working at a company that plans on giving all employees who started working for the company 10 or more years ago a slight longevity pay increase. Using date subtraction could work. However, your criteria would then be a number of days, and modifications might be difficult for someone who might need to perform a similar query in the future.

STEP 4 ≫   Another way to accomplish this would be to extract only the year portion of the date. The *DatePart function* is an Access function that examines a date and returns a portion of the date, and it works well for this case. DatePart returns a numeric value for the interval you have selected. You can find this function through the Expression Builder in the Date/Time category of Built-In Functions.

DatePart(interval, date, *firstdayofweek, firstweekofyear*)

Assuming the query is run in 2016, you would want the query to find anyone who has a HireDate in 2006 or earlier. If you could find just the year portion of the HireDate, you could easily subtract it from 2016 and only add a raise when the difference is greater than or equal to 10 years. The first part of this operation would be to extract the year from the HireDate, which can be done using DatePart: DatePart("yyyy", [HireDate]). Figure 5.36 shows the expression syntax in the Expression Builder, and Figure 5.37 shows the results.

FIGURE 5.36 DatePart Function Syntax

Function in Expression Builder

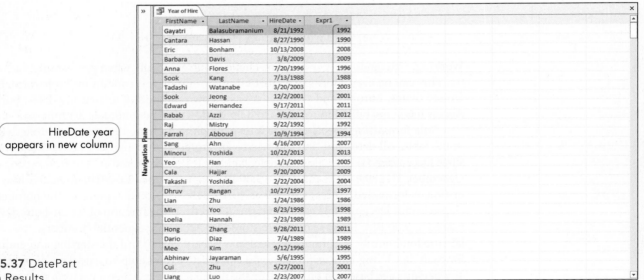

HireDate year appears in new column

FIGURE 5.37 DatePart Function Results

DatePart is not only used to extract the year; it can also be used to extract the month, day, and a number of other intervals as well. You could use this function, for example, to find all employees who started in the current month (say, January), and send them a card thanking them for being with the company another year.

The function always returns a numeric value, so if you extract the month, you get a number from 1 (representing January) through 12 (December). If you extract the weekday, you get a number from 1 (representing Sunday) through 7 (Saturday).

Table 5.1 shows the DatePart function parameters.

TABLE 5.1 Using the DatePart Function

Function Portion	Explanation
«interval»	The first argument, the interval, describes the portion of the date that you wish to return. You can use any of the following: "yyyy" Year "q" Quarter "m" Month "y" Day of year "d" Day "w" Weekday "ww" Week "h" Hour "n" Minute "s" Second
«date»	The second argument, the date, tells Access where to find the Date/Time information.
«firstdayofweek»	*Optional*. A constant that specifies the first day of the week. If not specified, Sunday is assumed.
«firstweekofyear»	*Optional*. A constant that specifies the first week of the year. If not specified, the first week is assumed to be the week in which January 1 occurs.

Here are some examples of the DatePart function being used on a date field named HireDate. For these examples, assume HireDate is 8/31/2017.

TABLE 5.2 Evaluating the DatePart Function

Function Portion	Resulting Value	Explanation
DatePart("yyyy",[HireDate])	2017	August 31, 2017, has a year of 2017.
DatePart("q",[HireDate])	3	Quarter 3 is July, August, and September.
DatePart("m",[HireDate])	8	August is the 8th month of the year.
DatePart("y",[HireDate])	243	August 31 is the 243rd day of the year.
DatePart("w",[HireDate])	4	August 31, 2017, is a Thursday.
DatePart("ww",[HireDate])	35	August 31, 2017, is in the 35th week of the year.

 TIP Displaying Month or Day Names

The numbers for months or days may be hard to read and not intuitive. However, a function to help with that exists. It makes sense to nest the results of your DatePart function within another function. If you want to specifically display the day of the week, the function WeekDay(«expression») would display the day of the week as a word. So, WeekDay(1) would return Sunday. Likewise, the function MonthName(«expression») would return the name of the month. For example, MonthName(3) would return March. This may make it easier for you to read.

Apply Criteria and Grouping to DatePart Results

Like any other field, a calculated field using DatePart can have criteria applied for it. For example, similar to our previous example, we could extract the month for our HireDate:

DatePart("m", [Employees]![HireDate])

If this were added as a field, it would display a number from 1 through 12 in the column. If you wanted to only display employees hired in April, for example, you would type the number 4 in the Criteria row. Upon running the query, you get a list of employees hired in April, regardless of the year.

In a previous chapter, you learned how to group by fields. This operation works well with the DatePart function. For example, if you wanted to see how many employees were hired by month, you could use the same example as before:

DatePart("m", [Employees]![HireDate])

Next, click the Totals button on the Query Tools Design tab, and then select Group By for this field. You would then add another field (HireDate, in this case) as the second column, and then set the Group By for that field to Count. You would end up with a list of months (1 through 12, representing January through December), each followed by the number of employees hired in that year.

In Hands-On Exercise 2, you will practice creating a parameter query. You will use advanced Expression Builder functions to perform calculations. You will perform date arithmetic as well.

Quick Concepts

1. What is the advantage to creating a parameter query? *p. 325*

2. What are two common uses for the Date function? *p. 329*

3. What does the IsNull function do? *p. 331*

4. Why is the expression a critical component of the IIf function? *p. 332*

5. Which function would you use if you needed to display just the year portion of a date? *p. 335*

2 Data Analysis Using Advanced Select Queries

After applying data validation rules to the tables, you will perform some advanced queries against the database. You will create a parameter query, use advanced Expression Builder functions, and use date arithmetic to manipulate the data.

Skills covered: Create a Parameter Query • Use Date and Round Functions • Use IIf and IsNull Functions • Perform Date Arithmetic

---

STEP 1 ≫ CREATE A PARAMETER QUERY

Tommy is hoping to create a query that will enable the volunteers to input the animal type and display all animals matching. He is hoping to also create a report based on that query. In addition, he would like to create a query to display all animals adopted in a certain date range. Refer to Figure 5.38 as you complete Step 1.

Step n: DateFound values are in August 2014

Step n: Twelve records are returned

FIGURE 5.38 Find By Date Results for August 2014 Animals

a. Open *a05h1Tommys_LastFirst* if you closed it at the end of Hands-On Exercise 1 and save it as **a05h2Tommys_LastFirst**, changing *h1* to *h2*.

b. Create a query using Query Design. Double-click the **Animals table** to add it to the query. Click **Close**.

c. Double-click each of the following fields to add them to the query: **AnimalName**, **AnimalType**, **Gender**, **Age**, **DateFound**, **Spayed/Neutered**, and **Notes**.

d. Type **[Enter Animal Type]** in the Criteria row for the AnimalType field.

e. Save the query as **Find Animal Type**. Run the query.

You are prompted to enter an animal type in a box labeled Enter Animal Type.

> **TROUBLESHOOTING:** If you are not prompted to Enter Animal Type, ensure your criterion for the AnimalType field is enclosed in brackets exactly as shown in step d.

f. Enter **Bird** at the prompt and click **OK**.

All nine birds in the database are displayed.

> **TROUBLESHOOTING:** If you get no results, ensure you typed [Enter Animal Type] in the correct field's criteria.

g. Close the Find Animal Type query.

h. Double-click the **Find Animal Type query** to run the query again. Enter **Cat** when prompted. Verify 86 records are displayed and close the Find Animal Type query.

i. Right-click the **Find Animal Type query** and select **Copy**. Right-click in a blank area of the Navigation Pane and select **Paste**. Name the query **Find By Date** and click **OK**.

j. Open the Find By Date query in Design view.

k. Remove the criterion from the AnimalType field.

l. Type **Between [Enter Start Date] and [Enter End Date]** on the Criteria row for the DateFound field.

m. Save the query. Run the query.

You will be prompted for one date, and then for a second date.

n. Type **8/1/2014** when prompted to Enter Start Date and click **OK**. Type **8/31/2014** when prompted to Enter End Date and click **OK**. Verify 12 animals are displayed, as shown in Figure 5.38 and close the query.

o. Click the **Find Animal Type query**. Click **Report** in the Reports group on the CREATE tab.

A report based on the Find Animal Type query is created, and you are prompted to Enter Animal Type.

p. Type **Bird** when prompted.

The same nine records displayed earlier appear in report form.

q. Save the report as **Animal Report** and close the report.

STEP 2 ≫ USE DATE AND ROUND FUNCTIONS

Tommy has some modifications to the database that you can achieve using advanced functions. You will assist him by setting a default date and rounding animal weights. Refer to Figure 5.39 as you complete Step 2.

AnimalName	AnimalType	Age	DateFound	Notes	Weight	Rounded
Leslie	Bird	1 year	6/22/2014		2.12	2
Edward	Cat	2 year	5/4/2014	White	12.04	12
Yolanda	Cat	6 weeks	9/16/2014	Black	12.58	13
Sully	Dog	5 years	7/12/2014	Bichon Frise	12.93	13
Emily	Bird	1 year	5/21/2014		2.13	2
Susan	Cat	3 year	7/18/2014	Black	12.47	12
Mark	Cat	6 weeks	3/3/2014	Orange	12.01	12
Tipsy	Cat	1 year	7/15/2014	Black with white boots	12.45	12
Christopher	Cat	2 years	11/21/2014	Black	12.46	12
Laura	Cat	2 years	9/28/2014	White	12.88	13
Leo	Cat	5 months	7/31/2014	Calico	7.44	7
Stephanie	Cat	5 years	6/2/2014	White	12.32	12
Lee	Bird	1 year	5/1/2014		2.11	2
Sylvia	Cat	2 years	1/4/2014	Calico	12.72	13

Step k: Column title set to Rounded

Steps h–j: Values rounded

Rouded Weights

FIGURE 5.39 Rounded Weights

a. Open the Animals table in Design view. Click the **DateFound field**.

b. Add **Date()** to the Default Value in Field Properties.

The default value for all new records is the current date.

c. Switch to Datasheet view. Save the changes when prompted. Scroll to the new record at the bottom of the table.

The first blank record has a default value of your current date. Note if you are working on this before 2014, your default date may be before some of the other dates.

d. Close the Animals table.

e. Create a new query using Query Design. Double-click the **Animals table** in the Show Table dialog box. Click **Close**.

f. Double-click the **AnimalName, AnimalType, Age, DateFound, Notes**, and **Weight fields** to add them to the query.

g. Click in the top row of the first column after the Weight field.

You will create a new column to round the Weight field.

h. Click **Builder** in the Query Setup group. Double-click **Functions**. Click **Built-In Functions** and click **Math** in the *Expression Categories* section of the Expression Builder.

i. Double-click **Round** in the *Expression Values* section.

Round(«number», «precision») displays in the Expression Builder.

j. Remove *«number», «precision»* from the expression and replace it with **Weight**.

Round(Weight) displays in the Expression Builder.

k. Click **OK**. Replace *Expr1* in your new column with **Rounded**. Run the query. Check the Rounded column against the Weight column to make sure animal weights are rounded to the nearest whole number. See Figure 5.39.

l. Save the query as **Rounded Weights** and close the query.

STEP 3 ≫ USE IIF AND ISNULL FUNCTIONS

Tommy hopes to find data entry errors in his database. Due to the sheer number of volunteers, he has noticed mistakes in the database, and he would like an automated query to find any pets that are listed as adopted but do not have an owner name. You will help him to accomplish this by nesting an IsNull function inside an IIf function. Refer to Figure 5.40 as you complete Step 3.

Step h: Column named ErrorCheck

Steps d–g: IIf function created

AnimalName	AnimalType	Adopted	OwnerName	OwnerPhone	DateOfAdoption	ErrorCheck
Leslie	Bird	✓	Barbara Stevens	(351) 962-5300	7/2/2014	Ok
Edward	Cat	✓	Veronica Chandler	(857) 670-2423	5/7/2014	Ok
Yolanda	Cat	✓	Terri Gonzalez	(711) 492-5550	10/5/2014	Ok
Sully	Dog	✓	Jigisha Bhalla	(236) 454-9264	8/8/2014	Ok
Susan	Cat	✓	Florence Blair	(300) 646-1104	8/11/2014	Ok
Christopher	Cat	✓	Stephanie Campbell	(351) 991-2011	12/19/2014	Ok
Leo	Cat	✓				Error
Stephanie	Cat	✓	Bernard Lane	(555) 433-4650	6/13/2014	Ok
Lee	Bird	✓	Tom Lyons	(351) 521-8818	5/29/2014	Ok
Marcus	Bird	✓	Joshua Harris	(998) 284-2499	8/6/2014	Ok
Judy	Cat	✓	Julie Cross	(300) 853-8707	1/17/2014	Ok
Rachel	Cat	✓	Ernest Hicks	(300) 871-1069	2/16/2014	Ok
Linda	Cat	✓	Juan Mckinney	(857) 820-9476	1/11/2014	Ok
Stephanie	Cat	✓	Gail Cole	(958) 734-2955	12/28/2014	Ok
Jill	Cat	✓				Error
Stephen	Cat	✓	Susan Gutierrez	(424) 750-3842	4/4/2014	Ok
Pearl	Bird	✓	Sarah Williamson	(822) 960-9675	10/15/2014	Ok
Rosemary	Cat	✓	Henry Snyder	(976) 828-7453	8/10/2014	Ok

FIGURE 5.40 Results of IIf Function

a. Create a new query in Query Design. Double-click the **Animals table**. Click **Close**. Double-click the **AnimalName, AnimalType, Adopted, OwnerName, OwnerPhone**, and **DateOfAdoption fields** to add them to the query.

You will use a combination of an IIf and IsNull function to find animals that are listed as adopted but do not have owners listed.

b. Type **Yes** in the Criteria row of the Adopted field.

You will limit your query results to animals that are listed as adopted.

c. Click in the top row of the first blank column following the DateOfAdoption column. Click **Builder**.

d. Double-click **Functions**. Click **Built-In Functions** and click **Program Flow** in the *Expression Categories* section of the Expression Builder. Double-click **IIf**.

IIf(«expression», «truepart», «falsepart») displays in the Expression Builder.

e. Click **«expression»**. Press **Delete**. Click **Inspection** in the *Expression Categories* section of the Expression Builder. Double-click **IsNull**.

IIf(IsNull(«expression»), «truepart», «falsepart») displays in the Expression Builder.

f. Click **«expression»**. Type **OwnerName**.

IIf(IsNull(OwnerName), «truepart», «falsepart») displays in the Expression Builder.

g. Click **«truepart»**. Type **"Error"**. Click **«falsepart»**. Type **"Ok"**.

IIf(IsNull(OwnerName), "Error", "Ok") displays in the Expression Builder.

h. Click **OK**. Replace *Expr1* with **ErrorCheck**. Run the query and compare the results to Figure 5.40.

The first Error message appears for Animal #7 (Leo). Notice Leo is listed as adopted but has no owner. Tommy can now review his records and fix the errors.

i. Save the query as **Data Entry Check**. Close the query.

STEP 4 ≫ PERFORM DATE ARITHMETIC

Tommy has been asked by a local animal control agency to provide a list of all animals that have been found in the month of January in any year. The agency is hoping to use this information to determine whether to add more part-time workers for January. You will need to help him get a list of all animals the shelter has collected during *any* January.

a. Create a new query in Query Design. Double-click the **Animals table**. Click **Close**. Double-click the **AnimalType, Gender, Age, DateFound, Weight**, and **Notes fields** to add them to the query.

b. Click the top row of the first blank column after the Notes field. Click Builder.

c. Double-click **Functions**. Click **Built-In Functions** and click **Date/Time** in the *Expression Categories* section of the Expression Builder. Double-click **DatePart**.

DatePart(«interval», «date», «firstdayofweek», «firstweekofyear») displays in the Expression Builder.

d. Click **«firstdayofweek»** and press **Delete**. Repeat the process for «firstweekofyear». Remove the extra commas as well.

DatePart(«interval», «date») displays in the Expression Builder.

e. Click **«interval»**. Type **"m"**. Click **«date»**. Type **DateFound**.

DatePart("m",DateFound) now appears in the Expression Builder.

f. Click **OK**. Replace *Expr1* with **Month**.

g. Run the query. Examine the new column.

The new column now contains a number corresponding to the number of the month of the year (for example, 1 for January and 12 for December).

h. Switch to Design view. Enter **1** in the Criteria row for the newly created column and run the query.

The five animals found in the month of January appear.

i. Save the query as **January Animals**. Close the query.

j. Close the database and exit Access. Submit the database based on your instructor's directions.

Chapter Objectives Review

After reading this chapter, you have accomplished the following objectives:

1. **Establish data validation.**
   - Establish required fields: Required fields cannot be left blank, and existing records do not have to be updated if you set this property.
   - Set default field values: Automatically enters a value in a field, which is useful if a majority of new records have the same value.
   - Set a validation rule and generate validation text: Validation rules limit the type or range of data that can be entered, and validation text provides more information when the user violates a validation rule.

2. **Create an input mask.**
   - Use the Input Mask Wizard: Input masks specify the exact format of the data entry. You can use the wizard to create common input masks such as Social Security number and phone number.

3. **Create and modify a lookup field.**
   - Create a lookup field: A field with a number of repeated values may be better suited as a lookup field, which provides the user with a finite list of values to choose from in a menu.
   - Modify a lookup field by adding and deleting values: Lookup field options are usually in a separate table, so changes can be performed in that table.

4. **Create a parameter query.**
   - Create a parameter query to provide flexibility: A parameter query is a select query where the user provides the criterion at run time. It enables you to create a query for one situation and then expand it into a query for unlimited situations.

   - Create a parameter report: Base a report on a query with parameters, and the same option to enter parameters is available. Used to extend the effectiveness of the query to a report.

5. **Use advanced functions in the Expression Builder.**
   - Use the Date function: Calculates the current date. Takes no parameters.
   - Use the Round function: Return a number rounded to a specific number of decimal places. Different precision levels are available by changing the precision parameter.
   - Use the IsNull function: Checks whether a field has no value.
   - Create conditional output with the IIf function: Evaluates an expression and displays one value when the expression is true and another value when the expression is false. The expression involves some sort of comparison that can be evaluated as yes or no. You can perform six types of comparisons: equal (=), not equal (<>), greater than (>), less than (<), greater than or equal to (>=), and less than or equal to (<=).
   - Nesting functions: Using one function within another function is known as nesting functions.

6. **Perform date arithmetic.**
   - Identify partial dates with the DatePart function: DatePart enables you to isolate part of a date (day of the week, week number, month, year, etc.).
   - Apply criteria and grouping to DatePart results: A calculated field using DatePart can have criteria applied for it. Grouping also works well with the DatePart function.

Key Terms Matching

Match the key terms with their definitions. Write the key term letter by the appropriate numbered definition.

a. Data validation
b. Date arithmetic
c. Date formatting
d. Date function
e. DatePart function
f. IIf function
g. Input mask
h. Input Mask Wizard

i. IsNull function
j. Lookup field
k. Lookup Wizard
l. Nesting functions
m. Parameter query
n. Round function
o. Validation rule

1. _____ A set of constraints or rules that help control how data is entered into a field. **p. 310**

2. _____ Restricts the data values that can be entered into a field. **p. 312**

3. _____ Enables you to restrict the data being input into a field by specifying the exact format of the data entry. **p. 313**

4. _____ Creates the menu of finite values by asking you six questions and using your answers to create the options list. **p. 316**

5. _____ Provides the user with a finite list of values to choose from in a menu. **p. 315**

6. _____ Frequently used to generate data restrictions for a field based on responses to a few questions. **p. 313**

7. _____ A select query where the user provides the criterion at run time. **p. 325**

8. _____ Calculates the current date. **p. 329**

9. _____ Returns a number rounded to a specific number of decimal places. **p. 330**

10. _____ Checks whether a field has no value. **p. 331**

11. _____ Evaluates an expression and displays one value when the expression is true and another value when the expression is false. **p. 331**

12. _____ Using one function within another function. **p. 334**

13. _____ Used to create expressions to calculate lapsed time. **p. 335**

14. _____ Affects the date's display without changing the actual underlying value in the table. **p. 335**

15. _____ An Access function that examines a date and returns a portion of the date. **p. 335**

Multiple Choice

1. Which of the following is not an example of a data validation technique?

   (a) Descriptive field names
   (b) Lookup fields
   (c) Default values
   (d) Input masks

2. To make a field required, you should:

   (a) Set the Required property in the Form Wizard.
   (b) Add an input mask.
   (c) Set the Required property in the Field Properties pane in the table's Design view.
   (d) Click the Required/Default command in the Table Design group.

3. Which field data type enables users to choose from a list of options while entering data?

   (a) Lookup field
   (b) Validation text
   (c) Input mask
   (d) Parameter

4. The string of characters !\(999") "000\-0000;0;_ represents which of the following?

   (a) Lookup field
   (b) Validation text
   (c) Input mask
   (d) Parameter

5. To alter the number of options in a lookup field, you should:

   (a) Add, change, or delete the records in the lookup table.
   (b) Add an input mask.
   (c) Change the validation text for the lookup field.
   (d) Delete the lookup field.

6. A parameter query enables you to:

   (a) Specify criteria for a field when you run the query.
   (b) Find and display specific parts of a date, for example the year.
   (c) Restrict the data a user enters into a field, such as requiring the data to appear as a phone number.
   (d) Perform mathematical operations, such as rounding.

7. Which of the following statements about the Round function is false?

   (a) The Round function has two parameters: the value you want to round and the precision.
   (b) A Round function with a precision of 1 rounds to the nearest integer.
   (c) A Round function without a precision parameter returns an integer.
   (d) Round(210.45,0) would return 210.

8. Which of the following statements is false?

   (a) The IsNull function works on date fields.
   (b) IsNull returns True if there is no value and False if there is a value.
   (c) A null value means that the value is zero for any type of field.
   (d) All of the above are true.

9. Which of the following is not a valid condition for an IIf function?

   (a) Age >= 17
   (b) TodaysDate − 90
   (c) City <> "Paterson"
   (d) All of the above are valid.

10. Which of the following cannot be extracted by the DatePart function?

    (a) Hours
    (b) Month
    (c) Years
    (d) All of the above can be extracted.

Practice Exercises

1 Physicians Center

The Paterson Physician Center has asked you to improve their data entry process. They want to create a form to enroll new physicians. Because the data entry personnel sometimes misspell the members' specializations, you decide to create a lookup table. If all of the specialty areas are entered uniformly, a query of the data will produce accurate results. Before you create the form, you decide to apply some of the data validation techniques you learned. You will also create a parameter query to assist a doctor in finding potential new volunteers. This exercise follows the same set of skills as used in Hands-On Exercise 1 in the chapter. Refer to Figure 5.41 as you complete this exercise.

Step n: Patients in study S07 excluded

Steps p–q: Volunteers born in 1968, 1969, and 1970 appear

FIGURE 5.41 High Cholesterol Query Results

First Name	Last Name	Phone Number	BirthDate	Cholesterol	StudyID
Feng	Gao	(555) 848-2655	9/8/1970	226	S01
Liang	Xu	(833) 601-5678	12/4/1968	220	S06
Daher	Elmira	(600) 518-2825	1/21/1969	238	S01
Patil	Abhinav	(600) 519-5180	11/22/1969	229	S04
Jeong	Kyung	(236) 748-9244	9/16/1968	215	S08
*				0	S00

High Cholesterol

a. Open *a05p1Physicians*. Save the database as **a05p1Physicians_LastFirst**.

b. Open the Physicians table in Design view.

c. Click **FirstName** in the table design grid and change the Required property to **Yes** in the Field Properties pane. Do the same for the LastName, State, PhoneNumber, and Specialization fields.

d. Save the table. Click **Yes** in response to all error messages that say *Data integrity rules have been changed* and *Existing data violates the new setting*.

e. Click the **PhoneNumber field** in the table design grid and click the **Input Mask** in the Field Properties in the bottom section of the window. Click ... on the right of the Input Mask field to start the Input Mask Wizard.

f. Click **Next** twice to accept the default mask and placeholder character.

g. Change the third screen to store data *With the symbols in the mask*. Click **Next**.

h. Click **Finish** on the final screen. Save the table and switch to Datasheet view.

i. Click the **Phone Number column** of the first record. Delete the existing phone number, type your phone number, and then press **Tab** to check for errors. Press **Esc** to exit the new record without saving.

j. Switch to Design view. Click the **Specialization field**. Change the Data Type box to **Lookup Wizard**.

k. Respond to the wizard as follows.
   - Select **I want the lookup field to get the values from another table or query**. Click **Next**.
   - Select **Table: Specialization** as the lookup table. Click **Next**.
   - Double-click **Specialization** in the Available Fields box to move it to the Selected Fields box. Click **Next**.
   - Click the arrow of the first sort box and select **Specialization**. Click **Next**.
   - Widen the column by dragging the right border to the right so all data is displayed. Click **Next**.
   - Click **Finish** to accept the default table name.
   - Click **Yes** to save the table.

l. Switch to Datasheet view. Click in the **Specialization field** and click the arrow to verify the new lookup field is working. For each physician, click the **Specialization arrow** and select the correct specialization as listed below. Once you have completed that, close the table.

First Name	Last Name	Specialization
Takeo	Yamada	Obstetrics
Qiturah	Hamade	Hematology
Kazuo	Yamaguchi	General Medicine
Farrah	Hariri	Cardiology
Guo	Sun	Internal Medicine
Arun	Jayaraman	Exercise Physiology
Donald	Anderson	General Medicine
Pola	Dallah	Cardiology
Cala	Hussein	Internal Medicine
Charles	Smith	Hematology
Kwan	Cho	Internal Medicine
Nabila	Azizi	Cardiology

m. Create a new query based on the Volunteers table. Select the **FirstName, LastName, PhoneNumber, BirthDate, Cholesterol**, and **StudyID fields**.

n. Change the Criteria row for the StudyID field to read <>7 so that the query excludes patients already in Study S07.

o. Change the Criteria row for the Cholesterol field to read >**200** so only patients with high cholesterol are displayed. Ensure the criteria appears on the same row as the StudyID criteria.

p. Change the criterion for the BirthDate field to read **Between [Start Date] and [End Date]** so the user is able to enter a start and end date. Ensure the criterion is on the same row as the StudyID and Cholesterol criteria.

q. Run the query. You will be prompted for a Start Date and End Date. Enter **1/1/1968** as the Start Date and **12/31/1970** as the End Date. You should see exactly five results. Save the query as **High Cholesterol**. See Figure 5.41.

r. Close the database. Close Access. Submit based on your instructor's directions.

2 Technical Support

Passaic County Technology Services (PCTS) provides technical support for a number of local companies. The human resources manager, Dora Marquez, has requested your assistance in creating a parameter query, a query that summarizes the calls by day of the week, and a query that rounds the hours a technician worked on a call. This exercise follows the same set of skills as used in Hands-On Exercise 2 in the chapter. Refer to Figure 5.42 as you complete this exercise.

FIGURE 5.42 Calls by Day Query Results

a. Open the database *a05p2PCTS* and save the database as **a05p2PCTS_LastFirst**.

b. Open the Calls table in Design view and click the **OpenedDate field**. Under *Field Properties*, change the default value to read **Date()** so the current date appears as the default. Change the field to **Required**. Save the table.

c. Switch to Datasheet view. Click **No** when prompted to test the existing data with the new rules. Click the **Last record button** at the bottom of the datasheet to verify the new record (marked with a *) shows today's date as the default value. Close the table.

d. Open the Calls By Type query in Design view. Click in the Criteria row of the CallTypeID field.

e. Type [**Enter Number of Call Type**] and run the query. Enter **1** when prompted to *Enter Number of Call Type*. Verify 29 records are displayed and save and close the query.

f. Create a new query in Query Design. Add the CallID from the Calls table.

g. Click **Insert Columns** in the Query Setup group of the Query Tools Design tab to insert a new column before the CallID field. Click in the top row of the newly inserted column and click **Builder** to launch the Expression Builder.

h. Double-click **Functions**. Click **Built-in Functions**. Click **Date/Time** and double-click **DatePart**.

i. Click «**interval**». Type "**w**" in place of the interval. Ensure you include the quotes.

j. Click «**date**». Type **OpenedDate** in place of the date.

k. Delete «firstdayofweek», «firstweekofyear», and the extra commas from the expression. The expression now reads *DatePart("w",OpenedDate)*.

l. Click **OK**. Replace *Expr1* that appears before the DatePart function with the word **Weekday**.

m. Click **Totals** in the Show/Hide group of the Query Tools Design tab.

n. Change the **Total row** for CallID to Count and run the query. Your results should show that Sunday (weekday 1) has the lowest volume of calls. Save the query as **Calls By Day** and close the query. See Figure 5.42.

o. Open the Customer Billing query in Design view. Click the first empty column (following the HoursLogged column) and launch Builder. Double-click **Functions**. Click **Built-in Functions**. Click **Math** and double-click **Round**.

p. Click «**number**» and replace it with **HoursLogged**. Click «**precision**» and replace it with **0**. Run the query and ensure the new column lists only whole numbers. Save and close the query.

q. Open the Call Status query in Design view. Click the top row of the OpenOrClosed column and click **Builder**.

r. Replace *[expression]* with **IsNull(ClosedDate)**, ensuring you do not delete the existing comma. Click **OK**.

s. Run the query. Notice the cases with no ClosedDate are listed as Open in the OpenOrClosed column, while the cases with a ClosedDate are listed as Closed. Save and close the query.

t. Close the database. Close Access. Submit based on your instructor's directions.

1 Hotel Chain

You are the general manager of a large hotel chain. Your establishment provides a variety of guest services ranging from rooms and conferences to weddings. Your staff need to improve their data entry accuracy, so you have decided to move to Microsoft Access and implement several data validation techniques. You also will take advantage of Access's Expression Builder to help analyze data.

a. Open *a05m1Hotel*. Save the database as **a05m1Hotel_LastFirst**.

b. Open the Members table in Design view. Add a phone number input mask to the Phone field. Save and close the table.

c. Open the Location table in Design view. Change the Required property for the City and Address fields to **Yes**.

d. Convert the Last Renovation field to a Lookup Wizard. Look the values up in the Renovation table. Save and close the Location table.

e. Open the Orders table in Design view. Add a validation rule that requires the value of the NumInParty field to be less than or equal to 75. Set validation text to **Party sizes cannot exceed 75.** then save and close the Orders table.

f. Create a copy of the Average By Day query. Name the new query **Average By Month**.

g. Replace the day grouping with a grouping by month. Use the appropriate formula with the correct parameters to achieve this. Display the name (e.g., January) for the month instead of the number (e.g., 1). Name the column **Month**.

h. Run the query. Save the query.

i. Create a copy of the Average By Month query. Name the new query **Average By Month and Year**.

j. Add a second grouping field so the results are grouped by month and year. Run the query. Verify your results show both an April 2017 average as well as an April 2018 average. Name the new field **Year**. Sort by Year in ascending order. Save and close the query.

k. Close the database. Close Access.

l. Submit based on your instructor's directions.

2 Northwind Traders

ANALYSIS CASE

You are the office manager of the Northwind Traders specialty food wholesaler. You need to modify the company's Access database to help produce more reliable information. You create a lookup customers form in which data cannot be modified by users. You also create queries and reports to validate data.

a. Open *a05m2Traders*. Save the database as **a05m2Traders_LastFirst**.

b. Open the Employees table in Design view. Add a phone number input mask to the HomePhone field.

c. Change the TitleOfCourtesy field to be a lookup field. Find values in the TitleOfCourtesy table. Sort by the TitleOfCourtesy field. Accept the default name. Save and close the table.

d. Open the TitleOfCourtesy table in Datasheet view. Add the titles **Sr.**, **Sra.**, and **Srta.** on separate lines, as the company has hired a Spanish-speaking representative and may hire more. Save and close the table. If you get a warning that data may be lost, click **OK**.

e. Open the Employees table in Datasheet view. Scroll to record 10 for Claudia Mendiola. Select **Srta.** for her TitleOfCourtesy by selecting it from the menu. Close the table.

f. Open the Customers table in Design view. Add an input mask to the CustomerID field so the field must be five nonnumeric characters in all uppercase.

g. Switch to Datasheet view. Locate the record for *Around the Horn*. Change the name of the company to **London Specialties**. Attempt to change the CustomerID to **99999**. If your input mask is working correctly, you will not be able to type it.

h. Change the CustomerID for London Specialties to **LONSP**. Close the table.

i. Create a copy of the Shipments By Vendor query. Name the query **Shipments By Vendor and Year**. Open the query in Design view.

j. Add a new field before Company Name. Calculate the year from the ShippedDate field and ensure the totals row is set to Group By. Name the column **Year**.

k. Add a parameter to the Year column so the user can enter a year at runtime and see one year's results at a time. Prompt the user to Enter Year. Save and close the query.

l. Open the Revenue query in Design view. Create a new field named **Net** that calculates the difference between Revenue and TotalCost. Round the Net field to the nearest dollar.

m. Add a new field to the Revenue query that displays *Profit* when the value of the Net field is greater than zero and *Loss* when it is less than or equal to zero. Name the field **ProfitOrLoss**.

n. Save and close the query.

⭐ **o.** Open Microsoft Word and open the *a05m2Traders* document from your data files. Save the document as **a05m2Traders_LastFirst**. Use the queries you created and modified to answer the questions found in the Word document. Save and close the document.

p. Close the database. Close Access.

q. Submit based on your instructor's directions.

3 Willow Insurance Agency

COLLABORATION CASE

Your team works together as database consultants. You have been contracted to assist the Willow Insurance Agency modify their Access database to produce more reliable information. You will individually make a copy of the database and implement what you believe are appropriate changes. You will then meet as a group, compare databases, and write a recommendation to the Willow Insurance Agency summarizing suggested changes.

a. Divide the tables in the Willow Insurance Agency database among your group members. The three tables found in the database are Employees, Location, and Titles. If you have three group members, each member chooses one table. If you have two members, one member should choose the Employees table, and the other should choose the Location and Titles tables.

b. Open *a05m3Willow* individually. Save the database as **a05m3Willow_LastFirst**.

c. Open Microsoft Word. Open *a05m3WillowAnalysis*. Save the file as **a05m3WillowAnalysis_LastFirst**.

d. Open your assigned table(s) in Design view. Examine the current data validation for each field where it exists. Is there an input mask? Is there a default value? Is there a validation rule? Are the fields required? Is there a lookup field?

e. Make changes to your assigned table(s) in the Access database, implementing what you feel are the appropriate data validation for each field. Save all changes and close the database.

f. Record whether you feel changes are suggested for each field and what changes you recommend in the Word document. Save and close the document.

g. Meet as a group once all group members have completed their analysis. Create a new Access database named **a05m3Willow_GroupName**. Import the updated tables from each group member's database. If you made changes such as adding a lookup field, ensure you import any tables you created as well.

h. Combine your Word documents into one document, showing the analysis for each table. Save the file as **a05m3WillowAnalysis_GroupName**. Ensure you fill in the team member names at the top of the Word document.

i. Discuss the results as a group. If the group feels any changes are necessary, adjust the Word document and the database to reflect these changes. Save all changes.

j. Exit Access and Word. Submit the four files—your individual analysis and database, as well as the group analysis and database—based on your instructor's directions.

Beyond the Classroom

Using Unfamiliar Functions

RESEARCH CASE

This chapter introduced you to some advanced Builder functions. You will use the Internet to find an unfamiliar function and also use a familiar function in a way you did not in this chapter. Open *a05b2Builder*. Save the database as **a05b2Builder_LastFirst**.

(1) Use a search engine to find out how to combine text values in Access using an expression. Using the information from the Internet, create a query based on the Customers table that combines the LastName and FirstName fields into one field that displays the last name, followed by a comma and a space, followed by the first name (e.g., Harris, Donald). Display the Phone field as the second column. Alphabetize by the created field. Save the query as **Phone List** and close the query.

(2) Create a query to display the name of the month (not the number) and sum of the balance for all accounts opened in each month (regardless of the year). *Hint:* The total balance for October should be $9,000.00, which will require some sort of grouping. Name the calculated column MonthOpened. Sort by the SumOfBalance field in descending order. Resize columns so all values are displayed. Save the query as **Total Balance By Month** and close the query.

Close the database. Close Access. Submit based on your instructor's directions.

Fixing a Query

DISASTER RECOVERY ✚

Anthony Carmelo, a co-worker in the Finance Department, has asked for your help with an Access query he is working on. The company gives all employees a 1 percent raise to their salary every five years they have been with the company. With your help, he was able to calculate the raise using a combination of Access functions. He is running the query on 1/1/2018, and it correctly grants a longevity increase for any employees who started in 2013, 2008, 2003, 1998, 1993, and 1998. He notices employees who left the company at some point are also being granted raises. Open the *a05b3Longevity* database and save it as **a05b3Longevity_LastFirst**. Open the Longevity Bonus query. Anthony is certain that he needs to add something to the Still Active field to check if the employee is still active; that is, that the employee does not have an end date.

He has most of the query working, but he cannot figure out how to ensure the EndDate field is empty in the StillActive field. The current expression, *IIf([EndDate]=Null,"Yes","No")*, always displays *No*. He believes if you can help him fix this expression to do what he is intending, the query will work. Change the StillActive field so it displays *Yes* for employees without an EndDate and *No* for employees with an EndDate.

Save and close the query, and close the database. Close Access. Submit based on your instructor's directions.

Job Search

SOFT SKILLS CASE 🅢

FROM SCRATCH

Amy Lee, human resources director for Moody Training, has a spreadsheet containing job applicants. She needs help converting the spreadsheet to a database and then performing some operations on the database.

(1) Start Access and create a new, blank desktop database. Save the file as **a05b4Applicants_LastFirst**. Import the Excel spreadsheet *a05b4Applicants*. Ensure that Access knows the first row contains column headings. Accept default data types. Select the SSN field as the primary key and save the table as **Applicants**.

(2) Amy would like a menu of degree types rather than having to type in B.S., B.A., and other degree types. Use the skills learned in this chapter to turn the HighestDegreeType field into a lookup field. Note: Seven degree types exist in the database that need to appear in the menu.

(3) Amy would like new records to have a default DateOfApplication set to today's date automatically and the SSN field to have an appropriate input mask applied to it.

(4) Amy noticed some applicants did not provide their degree. She would like a query (rather than a filter) to find the first name, last name, and e-mail address for all applicants with null degree names so they can be contacted via e-mail for clarification. She would like the query saved as **Missing Degrees**.

Close the database. Close Access. Submit based on your instructor's directions.

Capstone Exercise

You work as the database manager at Replacements, Ltd., located in Greensboro, North Carolina. Replacements, Ltd., has the world's largest selection of old and new dinnerware, including china, stoneware, crystal, glassware, silver, stainless steel, and collectibles. Your task is to add validation rules, create a form that data entry associates can use to add new items to the inventory, and create a new table to classify merchandise as china, crystal, or flatware. You will also use queries and reports to analyze existing data.

Database File Setup and Add New Table

You need to copy an original database file, rename the copied file, and then open the copied database to complete this capstone exercise. After you open the copied database, you will create a new table that will be the source for a lookup.

a. Open *a05c1Replace* and save it as **a05c1Replace_LastFirst**.

b. Use Design view to create a new table. Add **ProductLineID** as the first field name, with data type AutoNumber; add **ProductLineDescription** as the second field name, with data type Short Text and field size 10. Ensure ProductLineID is set as the primary key. Save the table and name it **Product Lines**. Add three records: **China**, **Flatware**, and **Crystal**. Close the table.

Establish Data Validation

You need to edit the Inventory table design to validate data. Specifically, you will set the ProductLineID and SKU fields to Required. You will also set a validation rule requiring OnHandQty to contain a value of 0 or higher.

a. Open the Inventory table in Design view.

b. Set the OnHandQty and ProductLineID fields to **Required**.

c. Establish a validation rule for the OnHandQty field that requires the value to be greater than or equal to zero.

d. Create validation text for the OnHandQty: **The value of this field must be 0 or greater.**

e. Save the table. Switch to Datasheet view and test the data with the new rules.

f. Change the OnHandValue in the first record to **–3**. The validation text appears.

g. Press **Esc** to restore the original OnHandValue value. Close the Inventory table.

Create an Input Mask

To help keep data input consistent, you will add input masks to the Phone fields in the Employees and Customer tables.

a. Open the Employees table in Design view.

b. Add a phone number input mask for the Phone field.

c. Save and close the table.

d. Open the Customer table in Design view.

e. Add a phone number input mask for the Phone field.

f. Save and close the table.

Create and Modify a Lookup Field

Create a lookup field in the Inventory table for ProductLineID. Use the new table you created previously as the source for the values in the lookup field.

a. Open the Inventory table in Design view.

b. Change the Data Type of the ProductLineID field to **Lookup Wizard**. Use the Product Lines table for the values in the lookup field, select both fields in the table, accept the default sort, hide the key field from the user, and then accept the default name *ProductLineID*.

c. Save the table. Switch to Datasheet view.

d. Change the product line to **Crystal** in the first record and click the second record. If the record updates successfully, change the first record back to **China**.

e. Close the table.

Create a Parameter Query

You need to modify an existing query to add a parameter so employees doing data entry can quickly get a list of inventory below a certain level.

a. Open the Find Low Quantities query in Design view.

b. Add criteria for the OnHandQty field. The user should be prompted to Enter Threshold. The query should display all results that are less than or equal to the threshold but greater than or equal to 1.

c. Run the query. Enter **2** when prompted to Enter Threshold. You should have two results.

d. Save and close the query.

Use Advanced Functions in the Builder

You will modify the Rounded Prices query to round retail values for items in the inventory. You will also create a query to display employees in need of a performance review.

a. Open the Rounded Prices query in Design view.

b. Create a new column to round the Retail price of each item to the nearest dollar. Name the field **RoundedRetail**.

c. Create a new column to display **Luxury** for all items that have a RoundedRetail value of $100 or more and **Everyday** for items that are less than $100. Name the field **Class**.

d. Run the query. Ensure the correct values appear.

e. Save and close the query.

f. Open the Overdue Reviews query in Design view.

g. Add a new column to determine if an employee's performance review is overdue. If the employee's DateOfLastReview is null, it should display **Overdue**. If not, it should display nothing. Name the column **ReviewStatus**.

h. Add criteria of **Overdue** to the column you just created, so only the employees who are Overdue display.

i. Run the query. Ensure only employees with null DateOfLastReview display.

j. Save and close the query.

Perform Date Arithmetic

Modify an existing query displaying daily totals to display monthly totals instead.

a. Open the Order Totals By Month query in Design view.

b. Change the first column so that instead of grouping by the order date, you group by the month. Use the DatePart function to extract the month from the date. Name the column **MonthNumber**.

c. Run the query. The first line should read 5 (as the month, representing May), with a total of $5,405.89.

d. Save and close the query.

e. Close the database. Close Access. Submit based on your instructor's directions.

Action and Specialized Queries

CHAPTER **6**

Moving Beyond the Select Query

Yuri Arcurs/Shutterstock

CASE STUDY | Replacement China, Inc.

Replacement China, Inc., is an international firm that sells china, crystal, and flatware replacement pieces. You are the database administrator for Replacement China, Inc., and need to perform several database management operations. The most urgent is the need to increase retail prices for a key manufacturer, Spode China, by 5 percent. You will use an update query to make this price increase; you will create other action queries to make additional changes to the firm's database.

Before you run the action queries, you decide to make a backup copy of the database. If a problem exists with any of the queries, you will be able to easily recover from the error by reverting to the backup copy. In addition to backing up the database as a precaution, you need to develop a method of verifying that each action query works properly. One method of verifying an action query is to check the values before running the update query and again after running it, ensuring that the values are updated properly.

You will also create another special type of query known as the crosstab query; a crosstab query will summarize data in the Replacement China, Inc., database and help the managers evaluate the sales and other company statistics. Finally, you will create two queries that will reveal tables with missing data and tables with duplicate data.

Action Queries

When you create a query, by default you are creating a select query. You begin your query design by selecting the necessary tables and then selecting the required fields to add to the query design grid. Select queries provide a subset of the data that answers most questions that users ask about the data in their databases. A select query is also flexible; you can update the underlying table data if you see an error or discover a blank field value. Another advantage of a select query is that you can create a query for one condition—for example, banquet sales in Boston hotels—and then copy the query, rename the copy, and change the criteria to extract data for a second city, for example, Miami.

Access provides four additional query types—update, append, make table, and delete—that you can use to add, edit, or delete data. The four queries are collectively referred to as action queries. An *action query* adds, edits, or deletes data in a database. You use these queries to update records that meet certain criteria, to append records to a table, to make a new table, and to delete specific records from a table. Because action queries change data, Access gives a warning when you attempt to run one. Access warns you that you are about to change data in the specified number of records and gives you a chance to cancel the changes.

TIP | Database Administrator Career

A database administrator (DBA) helps manage databases, including performing backups, security checks, and upgrades to keep data both safe and accessible. According to the U.S. Department of Labor (www.bls.gov/ooh/computer-and-information-technology/database-administrators.htm), you need a bachelor's degree in Management Information Technology, Information Systems, or Computer Science to work in this field. This Web site also contains salary information.

In this section, you will learn about action queries and how they are used to maintain databases. Specifically, you will create the following types of action queries: update, append, make table, and delete.

Determining When to Use an Action Query

Four main action queries can be used to maintain a database:

- **Update query.** An update query is used to update or change data automatically based on criteria that you specify. Rather than modifying data manually or using the find and replace tool, the update query is fast and accurate.

- **Append query.** An append query is used for adding records to an existing table. Records can be selected from various sources, such as external databases and spreadsheets. Rather than entering data manually or performing multiple copy-and-paste operations to a table, the append query is an automated process.

- **Make Table query.** A make table query automatically creates a new table from data that already exist in a database. You can create the new table in the current or another database. For example, a make table query can use criteria to make a table that archives older records that need to be stored outside of the current table. The process is automated and saves the trouble of tedious copy-and-paste operations. A make table query overwrites existing data in a table of the same name.

- **Delete query.** A delete query removes records from a table based on criteria that you specify. For example, after a make table query is run to create records in another table, you may want to remove those same records from the current table. The delete query saves the chore of having to locate and delete records manually.

The Replacement China, Inc., database, like most Access databases, requires some type of regular maintenance—usually performed by the DBA or another person assigned to these tasks. For example, customer orders that were entered last month but not filled might now be outdated. Over time, those outdated orders must be dealt with so they are not just taking up space in the database. One way to handle this type of outdated data is to move it from the primary order table to an inactive order table. You can accomplish this task using a make table query, an append query, and a delete query. First, design a make table query to create an inactive orders table based on existing data, create an append query to add future outdated orders to the inactive orders table, and then create a delete query to remove the outdated orders from the primary order table.

Another condition that exists in the Replacement China, Inc., database (and many Access databases) is null (i.e., blank) values in numeric data fields. In a list of products, each with a cost and a retail price, it is not uncommon for one of the fields to contain a null value. Access does not always calculate properly when a null is in the list of values. It is usually better to enter the value zero rather than have a null value. When null values exist, you can use an update query to replace null values with a zero. First, find all the records with null values using a select query, and then create an update query that will replace the null values with zeros. This is a good alternative to a manual or some other filter-and-replace operation. Once the update query has been created, it can be used on a regular basis to remedy this condition.

Recognize the Benefits of an Action Query

One situation that requires an action query is when an end user is required to enter the same information into many records. For example, at Replacement China, Inc., if all of the customers who had Julia as their sales representative are now going to be handled by Susan, then Julia will need to be replaced by Susan for each of her customers. An employee could complete this task manually, or you could create an action query and replace "Julia" with "Susan" automatically. To handle this situation, create a select query that lists all the customers who have Julia as their sales representative. Next, change the select query to an update query and enter Susan as the new sales representative. Run the update query, and the task is finished! Once an update query has been created, it can be used repeatedly or modified to handle different situations.

A student database in a college is another situation where an Access designer needs to use action queries. When students enroll in a school or program, they are classified as current students and are entered into the Students table. After graduation, the school likely moves them to a Graduates table. An append query is the easiest way to move records from one table to another. Create a select query to select all the records from the Students table in which the graduation date is not blank (i.e., the student *has* a graduation date). Change the select query to an append query, specify the Graduates table as the *append to* table, and then run the query. The students are now in the Graduates table. Use a delete query to remove the students from the Students table (to avoid storing duplicate data).

Back Up a Database When Testing an Action Query

STEP 1 ▶ Action queries locate and alter data that meet specific criteria. You cannot undo updates or deletions performed with an action query. Therefore, you should exercise caution when executing an action query. Before running an action query, it is best to back up the entire database. This provides you with some insurance in case you need to recover from a mistake. After the backup is made, you usually want to create a simple select query first to test your criteria and determine which data will be modified, appended, or deleted before switching to an action query. Once you run an action query, you are committing yourself to an irreversible change.

Updating Data with an Update Query

An *update query* changes the data values in one or more fields for all records that meet specific criteria. For example, the phone company announces that all of your customers in a specific area code will now have a different area code. You construct an update query to identify records of all customers who live in the specific area code and then change their existing area code to the new area code. Another example might be in a database storing information about student athletes and their academic eligibility. At the end of each semester, you would create an update query to identify all academically eligible athletes based on their grade point average (GPA). All athletes with a GPA of 2.5 or higher would be updated to eligible.

Create a Select Query Before Running an Update Query

Prior to updating data in a table, you may first want to locate the records that need to be modified. For example, you discover that one or more orders have a missing order date—key information required to process the order. To find other orders with a missing order date, you would first create a select query.

To create a select query, do the following:

1. Click Query Design in the Queries group on the CREATE tab.
2. Add the order data table to the query design and add all fields to the query design grid.
3. Add Is Null to the criterion of the order date field, as shown in Figure 6.1.
4. Run the query to see how many orders have a missing order date, as shown in Figure 6.2.

You could then ask a customer service employee to research the orders with missing dates, perhaps by talking with user 8580, the employee who entered the orders.

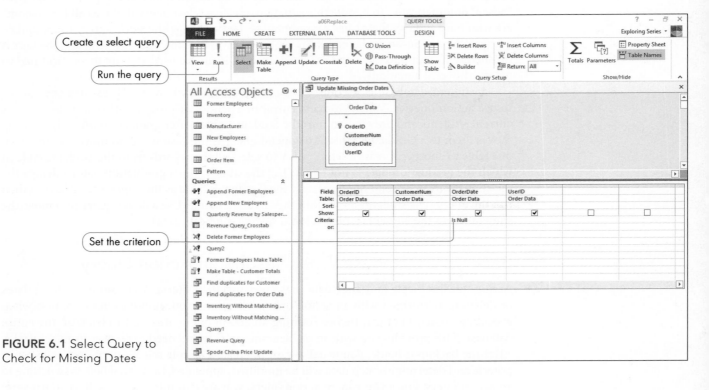

FIGURE 6.1 Select Query to Check for Missing Dates

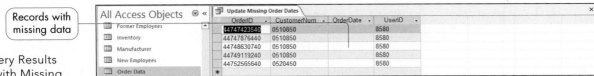

FIGURE 6.2 Query Results Show Records with Missing Dates

Convert a Select Query to an Update Query

STEP 2 Your goal is to update records with a missing order date. Once the records with a missing order date are found by a select query, you decide to convert it to an update query and insert the current date into any record with a blank order date so that the orders can be processed.

To create the update query, do the following:

1. View the select query in Design view (as shown in Figure 6.1).
2. Click Update in the Query Type group.
3. Enter the new value into the Update To row. In the missing order date example, type the Date() function into the Update To row of the OrderDate field (as shown in Figure 6.3).
4. Click Run in the Results group. (If you want to verify which records the update query will affect before running the query, test the query as described in the next section.)

The current date is inserted into the OrderDate field for all records with a missing order date.

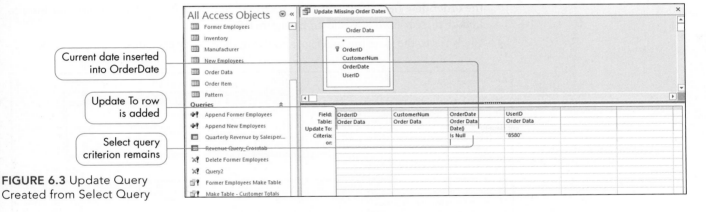

Current date inserted into OrderDate

Update To row is added

Select query criterion remains

FIGURE 6.3 Update Query Created from Select Query

Test an Update Query

STEP 3 You can test an update query (before clicking Run) and verify that the correct records will be updated by switching to Datasheet view first. Once an update query is run, you cannot undo the action, so it is important to view the eligible records beforehand.

To test an update query before running it, do the following:

From Design view, click View in the Results group and click Datasheet view.

Datasheet view will look different than usual—most of the columns that were showing in the Datasheet view of the select query are no longer showing in the Datasheet view of the update query (see Figure 6.4). Only the column and records that conform to the Update To criteria are showing. You can use this information to evaluate the number of records that will be updated when you run the update query. Look at the number of records shown in the navigation bar at the bottom of the Datasheet view. If the number of records is what you expect, then it is safe to run the update query.

FIGURE 6.4 Datasheet View
of an Update Query

To run the update query, do the following:

1. Return to the query Design view.
2. Verify that Update is selected in the Query Type group.
3. Click Run in the Results group. The five records will have the current date inserted into the order date field, after you click Yes to the Access message *Are you sure you want to update these records?* (as shown in Figure 6.5).
4. Click Yes to the warning message and the update query executes.

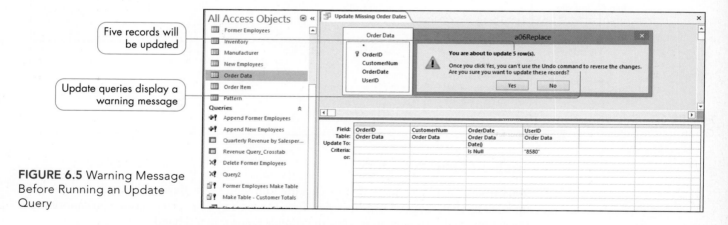

Five records will
be updated

Update queries display a
warning message

FIGURE 6.5 Warning Message
Before Running an Update
Query

TIP **Add a New Field Before Running an Update Query**

Backing up the database prior to running an update query is the best precaution. Additionally, there may be times when adding a new field to a table may be a practical option. For example, if you are reducing the values of retail prices by 15 percent, you lose the original prices after changing them with an update query. To avoid this, add a new field to the table named Retail Original (for example). Then create an update query that updates the Retail Original field with the current retail price. Next, run the update query to decrease the current retail prices by 15 percent. Now you have both the original retail price (Retail Original) and the new retail price (Retail New).

Verify an Update Query

Running an action query from Design view does not display a view of the results; Access simply returns you to the query design window. No records (with the new data) are displayed. One way to test the results would be to create a query to locate the updated records. Click Select in the Query Type group and modify the query's criteria to select the updated data. In the sample database, we inserted the current date into the missing order date fields. You would change the order date criterion from Is Null to today's date and run the query to view the corrected records.

Another method is to try to locate the original records prior to their being updated and discovering that those records no longer exist in their original state. In the example, you could select orders for User (employee) 8580 where the order dates are null. With Is Null as the criterion in the order date field, enter 8580 in the User ID criteria row and run the query. The query results show that there are no longer records for this user with missing (null) order dates (as shown in Figure 6.6).

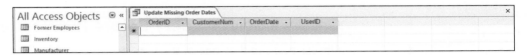

FIGURE 6.6 Verify the Data After an Update Query

TIP Do Not Rerun Action Queries

After you run an action query, it might appear that nothing has happened except that the warning box disappears. You might be tempted to click Run again—but you should not; you may find that data is changed again unnecessarily. For example, if you created an update query to lower the sale price of all products by 15 percent, entering *[Sale Price]* * .85 into the Update To row for the sale price field would work correctly. However, running the query a second time would lower the price an additional 15 percent from the current price. In this case, the total reduction would be a 27.75 percent discount (lower than the intended 15 percent).

Adding Records to a Table with an Append Query

STEP 4 》 Another type of action query is the append query. An **append query** copies records from one or more tables (the source) and adds them to an existing table (the destination). The appended records appear in the destination table in primary key order, or they are added to the bottom of the table if no primary key exists. If any appended record violates the primary key rule or another rule created for the destination table, the record is rejected. For example, you might use an append query to copy employee records in the Replacement China, Inc., database. Suppose the company hires new employees each week. The company may place new hires into a Candidates table until the background checks are complete. Once the checks are completed, the candidates can be appended to the Employees table and then deleted from the Candidates table. Moving records from one table to another can be accomplished with the combination of an append query and a delete query. Append queries are frequently used in conjunction with delete queries. If you use an append query to copy a record from one table to another, the original record still exists. The same data is now stored in two different places—a practice that must be avoided in a database. After the criteria for an append query are established, you can reuse the same criteria to create a delete query and delete the records from the source table. This is a common practice when working with append queries.

Often, organizations store the active records (today's or this week's activities) in one table and then append them to a more permanent table after they are completed. The tables involved with an append query—the source and destination—usually contain the same field names. In most cases, the data types of the source fields must match the data types of the destination fields. The rules for appending are as follows:

- Data types of the fields in both tables must match in most cases; however, some exceptions to this rule exist.

- All the normal rules for adding a new record to the destination table apply. For example, the records are not added if a value is missing in the source table when the field is required in the destination table.

- If a field from the source table does not exist in the destination table, Access leaves a blank in the Append To row, and you will need to manually specify the destination field name (or just delete the unneeded source field from the query design grid). If the destination table has non required fields that are not in the source table, the record appends, and the missing field values are blank.

- The destination table should not contain an AutoNumber field. An AutoNumber in the source table should append to a Number field in the destination table.

Create a Select Query Before Running an Append Query

Similar to an update query, the first step in creating an append query is to create a select query. You can use one or multiple tables for the data source. Next, select the fields you want to append from the table(s) to the query design grid. Enter the criteria to filter only the records you want to append. For example, if Replacement China, Inc., wanted to move its former employees from the Employees table to the Former Employees table, it could create a select query, and then add criteria to find employees where the termination date is not null. The results of this query are shown in Datasheet view in Figure 6.7.

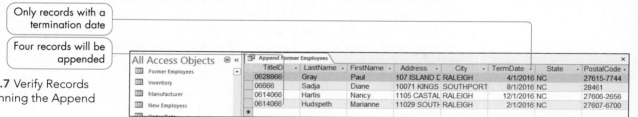

FIGURE 6.7 Verify Records Before Running the Append Query

Set Append To Fields in an Append Query

After you verify that the correct records are selected, switch to Design view, and then change the select query to an append query.

To convert the select query to an append query, do the following:

1. In Design view, click Append in the Query Type group.
2. Select the destination table using the table name arrow and click OK.

Figure 6.8 shows the Append dialog box that displays, in which you specify the destination table.

When you change to an append query, Access removes the Show row in the query design grid and adds the Append To row in its place. If the fields in the source and destination tables are the same, Access automatically inserts the correct field names into the Append To row, as shown in Figure 6.9.

FIGURE 6.8 Click Append to Create an Append Query

FIGURE 6.9 Source Fields Append to Destination Fields

Run an Append Query

If you need to verify the records to be appended, you can click View in the Results group to double-check in Datasheet view. After verifying the records, switch back to Design view.

To run an append query, do the following:

1. In Design view, click Run in the Results group. You will receive a warning message telling you that you are about to append the number of records selected, as shown in Figure 6.10.
2. Click Yes to continue. As with all the action queries, you cannot undo the action after it is run.
3. Save and close the append query (if required).
4. Open the destination table and verify that the appended records are in the table.

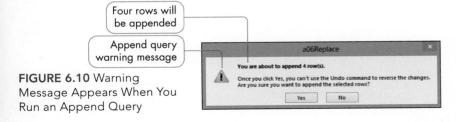

FIGURE 6.10 Warning Message Appears When You Run an Append Query

Creating a Table with a Make Table Query

The third type of action query is the make table query. A **make table query** selects records from one or more tables and uses them to create a new table. Suppose that your school has a large database that stores information about students. The database has information about the classes students are registered for each term, their majors, and their emergency contact information. The Business and Technology Department needs to know the names of the students enrolled in its programs. You can use a make table query to extract the Business and Technology Department student data and then use it to create a new table. Subsequent searches can be done on the new table, reducing the response time required by searching the larger database that contains all student records.

At Replacement China, Inc., the sales manager may want to know the total year-to-date orders for each customer. You could create a make table query that would insert this information into a new table—Customer Order Totals, for example.

Create a Make Table Query

STEP 5 ≫

The process of creating a make table query is very similar to creating an append query. The difference is that a make table query creates the structure of the table and then adds the records to the table. An append query requires the destination table to exist first; otherwise, it cannot append additional records. You can use the make table query to copy some or all records from a source table to a destination table even if the destination table does not exist. If the destination table exists and you run the make table query, Access prompts you before it deletes the original table. If you click Yes, Access deletes the source table and replaces it with data specified by the make table query.

To create a make table query, do the following:

1. Create a select query; specify the tables and field names that you want to add to the new table to the query design window.
2. Specify the criteria that will result in selecting the correct records for your new table.
3. In Design view, click Make Table in the Query Type group.
4. Specify the table name that you want to create in the Table Name box.
5. Click OK.

Figure 6.11 displays the setup for a make table query that will copy aggregate order data to a new table.

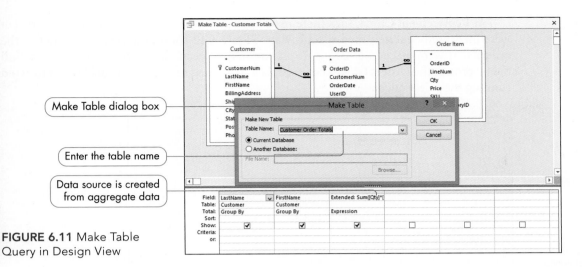

Make Table dialog box

Enter the table name

Data source is created from aggregate data

FIGURE 6.11 Make Table Query in Design View

Test and Run a Make Table Query

As with the other action queries, you should preview the datasheet prior to running the query to verify that the records are those that you intend to insert into a new table.

To test and run a make table query, do the following:

1. Click View in the Results group to view the records in Datasheet view.
2. After you verify that the records are correct, click View again to return to Design view.
3. Click Run in the Results group and Access displays a warning telling you that you are about to append records to a new table.
4. Click Yes and the new table is created.
5. Open the new table and verify the records are correct.
6. Save and close the query (if required).

If you run the same make table query at a later date, the first table is replaced with a new, up-to-date table.

Deleting Records with a Delete Query

STEP 6 >> The final type of action query is the delete query. A **delete query** selects records from a table, and then removes them from the table. Sometimes it is necessary to identify and delete data in a database. However, it should always be done with caution. For example, if you copy the Replacement China, Inc., database inactive customers from the Customers table to the Inactive Customers table using an append query, you will want to delete those records from the Customers table. Take precautions prior to running a delete query. If you create a backup copy of the database prior to running a delete query, you can always recover from an error.

Create a Delete Query

The delete query begins the same way as all of the other action queries, with a select query.

To create a delete query, do the following:

1. Create a select query; specify the tables and field names that you want to remove from the table in the query design window.
2. Specify the criteria in the fields that will result in deleting the correct records from your table.
3. In Design view, click Delete in the Query Type group.

At Replacement China, Inc., there may be times when they need to remove orders that were incorrectly entered on a specific date. Figure 6.12 shows the criterion to delete the orders that were placed on 6/10/2016. If you fail to specify a criterion, Access deletes all the records in the Orders table. Access displays a warning message and enables you to avoid running the delete query.

Add criteria as needed

FIGURE 6.12 Delete Query in Design View

Test and Run a Delete Query

As with the other action queries, always view the records to be deleted in Datasheet view prior to running the delete query. After you verify the number of records in the datasheet, run the query.

To run the delete query, do the following:

1. Switch to Design view, if you were testing the query in Datasheet view.
2. Click Run in the Results group to run the query and delete the records.
3. Click Yes when the warning message appears. Verify the results of the delete query by opening the table to confirm that the records were deleted.
4. Save and close the query (if required).

> **TIP** **Action Query Icons**
>
> Access denotes the action queries differently from select queries by displaying a specific icon for each action query type in the Navigation Pane (see Figure 6.13). This may prevent users from accidentally running an action query and getting unexpected results. For example, if an update query is created to increase prices by 10 percent, running the query a second time would increase those prices again. Exercise caution when running action queries.

Action query icons

FIGURE 6.13 Action Query Icons

You will experiment with creating and running action queries in Hands-On Exercise 1 using the data from Replacement China, Inc. You will run an update query to identify all of the products in inventory from a specified manufacturer and increase their prices by

5 percent. You will use an append query to add new employees to the Employees table. Next, you will make a table containing the employees who are no longer with the firm. You will use a delete query to remove the employees from the Employees table who no longer work for Replacement China, Inc.

Quick Concepts

1. What is a benefit of creating an append query? *p. 358*

2. What is a potential disadvantage of running an update query? *p. 362*

3. What is a good strategy for handling mistakes that can occur while running action queries? *p. 362*

Hands-On Exercises

Watch the Video for this Hands-On Exercise!

MyITLab®
HOE1 Training

1 Action Queries

Several maintenance tasks are required at Replacement China, Inc. Before work begins, you decide to back up the database to make it easy to recover from a mistake. Each task requires an action query. After you create and run each query, you verify the changes by checking the records in the modified table.

Skills covered: Back Up a Database When Testing an Action Query • Create an Update Query • Test an Update Query • Create an Append Query • Create a Make Table Query • Create a Delete Query

---

STEP 1 ▶ BACK UP A DATABASE WHEN TESTING AN ACTION QUERY

Create a backup copy of the Replacement China, Inc., database before you create any action queries. If you make a mistake along the way, revert to the original file and start again. Refer to Figure 6.14 as you complete Step 1.

Step b: Click Back Up Database

FIGURE 6.14 Create a Backup Copy of the Database

a. Open *a06h1Replace*. Click **Save As** on the FILE tab, click **Save As**, and then type **a06h1Replace_LastFirst**. Click **Save**.

> **TROUBLESHOOTING:** Throughout the remainder of this chapter and textbook, click Enable Content whenever you are working with student files.

> **TROUBLESHOOTING:** If you make any major mistakes in this exercise, you can close the file, repeat step a above, and then start over.

b. Click **Save As** on the FILE tab, and double-click **Back Up Database**.

Before you execute an action query, it is recommended that you make a backup copy of the entire database first. If a problem occurs, you can use the backup copy to recover.

c. Click **Save** to accept the default file name for the backup copy of the *a06h1Replace_LastFirst_date* database.

A backup copy of the database now exists in your default folder.

d. Verify the backup file exists in your default folder.

STEP 2 ≫ CREATE AN UPDATE QUERY

One of your manufacturers, Spode China, has increased its prices for the upcoming year. You decide to increase your retail prices as well. You create an update query to increase the retail price by 5 percent but only for items that are supplied by Spode China. Refer to Figure 6.15 as you complete Step 2.

FIGURE 6.15 Create an Update Query

a. Click **Query Design** in the Queries group on the CREATE tab.

The Show Table dialog box opens.

b. Double-click the **Inventory**, **Pattern**, and **Manufacturer tables** to add these tables to the query design space. Close the Show Table dialog box.

c. Add the SKU, OnHandQty, and Retail fields from the Inventory table, MfgID field from the Pattern table, and Alias field from the Manufacturer table to the design grid. Type **801190** in the **Criteria row** of the MfgID column.

You added the criteria to select only Spode China pieces to update the prices. The MfgID for Spode China is 801190.

d. Switch to Datasheet view and verify the correct records are selected.

The results include 1,129 Spode China records.

e. Switch to Design view. Click the **MfgID column** and click **Insert Columns** in the Query Setup group.

A new blank column appears between Retail and MfgID.

f. Type **Value: [OnHandQty]*[Retail]** in the first row of the new blank column. Click **Property Sheet** in the Show/Hide group. Select **Currency** from the list in the Format box and close the Property Sheet.

> You created a calculated field so that you can check the total value of the inventory before and after the update.

g. Switch to Datasheet view. Click **Totals** in the Records group. Advance to the last record.

h. Click in the **Total row** of the Value column, click the arrow, and then select **Sum**.

> The total of the Value column is $911,415.88. The value after the update should be $956,986.67 (911,415.88 × 1.05).

i. Click **View** to return to Design view. Click **Update** in the Query Type group.

> You changed the query type from a select to an update query. The Sort and Show rows are replaced by the Update To row in the grid.

j. Click the **Update To row** under the Retail field in the design grid. Type **[Retail] * 1.05**. With the Retail field selected, click **Property Sheet** in the Show/Hide group. Select **Currency** from the list in the Format box and close the Property Sheet.

> The expression will replace the current retail value with a value 5 percent higher.

k. Compare your screen to Figure 6.15.

STEP 3 ≫ TEST AN UPDATE QUERY

You created an update query to increase the retail price of Spode China products by 5 percent, but you want to verify the values before you run the query. Once you update the prices, you will not be able to undo the changes. Refer to Figure 6.16 as you complete Step 3.

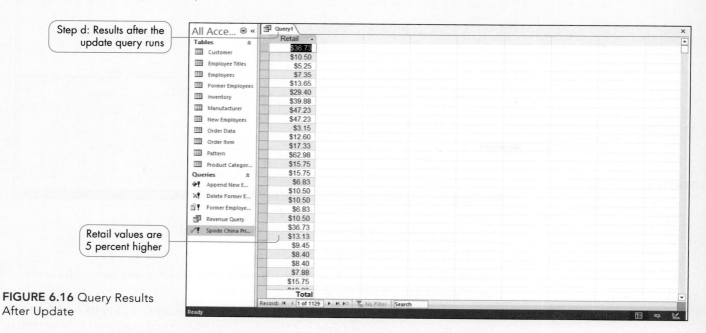

FIGURE 6.16 Query Results After Update

a. Switch to Datasheet view and examine the records before running the query.

> You should see a list of retail prices ($34.98, $10.00, $5.00, $7.00, etc.) but no other columns. Access only displays the columns that have a value in the Update To row. These are the current prices that will be updated.

b. Click **View** to return to Design view.

c. Click **Run** in the Results group to execute the query. Click **Yes** in response to the *You are about to update 1129 row(s)* warning.

> Although it may seem as though nothing happened, your prices have changed.

d. View the results in Datasheet view.

The first four retail prices are now $36.73, $10.50, $5.25, and $7.35, as shown in Figure 6.16. These prices are 5 percent higher than the original retail prices you saw in step a above.

e. Return to Design view. Click **Select** in the Query Type group.

f. Switch to Datasheet view.

The prices in the Retail column reflect the updated prices, and the bottom of the Retail column is now $956,986.67, which verifies that the update query worked correctly.

g. Return to Design view.

h. Click **Update** in the Query Type group to change back to an update query. Save the query as **Spode China Price Update**. Close the query.

The query icon in the Navigation Pane indicates the query is an update query.

STEP 4 ≫ CREATE AN APPEND QUERY

Replacement China, Inc., hired several new employees who were placed into the New Employees table for a 30-day probation period. The probation period is over, and now you need to add them to the Employees table. Refer to Figure 6.17 as you complete Step 4.

Step i: Append query will add four records

FIGURE 6.17 New Employees to Be Appended to the Employees Table

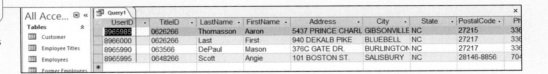

> **TROUBLESHOOTING:** You could make a backup copy of the database to revert back to in the event of an error. You backed up the database at the beginning of this exercise, but you may want another backup in case the append query causes a problem. If you complete this step on the same day as you completed the last step, Access adds _(1) to the end of the backup file name to distinguish it from the earlier file name.

a. Open the New Employees table in Datasheet view. Add yourself as a new record. Type **8966000** in the **UserID field**; **0626266** in the **TitleID field**; your last name, first name, address, city, state, postal code, and phone number in the respective name fields; and **9/11/2016** in the **HireDate field**.

b. Close the New Employees table.

c. Open the Employees table and note the total records in the navigation bar at the bottom of the window.

The navigation bar shows 115 current employees.

d. Close the Employees table.

e. Click **Query Design** in the Queries group on the CREATE tab. Double-click the **New Employees table**. Close the Show Table dialog box.

You have begun to create a select query.

f. Click **Append** in the Query Type group.

You need to change the query design to an append query to add the newly hired employees to the Employees table. The Append dialog box opens, prompting you to supply the destination table name.

g. Click the **Table Name arrow** and select **Employees**. Verify the Current Database option is selected and click **OK**.

The Append To row appears on the design grid, ready for you to add fields. You need all of the fields in the New Employees table added to the Employees table.

h. Double-click the title bar of the New Employees table in the top portion of the Design view window. All of the fields are selected. Drag the selected fields to the first field box in the design grid.

i. Click **View** in the Results group and preview the data you are about to append.

You should see 4 rows and 10 fields, as shown in Figure 6.17.

j. Click **View** in the Views group to return to Design view.

k. Click **Run** in the Results group to run the query. Click **Yes** in response to the *You are about to append 4 row(s)* warning.

l. Open the Employees table. Sort the table in descending order (Newest to Oldest) by the HireDate field and make sure the four newest records were added.

The Employees table should now contain a total of 119 employees. Your own name should be one of the top four records.

m. Click the **Query1 tab** and click **Save** on the Quick Access Toolbar. Save the query as **Append New Employees**. Close the open objects. Save the design of the New Employees table.

The query icon in the Navigation Pane indicates the query is an append query.

STEP 5 ⟫ CREATE A MAKE TABLE QUERY

Replacement China, Inc., needs to create a Former Employees table for all employees who are no longer with the company. The records of these former employees are currently stored in the Employees table. You need to move them to a Former Employees table. Refer to Figure 6.18 as you complete Step 5.

Step j: Nine records added to the Former Employees table

FIGURE 6.18 Use Make Table to Create a New Table

a. Click **Query Design** in the Queries group on the CREATE tab.

b. Double-click the **Employees table** to add it to the query. Close the Show Table dialog box.

Some of the employees listed in the Employees table no longer work for Replacement China, Inc. You need to retain this information but do not want these records included in the Employees table; the records will be stored in the archived Former Employees table.

c. Double-click the title bar of the Employees table in the top portion of the Design view window to select all the fields. Drag the selected fields to the first field box in the design grid.

d. Type **Is Not Null** in the **Criteria row** of the TermDate field.

This criterion will select only those employees with a value in the termination date field.

e. Display the results in Datasheet view.

You should find that nine employees are no longer with the company. These are the employees you want to move to a new table using a make table query.

f. Click **View** to switch back to Design view.

g. Click **Make Table** in the Query Type group.

The Make Table dialog box opens and asks that you name and provide storage location information for the new table. You want to archive this data, but the new table can reside in the same database.

h. Type **Former Employees** in the **Table Name box**. Make sure the Current Database option is selected. Click **OK**.

i. Click **Run** in the Results group to run the query. Click **Yes** in response to the *You are about to paste 9 row(s) into a new table* warning.

j. Examine the Navigation Pane to make sure that the new Former Employees table exists. Open the Former Employees table to verify the nine former employees are present, as shown in Figure 6.18. Close the table.

TROUBLESHOOTING: If your table did not come out properly, delete the query and the newly created table. You can try this query again by beginning from Step 5b. Be sure to check that the correct criterion is entered to locate employees with termination dates.

---

k. Save the query as **Former Employees Make Table**.

The query icon in the Navigation Pane indicates the query is a make table query.

l. Close the query.

STEP 6 ›› CREATE A DELETE QUERY

You moved the former employees from the Employees table to the Former Employees table in the Replacement China, Inc., database. Now you need to delete the former employees from the Employees table. It is not a good practice to have the same data stored in two different tables. Refer to Figure 6.19 as you complete Step 6.

FIGURE 6.19 Create a Delete Query to Remove Former Employees

a. Click **Query Design** in the Queries group on the CREATE tab.

b. Double-click the **Employees table** in the Show Table dialog box to add it to the query. Close the Show Table dialog box.

c. Drag the * from the Employees table to the first column of the query design grid.

The * field only takes up one column in the design grid. The * field represents all the fields in the Employees table. This is a shortcut for adding all of the fields to the design grid in one step rather than one by one.

d. Drag the **TermDate field** from the Employees table to the second column of the query design grid.

You need to add the TermDate a second time to use it to set the criteria for the select query.

e. Type **Is Not Null** in the **Criteria row** for the TermDate field. Click **View** to switch to Datasheet view.

You created a select query to make sure you have correctly identified the nine records for deletion prior to changing it to a delete query. Nine records are shown in Datasheet view.

f. Switch to Design view. Click **Delete** in the Query Type group.

The Delete row now contains From in the Employees.* column and Where in the TermDate column. This delete query will delete all records in the Employees table that have a termination date.

g. Click **Run** in the Results group. Click **Yes** in response to the *You are about to delete 9 row(s) from the specified table* warning.

You deleted the nine former employees from the Employees table.

h. Save the query as **Delete Former Employees**. Close the query.

i. Open the Employees table and verify that the total employees has been reduced from 119 to 110. Close the table.

j. Click **Compact & Repair Database** on the FILE tab.

k. Click **Save As** on the FILE tab, and double-click **Back Up Database**. Name the backup **a06h1Replace_LastFirst_date_(1)**.

You just created a backup of the database you used to complete Hands-On Exercise 1. The *a06h1Replace_LastFirst* database remains open. If you complete this step on the same day as you worked the last step, Access adds_*(1)* to the end of the backup file name to distinguish it from the earlier file name.

l. Keep the database open if you plan to continue with Hands-On Exercise 2. If not, close the database and exit Access.

Queries for Special Conditions

This section will improve your overall effectiveness with a database by introducing you to three types of queries that are used for special conditions.

A crosstab query calculates data using a sum, average, or other function and groups the results by two sets of values. In this section, you will learn how to construct a crosstab query that displays aggregate data in a row-and-column format where each row and column presents values that you select from your database. An unmatched record is a record in one table without a matching record in a related table. A duplicate record is one where the same information is entered extraneously in a table, usually by data entry error. You will also create two special queries: one to find unmatched records and one to find duplicate records.

Summarizing Data with a Crosstab Query

 You can present aggregate data to the user with a crosstab query. A *crosstab query* summarizes a data source into a grid of rows and columns; the intersection of each row and column displays the aggregate data. A crosstab query is usually created to show trends in values (e.g., sales) over time. For example, to evaluate the sales force at Replacement China, Inc., you might want to construct a crosstab query to examine the revenue generated by each salesperson over a specific period of time. The salespersons' names would be listed along the left side of the grid (the rows). The name of each quarter (or month, for example) would be listed along the top of the grid (the columns). The intersection of the rows and columns displays the total or average revenue for each salesperson for each quarter (or month) of the year. This intersecting cell is the heart of the crosstab query. Crosstab queries can be based on a table or a query.

Group and Summarize Data

The grouping in a crosstab query comes from the definitions of row and column headings. *Row headings* display field names along the left side of a crosstab query. *Column headings* display field names along the top of a crosstab query. The summarizing or aggregating data in a crosstab query is displayed at the intersection of the rows and columns. The type of data that is displayed depends on which aggregate function you choose when you create the crosstab query—count, sum, and average are a few examples. If you want to know the quarterly sales for each salesperson for the current year, use salesperson as the row heading, the order date as the column heading, and the total quarterly sales in dollars as the intersecting values. When you assign a date field to the column heading, Access gives you an option for summarizing by year, quarter, month, or date. You can also add rows to give the crosstab query additional levels of grouping.

> ## TIP Choosing a Data Source for a Crosstab Query
>
> Crosstab queries work best when you select a data source that has at least two grouping fields. For example, if you want to evaluate a baseball team's performance over the past five years, you could create a crosstab query. The rows could list the category of the game—preseason, conference, nonconference—and the columns could list each of the past five years. The intersection of each category with each year would give you the count of the games won. If you wish to break down the crosstab query even further, you could add the Home/Away field to the rows—the data would be grouped first by game category, and then by home/away games. Then, the query could provide some additional information about the team's effectiveness while playing at home or away.

Use the Crosstab Query Wizard

You will almost always use the Crosstab Query Wizard to build a crosstab query, although it can be built from scratch using the query design grid. As with any query wizard, you first need to identify the source of the data that will be the basis of the crosstab query. Unlike other queries, you can only reference one object (table or query) as the data source in a crosstab query. Therefore, if you want to use fields stored in different tables, you must first combine the required data in a query. Once the data are combined in a single source, you can create the crosstab query.

To create a crosstab query, do the following:

1. Click the Query Wizard in the Queries group on the CREATE tab.
2. When the New Query dialog box appears, select Crosstab Query Wizard.
3. Click OK, as shown in Figure 6.20.

FIGURE 6.20 Open the Crosstab Query Wizard

4. Identify the data source and click Next. You can display tables, queries, or a combination of both by selecting the appropriate view (see Figure 6.21).
5. In the next step, shown in Figure 6.22, identify up to three row heading fields. To make a selection, double-click the field name or click the > button. Click Next. Access limits the number of row heading fields to three and the number of column headings to one. You can have as many aggregate fields as you want, but more than two or three makes the crosstab query difficult to read.
6. Select the field for the column headings, as shown in Figure 6.23. Click Next.
7. If the field contains date data, the next window will ask for the date interval (see Figure 6.24). Click Next. In this example, the sales data for each salesperson will be summarized by quarter.
8. Choose the field to use in a calculation at the intersection of each row and column; then choose what type of aggregate function to apply, such as Avg, Count, or Sum. Click Next. Figure 6.25 shows the result of selecting the Revenue field and the Sum function.
9. Name the query and provide information on how you want to view the new query (see Figure 6.26).
10. Close the query.

FIGURE 6.21 Select the Crosstab Query Data Source

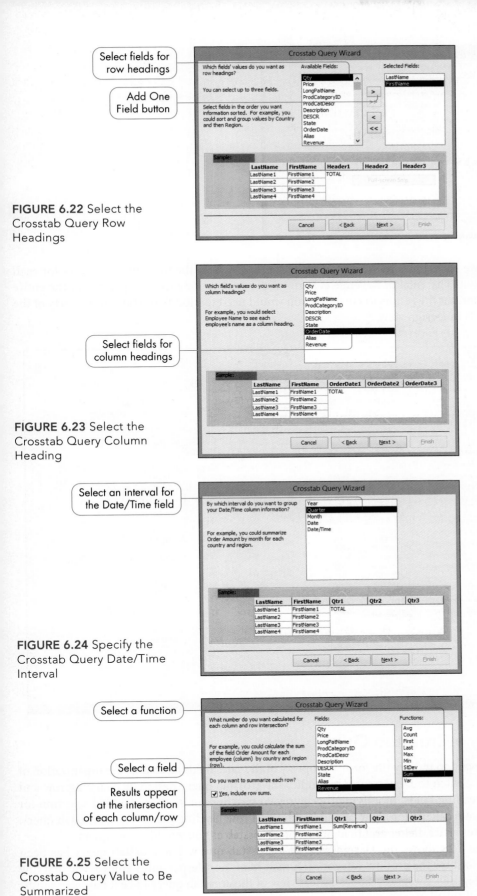

FIGURE 6.22 Select the Crosstab Query Row Headings

FIGURE 6.23 Select the Crosstab Query Column Heading

FIGURE 6.24 Specify the Crosstab Query Date/Time Interval

FIGURE 6.25 Select the Crosstab Query Value to Be Summarized

Name the query

Select to view or modify design

FIGURE 6.26 Name the Crosstab Query

Figure 6.27 shows the results of a crosstab query with the total quarterly sales for each salesperson. The Total of Revenue column displays totals for each salesperson for the entire year. To format the results as currency, you would need to modify the format property of the sales fields in Design view.

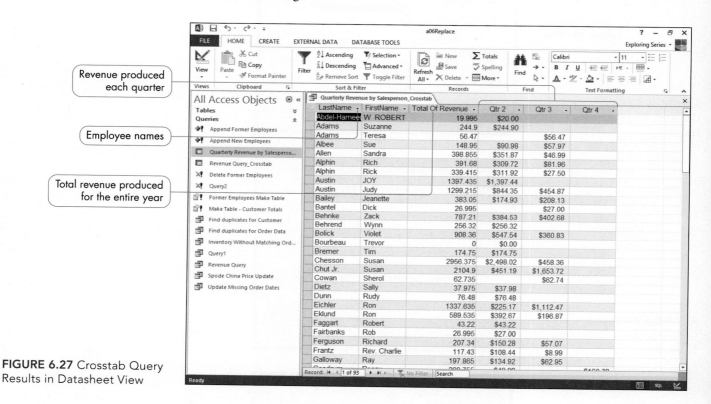

Revenue produced each quarter

Employee names

Total revenue produced for the entire year

FIGURE 6.27 Crosstab Query Results in Datasheet View

Modify a Crosstab Query

STEP 2 You may want to modify the format property of the sales fields or change the organization of the query. Switch to Design view to modify the crosstab query design by changing row and column heading fields, modifying the aggregate function, or altering the field selection for the aggregate calculation. You can add additional row heading fields to the crosstab query. Modify properties, fields, and field order for a crosstab as you would in any query.

Figure 6.28 shows the Design view of a crosstab query. The crosstab query has been modified to show the product category IDs instead of the salesperson's names as the first row heading. Figure 6.29 shows the Datasheet view of the crosstab query once it has been modified, and all calculations have been formatted as currency.

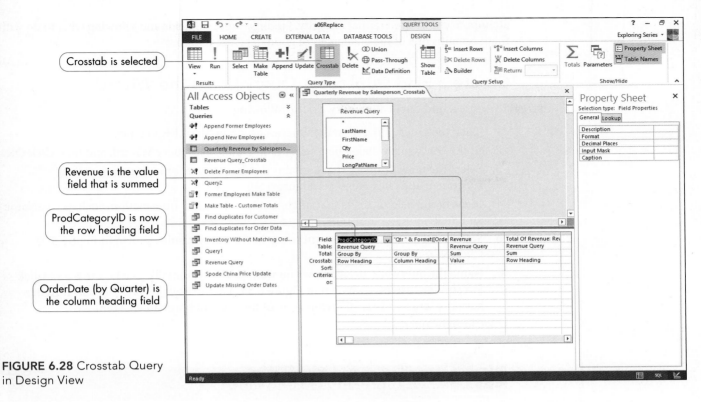

Crosstab is selected

Revenue is the value field that is summed

ProdCategoryID is now the row heading field

OrderDate (by Quarter) is the column heading field

FIGURE 6.28 Crosstab Query in Design View

FIGURE 6.29 Edited Crosstab Query in Datasheet View

Finding Duplicate Records with a Query

If two records with the same name and address are in a table, that may indicate a duplicate entry. You might expect Access to restrict a user from entering a record into a table with the same name and address; however, because many tables use unique values as the ID number for each record, as long as the ID is different, a user would be able to enter one, two, three, or more records with the same name and address. Access can create a query to display records that are potential duplicate records, for example, a duplicated order.

Sometimes data is entered more than once by mistake. However, not all duplicated data in a database is the result of an error. Some duplication occurs naturally. For example, the CustomerID field is the unique identifier in the Customer table; no two customers can have the same ID number. However, the CustomerID field also appears as a foreign key field in the Orders table. Because of the one-to-many relationship between the Customer table and the Orders table, the CustomerID can repeat in the Orders table. One customer may place many orders. Repeating data values in a foreign key on the many side of a one-to-many relationship is standard database design—duplication is expected.

Additionally, some data values repeat naturally in a table. The city field will contain many records with duplicating values. The LastName field may contain records with the same name, such as Smith, Lee, or Rodriguez. These duplicated data values are not errors. Not all duplicated data values are problematic; however, there may be occasions when you will need to find and manage unwanted duplicates.

Use a Find Duplicate Records Query

STEP 3 ▶ You can use a *find duplicates query* to help identify duplicate values in a table. If you inherit a poorly designed database and are unable to enforce referential integrity between tables, you can run a find duplicates query to identify the duplicate values in the primary key field candidate. Once you identify the problem records, you can fix or eliminate them and then attempt to enforce referential integrity. Finding duplicate fields and knowing what to do with them remains one of the challenges of good database design.

Create a Find Duplicates Query Using the Wizard

To create a find duplicates query, do the following:

1. Click the Query Wizard in the Queries group on the CREATE tab.
2. In the New Query dialog box, select Find Duplicates Query Wizard, and then click OK.
3. Select the table or query that contains the data source for your query, such as Customer, and click Next (see Figure 6.30).
4. Identify the field or fields that might contain duplicate information, such as LastName and FirstName, as shown in Figure 6.31. Click Next.
5. Select additional fields you want to see in the query results, shown in Figure 6.32. Click Next.
6. Name the query and decide how you want to view it initially (see Figure 6.33). Click Finish. The results are shown in Figure 6.34. The first two records for Susan Agner have the same address; therefore, one of them should probably be removed.
7. Close the query.

Deleting Duplicate Records

Use caution when deleting duplicate records. For example, if two customers in a table have the same exact details but unique ID (primary key) fields, records (such as orders) may be stored using both customer IDs. Be sure to ensure that when you delete the duplicated customer record, you do not delete associated orders in a related table. Associate the orders with the customer record that you are keeping.

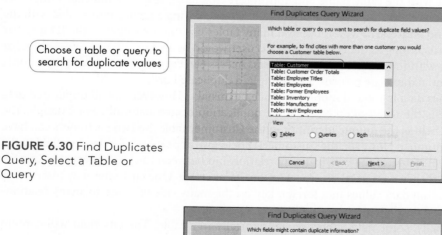

Choose a table or query to search for duplicate values

FIGURE 6.30 Find Duplicates Query, Select a Table or Query

Choose field(s) that might have duplicates

FIGURE 6.31 Find Duplicates Query, Select Fields

FIGURE 6.32 Find Duplicates Query, Select Additional Fields

Add fields to the query results

FIGURE 6.33 Name the Find Duplicates Query

Name the query

Duplicate customer Susan Agner

FIGURE 6.34 Duplicate Customers

Finding Unmatched Records with a Query

It is possible for a company to run reports that show which customers did *not* place an order in the past week, or in the previous month, or in the past 12 months, or ever. No matter how a company decides to handle this group of customers, it could be useful to know how many customers who receive their catalog have never placed an order. Access comes with a special query wizard that helps you find these customers. A *find unmatched query* compares records in two related tables and displays the records found in one table but not the other.

Use a Find Unmatched Query

STEP 4 >> Another use of a find unmatched query could be in a grade-book database. Your instructor might have a database that contains a Student table with all the relevant student information. The database would also have a Grades table that holds all the grades for each student. Throughout the semester, as students complete their assignments, the instructor enters the score for each assignment into the Grades table. Periodically, the instructor could run a report showing all the grades for each assignment and perhaps showing the average score at the bottom of the report. But this report would not include students who have not completed each assignment; these students could be identified with a find unmatched query.

The find unmatched query would require two tables (Students and Grades) with a common field (StudentID) where one of the tables is missing information (Grades). The find unmatched query could become the source for a Missing Assignments Report.

Create a Find Unmatched Query Using the Wizard

In the Replacement China, Inc., database, management may want to know which items in the inventory are obsolete. *Obsolete* could be defined as *items that the company stocks that have never been sold*. You can create a find unmatched query to identify these obsolete items.
To create an unmatched query, do the following:

1. Click the Query Wizard in the Queries group on the CREATE tab.
2. In the New Query dialog box, select the Find Unmatched Query Wizard, and then click OK.
3. Select the table that will serve as the primary table source for this query (see Figure 6.35). Click Next. The first table is the one with the records you want to see in the results—for example, the one with inventory items that have never sold.
4. Select the second table that contains the related records—for example, the table that can show whether or not an inventory item was sold (see Figure 6.36). Click Next.
5. Click the appropriate field in each field list, if necessary. Click Matching Fields to determine what is the matching field you want to use. Click Next. The find unmatched query only works if the two tables share a common field. Usually, the two tables are related to each other in a relationship, but a relationship is not required. Access automatically recognizes the common field (see Figure 6.37).
6. Identify which fields to display in the query output. Use the One Field arrow to move the fields you want from the *Available fields* box to the *Selected fields* box, as shown in Figure 6.38. Click Next. In this case, three fields have been selected for the query.
7. Name the query (see Figure 6.39), and then click Finish to view the results.

Figure 6.40 displays the query results.

Choose a table that contains records you want in the query results

FIGURE 6.35 To Find Unmatched Records, Choose a Primary Table First

Choose the table with related records

FIGURE 6.36 To Find Unmatched Records, Choose a Related Table Second

The results will show which items in the inventory have no sales. These items can be returned to the manufacturer, discounted in order to sell them, or used as a write-off.

TIP | Which Table Do I Choose First?

The first screen of the Find Unmatched Query Wizard asks you *Which table or query contains records you want in the query results?* Choosing this first table is not always an easy task. Select the table that contains records that may be unmatched. The second screen asks, *Which table or query contains the related records?* When you choose the second table, choose a table that shares a common field with the first one. If the two tables have more than one common field candidate, you will need to carefully select which fields you want Access to use. If you make a mistake, delete the query, start over, and then try reversing the order of the two tables.

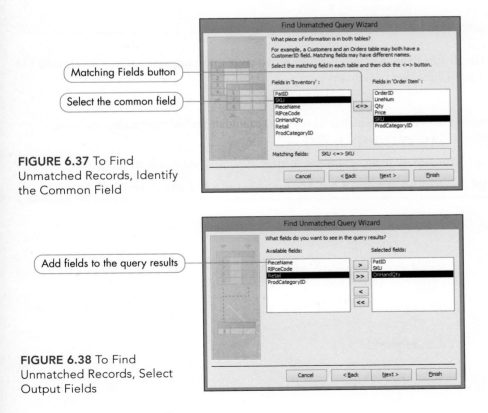

Matching Fields button

Select the common field

Add fields to the query results

FIGURE 6.37 To Find Unmatched Records, Identify the Common Field

FIGURE 6.38 To Find Unmatched Records, Select Output Fields

Name the query

FIGURE 6.39 Name the Find Unmatched Records Query

Inventory items that have not sold

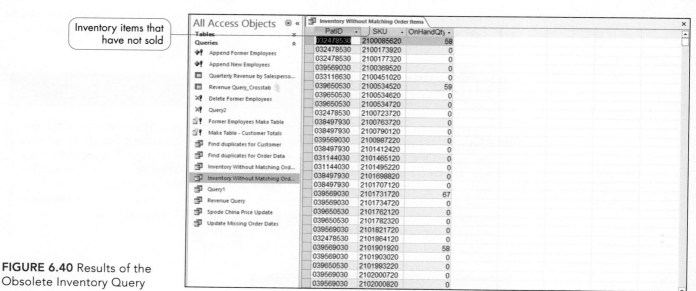

PatID	SKU	OnHandQty
032478530	2100085620	58
032478530	2100173920	0
032478530	2100177320	0
039569030	2100369520	0
033116630	2100451020	0
039650530	2100534520	59
039650530	2100534620	0
039650530	2100534720	0
032478530	2100723720	0
038497930	2100763720	0
038497930	2100790120	0
039569030	2100987220	0
038497930	2101412420	0
031144030	2101465120	0
031144030	2101495220	0
038497930	2101698820	0
038497930	2101707120	0
039569030	2101731720	67
039569030	2101734720	0
039650530	2101762120	0
039650530	2101782320	0
039569030	2101821720	0
032478530	2101864120	0
039569030	2101901920	58
039569030	2101903020	0
039650530	2101993220	0
039569030	2102000720	0
039569030	2102000820	0

All Access Objects
Tables
Queries
- Append Former Employees
- Append New Employees
- Quarterly Revenue by Salesperso...
- Revenue Query_Crosstab
- Delete Former Employees
- Query2
- Former Employees Make Table
- Make Table - Customer Totals
- Find duplicates for Customer
- Find duplicates for Order Data
- Inventory Without Matching Ord...
- Inventory Without Matching Ord...
- Query1
- Revenue Query
- Spode China Price Update
- Update Missing Order Dates

FIGURE 6.40 Results of the Obsolete Inventory Query

In Hands-On Exercise 2, you will improve your querying skills as you work with the Replacement China, Inc., database.

Quick
Concepts

1. How do you determine which field is a good candidate for the intersecting rows and columns in a crosstab query? *p. 377*

2. Why is it important to recognize and manage duplicate data in a database? *p. 381*

3. What is one situation where it could be useful to run a find unmatched query? *p. 383*

Hands-On Exercises

Watch the Video
for this Hands-
On Exercise!

MyITLab®
HOE2 Training

2 Queries for Special Conditions

Replacement China, Inc., has asked you to review their database and make a few improvements. You decide to create a crosstab query to help them look up employee information more easily. You also summarize their revenue data by state to help them analyze sales history. Finally, you check for unmatched data and duplicate data using the built-in query tools.

Skills covered: Use the Crosstab Query Wizard • Edit a Crosstab Query • Create a Find Duplicate Records Query Using the Wizard • Create a Find Unmatched Query Using the Wizard

STEP 1 ≫ USE THE CROSSTAB QUERY WIZARD

You need to analyze the revenue generated by each salesperson at Replacement China, Inc. You decide to break down the results by state. This type of summary can be accomplished using a crosstab query. Refer to Figure 6.41 as you complete Step 1.

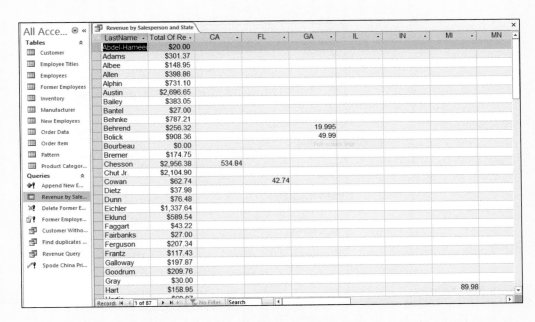

FIGURE 6.41 Crosstab Query Results

a. Open *a06h1Replace_LastFirst* if you closed it at the end of Hands-On Exercise 1. Click **Save As** on the FILE tab, click **Save As**, and then type **a06h2Replace_LastFirst**, changing *h1* to *h2*. Click **Save**.

b. Click **Query Wizard** in the Queries group on the CREATE tab.

c. Select the **Crosstab Query Wizard**. Click **OK**.

The Crosstab Query Wizard opens..

d. Click **Queries** in the *View* section of the Crosstab Query Wizard dialog box. Select **Query: Revenue Query**. Click **Next**.

You selected the Revenue query as the data source that contains revenue by salesperson and state for the crosstab query.

e. Double-click the **LastName field** in the Available Fields box to move it to the Selected Fields box. Click **Next**.

You selected the LastName field as the row heading. The query summarizes the data for each salesperson's last name.

f. Click the **State field** to select it as the column heading. Click **Next**.

You selected the State field as the column heading.

g. Click the **Revenue field** in the Fields box to select it as the summarizing field. Click **Sum** in the Functions box to specify which aggregate function to perform. Click **Next**.

You directed the crosstab query to show you the sum of revenue for each salesperson and for each state.

h. Change the query name to **Revenue by Salesperson and State**. Make sure the *View the query* option is selected. Click **Finish**.

i. Examine the results.

The data shows the sum of revenue for each salesperson in each state. However, the results are cumbersome to view. You will edit the crosstab query in the next step.

STEP 2 ≫ EDIT A CROSSTAB QUERY

The sales reps at Replacement China, Inc., would like to change the column heading field from State to ProdCategoryID. This will help the sales reps identify the sales for each product category and also reduce the number of columns in the crosstab query. Refer to Figure 6.42 as you complete Step 2.

LastName	Total Of Re	1	2	3
Abdel-Hamee	$20.00			19.995
Adams	$301.37	24.995	276.375	
Albee	$148.95	57.97	74.985	15.995
Allen	$398.86	16.995	97.48	284.38
Alphin	$731.10	230.915	316.385	183.795
Austin	$2,696.65	1257.525	742.005	697.12
Bailey	$383.05	0	174.925	208.125
Bantel	$27.00			26.995
Behnke	$787.21	200.18	491.515	95.515
Behrend	$256.32	126.35	46.99	82.98
Bolick	$908.36	515.845	184.555	207.96
Bourbeau	$0.00	0		
Bremer	$174.75	7.99	79.31	87.45
Chesson	$2,956.38	1399.245	963.945	593.185
Chut Jr.	$2,104.90	833.875	854.125	416.9
Cowan	$62.74	42.74	19.995	
Dietz	$37.98		37.975	
Dunn	$76.48	76.48		
Eichler	$1,337.64	719.055	505.82	112.76
Eklund	$589.54	121.915	74.95	392.67
Faggart	$43.22	9.995	33.225	
Fairbanks	$27.00	26.995		
Ferguson	$207.34	23.085	107.955	76.3
Frantz	$117.43	84.94		32.49
Galloway	$197.87	7.995	127.9	61.97
Goodrum	$209.76	71.975	88.29	49.49
Gray	$30.00			29.995
Hart	$158.95	68.965		89.98

Record: 1 of 87 · No Filter · Search

FIGURE 6.42 Revised Crosstab Query Results

a. Switch to Design view.

b. Click the arrow in the Field row of the State column in the query design grid and select **ProdCategoryID**.

The columns now show the product category IDs rather than the state names, reducing the number of columns.

c. Click in the **Total of Revenue field**, open the Property Sheet, and then change the Format field property on the General tab to **Currency**. Close the Property Sheet.

d. Click **Run** in the Results group to see the new results. Double-click the right border of the *Total of Revenue* column so all of the data displays.

e. Save the changes and close the query.

One of the data entry employees believes duplicate entries are present in the Pattern table. You create a query to look for duplicates in the LongPatName field in the Pattern table. If duplicates do exist, the company will need to move all orders to one Pattern and then delete the other Pattern. Refer to Figure 6.43 as you complete Step 3.

Step e: Two duplicates exist in the LongPatName field

FIGURE 6.43 Results of the Find Duplicate Records Query

a. Click **Query Wizard** on the CREATE tab and select **Find Duplicates Query Wizard** to create a find duplicates query. Click **OK**.

b. Click **Table: Pattern** (scroll down, if necessary). Click **Next**.

c. Double-click the **LongPatName** in the Available fields box to move it to the Duplicate-value fields box. Click **Next**.

d. Click **>>** to move the rest of the fields in the table from the Available fields box to the Additional query fields box. Click **Next**.

e. Click **Finish** to accept the default name, *Find duplicates for Pattern*, and the option to view the results.

The query runs and opens in Datasheet view. It contains four records showing two duplicate LongPatName fields.

f. Save the query. Close the query.

STEP 4 ≫ CREATE A FIND UNMATCHED QUERY USING THE WIZARD

The Marketing Manager at Replacement China, Inc., asked you to identify the customers who have not placed orders. You create a find unmatched query to find the customers who have no records in the Order Data table. Someone from the Marketing Department will contact these customers and offer them an incentive to place an order. Refer to Figure 6.44 as you complete Step 4.

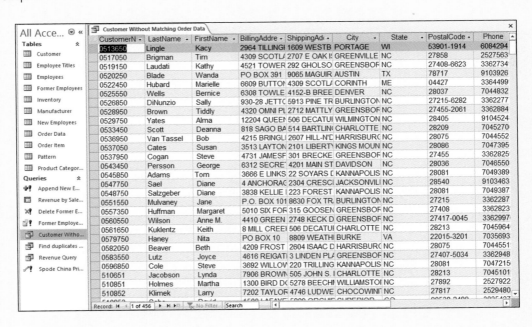

FIGURE 6.44 Customers Who Have Not Ordered

a. Click **Query Wizard** in the Queries group on the CREATE tab. Select the **Find Unmatched Query Wizard** in the New Query dialog box and click **OK**.

   You need to create a find unmatched query to find the customers who have not placed an order.

b. Click **Table: Customer** to select the Customer table. Click **Next**.

   You selected the Customer table as the first table. You will select the Order Data table next so you can find customers who have not ordered.

c. Click **Table: Order Data** and click **Next**.

   You selected the Order Data table as the second table so you can find customers who have not ordered.

d. Click **Next** at the next screen.

   Access identifies the common field (CustomerNum) that exists in both tables.

e. Click >> to add all of the fields to the query. Click **Next**.

f. Click **Finish** to accept the default name and the option to view the results.

   456 customers have not placed an order.

g. Save the query. Close the query.

h. Click **Compact & Repair Database** on the FILE tab.

i. Close the database. Close Access.

j. Submit based on your instructor's directions.

Chapter Objectives Review

After reading this chapter, you have accomplished the following objectives:

1. **Determine when to use an action query.**
   - Recognize the benefits of an action query: Action queries add, edit, or delete the data in a database. These four queries—update, append, make table, and delete—are used for updating records that meet certain criteria, for appending records to a table, for making a new table, and for deleting specific records from a table.
   - Back up a database when testing an action query: Action queries change data in your database, so it is important to back up your database in case it needs to be restored.

2. **Update data with an update query.**
   - Create a select query before running an update query: Create a select query to define the fields and criteria to be used in your update query.
   - Convert a select query to an update query: An update query changes the data values in one or more fields for all records that meet a specific criterion. The update query defines precisely how field values will be updated.
   - Test an update query: View the update query in Datasheet view to determine which records will be affected before you run it.
   - Verify an update query: Open the table to determine the results of the updates.

3. **Add records to a table with an append query.**
   - Create a select query before running an append query: Create a select query to define the fields and criteria to be used in your append query.
   - Set Append To fields in an append query: An append query selects records from one or more tables and adds them to another table. The append query will define precisely how fields and records will be appended.
   - Run an Append Query: If you need to verify the records to be appended, you can click View in the Results group to double-check in Datasheet view.

4. **Create a table with a make table query.**
   - Create a make table query: A make table query selects records from one or more tables and uses them to create a new table.

   - Test and run a make table query: View the make table query in Datasheet view to determine which records will be added to the new table before you run it.

5. **Delete records with a delete query.**
   - Create a delete query: A delete query selects records from a table and then removes them from the table.
   - Test and run a delete query: View the delete query in Datasheet view to determine which records will be deleted from the table before you run it.

6. **Summarize data with a crosstab query.**
   - Group and summarize data: A crosstab query summarizes a data source into a grid of rows and columns; the intersection of each row and column displays valuable aggregate data.
   - Use the Crosstab Query Wizard: The wizard guides you through the steps of creating the crosstab query, including setting the row and column headings.
   - Modify a crosstab query: In Design view, you can modify the row/column headings of the query, format fields, and summarize the data in different ways.

7. **Find duplicate records with a query.**
   - Use a find duplicate records query: The Find Duplicates Query Wizard is used to help identify duplicated values in a table. However, not all duplicated data in a database are the result of an error.
   - Create a find duplicates query using the wizard: The wizard guides you through the steps of creating the query, including identifying which fields to search for duplicated data.

8. **Find unmatched records with a query.**
   - Use a find unmatched query: The Find Unmatched Query Wizard creates a query that compares records in two related tables and returns the records found in one table but not the other.
   - Create a find unmatched query using the wizard: The wizard guides you through the steps of creating the query, including identifying which fields to search for unmatched data.

Key Terms Matching

Match the key terms with their definitions. Write the key term letter by the appropriate numbered definition.

a. Action query
b. Append query
c. Column headings
d. Crosstab query
e. Delete query

f. Find duplicates query
g. Find unmatched query
h. Make table query
i. Row headings
j. Update query

1. _____ A query that selects records from one or more tables (the source) and adds them to an existing table (the destination). **p. 363**

2. _____ A query that compares records in two related tables, and then displays the records found in one table but not the other. **p. 383**

3. _____ A query that summarizes a data source into a few key rows and columns; the intersection of each row and column displays aggregate data. **p. 377**

4. _____ A query that selects records from one or more tables and uses them to create a new table. **p. 366**

5. _____ The field names displayed along the left side of a crosstab query. **p. 377**

6. _____ A query that selects records from a table and then removes them from the table. **p. 367**

7. _____ The field name displayed at the top of a crosstab query. **p. 377**

8. _____ A query that adds, updates, or deletes data in a database. **p. 385**

9. _____ A query that changes the data values in one or more fields for all records that meet specific criteria. **p. 360**

10. _____ A query that helps you identify repeated values in a table. **p. 381**

Multiple Choice

1. Which one of the following tasks could not be completed with an action query?

   (a) Deleting records from a table
   (b) Updating records in a table
   (c) Displaying data based on a value entered at run time
   (d) Creating a new table based on a group of selected records

2. Which statement is true about action queries?

   (a) Users use action queries more frequently than database administrators.
   (b) You can run an action query as many times as you like.
   (c) A delete query is not an action query.
   (d) Action queries should be executed with caution because you cannot undo their changes.

3. Which query below is used as a basis to create the other three?

   (a) Select query
   (b) Update query
   (c) Delete query
   (d) Append query

4. Your company merged with another company, and now the two customer lists are combined into one table. Because the two companies had many of the same customers, the customer table now contains many duplicate customers with different account numbers. What is the best way to resolve this problem?

   (a) Delete duplicate customers manually.
   (b) Create a select query showing all customers in alphabetical order and then run a delete query to delete every other record.
   (c) It will not affect overall performance of the database to have duplicated records, so leave the table as is.
   (d) Use a find duplicates query to locate duplicate customers. Delete one of the duplicates.

5. Why is it important to monitor how many times an update query is executed?

   (a) Update queries are capable of changing values (such as prices) more than one time.
   (b) Update queries can be used to delete records from your tables.
   (c) It is not important; you can always undo the results of an update query.
   (d) An update query can erase your table and create a new one in its place.

6. Which statement is true about action queries?

   (a) An append query is usually run after an update query.
   (b) A delete query is usually run before an update query.
   (c) A delete query is usually run after an append query.
   (d) Make table queries are usually constructed from an update query.

7. Why would you use an update query?

   (a) Because users need to be able to select records based on varied selection criteria
   (b) To determine which records may need to be deleted from the database
   (c) To summarize the data in a firm's database to help managers evaluate their financial position
   (d) To increase retail prices in a firm's database

8. How do you create a crosstab query?

   (a) Click Crosstab Query on the Create tab.
   (b) Click Query Wizard and select Crosstab Query Wizard for the query type.
   (c) Click Crosstab Query on the Database Tools tab.
   (d) Create a select query and convert it to a crosstab query.

9. What is an unmatched record?

   (a) A record that contains the primary key in the one table
   (b) A record that requires deletion when running a delete query
   (c) A duplicated record that cannot be connected to a parent record
   (d) A record in one table without a matching record in a related table

10. What is the best way to find students who have not attended a certain class?

    (a) Create a select query of attendance and compare the results to the student roster.
    (b) Create a select query of attendance and use the query to create an update query.
    (c) Create a select query of attendance for the students in the class. Then create a find duplicates query using the attendance table.
    (d) Create a find unmatched query using the student and attendance tables.

Practice Exercises

1 National Bank

You are the DBA for a national bank. The bank has decided to decrease mortgage loans by a half percent. You use an update query to modify the mortgage rates. In addition, you decide to move all mortgages from the loans table to a new mortgages table. You delete the mortgages from the loans table after they are moved. This exercise follows the same set of skills as used in Hands-On Exercise 1 in the chapter. Refer to Figures 6.45 and 6.46 as you complete this exercise.

FIGURE 6.45 Update Query to Decrease Rates by 0.50 Percent

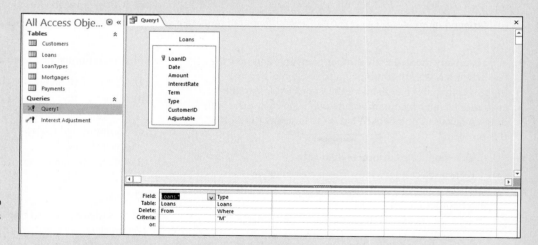

FIGURE 6.46 Query Design to Delete Mortgages from Loans Table

a. Open *a06p1Bank*. Click **Save As** on the FILE tab, click **Save As**, and then type **a06p1Bank_LastFirst**. Click **Save**.

b. Click **Query Design** in the Queries group on the CREATE tab. Double-click the **Loans table** in the Show Table dialog box to add it to the query. Close the Show Table dialog box.

c. Double-click the **LoanID**, **InterestRate**, and **Type fields**. Click **Run** in the Results group. Save the query as **Interest Adjustment**.

d. Switch to Design view. Type *M* in the **Criteria row** of the Type column.

   Entering *M* in the Criteria row of the Type column will isolate only those loans that are mortgages.

e. Click in the **Field row** of the fourth column and type **NewRate: [InterestRate] - 0.0050**. Press **Enter**.

   You have created a new field with the calculation for the new interest rate, which decreases by 0.50 percent.

f. Click **Property Sheet** in the Show/Hide group with the calculated field column selected. Change the Format property to **Percent**. Close the Property Sheet.

g. Click **Run** in the Results group and examine the results of the NewRate calculated field.

h. Switch to Design view. Click **Update** in the Query Type group. Click in the **Update To row** of the InterestRate field and type **[InterestRate] - 0.0050**.

   The update query changes the existing interest rates to the lower interest rates calculated in the NewRate field. Compare your query design to Figure 6.45.

i. Click **View** in the Results group to verify that 12 records will be updated. Switch back to Design view.

j. Click **Run** in the Results group. Click **Yes** in response to the Warning box. Save and close the query.

k. Open the Loans table and verify the Mortgage loan interest rates are 0.50 percent lower. Close the table.

l. Click **Query Design** in the Queries group on the CREATE tab. Double-click the **Loans table** in the Show Table dialog box. Close the Show Table dialog box.

m. Double-click the title bar of the Loans table to select all the fields and drag them to the first column in the design grid.

n. Click **Run** in the Results group to run the query.

o. Switch back to Design view. Type **M** in the **Criteria row** of the Type column. Click **Run** in the Results group to run the query.

   You only want to see the mortgages in the query results.

p. Switch back to Design view. Click **Make Table** in the Query Type group and type **Mortgages** as the new table name. Accept the default setting of Current Database and click **OK**.

q. Switch to Datasheet view to verify that only the 12 mortgage loans will be affected.

r. Switch to Design view. Click **Run** in the Results group. Click **Yes** in response to the Warning box.

s. Double-click the **Mortgages table** in the Navigation Pane. Verify that the 12 mortgages are in the table. Close the table.

t. Click **Delete** in the Query Type group on the DESIGN tab to change the make table query to a delete query.

u. Delete all the columns in the query design grid except the Type column.

   The Type column contains the criterion you need for the delete query.

v. Drag the * **field** from the Loans table to the first column in the query design grid.

   Compare your query design to Figure 6.46.

w. Click **Run** in the Results group. Click **Yes** in response to the Warning box.

x. Save the query as **Delete Mortgages Query**. Close the query.

y. Compact and repair the database. Close the database. Close Access.

z. Submit based on your instructor's directions.

2 Break Room Suppliers, Inc.

Break Room Suppliers, Inc., is a small service organization that provides coffee, tea, and snacks to local businesses. You have been asked to review the database and create several queries; these queries can be run periodically by the owner. This exercise follows the same set of skills as used in Hands-On Exercises 1 and 2 in the chapter. Refer to Figures 6.47 and 6.48 as you complete this exercise.

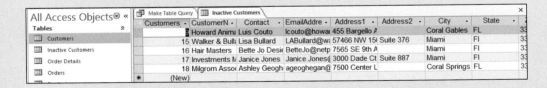

FIGURE 6.47 Inactive Customers Table

FIGURE 6.48 Crosstab Query
Showing Profit for Each City

City	Total Of Re ▾	2/1/2016 ▾	2/11/2016 ▾	2/12/2016 ▾	2/14/2016 ▾	2/19/2016 ▾	2/20/2016 ▾
Coconut Grove	$582.00					$118.50	
Coral Springs	$392.75						
Miami	$1,812.88	$301.50	$114.00	$50.13	$201.75	$34.00	$42.50

Profit Summary_Crosstab

a. Open *a06p2Coffee*. Click **Save As** on the FILE tab, click **Save As**, and then type **a06p2Coffee_LastFirst**. Click **Save**.

b. Double-click the **Sales Reps table** to open it. Replace *Your_Name* with your name. Close the table.

c. Click **Query Wizard** in the Queries group on the CREATE tab. Click **Find Unmatched Query Wizard**, click **OK**, and then answer the wizard questions as follows:

- Select **Table: Customers** as the first table. Click **Next**.
- Select **Table: Orders** as the second table. Click **Next**.
- Accept the CustomerID field as the common field. Click **Next**.
- Click >> to move all of the fields in the Available fields box to the Selected fields box. Click **Next**.
- Accept *Customers Without Matching Orders* as the query name and click **Finish** to display the four inactive customers. Leave the Customers Without Matching Orders query open.

d. Switch to Design view. Click **Make Table** in the Query Type group and follow these steps:

- Type **Inactive Customers** in the **Table Name box**. Click **OK**.
- Click **View** in the Results group to verify that four customers are shown.
- Click **View** to return to Design view.
- Click **Run** in the Results group to run the make table query.
- Click **Yes** in response to the Warning box.
- Click **Save As** on the FILE tab, click **Save Object As**, and then click **Save As**. Save the copy of the query with the name **Make Table Query**. Click **OK**.

e. Open the Inactive Customers table to verify that the four records have been archived. Close the table.

f. Ensure the Customers Without Matching Orders query is open. Click the **DESIGN tab**, click **Delete** in the Query Type group, and then follow these steps:

- Right-click the **Orders table** and select **Remove Table**.
- Type **9 Or 15 Or 16 Or 17** into the **Criteria row** of the CustomerID column.
- Click **View** in the Results group to verify that four customers are shown.
- Click **View** to return to Design view.
- Click **Run** in the Results group to run the delete query.
- Click **Yes** in response to the Warning box.
- Click **Save As** on the FILE tab, click **Save Object As**, and then click **Save As**. Save the copy of the query with the name **Delete Inactive Customers Query**.
- Close the query.

You have deleted the inactive customers (IDs 9, 15, 16, and 17) from the Customers table.

g. Create a copy of the Delete Inactive Customers Query and rename it as **Append Inactive Customers Query**.

- View the query in Design view.
- Click **Append** in the Query Type group. Append to Inactive Customers and click **OK**.
- Delete the existing criterion and type **5** into the **Criteria row** of the CustomerID column.
- Click **View** in the Results group to verify that one customer is shown.
- Click **View** to return to Design view.
- Click **Run** in the Results group to run the append query.
- Click **Yes** in response to the Warning box.
- Save and close the query.

You have appended CustomerID 5 to the Inactive Customers table, as shown in Figure 6.47. Note that because CustomerID is an AutoNumber field in the Inactive Customers table, the record will be renumbered when appended to that table.

h. Click **Query Wizard** in the Queries group on the CREATE tab. Click **Crosstab Query Wizard**, click **OK**, and then follow these steps:

- Click **Queries** in the *View* section.
- Click **Query: Profit Summary**. Click **Next**.
- Click **City** and click > to select it as the Row heading. Click **Next**.
- Click **OrderDate** to select it for the Column heading. Click **Next**.
- In the next screen, click **Date** and click **Next**.
- Click **Revenue** as the calculated field and click **Sum** as the aggregate function. Click **Next**.
- Click **Finish** to accept *Profit Summary_Crosstab* as the query name and view the query results. Compare your results to Figure 6.48.
- Save and close the query.

i. Click **Query Wizard** in the Queries group on the CREATE tab. Click **Find Duplicates Query Wizard**, click **OK**, and then follow these steps:

- Click **Table: Customers**. Click **Next**.
- Click **Contact** and click > to search for duplicates in this field. Click **Next**.
- Click >> to indicate you want to see all the additional fields. Click **Next**.
- Type **Find contact duplicates in Customers** as the query name. Click **Finish**.
- Close the query.

j. Compact and repair the database.

k. Close the database. Close Access.

l. Submit based on your instructor's directions.

1 Northwind Traders

Northwind Traders is a small international specialty foods distribution firm. Management has decided to close their North and South American operations and concentrate on their European markets. They have asked you to update certain customer records and to move all deactivated customers to another table. Once you move the records, you will delete them from the original table. Refer to Figure 6.49 as you complete this exercise.

FIGURE 6.49 Deactivated Customers Table Created with Action Queries

a. Open *a06m1Exporters*. Click **Save As** on the FILE tab, click **Save As**, and then type **a06m1Exporters_ LastFirst**. Click **Save**.

b. Create a select query based on all of the fields from the Customers table. Add criteria to show only customers in the USA. Run the query.

c. Change the query to an update query that replaces all instances of *USA* with **United States**. Run the query. Save the query as **Update US Customers**. Close the query.

d. Create a make table query that is based on all of the fields in the Customers table. Name the new table **Deactivated Customers**. Add criteria to select only United States customers. Run the query and save it as **Make Table Query**. Close the query.

e. Make a copy of the Make Table Query in the Navigation Pane and name the copy **Append Query**. Right-click the new **Append Query** and select **Design View** from the list.

f. Change the query type to **Append**. Append records to the Deactivated Customers table. Change the criteria of the Country field to **Venezuela**. Run the query. Save and close the query.

g. Make a copy of the Append Query in the Navigation Pane and name the copy **Delete Query**. Right-click the new **Delete Query** and choose **Design View** from the list.

h. Change the query type to **Delete**. Change the Country criteria to **United States Or Venezuela**. Delete all the columns in the query design grid except the Country column. Run the query. Save and close the query. Open the Deactivated Customers table to view the records added by the make table and append queries. Close the table.

i. Close the database. Close Access.

j. Submit based on your instructor's directions.

2 Hotel Chain

ANALYSIS CASE

You are assisting the general manager of a large hotel chain. You need to perform several tasks for the general manager including calculating the total revenue for each service for each city. You also need to find duplicate names in the members table. Refer to Figures 6.50 and 6.51 as you complete this exercise.

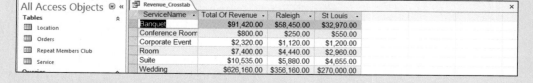

FIGURE 6.50 Crosstab Query Displays Revenue by Service and City

FIGURE 6.51 Raleigh Members Without Matching Orders

a. Open *a06m2Rewards*. Click **Save As** on the FILE tab, click **Save As**, and then type **a06m2Rewards_LastFirst**. Click **Save**.

b. Create a crosstab query based on the Revenue query. Use the ServiceName field for the row heading, the City field for the column heading, and the Revenue field for the column and row intersection. Sum the Revenue field. Save the query as **Revenue_Crosstab**.

c. Format the Revenue and Total of Revenue crosstab values as **Currency**. Run the query. Compare your results to Figure 6.50. Save and close the Revenue_Crosstab query.

DISCOVER

d. Create a copy of the Revenue_Crosstab query and save it as **Revenue_Crosstab2**.

e. Modify the query so that the City field is the row heading and the ServiceName field is the column heading. Run the query, save the query, and close it.

f. Create a find unmatched query that displays repeat members from Raleigh. Records from the Repeat Members Club table should display in the results. Include all fields from the table. Test the query and save it as **Raleigh Members Without Matching Orders**. Compare your results to Figure 6.51. Print the results of the query and submit to your instructor.

g. Create a copy of the Raleigh Members Without Matching Orders query and save it as **Charlotte Members Without Matching Orders**.

h. Modify the query so that Charlotte members who have not used any hotel services are displayed in the results.

i. Create a find duplicates query that displays any locations that have the same city and address. Display the LocationID field as an additional field in the query. Run the query and save it as **Find Duplicate Locations**.

j. Change the Address for LocationID 15 to **Downtown**, in the query results. Close the query.

k. Close the database. Close Access.

l. Submit based on your instructor's directions.

3 Car Dealership

COLLABORATION CASE

You have been asked to modify a car dealership database that tracks employee data, sales records, and vehicle information. You and your team will identify new hires in the database and move them to a separate table. You will summarize data in the database and locate unmatched records. Refer to Figure 6.52 as you complete this exercise.

FIGURE 6.52 Vehicles Without Matching Sales Agreements

a. Open *a06m3Collaboration*. Click **Save As** on the FILE tab, click **Save As**, and then type **a06m3Collaboration_GroupName**. As a team, study the existing database and the relationships between the tables. Open each table and study the data that you will be working with.

Assign the following two tasks to a team member:

b. Create a select query based on all of the fields from the Employees table. Add criteria to show only employees whose Active status is No. Run the query.

c. Convert the select query a make table query. Name the new table **Hires Not Activated**. Run the query and save it as **Make Table Query_LastFirst**. Close the query. Open the Hires Not Activated table to verify the results.

Assign the following three tasks to a team member:

d. Set the Active status of Employee ID 3 (Jim Delsor) to **No** in the Employees table. Close the table.

e. Make a copy of the Make Table Query_LastFirst in the Navigation Pane and name the copy **Append Query_LastFirst**. Right-click the new append query and choose **Design View** from the list.

f. Change the query type to **Append**. Append records to the Hires Not Activated table. Modify the criteria to select Employee ID 3 and delete the existing criterion. Run the query. Save and close the query.

Assign the following two tasks to a team member:

g. Make a copy of the Append Query_LastFirst in the Navigation Pane and name the copy **Delete Query_LastFirst**. Right-click the new delete query and choose **Design View** from the list.

h. Change the query type to **Delete**. Modify the criteria to show only employees whose Active status is No and delete the existing criterion. Run the query. Save and close the query. Open the Employees table and note that the inactive employees are deleted.

Assign the following two tasks to a team member:

i. Create a crosstab query based on the Available Inventory query. Use the VehicleMake field for the row heading, the VehicleYear field for the column heading, and the VehicleSalePrice field for the column and row intersection. Average the VehicleSalePrice field. Save the query as **Available Inventory_Crosstab_LastFirst**.

j. Set the caption of the Total Of VehicleSalePrice: [VehicleSalePrice] field to **Average Sale Price**. Save and close the query.

k. Collaborate with your team to determine what would be the best way to portray vehicles that have no sales agreement. Create an unmatched query to view these records, and include all of the fields from the Vehicles table. Accept the default query name. Finish and then close the query.

l. Compact and repair the database. Close the database. Exit Access. Submit the database based on your instructor's directions.

Find Duplicate Data in a Database

RESEARCH CASE

In this chapter, you learned about the difference between valid and invalid duplicates in a database. Go to www.microsoft.com and search for **duplicate data in Access 2013**. Locate the article *Find duplicate records with a query* that discusses the Find Duplicates Query Wizard. Read through the article and write a brief summary of your findings in a Word document; save the file as **a06b2Duplicate_LastFirst**. Close the document. Submit based on your instructor's directions.

Prohibit Duplicate Append

DISASTER RECOVERY

Northwind Traders is an international specialty foods distributor that relies on an Access 2013 database to process its orders. A make table query moved all the owners from the Customers table to a new Customer Owners table. A colleague converted the make table query to an append query and ran it again (expecting it would not add another set of records). Unfortunately, it did add a second set of owners to the table, and now every owner is duplicated. What is the best way to fix this problem? You need to retain the append query and run it once in a while in case a new owner was added to the database. Running the append query should not add any duplicate records to the Customer Owners table. Open *a06b3Food* and save it as **a06b3Food_LastFirst**. Correct the problem in the table. When you are finished, compact, repair, and close your database. Submit based on your instructor's directions.

Cover Letters and Resume Tips

SOFT SKILLS CASE **S**

You want to determine how many of the new employees in your database have no resumes on file with the Human Resources Department. You decide to create a make table query with their personal information so that they can be contacted by HR. Open *a6b4Resumes*. Save a copy of the database as **a6b4Resumes_FirstLast**. Create the query based on the New Employees table and include the following fields: FirstName, LastName, Email, DateOfHire, and ResumeOnFile (in that order). Hide the ResumeOnFile field in the query results. Set the query to create a table named **Missing Resume**. Save the query as **Missing Resume_Make Table**. Run the query to create the table and close the query. Close the database. Exit Access. Submit the database *a6b4Resumes_FirstLast* based on your instructor's directions.

Capstone Exercise

Northwind Traders is a small international gourmet foods whole-saler. You will update the database by increasing the price of all of the beverage and dairy products. You will make a table of discontinued products. You will also summarize profits by salesperson and category and identify products that have no orders.

Database File Setup

Open the original database file, save a copy with a new file name, and then open the copied database to complete this capstone exercise.

a. Open *a06c1Prices* and save it as **a06c1Prices_LastFirst**.

Identify and Update Selected Category Prices

Create a select query to identify all of the products in the beverage and dairy categories, and then create an update query to increase their prices.

a. Create a select query that includes the CategoryID and CategoryName from the Categories table and the UnitPrice and ProductName fields from the Products table. Run the query and note the CategoryIDs for Beverages and Dairy.

b. Add the appropriate CategoryID criterion to limit the query output to only Beverages.

c. Convert the query to an update query. Update the UnitPrice for beverages only by increasing it by 5 percent. View the query in Datasheet view prior to running it to make sure you are updating the correct records. Return to Design view and run the query.

d. Update the UnitPrice for dairy products only by increasing it by 4 percent. View the query in Datasheet view prior to running it to make sure you are updating the correct records. Return to Design view and run the query.

e. Save the query as **Update Prices**. Close the query.

Create a New Table

Identify the discontinued products and create a new table to store them.

a. Create a select query that identifies all of the discontinued products. Include all fields from the Products table.

b. Convert the select query to a make table query.

c. Name the new table **Discontinued Products**. Run the query.

d. Save the query as **Make Discontinued Products Table**. Close the query.

e. Make a copy of the Make Discontinued Products Table query and save it as **Append Discontinued Products Table**. Open the Append Discontinued Products Table query in Design view. Convert the make table query to an append query. The query will append to the Discontinued Products table.

f. Modify the criteria to append Boston Crab Meat as a product, using the SupplierID from the Products table. Run the query, save it, and then close it.

g. Make a copy of the Append Discontinued Products Table query and save it as **Delete Discontinued Products**. Open the Delete Discontinued Products query in Design view. Convert the append query to a delete query.

h. Modify the criteria to delete the discontinued products, as well as the record for Boston Crab Meat using its SupplierID (*Hint:* There will be two criteria). Run, save, and close the query.

Calculate Summary Statistics

Create a crosstab query that shows profits by salesperson and category.

a. Open the Profit query in Design view and add the **LastName field** from the Employees table to the last column of the design grid. Run, save, and close the query.

b. Use the query wizard to create a crosstab query based on the Profit query that shows total profit by LastName (row heading) and CategoryName (column heading). Name the query **Profit_Crosstab**.

c. Modify the query to display **CategoryName** as a row heading field and **LastName** as a column heading field. Run, save, and close the query.

Create a Find Unmatched Query

a. Create a query to find out if any of the products have no current order details. Add all of the fields from the Products table to the results.

b. Save the query as **Products With No Orders**. Run the query and close it.

c. Close the database. Close Access.

d. Submit based on your instructor's directions.

Access

Advanced Forms and Reports

CHAPTER 7

Moving Beyond the Basics

Yuri Arcurs/Shutterstock

OBJECTIVES | AFTER YOU READ THIS CHAPTER, YOU WILL BE ABLE TO:

CASE STUDY | Technical Services

Yellowstone County Technical Services is a small company that provides technical support for a number of businesses in Yellowstone County, Montana. As one of the company's supervisors, you have been tasked with updating the customer tracking database to expand the input and output capabilities of the system.

In your experience with the company, you have seen some of the common errors users make when performing data entry and have also seen what is effective and what is not effective in forms. In addition, you have seen which reports users utilize and have heard suggestions about changes they would like made.

Creating a database is difficult, but updating a database and making it more user-friendly can be the difference between a tool that is accepted and a tool that is rejected. As any good database administrator realizes, being proactive and helping users prevent errors is critical. In addition, finding ways to extract more information from the same amount of data is important as well. Being able to interpret and present the information in a database so management can use it can be what makes or breaks your career as a database administrator.

In your role as supervisor, you also want to lead your technicians by example, and implementing improvements in your database is a good start. After implementing the changes, you can use the database as a case study to train your technicians in effective database design.

Advanced Forms

For basic database solutions, a simple form created with the Form tool will handle most needs. However, at times you need to go beyond the basics. For example, you can create a form that enables users to look up information but not change it, thereby providing a measure of security. You do not have to worry about users accidentally changing data. You can change a field to a lookup field, finding values in another table or a list of values. However, there may be times where you do not need the lookup in the table but would like it in a form. This can be done through the use of a combo box. Another part of improving data entry is making a form easy to navigate. Sometimes when you tab through a form, you may not end up in the desired field. You can change the tab order in a form to make data entry more efficient. You can also create and manipulate subforms, which show related records from other tables. Part of your goal when administering a database is to make the database simple and powerful, and forms provide that functionality. You will use Design view to make most of the changes in this chapter.

Restricting Edits in a Form

One method of protecting data in a database is to restrict casual users from editing the data. Casual users may need access to the data to look up information such as a person's address or phone number or to review the details of an order. However, the people who need to look up information may be people you do not want adding, editing, and deleting records. When too many users make changes to the data, the data can become unreliable and difficult to maintain. If only a select group of users is allowed to enter and edit data, maintaining the integrity of the data is much easier.

Most databases have data entry forms. For example, a customer form might be created in a bank's database to enable customer information to be entered. If a mistake is made, data entry personnel can find the record with the mistake and fix the error. The form does not require permission or a password to make an edit. Perhaps other employees at the bank also need to look up information—for example, a phone number to contact a customer. The person making these calls will need to look up the phone number of a customer without making any changes to the data. When users need to look up information without making changes, it is best to create a copy of the original form and then restrict editing on the copy. A form that enables users to view but not change data is a ***read-only form***. Incorporating read-only forms in a database helps avoid accidental changes to data. You may ask why you would create a read-only form instead of simply creating a report. Remember that forms are preferred because they show one record at a time, and they enable searches.

In addition to setting the form so data cannot be changed, you as the designer have two other questions to answer. Do you want to allow users to delete records using this form? Do you want to allow users to add new records using this form? Even if a form has restricted editing, it still enables adding and deleting records. These options can be switched off as well.

Create a Read-Only Form

To create a read-only form, do the following:

STEP 1 » 1. Open the form in Layout view.
2. Click the Property Sheet in the Tools group on the DESIGN tab.
3. Select Form in the *Selection type* box at the top of the Property Sheet.
4. Click the Allow Edits property on the Data tab.
5. Change the Allow Edits property to No, as shown in Figure 7.1.
6. Change the Allow Additions and Allow Deletions properties to No (if desired).
7. Switch to Form view to test the form.

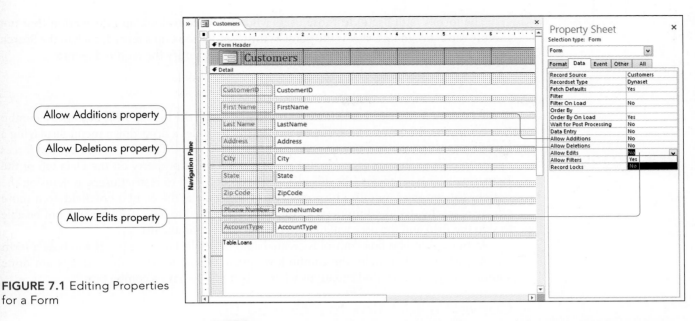

FIGURE 7.1 Editing Properties for a Form

TIP Change the Title for Read-Only Forms

It is suggested that you change the form title and name to indicate it is read-only. Otherwise, you can frustrate users who might open the form and wonder what they are doing wrong!

To test the changes to the form, switch to Form view, and then attempt to change the data in the first record. If you attempt to change the address, for example, nothing happens. In addition, if you changed the Allow Additions and Allow Deletions properties to No, you can see the results of this change when you attempt to click Delete in the Records group on the Home tab—Delete is no longer available. Normally, you add a record in a form by clicking the *New (blank) record* button in the navigation bar at the bottom of the form window. However, because the Allow Additions property is set to No, the option has been disabled. Figure 7.2 shows a read-only form. You will notice it is not obvious it is read-only. Editing the form title to indicate it is read-only will help.

FIGURE 7.2 Read-Only Form

The form is still useful to those users who only need to look up information (but not modify the data). In fact, that is the point of the form. To look up a record, click in the Search box in the navigation bar and type some key words to identify the required record.

Creating a Drop-Down Menu

If you create a form based on a table with a lookup field, the lookup field becomes a combo box control on the new form. A *combo box control* provides a drop-down menu displaying a list of options from which the user can choose a single value. The combo box control forces a user to choose an item from the list if the Limit To List property on the Data tab of the Property Sheet is set to Yes (the default). If you do not want to restrict users to items on the options list, set the Limit To List property to No. To make the combo box field even more effective, set the Required property of the underlying field to Yes—the user will not be able to skip the field and the user will have to choose an item on the list.

At times a combo box control is created automatically. For example, if you base a form on an existing lookup field, the combo box appears without extra effort. If it is not done automatically, you may find situations where it is useful to have a combo box.

Convert a Text Box to a Combo Box

At times, a text box on a form should be converted to a combo box. This can happen when the data you are collecting may not appear to contain repeating data at first. As you enter transactions over time, you may realize that a field does have repeating data and that a combo box may be appropriate. The desire to make input easier for the user should be weighed against creating a drop-down menu that is too long. For example, the state field will sometimes be a combo box. Fifty states and the District of Columbia make up the United States, and you may prefer not to have a drop-down menu containing 51 items. However, if the customers that are entered in your database are located in only a subset of the 50 states, you may be able to include a subset of the states.

Before you convert a text box to a combo box, you should first create a new table and enter the values for the option list, much like you do for lookup fields. Then, do the following:

STEP 2

1. Open the form in Design view (or Layout view) and right-click the text box you want to convert.
2. From the shortcut menu, click the Change To option and select Combo Box, as shown in Figure 7.3.

The field now displays with an arrow on the right side of the text box. It does not yet do anything, however.

FIGURE 7.3 Changing a Text Box to a Combo Box

Customize a Converted Combo Box

Once you have converted a text box to a combo box, you still have changes to make to enable the options. For example, you likely want to ensure that users can only enter values appearing on the menu. Though optional, these enable you to help improve data entry. Figure 7.4 shows three properties you can set to customize a combo box, and Figure 7.5 shows how a combo box appears in form view. To set a source for a combo box, do the following:

1. Switch to Design view of the form.
2. Click the Property Sheet in the Tools group on the DESIGN tab.
3. Select a Row Source on the Data tab.
4. Switch to Form view to test the combo box.

FIGURE 7.4 Customizing a Combo Box

FIGURE 7.5 Customized Combo Box in Form View

As described earlier, you may want to ensure your users only enter values that exist in the menu. To limit the values to the contents of the source table, do the following:

1. Switch to Design view of the form.
2. Click the Property Sheet in the Tools group on the DESIGN tab.
3. Change the Limit To List property to Yes on the Data tab.
4. Switch to Form view to test the combo box.

What if the available states have been restricted to the states that are represented by the customers, and a customer from a different state—one not on the list—takes out a loan? If you have set the Limit To List option, Access generates an error, as shown in Figure 7.6. Similar to lookup fields, storing values in a separate table makes it very easy to change the values allowed in a combo box if the values ever need changing. For example, you may have initially dealt with customers in Idaho, Montana, and Wyoming. If you ever need to add Oregon and Washington to the combo box, you can simply add new rows to the table storing the state names.

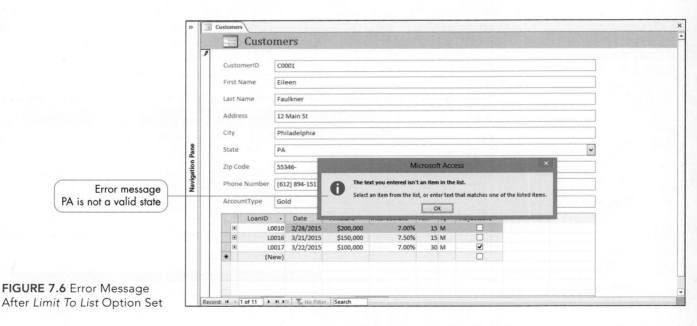

FIGURE 7.6 Error Message After *Limit To List* Option Set

You may also want to set a default value to appear on the form. If you have already set a value for a field on the table, it will appear in the form, but if not, you can set a default value on a form by doing the following:

1. Switch to Design view of the form.
2. Click the Property Sheet in the Tools group on the DESIGN tab.
3. Enter a Default Value on the Data tab.
4. Switch to Form view to test the combo box.

Setting the Tab Order

When entering data into a table, users press Tab to advance from one field to the next. Data cannot be entered out of order unless you click a field with the mouse instead of pressing Tab. The *tab order* is the sequential advancing in a form from one field or control to the next when you press Tab. When working with forms, the designer must remember to check the tab order before delivering the form to the end users; when a form is created, the initial tab order is not necessarily the order that is most useful to the user.

Set the Tab Order

STEP 3 » Sometimes, Access sets the tab order in a way that makes little sense. You may enter data in the first field, hit Tab, and end up in the bottom text box. This is something that frustrates users but is easily fixed. The first step you should take if this occurs is to have Access automatically set the tab order. To automatically set the tab order in a form, do the following:

1. Switch to Design view.
2. Click Tab Order in the Tools group on the DESIGN tab. This displays the Tab Order dialog box showing all the controls in each section of the form, as shown in Figure 7.7.
3. Click Detail to display the tab order for the fields.
4. Click Auto Order if the form has a Stacked layout and you want to enter data from top to bottom.
5. Click OK to accept the changes.

FIGURE 7.7 Tab Order Dialog Box

Access does its best to set the tab order properly, but at times it does not work as you might require. For example, Auto Order does not work well if you have a two-column form. If you need to create a customized tab order, do the following:

1. Switch to Design view.
2. Click Tab Order in the Tools group on the DESIGN tab.
3. Click Detail to display the tab order for the fields.
4. Click the field selector to the left of a field name, release the mouse, and then drag the field to the desired position in the tab order. For example, if two fields are next to each other but in the wrong order, click the second field, release the mouse, and then drag the second field on top of the first one.
5. Click OK to accept the changes.

Remove a Tab Stop

At times, you want the tab order to skip a field completely. For example, if you add a calculated field to the form, you would not want to stop at this field. Calculated fields do not require data entry. Another example occurs when you have an AutoNumber field as the primary key. Your user does not need to add data there, so it should not have a tab stop.

To remove the Tab Stop property of a field, do the following:

1. Switch to Layout view (or Design view).
2. Click the field you want to remove.
3. Click Property Sheet in the Tools group on the DESIGN tab stop.
4. Click the Other tab in the Property Sheet.
5. Locate the Tab Stop property and change the property setting to No, as shown in Figure 7.8.
6. Return to Form view and test the change by pressing Tab to advance through the fields on the form. The field you modified should be skipped when you press Tab.

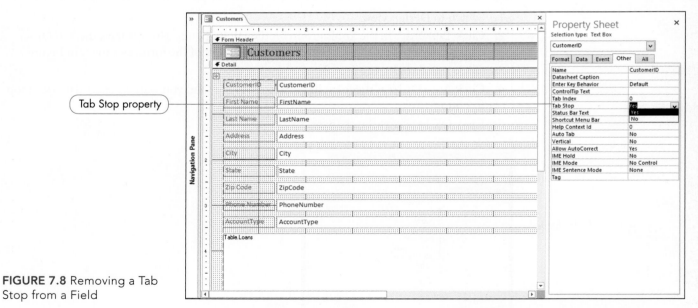

FIGURE 7.8 Removing a Tab Stop from a Field

Using Subforms

Relationships between tables usually exist in Access databases, which can lead to more complicated forms. How should you display records from related tables? Commonly, the main form displays records from a related table using a *subform*. Subforms are generally laid out in a tabular fashion and are used when a relationship exists between two tables, as shown in Figure 7.9.

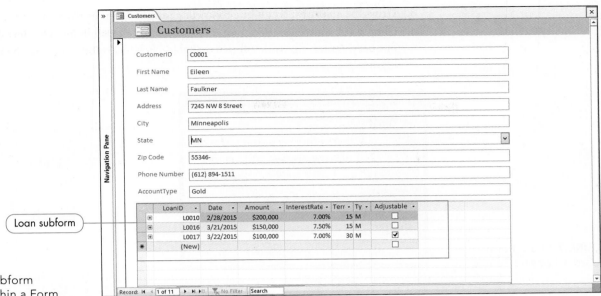

FIGURE 7.9 Subform Appearing Within a Form

Subforms are created by the Form tool automatically. They also can be created by the Form Wizard. If a relationship exists and you choose fields from two different tables using the Form Wizard, it automatically assumes you want a form with a subform. You can also manually add a subform to any form using the Subform/Subreport tool. To manually add a subform using the Subform/Subreport tool, do the following, assuming a relationship exists between the two tables:

STEP 4

1. Open the form in Design view.
2. Click the Subform/Subreport tool in the Controls group on the DESIGN tab, as shown in Figure 7.10. Depending on your screen resolution, you may need to click More.

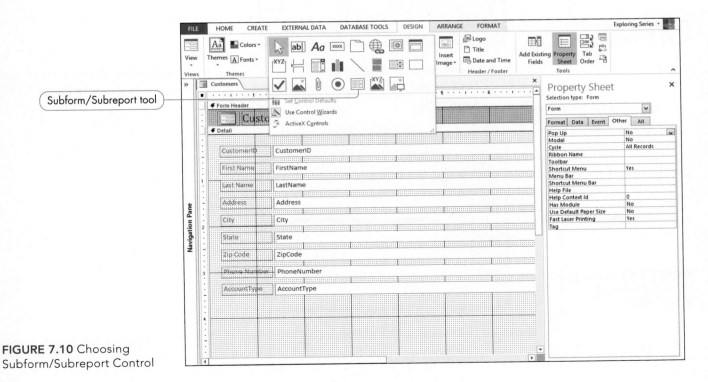

FIGURE 7.10 Choosing Subform/Subreport Control

3. Draw the subform. It can be resized later as needed.
4. Choose the source for the subform. You can use an existing form or view data in a table or query. Assuming you want to use a table, click that option and click Next, as shown in Figure 7.11.

FIGURE 7.11 SubForm Wizard: Choosing Source

5. Choose the appropriate fields from the table (or query) source, as shown in Figure 7.12. Click Next.

FIGURE 7.12 SubForm Wizard: Choosing Fields

6. Assuming a relationship exists between the two tables, you will be shown a connection between the tables. Choose the relationship you want to use, as shown in Figure 7.13. Click Next.

Suggested relationships

FIGURE 7.13 SubForm Wizard: Choosing Relationship

7. Accept the default name or create your own name for the subform. Click Finish. Your results will resemble Figure 7.14.

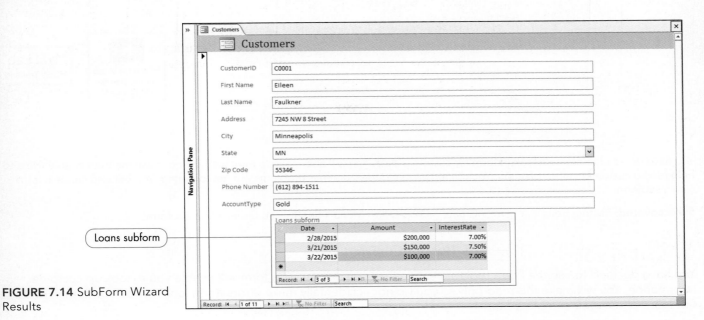

FIGURE 7.14 SubForm Wizard Results

Loans subform

You can change the size of the subform or the size of the fields in the subform as necessary. It will display in tabular fashion. The changes are easier to make in Layout view, as you can see the data as it appears in the subform.

Quick **Concepts** ✓

1. Why create a read-only copy of a form? *p. 404*

2. What does a combo box control do? *p. 406*

3. What is one reason the Auto Order option of the tab order may not work? *p. 409*

4. What does a subform do? *p. 410*

1 Advanced Forms

You have decided to create a lookup form for customer data. You will also create a form with a drop-down menu to enable users to help record customer call satisfaction. You will repair an old form that has problems with tab ordering. You will also create a form with a subform.

Skills covered: Restrict Edits in a Form • Create a Drop-Down Menu • Set the Tab Order • Use Subforms

STEP 1 ≫ RESTRICT EDITS IN A FORM

You have decided to use the Form tool to create a Customers form. This form will enable you to look up customer information. You will make this read-only so you do not accidentally make errors when looking up information. Refer to Figure 7.15 as you complete Step 1.

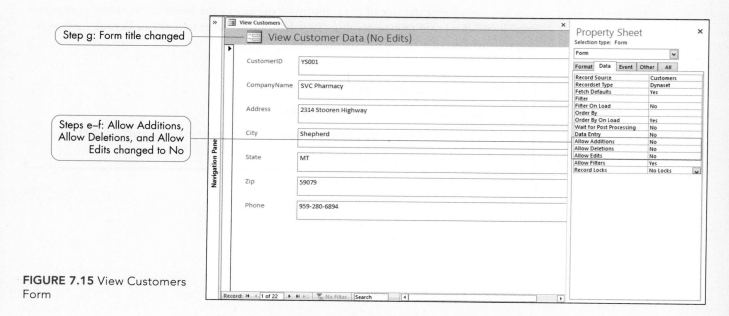

FIGURE 7.15 View Customers Form

a. Open *a07h1Yellowstone* and save it as **a07h1Yellowstone_LastFirst**.

b. Select the **Customers table** in the Navigation Pane. Click the **CREATE tab** and click **Form** in the Forms group.

   Access creates a new form based on the Customers table. The form opens in Layout view, ready to edit.

c. Click anywhere in the subform at the bottom of the window, click the border of the subform, and then press **Delete** to delete the subform.

> **TROUBLESHOOTING:** If you are prompted to confirm deleting of records, press No and ensure you have clicked the border before pressing Delete.

d. Click **Property Sheet** on the DESIGN tab in the Tools group if it is not already displayed.

   The Property Sheet displays on the right side of your screen.

e. Click the **Data tab**, if necessary. Click in the **Allow Edits box**, which currently displays *Yes*, and click the drop-down menu at the right. Change the value to **No**.

f. Repeat step e to change the **Allow Additions** and **Allow Deletions property values** to **No**. Close the Property Sheet.

g. Change the title of the form to **View Customer Data (No Edits)**. Compare your results to Figure 7.15.

h. Switch to Form view.

i. Attempt to type in the **CompanyName box**.

You should not be able to change the field value.

j. Attempt to add and delete a record.

You should not be able to add or delete a record.

k. Click **Save** in the Quick Access Toolbar and save the form as **View Customers**. Close the form.

STEP 2 ›› CREATE A DROP-DOWN MENU

You will use the Form tool to create an Access form to help manage customer call data. This form will enable you to record customer data. You will implement this using a drop-down menu. Refer to Figure 7.16 as you complete Step 2.

Step g: Row Source corresponds to values in CustomerSatisfaction table

FIGURE 7.16 Calls Drop-Down Form

a. Select the **Calls table** in the Navigation Pane. Click the **CREATE tab** and click **Form** in the Forms group.

Access creates a new form based on the Calls table.

b. Right-click the **CustomerSatisfaction text box**, click the **Change To option**, and then select **Combo Box**.

The CustomerSatisfaction text box changes to a combo box with an arrow on the right side of the box.

c. Click **Property Sheet** on the DESIGN tab in the Tools group if it is not already displayed.

d. Click the **Row Source property** on the Data tab of the Property Sheet, click the arrow, and then select **Satisfaction Results**.

e. Click the **Limit To List property** and change the value to **Yes**.

f. Switch to Form view.

g. Click in the **CustomerSatisfaction field**. Notice an arrow now appears on the right of the box. Click the arrow and notice values of 1, 2, 3, 4, and 5 appear, as shown in Figure 7.16.

h. Type the value **6** for the **CustomerSatisfaction field** and press **Tab**.

Access will display an error message that the text you entered is not a value on the list.

> **TROUBLESHOOTING:** If Access does permit the value to be entered, ensure you set the Limit To List property to Yes.

i. Click **OK**. Change the value for the first record's CustomerSatisfaction field to **2** and press **Tab**.

The value will save properly.

j. Save the form as **Calls Drop-Down**, and close the form.

STEP 3 ≫ SET THE TAB ORDER

The users of the current Edit Customers report have reported problems with the tab order. You will fix the tab order. You will also fix an old form so that the tabs appear in the correct order and remove a tab stop. Refer to Figure 7.17 as you complete Step 3.

Step i: Final tab order for Customers Old form

FIGURE 7.17 Tab Order for Customers Old Form

a. Open the Edit Customers form in Form view.

b. Click the **CustomerID box**. Press **Tab**.

When you press Tab, Access brings you to the State field.

c. Press **Tab** five more times, noticing where the cursor moves each time.

The fields are not displayed in a logical order.

d. Switch to Design view and click **Tab Order** in the Tools group on the DESIGN tab.

e. Click **Detail** and click **Auto Order**. Click **OK**.

Because this is a Stacked Layout form, Access changes the tab order so it moves down one field at a time.

f. Switch to Form view. Press **Tab** six times and verify that the tab order progresses in a logical order. Save and close the form.

g. Open the Customers Old form in Form view. Press **Tab**.

The form moves to the Phone field. You will switch the tab order so Phone appears last.

h. Switch to Design view. Click **Tab Order** in the Tools group on the DESIGN tab. Click **Detail** and click **Auto Order**.

Notice *Phone* is now at the beginning of the tab order, which is not the logical location for it.

i. Click the **Row Selector** to the left of the Phone field. Drag the **Phone field** beneath the Zip field. Your tab order should match Figure 7.17. Click **OK**.

j. Click the **CustomerID field**. Display the Property Sheet.

k. Click the **Other tab** in the Property Sheet. Locate the Tab Stop property and change the property setting to **No**.

You will no longer be able to access the CustomerID field by pressing Tab.

l. Switch to Form view. Tab through the fields, ensuring the fields display in the correct order and that pressing Tab does not bring you to the CustomerID field.

m. Save and close the form.

STEP 4 ≫ USE SUBFORMS

The Edit Customers form does not display the related call information for each customer. You will modify it so the subform containing the information appears. Refer to Figure 7.18 as you complete Step 4.

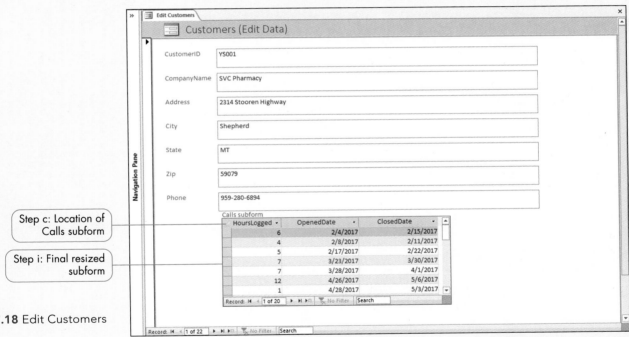

FIGURE 7.18 Edit Customers Subform

a. Open the Edit Customers form in Design view.

b. Click the **Subform/Subreport tool** in the Controls group on the DESIGN tab. If it is not visible, you may need to scroll or click the **More button** at the bottom-right of the Controls box.

c. Draw a box in the location shown in Figure 7.18. The size does not matter, as it will be resized later.

The Subform Wizard dialog box displays.

d. Select **Use existing Tables and Queries** and click **Next**.

e. Click the **Tables/Queries arrow** and select **Table: Calls**. Double-click the **HoursLogged**, **OpenedDate**, and **ClosedDate fields**. Click **Next**.

f. Click **Next** to accept the default relationship.

g. Accept the default Calls subform name and click **Finish**.

h. Switch to Layout view. Notice the Calls subform appears at the bottom of the screen.

i. Resize the subform and the fields to be approximately the size shown in Figure 7.18.

j. Save and close the form.

k. Keep the database open if you plan to continue with Hands-On Exercise 2. If not, close the database and exit Access.

Controls and Sections

As you work with tools to create and modify forms and reports, you will often need to switch between the three views in Access—Form or Report view, Layout view, and Design view. You use Layout view to perform most changes, but Design view gives you, as a designer, a higher level of control.

To lay out forms and reports, to display fields, and to display field labels, you use basic controls such as text boxes and labels. However, other types of controls exist. You can add formatting controls as well as controls that perform calculations using the same functions found in the Expression Builder.

In this section, you will examine the different form and report sections. As you learn how to create forms and reports, placing fields and labels in the correct section will become a habit. You may have to use trial and error at first, switching between different views until the form or report is working correctly.

The overlap between forms and reports will be easy to see. The same functionality applies to both, so the skills you use in forms can be applied to reports and vice versa.

Using Advanced Controls

Whether you are dealing with a form or report, some features are common to both. A number of common controls are available. When you use the form and report wizards to create basic objects, the resulting forms and reports contain a number of controls that you did not add yourself.

Both forms and reports have a text box control, which displays the data found in record source (often, a table). Although the term *text box* may imply it only displays Short Text values, it can display numeric data, currency, and dates, depending on the field's data type.

The label control is a word or phrase to describe the data associated with a text box. For a field in a form or report, the label control defaults to the caption you set for a field. If you have not set a caption for a field, the label will default to the field name.

Forms and reports also have layout controls. The layout control keeps the fields together in an orderly fashion, enabling you to move fields without having to worry about lining fields up.

Identify Control Types

Both label controls and text box controls are known as **bound controls**. A bound control is a control that is connected to a field in a table or query. Outside of computers, the term *bound* can refer to two objects tied together, so you can see where this term comes from. A bound control changes each time a new record is displayed, as the value is dynamic.

Forms and reports also contain **unbound controls**. An unbound control is a control not tied to a specific field. Generally, this refers to decorative elements, such as the title of the report. An unbound control stays the same as you switch between records. Some other examples of unbound controls are lines, pictures, and other non-data-related elements.

 TIP | **Remove the Tab Stop from Unbound Controls**

In most cases, you will want to remove the tab stop from an unbound control. Unbound controls do not require data entry, so there is no reason for the cursor to stop on them.

A *calculated control* contains an expression that generates a calculated result. Calculated controls can also be applied to forms or reports and include aggregate functions such as Sum, Min, Max, and Average. These are basic calculated controls. More advanced calculated controls can contain a combination of functions, constants, and field names from the record source. Figure 7.19 shows each of these types of controls.

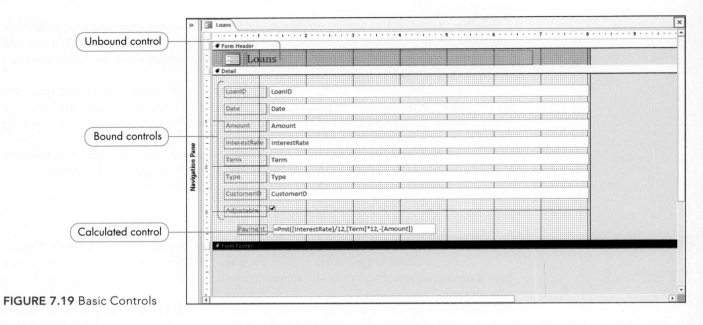

FIGURE 7.19 Basic Controls

Despite having the name *control* in the name, bound, unbound, and calculated controls are not found on the Controls group on the Design tab, which is available in Layout or Design view. Each of these is a category of controls. Recall a text box control is an example of a bound control because it is connected to a field.

Add Emphasis to a Form or Report

When using the Form or Report tools to create an automatic form or report, you have a number of default controls. The title, the form/report icon, and each field are examples. In addition, the form or report has a layout control.

If you want to add emphasis to your form or report, the Line control and Rectangle control are two options. The Line control will allow you to insert a line into your form or report, and the Rectangle will allow you to add a rectangle. After inserting these into an object, you can modify the shape to have a different line color, line thickness, and line type (such as dashed or dotted), and in the case of rectangles you can change the fill color. You will only find these options in Design view; they are not available in Layout view. To add a line or rectangle shape to a form or report, do the following:

1. Switch to Design view.
2. Click the DESIGN tab.
3. In the Controls group, select the Line or Rectangle control, as shown in Figure 7.20. You may need to click More or scroll to see this, depending on your screen configuration.
4. In the form or report, drag the mouse from the desired start point to the desired end point.

FIGURE 7.20 Advanced Controls

Your line or rectangle will appear. Once you have added a line or rectangle, you can format it by doing the following:

1. Switch to Design view.
2. Click the line or rectangle you wish to format.
3. Click the FORMAT tab.
4. In the Control Formatting group, choose the Shape Outline menu to change the color, thickness, and line type for the rectangle or line. Choose Shape Fill to add a fill color to a rectangle.

Add Text and Images to a Form or Report

Both forms and reports have the option to include text and images.

In addition to the existing label controls, you may wish to add some sort of explanatory text to a form or report. Instead of (or in addition to) a validation rule, you can add text providing guidance for your users. As this text is not tied to a specific field and is unchanging, it is considered a label. To add text to a form or report, do the following:

1. Switch to Design view.
2. Click the DESIGN tab.
3. In the Controls group, click the Label control, as shown in Figure 7.20. You may need to click More or scroll to see this, depending on your screen configuration.
4. Drag the mouse from the desired start point to the desired end point.
5. Type the text you would like to appear in the label.

Images can be useful especially when dealing with corporate forms and reports. Companies commonly use the same logo and colors on official publications. When creating a form or report, you can insert an image file containing the company logo or any other image. Often, the image is inserted in the Form Header or Report Header, so it displays once when printed or viewed on the screen. The Form Header and Report Header will be discussed further in this chapter. To add an image to a form or report, do the following:

1. Switch to Design view.
2. Click the DESIGN tab.
3. In the Controls group, click the Image control, as shown in Figure 7.20. You may need to click More or scroll to see this, depending on your screen configuration.
4. Drag the mouse from the desired start point to the desired end point. The Insert Picture dialog box appears.
5. Browse to the location containing the image and click Open.
6. Resize the image control as necessary.

Add a Calculated Control

Forms and reports based on a query can display calculated fields like any other field. However, some forms and reports are based on a table rather than a query. In this case, you can add a calculated field using a text box. The Expression Builder and its functions can be used similarly to how they are used in queries.

To add a calculated control to a form or report using the Expression Builder, do the following:

1. Switch to Design view.
2. Click the DESIGN tab.
3. In the Controls group, click the Text Box control, as shown in Figure 7.20. You may need to click More or scroll to see this, depending on your screen configuration.
4. Drag the mouse from the desired start point to the desired end point. The word *Unbound* appears in the text box. Access also displays a label by default. You can choose to delete or modify the label as necessary.
5. Display the Property Sheet.
6. Click the Data tab on the Property Sheet and click the Ellipsis (…) found next to the Control Source property to open the Expression Builder.
7. Create the desired expression.

Note that if you are comfortable with functions, you do not have to use the Expression Builder. You could simply type the formula into the text box, preceded by an equal sign. For example, you could type =Date() to show the current date.

If you want to format the results of the function (for example, change the number of decimal places for a numeric field), do the following:

1. Switch to Design view.
2. Click the text box you wish to format.
3. Click Property Sheet on the DESIGN tab in the Tools group.
4. To change the format, click the Format property on the Property Sheet's Format tab. To change decimal places for a numeric field, click the Decimal Places property.

Fix Layout Errors After Adding Controls

When dragging a new text box label to a report, you may find it puts the label in the same row as the data rows. If this happens, you can click Tabular Layout in the Table group of the Arrange tab while both the label and text box controls are selected.

Add a Page Break Control

Pagination can be important for forms and reports. Instead of being unsure where a page will break when printed, you can add a page break at a certain location. To add a page break to a form or report, do the following:

1. Open the report in Design view.
2. On the DESIGN tab, click the Insert Page Break control, as shown in Figure 7.20. You may need to click More or scroll to see this, depending on your screen configuration.
3. Click the mouse in the section of the form or report where you want the page break. When you click the Insert Page Break control, the mouse pointer changes to a crosshair with a small report (even in forms) icon.
4. After you click the form or report, a series of six dots appears on the left margin.

   To remove a page break, click the six dots and press Delete.

Using Sections

A *section* is a part of a form or report that can be manipulated separately from other parts of a form or report. Basic forms have three sections, and basic reports contain five sections. Sections are visible in Design view. Each section can be collapsed or expanded as needed.

Identify the Default Sections

STEP 3 ⟩⟩

STEP 4 ⟩⟩

One section common to forms and reports is the ***Form Header*** (for forms) or the ***Report Header*** (for reports). The *Form Header* section and the *Report Header* section are similar in that they are headers that display one time at the top of each form or report. This section contains the title by default. Column headings (labels) are also located in this section for reports as well as some types of forms. When a form or report is printed, the Form Header or Report Header displays only once immediately before the first record appearing on a printout.

Similarly, the ***Form Footer*** and ***Report Footer*** sections are footers that display one time at the bottom of the form or report. This section is left blank by default for forms and may contain some sort of aggregate function (such as Count) for a report. When a form or report is printed the Form Header or Form Footer appears once, in this case after the final record, regardless of the number of pages.

Another default section is the ***Page Header*** section. The Page Header is a header that appears once at the top of each page in a form or report. This is more commonly used for reports, as they are designed for printing. Page Headers are switched off by default for forms but can be switched on as necessary.

The ***Page Footer*** is a footer that appears once at the bottom of each page in a form or report. As with the Page Header, the Page Footer is much more common on reports. The Page Footer is also switched off by default for forms.

The distinction between the Form/Report and Page headers and footers can be confusing at first. If you had a 10-page form or report, each page would display a Page Header, while only the first page would display the Form/Report Header. Likewise, the same report would display the Page Footer on each page while displaying the Form/Report Footer once after the final record.

The ***Detail section*** displays the records in the record source. The *Detail* section displays in between the headers and footers sections in both forms and reports. Figure 7.21 shows the various form sections in Design view, and Figure 7.22 shows them as they appear when printed. Figure 7.23 shows the report sections in Design view, and Figure 7.24 shows them as they appear when printed.

FIGURE 7.21 Form Sections in Design View

FIGURE 7.22 Form Sections in Print Preview

FIGURE 7.23 Report Sections in Design View

Report Header (once at top of report)

Page Header (top of each page)

Report Footer (once at bottom of report)

Page Footer (bottom of each page)

FIGURE 7.24 Report Sections in Print Preview

Show, Hide, and Resize Sections

Forms and reports display the *Detail* and *Form/Report Header* and *Footer* sections by default. Reports also include the Page Header/Footer by default. Right-clicking a blank area of the form or report enables you to switch on or off sections. Note that when you switch a section off, it deletes all controls in the section. The header and footer sections are tied together; if you remove the Form or Report Header, the Form or Report Footer also disappears. See Figure 7.25 for an illustration in Form Design view and Figure 7.26 for Report Design view.

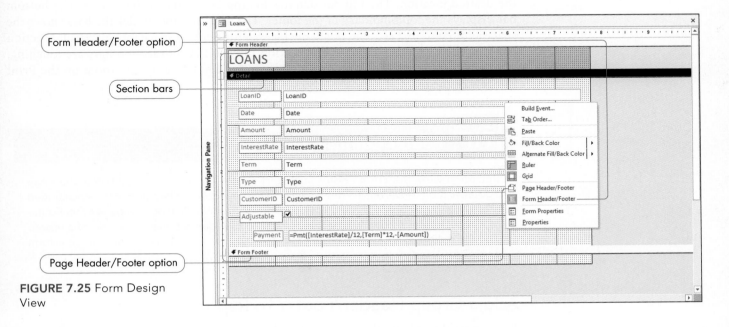

Form Header/Footer option

Section bars

Page Header/Footer option

FIGURE 7.25 Form Design View

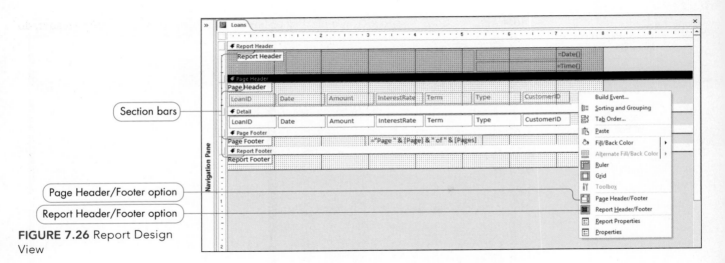

Section bars

Page Header/Footer option

Report Header/Footer option

FIGURE 7.26 Report Design View

In reports, although the *Detail* section cannot be removed, you can hide it from Print Preview, Layout view, and Design view. This is helpful when a report output, for example, contains data with totals at the end. For example, you may display the sum of the values in a field. If you only need to output the totals of each category and not the values of every record, this is a good option. To show Details only, click Hide Details in the Grouping & Totals group on the Design tab. Click Hide Details again to redisplay hidden details. Note that this option is not available for forms.

Within a form or report, you may want to change the height or width of portions of a section. The width is a global property. You cannot change the width of one section without changing it for the entire object. However, you can change the height of each section independently. In Figures 7.25 and 7.26, each gray **section bar** marks the top boundary of a section. Section bars appear gray in these figures, but they can appear in different colors based on your Office setup. You can expand or collapse the space between report sections by moving your mouse over the section bar and dragging to the desired location. The top bar denotes the top boundary of the header. The bottom bar displays the top boundary of the footer. The grid-like area under the bars shows the space allotted to that section. If you decide that the allotted space for a particular section is not needed, you can collapse that section fully so that the section bars are touching. The section remains in the report's design but will not take up any room on the Print Preview or the printed page.

 Footer Confusion

In Design view, the *Form Footer* or *Report Footer* section is located below the *Page Footer* section. However, in Print Preview, the Form Footer or Report Footer is positioned above the Page Footer. This may cause some confusion at first; however, the *Form Footer* or *Report Footer* section will be needed to produce grand totals at the end of a report. The Form Footer or Report Footer will only appear one time—at the end of a form or report.

Add a Group Header/Footer to Reports

The Report Wizard and the Group & Sort button are used to add grouping to a report. In addition to the five main sections previously listed, you can also add a custom *Group Header* and *Group Footer* section to a report. Because you cannot add grouping to forms, you will not have the option to add a Group Header or Footer to a form. To add a Group Header, do the following:

1. Switch to Layout view.
2. Click the Group & Sort button on the Grouping & Totals group of the DESIGN tab.
3. Click *Add a group* in the *Group, Sort, and Total* pane at the bottom of the screen.
4. Select the field to group by.
5. Note that even though you have done most work in this chapter in Design view, doing the grouping in Layout view saves you a few steps.

Once you have added grouping, a **Group Header** section appears just above the *Detail* section in Design view, along with the name of the field by which you are grouping. This section appears once each time the grouping field value changes, and the group header prints with the new value. For example, in a Loan report grouped by Type, the group header prints once for each Type, with the loans of that type following. If you select the Type field as a custom group, the section is named Type Header, as shown in Figure 7.27.

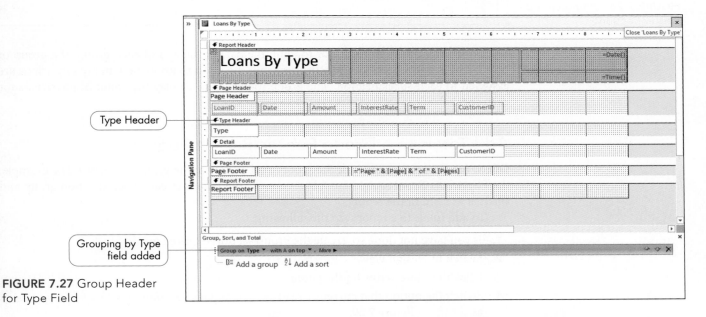

FIGURE 7.27 Group Header for Type Field

A **Group Footer** section does not show by default. It appears just below the *Detail* section in Design view, but only when you select this option in the *Group, Sort, and Total* pane. As with the Group Header, the Group Footer appears once for each distinct value in the grouping field. To display the Group Footer, do the following:

1. Switch to Layout or Design view.
2. Click the More arrow on the *Group, Sort, and Total* pane
3. Switch the option that currently reads *without a footer section* to *with a footer section*, as shown in Figure 7.28.

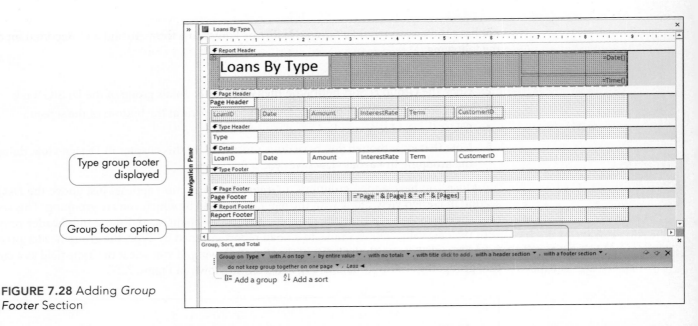

FIGURE 7.28 Adding *Group Footer* Section

The group footer is useful for totaling the data at the end of each group. If a group of physicians is part of a major practice, it would be good to know how many physicians are assigned to each specialization. The group footer could display the count of physicians for each specialization.

Add Totals to a Group Footer/Report Footer

Often, reports require totals at the group level and/or at the grand total level. For example, the Physicians Report might contain a count of physicians in each Specialization group and again at the end of the report.

To add totals to a report, do the following:

1. If you have not done so, create the group section required for the totals.
2. Switch to Design view.
3. Click the More arrow on the *Group, Sort, and Total* pane
4. Switch the option that currently reads *without a footer section* to *with a footer section*, as shown in Figure 7.29.

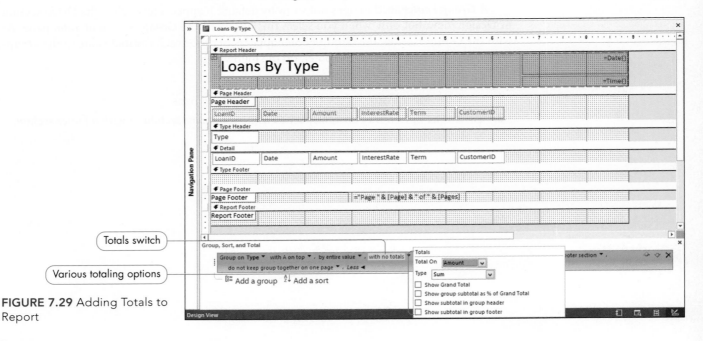

FIGURE 7.29 Adding Totals to Report

5. Select the appropriate total option. Figure 7.30 shows the count (Count Records) for the LoanID field added to the Type Footer and Report Footer.

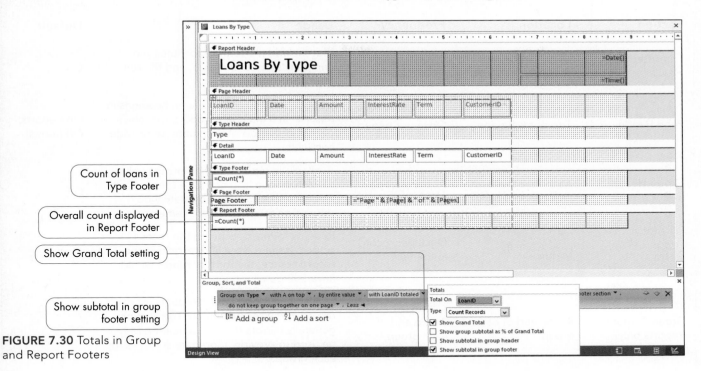

Count of loans in Type Footer

Overall count displayed in Report Footer

Show Grand Total setting

Show subtotal in group footer setting

FIGURE 7.30 Totals in Group and Report Footers

TIP | Add a Page Break to a Group Footer

A page break is commonly used in a group footer. Doing so causes each group to print on a separate page. For example, if you had a report grouped by customer, the report would print each customer's data on a separate page (rather than continuing with the next customer on the same page). This type of report is useful when the information is distributed to each customer. In the case that a customer's information takes up more than one page, the page break is inserted after each customer's information.

Section	Location	Frequency	Usage	Default
Form/Report Header	Top of the form/report	Once	May include the form/report title, the company's name and logo, and the run date and time.	On
Page Header	Top of each page	Once per page	Generally contains the column headings in reports. In a multipage report, the labels repeat at the top of each page to provide continuity.	On (reports) Off (forms)
Group Header (reports only)	At the start of each new group	At the start of each group	Available in reports only. Prints the value of each unique instance for a grouped field. A report grouped by state would print up to 50 unique state names.	Off
Detail	Middle	Once per record in the record source	Repeats for each record in the record source. If there were 500 records in the record source, the form or report would have 500 detail listings.	On
Group Footer (reports only)	At the end of each group	At the end of each group	Available in reports only. Repeats for each record in the record source. This section generally mirrors the group header. May be used to provide aggregate statistics for each group.	Off
Page Footer	Bottom of each page	Once per page	Generally used to print page numbers.	On (reports) Off (forms)
Form/Report Footer	End of the form/report	Once	Often used to print grand totals or other aggregate information for the records.	On

Quick Concepts ✓

1. What is the difference between controls in forms and controls in reports? *p. 419*

2. What is the difference between a bound control and an unbound control? *p. 419*

3. What is the purpose of a calculated control? *p. 420*

4. List the five default sections of a report. *p. 423*

5. What do the Group Header and Footer do? *pp. 426–427*

Hands-On Exercises

Watch the Video
for this Hands-
On Exercise!

MyITLab®
HOE2 Training

2 Controls and Sections

You have decided to modify reports to add calculations, and to modify the different header and footer sections of forms and reports to improve the print and on-screen readability.

Skills covered: Use Advanced Controls in Forms • Use Advanced Controls in Reports • Use Sections in Forms • Use Sections in Reports

---

STEP 1 ≫ USE ADVANCED CONTROLS IN FORMS

You will be making changes to an existing form and a calculated control to determine if a call is Open or Closed. Refer to Figure 7.31 as you complete Step 1.

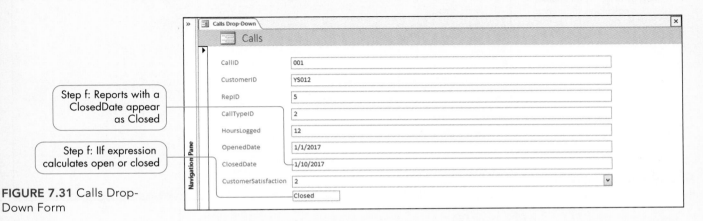

Step f: Reports with a ClosedDate appear as Closed

Step f: IIf expression calculates open or closed

FIGURE 7.31 Calls Drop-Down Form

a. Open *a07h1Yellowstone_LastFirst* if you closed it at the end of Hands-On Exercise 1. Save the database as **a07h2Yellowstone_LastFirst**, changing *h1* to *h2*.

b. Open the Calls Drop-Down form in Design view.

c. Drag the end of the *Detail* section (appearing right above the Form Footer) to about 4" on the vertical toolbar.

d. Click **Text Box** in the Controls group on the DESIGN tab. Click beneath the last control in the form to insert the control. It should be placed approximately where it appears in Figure 7.31.

> **TROUBLESHOOTING:** If you are unable to see the Text Box control, click the More button in the Controls group and select the Text Box control.

e. Display the Property Sheet. Click the **Data tab** on the Property Sheet, click in the **Control Source box**, and then click the **Ellipsis (…)** found next to the Control Source property.

f. Type **IIf(IsNull([ClosedDate]),"Open","Closed")** in the **Expression Builder**. Click **OK**.

This expression displays Open when the ClosedDate is null (in other words, when no value exists in the ClosedDate field) and Closed otherwise.

g. Delete the label for the new control. The control has a default name of *Text* followed by a two-digit number.

h. Switch to Form view. Ensure the first few records display *Closed.* Click the **Last Record Navigation button** and ensure the last record in the table has a value of *Open.*

i. Save and close the form.

STEP 2 ≫ USE ADVANCED CONTROLS IN REPORTS

You will make changes to an existing report to display the number of days each call has been open. Refer to Figure 7.32 as you complete Step 2.

Step h: Call 001 has been open 9 days

Step g: Days Open column calculates difference

FIGURE 7.32 Days Open Report with Calculation

a. Open the Days Open report in Design view.

b. Click the **Text Box control** in the Controls group on the DESIGN tab. Click to the right of the ClosedDate text box in the *Detail* section of the report to add a new field.

> **TROUBLESHOOTING**: If you are unable to see the Text Box control, click the More button in the Controls group and select the Text Box control.

c. Click the **Tabular button** in the Table group on the ARRANGE tab.

The new field lines up after the final column in the report.

d. Click the **label control** for the new column. Delete the existing text and type **Days Open.**

e. Click in the **text box control** for the new column. Display the Property Sheet.

f. Click the **Data tab** on the Property Sheet and click **Control Source**. Click the **Ellipses (. . .)** to launch the Expression Builder.

g. Type **=[ClosedDate]-[OpenedDate]** in the **Expression box**. Click **OK.**

h. Switch to Report view. Verify the calculation correctly displays the number of days each call was open, as shown in Figure 7.32.

i. Save and close the report.

You will adjust an existing form by adding a logo to the form header and adding a page header. Refer to Figure 7.33 as you complete Step 3.

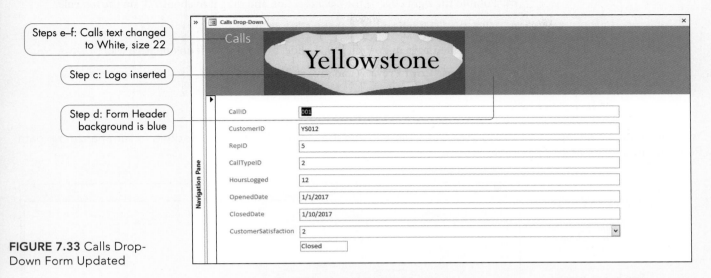

Steps e–f: Calls text changed to White, size 22

Step c: Logo inserted

Step d: Form Header background is blue

FIGURE 7.33 Calls Drop-Down Form Updated

a. Open the Calls Drop-Down form in Design view.

b. Click the **form logo** in the *Form Header* section and press **Delete**.

   The form logo disappears.

c. Click the **Image control** in the Controls group on the DESIGN tab. Click to the right of the word *Calls* in the Form Header. Browse to the location of your data files and select **a07h2Logo**.

   A logo for Yellowstone appears in the report header.

d. Click the grey background of the Form Header. Click the **Shape Fill arrow** in the Control Formatting group on the FORMAT tab. Select **Blue, Accent 1** (first row, fifth column).

e. Click the **Calls label**. Click the **Font Color arrow** in the Font group on the FORMAT tab. Select **White, Background 1**. Recall you can see the names for each color by pointing to a color and waiting for the ScreenTip to appear.

f. Click the **Font Size arrow** in the Font group on the FORMAT tab. Change the size to **22**.

g. Switch to Form view and compare your form to Figure 7.33.

h. Switch to Design view. Right-click a blank area and select **Page Header/Footer**.

   A *Page Header* section appears above the *Detail* section, and a *Page Footer* section appears below the *Detail* section.

i. Click the **Label control** in the Controls group on the DESIGN tab. Click the left side of the Page Footer. Type **Created by First Last**, replacing *First* with your first name and *Last* with your last name.

j. Switch to Form view.

   The page footer is not displayed because it will only appear when printed.

k. Click the **FILE tab** and click **Print**. Click **Print Preview**.

   The footer should appear on each page. You will notice the form is too wide to fit on one page left to right. When printed, this might lead to extra pages.

l. Switch to Design view. Click the **CallID text box** and change the width to **5.5"** on the top ruler.

All other controls resize as well.

m. Point to the right edge of the *Detail* section and drag it to about 7.5" on the top ruler.

n. Click the **FILE tab** and click **Print**. Click **Print Preview**.

As a printed page in Portrait is 8.5" wide, this will now fit on one page wide.

o. Click **Close Print Preview** and save and close the form.

STEP 4 ≫ USE SECTIONS IN REPORTS

You will create a new report based on the Calls table and use the Group Headers and Footers to summarize the data. Refer to Figure 7.34 as you complete Step 4.

Step e: RepID field resized

Step d: Report grouped by CallTypeID

Step h: Sum added to Group Footer

FIGURE 7.34 Final Calls By Type Report

a. Click the **Calls table**. Click the **Report tool** on the Reports group of the CREATE tab.

b. Delete the report icon from the Report Header.

c. Click **Group & Sort** in the Grouping & Totals group on the DESIGN tab if it is not already displayed.

The *Group, Sort, and Total* pane appears at the bottom of the report.

d. Click **Add a group** in the *Group, Sort and Total* pane and select **CallTypeID**.

The report will be grouped by the type of call.

e. Resize the RepID field width so it takes up only as much room as necessary.

The report should fit on one page, left to right.

f. Switch to Design view.

Notice a CallTypeID Header appears between the *Page Header* and *Detail* sections.

g. Click the **More arrow** in the *Group, Sort, and Total* pane. Click the **without a footer section arrow** and switch to **with a footer section**.

A CallTypeID footer appears between the *Detail* and *Page Footer* sections.

h. Click the **HoursLogged text box**. Click **Totals** in the Grouping & Totals group on the DESIGN tab and select **Sum**.

A Sum function appears in both the CallTypeID Footer and the Report Footer.

i. Resize the CallTypeID Footer and Report Footer to be about 1" tall.

j. Resize the text boxes for the new sum fields to be about double the current height.

k. Click the **Insert Page Break control** in the Controls group on the DESIGN tab. Click the bottom of the CallTypeID Footer.

Six small dots appear on the left of the CallTypeID Footer.

l. Display the report in Print Preview.

TROUBLESHOOTING: If you get an error message stating *The section width is greater than the page width, and there are no items in the additional space, so some pages may be blank.*, try making the rows slightly less tall.

All calls with a CallTypeID appear on page 1, with a total of 188 hours appearing on page 2. Scroll to page 4 and notice a total of 208 hours for all calls with a CallTypeID of 2. Your results should resemble Figure 7.34.

m. Save the report as **Calls By Type** and close the report.

n. Exit Access. Submit based on your instructor's directions.

Chapter Objectives Review

After reading this chapter, you have accomplished the following objectives:

1. **Restricting edits in a form.**
   - Create a read-only form: Read-only forms enable users to view but not change data to help prevent erroneous data entry.

2. **Creating a drop-down menu.**
   - Convert a text box to a combo box: A combo box control provides a drop-down menu that displays a list of options from which the user can choose a single value.
   - Customize a converted combo box: Information can be looked up in a table or, less commonly, added manually. You can restrict to only the provided values using the Limit To List option.

3. **Setting the tab order.**
   - Set the tab order: Tab enables users to advance from one field to the next in a form. The tab order is the sequential advancing in a form from one field or control to the next when you press Tab. Changing the tab order may become useful in some instances.
   - Remove a tab stop: Tab stops can be removed from any field. Oftentimes, they are removed from fields that do not require data entry.

4. **Using subforms.**
   - Form can display records from a related table using a subform.
   - Subforms are generally laid out in a tabular fashion and are used when a relationship exists between two tables.

5. **Using advanced controls.**
   - Identify control types: Label controls and text box controls are known as bound controls. A bound control is a control that is connected to a field in a table or query. An unbound control is a control not tied to a specific field, often decorative elements such as titles, lines, pictures, and other decorative objects.
   - Add emphasis to a form or report: The Line and Rectangle controls are among the options to add emphasis.
   - Add text and images to a form or report: Text can be added using a Label control, and images can be added using the Image control.

   - Add a calculated control: A calculated control is placed inside a text box that contains an expression that generates a calculated result and can contain functions, constants, or field names from the record source. Calculated controls can use the Expression Builder to help create complex expressions.
   - Fix layout errors after adding controls: When adding controls, you may need to add them to a layout to maintain a consistent layout.
   - Add a page break control: You can specify exactly where to add a page break using the Page Break control.

6. **Using sections.**
   - Identify the default sections: A section is a part of a form or report that can be manipulated separately from other parts of the form or report. They are viewable in Design view. The *Form Header* section and the *Report Header* section are headers that display one time at the top of each form or report. The Form Header and Report Header appear only once on printouts immediately before the first record appearing on a printout. *Form Footer* and *Report Footer* sections are footers that display one time at the bottom of the form or report. When a form or report is printed the Form Header and Form Footer appear once regardless of the number of pages. The Page Header is a header that appears once at the top of each page in a form or report. The Page Footer is a footer that appears once at the bottom of each page in a form or report. The *Detail* section displays the records in the record source.
   - Show, hide, and resize sections: You can show any missing section by right-clicking and selecting the missing section. Most sections can be hidden.
   - Add a Group Header/Footer to reports: The *Group Header* section appears just above the *Detail* section in Design view, along with the name of the field by which you are grouping. The *Group Header* section appears once each time the grouping field value changes. The *Group Footer* section appears just below the *Detail* section in Design view. Group Headers and Footers are only available in reports.
   - Add totals to a Group Footer/Report Footer: Group Footers (hidden by default) are commonly used for totals.

Key Terms Matching

Match the key terms with their definitions. Write the key term letter by the appropriate numbered definition.

a. Bound control
b. Calculated control
c. Combo box control
d. *Detail* section
e. Form Footer
f. Form Header
g. Group Footer
h. Group Header
i. Page Footer

j. Page Header
k. Read-only form
l. Report Footer
m. Report Header
n. Section
o. Section bar
p. Subform
q. Tab order
r. Unbound control

1. _____ A form that enables users to view but not change data. **p. 404**

2. _____ Provides a drop-down menu displaying a list of options from which the user can choose a single value. **p. 406**

3. _____ The sequential advancing in a form from one field or control to the next when you press Tab. **p. 409**

4. _____ Records displayed that are related to records in a main form. **p. 410**

5. _____ A control that is connected to a field in a table or query. **p. 419**

6. _____ A control not tied to a specific field. **p. 419**

7. _____ A control containing an expression that generates a calculated result. **p. 420**

8. _____ Part of a form or report that can be manipulated separately from other parts of the form or report. **p. 423**

9. _____ A header that displays once at the top of each form. **p. 423**

10. _____ A header that displays once at the top of each report. **p. 423**

11. _____ A footer that displays one time at the bottom of a form. **p. 423**

12. _____ A footer that displays one time at the bottom of a report. **p. 423**

13. _____ A header that appears once at the top of each page in a form or report. **p. 423**

14. _____ A footer that appears once at the bottom of each page in a form or report. **p. 423**

15. _____ Displays the records in the record source. **p. 423**

16. _____ Marks the top boundary of a section in a form or report. **p. 426**

17. _____ Appears just above the *Detail* section in Design view, along with the name of the field by which you are grouping. Appears once each time the grouping field value changes. **p. 427**

18. _____ Appears just below the *Detail* section in Design view. Appears once each time the grouping field value changes. **p. 427**

Multiple Choice

1. A form that is read-only enables you to:

   (a) Change formatting.

   (b) Change data.

   (c) View records.

   (d) All of the above

2. A combo box enables you to:

   (a) Add a drop-down menu.

   (b) Perform calculations.

   (c) Add headers to a form.

   (d) Create a read-only form.

3. Which of the following statements about tab order is false?

   (a) Tab order can be automatically assigned.

   (b) Fields can have their tab stop removed.

   (c) Tab order can be arranged in any order you want.

   (d) None of the above

4. Which of the following would most likely not be a subform?

   (a) A list of patients for a doctor

   (b) A list of orders for each customer

   (c) A list of employees for a location

   (d) A list of birth mothers for a child

5. A control connected to a field in a table or query is a(n):

   (a) Bound control.

   (b) Calculated control.

   (c) Rectangle control.

   (d) Unbound control.

6. A control containing =*Date()* is most likely to be a(n):

   (a) Bound control.

   (b) Calculated control.

   (c) Rectangle control.

   (d) Unbound control.

7. Which statement is false about controls?

   (a) The *Detail* section displays the values of records.

   (b) A label control is used for text, such as titles.

   (c) A calculated field is created with a text box control.

   (d) Forms cannot display calculated controls.

8. Which of the following prints once per report?

   (a) Form Header

   (b) Group Header

   (c) Page Header

   (d) Report Header

9. Which of the following prints on every page of a form?

   (a) Form Header

   (b) Group Header

   (c) Page Header

   (d) Report Header

10. Which of these is not available in an Access form?

    (a) *Detail* section

    (b) *Group Header* section

    (c) *Form Header* section

    (d) *Page Footer* section

1 La Vida Mocha

FROM SCRATCH

You are helping La Vida Mocha, a small coffee supply store, migrate to Access. You will help them add data validation and create two forms, one for data entry and one for viewing data. This exercise follows the same set of skills as used in Hands-On Exercises 1 and 2 in the chapter. Refer to Figure 7.35 as you complete this exercise.

Menu created

Label added

FIGURE 7.35 Edit Customers Form

a. Open Access and create a new database named **a07p1Coffee_LastFirst**.

b. Import the text file *a07p1States* into the database. Name the field **StateName** and choose the StateName field as the primary key. Save the table as **State**. Accept all other default properties.

c. Import the text file *a07p1Customers* into the database. Ensure you check the **First Row Contains Field Names option**, accept default field names, and choose **ID** when asked to select a primary key. Name the table **Customers**.

d. Click the **Customers table** in the Navigation pane. Click **Form** in the Forms group on the CREATE tab. Save the form as **Edit Customers**.

e. Right-click the **State text box**, select **Change To**, and then select **Combo Box**. Click the **Property Sheet button** in the Tools group on the DESIGN tab.

f. Change the **Row Source property** to **State**. Change the **Limit To List property** to **Yes**. Switch to Form view.

g. Change the City for the first customer to **Paterson**, the State to **NJ**, and the Zip to **07505**. You may notice the tab order does not work correctly for this form.

h. Switch to Design view. Click **Tab Order** in the Tools group on the DESIGN tab. Click the **Row Selector** to the left of the State field and drag it below the City field. Click **OK**.

i. Drag the **section bar** below the Form Footer down to approximately 1" on the vertical ruler.

j. Click the **Label control** in the Controls group on the DESIGN tab. Click in the top-left corner of the *Form Footer* section. Type the text **Private information. Print with care!** in the label.

k. Click the border of the label you created in step j to select the entire control. Click the **Font Size menu** in the Font group on the FORMAT tab. Change the font size for the Label control to **36**. Resize the control so all information is displayed on one line.

l. Click the **Font Color menu** in the Font group on the FORMAT tab. Select the **Black, Text 1 color** in the first row.

m. Click the **Background Color menu** in the Font group on the FORMAT tab. Select the **Gold, Accent 4 color** in the first row. Switch to Form view and compare your form to Figure 7.35.

n. Save and close the form. Create a copy of the form named **View Customers**. Open View Customers in Design view.

o. Change the title at the top of the form to **Customers (View Only)**.

p. Display the Property Sheet. Ensure the drop-down at the top of the Property Sheet displays *Form*. Click the **Data tab** and change the options **Allow Additions**, **Allow Deletions**, and **Allow Edits** to **No** to create a read-only form. Switch to Form view and ensure you cannot change data.

q. Save and close the form. Exit Access. Submit the database based on your instructor's directions.

2 Northwind Traders

You are a technical supervisor at Northwind Traders. The technician who handles most Access tasks just went on paternity leave, and he was unable to address user changes before going on leave. You will create a form and report based on user requests. This exercise follows the same set of skills as used in Hands-On Exercises 1 and 2 in the chapter. Refer to Figure 7.36 as you complete this exercise.

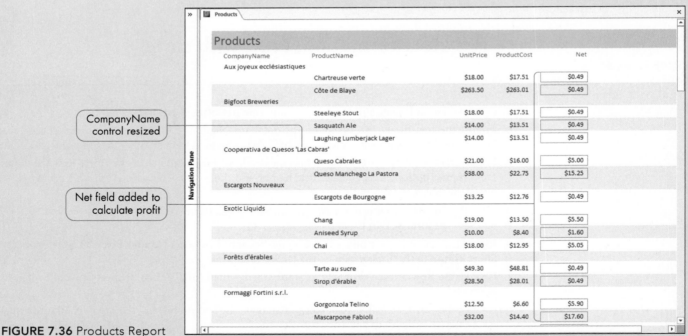

FIGURE 7.36 Products Report

a. Open *a07p2Traders*. Save the database as **a07p2Traders_LastFirst**.

b. Open the Products by Category form in Design view.

c. Use the section bar to increase the size of the *Detail* section to about 5" vertically.

d. Click the **Subform/Subreport tool** in the Controls group on the DESIGN tab. Click below the top-left corner of the Description label.

e. Answer the Subform Wizard as follows:

- Select **Use existing Tables and Queries** and click **Next**.
- Select **Table:Products** from the Tables/Queries list. Double-click the **ProductName**, **QuantityPerUnit**, **UnitPrice**, **UnitsInStock**, and **UnitsOnOrder fields**. Click **Next**.
- Select the default relationship (show Products for each record in Categories using CategoryID). Click **Next**.
- Accept the default name of *Products subform*. Click **Finish**.

f. Switch to Layout view. Resize the columns in the subform so all fields are displayed.

g. Save and close the form.

h. Open the Products report in Layout view. Click **Group & Sort** in the Grouping & Totals group on the DESIGN tab. Click **Add a group** in the *Group, Sort and Total* pane. Select **CompanyName**. Notice the CompanyName field is not wide enough to display all values.

i. Switch to Design view. Change the width of the CompanyName field (displayed in the CompanyName Header) to **4"** on the horizontal ruler.

j. Click the **Text Box control** in the Controls group on the DESIGN tab. Click to the right of the ProductCost box.

k. Click **Tabular** in the Table group on the ARRANGE tab.

l. Click in the label for the control created in step j. Change the text in the label from the existing text (which should be *Text* followed by two numbers) to **Net**.

m. Click the text box for the new field and type **=UnitPrice-ProductCost** in the box.

n. Display the Property Sheet by clicking the **Property Sheet button** in the Tools group on the DESIGN tab.

o. Click the **Format button** on the Property Sheet. Change the format to **Currency** and change the **Decimal Places property** to **2**.

p. Switch to Report view. Compare your report to Figure 7.36.

q. Save and close the report.

r. Close the database. Exit Access.

s. Submit based on your instructor's directions.

Mid-Level Exercises

1 Red Cliffs City Hotels

ANALYSIS CASE

You are the general manager of a large hotel chain. You track revenue by categories: hotel rooms, conference rooms, and weddings. You need to create a form that includes a drop-down menu for the state and the company logo in the header, uses the company colors, and has a correct tab order. You also plan on modifying a report so it displays the number of years that each customer has been a member.

a. Open *a07m1Rewards*. Save the database as **a07m1Rewards_LastFirst**.

b. Select the **Members table** and create a form using the Form tool. Save the form as **Maintain Members**.

c. Switch to Design view. Change the State text box to a combo box.

d. Change the Row Source to **States**.

e. Delete the form logo and the label control (containing the word *Members*) from the *Form Header* section.

f. Insert an Image control in the top-left corner of the *Form Header* section. Insert the **a07m1Logo** file.

DISCOVER

g. Change the background color of the *Detail* section to the orange color found in the first row (*Orange, Accent 6*). Note: Select all the labels by drawing a box around them in Design view. Change the font color of the labels to **Black, Text 1**. Change the border width of the labels to **4 pt** and the border color to **Blue, Accent 1**.

h. Switch to Form view. Ensure the form appears correctly. Verify the tab order works as expected by pressing **Tab** to visit each field. Save and close the form.

i. Open the Members By State report in Design view.

j. Add a formula in the **Time as Member box** to determine the number of years they have been a member. Use **#12/31/2017#** as the current date (recall dates must be surrounded by # signs), subtract the MemberSince field, and divide the result by **365**.

k. Change the format of the formula you created in step k to display as **Standard format** with 1 decimal place.

l. Add grouping by the State field. Ensure you remove the State label from the Page Header.

m. Switch to Report view. Ensure the values displayed make sense. For example, member Melissa Remaklus been a member since 11/8/2006, so she has been a member for slightly more than 11 years (assuming it is 12/31/2017).

n. Save and close the report.

o. Open the *a07m1Analysis* document in Word and save as **a07m1Analysis_LastFirst**. Use the database objects you created to answer the questions. Save and close the document.

p. Close the database. Exit Access. Submit based on your instructor's directions.

2 Replacement Parts

You are working as a stockperson in the warehouse for Replacement Parts. You have been given an internship in the information technology department. You have been tasked with making modifications to the company's database. As you are hoping to move from being a stockperson to being a member of the technology staff, you want to impress and go above and beyond what has been asked of you.

a. Open *a07m2Replace*. Save the database as **a07m2Replace_LastFirst**.

b. Create a new form based on the Employees table. Save the form as **Employees Lookup**.

c. Delete the subform. Change the form to be read-only, ensuring users cannot add, delete, or edit records.

d. Change the title in the Form Header to **Employees (Lookup Only)**. Save and close the form.

e. Open the Customer Orders report in Design view.

f. Insert the **a07m2Logo image** in the Report Header to the right of the Customer Orders text.

g. Display the Group Footer. Display the sum of the Qty field in the Group Footer. Add a label that displays **Total Qty Ordered** to the left of the Qty sum.

h. Add a new Text Box control after the Price field. Click **Tabular** in the Table group on the ARRANGE tab.

i. Change the label for the new control to **Line Total**. Add a formula in the text box to multiply the Qty field by the Price field.

j. Change the format of the Line Total to **Currency**.

k. Use the Line control to add a horizontal line at the bottom of the *Group Footer* section.

l. Switch to Report view and ensure the Total Qty Ordered values appear correctly. Switch to Design view.

m. Add a Sparse Dots border to the Total Qty Ordered text boxes. Add a Special Effect of **Shadowed**. Save and close the report.

n. Exit Access. Submit the database based on your instructor's directions.

---

3 Ramos Hospital

You are working for a local hospital in the information technology department. The founder, Waynet Ramos, has asked your team to help her put together some forms and reports. As she is very busy, she is hoping your team can independently develop some reports and work together to implement and revise them. After discussions with her, you realize she is asking for grouped reports.

a. Waynet needs a report based on which doctors are assigned to each patient, a report showing all medications and who they are prescribed to, and a report showing each patient with the medications they are on. Each group member will create one report.

b. Open Access and open *a07m3Ramos* individually. Save the file as **a07m3Ramos_LastFirst**. Each of you will create your report in an individual database.

c. Create a report using the Report Wizard based on the appropriate tables. Add grouping as necessary.

d. Save the report as **LastFirst**, replacing *Last* and *First* with your last and first names.

e. Make the report as attractive and useful as possible. You may want to perform tasks such as adding subtotals to the group or report footer, changing sorting, removing or add a layout control, changing formatting options, and changing the background color. Modify the report, save the changes, and then exit Access.

f. Meet as a group. Open *a07m3Ramos* and save the file as **a07m3Ramos_GroupName**.

g. Import the report from each of your databases.

Your *a07m3Ramos_GroupName* file will now have one report for each student.

h. Examine the reports each of you created.

i. Work with your group to improve the reports as necessary. Ensure that you take a critical eye to what your group members came up with and help them improve their report.

j. Save the changes and close all reports. Ensure each student has a copy of the final *a07m3Ramos_GroupName* database.

k. Exit Access and submit both the *a07m3Ramos_GroupName* and *a07m3Ramos_LastFirst* databases based on your instructor's directions.

Create a Tabbed Form

 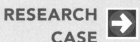

Cindy Livesey has a Web site at LivingRichWithCoupons.com where she posts coupon deals. She also has a coupon database that she maintains in Access, which she uses to keep track of her own stockpile. Cindy has contacted you, as one of the users of her Web site, to assist her in organizing the way she inputs coupons. Open the *a07b2Coupons* database and save it as **a07b2Coupons_LastFirst**.

1. Research tabbed forms in Access help or on the Internet. You will create a form based on the Products table, with a tabbed form below. The tabbed form will have two tabs. One tab should display the contents of the related Coupon table as a subform, and the second tab should display the Stockpile Information table. Save the form as **Coupon Reference**.

2. Cindy would like a field on the Stockpile Information tab to display *Yes* when it is time to restock and *No* when it is not. You can accomplish this by inserting a text box field and using the IIf function, displaying *Yes* when the NumberInStockpile is less than the RestockNumber field.

Close the database and close Access. Submit based on your instructor's directions.

Products Database

A new hire for your company is performing data entry for company products. Her system crashed, and the information technology department was able to restore the database from an old backup. She has asked you for help in fixing the database. She has noticed a few problems with the Products Ordered form:

1. The form's tab order does not work properly.

2. The Total On-Hand Value at the top of the page is used to display a value and no longer does. It used to display with two decimal places and no dollar sign. In addition, a lot of extra space exists at the top of the screen between the title and data.

3. The form no longer displays the current date and time at the top right of each page when printed.

4. The subform field widths are too small.

Open *a07b3Food* and save it as **a07b3Food_LastFirst**. Repair the errors above and save and close the database. Submit based on your instructor's directions.

Health Care Privacy

The Woodland Park Hospital is working on a database system to keep track of patients, illnesses, and the doctor assigned to treat the patient. As the technology lead on this project, the group evaluating the database would like your thoughts on how to implement forms and reports. The evaluating committee will be looking at the HIPAA Protected Health Information (PHI) regulation when deciding whether your solution is acceptable. Create forms and reports as specified below and examine the HIPAA PHI regulations. In addition, consider what information you think should be available for each type of user. Open *a07b4Medications* and save it as **a07b4Medications_LastFirst**. Create forms and reports to meet the following specifications. Choose only the fields that you think each group needs based on your research.

1. Doctors need a report showing patient information. Save the report as **Doctor Patient List** and ensure the report title is *Doctor Patient List* as well.

2. Nurses need a report showing medications, doses, and room numbers for each patient. Save the report as **Medications By Room** and change the report title to **Medications by Room**.

3. Front-desk personnel want to enter new patients using a form. Save the form as **Intake**.

4. The hospital needs to provide statistics about how many people are hospitalized with each type of illness to various agencies. Save the report as **Illness Statistics** and change the report title to **Illness Statistics** as well.

Exit Access. Submit the database based on your instructor's directions.

Capstone Exercise

The Human Resources department has asked you to assist them in updating the database they have been using. They need to create a form that can be used to find information but not change information. They have an existing form that they would like to enhance, and they need to be able to present supervisors with a list of employees who report to them. You will assist them in these tasks.

Database File Setup

You will save a copy of the original database and open the database to complete this capstone exercise.

a. Open *a07c1Prices*.

b. Save the database as **a07c1Prices_LastFirst**.

Restrict Edits in a Form

You will create a form to view employees. Use the Form tool to create the form, and then switch the form to be read-only.

a. Select the Employees table and use the Form tool to create a new form.

b. Change the title to **View Employees**.

c. Delete the Orders subform.

d. Change the **Allow Edits**, **Allow Additions**, and **Allow Deletions** settings to **No**.

e. View the form and data in Form view.

f. Save the form as **View Employees** and close the form.

Create a Drop-Down Menu and Set Tab Order

You will modify an existing form to implement a drop-down menu and fix the tab order.

a. Create a new table named **Countries**. Rename the default ID field to **Country** and change the data type to **Short Text**. Enter two records, **UK** and **USA**. Close the table.

b. Open the Update Employees form in Design view.

c. Change the Country field to a combo box.

d. Set the Row Source to **Countries** and the Limit To List property to **Yes**.

e. Fix the tab order so the Postal Code field comes before the Country field. Save and close the form.

Use Controls and Sections

You have been asked to add some privacy information to the bottom of the View Employees form and make some design changes. You have also been asked to create a report for managers that shows the name of all employees who work for them and calculates the number of years the employees have been employed at the company.

a. Open the View Employees form in Design view. Add a new label control in the left-side of the Form Footer that displays the text **Personnel information is considered private and printouts should be shredded after use**.

b. Change the font color to **Black, Text 1** and bold the text.

c. Save and close the form.

d. Create a new report based on the Employees table using the Report Wizard. Select the **FirstName, LastName, HireDate**, and **HomePhone fields**. Select all other default options.

e. Switch to Layout view. Add grouping by the ReportsTo field.

f. Switch to Design view. Display the Group Footer. Display the count of the First Name field in the Report Footer.

g. Add an Insert Page Break control at the bottom of the ReportsTo footer.

h. Resize the Home Phone field so the right side lines up with the 6" on the horizontal ruler.

i. Add a new Text Box control to the right of the Home Phone box. Use the Tabular button in the Table group on the ARRANGE tab to place it correctly.

j. Change the label for the field to **Years Employed**.

k. Add a formula in the text box to calculate the number of years the employee has been employed, assuming the current date is #12/31/2017#. Format the field as **Standard** with 1 decimal place.

l. Close and save the report. Close the database. Exit Access.

m. Submit based on your instructor's directions.

Get Connected

Exchanging Data Between Access and Other Applications

OBJECTIVES AFTER YOU READ THIS CHAPTER, YOU WILL BE ABLE TO:

1. Create a Hyperlink field p. 448

2. Add an Attachment field p. 450

3. Add attachment controls to forms and reports p. 453

4. Export data to Excel p. 463

5. Export data to Word p. 467

6. Export data to a PDF or XPS document p. 470

7. Export objects to another Access database p. 473

8. Link to an Access table p. 484

9. Link to an Excel spreadsheet p. 487

10. Import an Excel spreadsheet p. 490

11. Import a text file p. 493

CASE STUDY | Property Management Data Exchange

The Blackwood Maintenance Service (BMS) is a property management company located in Pineville, North Carolina. The owners would like to attract new customers by expanding the services they offer. Many of the properties that are maintained by BMS belong to residents' associations.

Your task is to contact the board members of each association and ask them if you can send information about the new services. You will also ask permission to send the homeowners a flyer by regular mail.

After contacting each association, you send the association manager a list of the new services that BMS can offer the homeowners. You also need to create a list of homeowners who BMS will contact by mail. You can prepare the information in a variety of ways, so you need to ask each association its preferred format. Information will also be sent to BMS in a variety of formats, and you will need to incorporate the new data into the database.

Connecting Access to External Files

In many cases, it is necessary or desirable to connect to data that exists apart from an Access database. Access provides several ways that you can access data, Web sites, or files from within your database. Access supports a *hyperlink* data type that enables you to quickly link to any file on your computer or to any Web page on the Internet. The data you enter as a hyperlink can be a path to any file on your computer, the location of a Web page on an intranet, an e-mail address, or a URL. A *uniform resource locator (URL)* is the location of a Web site or Web page on the Internet. When you click a hyperlink field value while in Datasheet view, Access launches the program required to display the file or Web page.

If you have a database that contains a Customers table, you can add a hyperlink field to store the Web site address of each customer. When you need information about the customer—the address, phone number, or contact information—you can quickly access the customer Web site by clicking the hyperlink. If the hyperlink is an e-mail address, Access launches a new e-mail window and automatically adds the customer's e-mail address into the To field. You can also link to an Excel spreadsheet that contains a list of the most recent invoices for the customer.

Access also offers you the option of attaching files to a record in a database through an attachment field. An attachment field enables you to attach multiple files of different types. Rather than links that direct you outside of your database, attachments are stored within the database file itself. No limit exists as to the number of files you can attach. For customers, you could attach a photo of the president or CEO, or a photo of a key contact that you work with. You can also attach other document formats, such as Word documents, including contracts or specifications for a product, or scanned documents that are in PDF format.

Users can easily interact with these documents by double-clicking on the appropriate attachment field. A dialog box appears with options to add, remove, open, or save a file. Choose the appropriate file, and then choose the action you want to take.

In this section, you will create a hyperlink field to store Web site addresses. In addition, you will learn how to attach photos and documents to records. Finally, you will learn how to attach files and use an attachment control in forms and reports.

Creating a Hyperlink Field

STEP 1 ≫ If you were working in a Customers table, you could add a Hyperlink field in Design view of the table to store the customers' Web sites. Figure 8.1 shows the hyperlink data type selection for the field name CustomerWebsite. After you add the hyperlink field, save the changes and switch to Datasheet view, where you can add the URLs, as shown in Figure 8.2.

Add a Hyperlink Field in Design View

To add a Hyperlink field in Access, do the following:

1. Open the table in Design view and add the new field name to the table.
2. Select Hyperlink from the Data Type list.
3. Save the changes and switch to Datasheet view.
4. Add the data values to the new hyperlink field.
5. Click a hyperlink value and Access launches the appropriate program, such as a Web browser or Excel, and enables you to interact with the file.
6. If you make any changes to the file, save the changes within the host application. For example, if you launch an Excel spreadsheet from within Access, you can make changes to the spreadsheet and then save your changes in Excel.

CustomerWebsite field added

Hyperlink data type

Customer Web site caption added

FIGURE 8.1 Creating a Hyperlink Field

Customer Web site URLs

Hyperlinks have a blue underline

FIGURE 8.2 Hyperlink Fields

Edit a Hyperlink in Datasheet View

STEP 2 ▶▶ When you attempt to edit a hyperlink by clicking it, you may accidentally launch the software application instead of just editing the hyperlink value.

To edit a hyperlink value, do the following:

1. Right-click the hyperlink field.
2. Point to *Hyperlink*.
3. Select Edit Hyperlink. The Edit Hyperlink dialog box displays as shown in Figure 8.3. Several options exist in the dialog box; however, the two options that are most commonly used are the *Text to display* box and the Address box.
4. In the *Text to display* box, change the *Text to display* value to modify what the user sees when he or she views the data in Datasheet view (for a table), Form view (for a form), or Print Preview (for a report).
5. In the Address box, enter the actual address that Access uses to locate and launch a file and open it with the appropriate software.
6. Click ScreenTip to create a ScreenTip that will display when you point your mouse over the hyperlink text. This is similar to the ScreenTips that appear when you hover your mouse over commands on the Ribbon.
7. Click OK.

Type text you want the user to see

Enter a ScreenTip (optional)

Type the URL for the Web site

FIGURE 8.3 Edit Hyperlink Dialog Box

 TIP | Working with a Hyperlink Field

Working with hyperlink fields can be frustrating for an end user. The user may accidentally click to open a program when he or she only wants to edit the hyperlink. For this reason, some database designers define hyperlink fields as text fields. Users can still store the URLs, e-mail addresses, and file name paths, but the references will not automatically launch any software. Users must copy and paste the references into the appropriate application.

To remove a hyperlink field, do the following:

1. Right-click the hyperlink field.
2. Point to *Hyperlink*.
3. Select Remove Hyperlink. Access will remove the current hyperlink without asking for confirmation.

Other options for manipulating a hyperlink field exist in the shortcut list that displays when you right-click a hyperlink; however, editing and removing a hyperlink field are the most commonly used.

Adding an Attachment Field

STEP 3 ≫

An Access database is primarily used to store and analyze data and to retrieve information. This data is usually typed directly into the tables or entered using an Access form. Sometimes you may want to store a reference to an external file—an image, a scanned document, an Excel spreadsheet, a PDF document—and then be able to open that file from within Access. These situations can be handled by adding an attachment field to a table. An *attachment field* is similar to an attachment in an e-mail; you can use an Access attachment to attach multiple files of any format and then launch those files from within Access. The files are actually copied into the database itself. Keep in mind that Access is not able to analyze the data within these external files; Access can only open the files. To review the documents, you need to use another program.

The size of your database grows when you attach files. Some file types are compressed by Access when you attach them (such as Excel and Word), and other file types increase the database size byte for byte (such as JPEG and other photo formats). You can monitor the increase in size using these steps:

1. Compact the database.
2. Check the size of the database file.
3. Add the file attachment.
4. Check the size of the database file again.

If the database grows too large, you can remove some attachments (such as JPEGs), resize the files, and reattach the files in a smaller format. JPEG attachments are one of the leading causes for "bloating" in an Access database. Remember to compact your database after you add and remove attachments.

Add an Attachment Field in Design View

If you were working with a Customers table and you wanted to store a photo of the owner, the office building, and the master contract in Access, in Design view you could add a new field named CustomerFiles and select the data type *Attachment*, as shown in Figure 8.4. Save the changes, and then switch to Datasheet view so you can add the files to the new attachment field. A paperclip icon with the number of files attached is shown in the New Attachment column. All records, except record 6, show (0) attachments because no files are attached yet (see Figure 8.5).

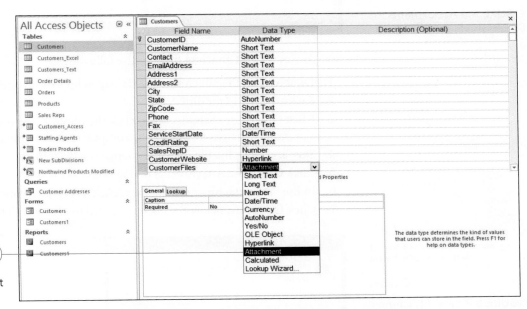

Attachment data type

FIGURE 8.4 Add an Attachment Field in Design View

Number of files is indicated in parentheses (2)

Paperclip icon indicates an Attachment field

FIGURE 8.5 Datasheet View Showing Attachments

Add or Edit Attachments in Datasheet View

STEP 4 » Suppose you have a database that stores all the customer information for your business. You want to store a photo of the owner, a photo of the exterior of the main building, a map with directions to the business, and a Word document containing the price structure for each company. The directions file was created using Google Maps and then saved as a PDF document. You can attach all of the files relating to each customer's record.

To attach a file to a record, do the following:

1. Double-click the attachment field's paperclip icon to open the Attachments dialog box, shown in Figure 8.6.
2. Click Add to add the first attachment.
3. Use the Choose File dialog box to locate and select the file.

4. Click Open to attach the file to the record.
5. Click Add again to add the next file and each additional file. In the previous example, you would need to click Add four times to add the two photos, the map, and the price structure document.
6. Click OK to close the Attachments dialog box. The paperclip icon would now show that (4) files are attached to the current record.
7. Click the record below the current record to save the attached files.

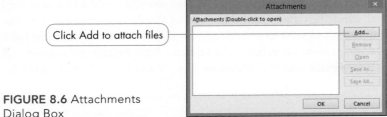

FIGURE 8.6 Attachments Dialog Box

To view or edit attached files, do the following:

1. Double-click the attachment field's paperclip icon to open the Attachments dialog box.
2. Select the file to modify.
3. Click Open. For example, if you click the photo of the owner, and then click Open, you can modify the photo using your computer's default picture manager software.
4. Save and close the file once the change has been made.
5. Click OK in the Attachments dialog box.
6. In the Save Attachment dialog box, click Yes to save your changes (see Figure 8.7).
7. Click the record below the current record to save the changes.

FIGURE 8.7 Save Attachment Message

Remove Attachments in Datasheet View

STEP 5 » To remove an attached file, do the following:

1. Double-click the attachment field's paperclip icon to open the Attachments dialog box.
2. Select the file to remove and click Remove.
3. Click OK.
4. Click the record below the current record to save the changes.

The number of files shown next to the paperclip is reduced by one.

TABLE 8.1	Using the Attachments Dialog Box
Add	Click to add one or more files to a record.
Remove	Click to remove previously attached files.
Open	Click to launch the appropriate application and open the file. If you try to close the Attachments dialog box with the file open, you will receive a warning that your changes may not be saved. If you are sure you have saved your changes, click OK. You will receive a message that the changes were saved to your hard drive in a temporary file. Access asks if you would like to save your updates to the database (see Figure 8.7).
Save As	Use to save the attached file to a local storage location. You must remember to add it back into the database if you make changes.
Save All	Save all of the attachments in a record to a local, temporary folder.

TIP Deleting Temporary Files

Each time you open an attachment file, Access creates a temporary file on your computer's hard drive. You can remove these temporary files by launching the desktop version of Windows Internet Explorer. Click Tools and select *Internet options*. On the General tab, click Delete in the *Browsing history* section. In the next dialog box, delete the temporary Internet files and Web site files and close the dialog box. Close the remaining dialog boxes to return to Internet Explorer.

Adding Attachment Controls to Forms and Reports

STEP 6 >> In a form or report, you can interact with attachments using an attachment control. An *attachment control* is a control that lets you manage attached files in forms and reports. In a form, the attachment control enables you to add, edit, and delete attachments the same way you can in a table. If the attachment is a photo, the control displays the photo as you navigate through the records. If the attachment is a document, you will only see an icon representing the application that was used to create the file. When you click an attachment control in Form view, the Attachment toolbar displays arrows that enable you to advance through the attachments. The Attachment toolbar also has a paperclip icon that you can click to open the Attachments dialog box. This dialog box is the same one that opens when you click an attachment field in a table.

In a report, the attachment field displays the first file only in Print Preview. If the first attachment is a photo, the control displays the photo; if the first file is a document, an icon representing the application is displayed. The Attachment toolbar does not appear in Print Preview. To see the Attachment toolbar and advance through multiple attachments in a report, close Print Preview, and then switch to Report view. Report view enables you to advance through multiple attachments. In a form, switch to Form view to work with the Attachment toolbar.

Add an Attachment Control to a Form

To add an attachment control to a form, do the following:

1. Open the form in Layout view.
2. Click Add Existing Fields in the Tools group on the DESIGN tab.
3. In the Field List, the attachment field appears as a parent field with three child fields. The expand symbol (+) enables you to expand and collapse the child fields.
4. Drag the parent field name to the form, and then drop it in the desired location, as shown in Figure 8.8. Access adds the bound attachment control and the associated label to the form.
5. Resize the bound control, if necessary, to ensure that the images display correctly.
6. Save your changes, and then switch to Form view to view your changes (see Figure 8.9).
7. Return to Layout view for additional modifications if necessary.

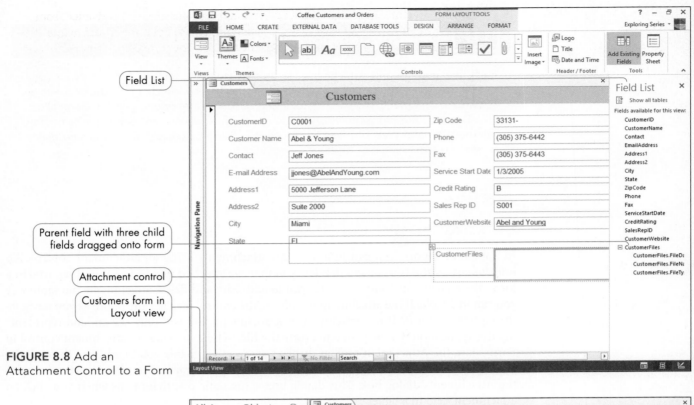

FIGURE 8.8 Add an Attachment Control to a Form

Field List

Parent field with three child fields dragged onto form

Attachment control

Customers form in Layout view

FIGURE 8.9 Attachment Control in Form View

Customers form in Form view

Attachment control displays image

Add an Attachment Field to a Report

STEP 7 ⟫ To add an attachment field to an existing report, do the following:

1. Open the report in Layout view.
2. Click Add Existing Fields in the Tools group on the DESIGN tab.
3. Drag the parent field name to the report, and then drop it in the desired location.
4. When the attachment control is in place, click the control to view the Attachment toolbar, as shown in Figure 8.10. Attachments can also be viewed in Report view of the report.

5. Using the Attachment toolbar, click the *next* and *previous* arrows to advance from one attachment to the next, or click the paperclip icon to open the Attachments dialog box. You should reduce the size of the attachment control in a report because a report usually displays multiple records on one page. If a user needs a larger view of a thumbnail, he or she can always review the photo in Layout view by opening the Attachments dialog box.

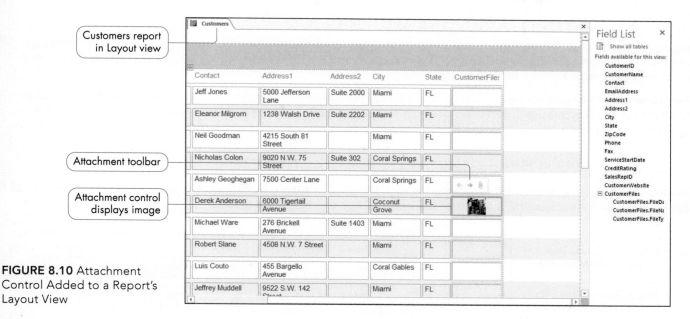

FIGURE 8.10 Attachment Control Added to a Report's Layout View

In Hands-On Exercise 1, you will work with the database from the Blackwood property management company. You will add and edit a Hyperlink field that will link properties to the appropriate school district's Web page. You will create and use an Attachment field (some with multiple attachments) in an Access table, and you will add attachment controls to a form and a report.

Quick Concepts ✓

1. What is the major difference between a linked file and an attachment? *p. 448*

2. What is a potential disadvantage of storing attachments in your databases? *p. 450*

3. In which view of a report is the Attachment toolbar available? *p. 453*

Hands-On Exercises

Watch the Video for this Hands-On Exercise!

MyITLab®
HOE1 Training

1 Connecting Access to External Files

Blackwood Maintenance Service wants to add a link to a Web site for each subdivision and a link to the school district that each subdivision resides in. You will also add a photo of each property that BMS now serves. Finally, you will add a photo and related documents to the record of each BMS agent.

Skills covered: Add a Hyperlink Field in Design View • Edit a Hyperlink in Datasheet View • Add an Attachment Field in Design View • Add or Edit Attachments in Datasheet View • Remove Attachments in Datasheet View • Add an Attachment Control in Layout View • Add an Attachment Field in a Form or Report

STEP 1 ≫ ADD A HYPERLINK FIELD IN DESIGN VIEW

Create a new field that will link to a Web site for each subdivision served by Blackwood. Also add a link to the school district Web site for each subdivision. Refer to Figure 8.11 as you complete Step 1.

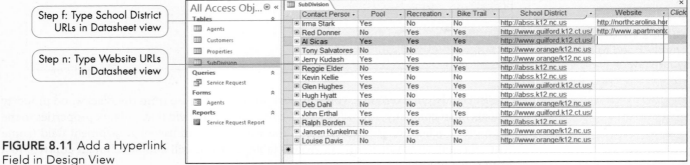

Step f: Type School District URLs in Datasheet view

Step n: Type Website URLs in Datasheet view

FIGURE 8.11 Add a Hyperlink Field in Design View

a. Open *a08h1Property*. Click the **FILE tab**, click **Save As**, click **Save As**, and then type **a08h1Property_LastFirst**. Click **Save**.

> **TROUBLESHOOTING:** Throughout the remainder of this chapter and textbook, click Enable Content whenever you are working with student files. If you make any major mistakes in this exercise, you can close the file, open *a08h1Property* again, and then start this exercise over.

b. Open the Agents table and replace *Your_Name* with your name in both the FirstName and LastName fields. Close the Agents table.

c. Open the SubDivision table in Design view. In the blank row below the BikeTrail field name, type **SchoolDistrict**. Click the **Data Type arrow** and select **Hyperlink**.

d. Type **School District** in the **Caption property box** in the Field Properties window in the bottom portion of the Table Design view.

e. Save the changes to the table. Switch to Datasheet view.

   You are ready to add the school districts' Web site addresses to the new hyperlink field.

f. Type **http://abss.k12.nc.us** into the **School District field** for records 1, 6, 7, 9, and 12.

   Fair Brook, North Point, Red Canyon, The Links, and The Pines are all located in the Alamance-Burlington School System.

g. Type **http://www.guilford.k12.ct.us** into the **School District field** for records 2, 3, 8, and 11.

King's Forest, Dale, Seeley Lake, and The Orchards are in the Guilford District.

h. Type **http://www.orange.k12.nc.us** into the **School District field** for the remaining records (records 4, 5, 10, 13, and 14).

The remaining subdivisions are in the Orange County School District.

> **TROUBLESHOOTING:** If you make a mistake, do not click in the School District field to correct it. Instead, click in the BikeTrail column and press Tab to select the field that contains an error. Retype the information.

i. Test the accuracy of the URLs by clicking the **School District hyperlink** in records 1 and 2. If the security window appears, click **Yes** to continue.

The browser opens and the school district's Web site opens. Close the browser window.

j. Widen the School District field so all the data is displayed, and then compare your screen to Figure 8.11.

k. Switch to Design view.

l. Type **Website** in the first blank field under *School District*. Select **Hyperlink** as the data type.

You added a second hyperlink field for each community's Web site.

m. Save the changes to the table. Switch to Datasheet view.

You are ready to add the community Web site addresses to the new hyperlink field.

n. Type **http://northcarolina.hometownlocator.com/nc/catawba/fairbrook.cfm** into the **Website field** of record 1.

This hyperlink points to the nearby community.

o. Type **http://www.apartmentguide.com/neighborhoods/North-carolina-Greensboro-Kings-Forests** into the **Website field** of record 2.

This hyperlink lists information about the surrounding community.

STEP 2 » EDIT A HYPERLINK IN DATASHEET VIEW

You realized that you entered an incorrect URL for the Guilford schools. The current URL links point to schools in Connecticut, not in North Carolina. You will fix the links in this step so that the URL links to schools in North Carolina. Refer to Figure 8.12 as you complete Step 2.

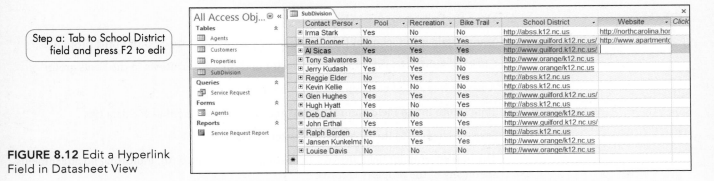

FIGURE 8.12 Edit a Hyperlink Field in Datasheet View

a. Click in the **BikeTrail column** of record 2 and press **Tab** to select the School District field. Press **F2** and edit the link so it reads **http://www.guilford.k12.nc.us**.

The *ct* segment of the hyperlink was changed to *nc*. The hyperlink is enclosed with pound signs (#), which Access uses to activate the link when clicked.

b. Click in the **BikeTrail column** of record 3 to save your changes. Test the new hyperlink by clicking the **School District field** in record 2, *http://www.guilford.k12.nc.us*.

The link now points to the correct school district. Close the browser window. You will use another method to edit the remaining Guilford URLs.

c. Right-click the **http://www.guilford.k12.ct.us** hyperlink in record 3, point to *Hyperlink*, and then select **Edit Hyperlink** from the shortcut menu.

The Edit Hyperlink dialog box opens.

d. Change the *ct* segment of the hyperlink to **nc** in the Address field at the bottom of the dialog box. Click **OK** to accept your changes and press the down arrow to save your changes.

The Text to display changes.

e. Test the modified URL by clicking **http://www.guilford.k12.nc.us hyperlink** in record 3.

The link now points to the correct school district. Close the browser window.

f. Edit the remaining Guilford URLs (change *ct* to **nc**) using the Edit Hyperlink dialog box. Compare your results to Figure 8.12.

g. Close the SubDivision table.

STEP 3 ≫ ADD AN ATTACHMENT FIELD IN DESIGN VIEW

BMS has collected photos of its properties for the past several years. The photos are stored in a folder where employees can access them as needed. The owners have asked you to create an attachment field so you can attach each photo to its corresponding property. Refer to Figure 8.13 as you complete Step 3.

Step c: Click Data Type in Photo field and select Attachment

FIGURE 8.13 Add an Attachment Field in Design View

a. Open the Properties table in Design view.

You will add an attachment field that enables you to attach the photos of the properties.

b. Click the **SubDivisionID field row selector** and click **Insert Rows** in the Tools group.

A new row is added between Listing and SubDivisionID.

c. Type **Photo** in the **Field Name column** and select **Attachment** as the data type.

d. Save the changes to the table design. Switch to Datasheet view.

The new attachment field displays a paperclip symbol with a (0), indicating no attachments are on any of the property records.

STEP 4 ≫ ADD OR EDIT ATTACHMENTS IN DATASHEET VIEW

In this step, you will attach the photos to the corresponding properties. Having these photos attached to the properties enables the agents to access them when working with the property owners. You will add 13 photos now and the other photos later. Refer to Figure 8.14 as you complete Step 4.

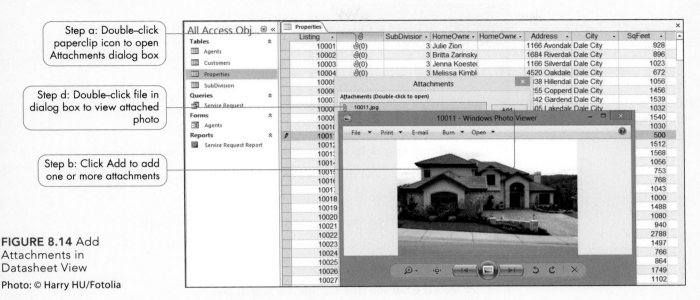

Step a: Double-click paperclip icon to open Attachments dialog box

Step d: Double-click file in dialog box to view attached photo

Step b: Click Add to add one or more attachments

FIGURE 8.14 Add Attachments in Datasheet View

Photo: © Harry HU/Fotolia

a. Double-click the **paperclip icon** in the Photo field in the record for listing 10011 to open the Attachments dialog box.

b. Click **Add**. Locate the *10011.jpg* photo found in the a08h1Photos folder. Double-click the file to add it to the Attachments dialog box.

The file displays in the Attachments dialog box.

c. Click **OK** to close the Attachments dialog box, and then click the record for listing 10012 to save the record.

d. Double-click the **paperclip** in record 11 to open the Attachments dialog box again. Double-click the *10011.jpg* photo to open your computer's default photo software.

Compare your screen to Figure 8.14.

e. Close the photo software and click **OK** in the Attachments dialog box.

f. Double-click the **paperclip** in listing 10043.

g. Click **Add** in the Attachment dialog box, and then locate and attach photo *10043.jpg* to the record. Click **OK**.

h. Double-click the **paperclip** in listing 10067 and attach photo *10067.jpg* to the record.

i. Add the corresponding photos to the following records: 10865, 10888, 10899, 10935, 10968, 11028, 11042, 11118, 11141, and 11171.

j. Select the record for listing 10025. Double-click the **paperclip** to open the Attachments dialog box. Click **Add** and add photo *10025a.jpg* to the Attachments dialog box. Before clicking OK to attach the photo, click **Add** in the Attachments dialog box to add a second attachment to the record. Double-click *10025b.jpg* to add it to the Attachments dialog box. Click **OK** to add both photo attachments to the record. Click the record for listing 10026 to save the record.

STEP 5 ≫ REMOVE ATTACHMENTS IN DATASHEET VIEW

One of the properties was sold, and the new owners are not going to use BMS to manage their property. You decide to remove the photos from this property. Refer to Figure 8.15 as you complete Step 5.

Step b: Click the image to select it

Step b: Click Remove to remove the image

FIGURE 8.15 Remove an Attachment in Datasheet View

a. Double-click the **paperclip** in listing 10025 to open the Attachments dialog box.

b. Click the first photo and click **Remove**.

c. Click the second photo and click **Remove**.

Both photos have been removed from the Attachments dialog box.

d. Click **OK** to close the Attachments dialog box and click the record below to save the record.

e. Close the Properties table.

f. Click the **FILE tab** and click **Compact & Repair Database**.

You decide to compact the database because adding and removing attachments can increase the size of the database.

STEP 6 ≫ ADD AN ATTACHMENT CONTROL IN LAYOUT VIEW

BMS asks you to create a report showing the properties with an outstanding service request. You decide to include a photo of each property, but only a thumbnail will appear in the report. Refer to Figure 8.16 as you complete Step 6.

Step h: Double-click Photo in the Field List Pane to add the image

FIGURE 8.16 Attachment Field in a Report

Photos: (From top) © Pavel Losevsky/Fotolia, © Pavel Losevsky/Fotolia, © Harry HU/Fotolia, © mbolina/Fotolia, © majeczka/Fotolia, © amelie/Fotolia, © qingwa/Fotolia

a. Open the Service Request query in Design view. Change the criterion from *Your_name* to your last name.

b. Switch to Datasheet view and examine the query results.

Thirteen properties display with you as the manager. The Photo field is missing; you must return to Design view to add it to the query design.

c. Switch to Design view.

d. Drag the **Photo field** from the Properties table and drop it into the first blank column in the query design grid.

> **TROUBLESHOOTING:** If you drag one of the three child fields, delete the column and try again. Make sure you add the parent photo field, the field with a (+) or (−) symbol to its left.

e. Switch to Datasheet view and examine the query results again. Save and close the query.

f. Double-click **Service Request Report** and switch to Layout view.

g. Click **Add Existing Fields** in the Tools group.

h. Click **Brookville** to select the City column. Double-click **Photo** in the Field List pane to add the field to the right side of the report.

> **TROUBLESHOOTING:** If you double-click one of the three child fields, click Undo and try again. Make sure you double-click the parent photo field, the field with a (+) or (−) symbol to its left.

The Photo field becomes the last column on the right of the report. Most of the photos are positioned on the right side of the right margin line. You will resize the other columns to reduce the layout width to one page.

i. Click **Add Existing Fields** in the Tools group to close the Field List window. Reduce the width of the Listing column by dragging the right border of the Listing column heading to the left.

j. Reduce the width of the City column until no photos are positioned on the second page.

k. View the report in Print Preview.

All the fields now fit onto one page.

l. Click **Close Print Preview** in the Close Preview group. Save and close the report.

STEP 7 ≫ USE AN ATTACHMENT FIELD IN A FORM OR REPORT

Blackwood wants to add a photo of each agent to the database. They also want to attach the latest performance evaluation to each employee's record. Refer to Figure 8.17 as you complete Step 7.

FIGURE 8.17 Attachment Field in a Form

Photo: © Rido/Fotolia

a. Open the Agents table in Design view. Add a field named **RelatedFiles** in the first blank row under *CellPhone*. Select **Attachment Data Type**. In the *Field Properties* section, type **Photo and Related Files** in the **Caption property**.

You added an attachment field to store the photo and performance review for each agent.

b. Save the table changes, and then switch to Datasheet view.

You need to attach a photo and a Word file for each employee.

c. Double-click the **paperclip** in the first record, for Juan Rosario. The Attachments dialog box opens. Click **Add**. Locate and open the *a08h1Agents* folder. Find and double-click *juan.jpg* to attach it. Click **OK** to close the Attachments dialog box and click another record to save the current record.

> The paperclip now shows that (1) file is attached to Juan's record. Next, add a photo and a Word file to Kia Hart's record.

d. Double-click the **paperclip** in Kia Hart's record to open the Attachments dialog box. Click **Add**. Locate the *kia.jpg* photo and attach it to the record by double-clicking the file. Click **Add** again and attach the document *Kia Hart Performance Evaluation*. Click **OK** to close the Attachments dialog box and click another record to save the current record.

> Kia's record should indicate (2) attachments.

e. Attach the remaining agents' photos to their records. Use the photo named *your_name* for your photo. Attach the *Your_Name Performance Evaluation* document to your record as well. Close the table.

f. Open the Agents form in Design view. Click the **ID field** to activate the Layout Selector (the small square with a cross inside, located to the left of the first field).

> You will move all the fields to the right.

g. Click **Layout Selector** and drag the fields as a group to the right.

> Use Figure 8.17 (the completed form) as a guide as you reposition the fields.

h. Click **Add Existing Fields** in the Tools group to open the Field List.

i. Drag the **RelatedFiles field** to the left of the fields you just moved.

> The field is added to the left side of the form. You need to reposition the label and the control separately.

j. Move the **RelatedFiles control** to the top of the form using the small solid square at the top-left of the control. Resize the control using Figure 8.17 (the completed form) as a guide.

> **TROUBLESHOOTING:** If the label follows the attachment control, release the mouse and try again. Verify you are dragging the attachment using the small solid square.

k. Drag the **Photo and Related Files label** to the bottom of the control, as shown in Figure 8.17. Click the **FORMAT tab** and click **Center** in the Font group to center align the label text.

l. Switch to Form view. Click **Next record** in the Navigation bar to advance to record 2, Kia Hart's record.

> This record has two attachments. The Word file displays as an icon, and the photo is not displayed.

m. Double-click the **Word icon** to open the Attachments dialog box. Click **Open**. Kia's overall rating is *Good*. Close the Word file. Click **Kia.jpg** and click **Open**. Close the photo file. Click **OK** in the Attachments dialog box.

n. Click the **Attachment control** to activate the Attachment toolbar. Click the **green arrow** to display the next attachment.

> Kia's photo displays.

o. Click **Next record** in the Navigation bar to advance to your record. Double-click the Attachment control to open the Attachments dialog box. Click each attachment and click **Open** to view each file. Close the Attachments dialog box when you are finished.

p. Save and close the form.

q. Click the **FILE tab** and click **Compact & Repair Database**.

r. Keep the database open if you plan to continue with Hand-On Exercise 2. If not, close the database and exit Access.

Exporting Data to Office and Other Applications

Using Access to collect and store data, to extract information, and to analyze information is useful for any organization. The accounting department of a company will always need to track sales, inventory, materials, and labor so it can report the financial statements to management each month. Access can handle this task. In addition, the sales department will need to process orders and track profitability based on each order and on categories of products. Access can handle this task as well. If management wants to know who its best customers are based on sales for the current year, Access can provide this information, too, using a query and a report.

But what happens when this information must be shared with the other departments or with other companies? How can the accountants deliver database information to others who might not be familiar with using Access or even have the software? One way to deliver information is via hard copies. However, this does not work if the recipient wants to manipulate the data him- or herself to analyze it further from a different angle. A common way to distribute data stored in an Access database is to export the data to another application.

In this section, you will learn how to export Access data to Excel and Word. Because these two applications are part of the Microsoft Office Suite, exporting from Access is straightforward. In addition to exporting to Excel and Word, this section will show you how to create a PDF or XPS document and how to export objects from one Access database to another Access database.

Exporting Data to Excel

Exporting data from Access to Excel is generally uncomplicated because the data in Access is usually structured in a manner that Excel understands. However, a few special situations exist when exporting to Excel; these situations will be discussed in the section that follows.

Select a Record Source to Export to Excel

If the record source you want to export to Excel is a table, such as the Customers table shown in Figure 8.18, then the export-to-Excel process is fast and easy. When you export a table to Excel, the field names become the column headings and the table records become the rows in the Excel spreadsheet.

To export a table to Excel, do the following:

1. Select the table in the Navigation Pane (or open the table first).
2. Click Excel in the Export group on the EXTERNAL DATA tab. Access opens the Export – Excel Spreadsheet dialog box to guide you through the export process.
3. Specify the file name and destination and the format for the exported file. Specify whether to export the data with formatting and layout. This option preserves most formatting and layout information applied in Access. Otherwise, the file opens using default Excel formatting.
4. Specify if you want to open the destination file after the export operation is complete. This option opens the resulting file. Otherwise, you would need to open it from within its application.
5. Specify if you want to export only the selected records (if you have selected one or more records in the datasheet).
6. Click OK.

When you export a table from Access, all of the columns and all the records in the table are exported, even if the table is open and not all of the data is visible (as shown in Figure 8.18). The end result is a new Excel worksheet containing all of the columns and all of the records in the Customers table, as shown in Figure 8.19.

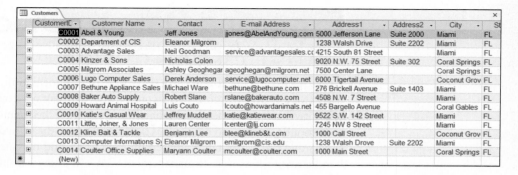

FIGURE 8.18 Customers Table in Access Before Exporting to Excel

FIGURE 8.19 Customers Table Exported to Excel

If you want to export only a subset of the Customers table, you can filter a table or select specific records before exporting. Alternatively, you could create a query to then export to Excel. For example, if you only need the address fields for customers in a certain zip code, you can create a query and then save it. Select the query, and then export the query records to Excel.

Export a Query to Excel

To export a query to Excel, do the following:

1. Select the query in the Navigation Pane (or open the query first).

2. Click Excel in the Export group on the EXTERNAL DATA tab. Access opens the Export – Excel Spreadsheet dialog box (shown in Figure 8.20) to guide you through the export process.

3. Specify the file name and destination and the format for the exported file.

4. Specify whether to export the data with formatting and layout.

5. Specify if you want to open the destination file after the export operation is complete (see Figure 8.21).

6. Specify if you want to export only the selected records (if you have selected one or more records in the datasheet).

7. Click OK.

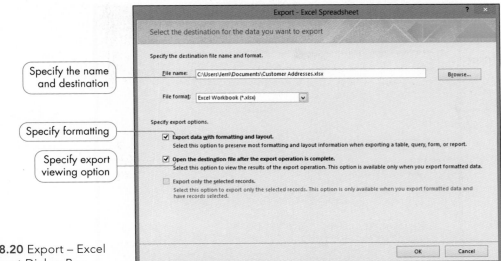

FIGURE 8.20 Export – Excel Spreadsheet Dialog Box

FIGURE 8.21 Customer Addresses Query Exported to Excel

The Excel spreadsheet will display. Once you are finished reviewing the exported Excel spreadsheet, and then return to the Access window, one final screen requires a response. In Figure 8.22, Access asks you, *Do you want to save these export steps?* Click the *Save export steps* check box if you want to repeat the same export process at a later time. Saving export steps is useful if you need to repeatedly export the same query. The saved steps are stored under Saved Exports in the Export group.

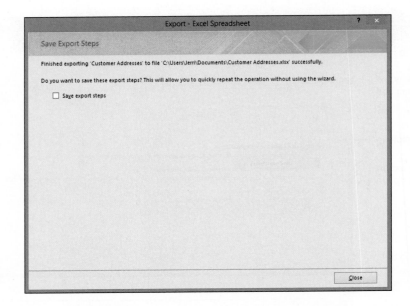

FIGURE 8.22 Save Export Steps Dialog Box

Export Forms and Reports to Excel

STEP 2» Exporting tables and queries to Excel usually yields predictable and consistent results. The main reason is the similarity between an Access datasheet and an Excel worksheet. Both have column headings, and both have multiple rows of data below the column headings. Most of the cells have data in them (blank cells are the exception). However, when you export forms and reports from Access to Excel, the results can be unpredictable. For example, if you export a form that contains Customers information and a subform showing the Orders for each customer, the Customers data exports but the Orders (subform data) does not. Furthermore, if you attempt to export a grouped report in Access, the grouping in Excel may not match the grouping in the Access report. You can either accept the results from the form or report, or redo the export using the underlying record source. The underlying tables and queries are more reliable than forms and reports. Figure 8.23 shows an Access form based on Customers and the related Orders for each customer. Figure 8.24 shows the same form after it is exported to Excel. The records from the related (Orders) table do not display.

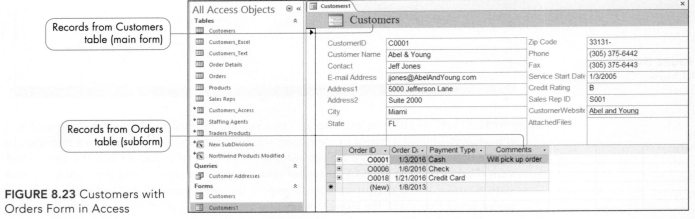

FIGURE 8.23 Customers with Orders Form in Access

Records from Customers table (main form)

Records from Orders table are missing

FIGURE 8.24 Customers with Orders Form Exported to Excel

Exporting Data to Word

Exporting data from Access to Word is similar to exporting data to Excel, except that you are not able to analyze the data as you can in Excel. Once the data is exported to Word, you will most likely use the data as is for reporting purposes rather than for analysis. Although you can modify the data in the table cells, those changes do not update the totals or other calculated fields (as they do in Excel).

The objects you select to export from Access to Word should have a tabular layout—tables, queries, and tabular reports fit this description. Although other object types do export to Word, the results are unpredictable and poorly formatted. If you are uncertain about which type of objects to export to Word, select any object in Access and export it to Word to see if it is properly formatted. If the data is usable, you can keep the Word document. If the data is not what you wanted, just close the file without saving and try again with a different layout.

When you export an object from Access to Word, Access creates a file in the RTF format. *Rich Text Format (RTF)* is a format that enables documents created in one software application to be opened with a different software application. The RTF format was introduced in 1987 by Microsoft and is now supported by Windows, Macintosh, open source, Unix, and other environments. RTF is a useful format for basic formatted text documents such as instruction manuals, résumés, letters, and other documents. These documents support special text formatting such as bold, italic, and underline. RTF documents also support left-, center-, and right-justified text. Furthermore, font specifications and document margins are supported in RTF documents.

When you export data from Access to Word, the RTF format is used and the file's extension will be .rtf. If you double-click the file, Windows opens Word by default and then displays the contents of the file. Word is the default software application for the RTF extension.

To convert an RTF file to a Word document, do the following:

1. From within Word, click the FILE tab.
2. Click Save As.
3. Change the *Save as type* to Word Document.

From that point forward, the document retains the Word format.

Select a Record Source to Export to Word

STEP 3 ≫ Similar to exporting to Excel, exporting Access tables and queries to Word is much simpler (as compared to exporting forms and reports). For example, if you need to add the Products table from an Access database into a Word document, as shown in Figure 8.25, the export-to-Word process is fast and easy. When you export a table to Word, Access creates an RTF file and inserts a table into the document. For the Products table, the field names become the column headings and the records become the table rows in the RTF file.

You can export tabular reports to Word; Access preserves the report's grouping aggregate functions. Some of the formatting may be lost. Columnar forms and reports do not export to Word properly; however, you can test the export of these objects to see if they produce usable data.

Click the More button, and then select Word from the list

FIGURE 8.25 Product Data in Access

Export Tables and Queries to Word

Exporting tables and queries to Word is similar to exporting tables and queries to Excel.

To export a table or query to Word, do the following:

1. Select the table or query in the Navigation Pane (or open the table or query first) and click the EXTERNAL DATA tab.
2. Click the More button in the Export group.
3. Select Word. Access opens the Export – RTF dialog box (shown in Figure 8.26) to guide you through the export process.

4. Specify the file name, destination, and format for the exported file.
5. Specify if you want to open the destination file after the export operation is complete (see Figure 8.26).
6. Specify if you want to export only the selected records (if you have selected one or more records in the datasheet).
7. Click OK.

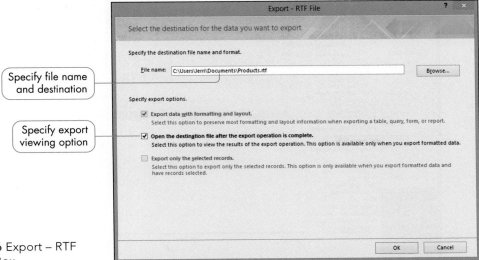

FIGURE 8.26 Export – RTF File Dialog Box

Modify an RTF File in Word

STEP 3 >

After you export an Access table to an RTF file, you can edit the file in Word and add additional text to the Products table content. If you need to send the products list to a few vendors to check current prices, you can insert a few blank lines above the Products table and type the To, From, and Subject lines as shown in Figure 8.27. Because the Products table was inserted at the top of the page, to insert lines above the table, click immediately before the first value in the first cell of the table and press Enter three times. The table moves down to make room for the To, From, and Subject lines. Type the rest of the information and save the document.

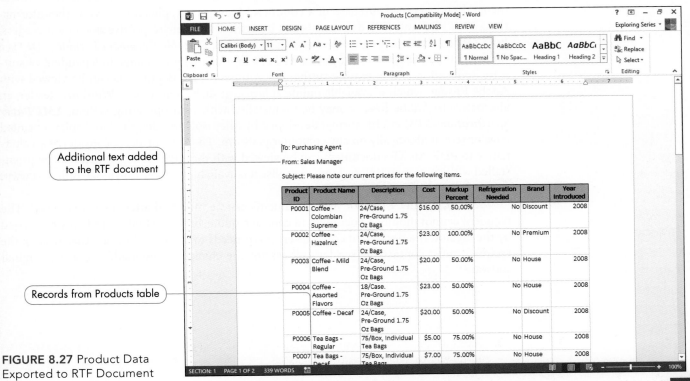

FIGURE 8.27 Product Data Exported to RTF Document

When you save an RTF file, you might want to change the file type to Word Document so that you can take full advantage of Word's features and formatting tools.

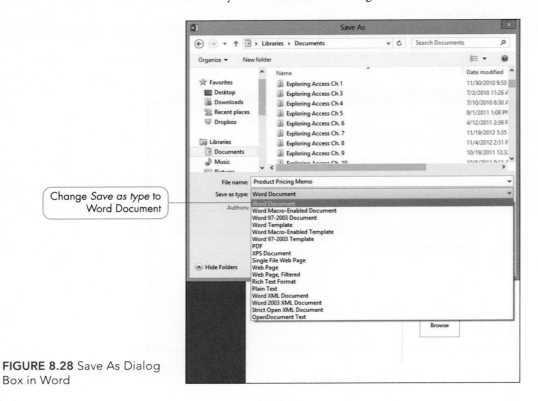

Change *Save as type* to Word Document

FIGURE 8.28 Save As Dialog Box in Word

Exporting Data to a PDF or XPS Document

Exporting data from Access to a PDF or XPS document is similar to exporting data to Word, except that you are not able to edit the exported documents. When you export from Access to Word or Excel, you can modify the exported files. This is not the case with PDF and XPS documents.

STEP 4 ≫

Two main reasons exist for exporting to a PDF or XPS document. First, these documents do not require purchase of a commercial software application to view the information. Both PDF and XPS documents can be opened by their respective document readers. Both readers are available as free downloads to users. *Portable Document Format (PDF)* is a file format created by Adobe Systems in 1993 for document exchange independent of software application and operating system environment. PDF documents can be viewed with Adobe Reader, which is available online at http://get.adobe.com/reader/. Windows Reader, an alternative to Adobe Reader, may be preinstalled with your operating system. *XML Paper Specification (XPS)* is a file format developed by Microsoft and designed to display a printed page onscreen identically on any computer platform. The XPS format is considered an alternative to PDF. An XPS document can be viewed with the XPS Viewer, which may be preinstalled with your operating system; otherwise it is available as a free download online at www.microsoft.com/whdc/xps/viewxps.mspx.

Second, neither PDF nor XPS documents can be modified after they are created. The recipient cannot modify a document (a contract, quote, or letter) that should only be revised by the creator. If a document contains errors or needs to be revised for another reason, the recipient must contact the sender and ask for the changes to be made using the original software.

Select an Object to Export

Tables, queries, forms, and reports can all be exported to a PDF or XPS document. However, the number of pages should be checked when the objects are exported. If you attempt to export one record in a form, you will be surprised to find the results contain all the records in the record source. Reports tend to be a good choice for creating PDF and XPS documents, particularly if they do not need modification or data analysis.

Export to a PDF or XPS Document

To export to a PDF or XPS document, do the following:

1. Select the object that you want to export and click the EXTERNAL DATA tab.
2. Click PDF or XPS in the Export group. The Publish as PDF or XPS dialog box opens, as shown in Figure 8.29.
3. Select the folder where the document should be saved, type the name of the exported document, and then select the document type, either PDF or XPS Document.
4. Click the *Open file after publishing* check box.
5. Click Publish to create the document.

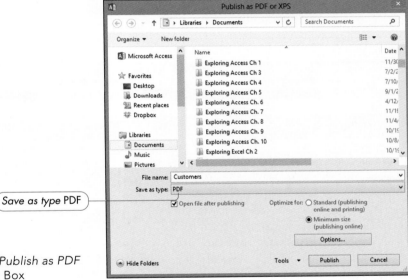

FIGURE 8.29 *Publish as PDF or XPS* Dialog Box

A document opens using the reader associated with the document type (PDF or XPS). The document contains multiple pages if the source has multiple pages. If the document is too wide, then two pages may be required to display one page of data. See Figure 8.30 as an example of a PDF document and Figure 8.31 as an example of an XPS document.

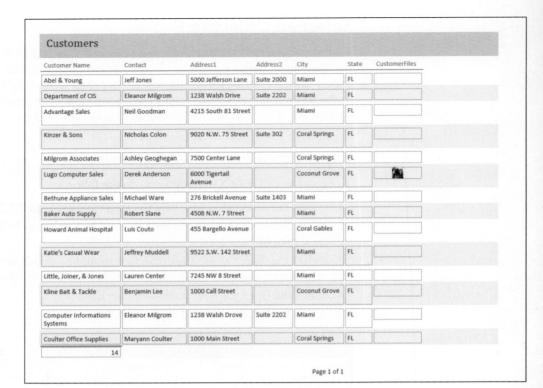

FIGURE 8.30 PDF Document Created from an Access Report

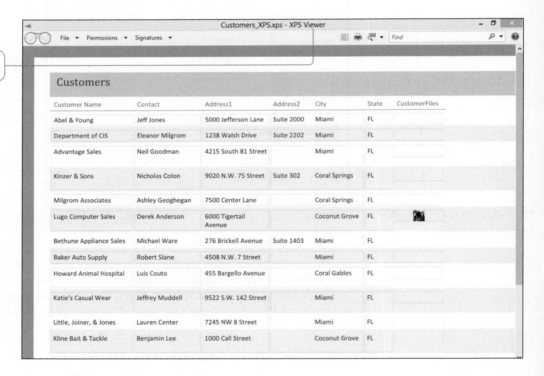

XPS documents are viewed with the XPS Viewer

FIGURE 8.31 XPS Document Created from an Access Report

TIP Viewing XPS Documents

XPS documents can be viewed with your browser (e.g., Internet Explorer) or Windows Reader if the XPS Viewer has not been installed. XPS documents are not as widely used and distributed as PDF documents. For that reason, PDF documents are the preferred format when exporting this type of document from Access.

Exporting Objects to Another Access Database

STEP 5 » After you create a database for one organization, you may be able to use the structure of some objects in a different database. For example, many business databases require an Employees table, a Customers table, and an Orders table. Companies also need a data-entry form for each of those three tables. There may be common reports that could also be exported from one database to another—for example, an Employee List report and a Customer List report. Exporting objects from one Access database to another saves time because you do not have to create the objects (tables, forms, reports) from scratch. You do not have to set the field names and data types (which Access refers to as the definition). You may have to modify the imported objects slightly to match the requirements of the new database.

When you export tables to another database, the Export dialog box asks if you want to export the data along with the definition. Usually, you will not want the data exported to the new database. After the tables are successfully exported, you can delete unwanted fields and add new fields to create the table structure you need for the new organization. Forms and reports need to be modified as well. Open the forms and reports in Layout view, and then delete any fields that were removed from the underlying tables. Add any new fields to the forms and reports that were added to the tables. You are now ready to populate the new tables either by adding data directly into the tables or by entering data using the forms.

Export Tables to Another Database

Before you can export a table to another database, you must first create the new database (or export the table to an existing database).

To create the new database, do the following:

1. Start Access and click *Blank desktop database* to create a new database.
2. Specify the location and type the name of the new database. You will have to navigate to the location of the new database when you export a table.
3. Click Create.
4. Close the blank target database.

To export a table from one database to another, do the following:

1. Select the table in the Navigation Pane.
2. Click the EXTERNAL DATA tab.
3. Click Access in the Export group.
4. The Export – Access Database dialog box appears (see Figure 8.32).
5. Click Browse to locate the destination file, click the file to select it, and then click Save.
6. Click OK to proceed to the next dialog box, shown in Figure 8.33. The second dialog box asks for the name of the table (you can accept the default name) and whether to export the Definition and Data or Definition Only.
7. Click OK in the second dialog box; the table is then exported to the destination database.
8. Return to the Access window. Close the Save Export Steps window without saving the steps.

To verify that the exported table is now in the destination database, locate and open the destination database. In the Navigation Pane, locate the exported table. Double-click the table to open it. After you verify the table was exported correctly, close the table, and then close the database. Return to the original database and export the next object.

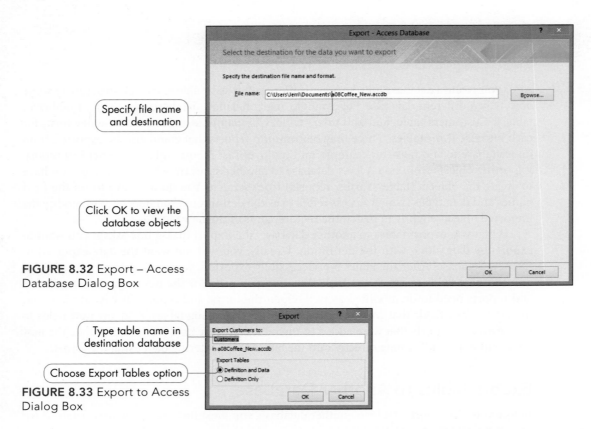

Specify file name and destination

Click OK to view the database objects

FIGURE 8.32 Export – Access Database Dialog Box

Type table name in destination database

Choose Export Tables option

FIGURE 8.33 Export to Access Dialog Box

Export Other Objects to Another Database

STEP 6>> To export other objects from one Access database to another, do the following:

1. Select the object (query, form, or report) in the Navigation Pane.
2. Click the EXTERNAL DATA tab.
3. Click Access in the Export group. The Export – Access Database dialog box appears (see Figure 8.32).
4. Click Browse to locate the destination file, click the file to select it, and then click Save.
5. Click OK to proceed to the next dialog box, shown in Figure 8.34. The second dialog box asks for the name of the object (you can accept the default name or type a new name).
6. Click OK in the second dialog box; the table is then exported to the destination database.
7. Return to the Access window. Close the Save Export Steps window without saving the steps.

Verify that the exported object is in the destination database by opening the destination database. In the Navigation Pane, locate the exported object. After you verify the object was exported correctly, return to the original database, and then open the original database to export the next object.

In Hands-On Exercise 2, you will export table data to Excel and export query data into Word using the same real estate database you used for Hands-On Exercise 1. You will also export data to a PDF document and export objects from the real estate database to another database. Verify that the objects were exported successfully by opening the destination database.

Type object name in destination database

FIGURE 8.34 Export Dialog Box for Form

Quick Concepts ✓

1. What is one advantage to exporting Access data to Excel? *p. 463*

2. Why would you want to have an Access report exported to PDF format? *p. 470*

3. Why would you decide to export the definition of a table to a different database, but not the data? *p. 473*

Hands-On Exercises

 Watch the Video for this Hands-On Exercise!

 MyITLab® HOE2 Training

2 Exporting Data to Office Applications

Blackwood Maintenance Service wants to contact the homeowners from the subdivisions they serve to tell them about their new services. You will create several formats, depending on the preference of the subdivision contact person. Some prefer an Excel spreadsheet, some prefer a Word document, one prefers PDF, and one prefers data in an Access table.

Skills covered: Export a Query to Excel • Export a Report to Excel • Export a Query to Word and Modify an RTF File in Word • Export to a PDF or XPS Document • Export a Table to Another Database • Export a Form to Another Database

---

STEP 1 ›› EXPORT A QUERY TO EXCEL

Create a new query that lists all the homeowners in The Woodlands subdivision and export it to an Excel spreadsheet. Refer to Figure 8.35 as you complete Step 1.

Woodlands owners in Excel

FIGURE 8.35 Woodlands Query Exported to Excel

a. Open *a08h1Property_LastFirst* if you closed it at the end of Hands-On Exercise 1. Click the **FILE tab**, click **Save As**, click **Save As**, and then type **a08h2Property_LastFirst**, changing the *h1* to *h2*.

> **TROUBLESHOOTING:** If you did not complete Hands-On Exercise 1, go back and complete it now. When you are finished, continue with Hands-On Exercise 2. If you make any major mistakes in this exercise, you can close the file, open *a08h1Property_LastFirst* again, and then start this exercise over.

b. Click the **CREATE tab** and click **Query Design** in the Queries group. Add the Properties table to the query design and close the Show Table dialog box.

c. Double-click the **SubDivisonID**, **Listing**, **HomeOwner**, **Address**, and **City fields** to add them to the query design grid.

d. Type **14** into the **Criteria row** of the SubDivisionID field. Uncheck the **Show check box**. Save the query as **The Woodlands Owners**.

You entered 14 in the Criteria row, which represents The Woodlands subdivision.

e. Run the query and widen the columns of the query so all the data values are visible.

When you export to Excel, the columns show all the data if the column widths are wide enough in Access.

f. Click the **EXTERNAL DATA tab** and click **Excel** in the Export group. Click **Browse** to choose the export location. Type **a08h2Woodlands_LastFirst** in the **File name box**. Click **Save**.

> **TROUBLESHOOTING:** If you inadvertently click Excel in the Import & Link group, cancel the dialog box and click Excel in the Export group.

g. Click the **Export data with formatting and layout** and **Open the destination file after the export operation is complete check boxes** in the Export – Excel Spreadsheet dialog box. Click **OK**.

A new Excel spreadsheet window opens showing The Woodlands owners' data.

> **TROUBLESHOOTING:** If you attempt to create an Excel file that already exists, Access warns you and asks you, *Do you want to replace the existing one?* If you attempt to create an Excel file that is already open, Access displays a warning, *Microsoft Office Access can't save the output data…* Close the open Excel file and try again.

h. Click **Microsoft Access** on the taskbar to return to Access. Click **Close** to close the Save Export Steps dialog box without saving.

i. Close the query. Save the query if you are asked.

j. Close the workbook and close Excel.

You need to send the Service Request Report to one of the BMS subcontractors. You will export the report to Excel. Refer to Figure 8.36 as you complete Step 2.

FIGURE 8.36 Report Exported to Excel

a. Double-click the **Service Request Report** in the Navigation Pane to open it.

You will export this report to Excel.

b. Click the **EXTERNAL DATA tab**.

c. Click **Excel** in the Export group.

d. Click **Browse**. Choose a location to save the export file. Change the file name to **a08h2Service_LastFirst**. Click **Save**. Click the **Open the destination file after the export operation is complete check box** in the Export – Excel Spreadsheet dialog box. Click **OK**.

A new Excel spreadsheet window opens, showing the Service Request Report data. The photos are missing, and the report title was deleted.

e. Click **Microsoft Access** on the taskbar to return to Access. Click **Close** to close the Save Export Steps dialog box without saving.

Compare the Excel report with your report in Access.

f. Close the report.

g. Close the workbook and close Excel.

You will need to create a query showing all homes with a tile roof built in or before 1997; these roofs may need to be repaired or replaced. Export the query results to Word. Modify the exported document to include the typical memo elements. Refer to Figure 8.37 as you complete Step 3.

Step h: Press Enter in Word document, and type to modify the RTF file

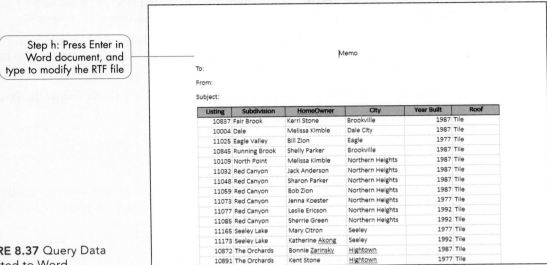

Memo

To:

From:

Subject:

Listing	Subdivision	HomeOwner	City	Year Built	Roof
10837	Fair Brook	Kerri Stone	Brookville	1987	Tile
10004	Dale	Melissa Kimble	Dale City	1987	Tile
11025	Eagle Valley	Bill Zion	Eagle	1977	Tile
10845	Running Brook	Shelly Parker	Brookville	1987	Tile
10109	North Point	Melissa Kimble	Northern Heights	1987	Tile
11032	Red Canyon	Jack Anderson	Northern Heights	1987	Tile
11048	Red Canyon	Sharon Parker	Northern Heights	1987	Tile
11059	Red Canyon	Bob Zion	Northern Heights	1987	Tile
11073	Red Canyon	Jenna Koester	Northern Heights	1977	Tile
11077	Red Canyon	Leslie Ericson	Northern Heights	1992	Tile
11085	Red Canyon	Sherrie Green	Northern Heights	1992	Tile
11165	Seeley Lake	Mary Citron	Seeley	1977	Tile
11173	Seeley Lake	Katherine Akong	Seeley	1992	Tile
10872	The Orchards	Bonnie Zarinsky	Hightown	1987	Tile
10891	The Orchards	Kent Stone	Hightown	1977	Tile

FIGURE 8.37 Query Data Exported to Word

a. Click the **CREATE tab** and click **Query Design** in the Queries group. Add the Properties table and the SubDivision table to the query design and close the Show Table dialog box.

b. Double-click the fields **Listing, HomeOwner, City, YearBuilt,** and **Roof** in the Properties table and drag **SubDivision** from the SubDivision table to the second column in the query design grid.

The other fields shift to the right to make room for the SubDivision field.

> **TROUBLESHOOTING:** If you inadvertently add the SubDivision field to the last column of the query design grid, point over the thin gray bar above the field name and when the downward-pointing arrow appears, click to select the column. Point in the selected column and click and drag to move the column into the correct position.

c. Type **Tile** in the **Criteria row** of the Roof column and type **<=1997** in the **Criteria row** of the YearBuilt column.

You only want to see properties with a tile roof that were built on or before 1997.

d. Save the query as **Properties Built on or Before 1997**.

e. Run the query. Widen the columns of the query so all the data values are visible.

When you export to Word, the columns show all the data if the column widths are wide enough in Access and the total width of the exported table does not exceed the Word document width.

f. Click the **EXTERNAL DATA tab**, click the **More button** in the Export group, and then select **Word** from the displayed list.

You will use the list of properties to create a memo to send to the roofer so he can inspect the roofs for damage.

g. Click **Browse** to choose a location to save the export file. Type **a08h2Sub_LastFirst** in the **File name box**. Click **Save**. Click the **Open the destination file after the export operation is complete check box** in the Export – RTF File dialog box. Click **OK**.

A new Word window opens, showing the Properties Built on or Before 1997 data.

> **TROUBLESHOOTING:** If you attempt to create a Word file that already exists, Access warns you and asks you, *Do you want to replace the existing one?* If you attempt to create a Word file that is already open, Access displays a warning, *Microsoft Office Access can't save the output data…* Close the open Word file and try again.

h. Press **Enter** one time in Word, type **Memo**. Press **Enter** and type **To:**. Press **Enter**, type **From:**, press **Enter**, type **Subject:**, and then center *Memo*, as shown in Figure 8.37.

i. Click the **FILE tab** and click **Save As** to save the new Word document as **a08h2Sub_ LastFirst**. Change the *Save as type* to **Word Document**. Click **OK** in the warning dialog box. Close Word.

j. Click **Access** in the Windows taskbar to return to Access. Click **Close** to close the Save Export Steps dialog box without saving.

k. Close the query. Save the query if you are asked.

STEP 4 » EXPORT TO A PDF OR XPS DOCUMENT

You need to send the Service Request Report to one of the BMS contractors. The contractor asks that you send him the report in a PDF format file because he does not own Microsoft Office. Refer to Figure 8.38 as you complete Step 4.

FIGURE 8.38 Service Request Report Exported to PDF

Photos: (Left) © Pavel Losevsky/ Fotolia; (Right, from bottom) © qingwa/Fotolia, © Maisna/Fotolia, © pics721/Fotolia, © Nomad_Soul/ Fotolia, © Pavel Losevsky/Fotolia

a. Select the **Service Request Report** in the Navigation Pane.

You will use this report to create a PDF document.

b. Click the **EXTERNAL DATA tab** and click **PDF or XPS** in the Export group.

c. Navigate to the folder where you are saving your files.

d. Change the file name to **a08h2Service_LastFirst** and select **PDF** for the *Save as type*. Click **Publish**.

A new PDF document is created in the folder where you are saving your files.

e. Click **Close** to close the Save Export Steps dialog box without saving.

f. Close the report.

Blackwood's landscaping contractor asked you for a list of all properties for which BMS provides landscaping services. Because his office manager knows Access, he asks you to send him the information in an Access database. Refer to Figure 8.39 as you complete Step 5.

FIGURE 8.39 Destination Database with the Properties Table

a. Close the *a08h2Property_LastFirst* database, if necessary. Open the *a08h2Propexport* database. Save it as **a08h2Propexport_LastFirst** in the folder where you are saving your solution files. Verify that this database does not contain any tables. Close *a08h2Propexport_LastFirst*. Open *a08h2Property_LastFirst*. Select, but do not open, the **Properties table** in the Navigation Pane.

b. Click the **EXTERNAL DATA tab** and click **Access** in the Export group.

The Export – Access Database dialog box appears.

c. Click **Browse** to locate the destination database file. Select the *a08h2Propexport_LastFirst* database and click **Save**. When you return to the Export – Access Database dialog box, click **OK**.

The Export dialog box displays, asking for additional information about the table you are exporting.

d. Confirm that *Properties* is in the *Export Properties to* box. Accept the **Definition and Data option**. Click **OK**.

You are sending the properties data to the landscaping contractor, and he will need all of the properties data.

e. Click **Close** to close the Save Export Steps dialog box without saving.

The table should have been exported, and next you want to verify that it is in the destination database.

f. Close *a08h2Property_LastFirst*. Locate *a08h2Propexport_LastFirst* and open the database. Open the Properties table.

Compare your findings to Figure 8.39.

g. Close the *a08h2Propexport_LastFirst* database.

h. Open the *a08h2Property_LastFirst* database.

The landscaping contractor would like you to send him a form to make it easier to work with the properties data. You will use the Form Tool to quickly make a form with stacked layout. You will export the form to the same destination database as in Step 5. Refer to Figure 8.40 as you complete Step 6.

FIGURE 8.40 Destination Database with the Properties Form

a. Click to select the **Properties table** in the Navigation Pane in the *a08h2Property_LastFirst* database.

b. Click the **CREATE tab** and click **Form** in the Forms group.

Access creates a new stacked layout form based on the Properties table.

c. Reduce the width of the Listing control by clicking on the right border and dragging it to the left. Reduce the width by 50%.

d. Select the last four fields (text box and label)—**DateServiceStarted**, **RequestForService**, **SellingAgent**, and **ListingAgent**—one at a time and press **Delete** to delete the fields from the form.

e. Save the form as **Properties Form**. Close the form. Select the **Properties Form** in the Navigation Pane.

f. Click the **EXTERNAL DATA tab** and click **Access** in the Export group.

The Export – Access Database dialog box appears.

g. Click **Browse** to locate the destination database file. Select the *a08h2Propexport_LastFirst* database and click **Save**. When you return to the Export – Access Database dialog box, click **OK**.

The Export dialog box appears, asking you to type the name of the form you are exporting.

h. Confirm that *Properties Form* is in the *Export Properties Form to* box. Click **OK**.

You accept the default name Properties Form.

i. Click **Close** to close the Save Export Steps dialog box without saving.

The form should have been exported, and next you want to verify that it is in the destination database.

j. Close the *a08h2Property_LastFirst* database. Locate *a08h2Propexport_LastFirst* and open the database. Verify the Properties Form is in the database.

Compare your screen to Figure 8.40.

k. Open the form to view the data.

l. Close the form.

m. Click the **FILE tab** and click **Compact & Repair Database**.

n. If you plan to continue with Hands-On Exercise 3, close the database but keep Access open.

Importing Data into Access

In the previous section, you learned about the benefits of exporting information from Access to Excel, from Access to Word, from Access to PDF or XPS, and from one Access database to another Access database. Sometimes you need the opposite process—*importing* data into Access, which enables you to copy external data into your database without linking it to its source file. A variety of data formats can be imported into Access. You will learn how to import the three most common formats: Access, Excel, and text.

When you work with Access, most of the data entry is achieved by typing directly into the tables or forms. However, at times, you may want to import Access database objects from another database into your Access database. If the other objects are tables, you can import the table from the other database into your database and then append that data to your tables. When you append the data to your tables, you may only need a subset of the fields, and you may also use criteria to limit the number of records you append. Create a form or a report based on the imported data if you plan to use the information as stand-alone data (with no connection to the other tables in the database).

You may also receive data in an Excel spreadsheet that can be imported directly into your Access database. Once the data is imported into Access, you can append that data to another table and consequently save a lot of data-entry time. Alternatively, you can use the imported Excel data as a stand-alone table; a stand-alone table can be used to create other objects—queries, forms, or reports.

You may also want to import and use text files in your Access databases rather than typing the data that originates from this type of source file.

In this section, you will learn how to link data from one Access database to another. You will also learn to access data in Excel when using Access by creating a link to and importing an Excel worksheet. Finally, you will learn how to import data into Access using a Text file.

Linking to an Access Table

When a table in another database is relevant to your database, two options are available. One is that you can import the table from the external database into your database; the other is to create a link to a table in another Access database. Importing a table from an external database increases the size of your database; the table could be so large that your database may run less efficiently. *Linking* lets you connect to a table without having to import the table data into your database. You can only link to the tables in another Access database; you cannot link to queries, forms, reports, macros, or modules.

When you link to a table in another Access database, Access creates a new table, called a *linked table*, which maintains a connection to the source table. You cannot change the structure of a linked table in the destination database (e.g., you cannot add or delete a field in a linked table, and you cannot modify the data type of a field). Any changes you make to the data in the source database are reflected in the linked table in the destination database, and vice versa.

A link to an Access table enables edits to the table in the source database from within the destination database. This is in contrast to a link to an Excel spreadsheet. You cannot edit a linked spreadsheet from within Access. The ability to link to Access tables is important because databases are sometimes intentionally split so that nontable objects reside in one database, whereas tables reside in another. To join the two databases, links are created from the database *without* tables to the database *with* tables. Users can add, delete, and edit data (in the linked tables) as if the tables resided in the first database (when they actually reside in the second).

Examine the Tables in the Source Database

STEP 1 >> Before you link to tables in another Access database, it is best to examine the tables in the source database first. To examine the Access tables, open the source database—the same way you open any Access database—and examine the data in the table(s). Double-click the table that contains the information you need, as shown in Figure 8.41. Make sure the contents, field names, and other elements are correct prior to linking to the table.

FIGURE 8.41 Products Table in External Database

If the data in the source table looks like it is generally compatible with a table in your database, you can add the linked data to your table. To add the new data into your existing table, you can append all or only a subset of the new table records to your table. You accomplish this by creating an append query based on the linked Access table. An append query is a special query that adds records to an existing table.

Link to an Access Table

STEP 2 >> After you examine the data in the source table—the data you want to link to Access—you are ready to create a link from within your Access database.

To link to an Access table in another database, do the following:

1. Click the EXTERNAL DATA tab.
2. Click Access in the Import & Link group. The Get External Data – Access Database dialog box opens, as shown in Figure 8.42.
3. Click *Link to the data source by creating a linked table.*
4. Click Browse to locate the Access database you want to link to.
5. Click the file to select it and click Open to specify this file as the source of the data.
6. Click the *Link to the data source by creating a linked table* option and click OK. The Link Tables dialog box appears, as shown in Figure 8.43.
7. Select the table you want to link to and click OK. Click Select All if the database contains multiple tables and you want to link to all of them.

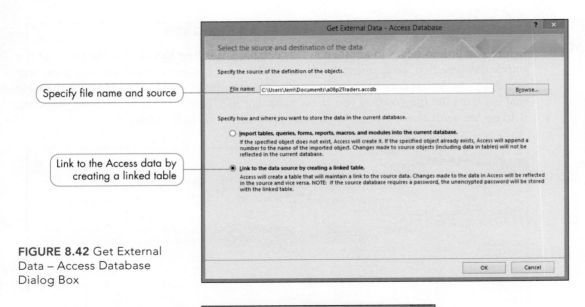

Specify file name and source

Link to the Access data by creating a linked table

FIGURE 8.42 Get External Data – Access Database Dialog Box

Select Products table

FIGURE 8.43 Link Tables Dialog Box

Once the link is created, you will see a special arrow icon next to the table name in the Navigation Pane that indicates the table is linked to an Access table (see Figure 8.44). Because the name of the linked table, Products, is the same as that of a table that already exists in your Access database, Access adds the number 1 to the end of the table name. Therefore, Access renames the linked table Products1. If you link to another table with the same name, Products, Access renames the third table Products2. To distinguish the linked Products table from the existing Products table, the second table could be renamed (as Traders Products, for example), as shown in Figure 8.45.

Linked Access table icon

FIGURE 8.44 Link to Access Table

FIGURE 8.45 Link to Access Table—Renamed

Linking to an Excel Spreadsheet

If you have an Access database and you want to import data from an Excel spreadsheet that contains information related to your database, you have three options. You can manually enter the information contained in the spreadsheet into the database tables; you can create a link from Access to Excel that enables you to update tables or create reports based on the data in the Excel spreadsheet; or you can import the data into your Access database to manipulate the data prior to appending it to the tables.

Linking and importing may appear to produce the same results; however, some differences do exist with regard to the resulting size of the database and the ability to modify data. Linking enables you to view the Excel data without increasing the size of the Access database. Importing a large Excel worksheet may increase the Access database substantially (linking to the same spreadsheet does not affect the size of the Access file). Importing an Excel sheet enables you to modify the data prior to appending it to a table. Linking does not enable you to update data from within Access; if errors exist in the worksheet, you must correct the errors in Excel and redisplay the linked table in Access.

Verify the Format of an Excel Spreadsheet

You find that some new property subdivisions are opening in your region, and you may want to target them for new business. You have obtained a spreadsheet that contains initial details, and you want to add the new data to your database. First open the spreadsheet in Excel and examine the data, as shown in Figure 8.46.

FIGURE 8.46 Property SubDivisions Spreadsheet to Import into Access

STEP 3》

Before linking to the spreadsheet, you want to be sure the data is organized so that the import will be successful. The data should be in continuous rows and columns with no blank rows, columns, or extraneous explanatory text. Ideally, the column headings and data formats should be an exact match to those in your database and in the same order, particularly if you are planning to merge the linked spreadsheet into an existing table. The data in the Excel spreadsheet contains titles in cells A1 and A2 and a blank row in row 3. These first three rows will not import properly and should be deleted prior to importing the data. However, it is a good idea to create a backup copy of the original spreadsheet before deleting the rows. This enables you to look up the original data in case this information is needed at another time. In the sheet to be linked, delete the title and blank rows, then save and close the Excel spreadsheet. The results should match those shown in Figure 8.47.

FIGURE 8.47 Excel Spreadsheet After Modification

Link to an Excel Spreadsheet

STEP 4 » After you modify the Excel spreadsheet so the data will properly link to Access, you are ready to create a link from within Access.

To link the Excel spreadsheet to Access, do the following:

1. Click the EXTERNAL DATA tab and click Excel in the Import & Link group. The Get External Data – Excel Spreadsheet dialog box launches as shown in Figure 8.48.
2. Click Browse to locate the Excel file you want to link to, click the file to select it, and then click Open to specify this file as the source of the data.
3. Click the *Link to the data source...* option and click OK. The Link Spreadsheet Wizard launches as shown in Figure 8.49.
4. Select the worksheet from the list of worksheets shown at the top of the dialog box and click Next.
5. Click First Row Contains Column Headings and click Next. The column headings of the Excel spreadsheet become the field names in the Access table.
6. Enter the new table name in the Linked Table Name box, as shown in Figure 8.50, and click Finish.

Because Access can only link to one sheet at a time, you might have to create multiple links, one for each worksheet. Make sure you label the links with descriptive names.

FIGURE 8.48 Get External Data – Excel Spreadsheet Dialog Box

FIGURE 8.49 Link Spreadsheet Wizard

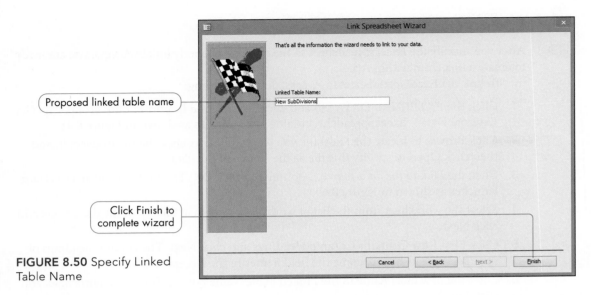

Proposed linked table name

Click Finish to complete wizard

FIGURE 8.50 Specify Linked Table Name

Once the link is created, you will see a special arrow icon next to the table name in the Navigation Pane that indicates the table is linked to the Excel file (see Figure 8.51). Double-click the table name and the table opens. The data looks similar to data in the other tables, even though the data resides in an external Excel file. Although you have the linked table open in Access, you can still open the file in Excel (and vice versa).

Linked Excel table icon

FIGURE 8.51 Icon Indicates Linked Excel Table

Importing an Excel Spreadsheet

Suppose you receive data in an Excel spreadsheet from another branch of your company and want to work with it in your Access database. In addition to linking to an Excel spreadsheet, you can import a spreadsheet into your Access database. Importing a large Excel worksheet may increase the database file size substantially; however, one reason why you would import an Excel spreadsheet is because you have more control over the imported data. The imported spreadsheet is actually a copy of the original spreadsheet, with no dependency on the external source. For that reason you are able to manipulate the data as necessary once it is available in your database.

TIP | Appending Excel Data to Your Database

When importing a spreadsheet into your database, if a comparable table exists, you can choose to append a copy of the Excel records to the table. In the Get External Data – Excel Spreadsheet dialog box, click the *Append a copy of the records to the table* option and select the table to which you want the records added.

Examine the Spreadsheet Before Importing

STEP 5 »

Always examine the Excel spreadsheet (as shown in Figure 8.52) before attempting to import it into Access. You want to be sure there are no extra rows of data that do not comply with the format of an Access table. You also need to delete any blank rows to ensure that the data to import is continuous and check that the column headings appear in the first row of the spreadsheet.

FIGURE 8.52 Excel Spreadsheet to Be Imported

Import a Spreadsheet into Access

After you examine the Excel spreadsheet to determine that the data will properly import to Access, you are ready to create the imported table.

To import the Excel spreadsheet to Access, do the following:

1. Click the EXTERNAL DATA tab.
2. Click Excel in the Import & Link group. The Get External Data – Excel Spreadsheet dialog box launches as shown in Figure 8.48.
3. Click Browse to locate the Excel file you want to import, click the file to select it, and then click Open to specify this file as the source of the data.
4. Click the *Import the source data...* option and click OK. The Import Spreadsheet Wizard launches.
5. Select the worksheet from the list of worksheets shown at the top of the dialog box (if necessary) and click Next.
6. Click the First Row Contains Column Headings check box and click Next two times (see Figure 8.53). The column headings of the Excel spreadsheet become the field names in the Access table.
7. Click the *Choose my own primary key* option if the imported data has a field that is acceptable as a primary key (as shown in Figure 8.54) and click Next. Access sets the value in the first column of the spreadsheet (for example, CustomerID) as the primary key field of the table. You can also allow Access to set the primary key if no value that is eligible to be a key field exists, or to set no primary key at all.
8. Enter the new table name in the Import to Table box, as shown in Figure 8.55, and click Finish.
9. Click Close when prompted to Save Import Steps.

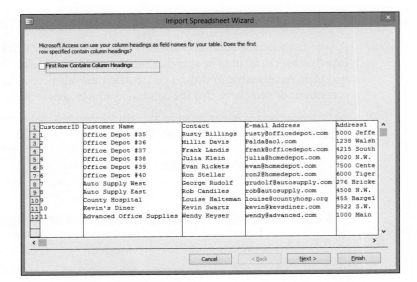

FIGURE 8.53 Import
Spreadsheet Wizard

FIGURE 8.54 Choose My Own
Primary Key Option

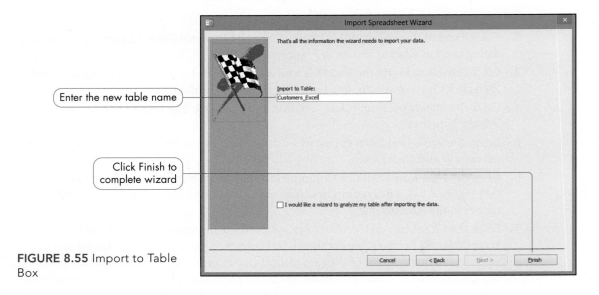

Enter the new table name

Click Finish to
complete wizard

FIGURE 8.55 Import to Table
Box

Importing a Text File

In the preceding examples, you learned how to link to a table in another Access database and to link to and import an Excel spreadsheet. In this example, you will import a text file directly into your existing Access database. *Text files* are common methods of exchanging information between two computer systems. Text files are usually created by computer software, not manually by humans, and usually contain consistent formatting.

The two most common text file types are comma-separated values (CSV) and fixed-length files. *CSV text files* use a comma to separate one column from the next column, enabling the receiving software to distinguish one set of field values from the next. *Fixed-length text files* allocate a certain number of characters for each field. A fixed-length file containing company data might contain the fields Company Name with 25 characters allocated, Address with 20 characters allocated, City with 20 characters allocated, Region with 2 characters allocated, and Postal Code with 10 characters allocated. Any values with fewer than the allocated characters have spaces added to the end of the value, and any value that is longer than its allocated characters is cut off at the position where the characters exceed the maximum allowed.

Examine the Text File Before Importing

STEP 6 ⟫ If you receive a text file that needs to be imported into Access, you should examine the file first before performing the import routine. You need to confirm that the contents of the text file are relevant to your database. Also, verify that the format of the file is consistent and that the fields and data values correspond to your Access tables. A text file of the CSV type usually has a .csv extension. If you double-click a CSV file, Excel, the default software application associated with CSV files, opens the file. You can examine the file using Excel. To see the file in its native format, right-click the file, click *Open with*, and then click Notepad from the shortcut menu.

For example, suppose the file NewCustomers.csv contains a list of new prospects for your company. Rather than open the file using the default software, Excel, you could open the file in Notepad to view the comma-separated text.

To open the CSV file in Notepad, do the following:

1. Right-click the file in File Explorer.
2. Point to *Open with*.
3. Click Notepad. The file opens in Notepad, as shown in Figure 8.56.

The data contains field names in the first row—Customer ID, Customer Name, Contact, and so forth—with data values starting in the second row. Each row contains commas separating one column from the next.

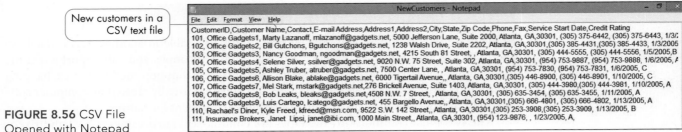

New customers in a CSV text file

FIGURE 8.56 CSV File
Opened with Notepad

Import a Text File into Access

STEP 7 » After you examine the data in the CSV file you are ready to import the data into your Access database.

To import a text file into an Access database, do the following:

1. Click the EXTERNAL DATA tab.
2. Click Text File in the Import & Link group. The Get External Data – Text File dialog box launches, as shown in Figure 8.57.
3. Click Browse to locate the CSV file you want to import (e.g., NewCustomers.csv), click the file to select it, and then click Open to specify this file as the source of the data.
4. Click the *Import the source data into a new table...* option and click OK. The Import Text Wizard dialog box appears as shown in Figure 8.58.
5. Click Next to proceed through the questions in the wizard.
6. Click the *First row contains field names* check box and click Next two times.
7. Click the *Choose my own primary key* option and click Next. Access sets the value in the first field name of the text file, if it is acceptable, as the primary key field of the table. You can also allow Access to set the primary key if no value that is eligible to be a key field exists, or to set no primary key at all.
8. Enter the new table name in the *Import to Table* box and click Finish.
9. Click Close when shown the Save Import Steps prompt. The new table appears in the Navigation Pane, as shown in Figure 8.59.

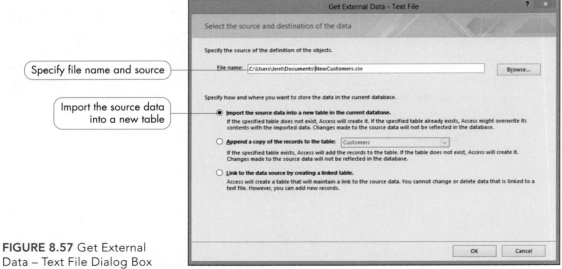

Specify file name and source

Import the source data into a new table

FIGURE 8.57 Get External
Data – Text File Dialog Box

Fields are comma separated

Data to be imported

FIGURE 8.58 Import Text Wizard

FIGURE 8.59 Table Imported from CSV File

New imported table

Quick
Concepts

1. What would be a benefit of importing a spreadsheet into your database rather than linking it? *p. 490*

2. Why is it important to examine a spreadsheet before importing it into Access? *p. 491*

3. How is the data organized in a CSV file? *p. 493*

Hands-On Exercises

3 Importing Data into Access

Blackwood Maintenance Service is adding additional subdivisions to its portfolio. It will need several new employees to manage the new subdivisions—you will review the list of agents provided in an Access database and link it to the BMS database. BMS has obtained some subdivision information in an Excel spreadsheet, which you will link and import to the database. Another spreadsheet containing potential properties to be inspected also needs to be imported. Finally, BMS purchased a list of properties that might need its services. You need to import the CSV list into the current database.

Skills covered: Examine the Tables in the Source Database • Link to an Access Table • Verify the Format of an Excel Spreadsheet • Link to an Excel Spreadsheet • Examine and Import a Spreadsheet into Access • Examine the Text File Before Importing • Import a Text File into Access

---

STEP 1 ≫ EXAMINE THE TABLES IN THE SOURCE DATABASE

BMS needs to hire additional agents. It received an Access database from a staffing company with a list of possible agents. You will need to review the data first before you add the data to the Blackwood database. Refer to Figure 8.60 as you complete Step 1.

FIGURE 8.60 Open the New Database and Table

a. Open the *a08h3Propstaff* database file.

Access opens the *a08h3Propstaff* database, and the staffing agents table displays in the Navigation Pane.

b. Open the Staffing Agents table in Datasheet view.

Thirteen agents are in the table.

c. Close the Staffing Agents table. Click the **FILE tab**, click **Save As**, click **Save As**, and then type **a08h3Propstaff_LastFirst**. Save the database in the folder where you are saving your solution files. Close the database.

STEP 2 ≫ LINK TO AN ACCESS TABLE

After examining the data from the staffing company, Blackwood wants to link the data to its database. You will create a link to the table in the staffing database; you will then append the data into the Agents table in the Blackwood database. Refer to Figure 8.61 as you complete Step 2.

Step I: Click to append new staffing agents

FIGURE 8.61 Append Staffing Agents to Agents Table

a. Open *a08h2Property_LastFirst*. Click the **FILE tab**, click **Save As**, click **Save As**, and then type **a08h3Property_LastFirst**, changing the *h2* to *h3*.

> **TROUBLESHOOTING:** If you did not complete Hands-On Exercises 1 and 2, go back and complete them now. When you are finished, continue with Hands-On Exercise 3.

b. Click the **EXTERNAL DATA tab** in the *a08h3Property_LastFirst* database and click **Access** in the Import & Link group.

c. Click **Browse** to locate the *a08h3Propstaff_LastFirst* database. Click the file to select it and click **Open**.

d. Select the **Link to the data source… option** and click **OK**.

e. Select the **Staffing Agents table** in the Link Tables dialog box and click **OK**.

   You created a link to the Staffing Agents table in the staffing database.

f. Double-click the **Staffing Agents table** in the Navigation Pane.

   You are now prepared to add the new agents to the Agents table so that all of the agents can be merged into one table.

g. Close the Staffing Agents table.

h. Click the **CREATE tab** and click **Query Design** in the Queries group. Add Staffing Agents to the query design and close the Show Table dialog box.

   You created a select query, which you will convert to an append query.

i. Double-click the title bar of the Staffing Agents table to select all the fields. Drag the fields to the query design grid.

j. Switch to Datasheet view.

   The new staffing agents are listed as expected.

k. Switch back to Design view.

l. Click **Append** in the Query Type group and select **Agents** using the Table Name arrow. Click **OK**.

   The *Append to* row appears in the query design grid with the corresponding field names listed. Some of the new IDs are the same as the existing IDs. You decide to remove the ID field from the append query.

m. Click the column selector at the top of the ID column. Press **Delete** to remove the column.

n. Click **Run** in the Results group to add the staffing agents to the Agents table. Click **Yes** in the message that says you are about to append 13 rows to the Agents table.

o. Save the query with the name **Append Staffing Agents**. Close the query.

p. Double-click the **Agents table** to verify the new agents are in the table.

The ID numbers of the appended agents are automatically assigned by the Agents table, as the ID field has the data type AutoNumber. Note that some of the missing data, such as home phone numbers, will need to be added later.

q. Close the table.

STEP 3 >> VERIFY THE FORMAT OF AN EXCEL SPREADSHEET

You will open the list of new subdivisions that BMS received in an Excel spreadsheet format and decide whether you want to add the information to your existing subdivision table. Refer to Figure 8.62 as you complete Step 3.

FIGURE 8.62 Copied Excel Worksheet to Be Modified

a. Open the Excel workbook *a08h3Propsub*. Click the **FILE tab**, click **Save As**, click **Save As**, click **Browse** to navigate to correct folder, click enter the file name **a08h3Propsub_LastFirst**, and then click Save.

You need to decide if the data will fit into the existing subdivision table and whether the data is formatted properly and does not contain extraneous rows.

b. Click **Enable Editing** in the Excel window, if necessary. Right-click the **Sheet1 tab**. Select **Move or Copy**. Select **Sheet2** in the *Before sheet:* box and click the **Create a copy check box**. Click **OK**. Double-click the copied sheet tab, rename the worksheet **New SubDivisions**, and then press **Enter**.

The new worksheet is the second worksheet.

c. Click the **New SubDivisions tab**, if necessary. Select the first three rows of the worksheet. Click **Delete** in the Cells group on the HOME tab, as shown in Figure 8.62.

The first row of a spreadsheet must contain column headings that can be recognized as field names by Access.

d. Click **cell A17**, which contains *The contact for Hawk Valley just resigned.* Press **Delete**.

There should not be any data after the last row of formatted data.

e. Save and close the workbook, and exit Excel.

The Excel spreadsheet can now be linked to the Access database.

STEP 4 ≫ LINK TO AN EXCEL SPREADSHEET

You decide to create a link to the new subdivisions worksheet. You will then import the data into your Access database. You will use the linked worksheet to create a new table in the database. If the linked Excel spreadsheet is updated later, you could run the Make Table query to overwrite the table with the new data. Refer to Figure 8.63 as you complete Step 4.

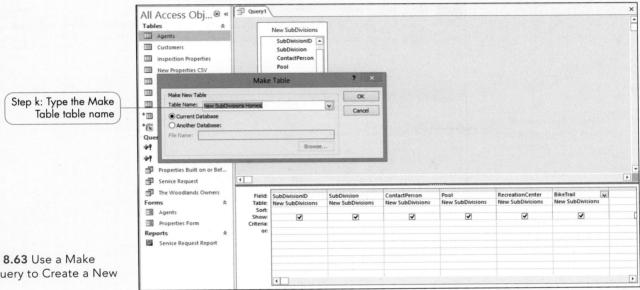

FIGURE 8.63 Use a Make Table Query to Create a New Table

a. Click **Access** in the Windows taskbar and click the **EXTERNAL DATA tab**.

b. Click **Excel** in the Import & Link group.

c. Click **Browse** to locate the spreadsheet *a08h3Propsub_LastFirst*. Click **Open**.

d. Select the **Link to the data source… option** and click **OK**.

e. Select **New SubDivisions** in the Show Worksheets box of the Link Spreadsheet Wizard. Click **Next**.

You chose the revised worksheet for the link.

f. Click the **First Row Contains Column Headings check box**. Click **Next**.

g. Accept the name *New SubDivisions* for the Access linked table name. Click **Finish**. Click **OK** in the message box that appears.

The Excel linked icon appears next to the New SubDivisions table.

h. Click the **CREATE tab** and click **Query Design** in the Queries group. Add the New SubDivisions table to the query design and close the Show Table dialog box.

You decide to create a new table from the linked spreadsheet using a Make Table query.

i. Add all the fields from the New SubDivisions table to the query design grid. Switch to Datasheet view to examine the records.

j. Switch back to Design view.

k. Click **Make Table** in the Query Type group. Type **New SubDivisions Homes** in the **Table Name box**, as shown in Figure 8.63. With the Current Database option selected, click **OK**. Click **Run** in the Results group and click **Yes** to the warning message. Close the Make Table query without saving the changes.

The Excel spreadsheet data is now an Access table.

STEP 5 ≫ EXAMINE AND IMPORT A SPREADSHEET INTO ACCESS

Blackwood received an Excel spreadsheet containing a list of potential new properties to be inspected. You need to examine the data prior to adding it to BMS's database; for now, the imported data will be used as a stand-alone table. Refer to Figures 8.64 and 8.65 as you complete Step 5.

Step a: The spreadsheet conforms to the format of an Access table

FIGURE 8.64 Spreadsheet to Be Imported into Access

Step i: Click the *Choose my own primary key* option

FIGURE 8.65 Importing a Spreadsheet into Access

a. Open the *a08h3Propinspect* workbook.

The spreadsheet conforms to the format of an Access table, so you do not need to make any changes to it at this time.

b. Close the workbook and exit Excel without making any changes to the file.

c. Click **Access** in the Windows taskbar and click the **EXTERNAL DATA tab**.

d. Click **Excel** in the Import & Link group.

e. Click **Browse** to locate the spreadsheet *a08h3Propinspect*. Click **Open**.

f. Select the **Import the source data into a new table in the current database option** and click **OK**.

g. Ensure *First Row Contains Column Headings* is checked and click **Next** in the Import Spreadsheet Wizard.

The first row of the spreadsheet contains column headings that will be used as the field names for the Access table.

h. Click **Next**.

i. Click the **Choose my own primary key option** and click **Next**.

Access sets the value in the first column of the spreadsheet, Listing, as the primary key field of the table.

j. Enter the new table name, **Inspection Properties**, in the *Import to Table* box and click **Finish**.

k. Click **Close** in the Save Import Steps dialog box.

The imported table appears in the Navigation Pane.

STEP 6 ≫ EXAMINE THE TEXT FILE BEFORE IMPORTING

Blackwood wants to add additional properties to its database. You want to examine the data prior to adding it to the database. The new data is in a text file. Refer to Figure 8.66 as you complete Step 6.

FIGURE 8.66 CSV File Opened in Notepad

a. Open *a08h3Propnew.csv*.

b. Exit Excel without making any changes to the file.

c. Right-click the *a08h3Propnew.csv* file in File Explorer, choose **Open with**, and then click **Notepad** from the shortcut menu.

You decide to examine the file in its native format using Notepad. The file has consistent formatting for importing into Access.

d. Close Notepad.

STEP 7 ≫ IMPORT A TEXT FILE INTO ACCESS

The BMS owners want to import and then append these properties to the Properties table in the Blackwood database. The Listing values will have to be modified when the data is appended so that they are higher than the existing values in the table. Refer to Figure 8.67 as you complete Step 7.

FIGURE 8.67 Append CSV Records to an Access Table

Step o: Select Properties using the Table Name arrow

a. Return to Access. Click the **EXTERNAL DATA tab**.

b. Click **Text File** in the Import & Link group.

c. Click **Browse** to locate the *a08h3Propnew.csv* file. Click **Open**.

d. Select the **Import the source data into a new table in the current database option** and click **OK**.

The Import Text Wizard starts. Delimited should be selected by default.

e. Click **Next** to accept the default options in this dialog box.

f. Click the **First Row Contains Field Names check box**. Click **Next**.

g. Click **Next** to accept the default field options in this dialog box.

h. Click the **No Primary Key option**. Click **Next**.

When the records are appended into an existing table in your database, a unique value is assigned to each of the imported records.

i. Enter the new table name, **New Properties CSV**, in the *Import to Table* box and click **Finish**.

j. Click **Close** in the Save Import Steps dialog box.

The imported table appears in the Navigation Pane.

k. Click the **CREATE tab** and click **Query Design** in the Queries group. Add **New Properties CSV** to the query design and close the Show Table dialog box.

You created a select query, which you will convert to an append query.

l. Double-click the title bar of the New Properties CSV table to select all the fields. Drag the fields to the query design grid.

m. Switch to Datasheet view.

The new properties are listed as expected.

n. Switch to Design view.

o. Click **Append** in the Query Type group and select **Properties** using the Table Name arrow. Click **OK**.

The *Append to* row appears in the design grid with the corresponding field names listed. The new listing values need to be modified so they conform to the format of the existing listings. You decide to add 11300 to each new listing number using a calculated field.

p. Select the **Listing field name** in the first column. Type the calculated field: **Listing2: [Listing] + 11300**.

q. Switch to Datasheet view to see the results of the calculated field.

All of the listing values are now higher than the listing numbers of the existing properties.

r. Switch to Design view.

s. Click **Run** in the Results group to add the new (Davidson) properties to the Properties table.

t. Click **Yes** in response to the *You are about to append 58 row(s)* message.

u. Save the query with the name **Append Davidson Properties**. Close the query.

v. Click the **FILE tab** and click **Compact & Repair Database**.

w. Close the database. Exit Access.

x. Submit *a08h3Property_LastFirst* based on your instructor's directions.

Chapter Objectives Review

After reading this chapter, you have accomplished the following objectives:

1. **Create a hyperlink field.**
   - Add a hyperlink field in Design view: A hyperlink in a table or form launches the appropriate software and enables you to interact with the file.
   - Edit a hyperlink field in Datasheet view: Edit a hyperlink value if it navigates to an incorrect Web page, file, or location.

2. **Add an attachment field.**
   - Add an attachment field in Design view: An attachment field stores a reference to an external file, and you can open that file from within Access.
   - Add or edit attachments in Datasheet view: Manage your attachments from the datasheet using the Attachments dialog box.
   - Remove attachments in Datasheet view: Attachments can be removed using the Attachments dialog box.

3. **Add attachment controls to forms and reports.**
   - Add an attachment control to a form: An attachment control lets you manage attached files in forms.
   - Add an attachment field to a report: You can also manage attached files in reports. In a report, only the first file displays in Print Preview, and you have to navigate to the others.

4. **Export data to Excel.**
   - Select a record source to export to Excel: Tables, queries, forms, and reports can all be exported to Excel if their formats are compatible with spreadsheets.
   - Export a query to Excel: Tables and queries tend to export well to Excel as their datasheet formats are compatible with spreadsheets.
   - Export forms and reports to Excel: Subforms or grouped data may not export or display correctly.

5. **Export data to Word.**
   - Select a record source to export to Word: Data that has been exported to Word cannot always be modified or analyzed.
   - Export tables and queries to Word: Export objects that have a tabular layout (e.g., tables and queries).
   - Modify an RTF file in Word: When an object is exported to Word, Access creates a file in Rich Text Format that opens in Word by default.

6. **Export data to a PDF or XPS document.**
   - Select an object to export: You are not able to edit the data exported to a PDF or XPS document.
   - Export to a PDF or XPS document: PDF and XPS documents can be opened by their respective readers.

7. **Export objects to another Access database.**
   - Export tables to another database: After you create a table for one database, you may be able to use it again (definition or both definition and data) for your next database.
   - Export other objects to another database: There may be common queries, forms, or reports that could also be exported from one database to another.

8. **Link to an Access table.**
   - Examine the tables in the source database: Ensure that the data and format are relevant to your database.
   - Link to an Access table: Linking lets you connect to a table without having to import the table data into your database.

9. **Link to an Excel spreadsheet.**
   - Verify the format of an Excel spreadsheet: Ensure that the data will display properly in Access; delete extraneous or blank rows.
   - Link to an Excel spreadsheet: Create a link from Access to Excel that enables you to view Excel data in Access.

10. **Import an Excel spreadsheet.**
    - Examine the spreadsheet before importing: Ensure that the data will display properly in Access.
    - Import a spreadsheet into Access: Import the data into your Access database to evaluate it before appending it to the tables.

11. **Import a text file.**
    - Examine the text file before importing: Ensure that the data is eligible to be separated into columns and is consistent from row to row.
    - Import a text file into Access: You are able to manipulate the data after it is imported into Access without changing the original text file.

Key Terms Matching

Match the key terms with their definitions. Write the key term letter by the appropriate numbered definition.

a. Attachment control
b. Attachment field
c. CSV text file
d. Fixed-length text file
e. Hyperlink
f. Importing

g. Linking
h. Portable Document Format (PDF)
i. Rich Text Format (RTF)
j. Text file
k. Uniform resource locator (URL)
l. XML Paper Specification (XPS)

1. _____ A file format developed by Microsoft and designed to display a printed page onscreen identically on any computer platform. **p. 470**

2. _____ Uses a comma to separate one column from the next column, enabling the receiving software to distinguish one set of field values from the next. **p. 493**

3. _____ Data type that enables you to quickly link to any file on your computer or to any Web page on the Internet. **p. 448**

4. _____ A common method of exchanging data between two computer systems. **p. 493**

5. _____ The location of a Web site or Web page on the Internet. **p. 448**

6. _____ Process that enables you connect to a table without having to import the table data into your database. **p. 484**

7. _____ A format that enables documents created in one software application to be opened with a different software application. **p. 467**

8. _____ This process may result in increasing the size of the Access database substantially. **p. 448**

9. _____ A file format created by Adobe Systems for document exchange independent of software application and operating system environment. **p. 470**

10. _____ Similar to an attachment in an e-mail; you can use it to attach multiple files of any format and then launch those files from within Access. **p. 450**

11. _____ Allocates a certain number of characters for each field. **p. 493**

12. _____ A control that lets you manage attached files in forms and reports. **p. 453**

Multiple Choice

1. Which statement about hyperlink fields is false?

   (a) Hyperlinks can launch Web pages on the Internet.
   (b) Hyperlinks can launch Excel spreadsheets.
   (c) Editing a hyperlink must be done in Design view.
   (d) Hyperlinks can be modified using the right-click option.

2. Which statement about attachments is true?

   (a) You can attach only one file per record in a table.
   (b) You can use attachment files in forms and reports, but you must first define them in the table.
   (c) Attached photos display as thumbnails in queries.
   (d) Attachment files do not increase the size of an Access database.

3. You need to attach an employee's most recent performance review to her record in the Employees table. What is the correct action?

   (a) Open the Employees table, add an OLE field, and then attach the document to the employee's record in Datasheet view of the table.
   (b) Open the Employees table, add an attachment field, and then attach the document to the employee's record in Design view of the table.
   (c) Open the Employees table, add an attachment field, and then attach the document to the employee's record in Datasheet view of the table.
   (d) Open the Employees table, add a hyperlink field, and then attach the document to the employee's record in Datasheet view of the table.

4. What is the primary difference between an imported table and a linked table?

   (a) Data in an imported table can be modified from Access; data in a linked table cannot be modified.
   (b) Both types increase the size of the database.
   (c) Users cannot create queries with a linked table.
   (d) The data in imported tables resides inside the database; the data in linked tables resides outside the database.

5. You have exported an Access table to Excel because:

   (a) You cannot create reports in Access.
   (b) It can be analyzed by a user who does not know Access or own the software.

   (c) Data cannot be sorted or filtered in Access.
   (d) The Access database has grown too large.

6. What is the default format when you export data to Word?

   (a) PDF
   (b) RTF
   (c) DOC
   (d) DOCX

7. What is the main difference between a PDF document and an XPS document?

   (a) PDF does not require reader software to open the documents.
   (b) PDF documents can be opened with an Internet browser.
   (c) XPS documents show a replica of what the printed document looks like.
   (d) One format was created by Adobe (PDF) and the other by Microsoft (XPS).

8. You have imported an Excel spreadsheet named *Inventory* into your database. It displays in the Navigation Pane as

   (a) The Inventory table.
   (b) The Inventory form.
   (c) The Inventory report.
   (d) A linked table.

9. Which type of objects can be exported from one database to another?

   (a) Tables only
   (b) Tables and queries
   (c) All objects
   (d) Reports only

10. Importing a text file

    (a) Requires the Import Wizard.
    (b) Can only be done with a CSV file.
    (c) Is limited to files with 999 rows or less.
    (d) Is similar to importing a Word file.

1 Houston Bank Customer Updates

As database administrator for Houston Bank, your manager wants you to attach photos of the customers to the records in the Customers table. You will create an attachment field in the Customers table and then attach the photos to each record. You will also create an e-mail field for the customers and add your own e-mail address to the table. This exercise follows the same set of skills as used in Hands-On Exercise 1 in the chapter. Refer to Figure 8.68 as you complete this exercise.

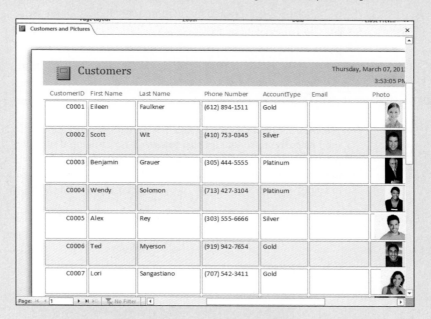

FIGURE 8.68 Hyperlink and Attachment Control in a Report

Photos: (From top) Fotolia, Fotolia, © carlos Restrepo/Fotolia, © Paul Hill/Fotolia, © Rido/Fotolia, Fotolia, © Rido/Fotolia

a. Open *a08p1Bank*. Click the **FILE tab**, click **Save As**, click **Save As**, and then type **a08p1Bank_LastFirst**. Click **Save**.

b. Open the Customers table in Datasheet view and replace *Your_Name* with your name. Switch to Design view.

c. Type **Email** in the first blank row of the Field Name column. Select **Hyperlink** as the Data Type.

d. Add another field, **Photo**, under *Email*, and then select **Attachment** as the Data Type.

e. Save the table. Switch to Datasheet view.

f. Type your e-mail address into the Email column of the eighth record.

g. Double-click the **paperclip** in the first record. Click **Add** in the Attachments dialog box. Locate and open the *a08p1Customer_photos* folder. Double-click the file named *C0001.jpg* to attach it to the record and click **OK** in the Attachments dialog box.

h. Double-click the **paperclip** in the second record. Click **Add**. Double-click the file named *C0002.jpg* to attach it to the record and click **OK**.

i. Repeat until all of the records have photos attached. Use either the provided picture for record 8 or attach a photo of yourself.

j. Click the **CREATE tab** and click **Report** in the Reports group to create a new report.

k. Modify the report in Layout view. Delete the Address, City, State, and Zip Code columns by clicking each column heading, pressing **Shift**, clicking the first text box below it, and then pressing **Delete**. Delete the empty columns by clicking the column heading of each one and pressing **Delete**.

l. Shrink the remaining columns so all of the fields will fit on one page. Display the report in Print Preview to verify that all columns fit on one page.

TROUBLESHOOTING: If empty columns remain in the report in Layout view, click the empty column heading of each one and press Delete. If the report does not fit onto one page, switch to Design view and drag the page numbers text box to the left. Then reduce the width of the report grid until the report fits on one page.

m. Save the report as **Customers and Pictures**. Close the report. Close the Customers table.

n. Click the **FILE tab** and click **Compact & Repair Database**.

o. Close the database. Exit Access.

p. Submit based on your instructor's directions.

2 International Gourmet Traders

The International Gourmet Traders is a small specialty foods distribution firm. Management wants to send its current product line list to several new potential suppliers. You will need to create several output formats for the product line list so that the new suppliers can receive the information in any one of the following formats: Excel, Word, PDF, or Access. This exercise follows the same set of skills as used in Hands-On Exercise 2 in the chapter. Refer to Figure 8.69 as you complete this exercise.

To: Product Suppliers

From: International Gourmet Traders

Subject: Request for competitive products

Category Name	ProductName	Wholesale Cost	UnitsInStock
Beverages	Chai	$12.95	39
Beverages	Chang	$13.50	17
Beverages	Chartreuse verte	$17.51	69
Beverages	Côte de Blaye	$263.01	17
Beverages	Ipoh Coffee	$45.51	17
Beverages	Lakkalikööri	$17.51	57
Beverages	Laughing Lumberjack Lager	$13.51	52
Beverages	Outback Lager	$14.51	15
Beverages	Rhönbräu Klosterbier	$7.26	125
Beverages	Sasquatch Ale	$13.51	111
Beverages	Steeleye Stout	$17.51	20
Condiments	Aniseed Syrup	$8.40	13
Condiments	Chef Anton's Cajun Seasoning	$15.50	53
Condiments	Genen Shouyu	$9.99	39
Condiments	Grandma's Boysenberry Spread	$19.00	120

FIGURE 8.69 Product Pricing Request in Word Format

a. Open *a08p2Traders*. Click the **FILE tab**, click **Save As**, click **Save As**, and then type **a08p2Traders_LastFirst**. Click **Save**.

b. Open the Current Product Line query, examine the records in Datasheet view, and then close the query. Verify that the Current Product Line query is selected in the Navigation Pane before you complete each step below.

c. Export the product information to an Excel format as follows:

- Click the **EXTERNAL DATA tab**.
- Click **Excel** in the Export group.
- Click **Browse** to open the File Save dialog box.
- Navigate to the location where you are saving your files.
- Type **a08p2Prodline_LastFirst** as the file name.
- Verify that the *Save as type* is set as Excel Workbook.
- Click **Save** to return to the Export – Excel Spreadsheet dialog box.
- Click the **Export data with formatting…** and **Open the destination file… check boxes**.
- Click **OK**.

- Verify that the data exported correctly to Excel and exit Excel. (The Excel file is automatically saved.)
- Click **Close** in the Save Export Steps dialog box in Access.

d. Export the product information to a Word format as follows:
- Click the **EXTERNAL DATA tab**.
- Click the **More button** in the Export group and select **Word** from the list.
- Click **Browse** to open the File Save dialog box.
  - Navigate to the location where you are saving your files.
  - Type **a08p2Prodline_LastFirst** as the file name.
  - Verify that the *Save as type* is set as Rich Text Format.
  - Click **Save** to return to the Export – RTF File dialog box.
- Click the **Open the destination file… check box**.
- Click **OK**.
- Verify that the data exported correctly to Word, press **Enter**, and then type the To, From, and Subject lines as shown in Figure 8.69.
- Click the **FILE tab** and click **Save As**.
- Navigate to the location where you are saving your files and type **a08p2Prodline_LastFirst** as the file name.
- Change the file type to Word Document.
- Click **Save**. Click **OK** in the compatibility message box.
- Close the Word document.
- Click **Close** in the Save Export Steps dialog box in Access.

e. Export the product information to a PDF format as follows:
- Click the **EXTERNAL DATA tab**.
- Click **PDF or XPS** in the Export group.
- Navigate to the location where you are saving your files.
- Type **a08p2Prodline_LastFirst** as the file name.
- Verify that the *Save as type* is set to PDF.
- Click **Publish**.
- Verify that the data exported correctly. Navigate to where you are saving your files in File Explorer and double-click the file to open it in your reader software.

> **TROUBLESHOOTING:** If all of the columns do not fit onto one page, return to the Current Product Line query and reduce the column widths. Publish to PDF again.

- Close the reader program.
- Click **Close** in the Save Export Steps dialog box in Access.

f. To export the product information to another Access database, follow these steps:
- Open the Current Product Line query in Design view.
- Click **Make Table** in the Query Type group to create a new table.
- Type **Products to Export** in the **Table Name box**, and with the Current Database option selected, click **OK**.
- Click **Run** in the Results group.
- Click **Yes** in response to the *You are about to paste 68 rows* message.
- Click the **FILE tab**, click **Save As**, click **Save Object As**, and then click **Save As**.
- Type **Make Table Products in Stock** as the query name and click **OK**. Close the query.
- Select the **Products to Export table** in the Navigation Pane and click the **EXTERNAL DATA tab**.
- Use File Explorer to locate and open *a08p2Prodstock*. Save it as **a08p2Prodstock_LastFirst**.
- Close *a08p2Prodstock_LastFirst* and return to the *a08p2Traders_LastFirst* database.
- Click **Access** in the Export group.
- Click **Browse** in the Export – Access Database dialog box.
  - Locate and select the *a08p2Prodstock_LastFirst* file.
  - Click **Save** to return to the Export – Access Database dialog box.

- Click **OK**.
- Click **OK** to accept the *Products to Export* table name and the *Definition and Data* option.
- Click **Close** in the Save Export Steps dialog box.

g. Click the **FILE tab** and click **Compact & Repair Database**.

h. Close the database.

i. Open the *a08p2Prodstock_LastFirst* database. Verify that the table exported correctly.

j. Close the database. Exit Access.

k. Submit based on your instructor's directions.

3 Break Room Suppliers, Inc.

Break Room Suppliers, Inc., provides coffee, tea, beverages, and snacks to businesses in its area. In an effort to expand their business, the owners have purchased several customer-prospect lists. You will need to link and import the prospect lists into Access so the owners can determine how best to use them in their database. You will also import an Excel spreadsheet containing newly developed sales rep information. This exercise follows the same set of skills as used in Hands-On Exercise 3 in the chapter. Refer to Figure 8.70 as you complete this exercise.

FIGURE 8.70 Customers Imported from Another Access Database

a. Open *a08p3Coffee*. Click the **FILE tab**, click **Save As**, click **Save As**, and then type **a08p3Coffee_LastFirst**. Click **Save**.

b. Click the **EXTERNAL DATA tab** and click **Excel** in the Import & Link group.

c. Click **Browse** in the Get External Data – Excel Spreadsheet dialog box and locate the file *a08p3Custexcel*.

d. Select the file and click **Open** to return to the Get External Data dialog box.

e. Click the **Link to the data source by creating a linked table option**. Click **OK**.

f. Click the **First Row Contains Column Headings check box**. Click **Next**.

g. Confirm **Customers_Excel** is the Linked Table Name. Click **Finish**. Click **OK** in the message box.

h. Double-click the **Customers_Excel table** in the Navigation Pane to view the customer records. Close the table.

i. Click the **EXTERNAL DATA tab** and click **Excel** in the Import & Link group.

j. Click **Browse** in the Get External Data – Excel Spreadsheet dialog box and locate the file *a08p3Repsexcel*.

k. Select the file and click **Open** to return to the Get External Data dialog box.

l. Click the **Import the source data into a new table in the current database option**. Click **OK**.

m. Click the **First Row Contains Column Headings check box**. Click **Next** two times.

n. Click the **Choose my own primary key option**. Click **Next**.

o. Confirm **Sales Reps** is the *Import to Table* name. Click **Finish**. Click **Close** in the Save Import Steps dialog box.

p. Double-click the **Sales Reps table** in the Navigation Pane to view the records. Close the table.

q. Click **Access** in the Import & Link group on the EXTERNAL DATA tab.

r. Click **Browse** in the Get External Data – Access Database dialog box and locate the file *a08p3Custaccess*.

s. Select the file and click **Open** to return to the Get External Data dialog box.

t. Click the **Link to the data source by creating a linked table option**. Click **OK**.

u. Click **Customers_Access** in the Link Tables dialog box. Click **OK**.

v. Double-click the **Customers_Access table** in the Navigation Pane to view the customer records. Close the table.

w. Click **Text File** in the Import & Link group on the External Data tab.

x. Click **Browse** in the Get External Data – Text File dialog box and locate the file *a08p3Custtext.csv*.

y. Select the file and click **Open** to return to the Get External Data dialog box. Verify that the *Import the source data into a new table in the current database* option is selected. Click **OK**.

z. Click **Next** when the Import Text Wizard appears.

aa. Click the **First Row Contains Field Names check box**. Click **Next**.

bb. Click **Next** to confirm the field options.

cc. Click the **No primary key option** in the next dialog box. Click **Next**.

dd. Change the *Import to Table* name to **Customers_Text**. Click **Finish**. Click **Close** in the Save Import Steps dialog box. Close the window.

ee. Double-click the **Customers_Text table** in the Navigation Pane to view the customer records. Close the table.

ff. Click the **FILE tab** and click **Compact & Repair Database**.

gg. Close the database. Exit Access.

hh. Submit based on your instructor's directions.

1 Morrison Arboretum

ANALYSIS CASE

The Morrison Arboretum at NC University wants to add a few new features to its database. They want to add photos of the plants to the Plant Descriptions table and a hyperlink field that points to a Web site that describes each plant. You also need to create a report showing the plant names, the corresponding hyperlinks, and the plant photos. You will export this report to Word, but because you notice that the photos will not export to Word, you will publish the report as a PDF document to distribute via e-mail to members. Finally, you will export a query to Excel to be used as a mailing list. Refer to Figure 8.71 as you complete this exercise.

FIGURE 8.71 Navigation Pane with Report and Linked Table

a. Open the file *a08m1Arbor*. Save it as **a08m1Arbor_LastFirst**.

b. Create a new hyperlink field named **PlantLink** in the Plant Descriptions table below the PlantName field.

c. Create a new attachment field named **Picture** in the Plant Descriptions table below the PlantLink field.

DISCOVER

d. Visit Wikipedia.org and perform a search on **viburnum**. Copy the URL and paste it into the correct PlantLink field in Datasheet view.

e. Use the Attachments dialog box to add the appropriate photo for each plant. The photos are in the folder named *a08m1Plant_Photos*.

f. Create a basic report based on the Plant Descriptions table. Set the title of the report as **Plants with Links and Pictures**.

 g. Center the report title text in the control and delete the logo to the left of the title control. Save the report as **Plants with Photos**. Close the report. Export the *Plants with Photos* report to Word and save the document as **a08m1Plants_LastFirst**. Note that no pictures were exported and close Word. Close the Save Export Steps dialog box without saving the export steps. Write a short paragraph in Word that discusses why it could be useful to save the export steps. Use Access Help as necessary to research this feature. Save the document as **a08m1Exports_LastFirst**.

h. Publish the report in PDF format and save the document as **a08m1Plants_LastFirst**. View the PDF report in your reader program, note that the pictures were exported, and then close the reader. Close the Save Export Steps dialog box without saving the export steps.

i. Export the query ENewsletter Members to Excel to use as mailing list and save the workbook as **a08m1Email_LastFirst**. Review the exported data and close Excel. Close the Save Export Steps dialog box without saving the export steps. Import the Excel spreadsheet back into the database as a linked table named **ENewsletter List**, using the first row headings as field names.

j. Open the ENewsletter List table and close the table. Compact and repair the database.

k. Close the database. Exit Access.

l. Submit based on your instructor's directions.

**ANALYSIS
CASE**

As the database manager of a hotel chain, you monitor the services ordered using a summary query. The hotel chain's manager asks you to send him a summary of the Raleigh location orders as an Excel spreadsheet. He also asks you to export the Repeat Members Club table to a different database. Several hotels in Los Angeles are for sale, and you decide to import their order data to determine their activity levels. Refer to Figure 8.72 as you complete this exercise.

FIGURE 8.72 Navigation Pane with Linked and Imported Data

a. Open *a08m2Hotel* and save it as **a08m2Hotel_LastFirst** in the folder where you are saving your files. Open *a08m2Hotelexport*. Save the database as **a08m2Hotelexport_LastFirst**. Close *a08h2Hotelexport_LastFirst* and return to the *a08m2Hotel_LastFirst* database.

b. Export the Repeat Members Club table to another Access database, *a08m2Hotelexport_LastFirst*. Verify that the table was exported correctly and return to the *a08m2Hotel_LastFirst* database. Do not save the export steps.

c. Modify the *Summary by ServiceID* query so that it displays only orders from location 3 (which is Raleigh). Save, run, and then close the query. Export the query to Excel and save the workbook as **a08m2Raleighorders_LastFirst** in the folder where you are saving your solution files.

d. Review the exported data and close Excel. Do not save the export steps. Import the Excel spreadsheet back into the database as a linked table named **Raleigh Property Updates**, with the first row headings as field names. Open the Raleigh Property Updates table and close the table. Do not save the import steps.

e. Open *a08m2Ordersexcel.xslx*. Exit Excel and return to *a08m2Hotel_LastFirst*. Import the Excel spreadsheet as a table named *Orders_Excel* with the first row as column headings and OrderID as the primary key field. Do not save the import steps.

f. Open *a08m2Ordersaccess*. Close *a08m2Ordersaccess* and return to *a08m2Hotel_LastFirst*. Create a link to the *Orders_Access* table in the *a08m2Ordersaccess* database. Do not save the import steps.

g. Open *a08m2Orderstext.csv*. Exit Excel and return to *a08m2Hotel_LastFirst*. Import the data as **Orders_Text** from the *a08m2Orderstext.csv* text file using the first row headings as field names and **OrderID** as the primary key field into the database. Do not save the import steps.

 h. Save a copy of the file *a08m2Orderstext* as **a08m2Orderstext_LastFirst** with the text file format (.txt). Edit the file using the Notepad program to delete the first record, *OrderID 4001*, and reimport the modified text file into your database as **Orders_Text**. Overwrite the original table when prompted. Write a short paragraph in Word that explains why it is important to edit a text file before it is imported into Access. Save the document as **a08m2Orderstext_LastFirst**.

i. Compact and repair the database. Close the database. Exit Access.

j. Submit based on your instructor's directions.

3 | Loan-Tracking Database

COLLABORATION CASE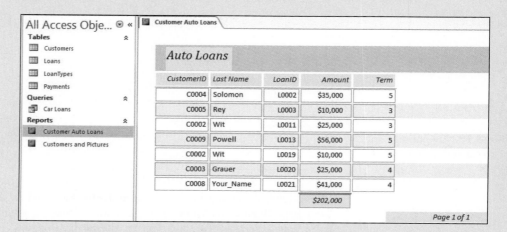

You have been asked to modify a loan-tracking database that tracks customer data, loan records, and payment information. You and your team will modify and import a spreadsheet and a text file into the database. You will add a hyperlink field that will store an e-mail address for each customer. You will then use imported data to create a query in the database, create a report based on the query, and then export the report to a Word document. Refer to Figure 8.73 as you complete this exercise.

FIGURE 8.73 Customer Auto Loans Report Includes Imported Data

All Access Obje... ⊙ «

Tables ⌃
- Customers
- Loans
- LoanTypes
- Payments

Queries ⌃
- Car Loans

Reports ⌃
- Customer Auto Loans
- Customers and Pictures

Customer Auto Loans

Auto Loans

CustomerID	Last Name	LoanID	Amount	Term
C0004	Solomon	L0002	$35,000	5
C0005	Rey	L0003	$10,000	3
C0002	Wit	L0011	$25,000	3
C0009	Powell	L0013	$56,000	5
C0002	Wit	L0019	$10,000	5
C0003	Grauer	L0020	$25,000	4
C0008	Your_Name	L0021	$41,000	4
			$202,000	

Page 1 of 1

a. Open *a08m3Collaboration* and save it as **a08m3Collaboration_GroupName**. As a team, study the existing database and the relationship between the Customers and Loans tables. You will add two new tables to the database by importing external data.

Assign the next two tasks to a team member.

b. Open the text file named *a08m3LoanTypes.txt* and save a copy of the file as *a08m3LoanTypes_LastFirst.txt*. Modify the text file so that instead of the existing separators, commas will specify where the values should be separated. Save your changes.

c. Create a table in the database by importing the modified text file named *a08m3LoanTypes_LastFirst.txt*. Use the first row of the file as field names and **Type** as the primary key and name the table **LoanTypes**. Accept all other default options. Do not save the import steps.

Assign the next two tasks to a team member.

d. Open the workbook named *a08m3Payments* and save a copy of the file as *a08m3Payments_LastFirst*. Modify the workbook so that it will import properly to an Access database. Save your changes.

e. Create a new table in the database by importing the workbook named *a08m3Payments_LastFirst*. Use the first row of the worksheet as column headings, ensure that PaymentID is set as the primary key, and them import the table as **Payments**. Accept all other default options. Do not save the import steps. Change the field size of the LoanID field to Long Integer. If a warning message appears, proceed with the change and then save and close the table.

Assign the next two tasks to a team member.

f. Add a Hyperlink field named **EmailAddress** below the PhoneNumber field in the Customers table.

g. Enter your own first and last names and your personal e-mail address in the appropriate fields for record C0008. Remove the existing attachment from the Photo field and add your own personal photo. Close the table.

Assign the next two tasks to a team member.

h. Add the LoanTypes and Payment tables to the Relationships window. Create a relationship between the Loans and Payments table, enforcing referential integrity. Create a relationship between LoanTypes and Loans, enforcing referential integrity. Save and close the Relationships window.

i. Create a query in Design view. Add the Customers, Loans, and LoanTypes tables to the query window. Add the following fields in this order: CustomerID, LastName, LoanID, Amount, Term, and LoanName. Set the criteria so that customers who have car loans will display in the results. Run the query, save it as **Car Loans**, and then close it.

j. Collaborate with your team to determine what would be the best way to portray the Car Loans query results in a report. Create the report and format it appropriately. Adjust the column widths so that they all fit within the page but the data is still visible. Delete the LoanName column and the Date and Time fields from the report.

k. Switch to Design view and move the page numbering control to the left so that its right edge is just inside the 7-inch mark on the horizontal ruler. Drag the right edge of the report to the left so that it is just inside the 7-inch mark on the ruler. View the report in Print Preview; the report should consist of one page.

l. Modify the report title as **Auto Loans** and delete the logo to the left of the title, if necessary

m. Save the report as **a08m3CustomerAutoLoans_LastFirst** and close the report. Export the report as a Word document using the same name and save it as a Word document. Close the report and exit Word. Do not save the export steps.

n. Compact and repair the database. Close the database. Exit Access. Submit the database and documents based on your instructor's directions.

Beyond the Classroom

Exporting from Access
RESEARCH CASE

The *a08b2China* file contains data from an international china, crystal, flatware, and collectibles firm. This chapter introduced you to the power of data sharing. You now know how to import and export data using many different types of file formats. The database contains a query, Orders More Than $150, which displays revenue information. Export the query and save it as a Word document as **a08b2China_LastFirst**. At the top of the document, write a brief memo to your instructor that lists at least five formats that are available for exporting data from Access. Use the Internet to research which formats are most popular among computer users. Add that information to your memo. Exit Word, close the database, and then exit Access. Submit the Word document based on your instructor's directions.

Exporting to Word
DISASTER RECOVERY

Your colleague needs you to export a report from Access to Word to provide him with the most recent sales data. Open *a08b3Real*. Export the Sales Report to Word. Save the Word document as **a08b3Real_LastFirst**. Compact, repair, and then close the database. Exit Access. Submit the Word document based on your instructor's directions.

Workplace Etiquette
SOFT SKILLS CASE

You want to determine how many of the new employees in the *a08b4Etiquette* database require a workplace etiquette in-service. Open *a08b4Etiquette*. Modify the Require Etiquette Inservice query so that only employees who have *not* had etiquette training display in the results. Export the query results to Excel. Save the Excel workbook as **Require Etiquette Inservice_LastFirst**. Close Excel. Compact, repair, and then close the database. Exit Access. Submit the Excel workbook based on your instructor's directions.

Capstone Exercise

You work as an associate database manager at Replacement China, Inc. This firm specializes in finding difficult-to-replace, no-longer-manufactured china, crystal, silver, and collectibles. You need to add a hyperlink field that will store a URL for each manufacturer's Web site. The HR department manager wants to store a photo and the most recent performance review for each employee. You also need to export select inventory items in three different formats. Finally, you will import information from Excel, Access, and text files. Compact and repair the database and make a backup of it when you are finished.

Database File Setup

Make a copy of the original database file, rename the copy, and then open the copy. After you open the copied database, you will replace an existing employee's name with your name.

a. Open *a08c1Replace* and save it as **a08c1Replace_LastFirst**.

b. Open the Employees table.

c. Navigate to record 21 and replace *Your_Name* with your name. Save the record and close the table.

Create Attachment and Hyperlink Fields

Add a hyperlink field to the Manufacturer table to store each company's Web site address. Add an attachment field to the Employees table to store the employee's performance reviews and photos.

a. Create a new field in the Manufacturer table after RlMfgCode named **Website** with the Hyperlink data type. Save the table.

b. Switch to Datasheet view, add the Web site **http://www.lenox.com** to the Lenox China record (7), and then add **http://www.waterford.com** to the Waterford Crystal record (14). Click each link to make sure it launches a browser and locates the appropriate Web site. Close the table.

c. Create a new field in the Employees table after HireDate named **Files** with the Attachment data type. Save the table.

d. Switch to Datasheet view and use the Find command to locate the record for UserID 822680. Add the Word document named *822680.doc* and the picture file named *822680.jpg* to the Files field. The files you need are in the a08c1Reviews folder. Additional attachments will be added in the future.

e. Create a basic form based on the Employees table that will open in Layout view. Delete the subform. Navigate to the record for UserID 822680 (record 21) and use the Attachment toolbar to display the Word document and the picture file.

f. Save the form as **Employees**. Close the form and the table.

Export a Filtered Table to Excel, Word, and PDF

You need to filter the Inventory table and then export the records to three formats: Excel, Word, and PDF. This information will be used to get prices on items that have no on-hand quantity.

a. Use *Filter by Selection* to display records in the Inventory table where the Category equals *Crystal*. Filter the records further to display Crystal where the OH (on-hand) value equals *0* (three records will display). Leave the filtered table open for the next three steps.

b. Export the filtered records to an Excel file. Save the file as **a08c1Crystal_LastFirst**. Do not save the export steps.

c. Export the same filtered records to a Word file. Press **Enter** one time and add the title **Crystal with 0 on hand** to the Word file. Save the file as a Word document with the name **a08c1Crystal_LastFirst**. Do not save the export steps.

d. Export the filtered records to a PDF document. Save the file as **a08c1Crystal_LastFirst**. Do not save the export steps.

e. Close the Inventory table without saving the changes.

Import and Link Data from Excel, Access, and a Text File

You need to import new customer records from Excel and Access. You also will import customer records from a text file.

a. Create a linked table in the database by importing the workbook named *a08c1Customers*. Use the first row of the Customers1 worksheet as row headings and accept all other default options.

b. Create a linked table in the database by importing the Customers2 table from the database named *a08c1Customers*.

c. Create a table in the database by importing the text file named *a08c1Textcust.csv*. Use the first row of the file as field names, **CustomerNum** as the primary key, and name the table **Customers Text**. Accept all other default options.

d. Compact and repair the database.

e. Close the database. Exit Access.

f. Submit based on your instructor's directions.

Fine-Tuning the Database

Analyzing and Improving Database Performance

CHAPTER 9

Yuri Arcurs/Shutterstock

OBJECTIVES AFTER YOU READ THIS CHAPTER, YOU WILL BE ABLE TO:

1. Verify first normal form p. 520

2. Verify second normal form p. 523

3. Verify third normal form p. 524

4. Create relationships p. 526

5. Use the Database Documenter tool p. 531

6. Use the Performance Analyzer tool p. 533

7. Use the Table Analyzer tool p. 535

8. Use the Database Splitter tool p. 538

9. Create a menu system p. 545

10. Encrypt and password-protect a database p. 548

11. Digitally sign and publish a database p. 550

12. Save a database as an ACCDE file p. 551

CASE STUDY | The Metropolitan Zoo

Your job as the information manager of the Metropolitan Zoo is to maintain the records for all of the animals at the zoo. The zoo maintains its records in an Access 2013 database, which you have been using for the past two months. The database was created by a former employee who learned about Access by taking a night course at a local community college. The forms and reports have been working well, according to Director of Field Programs, Selene Platt. Selene has worked at the Metropolitan Zoo for 27 years, and she provides you with the information about each animal. She hired you to help with the daily upkeep of the database; she also wants to evaluate the design and performance of the database.

Your tasks include entering new animals, updating changes to existing records, and archiving records for animals that leave the zoo. As you work with the Access database and become familiar with the tables, the table relationships, the data-entry forms, and the reports, you start to look for ways to improve the performance of the database. You also look for ways to protect the data that already exists in the database. These improvements will help you complete the daily tasks of the database; they may also help your boss, Selene, get faster and more reliable results from the database.

Database Normalization

In an earlier chapter, you used common sense to determine which fields to include in each table. The process changes when you deal with a more complex system. Database designers generally start by performing customer interviews, reviewing existing documents, examining existing files, and applying their own knowledge to create a list of potential fields. They then identify potential primary keys and divide the fields into tables. They then go through a process to refine the tables and remove issues. *Normalization* is the formal process of deciding which fields should be grouped together into which tables. Experienced database designers may instinctively create tables that follow the rules of normalization. Less experienced designers generally use the process of normalization to guide them in the process of creating the database. The benefits of normalization are:

- Minimization of data redundancy
- Improvement of referential integrity enforcement
- Ease of maintaining data (add, update, delete)
- Accommodation of future growth of a database

Though this sounds straightforward, it can present challenges. Many colleges and universities have multiple graduate-level database classes to train future database designers in this process.

Following the rules of normalization while creating tables in Access helps you design tables that are free from anomalies. An *anomaly* is an error or inconsistency within a database. Many times, these errors occur when you add, edit, and delete data. Assume a spreadsheet is keeping track of company orders, one order per row. Repeat customers would lead to multiple references to the same customer. Mixed in among thousands of orders, we might have the following information for customer Faten Bader:

9/1/15	Faten Bader	West Paterson, NJ	#456789	3	$12.50
9/10/15	Faten Bader	West Paterson, NJ	#894561	1	$2.95
9/25/15	Faten Bader	West Paterson, NJ	#981156	1	$.95

Faten may call in and change her address, saying her town name changed from West Paterson to Woodland Park, and this introduces an update problem (anomaly). How does the database know which record to update—the first, the second, the third, or all three? A user might try to update the records manually, but this might produce an anomaly as well if only one or two of the three records are changed. If the town's name has changed, should it change for all other customers?

In this section, you will learn the first three rules of normalization. These rules are known as *normal forms* and indicate the current state of a table. The first three normal forms are referred to as first normal form (1NF), second normal form (2NF), and third normal form (3NF). By definition, a table cannot be in 2NF unless it is already in 1NF, and it cannot be in 3NF unless it is in 2NF.

A table that meets 1NF criteria is better than a table that does not. Similarly, a table that meets 2NF criteria is better than a table that is in 1NF, and a table that meets 3NF criteria is better than a table that is in 2NF. There are five normal forms; however, the majority of database designs only require the first three normal forms.

Verifying First Normal Form

STEP 1 » First normal form is the first rule to identify and correct. It can be demonstrated by using an Excel spreadsheet that contains information about authors, books, and publishers (see Figure 9.1). In the spreadsheet, Dan Brown is listed as an AuthorName in column C; the titles of the books that Brown authored are listed on row 5 in column D. The remaining fields contain additional information related to the books. This example would not pass the

1NF test because column D—including the books that Brown authored—has multiple values in a single cell. Brown, the author, is listed once, and the books he wrote are listed in one cell. Even titles on two lines in the same cell are considered multiple values in one cell. If this Excel spreadsheet were imported into Access, the corresponding Access table with repeating groups would be as shown in Figure 9.2. This table shows the same condition with repeating values in the Title field. Repeating groups are not allowed in a normalized table.

Two values in the same cell

FIGURE 9.1 Excel Spreadsheet with Repeating Groups

Two values in the same record

FIGURE 9.2 Access Table with Repeating Groups

We define *first normal form (1NF)* as a table that contains no repeating groups or repeating columns. In the book example, the Title column might be replaced with Title1, Title2, and Title3. This might appear to correct the repeating groups problem because each cell contains one piece of information; however, this type of design still violates 1NF and must be corrected. In this example, it is still difficult to find data efficiently.

TIP   Multivalued Data Types in Access

Access enables you to create a multivalued field using the Lookup Wizard data type. This data type enables you to enter multiple values into a single field for one record. This data type may appear to break the rules of 1NF, but remember that multivalued fields are handled with special invisible tables Access creates in the background. Although multivalued fields can be useful at times, remember to avoid them if you plan to upgrade to a more powerful database (e.g., SQL Server) in the future.

There are several problems with tables that have repeating groups—it is difficult to add new entries, it is difficult to update existing entries, and it is difficult to properly extract information when running queries. For example, if you want see the information for *Digital Fortress*, you could create a filter or query searching for those results. However, Access considers them to be part of the same record, and you would also see the book *The Lost Symbol*. As a matter of fact, when you attempt to filter your data (as shown in Figure 9.3), you would immediately notice the two book names listed as one piece of data. Similar problems would exist with queries searching for a specific book. In other words, there is no easy way to only show the information for *Digital Fortress*. This occurs because all the books by one author are contained in the same record.

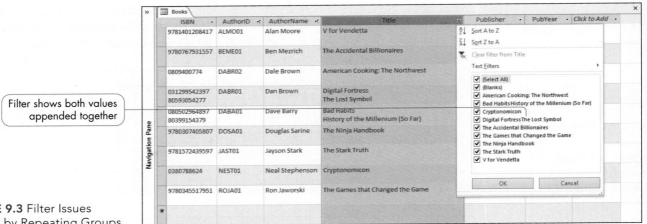

Filter shows both values appended together

FIGURE 9.3 Filter Issues Caused by Repeating Groups

To fix a table that has repeating groups, simply make sure each unique piece of information is on a separate row. Any columns should have the missing information added, even if this leads to repetition. You would need to do this in Excel before importing to Access, or alternately add rows in Access and separate the repeating data into individual rows.

Figure 9.4 shows the Books table in Access after it has been put into first normal form; the single Brown row has been split into two rows, and the books by the same author have been separated. Now each book has its own record.

At this point, although the table is in 1NF, it still has redundancy issues. In fact, we have introduced redundancy into our table. However, because normalization is a process, further normalization will remove the introduced redundancies.

Books

ISBN	AuthorID	AuthorName	Title	Publisher	PubYear
9781401208417	ALMO01	Alan Moore	V for Vendetta	DC Comics	2005
9780767931557	BEME01	Ben Mezrich	The Accidental Billionaires	Anchor Books	2009
9780399154379	DABA01	Dave Barry	History of the Millenium (So Far)	G. P. Putman's Sons	2007
0805029648	DABA01	Dave Barry	Bad Habits	Henry Holt & Co.	1987
9780593054277	DABR01	Dan Brown	The Lost Symbol	Doubleday	2009
0312995423	DABR01	Dan Brown	Digital Fortress	St. Martin	1998
0809400774	DABR02	Dale Brown	American Cooking: The Northwest	Time Life	1970
9780307405807	DOSA01	Douglas Sarine	The Ninja Handbook	Three Rivers Press	2008
9781572439597	JAST01	Jayson Stark	The Stark Truth	Triumph Books	2007
0380788624	NEST01	Neal Stephenson	Cryptonomicon	Perennial	1999
9780345517951	ROJA01	Ron Jaworski	The Games that Changed the Game	ESPN Books	2010

Two records created from original

FIGURE 9.4 Books Table in First Normal Form

The following situations may violate 1NF:

- Multiple values in the same field separated by commas or some other identifier
  - An Authors field listing **Poatsy, Krebs, Cameron, and Williams** is a violation of 1NF.
  - An Address2 field listing **Paterson, NJ 07501** is a violation of 1NF.
  - A Teaching field that contains the following values for the same class, on two lines is a violation of 1NF:
    Cameron
    Siegel
- Multiple columns in the same record containing the same sort of data
  - A table with an Author1 field set to **Poatsy**, Author2 field set to **Krebs**, Author3 field set to **Cameron**, and Author4 field set to **Williams** is a violation of 1NF.

Our focus will be on the more obvious examples, such as multiple values in the field separated by commas or values on separate lines.

Verifying Second Normal Form

STEP 2 » A table is in *second normal form (2NF)* if it meets 1NF criteria and all non-key fields are functionally dependent on the entire primary key. *Functional dependency* occurs when the value of one field is determined by the value of another. A *non-key field* is any field that is not part of the primary key. Therefore, a table with a single-field primary key is usually in 2NF. Because many tables have a single-field primary key, 2NF often requires no changes to a table. However, some tables have a *composite key*, a primary key that is made of two or more fields. Tables with a composite key may require some changes.

Most bookstore databases contain information about location and quantity in stock. Therefore, we have expanded the earlier example to include three extra fields, as shown in Figure 9.5. For the purposes of this example, assume the bookstore has two locations, one in Paterson and one in Wanaque. Because this more realistic version of the table has the location added, a problem now exists. Notice in Figure 9.5 that the ISBN cannot be the primary key for this table because the same book (with the same ISBN) can appear in both locations. In this case, a good option is to use a combination of two fields as the primary key. The composite key for this table would be ISBN plus the location, which uniquely identifies each row.

Because this table has a composite key, you need to ensure all fields are functionally dependent on the entire primary key. To find out the number of books on hand for any specific title, you need to know both the ISBN and the location. Likewise, to find the aisle in which a book is stored, you would need both the ISBN and the location. However, a book's title is independent of the location. Regardless of whether it is in Paterson or Wanaque, the book with an ISBN of 0312995423 is always *Digital Fortress*. The same goes for the rest of the fields. Notice in Figure 9.5 that all the information related to the book *Digital Fortress* is repeated—the AuthorName, Title, Publisher, and PubYear. One data-entry error can lead to inconsistent data.

Data repeated for *Digital Fortress*

Digital Fortress locations

ISBN	AuthorID	AuthorName	Title	Publisher	PubYear	Location	OnHand	Aisle
0312995423	DABR01	Dan Brown	Digital Fortress	St. Martin	1998	Paterson	2	5
0312995423	DABR01	Dan Brown	Digital Fortress	St. Martin	1998	Wanaque	3	1
0380788624	NEST01	Neal Stephenson	Cryptonomicon	Perennial	1999	Paterson	1	1
0805029648	DABA01	Dave Barry	Bad Habits	Henry Holt & Co.	1987	Wanaque	1	4
0809400774	DABR02	Dale Brown	American Cooking: The Northwest	Time Life	1970	Paterson	1	8
9780307405807	DOSA01	Douglas Sarine	The Ninja Handbook	Three Rivers Press	2008	Paterson	1	3
9780345517951	ROJA01	Ron Jaworski	The Games that Changed the Game	ESPN Books	2010	Paterson	2	1
9780399154379	DABA01	Dave Barry	History of the Millenium (So Far)	G. P. Putman's Sons	2007	Wanaque	1	2
9780593054277	DABR01	Dan Brown	The Lost Symbol	Doubleday	2009	Paterson	11	3
9780593054277	DABR01	Dan Brown	The Lost Symbol	Doubleday	2009	Wanaque	5	4
9780767931557	BEME01	Ben Mezrich	The Accidental Billionaires	Anchor Books	2009	Paterson	11	5
9780767931557	BEME01	Ben Mezrich	The Accidental Billionaires	Anchor Books	2009	Wanaque	6	5
9781401208417	ALMO01	Alan Moore	V for Vendetta	DC Comics	2005	Paterson	2	5
9781572439597	JAST01	Jayson Stark	The Stark Truth	Triumph Books	2007	Wanaque	1	6
							0	

FIGURE 9.5 Books Table Including Location and Stock Information

If you look up the ISBN 0312995423, whether in this database, on an online bookstore such as Amazon, or in a Barnes & Noble retail store, you should always find the same title, publisher, and author name of the book. Therefore, the title, publisher, and author name are functionally dependent on the ISBN, not the combination of ISBN and location. In other words, these fields are each characteristics of the book.

Amazon may have the same book in its inventory as our bookstore in Paterson, but the book's location, the number on hand, and the aisle will be different or possibly not present. This is because the location, number on hand, and the aisle are not characteristics of the book. Instead, these are characteristics of the book as it exists in a bookstore.

Second normal form tells you that when fields are functionally dependent upon part of a primary key, you need to remove those fields from the table. Most of the time, this results in new tables, though it is possible to move fields into another existing table.

To resolve the problem, you need to create two tables. The first table you will name Books. The Books table should contain the fields ISBN, AuthorID, AuthorName, Title, Publisher, and PubYear. The primary key of this table is ISBN. See Figure 9.6.

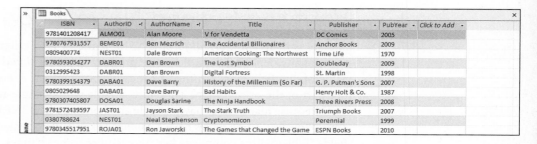

FIGURE 9.6 Books Table in Second Normal Form

The second table you will name Stock. This table contains the fields ISBN, Location, OnHand, and Aisle, as shown in Figure 9.7. The primary key for this table is a composite key, the combination of ISBN and Location.

FIGURE 9.7 Newly Created Stock Table

Notice that the data, once divided into two tables, has less repetition of book information.

TIP Other Issues Fixed by Second Normal Form

For simplicity's sake, this example has focused on composite key issues. There are other situations in which 2NF may require changes. In Figure 9.5, just adding an AutoNumber field labelled as the primary key would not solve the issue that the ISBN would still determine some of the information, and the combination of ISBN and location would determine some of the information. Examples will focus on the composite key issues that 2NF fixes.

Verifying Third Normal Form

STEP 3 A table is in *third normal form (3NF)* if it meets 2NF criteria and no transitive dependencies exist. *Transitive dependencies* occur when the value of one non-key field is functionally dependent on the value of another non-key field. AuthorName in the example is dependent on AuthorID and, therefore, is an example of a transitive dependency. Whenever you know the AuthorID, the AuthorName is automatically known. Therefore, to conform to 3NF, AuthorName must be moved to another table, as shown in Figure 9.8. The new table contains two fields: AuthorID and AuthorName. The Books table can now reference the author using the AuthorID field, as shown in Figure 9.9. The Books table is in 3NF because the transitive dependency was removed. In effect, moving to 3NF requires some work, as a new table often needs to be created and data moved. For a large database, this may require creation of a Make Table query (see the *Action Queries* section of this textbook for more information). In the worst case, this could require large amounts of tedious data entry. However, the trade-off is less repeated data, which leads to fewer anomalies. For example, if you had a typographical error for an author's name (say, Steven King instead of Stephen King), you would only need to change the spelling in one place to correct it.

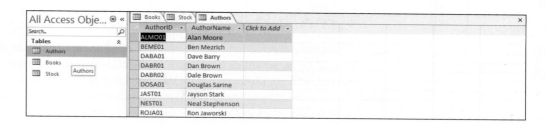

FIGURE 9.8 Newly Created Author Table

FIGURE 9.9 Books Table in Third Normal Form

Another way to handle a conversion to 3NF is to delete fields that may not be necessary. In this specific case, you probably want to keep the AuthorID. In other cases, ask yourself if there is an extra field that can be eliminated. Table 9.1 presents a summary of the three normal forms covered in this chapter.

TABLE 9.1   Normalization Summary

Form	What It Does	Notes
First Normal Form	Removes repeating groups	Introduces redundancy, which is fixed by later normal forms.
Second Normal Form	Removes dependencies on part of a composite primary key	Commonly an issue when a table has a composite key. If the primary key is a single field, a table is usually in 2NF. Changes usually result in added tables.
Third Normal Form	Removes dependencies on any field that is not a primary key	Changes usually result in new tables.

TIP   City, State, ZIP, 3NF?

For most locations in the United States, if you have the ZIP code, you can look up the city and state. This might lead you to believe that this is a transitive dependency. However, on some rare occasions this is not true. For example, the ZIP code 42223 covers parts of Christian County, Kentucky, and Montgomery County, Tennessee. In this case, the same ZIP code not only crosses county borders, it also crosses state lines! Note that in this case, this oddity has to do with an army base that crosses state borders. Due to issues such as these, it is safe to consider a database with the city, state, and ZIP in the same table to be in 3NF.

On the other hand, if you have two customers who live in North Brunswick, NJ, one person doing data entry might type it into the database as North Brunswick and the other may abbreviate it as N Brunswick. If you created a filter or query to locate all towns listed as North Brunswick, only one of those two customers would appear. The argument for putting ZIP in a separate table is to avoid issues such as that.

Creating Relationships

STEP 4 » If you have created new tables, you will need to create relationships between the tables. This should be done after completion of the normalization process. The tables should be connected, and the Enforce Referential Integrity option should be checked. Figure 9.10 shows the relationships in the Books database after normalization. This is not done automatically, so you should set this up as you did in an earlier chapter.

Creating relationships can also be a way to test your normalization. Normalization should not result in data loss, so if you cannot create a relationship between the tables, there is likely an issue with the way you have normalized.

FIGURE 9.10 Relationships in Books Database

In Hands-On Exercise 1, you will work with the Metropolitan Zoo's database to make sure its tables are normalized. The database has been functioning for over two years, so you will have to preserve the existing data when you modify any table. Your boss will work with you to determine which information is important and which data can be discarded.

Quick Concepts

1. What is the purpose of normalizing a database? *p. 520*

2. What problems does first normal form fix? *p. 521*

3. What problems does second normal form fix? *p. 523*

4. What problems does third normal form fix? *p. 524*

Hands-On Exercise

Watch the Video
for this Hands-
On Exercise!

MyITLab®
HOE1 Training

1 Database Normalization

Your job at the Metropolitan Zoo has been fun and challenging. You have been making daily updates to the zoo's database with the help of your boss, Selene Platt. Based on your understanding of the rules of normalization, you decide to recommend some design changes to the database.

Skills covered: Verify First Normal Form • Verify Second Normal Form • Verify Third Normal Form • Create Relationships

STEP 1 ≫ VERIFY FIRST NORMAL FORM

Your boss has asked you to review the table structure to see if any changes should be made. You decide to apply the rules of normalization to the Animals table, starting with 1NF—eliminate any repeating groups. Refer to Figures 9.11–9.13 as you complete Step 1.

Animals

AnimalName	AnimalType	Diet	Endangered	Origin	ExhibitID	TrainerID	TrainerName
Anny	Mockingbird	Insects	☐	North America	1	1	Asha
Cara	Manatee	Plants	☐	Central America	1	1	Asha
Dietre	Clouded Leopard	Small animals	☐	Southeast Asia	1	2	Keisha
Sindall	Bengal Tiger	Animals, Fish	☑	India	1	4	Ruben
Perenolde	Komodo Dragon	Deer, Boar	☑	Indonesia	1	1	Asha
Rakshiri	Bengal Tiger	Animals, Fish	☑	India	1	4	Ruben
Bronstein	Komodo Dragon	Deer, Boar	☑	Indonesia	1	3	Elizabeth
Stampy	Elephant	Plant parts, Grass	☐	Africa	2	3	Elizabeth
Farunn	Grey Rhinoceros	Plants	☑	Africa	2	2	Keisha
Uhkloc	Gorilla	Leaves, Fruit	☐	Central Africa	2	4	Ruben
Zhevra	Zebra	Plants	☐	South Africa	2	4	Ruben
Cassandra	Ostrich	Alfalfa	☐	Africa	2	2	Keisha
Palom	Black Rhinoceros	Plants	☑	Africa	2	2	Keisha
Archie	Zebra	Plants	☐	South Africa	2	3	Elizabeth
Sophie	Giraffe	Leaves, Stems	☑	West Africa	2	2	Keisha
Cassandra	Emerald Tree Boa	Mice, Birds	☐	South America	3	1	Asha
Khamen	Cuban Crocodile	Fish, Small animals	☑	Cuba	3	3	Elizabeth
Pocho	Cuban Crocodile	Fish, Small animals	☑	Cuba	3	4	Ruben

Step b: Repeating groups found in Diet field separated by comma

FIGURE 9.11 Animals Table Before Normalization

Animals

AnimalName	AnimalType	Endangered	Origin	ExhibitID	TrainerID	TrainerName
Cassandra	Emerald Tree Boa	☐	South America	3	1	Asha
Anny	Mockingbird	☐	North America	1	1	Asha
Cara	Manatee	☐	Central America	1	1	Asha
Perenolde	Komodo Dragon	☑	Indonesia	1	1	Asha
Dietre	Clouded Leopard	☐	Southeast Asia	1	2	Keisha
Farunn	Grey Rhinoceros	☑	Africa	2	2	Keisha
Cassandra	Ostrich	☐	Africa	2	2	Keisha
Palom	Black Rhinoceros	☑	Africa	2	2	Keisha
Sophie	Giraffe	☑	West Africa	2	2	Keisha
Stampy	Elephant	☐	Africa	2	3	Elizabeth
Khamen	Cuban Crocodile	☑	Cuba	3	3	Elizabeth
Archie	Zebra	☐	South Africa	2	3	Elizabeth
Bronstein	Komodo Dragon	☑	Indonesia	1	3	Elizabeth
Sindall	Bengal Tiger	☑	India	1	4	Ruben
Uhkloc	Gorilla	☐	Central Africa	2	4	Ruben
Zhevra	Zebra	☐	South Africa	2	4	Ruben
Rakshiri	Bengal Tiger	☑	India	1	4	Ruben
Pocho	Cuban Crocodile	☑	Cuba	3	4	Ruben

Step c: Diet field removed from table—was previously after AnimalType field

FIGURE 9.12 Animals Table in First Normal Form

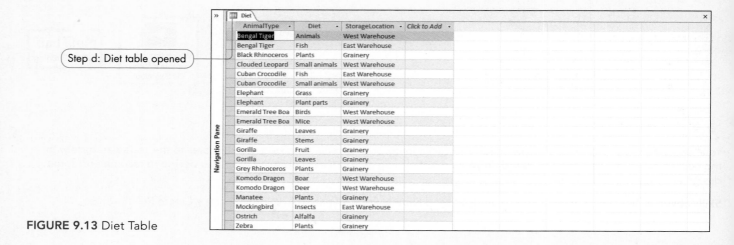

Step d: Diet table opened

FIGURE 9.13 Diet Table

a. Open *a09h1Zoo*. Save the database as **a09h1Zoo_LastFirst**.

> **TROUBLESHOOTING:** If you make any major mistakes in this exercise, you can close the *a09h1Zoo_LastFirst* file and repeat the exercise.

b. Open the Animals table in Datasheet view. Look for repeating groups in the Animals table.

Examining Figure 9.11, you can see the Diet field has multiple values separated by commas. This qualifies as a repeating group. This information needs to be added to a new table and removed from this table. For simplicity's sake, the information for animal diets has been added to a table called Diet, so you will only need to remove the Diet field from the Animal table to conform to 1NF.

c. Delete the Diet field in the Animals table. Click **Yes** when asked for confirmation.

Your Animals table should now match Figure 9.12, and the table now meets 1NF criteria. You deleted the Diet field because it contained repeating values. Repeating values violate 1NF.

d. Open the Diet table in Datasheet view.

For the purposes of this exercise, the data is already in the Diet table as shown in Figure 9.13. This table has been provided to expedite the normalization process.

STEP 2 » VERIFY SECOND NORMAL FORM

After you remove the Diet field, you will examine the Animals table to apply the second normalization rule. Refer to Figures 9.14 and 9.15 as you complete Step 2.

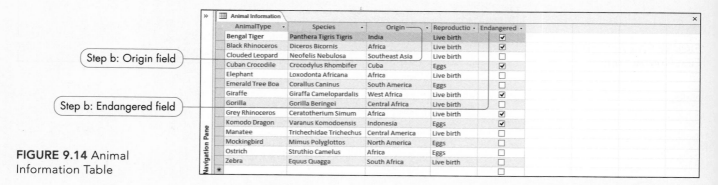

Step b: Origin field

Step b: Endangered field

FIGURE 9.14 Animal Information Table

Step d: Origin and Endangered fields removed

FIGURE 9.15 Animals Table in Second Normal Form

a. Switch to Design view, if necessary, for the Animals table. Notice this table has a composite key. Examine the Animals table to look for any non-key fields that are not functionally dependent on the entire primary key.

The primary key for this table is a composite key. Notice in Figure 9.12 that there are two animals named Cassandra, so the combination of AnimalName and AnimalType is the only way to uniquely identify any animal. As there is a composite key in this table, you must check to make sure it is in 2NF.

Origin, Diet, and Endangered are all determined by AnimalType and are attributes of a type of animal, not a specific animal. ExhibitID, TrainerID, and TrainerName are attributes of a specific animal.

b. Open the Animal Information table in Datasheet view. Note this table includes the Origin and Endangered fields as well as other fields regarding animals. See Figure 9.14.

In reality, you may have to create a separate table for this information, but this table is provided to avoid tedious data entry.

c. Close the Animal Information table.

d. Examine the Animals table. This table is not in 2NF because some fields are dependent on part of the primary key. Delete the Origin and Endangered fields, clicking **Yes** in response to the warning.

You delete these two fields because they are not functionally dependent on the entire primary key.

e. Save the Animals table. Switch to Datasheet view.

Your table should match Figure 9.15.

All the remaining fields are functionally dependent on the entire primary key. Therefore, the table now meets 2NF criteria.

STEP 3 ›› VERIFY THIRD NORMAL FORM

The final step to improve the zoo's Animals table is to apply 3NF: the value of a non-key field cannot be functionally dependent on the value of another non-key field.

a. Switch to the Datasheet view for the Animals table. Look for any non-key field values that are functionally dependent on another non-key field value.

TrainerName (non-key) is functionally dependent on TrainerID (non-key). If you know the TrainerID, you automatically know the TrainerName. For example, if you enter value 1 for the TrainerID, then the trainer's name will always be Asha. A Trainers table already exists.

b. Switch to Design view in the Animals table.

c. Delete the TrainerName field, clicking **Yes** in response to the warning.

You delete the TrainerName field because it is functionally dependent on the TrainerID field and therefore is not allowed in the Animals table. Normally, this would then require you to set up a new table, but as you already have a Trainers table, you can simply delete the TrainerName field. Note that this may not always be the case.

d. Save and close the Animals table.

The table now meets 3NF criteria.

STEP 4 ≫ CREATE RELATIONSHIPS

You will now create relationships for the tables in the database. Because there are three tables with the AnimalType field, there may be some confusion as to how to establish the proper relationships between tables to ensure proper database function.

a. Click **Relationships** in the Relationships group on the DATABASE TOOLS tab to show the Relationships window.

> **TROUBLESHOOTING:** If all the tables are not closed, you will get a warning about tables being locked. If you receive this warning, exit the Relationships window, close all open tables, and repeat step a.

b. Click **Show Table**. Add each of the four tables to the layout and close the Show Table dialog box.

c. Drag the **AnimalType field** from the Animal Information table to the AnimalType field in the Animals table.

The Animals and Animal Information tables are related by the common AnimalType field.

d. Select the **Enforce Referential Integrity** and **Cascade Update Related Fields options**. Click **Create** to create this relationship.

e. Repeat steps c and d to connect the AnimalType field in the Animal Information table to the AnimalType field in the Diet table.

You may also notice the Animals and Trainers tables are not yet linked. You are leaving these tables unlinked intentionally.

f. Save the relationships and close the Relationships window.

g. Keep the database open if you plan to continue with Hands-On Exercise 2. If not, close the database and exit Access.

Built-In Analysis and Design Tools

A supervisor asks you to create a survey in the database to store suggestions from visitors about their experience while visiting the zoo. Then another department hears about the survey and asks you to add their items to the survey. As new tables, queries, forms, and reports are added to the database, its performance may decline. This slower performance may be due to the fact that Access databases are often created by users—sales managers, accountants, scientists, and production managers—who lack formal training about how to design an Access database. For example, a scientist who creates a database with 10 tables might not understand how to join the tables to produce efficient results.

Even if a database is in 3NF, deficiencies that cause the database to perform poorly may exist. For example, even though the rules of normalization dictate how to design tables, setting relationships may be applied incorrectly. This affects performance. Some IT administrators may try to compensate for a poorly designed database by migrating to an enterprise-level Database Management System (DBMS), such as Microsoft SQL Server or Oracle.

Moving to a DBMS may have a positive net effect on the speed of processing; however, the design problems that existed in Access will still exist. It is best to resolve the design issues first (in Access) and then evaluate whether Access can handle the processing demands of the database. If it can, other reasons to use Access rather than move to an enterprise-level DBMS may exist. These reasons include wizards to help create tables, forms, and reports and a graphical user interface (GUI) that is intuitive to Access users. Also, Access can run on a desktop computer and does not require its own dedicated server as enterprise-level DBMS programs do. Another reason is cost. Microsoft SQL Server and Oracle are much more expensive than Access. If you recommend migrating to one of those solutions, it is best to be sure it is worth the investment.

Sometimes, you can fix problems using the built-in Access tools. For example, you can split an Access database into two database files. If a number of users are accessing the same database, splitting the database may improve performance. One file would contain all the tables and reside on a server, while the other would reside with each user. Users could create their own queries, forms, and reports on their local machines but still access the same data everyone else is using. This could save your company money, which is always a plus.

Access provides three useful tools that database administrators can use to improve the performance of a database—the Database Documenter tool, the Performance Analyzer tool (found as the Analyze Performance icon), and the Table Analyzer tool (found as the Analyze Table icon). In this section, you will learn how to use these three tools, which can be found in the Analyze group on the Database Tools tab, as shown in Figure 9.16. Also in this section, you will learn how to split an Access database into two databases using the Database Splitter tool. The Database Splitter tool is shown in Figure 9.16 on the Database Tools tab, in the Move Data group, with the name Access Database.

Database Splitter tool

Database analysis tools

FIGURE 9.16 Database Analysis Tools

Using the Database Documenter Tool

STEP 1 ≫   The **Database Documenter** creates a report that contains detailed information for each selected object. When you run the Database Documenter, you can specify which object group you want to see and which specific objects within the selected group you want to document. The Documenter creates a report showing the field names, data types, properties, indexes, and permissions for each of the selected tables. If you run the Documenter for the entire zoo database, the report generated is between 15 and 20 pages long. In other words, the important information can get lost, so it is important to choose only the information you want to see. A common use for the Database Documenter is to verify and update the properties of one object using a printout of the properties of another similar object.

Start the Database Documenter

To use the Database Documenter, click Database Documenter in the Analyze group on the Database Tools tab. The Documenter dialog box opens so that you can select objects to include in the report (see Figure 9.17). Each tab in the Documenter dialog box represents a database object that can be documented. After you select the objects you want to analyze, click OK to generate the report.

FIGURE 9.17 Database Documenter Dialog Box

The Documenter creates a report that contains detailed information about the tables and other selected objects in your database; the report opens in Print Preview mode, as shown in Figure 9.18. This shows a large amount of detail about the table and fields, likely more than you need for the type of analysis you are performing. Access enables you to specify which items to include and which to skip. To select the items to be included, click Options, as shown in Figure 9.17. Once you click Options, the Print Table Definition dialog box displays; using the options available, specify which items you want to see on the report. For example, if you want to minimize the information on the report, uncheck all the *Include for Table* items, select the second option in the *Include for Fields* section, and then select nothing in the *Include for Indexes* section (see Figure 9.19). The result is a report that is 4 or 5 pages long, as compared to 20 pages when all the items were checked.

FIGURE 9.18 Database Documenter Report

Although the Documenter starts in Print Preview mode, also notice on the Print Preview tab options to save the report in a number of formats, including as a PDF or XPS file. This is especially useful if you need to share the results of a report with someone else electronically. See Table 9.2 for more details about the Database Documenter options.

Table detail level

Field detail level

Index detail level

FIGURE 9.19 Print Table Definition Dialog Box

TABLE 9.2 Database Documenter Options	
Option	**Function**
Include for Table: Properties	Options for table properties, including coloring, number of records, and date of last update.
Include for Table: Relationships	Documents table relationships, including which fields are common between tables and type of relationship, such as one to many.
Include for Table: Permissions by Users and Group	Shows permissions for the tables based on users and/or groups. If your database does not have user-based permissions, this is not worth leaving checked.
Include for Fields: Nothing	Includes no detail about the fields in the selected tables.
Include for Fields: Names, Data Types, and Sizes	Includes field names, data types and field sizes for each field in the selected tables.
Include for Fields: Names, Data Types, Sizes, and Properties	Includes field names, data type, and field size for each field in the selected tables and options such as whether a zero-length value (or null value) is allowed, column width, and text alignment. This makes the report much longer.
Include for Indexes: Nothing	Includes no detail about the indexes in the selected tables.
Include for Indexes: Names and Fields	Includes the names of all indexes and the fields with which they are associated.
Include for Indexes: Names, Fields, and Properties	Includes the names of all indexes, the fields they are associated with, and the index properties, including the number of distinct index values and whether the index is required and must be unique. This makes the report much longer.

Using the Performance Analyzer Tool

STEP 2》 The Database Documenter is useful for listing the properties of each object in a database. However, the Documenter does not identify any flaws in the design of the database. To evaluate the design of the database, you can use the Performance Analyzer. The **Performance Analyzer** evaluates a database and makes recommendations for optimizing the database. Figure 9.20 shows the Performance Analyzer dialog box, where you can select what you would like to analyze.

All Object Types tab

All objects are selected

FIGURE 9.20 Performance Analyzer Dialog Box

The Performance Analyzer lists three kinds of analysis results—recommendations, suggestions, and ideas (see Figure 9.21). When you click an item in the Analysis Results list, information about the proposed optimization is displayed in the Analysis Notes box. Suggestion optimizations have potential trade-offs that you should consider before performing them. To view a description of the trade-offs, click a suggestion in the list and read the information in the Analysis Notes box. Access can perform recommendations and suggestions automatically for you; idea optimizations must be performed manually by you.

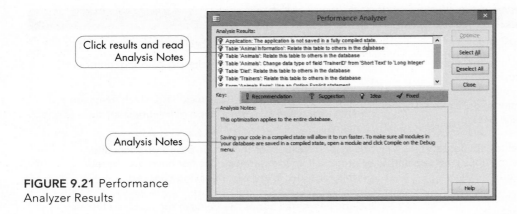

Click results and read Analysis Notes

Analysis Notes

FIGURE 9.21 Performance Analyzer Results

Start the Performance Analyzer

To launch the Performance Analyzer, click Analyze Performance in the Analyze group on the Database Tools tab (refer to Figure 9.16) to display the Performance Analyzer dialog box shown in Figure 9.20. The Tables tab is selected by default. There are tabs for Queries, Forms, Reports, Macros, Modules, Current Database, and All Object Types. Often, the tables are the cause of slowdowns in databases, so the Tables tab is usually the first place to start analyzing performance. Performing searches using queries on poorly designed tables can result in performance issues. The Performance Analyzer attempts to find these issues.

If users inform you that the database generally runs slowly (e.g., reports take a long time to complete), you might choose to analyze the All Object Types tab in an attempt to improve performance. It is possible that forms and reports can have issues as well.

After you select objects for analysis and click OK in the Performance Analyzer dialog box, the dialog box displays an Analysis Notes box, as shown in Figure 9.21. The analysis results in three different types of potential solutions. An Analysis Note provides a brief description of a potential problem and its possible solution. Table 9.3 shows more detail about the three result types you may see if you run the Performance Analyzer.

TABLE 9.3	Performance Analyzer Result Types
Recommendation	Read the Analysis Notes, click the specific recommendation, and then click Optimize. The item's icon changes to Fixed after optimization.
Suggestion	Read the Analysis Notes, click the specific suggestion, and then click Optimize. The item's icon changes to Fixed after optimization.
Idea	Read the Analysis Notes and determine how you will manually implement this idea into your database. Access does not optimize ideas, as these materially change the database design. These require manual changes.

You optimize the database by clicking the result items and then clicking Optimize after you read the Analysis Notes. On occasion, you will find that an optimization results in a trade-off that affects your database in ways you might not consider. For example, changing an existing field named TrainerID with a data type of Short Text to a data type of Long Integer may erase existing data that does not fit the new data type. You may have TrainerIDs that are nonnumeric, and these would be erased from the database. However, changing data types as recommended does improve performance.

Also note that the Performance Analyzer does not catch all problems. Though a useful tool, the Performance Analyzer may miss some issues, so think of this tool as a supplement to your own analysis, not a replacement for it.

TIP | Back Up Database Before Optimizing It

Before optimizing your database by using the recommendations, suggestions, and ideas of the Performance Analyzer, it is best to back up your database. That way, you can revert back to the copy if the optimization yields unexpected results. It is also a good practice to read the Analysis Notes before executing any of the analysis recommendations or suggestions.

Add an Index

An item that appears frequently in the Analysis Notes box is *Add an index*. This is a simple change to a field (or fields) in a table that could improve performance when implemented. An **index** reduces the time it takes to run queries and reports. It is similar to the index in the back of this textbook. Generally, you should add an index to any field that will be searched often. For example, in a college database, a student's name would likely be indexed, but not a phone number. However, in a cell phone service provider's database, a phone number would probably be indexed because customer service representatives might use it to find a customer.

On one hand, for reports and queries with a large record source, adding an index can save substantial time. On the other hand, adding more indexes to a table can decrease database performance because each time you add a new record to a database the index must be sorted. In a large database, this may result in a longer wait time before a record is saved. A database of the size of the zoo database may not need an index, but in a larger project this is a common suggestion.

Using the Table Analyzer Tool

STEP 3 ⟫ The **Table Analyzer** analyzes the tables in a database and normalizes them for you. Normalizing an existing table involves splitting a table into smaller, related tables, with each table focused on a single topic of information, as you did in the first section of this chapter.

As stated earlier, a normalized database has a number of advantages over an unnormalized one. First, updating information is faster and easier because fewer data changes are required.

Second, only the minimum information is stored; therefore, the database is smaller. Finally, a normalized database holds more reliable data because data is stored in only one place.

Although the Table Analyzer helps you create a normalized database, you may want to modify the decisions the Table Analyzer makes if you have database design experience. You can rename tables, split tables, rearrange fields in tables, and create relationships between tables. You can modify Table Analyzer decisions during every step of the normalization process.

Start the Table Analyzer

To start the Table Analyzer, click Analyze Table in the Analyze group on the Database Tools tab. Step one of the Table Analyzer Wizard opens with an explanation of the pitfalls of duplicating information. The output from this process should be tables that pass through normalization, resulting in the creation of additional tables in your database. The Table Analyzer Wizard explains problems for which it will search, describes how it will attempt to fix problems it identifies, and asks you to identify a table for analysis. You can take some control of the process by deciding which fields should be included in new tables created by the Table Analyzer Wizard, or you can choose to let the wizard decide on your behalf.

You could advance through the entire Table Analyzer Wizard accepting the defaults, but this is uncommon. The wizard will offer suggestions, but it is best to think about whether they make sense in your database. It is best to run the Table Analyzer before you attempt any normalization. If you have already created tables and have an incomplete normalization, you may not get a solid recommendation.

Step Through the Table Analyzer Wizard

If you choose to let the Table Analyzer Wizard normalize the tables in your database, the Table Analyzer Wizard runs through the following process:

Step 1. The Table Analyzer Wizard asks you to choose a table (see Figure 9.22). The wizard then breaks the table into a set of smaller tables. Each of these smaller tables contains the minimum set of information that should be grouped together.

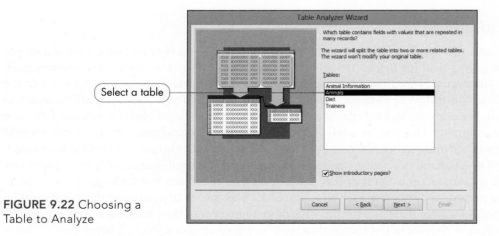

FIGURE 9.22 Choosing a Table to Analyze

Step 2. You can direct the wizard to decide what fields go in what tables, as shown in Figure 9.23. The other option is for you to decide how to divide the table into smaller tables. Access makes a recommendation, but if you prefer, you can do the breakdown yourself.

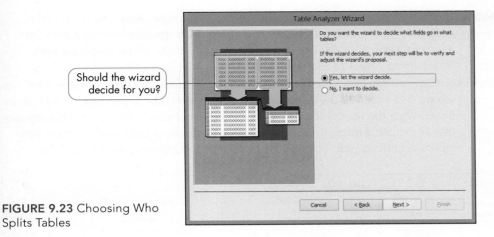

FIGURE 9.23 Choosing Who Splits Tables

Should the wizard decide for you?

Step 3. If you tell the wizard to decide for you, the wizard divides the table and creates relationships that control how the new tables are linked, as shown in Figure 9.24. These relationships enforce referential integrity (data consistency) with cascading updates. The wizard does not automatically add cascading deletes to the relationships because of the risk that you may accidentally delete large portions of data. You can rename the tables in this step. If you prefer to set the cascading deletes option, you must do so yourself.

Rename proposed tables from default names

Fields can be dragged from table to table

FIGURE 9.24 Confirming Relationships and Table Names

Step 4. The wizard proposes tables and fields, and asks you to confirm the primary keys in each table, as shown in Figure 9.25.

Generate a primary key

Change primary key to selected field

Primary keys are identified

FIGURE 9.25 Confirming Primary Keys

Step 5. In the next step, the wizard searches the new tables for inconsistent data (for example, the same customer with two different phone numbers) and presents a list of records that you can change or accept. If there are no problems with inconsistent data, this step does not appear.

Step 6. Finally, you can choose to create a query that simulates the original table. The wizard first backs up the original table and renames it by appending "_OLD" to its name. Then the wizard creates a query using the original table name. This ensures that any existing forms or reports based on the original table work with the new table structure as well. The results of the wizard might resemble Figure 9.26.

AnimalName	AnimalType	Origin	Endangered	ExhibitID	Lookup to N	ID	Click to Add
Anny	Mockingbird	North America	0	1	1, Asha	1	
Archie	Zebra	South Africa	0	2	3, Elizabeth	2	
Bronstein	Komodo Drago	Indonesia	-1	1	3, Elizabeth	3	
Cara	Manatee	Central Americ	0	1	1, Asha	4	
Cassandra	Emerald Tree E	South America	0	3	1, Asha	5	
Cassandra	Ostrich	Africa	0	2	2, Keisha	6	
Dietre	Clouded Leopa	Southeast Asia	0	1	2, Keisha	7	
Farunn	White Rhinoce	Africa	-1	2	2, Keisha	8	
Khamen	Cuban Crocodil	Cuba	-1	3	3, Elizabeth	9	
Palom	Black Rhinocer	Africa	-1	2	2, Keisha	10	
Perenolde	Komodo Drago	Indonesia	-1	1	1, Asha	11	
Pocho	Cuban Crocodil	Cuba	-1	3	4, Ruben	12	
Rakshiri	Bengal Tiger	India	-1	1	4, Ruben	13	
Sindall	Bengal Tiger	India	-1	1	4, Ruben	14	
Sophie	Giraffe	West Africa	-1	2	2, Keisha	15	
Stampy	Elephant	Africa	0	2	3, Elizabeth	16	
Uhkloc	Gorilla	Central Africa	0	2	4, Ruben	17	
Zhevra	Zebra	South Africa	0	2	4, Ruben	18	

All Access Ob... » — Tables: Animal Information, Animals_OLD, Diet, New Animals, New Trainers, Trainers. Queries: Animals. Forms: Animals Form, Trainers Form. Reports: Metropolitan Zoo Trainers.

FIGURE 9.26 New Animals Table

As you can see from Figure 9.27, the underlying tables may look messier than the ones you created through normalization. However, if you do not know how to perform normalization, or if the database is straightforward, the analyzer tool would be preferable. Either way, it is important to check the tables Access recommends and not just accept them without viewing.

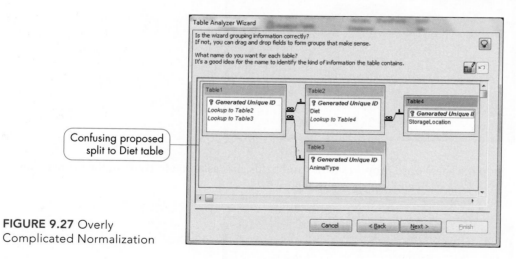

Confusing proposed split to Diet table

FIGURE 9.27 Overly Complicated Normalization

After the Table Analyzer Wizard is finished, examine the new table structure. Click the Database Tools tab and click Relationships in the Relationships group. From there, you can review and modify the table relationships as needed.

Using the Database Splitter Tool

STEP 4 »
A single-file Access database may work fine for a small office with a handful of users. However, when the number of users grows beyond that, you can use the **Database Splitter** tool, which enables you to split a database into two files: a back-end and a front-end database. A **back-end database** contains the tables of the database. A **front-end database** contains the queries, forms, and reports of the database. The two databases are connected, with the forms, queries, and

reports stored in the front-end database and the tables stored in the back-end database. You could then have multiple front-end databases using one back-end database.

The main reason to split an Access database is to improve development and maintenance. When a developer works with a single-file Access database, all users must exit the database while the developer makes changes. This can be inefficient for the developer and disruptive for the users. The front end of a split database can be modified while users continue to work. Once the changes to the front end are completed, the new file is distributed to the users (to replace the existing front-end database file).

This approach offers other advantages as well. Splitting the database may improve the speed at which the database processes data and returns results. A report that takes two minutes to display in a single-file database may take only one minute in a split database. There are many other reasons to support splitting a database into two files, as outlined in Table 9.4. The back-end database is typically placed on a server, and a front-end database is placed on each individual user's computer. The front-end database contains links to the tables in the back end.

TABLE 9.4	Reasons to Split an Access Database into Two Files
Improved Performance	The performance of the database usually improves because only the data is sent across the network—not the queries, forms, reports, macros, and modules.
Greater Data Availability	When only the data is sent across the network, database edits are completed more quickly, which makes the data available quicker.
Enhanced Security	If you store the back-end database on a server, you can use the server's security features to help protect your data. Because users access the back-end database by using linked tables, it is less likely that intruders can obtain unauthorized access to the data.
Improved Reliability	If a user encounters a problem and the database closes unexpectedly, any database file corruption is usually limited to the front-end database. Because the user only accesses data in the back-end database by using linked tables, the back-end database file is much less likely to become corrupted. In addition, servers are generally backed up in a business environment; a client machine may not be.
Flexible Development Environment	Because each user works with a separate copy of the front-end database, each user can independently develop queries, forms, reports, and other database objects without affecting other users. Also, developers can distribute an updated version of the front-end database without affecting the data in the back-end database.

Start the Database Splitter

The Database Splitter is not identified by name on the Access Ribbon. To start the Database Splitter, click the Database Tools tab and click Access Database in the Move Data group. The first screen explains what the Database Splitter Wizard does and gives a brief summary of the benefits of a split database. The Database Splitter starts as shown in Figure 9.28.

Split Database

FIGURE 9.28 Database Splitter Wizard

In the next step, the wizard asks you to name the new back-end database. Designate the database name and location for the back-end database or just accept the default file name that Access suggests—the original name plus the suffix "be" for "back-end" (see Figure 9.29).

Work with the Front-End Database

After Access creates the back end, the front-end database remains open. The tables that existed in the original database have been replaced with linked tables with the same table names. Linked tables have an arrow icon to indicate they are linked to another Access database (see Figure 9.30). When you point to a table name, a ScreenTip shows the path to the physical table to which your front-end database is linked. As you add data to the linked tables using the front-end database, the data becomes available to other users of the back-end tables.

Note that if you use the front-end database on a different machine, or if you move the files into a different folder, you may get an error stating the file path is not valid. The back-end database is generally stored on a networked server, so this is not an issue in the real world unless the file is moved on the server.

Create Back-end Database dialog box

Name has _be appended to database name by default

FIGURE 9.29 Naming the Back-End Database

Arrow icons represent linked tables

FIGURE 9.30 Linked Tables

In Hands-On Exercise 2, you will use the built-in analysis and design tools to analyze a database. You will also split a database into a front end and a back end.

Quick Concepts

1. Describe three reasons to use the Database Documenter tool. ***p. 531***

2. Define the three possible analyzer result types the Performance Analyzer tool might propose. ***p. 534***

3. How does the Table Analyzer tool make you more productive? ***p. 535***

4. Why would a database administrator choose to split a database? ***p. 538***

Hands-On Exercise

2 Built-In Analysis and Design Tools

The Metropolitan Zoo database has been working well, but you decide to examine the database to see if more improvements can be made. You use the built-in tools to analyze the database; you also decide to split the database into two files. Before you begin, you make a copy of the database so the original format will be safe in case you make a mistake.

Skills covered: Use the Database Documenter Tool • Use the Performance Analyzer Tool • Use the Table Analyzer Tool • Use the Database Splitter Tool

STEP 1 >> USE THE DATABASE DOCUMENTER TOOL

You will create a report with the Database Documenter to show information on relationships. You will save this report as a PDF file. Refer to Figure 9.31 and Figure 9.32 as you complete Step 1.

Step d: Correct options for exercise

FIGURE 9.31 Database Splitter Options

Step e: Ensure *Save as type* is PDF

FIGURE 9.32 Saving Report as PDF

a. Open *a09h1Zoo_LastFirst* if you closed it at the end of Hands-On Exercise 1. Save the database as **a09h2Zoo_LastFirst**, changing *h1* to *h2*. Click **Save**.

b. Click **Database Documenter** in the Analyze group on the DATABASE TOOLS tab. Click the **All Objects Types tab**.

c. Click **Select All** on the All Object Types tab and click **Options**.

d. Check the **Relationships box** in the *Include for Table* section. Uncheck checkboxes for *Properties* and *Permission by User and Group*, if necessary. Click **Nothing** in the *Include for Fields* section and click **Nothing** in the *Include for Indexes* section. Your dialog box should resemble Figure 9.31. Click **OK**. Click **OK** to run the report.

You have changed the options so only the required information is present in the report.

e. Select **PDF or XPS** in the Data group on the PRINT PREVIEW tab. Select **PDF** as the option for *Save as type* and type **a09h2ZooDocumenter_LastFirst** for the file name. Click **Publish** to save the file, as shown in Figure 9.32.

This enables you to save the report.

> **TROUBLESHOOTING:** After saving the report, it may open in Adobe Reader or Adobe Acrobat. If this happens, close the program and return to Access.

f. Click **Close** on the next screen, which asks you if you want to save the steps.

g. Click **Close Print Preview** in the Close Preview group to close the report.

STEP 2 ≫ USE THE PERFORMANCE ANALYZER TOOL

To evaluate the performance of the zoo database, you decide to run the Performance Analyzer tool. You run the analyzer and then review the recommendations, suggestions, and ideas in the results. You will implement some of the results. Refer to Figure 9.33 as you complete Step 2.

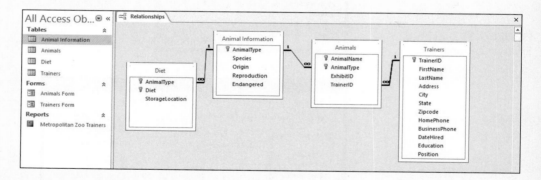

FIGURE 9.33 Final Relationships for Zoo Database

a. Click the **DATABASE TOOLS tab** and click **Analyze Performance** in the Analyze group.

b. Click the **All Object Types tab**, click **Select All**, and then click **OK** to start the Performance Analyzer.

The results window displays ideas to improve the zoo database.

c. Review the results of the Performance Analyzer and take note of the idea regarding relating Trainers to another table. Click **Close** to close the Performance Analyzer dialog box.

You decide to establish relationships between the Trainers and Animals tables.

d. Click **Relationships** in the Relationships group on the DATABASE TOOLS tab and create a relationship between the Trainers and Animals tables, using the common field TrainerID. Ensure the Enforce Referential Integrity and Cascade Update Related Fields options are set.

Your relationships should now match Figure 9.33. The tables may appear in a different order or of a different height in your database.

e. Save and close the Relationships window.

f. Repeat the procedure in steps a and b above to run the Performance Analyzer again and see if the results are different this time.

The idea to relate tables is gone.

g. Close the Performance Analyzer dialog box.

STEP 3 » USE THE TABLE ANALYZER TOOL

You decide to test the design of the tables in the zoo database. To do this, you will open an older version of the database, run the Table Analyzer, and then compare the results to the current database. Refer to Figure 9.34 as you complete Step 3.

FIGURE 9.34 Relationship Suggested by Performance Analyzer

a. Open *a09h2ZooAnalyzer*. Save the database as **a09h2ZooAnalyzer_LastFirst**.

b. Click the **DATABASE TOOLS tab** and click **Analyze Table** in the Analyze group.

The Table Analyzer Wizard starts.

c. Click **Next** twice.

Access shows a screen asking you to select tables.

d. Select the **ZooAnimals table**. Click **Next** twice.

The ZooAnimals table has been split into three tables.

e. Click the **Rename Table icon**, type **Animals** as the name of Table1, and then click **OK**. Select **Table2** and use the same steps to rename Table2 **Animal Information**. Select **Table3** and rename it **Trainers**. Click **Next**.

f. Click the **AnimalID field** in the Animals table and click the **Set Unique Identifier icon** to set the primary key. Click the **AnimalType field** in the Animal Information table and use the same process to set the primary key. Click **Next**.

Note that Access correctly identified the primary key for the Trainers table, so there is no need to set that manually.

g. Select the **No, don't create the query option** and click **Finish**. Click **OK** in response to the warning message.

This normalization is similar to the one you did in Hands-On Exercise 1, but it did not fix the repeating groups issue in the Diet field. However, if you had no understanding of normalization, using the Table Analyzer helps achieve the goal of reducing data redundancies.

h. Close the database.

i. Submit based on your instructor's directions.

You decide to split the zoo database to see if the performance of the database improves. You use the Database Splitter to divide the database into a front-end and a back-end file.

a. Open *a09h2Zoo_LastFirst*. Save the database as **a09h2ZooSplit_LastFirst**.

The new database is displayed.

b. Click the **DATABASE TOOLS tab** and click **Access Database** in the Move Data group.

The Database Splitter Wizard starts.

c. Click **Split Database**. Accept *a09h2ZooSplit_LastFirst_be* as the file name and click **Split**.

The Database Splitter splits the database into two files.

d. Click **OK**.

The database is split successfully.

e. Open the tables and the other objects to verify the database is working properly.

f. Close the database. Close Access.

g. Submit based on your instructor's directions.

Database Security

Computer security can be defined as the protection of data from unauthorized access, change, or destruction and can be divided into two general categories: physical security and logical security. Physical security involves protecting assets you can touch, such as computers, storage devices, backup tapes, and the office safe. Logical security protects the information that resides on the physical devices, including databases and other computer software. Security measures need to be taken to protect your assets against both physical and logical threats.

Database security is a specialty within computer security that protects a database application from unintended use. Unintended use includes unauthorized viewing of data, unauthorized copying and selling of data, malicious attacks, destruction of data by employees, and inadvertent mistakes made by employees.

In this section, you will learn several techniques available in Access to keep your database application safe. These techniques include:

- Creating a navigation form.
- Encrypting and password protecting a database.
- Digitally signing and publishing the database.
- Saving a database as an ACCDE file.

Creating a Menu System

Most database users prefer a menu system for opening and closing forms and reports, especially forms and reports that are used every day. This can be accomplished using a *navigation form*, which is a tabbed menu system that ties the objects in the database together so that the database is easy to use. The interface displays a menu enabling a nontechnical person to open the various objects within the database and to move easily from one object to another. The form is quite powerful, but it is also easy to create. When you create a navigation form, you simply drag and drop forms and reports onto tabs. An added benefit of a navigation form is that it can be easily converted to a Web form if the Access database is deployed on a company intranet or on the Internet. Navigation forms have the look and feel of a web form.

TIP | Switchboards: Another Menu System

Navigation forms were introduced in Access 2010. Before that point, users would use a switchboard to do what the navigation form accomplishes. If you are using a database that is more established, you may find a switchboard as the primary method of interacting with the database rather than a navigation form.

Microsoft removed the Switchboard Manager from the Ribbon when it introduced navigation forms. If you ever need to create or manage a switchboard, follow these steps to display the Switchboard Manager:

1. Click the FILE tab and click Options.
2. Click Customize Ribbon.
3. Select All Commands from the *Choose commands from* option. See Figure 9.35.
4. Scroll down until you see Switchboard Manager.
5. Select Switchboard Manager.
6. On the right, expand the Database Tools group.
7. Click Database Tools.
8. Click New Group.
9. Rename *New Group* as Switchboard.
10. Click Switchboard (Custom).
11. Click Add. The Switchboard Manager is added to the Ribbon as shown in Figure 9.36.

FIGURE 9.35 Adding Switchboard Manager to Ribbon

- Select All Commands
- Customize Ribbon
- Select Switchboard Manager and click Add
- Find Switchboard Manager
- Add a new group

- Switchboard Manager

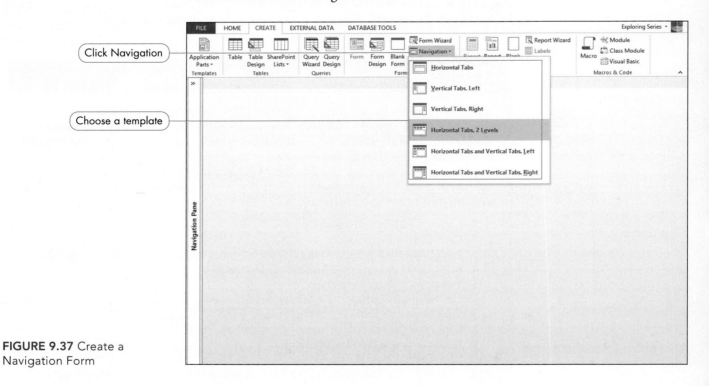

FIGURE 9.36 Switchboard Manager Added to Ribbon

To create a navigation form, click the Create tab and click Navigation in the Forms group. Select one of the six preset templates (as shown in Figure 9.37) and Access creates the basic structure of the navigation form.

- Click Navigation
- Choose a template

FIGURE 9.37 Create a Navigation Form

Create a Navigation Form

For example, choose the first template on the list, Horizontal Tabs, and Access creates a navigation form with [Add New] at the top-left corner of the page. Drag an object from the Navigation Pane onto [Add New], and Access displays the object in the main viewing area, as shown in Figure 9.38. Drag the next object from the Navigation Pane onto [Add New] and Access displays that object. Continue adding the remainder of the objects you want on the navigation form. Switch to Form view and click each tab to view and test each object (see Figure 9.38). Save and close the form.

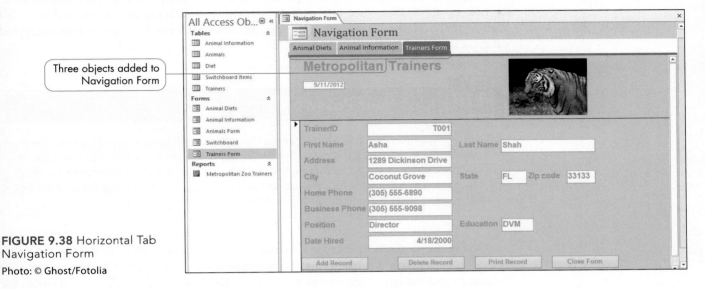

FIGURE 9.38 Horizontal Tab Navigation Form

Photo: © Ghost/Fotolia

Start a Navigation Form Automatically

To start the navigation form automatically when the database starts, click the File tab and click Options. Click Current Database and select the name of the navigation form using the Display Form option, as shown in Figure 9.39. Click OK to close the Access Options window.

Note that any form, not only a navigation form, can be set to display automatically. Also note that this applies to the current database, so each database can have different forms set to launch on startup.

FIGURE 9.39 Launching a Form When Database Opens

Encrypting and Password Protecting
a Database

Access 2013 incorporates encryption methods to help keep your databases secure. *Encryption* is the process of altering digital information using an algorithm to make it unreadable to anyone except those who possess the key (password). As the point of encryption is to protect your data, you need to choose a password when setting up encryption. Encrypting a database makes its contents unreadable to other programs and is especially useful if you intend to distribute your database via e-mail or store your database on removable media such as a USB flash drive. Because millions of secret codes (or passwords) can be generated, an encrypted database is difficult to break.

TIP Lost Your Password?

There are a number of software applications that attempt to find a password for a database. However, the more secure the password, the longer it takes to recover. It may take days or weeks for a password to be recovered, but that is better than losing data permanently. Also keep in mind that the same tool you can use to recover a legitimately lost password can be used by anyone, so a strong password helps prevent unauthorized access.

One of the methods to encrypt a database is to assign a password to the file. Adding a password to an Access database prevents unauthorized access to the file. Passwords typically include a combination of letters and numbers. A good password should be impossible for unauthorized users to guess. For example, use at least eight characters that combine uppercase and lowercase letters, numbers, and symbols to make the password more difficult for others to guess. An example of a weak password is Eric1999 (the author's name and year of graduation). A stronger password is Exp2013@r$. Be sure to record the passwords you assign to your database.

TIP Password Security

The purpose of the password is to keep unauthorized users from using the database. If you create a password that uses letters, numbers, and symbols, make sure your own password does not keep you from accessing your own data!

Writing down the password on a sticky note and leaving it on your monitor is not a good choice for protecting a truly secure password. If you write down your passwords, store them in a secure location such as a locked file cabinet or a safe.

You can download or purchase a client tool to manage your passwords or use a secure online password manager. Of course, tools like that require a password, so make sure you do not forget the password that protects your passwords.

Adding a password and encryption to a database is easily done, but it requires that the database be opened in exclusive mode. *Open Exclusive* mode guarantees that you are the only one currently using the database. To open a database with exclusive access, click the File tab, click Open, click Computer, and then click Browse to display the Open dialog box. Locate the database you want to open, click the Open arrow at the bottom of the dialog box, and then select Open Exclusive from the list (see Figure 9.40).

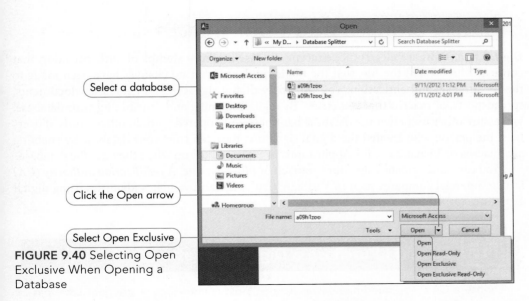

Select a database

Click the Open arrow

Select Open Exclusive

FIGURE 9.40 Selecting Open Exclusive When Opening a Database

After opening a database in exclusive mode, you are ready to assign a password. To accomplish this, click the File tab, click Info, and then click *Encrypt with Password*, as shown in Figure 9.41. The Set Database Password dialog box opens so that you can enter and verify a password. The database is encrypted when you click OK in the Set Database Password dialog box. Once you have set the password, close the database and then open it again without exclusive access. When you open the database, the Password Required dialog box appears. You must type the correct password and click OK to open the database.

Encrypt with Password

FIGURE 9.41 Adding Password to Encrypt Database

Removing a Password

If you want to remove a password, you must open the database using the Open Exclusive option. Click the File tab, click Info, and then click Decrypt Database. In the Unset Database Password dialog box, type the password and click OK. The database password has been removed. You need the database password to do this, of course.

Digitally Signing and Publishing a Database

STEP 3 ❯❯ *Digital signatures* are electronic, encryption-based, secure stamps of authentication that confirm who created the file, that the file is valid, and that no changes have been made to the file after its authentication. You can apply digital signatures to databases, documents, spreadsheets, or macros that you create. By digitally signing and distributing your database, you assure other users that the database has not been tampered with. In other words, if users trust the person who created the digital signature, they can trust your database by enabling any macros or Visual Basic for Applications (VBA) code to run when they use the database.

You can either create a signature yourself or purchase one. A *certification authority (CA)* is a commercial company, such as VeriSign, that issues and validates identities using digital signatures for a fee.

TIP Should I Purchase a Digital Signature?

Choose a CA if you need high-level security. Most countries have stringent laws that regulate CAs so that purchasers can be sure that their digital signatures are valid. Many software manufacturers purchase digital signatures, so when you install their software, you are shown the name of the software publisher. As only the publisher can digitally sign the software, the signature enables users to trust the source of software.

Digital signatures are also used in banking and other fields. If you have a need to assure others that you are the sender of a file and it has not been tampered with, a digital certificate might be a better choice than self-certification. Having an independent group verifying your identity and preventing digital forgeries may be worth the cost.

Use the SelfCert Tool

If you do not have a security certificate from a commercial vendor, you can create one by using the SelfCert tool (included with Microsoft Office).

To create a self-signed certificate, complete the following:

1. From the Start screen, type *Digital Certificate for VBA Projects*. Click the tool to start it.
2. Type a name for the new certificate into the *Your certificate's name* box.
3. Click OK twice.

If the Digital Certificate for VBA Projects tool does not appear on the Start screen, it is possible it was not installed to the Start screen. If not, use File Explorer to navigate to the following location: C:\Program Files\Microsoft Office\Office15. In that folder, double-click SelfCert.exe and complete steps 2 and 3 above.

You can attach your certificate to a database immediately before you distribute it to your users. Keep in mind that a digital signature does not prove that you own the database. By use of a timestamp, it can prove that you were the last person to modify it. You provide the timestamp information to others when you distribute, or publish, your database. By examining the timestamp on your database, you can prove that it has or has not been modified since you applied your signature. A *timestamp* is a combination of the date and time that is encrypted as part of the digital signature. For a timestamp to be truly valid to others, it must be passed through a timestamping service provider. Again, this can be a commercial entity or a server located on your network. Further discussion of this process is outside the scope of this textbook.

Apply a Digital Signature

You can digitally sign and publish your database simultaneously from within Access 2013. To digitally sign and publish your database, click the File tab, click Save As, and then double-click *Package and Sign*. If the Select Certificate dialog box opens, select an existing certificate and click OK. The database is packaged and converted to the .accdc file format and digitally signed with your certificate.

Saving a Database as an ACCDE File

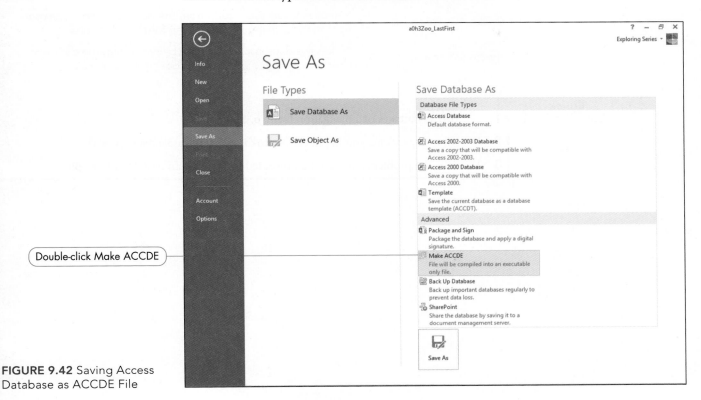

STEP 4 » Access 2013 enables the use of the file extension .accde. Creating an *Access Database Executable (ACCDE)* file will remove all VBA source code, prohibit users from making design and name changes to forms or reports within the database, and prohibit users from creating new forms and reports. Users can execute the VBA code, but they cannot modify it. The ACCDE file type was first introduced in Access 2007.

FIGURE 9.42 Saving Access Database as ACCDE File

Create an ACCDE File

You can create a database with the .accde file extension within Access 2013. This is a simple process that saves your existing database with the new file extension, making a copy of the last saved edition of your database. To create an ACCDE file, click the File tab, click Save As, and then double-click Make ACCDE (see Figure 9.42). The Save As dialog box opens. The *File name* box displays the same main name as the original database with the .accde extension. The *Save as type* box displays *ACCDE File (*.accde)*. Click Save to save the database with the .accde file format. Note you cannot create an ACCDE file unless you have clicked the Enable Content button. As ACCDE files can cause potentially dangerous code to be executed, you first need to assure Access the file is trustworthy.

If you do not have exclusive use of the database before you convert the database to the .accde file format, you receive a message telling you that another user has the database open. The process stops.

Keep the Original Database File Safe

When the database has been converted to .accde, it cannot be converted back to its source format (.accdb). Therefore, keep your original database—the database as it existed when it was converted to the .accde file format—in a safe place. This backup is needed if one or more of its objects (forms, reports, or VBA code) needs to be changed. Without your original database, you would not be able to make these changes. You would be forced to create the database again. Users would not be able to alter the design of forms and reports, nor would they be able to change the VBA code.

In Hands-On Exercise 3, you will practice all of the security measures discussed in this section. Table 9.5 recaps the highlights from this section.

TABLE 9.5	Security Measures and Their Intended Results
Digital Signature	Provides proof to others of when you last modified the database. Not very secure without password protection.
Make ACCDE	Removes Visual Basic code from the database and stops users from making changes to database forms and reports.
Password Protect	Makes the database unreadable by encrypting the database. Users must enter a password to open the database.

Quick Concepts

1. List two advantages of a navigation form. *p. 545*

2. Describe two reasons you might choose to digitally sign a database. *p. 550*

3. Describe the problems that can be prevented by creating an ACCDE file. *p. 551*

Hands-On Exercise

3 Database Security

Management has asked you for a plan to protect the database from accidental deletes, intrusions, and theft. You decide to put several safety and security measures into action, including the addition of a password to protect against unauthorized use of the database.

Skills covered: Create a Menu System • Encrypt and Password-Protect a Database • Digitally Sign and Publish a Database • Save a Database as an ACCDE File

STEP 1 >> CREATE A MENU SYSTEM

You decide to create a navigation form to make it easier to open the daily forms and reports. You ask the employees which objects they use the most, and then add them to the navigation form. You decide to use the Horizontal Tabs template. Refer to Figure 9.43 as you complete Step 1.

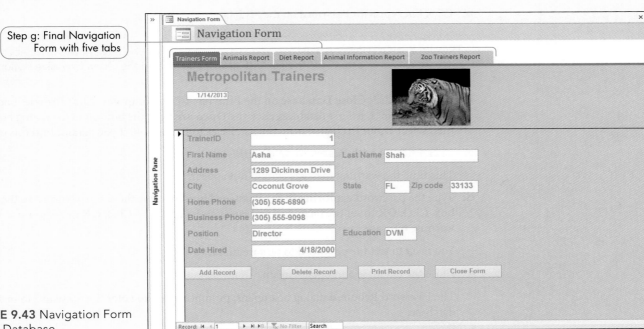

Step g: Final Navigation Form with five tabs

FIGURE 9.43 Navigation Form in Zoo Database

a. Open *a09h2Zoo_LastFirst*. Save the database as **a09h3Zoo_LastFirst**, changing *h2* to *h3*.

b. Select the **Animals table** and create a basic report using the Report tool. Save the report as **Animals Report**. Close the report.

c. Repeat step b to create a report based on the Diet table. Save the report as **Diet Report**. Close the report.

d. Repeat step b to create a report based on the Animal Information table. Save the report as **Animal Information Report**. Close the report.

e. Click the **CREATE tab** and click **Navigation** in the Forms group. Select the **Horizontal Tabs option** (the first item on the list).

A new Horizontal Tabs navigation form appears in the workspace.

f. Drag the **Trainers Form** from the Navigation Pane to [Add New].

g. Repeat step g to add Animals Report, Diet Report, Animal Information Report, and Zoo Trainers Report, in that order.

> **TROUBLESHOOTING:** If the Field List appears and covers your form, you can close it.

    h. Switch to Form view and test the navigation form by clicking each tab.

        Compare your results to Figure 9.43.

    i. Save and close the navigation form with the default name.

STEP 2 ≫ ENCRYPT AND PASSWORD-PROTECT A DATABASE

Selene asked you to add a password to the database. Several new employees have just been hired, and she wants to restrict their access to the database for the first six weeks. You discuss the password with Selene and decide to use a combination of letters, numbers, and symbols. Refer to Figure 9.44 as you complete Step 2.

Step f: Password masked by asterisks

FIGURE 9.44 Database Password Established

    a. Click **Encrypt with Password** on the FILE tab.

> **TROUBLESHOOTING:** A message appears telling you that you must have the database open for exclusive use. Close the file and open it again using the Open Exclusive option.

    b. Click **OK**. Click **Close Database** on the FILE tab. Click **Computer**. Click **Browse**. Locate the *a09h3Zoo_LastFirst* database, click the **Open arrow** at the bottom of the dialog box, and then select **Open Exclusive** from the list. Refer to Figure 9.40 if you cannot find this option.

    c. Click **Encrypt with Password** on the FILE tab.

        This time the warning message should not appear.

    d. Type the password **exploring** in the **Password box** and type the same password in the **Verify box**. Click **OK** to set the password and encrypt the database. Click **OK** in response to the warning message.

        You need to test the password to be sure that it works.

    e. Close the database and open it again.

        The Password Required dialog box opens, prompting you to enter the password to open the database.

    f. Type **exploring** in the **Enter database password box** and click **OK**.

STEP 3 ≫ DIGITALLY SIGN AND PUBLISH A DATABASE

You suggest to Selene that she add a digital signature to the database. You explain that the database content will be trusted when users from other departments start to use it. Refer to Figure 9.45 as you complete Step 3.

Step b: Create a name for your certificate

FIGURE 9.45 Digitally Signing the Database

a. Type **Digital Certificate for VBA Projects** in the **Start screen**. Click the tool to start it.

> **TROUBLESHOOTING:** If Digital Certificate for VBA Projects is not linked on your Start screen, use File Explorer to browse to the C:\Program Files\Microsoft Office\Office15 folder. Double-click SelfCert.exe.

b. Type your full name in the **Your certificate's name box** and click **OK**.

The *Your Name Success* dialog box appears, confirming that you successfully created a new certificate.

c. Click **OK**.

d. Click **Save As** on the FILE tab, and double-click **Package and Sign**.

e. Select the certificate you created in step b, if prompted. Click **OK**.

A new ACCDC file name is suggested using the current database.

f. Click **Create** to accept the new database name with the attached certificate.

A digitally signed database is created in the background; the original database remains open.

STEP 4 ≫ DIGITALLY SIGN A DATABASE

You decide to make the database more secure digitally signing it and saving it as an ACCDE file. This type of file prohibits the zoo employees from making changes by mistake (or intentionally). Refer to Figure 9.42 as you complete Step 4.

a. Click **Save As** on the FILE tab, and then double-click **Make ACCDE**.

The Save As dialog box opens. The default *Save as type* is ACCDE File (*.accde), and the suggested file name is *a09h3Zoo_LastFirst.accde*.

> **TROUBLESHOOTING:** If your file extensions are hidden, your file name will not show *accde* on the end of the file. Make sure the *Save as type* is ACCDE File.

b. Click **Save** to create the *a09h3Zoo_LastFirst.accde* database file.

c. Click **Close** on the FILE tab.

d. Locate and open the *a09h3Zoo_LastFirst.accde* file you created.

You are prompted for the database password. After you type the password, click Open if a security notice appears.

e. Test the ACCDE file by opening the Animals Form. Right-click the **ANIMALS FORM tab** and observe that *Design View* and *Layout View* are is missing from the shortcut menu.

f. Close the form.

g. Close the file and exit Access.

h. Submit based on your instructor's directions.

Chapter Objectives Review

After reading this chapter, you have accomplished the following objectives:

1. **Verify first normal form**
   - The first step to normalizing a table, which removes repeating groups.

2. **Verify second normal form**
   - Requires 1NF. Criteria is that all non-key fields must be functionally dependent on the entire primary key. If no composite key exists, the table is often in 2NF.

3. **Verify third normal form**
   - Requires 2NF. Removes transitive dependencies, or dependencies on non-key fields.

4. **Create relationships**
   - After normalization, relationships exist between your tables. If a table cannot be connected to others, there is likely a problem with your normalization.

5. **Use the Database Documenter tool**
   - Start the Database Documenter: Database Documenter creates a report containing detailed information for each selected object. Database Documenter can be run on specific objects (for example, only tables, or only forms and reports). Users can select varying levels of detail.

6. **Use the Performance Analyzer tool**
   - Start the Performance Analyzer: Performance Analyzer evaluates a database and makes optimization recommendations.
   - Add an index: Performance Analyzer may recommend adding an index, which will speed up searches such as queries or filters.

7. **Use the Table Analyzer tool**
   - Start the Table Analyzer: The Table Analyzer guides the user through the normalization process. This is a great tool for users with no experience with normalization.
   - Step through the Table Analyzer Wizard: The wizard enables you to split tables, rename newly created tables, rearrange fields in the new tables, and create relationships.

8. **Use the Database Splitter tool**
   - Start the Database Splitter tool: The Database Splitter tool is useful when the number of database users grows beyond a few. The tool splits a database into two files—a front-end database containing queries, forms, and reports, and a back-end database containing tables. Splitting a database may improve the speed of data processing. The back-end database is generally on a server.
   - Work with the front-end database: The front-end database is typically on each user's machine. The front-end database enables users to create their own queries, forms, and reports if necessary. The front end links to back-end tables, which can be shared between users.

9. **Create a menu system**
   - Create a Navigation form: Navigation forms help users open important forms and reports quickly. Choose one of six prebuilt layouts. Drag and drop forms and reports directly on tabs. A navigation form can be easily converted to a Web form.
   - Starting a Navigation form automatically: Navigation forms can start automatically when a database opens to help provide guidance to users.

10. **Encrypt and password-protect a database**
    - Encryption alters digital information using an algorithm, making it unreadable without the key (secret code). Encrypted databases are very difficult to break in to. Encryption is suggested especially if a database is sent via e-mail or put on removable storage such as a USB drive.

11. **Digitally sign and publish a database**
    - Use the SelfCert tool: SelfCert creates a personal signature. The signature can be applied to databases as well as other Office files.
    - Apply a digital signature: Once a certificate is created, it can be applied to a database. Doing so creates an ACCDC file, indicating it has been digitally signed.

12. **Save a database as an ACCDE file**
    - Create an ACCDE file: An ACCDE file is an executable form of the database—objects such as forms, reports, and VBA code cannot be changed. Saving as an ACCDE file adds an extra layer of protection.
    - Keep the original database file safe: Once created, an ACCDE file does not let you modify objects (forms, reports, and VBA code), so the original ACCDB must be kept safe. If the ACCDB file disappears, you will have to recreate your database objects.

Key Terms Matching

Match the key terms with their definitions. Write the key term letter by the appropriate numbered definition.

a. Access Database Executable (ACCDE)
b. Anomaly
c. Back-end database
d. Certification authority (CA)
e. Composite key
f. Database Documenter
g. Database Splitter
h. Digital signatures
i. Encryption
j. First normal form (1NF)

k. Front-end database
l. Functional dependency
m. Navigation form
n. Non-key field
o. Normalization
p. Performance Analyzer
q. Second normal form (2NF)
r. Table Analyzer
s. Third normal form (3NF)
t. Transitive dependencies

1. _____ A commercial company, such as VeriSign, that issues and validates identities using digital signatures for a fee. **p. 550**

2. _____ A file that has had all VBA source code removed, prohibits users from making design and name changes to forms or reports within the database, and prohibits users from creating new forms and reports. **p. 551**

3. _____ A tabbed menu that ties the objects in the database together so that the database is easy to use. **p. 545**

4. _____ A primary key that is made up of two or more fields. **p. 523**

5. _____ A tool that creates a report containing detailed information for each selected object. **p. 531**

6. _____ An error or inconsistency that occurs when you add, edit, and delete data. **p. 520**

7. _____ Analyzes the tables in a database and normalizes them for you. **p. 535**

8. _____ Any field that is not part of the primary key. **p. 523**

9. _____ Contains the queries, forms, and reports of the database. **p. 538**

10. _____ Contains the tables of the database. Often stored on a server or network location. **p. 538**

11. _____ Electronic, encryption-based, secure stamps of authentication that confirm who created the file, that the file is valid, and that no changes have been made to the file after its authentication. **p. 549**

12. _____ Enables you to split a database into two files—a back-end database, which contains the data tables, and a front-end database. **p. 538**

13. _____ Evaluates a database and then makes recommendations for optimizing the database. **p. 533**

14. _____ Occur when the value of one non-key field is functionally dependent on the value of another non-key field. **p. 524**

15. _____ Satisfied when a table contains no repeating groups or repeating columns. **p. 521**

16. _____ Satisfied when a table meets 2NF criteria and no transitive dependencies exist. **p. 534**

17. _____ Satisfied when a table that meets 1NF criteria and all non-key fields are functionally dependent on the entire primary key. **p. 523**

18. _____ The formal process of deciding which fields should be grouped together into which tables. **p. 520**

19. _____ The process of altering digital information using an algorithm to make it unreadable to anyone except those who possess the key (or secret code). **p. 547**

20. _____ When the value of one field is determined by the value of another. **p. 523**

Multiple Choice

1. Which of the following statements about normalization is false?

    (a) A database in 3NF must also be in 1NF.

    (b) There are only three normal forms.

    (c) Normalization reduces redundancy.

    (d) The Table Analyzer can help normalize tables.

2. A table is considered the most normalized when it is in which form?

    (a) 2NF

    (b) 1NF

    (c) 3NF

    (d) Unnormalized

3. Normalization can be defined as:

    (a) Eliminating repetition of data.

    (b) Adding a layer of security to a database.

    (c) Transforming tables into forms.

    (d) A database with multiple tables.

4. The Performance Analyzer:

    (a) Lists the properties of every object in the database.

    (b) Locates places where the database can be optimized.

    (c) Searches for rows of repeating data and suggests design changes to improve performance.

    (d) Is a wizard that provides step-by-step instructions on the creation of tables and forms.

5. The Database Documenter:

    (a) Lists the properties of every object in the database.

    (b) Locates places where the database can be optimized.

    (c) Searches for rows of repeating data and suggests design changes to improve performance.

    (d) Is a wizard that provides step-by-step instructions on the creation of tables and forms.

6. The Table Analyzer:

    (a) Lists the properties of every object in the database.

    (b) Locates places where the database can be optimized.

    (c) Normalizes a database.

    (d) Is a wizard that provides step-by-step instructions on the creation of tables and forms.

7. Which of the following describes a digital signature?

    (a) A scanned copy of the database owner's signature

    (b) Provided by Microsoft when you purchase Office 2013

    (c) Provides a timestamp that can help prove who last modified the database

    (d) An e-mail that details who last made changes to the attached database

8. Which of the following is true about encrypted databases?

    (a) Database encryption alters the contents of the database so that it cannot be opened without a password.

    (b) Encrypted databases can be broken into with ease.

    (c) The contents of encrypted databases cannot be modified.

    (d) Databases can be encrypted but not have a password assigned.

9. Which password is strongest?

    (a) MyAuntSally

    (b) Ginger125

    (c) Mypassword11

    (d) 5*m6notX

10. You open a database with exclusive access. What can other users do?

    (a) Other users can open the database and make changes to it.

    (b) Other users cannot open the database when it is already open with exclusive access.

    (c) No rules apply. Exclusive access is a database setting that can be turned on or off.

    (d) Other users can open but cannot modify the database.

Practice Exercises

1 Info Labs

Info Labs, a clinical studies company in Mississippi, employs 14 employees; most employees fall in the categories of manager, account rep, or trainee. The employee database holds information about each employee, including their salary and gender, their title, and their location. You have been asked to review the database to see if the employee table was designed properly. This exercise follows the same set of skills as used in Hands-On Exercises 1 and 2 in the chapter. Refer to Figure 9.46 as you complete this exercise.

FIGURE 9.46 Relationships in Clinic Database

Step o: Two one-to-many relationships

a. Open *a09p1Clinic*. Save the database as **a09p1Clinic_LastFirst**.

b. Open the Employees table in Datasheet view and examine the data. Determine if the data meets the three normalization rules: 1NF, 2NF, and 3NF.

c. Close the Employees table. You decide to use the Table Analyzer for help with normalizing the Employees table.

d. Click **Analyze Table** in the Analyze group on the DATABASE TOOLS tab. When the first wizard screen appears, click **Next** twice.

e. Select the **Employees table** when the *Which table contains fields with values that are repeated in many records* screen appears. Click **Next** twice.

f. Verify the Employees table has been split into three tables on the next screen.

g. Click **Table1**, click the **Rename Table icon**, and then type **Employee Profiles** as the new name of this table. Click **OK**.

h. Click **Table2**, click the **Rename Table icon**, and then type **Locations** as the new name of this table. Click **OK**.

i. Click **Table3**, click the **Rename Table icon**, and then type **Titles** as the new name of this table. Click **OK**.

j. Click **Next**.

k. Click **LocationID** in the Locations table and click the **Set Unique Identifier icon** to set LocationID as the primary key.

l. Click **EmployeeID** in the EmployeeProfiles table and click the **Set Unique Identifier icon** to set EmployeeID as the primary key.

m. Click **Next**. Select the **No, don't create the query option**. Click **Finish**. Click **OK** when the information message appears.

n. Review the new tables and confirm that the Analyzer moved fields from the Employees table into the two new lookup tables. Close all the tables.

o. Click **Relationships** on the DATABASE TOOLS tab in the Relationships group. Click **All Relationships** to reveal the relationships created by the Table Analyzer. Close the Relationships window and click **No**.

p. Click **Info** on the FILE tab, and click **Encrypt with Password**. Access displays the message *You must have the database open for exclusive use.* Click **OK**. Close the database. Use the Open Exclusive option to open the database.

q. Click **Info** on the FILE tab, and click **Encrypt with Password**. Use **exploring** as the password, in all lowercase letters. Click **OK**. Click **OK** in response to the *Row level locking will be ignored* message.

r. Close the database and reopen it. Type **exploring** in the **Enter database password box**. Close the database and close Access.

s. Submit based on your instructor's directions.

2 Metropolitan Zoo Members

The Metropolitan Zoo invites its patrons to become members of the zoo. For a donation of $50 per year for an individual, or $100 for a family membership, members are entitled to special discounts and member-only promotions. For example, when the pygmy hippos were delivered to the zoo, members were allowed to observe their arrival before the rest of the public. Your task is to review the members database to review the tables for normalization errors, check the performance, to create a lookup field, and then save the database as an ACCDE file. This exercise follows the same set of skills as used in Hands-On Exercises 1–3 in the chapter. Refer to Figures 9.47 and 9.48 as you complete this exercise.

FIGURE 9.47 Lookup Field in Membership Table

FIGURE 9.48 Navigation Form in Members Database

a. Open *a09p2Members*. Save the database as **a09p2Members_LastFirst**.

b. Open the Members table and examine the data. Determine if the data meets the three normalization rules: 1NF, 2NF, and 3NF.

c. Close the Members table. You decide to normalize the table manually.

d. Click **Query Design** in the Queries group on the CREATE tab. Add the Members table to the query design and close the Show Table dialog box.

e. Add the MembershipTypeID, MembershipTypeName, and MembershipDonation fields to the query design grid. Run the query. Take note of the repeating rows of data.

f. Switch to Design view. Click **Totals** in the Show/Hide group to eliminate the duplicate rows. Run the query. Only the unique rows show in the results.

g. Switch to Design view. Click **Make Table** in the Query Type group and type **MemberTypes** in the **Table Name box**. Click **OK**. Click **Run** in the Results group to create the MemberTypes table. Click **Yes** to the warning message. You created a second table (MemberTypes) to help normalize the Members table.

h. Save the query as **Create Member Types**. Close the query.

i. Open the MemberTypes table in Design view. Set the MembershipTypeID field as the primary key. Save and close the table.

j. Open the Members table in Design view and use the Lookup Wizard to join the Members table to the MemberTypes table in a relationship. Complete the following steps:

- Change the MembershipTypeID Data Type to *Lookup Wizard*.
- Click **Next** in the first Lookup Wizard step, select the **MemberTypes table** in the next step, and then click **Next**.
- Click the >> **button** to include all fields in the Lookup field. Click **Next** three times.
- Click **Finish** and click **Yes** to save the table. The two tables are now joined using the MembershipTypeID field.

k. Switch to Datasheet view. Click the **MembershipTypeID field** in the first row and verify the Lookup field is working. Next, you will delete the redundant fields in the Members table.

l. Switch to Design view. Select the **MembershipTypeName** and **MembershipDonation fields**. Click **Delete Rows** in the Tools group. Click **Yes** to confirm the deletion. Save and close the table.

m. Create a basic form using the Form button for each of the three tables in the database using the Form tool. Delete any subforms that appear automatically.

n. Create a basic report based on the Members table using the Report tool. Include MemberID, LastName, FirstName, EmailAddress, Phone, City, and StateOrProvince, in that order.

o. Use these four new objects to create a navigation form using the Horizontal Tabs template (see Figure 9.45). Edit the fourth tab and change the caption to **Members Report**. Close the Navigation Pane. Switch to Form view and test the new navigation form. Close the navigation form.

p. Click the **DATABASE TOOLS tab** and click **Analyze Performance**. Click the **All Object Types tab**, click **Select All**, and then click **OK**. The first idea in the Results window suggests you save your application as an MDE file, which is called ACCDE in Access 2013.

q. Close the Results dialog box.

r. Click **Save As** on the FILE tab, and double-click **Make ACCDE**. Click **Save**. The ACCDE file is saved in the same location as the original file with the same name, *a09p2Members_LastFirst*.

s. Close the database and close Access.

t. Submit based on your instructor's directions.

Mid-Level Exercises

1 | The Computer Store

ANALYSIS CASE

The Computer Store, based in Florida, sells computer products to individuals and businesses. You have been hired to assist with the daily computer operations, including management of the order processing database. Your assignment is to analyze the database, create a front end for the users, and transfer the tables to a back-end database. After splitting the database, you recommend a navigation form to open the database objects. Refer to Figure 9.49 as you complete this exercise.

FIGURE 9.49 Navigation Form in Computers Database

a. Open *a09m1Computers*. Click **Save Database As** on the FILE tab, and type **a09m1Computers_LastFirst**. Click **Save**.

b. Open the Database Documenter. Click **Options** and ensure none of the Include for Table items are selected. Select the **Names, Data Types, and Sizes option** in the *Include for Fields* section and select nothing in the *Include for Indexes* section. Click **OK**. Click the **Customers check box** and click **OK**. In the generated report, take note of the Size (the third column) of each field. Notice the values for the ZipCode and PhoneNumber field sizes in the Customers table. Close the generated report after viewing it.

 c. Open the Customers table in Design view and increase the field size to an appropriate size. The field size should be large enough to accommodate all data but small enough so users can not enter extra characters. Save and close the table.

d. Click **Access Database** in the Move Data group and click **Split Database** to split the database into a front-end and a back-end database. Keep the default back-end name, which adds the suffix *be* to the current database name. The front-end Navigation Pane shows linked table icons, similar to those in Figure 9.30.

e. Open the Customers table and type your name as the next customer. Close the table. Open the back-end database and verify your name is in the Customers table. Close the back-end database.

> **TROUBLESHOOTING:** If you use the front-end database on another machine, you may get an error stating the file path is not valid. Use the techniques learned in a previous chapter to link the front-end database to the back-end database.

f. Open the front-end database again and create three objects: a Customers form using the Customers table, a Products form using the Products table, and a Customer List report using the Customers table.

g. Create a navigation form using the Vertical Tabs, Left template. Add the Customers form, followed by the Products form, followed by the Customer List report, followed by the Products List report.

h. Test the navigation form in Form view (compare to Figure 9.49). Save and close the form.

i. Add the navigation form to the Display Form option in the Access Options page so the navigation form opens when the database opens. Test the feature by closing and opening the database. Refer to Figure 9.37 if necessary.

j. Close the database.

k. Submit based on your instructor's directions.

<table>
<tr><td>2</td><td>Boats for All Seasons</td></tr>
</table>

The owners of Boats for All Seasons would like to improve their database. They would like to add some additional forms and reports and also modify their main table. They are having a problem because customers who bought boats from them years ago are returning to purchase again. The owners are unsure how to record a second transaction for the same customer. After the modifications are completed, they would like you to create a navigation form and also make suggestions for making the database more secure. Refer to Figure 9.50 as you complete this exercise.

FIGURE 9.50 Deleting Redundant Fields in Customers Table

a. Open *a09m2Boats*. Save the database as **a09m2Boats_LastFirst**.

b. Open the Customers table and review the contents of the table. Make a list of any problems that may cause data-entry errors. Does the table need to be normalized? You will split the customers table into two tables: the Customers table and the BoatPurchases table.

c. Open the Customer Purchases query and examine the results. The owners are trying to use this query to enter purchases. They are confused because the boat purchase data is comingled with the Customers table. Also, some of the customers are still prospects and have not even purchased a boat yet. You will fix the problem in the steps below.

d. Modify the Customer Purchases query so it only shows fields with values. Run the query. Your query should list only customers who purchased a boat (56 records).

e. Switch to Design view. Click **Make Table** and type **BoatPurchases** in the **Table name box**. Click **OK**. Run the query and click **Yes** at the warning. Save and close the query.

f. Open the BoatPurchases table in Design view and change the CustomerID Data Type to **Number**. Save the table and switch to Datasheet view. Sort the records by CustomerID, locate the three customers who purchased more than one boat (Billingslea, Mcdowell, and Windon), and then update their CustomerIDs so that both purchases show the smaller ID. For example, change the second Billingslea CustomerID from *62* to **2**.

g. Change the CustomerID field in the BoatPurchases table to a Lookup Wizard displaying CustomerID, LastName, and FirstName, sorted by LastName and then by FirstName. Hide the key column. Save the table and click **Yes** at the prompt. Your field should show the customer LastName and FirstName when you click in the CustomerID field.

h. Switch to Datasheet view. Verify that the name in column 1 matches the names in columns 2 and 3. If it does, switch to Design view and delete the **LastName** and **FirstName fields**. These two fields were for reference only until you verified the data matched the column 1 data. Save and close the BoatPurchases table.

i. Open the Customers table in Design view and delete the **BoatType**, **BoatPurchaseDate**, and **BoatPurchaseAmount fields**. This information is not needed in the Customers table because it now exists in the BoatPurchases table.

j. Save the table and switch to Datasheet view. Sort the table by Ascending LastName. Locate the three customers who purchased more than one boat (Billingslea, Mcdowell, and Windon) and delete the three duplicate records with the larger CustomerID. For example, delete the second Billingslea record with a CustomerID of *62*.

k. Close the database and reopen it using the Open Exclusive option. Encrypt the database with a password of **exploring**.

l. Create a new form and a new report using the BoatPurchases table.

m. Use the information in the *Add the Switchboard Manager* section to create a switchboard using the Switchboard Manager. Add the Boat Purchases form, the Boat Purchases report, the Customer Data Entry form, and the Customers and Prospects report to the switchboard. Modify the Access options so the switchboard automatically opens when the database opens. Close and reopen the database to test the switchboard.

n. Click **Save As** on the FILE tab, and make an ACCDE file. The ACCDE file is saved in the same location as the original file.

o. Close the database and close Access.

p. Submit based on your instructor's directions.

3 | Normalizing a Database

The Specialty Foods, Ltd., company has a large database that has not been normalized. The company's recent hires have been given the task of trying to normalize the database.

a. Open the *a09m3Orders* database and save it as **a09m3Orders_GroupName**. (This step should be completed by only one person in your group. Replace *GroupName* with the name or number assigned to your group by your instructor.)

b. Examine the contents of the CustomerOrders table. Create a list of fields in the database. This database, with over 2,100 rows of information, contains a large amount of redundancy. Some companies, Specialty Foods included, create a database and do not normalize until the amount of data becomes unmanageable.

c. Each member of the group should take the list of fields, examine them separately, and create an initial guess as to what the final tables will look like. Be sure to identify potential primary keys for each table.

d. Come together as a group and discuss your proposals. Reach a consensus on the final design. Put this aside for the moment.

e. Each student should separately attempt to convert the database from the unnormalized state to 1NF.

f. Come together as a group and discuss your proposals. Reach a consensus on the design after 1NF. Be sure to identify primary keys. Open Microsoft Word and open *a09m3Normalization*. Record your proposal in the section labeled *First Normal Form* and save it as **a09m3Normalization_GroupName**. For example, the table titles shown in Figure 9.46 would be described like this:

Table Name: Titles

Fields: TitleID, TitleDesc

Primary Key: TitleID

g. Attempt to convert the database from the 1NF group settled on in step f to 2NF. Do this separately.

h. Come together as a group and discuss your proposals. Reach a consensus on the design after 2NF. Be sure to identify primary keys. Record the proposal in the *a09m3Normalization_GroupName* document in the section labeled *Second Normal Form*.

i. Each student should separately attempt to convert the database from the 2NF the group settled on in step h to 3NF.

j. Come together as a group and discuss your proposals. Reach a consensus on the design after 3NF. Be sure to identify primary keys. Record the proposal in the *a09m3Normalization_GroupName* document in the section labeled *Third Normal Form*.

k. Run the Analyze Table tool in Access on the CustomerOrders table. Name the tables appropriately. Accept the default primary keys proposed. Do not create a query when prompted. Examine the tables created and the relationships between the tables. Discuss as a group what (if anything) differs between your proposal and that proposed by Access. In the *a09m3Normalization_GroupName* document in the *Comparison* section, summarize the differences and attempt to explain why Access has different results than your proposal. Given the choice, would you use your proposal or the one provided by Access? Why?

l. Exit Word. Exit Access. Submit the Word document and the Access database based on your instructor's directions.

Beyond the Classroom

Switchboard Versus Navigation Form

RESEARCH CASE →

Your company uses an Access 2013 database to store its customer and sales information. The Accounting Department uses and maintains this database. Three other departments—Marketing, Sales, and Production—also need access to the database. Some users have asked for a switchboard, and others have asked for a navigation form. The accounting department does not have experience with creating either of these forms. Your assignment is to do online research to determine which menu system is better for your company: a switchboard or a navigation form. Create a Word document named **a09b2Switchboard_LastFirst**, giving a brief summary of the two menu systems and recommending which one is better for the company.

Troubleshoot: ACCDE File Errors

DISASTER RECOVERY +

Keith Hernandez, the manager of a local collectibles store, has contacted you about a database issue he has. His former technology support person set up a database for him on his USB flash drive. When he brought the file home, he was shown the following error:

> The database was created with the 32-bit version of Access. Please open it with the 32-bit version of Microsoft Access.

He tried then recreating the ACCDE from his home machine, but when he brought it to work, he was given the following error:

> The database was created with the 64-bit version of Access. Please open it with the 64-bit version of Microsoft Access.

Keith is frustrated and is hoping you can find out if there is a way for him to create an Access Database Executable that works on both the 32-bit and 64-bit versions of the program. If there is no way to do this, he is hoping you might have recommendations on how he should work with these ACCDE files. Write up your findings in a Word document and save it as **a09b3Collect_LastFirst**. Note he does not want you to fix the issue; he is just interested in finding out if this can be done or not. Keith has provided you with *a09b3Collect* (the original database), *a09b3Collect64* (which works on 64-bit editions of Access but not 32-bit editions), and *a09b3Collect32* (which works on 32-bit editions of Access but not 64-bit editions). However, you should only submit the final Word document to your instructor.

Interview Questions

SOFT SKILLS CASE S

You are a database administrator at a large company. The company is hiring a new entry-level database administrator, and your supervisor, Keith Mast, has asked you to draft questions to be asked during the interview. Specifically, he would like questions that an entry-level person should be expected to answer. You have decided you will ask them a question about normalization, another about database performance, a third about splitting databases, and a fourth about encryption. Your boss has asked to see the questions (and ideal answers) before the interview. Create a new Word document named **a09b4Interview_LastFirst**. Create the four questions you would ask an interviewee to explain during an interview, and provide optimal answers for the four questions. Submit based on your instructor's directions.

Capstone Exercise

Your company handles room registration, speaker coordination, and other functions for national conferences that are held at your campus throughout the year. The sales department mails schedules to speakers and building coordinators. The speaker database was modified by unauthorized personnel, and some of the changes need to be reversed. For example, all of the relationships were deleted; they need to be recreated. You have been asked to analyze the database, fix the relationships, and make the database more secure to avoid this situation in the future. The database tables may already be normalized; however, you need to examine the tables to verify this.

Restore Database Relationships

You open the original database and use Save As to create a copy of the original.

a. Open *a09c1NatConf* and save the database as **a09c1NatConf_LastFirst**.

b. Open each table in the database and look for normalization errors.

c. Open the Relationships window. Notice there are currently no relationships.

d. Add the Speakers, SessionSpeaker, Sessions, and Rooms tables to the Relationships window. Restore relationships by dragging the primary key from the primary table onto the foreign key of a related table.

e. Enforce *Referential Integrity* and *Cascade Update Related Fields* for each relationship you create.

f. Save the changes and close the Relationships window.

Analyze Database Performance

You want to verify that the database performs properly when it is used in a production environment. Run Performance Analyzer and take note of the recommendations, suggestions, and ideas in the analysis results.

a. Open the Performance Analyzer dialog box, click the **All Object Types tab**, click **Select All**, and then click **OK**.

b. Verify that the first item on the list (an idea) suggests creating an MDE file, which is called ACCDE in Access 2013. You will create an ACCDE file later.

c. Verify the third item on the list (an idea) suggests you change the data type of RoomID in the Sessions table from *Short Text* to **Long Integer**. You decide not to make this change.

> **TROUBLESHOOTING:** If changing the data type of RoomID is not the third idea, ensure you set the options properly in step a.

d. Close the Performance Analyzer.

Split the Database

Splitting the database by creating a back end and a front end enables users to customize their individual front-end databases; the back end (the tables) remains safe and secure.

a. Split the database, accepting the default back-end name *a09c1NatConf_LastFirst_be*. The front-end copy of the database remains open.

b. Look for the linked tables in the front-end copy of the database.

Create the Navigation Form

You need to create a navigation form that displays a new form and the three reports in the database. Add the navigation form to the Display Form option to make the navigation form appear whenever the database opens.

a. Create a new form based on the Speakers table.

b. Save the form as **Add or Edit Speakers**.

c. Create a navigation form based on the Horizontal Tabs template.

d. Drag the new **Add or Edit Speakers form** to the first tab position.

e. Drag the reports to fill the next three tab positions.

f. Switch to Form view and test the navigation form. Save the navigation form with the default name and close it.

g. Set the database to open the navigation form when the database opens. This setting can be found in Options on the FILE tab. Click the **Current Database tab** and update the Display Form option.

h. Test the navigation form by closing and then reopening the database.

Encrypt the Database with a Password and Create the ACCDE File

Make sure you have the database open with exclusive access before completing these steps. You need to encrypt the front-end database with a password. In addition, you want to convert the front-end database to the ACCDE file format.

a. Display the Set Database Password dialog box.

b. Set the database password to **exploring**. Type the same password in both text boxes. Click **OK** at the next prompt.

c. Close and reopen the database to test the password.

d. Convert the front-end database to an ACCDE file format. A new database file with extension .accde is created in the background.

e. Close the database. Close Access.

f. Submit based on your instructor's directions.

Using Macros and SQL in Access

CHAPTER **10**

Advanced Techniques

Yuri Arcurs/Shutterstock

CASE STUDY | Retirement Plan Helps Retain Employees

Terry Jackson, owner of Sunshine Therapy Club in Chicago, Illinois, offers her full-time employees a generous benefits package. In addition to a health care plan, paid vacation, and paid holidays, she also offers a 401k retirement plan to all full-time employees who have been employed for at least 90 days. Employees can contribute a percentage of their wages to 401k accounts and receive a tax deduction on their federal, state, and local tax returns. Employees can set the amount of their contribution anywhere between 1% and 15% of their weekly pay. For employees who have been with the company for at least one year, the company will match the employees' contributions up to 5%.

You have been asked to assist Associate Director Nancy Williams with verifying the accuracy of the Sunshine employee data and the employee contributions and ensuring that they fall within the plan guidelines. For example, only employees who have worked for the company at least one year are eligible for the company match. In addition, the plan must meet the minimum standard of employee participation. Terry would also like to receive a weekly report that shows the contribution per employee and the total contribution for the week. She would also like to see the company match per employee and the total company match for the week.

You decide to use macros and data macros to verify the plan is in compliance each week rather than wait until the end of a quarter or year. Any problems can then be corrected immediately. Data macros will also be utilized to verify data entry and alert the user if data is outside the normal plan parameters. You will also construct several SQL statements to use as the record source for several reports.

Macro Design

Access provides developers with a variety of built-in tools to create tables, queries, forms, and reports. However, sometimes a developer needs to have more control over how the objects in a database behave individually or in relation to other objects. This type of functionality can be accomplished through programming code. Access provides two methods of programming—creating macros and creating procedures using Visual Basic for Applications (VBA). In general, it is easier to create a macro than a VBA procedure because Access includes an automated tool for creating macros, the Macro Designer. VBA will not be covered in detail in this chapter; however macros can be converted to VBA without having to write any complex programming code whatsoever.

In this section, you will learn how to create two types of macros: stand-alone macros and embedded macros. You will also learn how Access creates macros for you when you add a command button to a form.

Understanding the Purpose of a Macro

STEP 1 ▶▶ A *macro* is a series of actions that can be programmed to automate tasks. Macros can be used to automate a repetitive task or perform a specific action. You can use macros to group a series of commands and instructions into a single command to accomplish repetitive or routine tasks automatically. After you create a macro, you initiate all its tasks by running the macro. For example, if you import the same Excel workbook data into Access each week, you could create a macro to help you accomplish this task. Or you might want to add a button to a form to run the same report each week. Access creates macros automatically for you when you add certain controls to a form or report, for example, if you create a command button in a form to run a report or print a customer order. Access uses embedded macros to enable the buttons to function.

Access supports two categories of macros: stand-alone macros and embedded macros. A *stand-alone macro* is a database object that you create and use independently of other controls or objects. Stand-alone macros display as objects in the Navigation Pane. Figure 10.1 shows three stand-alone macros.

Stand–alone macros display in the Navigation Pane

FIGURE 10.1 Stand-Alone Macros

An *embedded macro* is a macro that executes when an event attached to a control or object occurs. An *event* occurs when a user enters, edits, or deletes data; events also occur when users open, use, and close forms and reports. After Update is an example of an event attached to a control. After Update is triggered each time you enter (update) data into a field on a form. On Close is another example of an event attached to an object. Whenever you close a form or a report, the On Close event is triggered and Access executes the steps stored in the macro associated with the On Close event.

Another common use of an embedded macro is to validate the data in a field or a record. When a user enters data into a field, the After Update event is activated. You can attach an embedded macro to the After Update event and evaluate the data entered to verify that it falls within a set of parameters. For example, if a user enters a series of 401k contributions, a macro could verify that the amounts are positive values and that the contributions are equal to or less than 15% of an employee's salary.

Table 10.1 summarizes the two macro types supported by Access.

TABLE 10.1 Access Macro Types	
Macro Type	**Description**
Stand-alone macro	A macro that is a separate object in the Access database. A stand-alone macro displays in the Navigation Pane and can be run independently. Stand-alone macros are also available to any control or object in the database.
Embedded macro	A macro that is embedded in a specific object or control. An embedded macro does not display in the Navigation Pane. Use an embedded macro when only one object needs to run the macro.

Creating a Stand-Alone Macro

STEP 2 >> A stand-alone macro, as stated earlier, displays as an object in the Navigation Pane and can be run independently of other objects. You use the Macro Designer to create a stand-alone macro.

To create a macro using the Macro Designer, do the following:

1. Click the CREATE tab.
2. Click Macro in the Macros & Code group. The Macro Designer is displayed, as shown in Figure 10.2. In this figure, the Navigation Pane is on the left, the build-a-macro area is in the middle, and the Action Catalog is on the right. The Action Catalog can be used as a reference as you design a macro; you can also locate an action in the Action Catalog and double-click it (or drag it) to add it to the macro.
3. Specify the arguments you want for the action or actions you added to the macro.
4. When you finish building the macro, click Save.
5. Type a descriptive name for the macro. The macro name will display in the Navigation Pane, as shown in Figure 10.1.
6. To run a stand-alone macro, double-click the macro name in the Navigation Pane.

FIGURE 10.2 Macro Builder

To edit an existing stand-alone macro using the Macro Designer, do the following:

1. Right-click the macro name in the Navigation Pane.
2. Select Design View from the shortcut menu.
3. After modifying, adding, or deleting macro actions, save and close the macro.

Using the Macro Designer

STEP 3 >> The *Macro Designer* enables you to create and edit macros. Macro Designer was designed to make it easier to create macros, to modify macros, and to add or delete actions from macros. You can use any of the following four methods for adding actions to a macro with the Macro Designer:

- Click the Add New Action arrow and choose the action you want to add to your macro.
- Type the action name directly into the Add New Action box; Access autocompletes the action name as you type.
- Locate an action in the Action Catalog and double-click it to add it to the macro.
- Drag the action from the Action Catalog into the macro.

Access executes the actions in the order in which you list them.

Next, specify the arguments you want for the action or actions you added to the macro. An *argument* is a variable, constant, or expression that is needed to produce the output for an action. For example, you may want to add a MessageBox action to the macro to display a message to users when the macro runs. The MessageBox action contains four arguments, one of which is required. To see a short description of each argument, point to the argument box, and Access displays a short explanation of the argument. The MessageBox action contains the arguments Message, Beep, Type, and Title, as shown in Figure 10.3.

MessageBox has four arguments: Message, Beep, Type, and Title

FIGURE 10.3 Macro Action with Arguments

You can also create an action by dragging a database object from the Navigation Pane to an empty row in the Macro Designer. If you drag a table, query, form, or report to the Macro Designer, Access adds an action that opens the table, query, form, or report. If you drag a macro to the Macro Designer, Access adds an action that runs the macro. Figure 10.4 shows the results of dragging the Employee form from the Navigation Pane into a new macro.

OpenForm action added by Access

Employee form added from the Navigation Pane

FIGURE 10.4 Drag the Employee Form into a Macro

Attaching an Embedded Macro to an Event

STEP 4 Embedded macros are always attached to an event of a control on a form or report, or to an event of the form or report object itself.

Access provides two methods to create an embedded macro. First, you can use a wizard, such as the Command Button Wizard, and let Access create the macro for you. Or you can add a macro to an existing control manually by clicking the ellipsis (…) in the event box of the control or object you are manipulating. When you add a macro to an event (such as the On Click event of a button), Access embeds a macro in the object or control as shown in Figure 10.5. Regardless of which method you use, the Event tab in the object's Property Sheet enables you to open and edit the embedded macro. Figure 10.5 shows how an embedded macro displays in the Property Sheet for a control.

Command Button Property Sheet

Embedded macro attached to On Click event

Command button control

FIGURE 10.5 Embedded Macro

To attach an embedded macro, first open the form or report in Design view. You can attach a macro to an event using one of two methods. The first method is by adding a command button control that automatically creates an embedded macro for you. The command button control creates an embedded macro automatically using the Command Button Wizard. After the wizard is finished, an embedded macro is inserted into the On Click event property of the button. The second method is to attach an embedded macro to an event.

STEP 5

To attach an embedded macro to an event, do the following:

1. Open the object in Design view and open the Property Sheet.
2. Click the control you want to add the macro to and click in the desired event property box on the Event tab. When you click in an event property box, the ellipsis (…) displays on the right side of the box, as shown in Figure 10.6.
3. Click the ellipsis (…), click Macro Builder, and then click OK.

The Macro Designer opens, and you can add actions using the same methods you used for the stand-alone macro. For example, you can create a macro to compute employee 401k contributions. The macro can display a message after the 401k Contribution is selected, informing the employee (or the user) the amount that will be deducted each paycheck (by displaying the 401k Contribution Percent *times* the weekly Salary).

TIP Editing an Embedded Macro

To edit an embedded macro, open the form or report in Design view. Next, open the Property Sheet, and then click the event property that contains the embedded macro. Click the ellipsis (…), and Access opens the Macro Designer and displays the actions associated with the macro. Modify the embedded macro, click Save, and then close when finished. The macro remains embedded in the object.

Select the Macro Builder in the Choose Builder dialog box

After Update event is selected

Click Build

FIGURE 10.6 Create an Embedded Macro

TIP | Converting a Macro to VBA

Although VBA is not covered in this textbook, it is helpful to know that macros can be converted to VBA. At times, VBA may be a better choice for automating an Access object, as VBA enables more complex functionality. However, rather than creating VBA code from scratch, you can convert an existing macro to VBA and then modify the VBA code as needed.

To convert a stand-alone macro to VBA, open the macro in Design view. While in Design view, click Convert Macros to Visual Basic in the Tools group on the Design tab, as shown in Figure 10.7. A new module is created with the VBA required to perform the same automated tasks as the original macro. The module displays in the Navigation Pane of the database.

Convert Macros to Visual Basic button

FIGURE 10.7 Convert a Macro to VBA

In Hands-On Exercise 1, you will create stand-alone and embedded macros. You will also practice using the Macro Designer.

Quick
Concepts

1. What is the difference between a stand-alone and an embedded macro? ***pp. 570–571***

2. How would you edit an existing stand-alone macro? ***p. 573***

3. What is the advantage of using the Command Button control to create an embedded macro? ***p. 574***

Hands-On Exercises

1 Macro Design

You were hired to help Nancy administer the 401k plan at Sunshine Therapy Club. After you examine the design of the database, you decide to use stand-alone and embedded macros to open the forms and reports that Nancy uses to administer the plan. Because macros are powerful and can accidentally harm a database, you decide to make a copy of the original database and work with the copy.

Skills covered: Understand the Purpose of a Macro • Create a Stand-Alone Macro • Use the Macro Designer • Attach an Embedded Macro to an Event • Attach an Embedded Macro to a Report Event

STEP 1 ≫ UNDERSTAND THE PURPOSE OF A MACRO

Because this is your first time working with the Sunshine Therapy Club database, you examine the current database by opening each table in Datasheet view. Next, you will open the Relationships window to see which tables are related. You will also open the forms and reports that are used frequently and determine that a macro can be created to open several objects automatically. Refer to Figure 10.8 as you complete Step 1.

FIGURE 10.8 Sunshine Objects Open

a. Open *a10h1Sunshine*. Click the **FILE tab**, click **Save As**, click **Save As**, and then type **a10h1Sunshine_LastFirst**. Click **Save** and click **Enable Content**.

> **TROUBLESHOOTING:** If you make any major mistakes in this exercise, you can close the file and start over.

b. Open the Employee table in Datasheet view and examine the records. Open the Contribution table and examine the records. Open the remaining tables and examine the records. Close all tables.

You examine the data in each table to get acquainted with the database. The Contribution table contains the 401k contributions for each employee. The Employee table contains personal information for each employee.

c. Click the **DATABASE TOOLS tab** and click **Relationships** in the Relationships group to open the Relationships window.

You examine the table relationships to help you understand the data entry rules of the database. The Employee table contains a unique Social Security number (SSN) for each employee. The Contribution table contains an SSN field, but multiple contributions can be entered for each SSN.

d. Close the Relationships window. Open the Employee table and add your data as a new record to the table. Type the following data when you enter your record:

SSN	999-99-9999 *(do not type the dashes)*
LastName	*your last name*
FirstName	*your first name*
Gender	*your gender*
Other fields	*the same data as Amanda Smith's record*

e. Close the Employee table.

f. Open the Contribution Summary by Job Title query and review the contributions by job title.

Terry will use this information to track which employees are participating in the plan.

g. Open the Contribution Details form and scroll to the bottom of the data. Add three new entries using the following data:

SSN	PayDate	GrossPay	EmployeeContribution	CompanyMatch
999-99-9999	10/15/2016	$4,583.33	$458.33	$45.83
999-99-9999	11/15/2016	$4,583.33	$458.33	$45.83
999-99-9999	12/15/2016	$4,583.33	$458.33	$45.83

h. Open the Employees form. Advance to your record by clicking **Last record** in the Navigation Bar. Change the **HireDate** to today's date.

The HireDate will be used later to calculate the length of employment.

i. Open the Detail Report. Locate your record (the last record of the report) and find your Emp Total percent. Your contribution is 1.99%.

j. Compare your database to Figure 10.8. Close all open objects.

STEP 2 ≫ CREATE A STAND-ALONE MACRO

Nancy would like to easily open the four objects that are used every day. You create a stand-alone macro to automatically open the four objects used in Step 1. Refer to Figure 10.9 as you complete Step 2.

FIGURE 10.9 Use Macro Designer to Create a Stand-Alone Macro

a. Click the **CREATE tab** and click **Macro** in the Macros & Code group.

The Macro Designer opens.

b. Click the **Add New Action arrow** and select **OpenQuery** from the list of options.

The OpenQuery arguments are displayed. The OpenQuery action will open a query automatically.

c. Click the arrow at the end of each box and select the following arguments:

Query Name Contribution Summary by Job Title
View Datasheet *(default)*
Data Mode Read Only

d. Save the macro as **Open 4 Objects**. Close the macro.

The Open 4 Objects macro now displays in the Macros Group in the Navigation Pane.

e. Double-click the **Open 4 Objects macro** to run it.

Only one object, the *Contribution Summary by Job Title* query, opens.

f. Close the query.

You created and tested a stand-alone macro in the previous step. Because the macro works correctly so far, you decide to edit the macro and add the other three objects. All four objects will open when you run the Open 4 Objects macro. Refer to Figure 10.10 as you complete Step 3.

Step h: Run a macro

Macro Builder shows all four actions

FIGURE 10.10 Use Macro Designer to Edit a Stand-Alone Macro

a. Right-click the **Open 4 Objects macro** in the Navigation Pane and select **Design View** from the shortcut menu.

The Macro Designer opens.

b. Click in the **Add New Action box** and type **OpenForm**. Press **Enter**.

You can type any action into the Add New Action box or select an action from the list. When you type an action, AutoComplete is enabled so you only have to type the first few letters of the action. The OpenForm arguments are displayed.

c. Select the following arguments:

Form Name	Contribution Details
View	Form *(default)*
Window Mode	Normal *(default)*

The remaining arguments can be left blank.

d. Click in the **Add New Action box** and type **OpenForm**. Press **Enter**.

The OpenForm arguments are displayed for the second form.

e. Select the following arguments:

Form Name	Employees
View	Form *(default)*
Window Mode	Normal *(default)*

The remaining arguments can be left blank.

f. Click in the **Add New Action box**, click the **Add New Action arrow**, and then click **OpenReport**.

The OpenReport arguments are displayed for the report.

g. Select the following arguments:

Report Name	Detail Report
View	Report *(default)*
Window Mode	Normal *(default)*

The remaining arguments can be left blank. You have added an OpenQuery, two OpenForms, and one OpenReport action to the macro.

h. Save the macro. Click **Run** in the Tools group on the DESIGN tab.

The Open 4 Objects macro runs and opens the four objects one after the other.

i. Close the four objects and close the macro.

STEP 4 ≫ ATTACH AN EMBEDDED MACRO TO AN EVENT

You created a stand-alone macro. Next, you will create an embedded macro attached to a control on a form. You will add a command button to the main menu with an embedded macro; the macro will open the Parameter Query when the button is clicked. The Parameter Query will prompt the user to enter a minimum salary and then display employees who earn at least that amount. Refer to Figure 10.11 as you complete Step 4.

Step 1: Embedded macro in the On Click event

FIGURE 10.11 Create an Embedded Macro Using the Command Button Wizard

Photo: © Yuri Arcurs/Fotolia

a. Double-click **Parameter Query** in the Navigation Pane. When prompted, enter **70000** and press **Enter**. Close the query.

The query displayed employees who earn at least $70,000.00.

b. Right-click the **Main Menu form** in the Navigation Pane and select **Design View** from the shortcut menu.

The Main Menu opens in Design view.

c. Click the **Button control** in the Controls group on the FORM DESIGN TOOLS DESIGN tab and click in the space between the Contribution Details and Detail Report buttons.

The Command Button Wizard opens.

d. Select **Miscellaneous** from the Categories list and select **Run Query** from the Actions list. Click **Next**.

e. Click **Parameter Query** and click **Next**.

f. Select the **Text option** and type **Parameter Query** as the display text. Click **Next**.

g. Type **cmdParameterQuery** as the name for the button. Click **Finish**.

h. Click **Property Sheet** in the Tools group on the DESIGN tab with the button selected. On the Format tab in the Property Sheet, set the button width to **2.25"** and the height to **.25"**. Click the **Font Size arrow** to select **12**. Leave the Property Sheet open. Click and drag the **Parameter Query button** so that its left edge is aligned with the left edge of the buttons above and below it.

i. Switch to Form view and click **Parameter Query**.

The query opens and asks for the minimum salary amount.

j. Type **70000** and press **Enter**.

The query results display all the employees with a salary of at least $70,000.

k. Close the query and switch to the Design view of the Main Menu form. Click **Parameter Query** (if necessary) and click the **Event tab** in the Property Sheet.

The embedded macro displays in the On Click event.

l. Click the **ellipsis (…)** on the right side of the On Click property. The Macro Designer opens and enables you to modify the embedded macro. Close the Macro Designer.

m. Save and close the Main Menu form.

STEP 5 ≫ ATTACH AN EMBEDDED MACRO TO A REPORT EVENT

Terry asks you to prompt the employees each time they run the Detail Report. She wants to remind them to give the report to her every Friday. Refer to Figure 10.12 as you complete Step 5.

FIGURE 10.12 Message Appears When the Report Opens

a. Right-click the **Detail Report** in the Navigation Pane and select **Design View** from the shortcut menu.

The Detail Report opens in Design view.

b. Open the Property Sheet, if necessary. Click the **Event tab** on the Property Sheet.

c. Click the **ellipsis (…)** on the right side of the On Open property box. The Macro Builder option should be selected by default. Click **OK**.

The Macro Designer opens and enables you to create an embedded macro.

d. Click the **Add New Action arrow** in the Add New Action box and click **MessageBox**.

The MessageBox arguments are displayed.

e. Type **Please deliver this report to Terry every Friday.** (include the period) in the **Message box**.

f. Verify that *Yes* is in the Beep box. Select **Information** in the Type box. Type **Check employee contributions** in the **Title box**.

g. Save and close the macro. With the report in Design view, click **View** and click **Print Preview** in the Views group to test the macro.

A message displays immediately, reminding you to give the report to Terry every Friday.

h. Click **OK**, close Print Preview, and then save and close the report.

i. Keep the database open if you plan to continue with Hands-On Exercise 2. If not, close the database and exit Access.

Data Macros

A data macro executes a series of actions when a table event occurs or whenever a named data macro is executed. A table event occurs naturally as users enter, edit, and delete table data. *Data macros* attach programming logic to tables; they also enable organizations to apply business logic to a database. Business logic describes the policies and procedures established by an organization. For example, you may want a macro to compare the values in two different fields when data is entered and perform an action as a result. When a form is based on a table that contains a data macro, the form contains the same business logic and the same results of the data macro as the table.

Data macros, like stand-alone macros and embedded macros, use the Macro Designer. The actions available in the Macro Designer are different for data macros than for stand-alone or embedded macros; however, the user interface is the same for each macro type. If you become proficient in creating one type of macro, you will be proficient in creating the other types as well.

In this section, you will learn data validation techniques using data macros. You will learn how to create event-driven data macros and named data macros. You will also see the similarity between data macros and other macros, and identify when to use which type.

Identifying When to Use a Data Macro

STEP 1 ≫ You can use data macros to validate and ensure the accuracy of data in a table. You learned how to use a validation rule to apply business logic to one field in a table. However, when business logic requires the comparison of two or more fields to intercept data entry errors, you need to use a data macro. In the case study, you might want to validate a contribution rate (field 1) based on an employee's position (field 2) and an employee's hire date (field 3). To automate this type of business logic easily, a data macro is required.

A few examples of when you might add a data macro to a table are as follows:

- Verifying that a customer has no outstanding invoices before placing a new order
- Keeping a log of any changes made to a specific table
- Sending a confirmation e-mail when a contributor makes a donation
- Maintaining a backup table

Data macros can only be used with table events. You cannot use a data macro with other objects; however, as stated earlier, a form based on a table that contains a data macro inherits the logic of the table. Two main types of data macros exist—event-driven data macros and named data macros. Event-driven data macros are triggered by table events; named data macros can be run from anywhere in the database. After you practice adding a few data macros, you will begin to see the power they add to a database.

Creating an Event-Driven Data Macro

STEP 2 ≫ Table events occur naturally as users enter, edit, and delete table data. Event-driven data macros, such as After Delete or Before Change, can be programmed to run before or after a table event occurs.

To attach a data macro to a table event, do the following:

1. Open the table you want to add the data macro to in Design view.
2. Click Create Data Macros in the Field, Record & Table Events group on the DESIGN tab, as shown in Figure 10.13.

3. Click the event to which you want to attach the macro. For example, to create a data macro that runs before you save a record, click Before Change.

4. Add macro actions using the Macro Designer. If a macro was previously created for this event, Access displays the existing macro actions.

5. Save and close the macro.

FIGURE 10.13 Data Macro Events

STEP 3 >>

In order to test the effect of a data macro, open the table to which the macro was added, and then add, delete, or update a record in order to trigger the macro. For example, if you attached a macro to the Before Change event, open the table, modify the data, and then advance to the next record to save the changes and to trigger the Before Change event. The data macro will run and execute the actions you created.

Creating a Named Data Macro

STEP 4 >>

In addition to creating data macros that are triggered by events, Access enables you to create named data macros. You can access these macros from anywhere in the database, including running them from within another macro.

To create a named data macro, do the following:

1. In Design view, click Create Data Macros in the Field, Record & Table Events group and select Create Named Macro from the list (see Figure 10.14).

FIGURE 10.14 Create a Named Data Macro

The Macro Designer displays so you can create the macro logic (see Figure 10.15). After you create a named data macro, save the macro with a descriptive name, such as DataMacro-Email. You will then be able to run the data macro from inside another macro using the RunDataMacro action. Figure 10.16 shows a data macro attached to the After Update event of the Employee table. The macro sends an e-mail to the database administrator each time the Employee table is updated. The data macro could also be attached to an event in an employees form that is dependent on the Employee table.

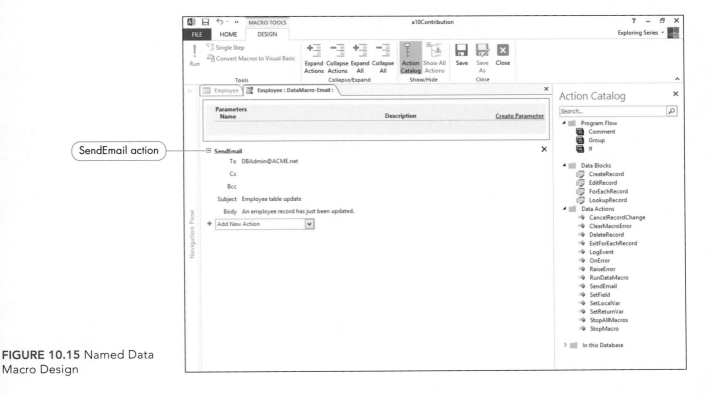

FIGURE 10.15 Named Data Macro Design

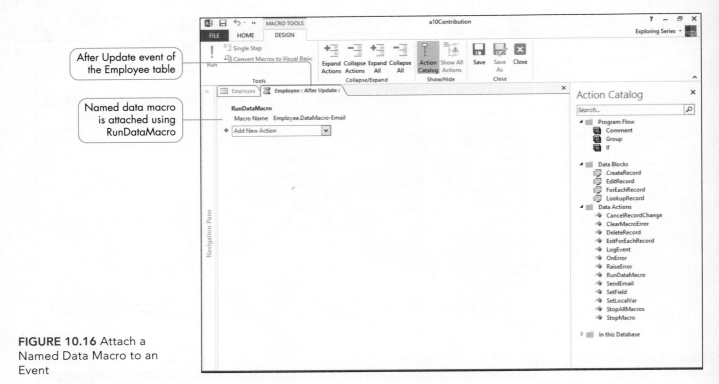

After Update event of the Employee table

Named data macro is attached using RunDataMacro

FIGURE 10.16 Attach a Named Data Macro to an Event

Quick
Concepts

1. When does a data macro run? *p. 583*

2. Why would you use a data macro? Name a specific reason. *p. 583*

3. When does an event-driven macro run? *p. 583*

Hands-On Exercises

2 Data Macros

You decide to demonstrate the power of data macros to Terry and Nancy. You will show them how data macros help reduce data entry errors by intercepting and changing incorrect data before it is added to a table. Although data macros are only created from within tables, you will demonstrate that named data macros can also be used with other objects in the database. You will create a named data macro in a table to send an e-mail, and then attach the same named data macro to a form.

Skills covered: Identify When to Use a Data Macro • Create a Before Change Data Macro • Test and Modify a Data Macro • Create a Named Data Macro • Attach a Named Data Macro to a Form

---

STEP 1 ≫ IDENTIFY WHEN TO USE A DATA MACRO

Certain tasks are completed manually, which lend themselves to using a data macro. A data macro will save time, and if set up correctly will never fail. In this exercise, you will identify an opportunity to create a data macro in the Employee table. Refer to Figure 10.17 as you complete Step 1.

> **Step e: Add and update the EligibleForMatch field**

	JobCode	HireDate	CountyID	Salary	401K	Active	EligibleForM	Click to Add
⊞	100	7/17/2010	3	$58,000.00	0.03	☑	☑	
⊞	150	7/16/2016	1	$77,000.00	0.05	☑	☐	
⊞	200	2/15/2009	2	$87,000.00	0.06	☑	☑	
⊞	150	3/13/2011	4	$81,000.00	0.02	☑	☑	
⊞	100	6/10/2016	3	$54,250.00	0.03	☑	☐	
⊞	250	9/6/2009	1	$87,600.00	0	☑	☑	
⊞	200	8/7/2008	4	$88,000.00	0.04	☑	☑	
⊞	100	11/11/2011	2	$64,000.00	0	☑	☑	
⊞	100	2/1/2011	1	$55,000.00	0.02	☑	☑	
⊞	100	4/8/2012	3	$54,200.00	0.04	☑	☑	
⊞	100	5/19/2009	3	$61,000.00	0.03	☑	☑	
⊞	150	6/3/2008	4	$78,000.00	0.1	☑	☑	
⊞	200	3/4/2010	3	$89,500.00	0.05	☑	☑	
⊞	150	12/31/2012	2	$58,500.00	0.08	☑	☐	
⊞	250	9/30/2008	4	$90,500.00	0.02	☑	☑	
⊞	150	1/10/2011	4	$76,600.00	0.03	☑	☑	
⊞	250	6/1/2009	1	$91,200.00	0.09	☑	☑	
⊞	100	4/14/2016	3	$55,000.00	0.04	☑	☐	
⊞	100	12/5/2016	3	$55,000.00	0.05	☑	☐	
*						☐	☐	

All Access Objects:
- Tables: Contribution, County, Employee, JobCode, ZipCode
- Queries: Contribution Summary by Job Ti..., Parameter Query
- Forms: Contribution Details, Employees, Main Menu
- Reports: Detail Report
- Macros: Open 4 Objects

FIGURE 10.17 Identify When to Use a Data Macro

a. Open *a10h1Sunshine_LastFirst* if you closed it after completing Hands-On Exercise 1. Click the **FILE tab**, click **Save As**, click **Save As**, and then type **a10h2Sunshine_LastFirst**, changing *h1* to *h2*. Click **Save**.

b. Open the Employee table in Design view.

c. Add a new field, **EligibleForMatch**, with data type **Yes/No**, to the table. Save the table.

  You will use the new field to indicate which employees are eligible for the company 401k matching contribution.

d. Switch to Datasheet view.

e. Update the first 10 records to indicate whether or not they are eligible for the company match. If an employee has been employed for at least one year, check the **EligibleForMatch check box**.

> **TROUBLESHOOTING:** Ensure that your own record contains today's date as the date of hire. As you have only joined the organization today, you will not be eligible for the company match.

Next, you will create a data macro to update the EligibleForMatch field. A data macro will update the EligibleForMatch check box each time a record changes.

STEP 2 ≫ CREATE A BEFORE CHANGE DATA MACRO

The EligibleForMatch check box can be updated automatically by a data macro based on the HireDate because the same eligibility rule applies to all employees. To eliminate the possibility of entry errors, you will use the Before Change event to update the eligibility of an employee automatically. Refer to Figure 10.18 as you complete Step 2.

FIGURE 10.18 Before Change Data Macro

a. Switch to Design view. Click **Create Data Macros** in the Field, Record & Table Events group on the DESIGN tab and click **Before Change**.

   The Macro Designer displays.

b. Drag the **If statement** from the Program Flow folder in the Action Catalog to the Add New Action box in the Macro.

   The structure of the If statement is added to the macro.

c. Type **(Date() – [HireDate]) >= 365** in the **Conditional expression box**.

   The expression determines if the employee has been employed at least one year (or 365 days) by subtracting the employee's hire date from today's date and then evaluating that difference to determine if it is greater than or equal to 365. If true, the macro will set the value of the EligibleForMatch field to Yes.

d. Select **SetField** from the Add New Action arrow within the If action.

   The SetField arguments are added to the macro.

e. Type **el** in the **Name box** (and Access displays *EligibleForMatch*, the field name it predicts you are looking for). Press **Tab** to accept the EligibleForMatch field.

f. Type **yes** in the **Value box**.

   Access checks the EligibleForMatch check box if the length of employment expression evaluates to true.

g. Save and close the macro. Save the Employee table.

STEP 3 ›› TEST AND MODIFY A DATA MACRO

You decide to test the Before Change macro using the rest of the employee records (11–19). Change one field in each record in order to trigger the Before Change event and verify the macro correctly updates the EligibleForMatch check box. You will also add an extra condition to the If statement in the macro that will update the check box if the employee is not eligible for the match. Refer to Figure 10.19 as you complete Step 3.

FIGURE 10.19 Data Macro with Else Statement Added

a. Switch to Datasheet view.

To test the accuracy of the data macro, you will retype the 401k (percent) for records 11 through 19 in order to trigger the Before Change event. The macro automatically selects the EligibleForMatch check box for the appropriate records. Later, when new records are added to the table, the macro will run each time a record is entered.

b. Type **0.03** in the **401K column** of record 11 (Sally Keller). Click in the **401K column** of row 12.

Because employee Sally Keller was hired on 5/19/2009, she is eligible for the 401k match. The data macro checks the check box.

c. Type **0.1** in the **401K column** of record 12. Click in the **401K column** of row 13.

Because employee Samantha Jackson was hired on 6/3/2008, she is eligible for the 401k match. The data macro checks the check box.

d. Repeat the process for the remaining records.

You wonder if the macro would uncheck an employee with an incorrectly checked EligibleForMatch check box. You decide to test the data macro for this condition.

e. Click the **EligibleForMatch check box** for your record and press ⬇ to trigger the macro.

You realize that the check box remains checked even though you are not eligible. You decide to modify the data macro to update the check box if the employee is not eligible for the match.

f. Switch to Design view. Click **Create Data Macros** in the Field, Record & Table Events group on the TABLE TOOLS DESIGN tab and click **Before Change**.

The Macro Designer displays showing the If statement you set up earlier.

g. Click the **If statement** and click the **Add Else hyperlink** to add the Else statement.

You will add another SetField statement to uncheck the EligibleForMatch check box when employees are employed for less than one year.

h. Type **s** in the **Add New Action box** (and Access displays *SetField*, the action it thinks you are looking for). Press **Tab** to accept the SetField action.

i. Type **el** in the **Name box** (and Access displays *EligibleForMatch*). Press **Tab** to accept the field EligibleForMatch.

j. Type **no** in the **Value box**.

Access will uncheck the eligible check box if the length of employment expression evaluates to false.

> **TROUBLESHOOTING:** Access attempts to add the Now function when you type no. Press Esc.

---

k. Save the macro. Close the macro. Save the Employee table.

l. Switch to Datasheet view, locate your record, and then change your proposed 401K contribution to **0.05**. Press ⬇ to save your change.

The check box is unchecked by the data macro because you are not eligible for the match.

STEP 4 ≫ CREATE A NAMED DATA MACRO

Terry wants to be notified when any changes are made to the Employee table. You decide to create a named data macro that will send an e-mail to her whenever a change is made to the Employee table. Refer to Figure 10.20 as you complete Step 4.

FIGURE 10.20 Create a Named Data Macro

a. Switch to Design view. Click **Create Data Macros** and click **Create Named Macro** in the Field, Record & Table Events group on the TABLE TOOLS DESIGN tab.

The Macro Designer displays.

b. Drag the **SendEmail action** from the Data Actions folder in the Action Catalog to the Add New Action box.

The SendEmail action and its five arguments are added to the macro.

c. Type your e-mail address in the **To argument box**. Skip the Cc and Bcc arguments.

> **TROUBLESHOOTING:** Your instructor may provide you with an alternate e-mail address to complete this step.

d. Type **Sunshine Database Alert** in the **Subject argument box**.

e. Type **The Employee table has been altered.** (include the period) in the **Body argument box**.

f. Save the macro as **DataMacro-SendEmail**. Close the macro.

g. Save the Employee table. Close the table.

STEP 5 ≫ ATTACH A NAMED DATA MACRO TO A FORM

You will attach the named data macro to a form event because many updates to the Employee table will be done through the Employees form. You decide to use the After Update event as the trigger for the send e-mail macro. Refer to Figure 10.21 as you complete Step 5.

FIGURE 10.21 Test a SendEmail Named Data Macro

a. Open the Employees form in Design view.

b. Click **After Update** on the Event tab of the Property Sheet.

The ellipsis (…) displays on the right side of the After Update event.

c. Click the **ellipsis (…)**, click **Macro Builder** if necessary, and then click **OK**.

The Macro Designer displays.

d. Click the **Add New Action arrow** and select the **RunDataMacro action** from the list.

e. Select **Employee.DataMacro-SendEmail** using the Macro Name arrow.

f. Save and close the macro.

g. Save the Employees form and switch to Form view.

h. Type the existing 401k percent in the **401K field** of the first record (Timothy Williams).

i. Press **Tab** twice to advance to the second employee.

As soon as you move to the second employee, the After Update event is triggered and the SendEmail macro is activated. Access attempts to send an e-mail using the parameters you typed in Step 4.

TROUBLESHOOTING: If an e-mail client is not set up on the computer you are using, you may have to cancel this step and stop the macro. When your computer is correctly configured to send the e-mail, the macro will run as expected.

---

j. Click **OK** if you receive the warning message shown in Figure 10.21. Click **OK** again and click **Stop All Macros**.

If the warning message was not received as shown in Figure 10.21, click **Allow**. Check your e-mail after a few minutes to see if you received the Sunshine Database Alert message.

k. Save and close the form.

l. Keep the database open if you plan to continue with Hands-On Exercise 3. If not, close the database and exit Access.

Structured Query Language

Until now, whenever you wanted to ask a question about the data in a database, you created a query using the query Design view. The query Design view enables you to select the tables you need and select the required fields from those tables. You can also add criteria and sorting in the query design grid. Whenever you create a query using the query Design view, you create a Structured Query Language (SQL) statement simultaneously. Access stores the SQL statement in the background. In this section, you will learn the basics of SQL, the correlation between query Design view and SQL view, and how to use an SQL statement in forms and reports.

Understanding the Fundamentals of SQL

STEP 1 *Structured Query Language (SQL)* is the industry-standard language for defining, manipulating, and retrieving the data in a database. SQL was developed at IBM in the early 1970s. Since then, Microsoft has developed its own version of SQL for Microsoft Access, which varies slightly from the industry-standard SQL language. Although you can use SQL to create and modify tables, this section will be limited to the retrieval of data. All of the queries you created so far in this textbook were created using the query Design view; however, they could have been created using SQL. In fact, all Access queries use an SQL statement—behind the scenes—to extract data from tables.

When you learn SQL, you are learning the data retrieval and data manipulation language of all the industry-leading databases—SQL Server, Oracle, and Sybase, to name a few. If you learn SQL in Access, your skills will be useful when you work in these other database environments. SQL is also used to extract data from a Web database.

Figure 10.22 shows a basic query that was created using the query Design view. This query extracts all records from the Contribution table for the employee with SSN 456667778. Figure 10.23 shows the results in Datasheet view; the results contain 12 records. You can switch to SQL view to examine the statements generated by any query you create. To switch to SQL view from any query view, click the View arrow, and then select SQL View (see Figure 10.23).

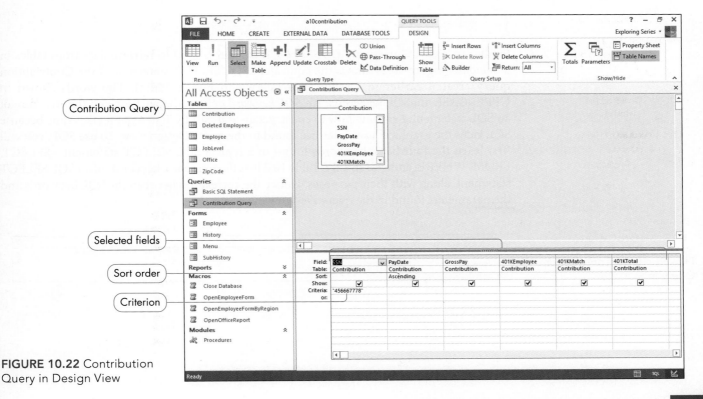

FIGURE 10.22 Contribution Query in Design View

FIGURE 10.23 Contribution Query in Datasheet View

TIP | SQL View

When you are working with queries in Access, you can switch to SQL view using three methods. You can click the View arrow and select SQL View from the list of options, you can right-click the query tab and select SQL View from this list, or, from the open query, you can click the small SQL icon at the bottom right of the Access window.

Interpreting an SQL SELECT Statement

STEP 2 >> Similar to a select query, an *SQL SELECT statement* is used to retrieve data from tables in a database. Figure 10.24 shows the equivalent SQL SELECT statement of the Contribution query created earlier in Design view (shown in Figure 10.22). The words shown in UPPERCASE are SQL keywords. An *SQL keyword* defines the purpose and the structure of an SQL statement. Learning how to construct an SQL SELECT statement takes time because SQL lacks the graphical user interface found in the query Design view. To use SQL, you will first learn the four basic keywords found in a typical SQL SELECT statement—SELECT, FROM, WHERE, and ORDER BY. Table 10.2 lists the four basic keywords of an SQL SELECT statement, along with their purposes. Notice the correlation between the SQL keywords and the parameters found in the query Design view.

FIGURE 10.24 Contribution Query in SQL View

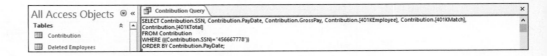

Keyword	Purpose
TABLE 10.2	**Four Basic Keywords of an SQL SELECT Statement and Their Purposes**
SELECT	Specifies the fields to include in the query
FROM	Specifies the table or tables where the fields can be found
WHERE	Sets the criteria for the rows in the results
ORDER BY	Determines how the rows will be sorted

Dissect an SQL SELECT Statement: SELECT and FROM Keywords

The **SELECT keyword** instructs Access to return the specific fields from one or more tables (or queries). When a query or expression containing a SELECT statement is executed, Access searches the specified table (or tables), extracts the designated data, and displays the results. The **FROM keyword** specifies the table (or tables) that will be searched. In Figure 10.24, the SQL statement begins as follows:

SELECT Contribution.SSN, Contribution.PayDate, Contribution.GrossPay,

Contribution.[401KEmployee], Contribution.[401KMatch],

Contribution.[401KTotal]

FROM Contribution

In the statement above, field names are listed after the SELECT statement and are separated by commas. If two fields from two different tables have the same name, the table name prefix followed by a dot is required. In the above example, *Contribution.* appears before each field name because the same field names appear in other tables in the database. Some field names, such as 401KEmployee, 401KMatch, and 401KTotal, are enclosed by brackets [ ] when a field name has a leading numeric character. In the above example, the FROM command is instructing Access to pull data from the Contribution table.

Instead of specifying the individual field names in SQL, you can use the asterisk character (*) to select all of the fields in a table. For example, the following SELECT statement returns all fields and records from the Contribution table and displays the results in a datasheet:

SELECT *

FROM Contribution;

Dissect an SQL Statement: WHERE Keyword

After you select the tables and fields using SELECT and FROM, you can then filter the resulting records using the WHERE keyword. The **WHERE keyword** specifies the criteria that records must match to be included in the results. If your query does not include the WHERE keyword, the query will return all records from the table(s). In Figure 10.24, the SQL statement contains the following clause:

WHERE (((Contribution.SSN)="456667778"))

In this example, the WHERE clause specifies that only records with SSN equal to 456667778 will display in the results. Because the SSN field is a text field, the quotes are required around the SSN criterion.

Dissect an SQL Statement: ORDER BY Keyword

Typically, you want the query results to be arranged in a particular order. The **ORDER BY keyword** is used to sort the records by a certain field in either ascending or descending order. The ORDER BY clause must be added to the end of an SQL statement after the WHERE clause. In Figure 10.24, the SQL statement contains the following clause:

`ORDER BY Contribution.PayDate;`

In the statement above, the ORDER BY clause sorts the records in ascending order by PayDate. To sort in descending order, add DESC to the end of the ORDER BY clause. To sort the above records beginning with the most recent pay date, the statement would become as follows:

`ORDER BY Contribution.PayDate DESC;`

Learn Advanced SQL Statements

The easiest way to learn more advanced SQL statements is to create Access queries in Design view and then view the SQL statement in SQL view. Although some statements might seem complex at first, the more you work with SQL, the easier it will become to understand SQL statements. You will begin to recognize that each SQL statement contains a shared syntax. For example, most SQL statements begin with SELECT and end with a semicolon (;).

Action queries can also be translated into SQL statements. Update queries, Append queries, Make Table queries, and Delete queries each have their equivalent SQL keywords and syntax. For example, suppose you wanted to add all the records in Figure 10.23 to a new table named Archive. To do this, you would create a Make Table query. The equivalent SQL statement would be:

`SELECT Contribution.SSN, Contribution.PayDate, Contribution.GrossPay,`

`Contribution.[401KEmployee], Contribution.[401KMatch],`

`Contribution.[401KTotal] INTO Archive`

`FROM Contribution`

`WHERE (((Contribution.SSN)="456667778"))`

`ORDER BY Contribution.PayDate;`

Using an SQL SELECT Statement as a Record Source

When you create a form or a report in Access, the first step is to choose a record source in the Navigation Pane. The record source can be either a table or a query, depending on the complexity of the data. The next step is to click the Create tab and choose the Form tool, Report tool, or another tool so that Access can create the new object. A sample report based on the Contribution table is shown in Figure 10.25.

FIGURE 10.25 Contribution Report Created with Contribution Table

Create an SQL Record Source for a Report

Based on the information you learned about SQL in this section, you should be able to create an SQL record source for a report. You know that the basic structure of an SQL statement is as follows:

SELECT field names

FROM table name

WHERE specified criteria must be met

ORDER BY field name;

STEP 3 ≫   The sample Contribution report, as shown in Figure 10.25, contains all of the records from the Contribution table; therefore no WHERE clause is required. The records are not sorted in a different order than the SSN order found in the Contribution table, so no ORDER BY clause is needed. Based on this information, the SQL statement for the record source of the Contribution report is as follows:

SELECT *

FROM Contribution;

Add an SQL Record Source to a Report

Now that you know the SQL record source for the Contribution report, you can replace the existing record source (the Contribution table) with the SQL statement. The following are reasons for using an SQL statement for a record source:

- You can create a form or report without creating a new query (because the record source is contained in the object).

- It is easier to transfer a form or report to another database (because the record source is contained in the object).

- You can construct the record source of a report at run-time using VBA (based on user input).

To replace a report's record source, do the following:

1. Open the report in Design view and open the Property Sheet.
2. Select Report using the Selection arrow at the top of the Property Sheet.
3. Click the DATA tab and click in the Record Source property box.
4. Delete the existing value (for example, Contribution) from the Record Source and type the SQL statement, such as *SELECT * FROM Contribution;* in its place, as shown in Figure 10.26.
5. Click View in the Views group on the DESIGN tab to display the Contribution report in Print Preview to test the change.

For example, in the sample Contribution report, you could open the report in Design view, and then open the Property Sheet. Locate the Record Source property on the Data tab, and then paste the SQL statement from the Contribution query (as shown in Figure 10.24) into the Record Source property box. View the report in Print Preview, as shown in Figure 10.27.

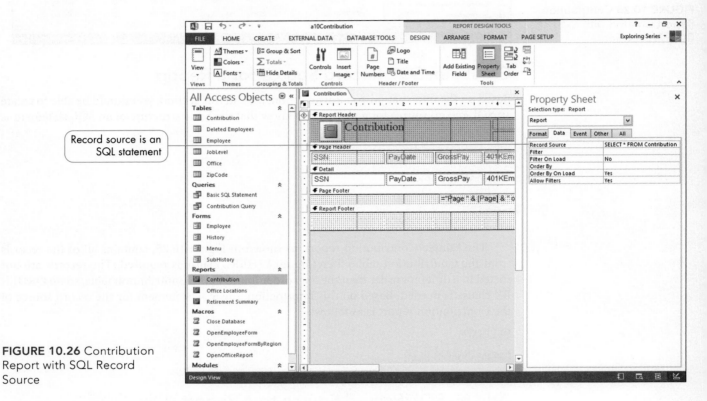

FIGURE 10.26 Contribution Report with SQL Record Source

Contribution Report for a specific SSN

FIGURE 10.27 Contribution Report with Modified SQL Record Source

Copy an SQL Statement from SQL View

The query discussed earlier, shown in Figure 10.22, contains SSN criteria and is sorted by PayDate. When you switch the query to SQL view, as shown in Figure 10.24, the SQL statement is displayed. Because the SQL statement is in text format, you can copy the statement and paste it into the record source of a report.

TIP | A Lengthy SQL Statement

When you paste an SQL statement into a record source, it might appear that the statement will not fit into the property box. However, the Record Source property can hold most SQL statements, including those statements that are very long. Use Shift+F2 to open the Zoom window to view or paste a lengthy SQL statement.

Quick **Concepts**

1. What is the purpose of Structured Query Language (SQL)? **p. 593**

2. What is the purpose of the SQL SELECT statement? **p. 594**

3. Why would you use an SQL statement as a record source for a report? **p. 597**

Hands-On Exercises

Watch the Video for this Hands-On Exercise!

MyITLab®
HOE3 Training

3 Structured Query Language

SQL will only be used in the Sunshine database in special circumstances. You suggest to Nancy that you use an SQL statement for the record source of two reports. You explain that an SQL statement can be used in place of a table or query record source.

Skills covered: Understand the Fundamentals of SQL • Create a Query and View the Equivalent SQL Statement • Using an SQL SELECT Statement as a Record Source

STEP 1 ▶▶ UNDERSTAND THE FUNDAMENTALS OF SQL

You need a query that will display employees who are social workers, and you have decided to try creating it in SQL before making any changes to the Sunshine objects. You create a new query, and then immediately switch to SQL view, where you can practice writing an SQL statement. Refer to Figure 10.28 as you complete Step 1.

FIGURE 10.28 Basic SQL Statement

a. Open *a10h2Sunshine_LastFirst* if you closed it at the end of Hands-On Exercise 2. Click the **FILE tab**, click **Save As**, click **Save As**, and then type **a10h3Sunshine_LastFirst**, changing *h2* to *h3*. Click **Save**.

b. Click the **CREATE tab** and click **Query Design** in the Queries group.

The Show Table dialog box displays.

c. Close the Show Table dialog box without adding any tables.

You will create a query using SQL statements rather than the usual query design interface.

d. Click **SQL** in the Results group.

The abbreviated SELECT statement displays in the SQL window.

e. Move the insertion point after *SELECT* and before the semicolon (;). Complete the following SQL statement in the SQL window and click **Run** in the Results group.

SELECT *
FROM Employee;

The records for all 19 employees are displayed in the results. All fields from the Employee table also display.

f. Click the **View arrow** and select **SQL View** from the list of options.

The current SQL statement displays in the SQL window.

g. Move the insertion point before the semicolon (;), revise the SQL statement as shown below, and then click **Run**.

> SELECT *
> FROM Employee
> WHERE JobCode = 100;

You added a WHERE clause to extract only the employees who are social workers (JobCode = 100). Only eight employees are displayed in the results.

h. Click the **View arrow** and select **SQL View**. Move the insertion point before the semicolon (;), revise the SQL statement as shown below, and then click **Run**.

> SELECT *
> FROM Employee
> WHERE JobCode = 100
> ORDER BY HireDate;

The same eight employees are displayed in the results, except now they display in HireDate order.

i. Save the query as **HireDateSQL Statement**. Close the query.

STEP 2 ≫ CREATE A QUERY AND VIEW THE EQUIVALENT SQL STATEMENT

You need to create a query that will show all the 401k contributions for Cook County employees. You want to see the equivalent SQL statement after you create the query in Design view first. Refer to Figure 10.29 as you complete Step 2.

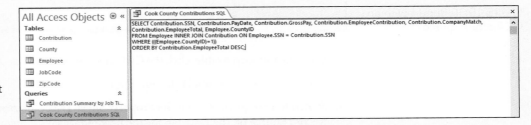

FIGURE 10.29 SQL Statement to Extract Cook County Contributions

a. Click the **CREATE tab** and click **Query Design** in the Queries group.

The Show Table dialog box displays.

b. Add the Contribution and Employee tables to the Query design using the Show Table dialog box and close the Show Table dialog box.

c. Add all the fields from the Contribution table to the query design grid. Add the CountyID field from the Employee table. Run the query.

All the fields of all 219 contributions are displayed in the results. You need to add the criterion for Cook County.

d. Switch to Design view and type **1** in the **CountyID criteria row**. Run the query.

The numeral 1 is the Cook County ID and is used as the criterion for the search. Forty-eight contributions now display in the results. You need to sort the results by descending EmployeeTotal amount.

e. Switch to Design view and select **Descending** from the EmployeeTotal sort row. Run the query.

The same 48 contributions are now displayed in descending EmployeeTotal order.

f. Switch to SQL view to see the equivalent SQL statement.

You learned how to create a query in Design view first and viewed the equivalent SQL statement in SQL view.

g. Save the query as **Cook County Contributions SQL**. Close the query.

STEP 3 >> USING AN SQL SELECT STATEMENT AS A RECORD SOURCE

Terry asks you to create an employee report sorted by the JobCode field. You decide to create the report based on the Employee table using the Report tool. You will then replace the Employee table record source with an SQL statement. Refer to Figure 10.30 as you complete Step 3.

FIGURE 10.30 Report with an SQL Record Source

a. Click the **Employee table**, click the **CREATE tab**, and then click **Report** in the Reports group.

Access creates a new tabular layout report.

b. Switch to Design view, open the Property Sheet, select the report, and then verify that the Record Source on the Data tab for the new report says *Employee*. Close the Property Sheet.

c. Click the **CREATE tab** and click **Query Design** in the Queries group.

The Show Table dialog box displays.

d. Add the Employee table to the query design using the Show Table dialog box. Close the Show Table dialog box.

e. Add the * field from the Employee table to the query design grid. Run the query.

Nineteen employees are displayed in the results.

f. Switch to Design view and add the JobCode field to the query design grid. Uncheck the **Show box** for JobCode and type >150 in the JobCode criteria.. Run the query.

The query displays 6 employees whose job code is greater than 150.

g. Switch to SQL view and copy the statement in the SQL window.

h. Click the **EMPLOYEE tab** and open the Property Sheet. Delete the existing Record Source and paste the SQL statement you copied into the box. Press **Shift+F2** and compare your statement to Figure 10.30.

i. Close the Zoom dialog box and open the report in Print Preview to test the new record source.

Because the report contains all the fields for the 6 employees, the report does not fit onto one page; however, you can leave the report as is.

j. Save the report as **Employee Report** and close it.

k. Close the query without saving it.

Chapter Objectives Review

After reading this chapter, you have accomplished the following objectives:

1. Understand the purpose of a macro.

- Understanding the purpose of a macro: A macro is an Access object that enables you to execute an action or series of actions based on the status of a button, a form, or a report. A macro can be run to accomplish repetitive or routine tasks automatically.

2. Create a stand-alone macro.

- Creating a stand-alone macro: A stand-alone macro displays as an object in the Navigation Pane and can be run independently of other objects. You use the Macro Designer to create a stand-alone macro. To run a stand-alone macro, double-click the macro name in the Navigation Pane.

3. Use the Macro Designer.

- Using the Macro Designer: The Macro Designer is a tool in Access that makes it easier to create and edit macros. The user interface simplifies the tasks of adding actions and parameters while building macros.

4. Attach an embedded macro to an event.

- Attaching an embedded macro to an event: Embedded macros are always attached to an event of a control on a form or report, or to an event of the form or report object itself. They can only be run from within the object itself.
- Attach an embedded macro to a report event: You can create a control that automatically creates an embedded macro for you (such as the command button control) or attach an embedded macro to an event by clicking the ellipsis (…) in the Property Sheet. A command button can be placed on a report that will print the report, close it, or close the database automatically.

5. Identify when to use a data macro.

- Identifying when to use a data macro: Data macros are only used with table events. You might add a data macro to a table to verify that a customer has no outstanding invoices before placing a new order, to keep a log of any changes made to a specific table, or to send a confirmation e-mail when a contributor makes a donation. A form based on a table that contains a data macro inherits the logic of the table.

6. Create an event-driven data macro.

- Creating an event-driven macro: Event-driven data macros are triggered when a table event, such as After Delete or Before Change, occurs.

- Testing and modifying a data macro: To attach a data macro to a table event, open the table you want to add the data macro to (in Design view) and click Create Data Macros in the Field, Record & Table Events group on the Design tab; to modify a data macro, reopen the macro and edit as needed.

7. Create a named data macro.

- Creating a named data macro: You can access these macros from anywhere in the database. You can run the named data macro from inside another macro using the RunDataMacro action.
- Attaching a named data macro to a Form: A named data macro can be run from within a form, for example, after a record is updated, an e-mail can be automatically generated.

8. Understand the fundamentals of SQL.

- Understanding the fundamentals of SQL: Structured Query Language (SQL) is the industry-standard language for defining, manipulating, and retrieving the data in a database. In fact, all Access queries use an SQL SELECT statement—behind the scenes—to extract data from tables.

9. Interpret an SQL SELECT statement.

- Interpreting an SQL SELECT statement: When you view an SQL SELECT statement in SQL view, the words shown in UPPERCASE are SQL keywords. An SQL keyword defines the purpose and the structure of an SQL statement. The four basic keywords found in a typical SQL SELECT statement are SELECT, FROM, WHERE, and ORDER BY.

10. Use an SQL SELECT statement as a record source.

- Creating a query and viewing the equivalent SQL statement: Once a query is created using Design view, the SQL statements can be viewed by switching to SQL view. A correlation exists between each SQL statement and a query parameter.
- Using an SQL statement as a record source: You can also use an SQL SELECT statement as the record source for a form or a report rather than a table or a query. Locate the Record Source property of the form or report and either type an SQL statement into the property box or copy and paste a statement from the SQL view window.

Key Terms Matching

Match the key terms with their definitions. Write the key term letter by the appropriate numbered definition.

a. Argument
b. Embedded macro
c. Event
d. Data macro
e. FROM keyword
f. Macro
g. Macro Designer

h. ORDER BY keyword
i. SELECT keyword
j. SQL keyword
k. SQL SELECT statement
l. Stand-alone macro
m. Structured Query Language (SQL)
n. WHERE keyword

1. _____ A series of actions that can be programmed to automate tasks. **p. 570**

2. _____ Database object that you create and use independently of other controls or objects. **p. 570**

3. _____ Occurs when a user enters, edits, or deletes data; also occurs when a user opens, uses, or closes a form or report. **p. 571**

4. _____ A macro that executes when an event attached to a control or object occurs. **p. 571**

5. _____ User interface that enables you to create and edit macros. **p. 572**

6. _____ A variable, constant, or expression that is needed to produce the output for an action. **p. 572**

7. _____ The industry-standard language for defining, manipulating, and retrieving the data in a database. **p. 593**

8. _____ Defines the purpose and the structure of an SQL statement. **p. 594**

9. _____ Block of text that is used to retrieve data from the tables in a database. **p. 594**

10. _____ The keyword that specifies the table (or tables) that will be searched. **p. 595**

11. _____ The keyword that instructs Access to return the specific fields from one or more tables. **p. 595**

12. _____ The keyword that is used to sort the records by a certain field in either ascending or descending order. **p. 596**

13. _____ The keyword that specifies the criteria that records must match to be included in the results. **p. 595**

14. _____ Executes a series of actions when a table event occurs. **p. 583**

Multiple Choice

1. Which statement about macros is false?

(a) Access supports embedded macros.

(b) Macros can be used with tables.

(c) The Macro Designer makes it easier to create macros.

(d) All macros display in the Navigation Pane.

2. Which tool automatically creates an embedded macro?

(a) Macro Designer

(b) Command Button Wizard

(c) Report Wizard

(d) Form Wizard

3. Which statement is true about a stand-alone macro?

(a) A stand-alone macro is created with the Macro Designer.

(b) Stand-alone macros exist outside the database.

(c) Stand-alone macros contain VBA code.

(d) Stand-alone macros can only be used in a table.

4. Which of these is a variable, constant, or expression that is needed to produce the output for a macro action?

(a) Command

(b) Statement

(c) Argument

(d) Event

5. Which statement is false for a named data macro?

(a) It must be created in a table.

(b) It cannot be attached to an event.

(c) It can be modified using the Macro Designer.

(d) It can be referenced using RunDataMacro.

6. Which is not a valid event?

(a) Before Update

(b) On Close

(c) If Open

(d) After Insert

7. Which statement is not true about SQL?

(a) It was invented originally by Microsoft.

(b) When you create a query, SQL is created automatically.

(c) SELECT statements retrieve data from tables.

(d) SQL lacks a graphical user interface.

8. Which SQL keyword returns a subset of the table records based on criteria?

(a) SELECT

(b) FROM

(c) WHERE

(d) ORDER BY

9. Which character is required at the end of an SQL statement?

(a) >

(b) :

(c) "

(d) ;

10. Which of the following is not a valid record source for a report?

(a) A query

(b) A SELECT statement

(c) A table

(d) A macro

Practice Exercises

1 Advertising Specialists, Inc.

Advertising Specialists, Inc., is a leading advertising agency with offices in Atlanta, Chicago, Miami, and Boston. The company has asked you to create a new form named Chicago Employees that only contains employees in Chicago. You have also been asked to create a menu that users can use to open the three reports and one form. First, you will create a macro that opens the Switchboard Manager (the feature that enables you to create a menu system). However, you will then decide to use the Form Design to create a menu manually instead. This exercise follows the same set of skills as used in Hands-On Exercises 1 and 3 in the chapter. Refer to Figure 10.31 as you complete this exercise.

FIGURE 10.31 Menu Created with Command Buttons

a. Open *a10p1Advertise*. Click the **FILE tab**, click **Save As**, click **Save As**, and then type **a10p1Advertise_LastFirst**. Click **Save**.

b. Open the Employees table and add yourself as a new record. Type **88888** as your EmployeeID. Type your last name, first name, and gender. Use the same values as the previous record (Marder) to complete the remaining fields. Close the table.

c. Open the Employees form in Design view. Click the **FILE tab**, click **Save As**, click **Save Object As**, and then click **Save As**. Type **Chicago Employees** in the **Save As dialog box** and click **OK**.

d. Open the Property Sheet, click the **Data tab**, and then click the **Record Source property**. Press **Shift+F2** to see a zoom view of the record source property.

e. Type **Select * From Employees Where LocationID="L03"** in the **Record Source property** to replace the Employees table with an SQL statement.

f. Click **OK** and save the form. Switch to Form view. Advance through all the records to verify that only Chicago (L03) employees are showing. Close the form.

g. Add the Switchboard Manager to the database by creating a macro as follows:
- Click the **CREATE tab** and click **Macro**.
- Type **RunMenuCommand** in the **Add New Action box**. Press **Enter**.
- Type **SwitchboardManager** in the **Command box**.
- Save the macro as **Switchboard Manager**.
- Close the Macro Designer.

h. Double-click the **Switchboard Manager macro** in the Navigation Pane. The Switchboard Manager starts, but you decide not to create a switchboard. When the warning message displays, click **No** to close the dialog box.

You decide to use Form Design and create a menu manually.

i. Click the **CREATE tab** and click **Form Design** in the Forms group.

j. Add the following labels, using Figure 10.31 as a guide:
   - A title label: **Advertising Specialists, Inc. Employee Database**
   - A subtitle label: **Forms**
   - A subtitle label: **Reports**

k. Use the Command Button Wizard to add the following buttons, using Figure 10.31 as a guide:
   - A button to open the Employees form. Set the text to display on the button as **Employees** and name the button **cmdEmployees**. Adjust the button position and size as shown.
   - A button to open the Employee Master List report. Set the text to display on the button as **Employee Master List** and name the button **cmdMasterEmployee**. Adjust the button position and size as shown.
   - A button to open the Employees by Location report. Set the text to display on the button as **Employees (by Location)** and name the button **cmdEmployeesLocation**. Adjust the button position and size as shown.
   - A button to open the Employees by Title report. Set the text to display on the button as **Employees (by Title)** and name the button **cmdEmployeesTitle**. Adjust the button position and size as shown.

l. Add the following button, using Figure 10.31 as a guide:
   - A button to quit the application. Set the text to display on the button as **Exit Access** and name the button **cmdExitAccess**. Adjust the button position and size as shown.

m. Add the following design elements, using Figure 10.31 as a guide:
   - A rectangle surrounding the title and the subtitle labels.
   - A label at the bottom of the report: **Designed by** *your name*.

n. Save the form with the name **Menu**.

o. View the Menu form in Form view. Click each button to test the functionality. Click the **Exit Access button** to test it; if Access closes, then your testing is complete.

p. Close Access.

q. Submit based on your instructor's directions.

2 Reliable Insurance, Inc.

Reliable Insurance, Inc., has decided to raise the salary of any employee with a good performance rating by 5%. You will create a data macro to help them implement this new policy. The company also creates a spreadsheet containing all employees from location L01 (Atlanta). The spreadsheet is faxed to the corporate office each month. The office manager would like to automate this process with a macro. This exercise follows the same set of skills used in Hands-On Exercises 1 and 2 in the chapter. Refer to Figure 10.32 as you complete this exercise.

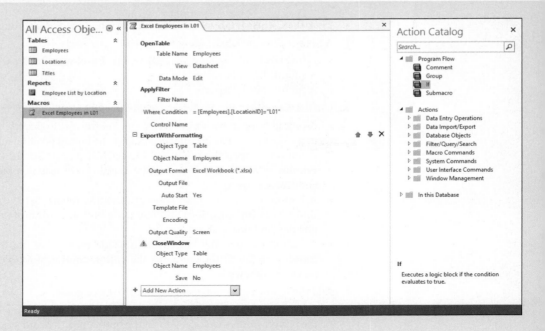

FIGURE 10.32 Macro to Export Data to Excel

a. Open *a10p2Reliable*. Click the **FILE tab**, click **Save As**, click **Save As**, and then type **a10p2Reliable_LastFirst**. Click **Save**.

b. Open the Employees table and add yourself as a new record. Type **88888** as your EmployeeID. Type your last name, first name, and gender. Type **L01** for your location. Use the same values as the previous record (Marder) to complete the remaining fields.

c. Switch to Design view and add a new field under the Salary field, called **SalaryAdjusted**, with data type **Currency**. Save the table.

d. Click **Create Data Macros** in the Field, Record & Table Events group and click the **Before Change event**. The Macro Designer opens. Follow these steps:

• Drag the **If statement** from the Program Flow folder in the Action Catalog to the Add New Action box in the Macro.
• Type **[Performance] = "Good"** in the **Conditional expression box**.
• Select **SetField** using the Add New Action arrow.
• Type **SalaryAdjusted** in the **Name box**.
• Type **[Salary]*1.05** in the **Value box**.
• Click the **Add Else command**.
• Select **SetField** using the Add New Action arrow.
• Type **SalaryAdjusted** in the **Name box**.
• Type **[Salary]** in the **Value box**.
• Save the Data Macro.
• Close the Data Macro.
• Save the table.

e. Switch to Datasheet view. Retype **Good** in the **Performance field** of the third employee (Johnson). Press ⬇ to move to the next record and activate the data macro.

The new increased salary displays in the SalaryAdjusted field.

f. Repeat the process for all Good employees and upgrade your performance from Average to Good and press ⬇. Close the table.

g. Click the **CREATE tab** and click **Macro** in the Macros & Code group to open the Macro Designer. You will create a macro to show employees with location L01.

h. Click in the **Add New Action box** and type **OpenTable**. Press **Enter**.

i. Add the following arguments:

Table Name	Employees
View	Datasheet *(default)*
Data Mode	Edit *(default)*

j. Click in the **Add New Action box** and type **ApplyFilter**. Press **Enter**.

k. Add the following arguments:

Filter Name	*(blank)*
Where Condition	[Employees].[LocationID]="L01"
Control Name	*(blank)*

l. Save the macro as **Excel Employees in L01**. Click **Run** in the Tools group to test the macro results so far. If the macro is working, the Employees table should open with only the L01 employees displayed. Close the filtered Employees table.

m. Click in the **Add New Action box** and type **ExportWithFormatting**. Press **Enter**.

n. Add the following arguments:

Object Type	Table *(default)*
Object Name	Employees
Output Format	Excel Workbook (*.xlsx)
Output File	*(optional: enter a file name and path)*
Auto Start	Yes
Template File	*(blank)*
Encoding	*(blank)*
Output Quality	Screen

o. Click in the **Add New Action box** and type **CloseWindow**. Press **Enter**.

p. Add the following arguments:

Object Type	Table
Object Name	Employees
Save	No

q. Save the macro. Close the macro. Run the macro by double-clicking the macro name in the Navigation Pane. The results should export the L01 employees to an Excel spreadsheet (you must designate the location if you left the Output File blank above). Close the spreadsheet, and the macro closes the Employees table.

r. Close Access.

s. Submit based on your instructor's directions.

Mid-Level Exercises

1 Northwind Exporters

ANALYSIS CASE

Northwind Exporters provides specialty foods to businesses around the world. You have been asked to filter the orders form so that each employee can see only his or her orders. You will also filter a report using an SQL statement. Refer to Figure 10.33 as you complete this exercise.

FIGURE 10.33 Filtering with an Embedded Macro

a. Open *a10m1Exporters*. Click the **FILE tab**, click **Save As**, click **Save As**, and then type **a10m1Exporters_LastFirst**. Click **Save**.

b. Open the Employees table and note that nine employees are shown. Close the table.

c. Open the Orders form. Advance through the orders using the Navigation Bar at the bottom of the form. Notice that the EmployeeID value is different for each order. Switch to Design view.

d. Add the first button to the form as shown in Figure 10.33. Click **Cancel** when the Command Button Wizard displays. Open the Property Sheet. Set the caption of the command button to **1**. Set the size of the button to **.25"** high and **.25"** wide.

   You are planning to create an embedded macro to filter the order records for Employee ID 1 when the command button is clicked.

e. Click the new **1 button** and in the Property Sheet, click the **On Click event**. Click the **ellipsis (…)** and with Macro Builder selected, click **OK** when the Choose Builder dialog box displays.

   The Macro Designer displays.

f. Type **ApplyFilter** in the **Add New Action box**. Type **[EmployeeID]=1** in the **Where Condition box**. Save and close the macro.

g. Switch to Form view and notice the total orders (50) as indicated in the Navigation Bar at the bottom of the form. Click **1** and notice the total orders (4) for EmployeeID 1 in the Navigation Bar. Advance through the orders, and then verify the EmployeeID is 1 for each order.

h. Switch to Design view, copy the **1 button**, paste it to the right of button 1, and then set **2** as the caption. In the Property Sheet, with button 2 selected, click the **On Click event**, and then click the **ellipsis (…)**. Modify the Where Condition box so it reads **2** instead of *1*. Test the new button in Form view.

i. Add buttons 3 to 6 using the same method as in step h.

DISCOVER

j. Create a seventh button with the caption **X** to remove the filters so all the orders will display in the form. Test each new button in Form view when finished and save the form.

k. Select the seven buttons. Click **Align** in the Sizing & Ordering group on the ARRANGE tab to align the tops of the seven buttons. Increase the horizontal spacing between the buttons so that about two dots of space remain between them. Save and close the form.

l. Open the Customers report and take note of the range of countries represented.

m. Switch to Design view. Open the Property Sheet, select the report, and then, on the DATA tab, click the **Record Source property**. Type **SELECT * FROM Customers WHERE Country = [Enter a country];** in the record source in place of the Customers table.

n. Save the report. Switch to Print Preview and type **USA** in the **Enter Parameter Value dialog box**. Click **OK** and close the report. Close Access.

★ **o.** State why you think it might be important to create a report that enables you to make selections according to the country code. Write a brief paragraph or two stating your reasons in a Word document and submit it to your instructor with the file name *a10m1Exporters.docx*.

p. Submit based on your instructor's directions.

---

2 Payroll Service, Inc.

ANALYSIS CASE

Payroll Service, Inc., provides payroll services to mid-sized businesses in Massachusetts, Illinois, Colorado, and California. You have been assigned to help the company set up business logic rules using macros and data macros. Your first task is to restrict the number of exemptions an employee can claim (based on marital status). You begin by restricting single employees to only one exemption. You will also create a macro that will e-mail the current list of employees to the main office. The main office needs the list in HTML format. Finally, you will create an SQL record source for a report. Refer to Figure 10.34 as you complete this exercise.

FIGURE 10.34 Stand-Alone Macro Sends a Database Object

a. Open *a10m2Salaries*. Click the **FILE tab**, click **Save As**, click **Save As**, and then type **a10m2Salaries_LastFirst**. Click **Save**.

b. Open the Employee table in Design view. Click **Create Data Macros** in the Field, Record & Table Events group and click the **Before Change event**.

The Macro Designer displays.

c. Drag the **If statement** from the Program Flow folder in the Action Catalog to the Add New Action box in the macro.

- Type **[MaritalStatus] = "single"** in the **Conditional expression box**.
- Select **SetField** from the Add New Action arrow.
- Type **Exemptions** in the **Name box**.
- Type **1** in the **Value box**.
- Save the Data Macro.
- Close the Data Macro.
- Save the table.

d. Switch to Datasheet view. In the first record, type **2** in the **Exemptions field**. Press ⬇ to move to the second row to trigger the Before Change event and the data macro. The number *2* changes to *1*. Repeat the test on the second record. Close the table.

e. Click the **CREATE tab** and click **Macro** in the Macros & Code group to open the Macro Designer.

f. Click in the **Add New Action box** and type **EmailDatabaseObject**. Press **Enter**.

g. Add the following arguments:

Object Type	Table *(default)*
Object Name	Employee
Output Format	HTML (*.htm; *.html)
To	*your e-mail address*
Cc	*(blank)*
Bcc	*(blank)*
Subject	E-mail Employee Table
Message Text	The Employee table is attached in HTML format.
Edit Message	No
Template File	*(blank)*

h. Save the macro with the name **Email Table**. Close the macro.

The macro now displays in the Navigation Pane.

i. Double-click the **Email Table macro**. The macro runs and attempts to send the Employee table as an attachment. Click **OK** if you receive the Microsoft Outlook warning message, as shown in Figure 10.21. Click **OK** again and click **Stop All Macros**.

If the warning message was not received, click **Allow**. Check your e-mail after a few minutes to see if you received the E-mail Employee Table message.

  DISCOVER

j. Open the Salaries by Gender report in Design view. Open the Property Sheet and verify the Record Source property contains *Employee*. Determine from the database which job code refers to which job title. Note the job code for Associate Consultant and the data type for this field.

★ **k.** Type an SQL statement into the Record Source property. The report should include all records from the Employee table except Associate Consultants. Switch to Print Preview and verify the report contains 10 records with the overall average salary of $79,650.00. Save the report.

l. Close the report. Close Access.

m. Submit based on your instructor's directions.

---

3 | **Loan Analysis**

COLLABORATION CASE

In the following exercise, you will create a data macro to send an e-mail message if the loan for a customer is set to Adjustable. Then you will modify the SQL record source for a query to change its criterion. Finally, you will modify a report based on the modified query.

a. Open *a10m3Collaboration* and save it as **a10m3Collaboration_GroupName**. As a team, study the existing database and the relationship between the Customers and Loans tables.

Assign the following tasks to a team member:

b. Open the Loans table in Design view. Create an embedded After Update data macro. Create an If statement that will determine if the loan is set to Adjustable. If true, send an e-mail to yourself with the following information:

Subject: **Adjustable vs. Fixed Rates**

Body: **Please check our recently lowered fixed interest rate for this loan**.

Save and close the macro.

c. View the Loans table in Datasheet view. Save the table when prompted. In the record for L0001, set the Adjustable field to *Yes* by clicking in the check box and pressing ⬇ to update the record. The update causes an e-mail to be sent to you if your computer is configured to do so. Otherwise, click **OK** in the Microsoft Outlook message box. Close the Loans table.

Assign the following task to a team member:

d. Open the Car Loans query in SQL view. Set the criterion so that the query displays mortgage loans. Return to Design view, observe the change, and then run the query. Save and close the query, and then rename it as **Mortgage Loans**.

Assign the following tasks to a team member:

e. Open the Customers table. For Customer C0008, add your first and last names and e-mail address to the table. Close the table.

f. Rename the Customer Auto Loans report as **Customer Mortgage Loans**. Open the report.

g. Collaborate with your team to determine what would be the best way to portray the Customer Mortgage Loans report. Make any design changes you see fit. Modify the report title to **Mortgage Loans**. Sort the records first by Last Name and then by Amount in ascending order.

h. View the report in Print Preview; the report should consist of one page. Save and close the report. Export the report as a Word document using the same name and save it as a Word document. Close the report and exit Word. Do not save the export steps.

i. Close the database. Exit Access. Submit the database and documents based on your instructor's directions.

Advanced SQL

RESEARCH CASE

Find a Web site that will teach you some additional SQL statements. Research the correct keywords to join two tables together. For example, find out how to list all of the fields and records from the Orders table and add the Customer Name field from the Customers table in the first column of the query results. Open the *a10b2Orders* database, save it as **a10b2Orders_LastFirst**, and then practice creating the SQL statements. Create a query in SQL view that performs the required task and save it as Orders by Customer. Submit the database *a10b2Orders_LastFirst* based on your instructor's directions.

Troubleshoot: Fix a Macro

DISASTER RECOVERY

Open the *a10b3Bonus* database and save the database as **a10b3Bonus_LastFirst**. A macro named Macro—Open Objects was created to open the Employees table, the Employees Form, and the Employees Report. The macro is not working properly; the third object does not display at all, and the first two objects are read-only—you want them to open in edit mode. Analyze the macro, diagnose the problems, and then fix the problems. Save and run the macro to ensure that it works properly. Submit the database *a10b3Bonus_LastFirst* based on your instructor's directions.

Meetings

SOFT SKILLS CASE

You want to determine how many of the new employees in your database will attend orientation meetings on specific dates. You decide to create a command button to run a macro from a form that will display query results with meeting attendees. Open *a10b4Meetings*. Save a copy of the database as **a10b4Meetings_LastFirst**. In the New Employees Data Entry form, create a command button that will open the Orientation Meeting query. Place the button at the 5" mark on the horizontal ruler, aligned with the top of the SSN control. Set the caption of the button as **Run Orientation Meeting** and name the button **cmdOrientation**. Set the width of the button to **1.75"**. Test the button in Form view. When prompted, enter the meeting date of **11/5/2018**. Close the query. Save and close the form, and close the database. Exit Access. Submit the database *a10b4Meetings_LastFirst* based on your instructor's directions.

Capstone Exercise

You are employed at Specialty Foods, Ltd., a small international gourmet foods distributor. The company has asked you to modify the database and improve the reliability of the data entry process. You decide to create a few macros and also add a menu for the common forms and reports. You will also modify the record source of one of the reports.

Database File Setup

a. Open *a10c1Specialty*, click the **FILE tab**, click **Save As**, click **Save As**, and then type **a10c1Specialty_LastFirst**. Click **Save**.

Create an Event-Driven Data Macro

A new field, ExpectedShipDate, was added to the Orders table. You will populate this new field when a new order is added using a Data Macro.

a. Open the Orders table in Datasheet view, observe the data, and then switch to Design view.

b. Create a data macro attached to the Before Change event.

c. Use the SetField Action to populate the ExpectedShipDate in the table. The ExpectedShipDate will always be 10 days after the OrderDate.

d. Save the macro. Close the macro. Save the table.

Test the Data Macro

Change a value in the first record, and then move to the second record to trigger the macro.

a. Switch to Datasheet view of the Orders table.

b. Retype the OrderDate in the first record (Order No 10248) and press ⬇. The macro will be triggered and automatically fill in the ExpectedShipDate with a date 10 days after the OrderDate.

c. Repeat the test on the second and third records (10249 and 10250). Close the table.

Create a Menu Form

Create a menu form using the Form Design view. Add three command buttons for the three forms in the database, and then add three command buttons for the three reports in the database.

a. Open the Main Menu form in Design view.

b. Add three buttons below the Forms label that will open the three forms in the database: Enter Customers, Enter Employees, and Enter Suppliers (in that order). Set the first one at the 2" mark on the vertical ruler and the 1" mark on the horizontal ruler. Set the height of the button to **0.5"** and the width to **1"**. The first button should have the caption **Enter Customers** with the button named as **cmdEnterCustomers**.

c. Repeat the same procedure for Enter Employees and Enter Suppliers, setting each button immediately below the one before it.

d. Add three buttons below the Reports label that will print preview the three reports in the database: Employees, Orders, and Products (in that order). Set the first one at the 2" mark on the vertical ruler and the 4" mark on the horizontal ruler. Set the height of the button to **0.5"** and the width to **1"**. The first button should have the caption **Employees** with the button named as **cmdEmployees**.

e. Repeat the same procedure for Orders and Products, setting each button immediately below the one before it.

f. Save the form, switch to Form view, and then test the buttons. Close all objects except the Main Menu form.

g. Switch to Design view, add an **Exit button** that exits Access to the top-right corner of the form, at the 0" mark on the vertical ruler and the 5" mark on the horizontal ruler, with a height of **0.5"** and a width of **1"**. Name the button **cmdExit**.

h. Apply the **Slice theme** to the Main Menu form only. Save the form, switch to Form view, and then test the Exit button. Reopen the database.

Add an SQL Statement as a Record Source

You need to modify the records in the Employees report. Modify the record source so that only employees with a Sales position display in the report.

a. Open the Employees report in Design view. Open the Property Sheet and click the **Record Source box**.

b. Type an SQL statement into the Record Source property of the report. The statement should select all fields (*) for employees with the Sales Representative title. Save the report.

c. Test the report in Print Preview and close the report. Close Access.

d. Submit based on your instructor's directions.

Access Introductory Application Capstone Exercise

You were recently hired by your local college to help with registering all transfer students. The college's Transfer Counseling Department is a one-stop location for transfer students to come with questions. They have been working with Excel spreadsheets generated by the Information Technology department, but they are hoping to do more with an Access database. They have had a number of problems, including employees putting information in the wrong fields, putting information in the wrong format, and creating incorrect formulas. They are also hoping for more consistent ways of finding information, as well as being able to generate reports. Your tasks include importing an existing Excel worksheet as a table into your Access database; modifying the table; creating a relationship between two tables; creating queries with calculated fields, functions, and totals; creating a form for input; and creating a report.

Set Up the Database File and Import an Excel Worksheet

To start, you have been provided with a database the Information Technology department created. The database has one table and one form. You will be importing an Excel spreadsheet into a table and creating a primary key.

a. Start Access. Open *a00c1College* and save the database as **a00c1College_LastFirst**.

b. Import the *a00c1Transfer* Excel workbook into a table named **Transfer Schools**. While importing the data, choose **StudentID** as the primary key field. Ensure *StudentID* has a data type of Short Text.

Modify a Table

Now that you have imported the data from the spreadsheet, you will modify the field properties in the Transfer Schools table and demonstrate sorting.

a. Set the StudentID field size to **10**.

b. Remove the @ symbol from the StudentID format property.

c. Change the AdmittingSchool field size to **75**.

d. Change the RegistrationFee and TuitionDue fields to have **0** decimal places.

e. Switch to Datasheet View. Resize all columns so all data are displayed.

f. Sort the Transfer Schools table on the CreditsTransferred field in ascending order.

g. Save and close the table.

Create Relationships

Now that the table is imported and modified, you will create a relationship between the two tables.

a. Add the Transfer Schools and Transfer Students tables to the Relationships window.

b. Create a one-to-one relationship between the StudentID field in the Transfer Students (primary) table and the StudentID field in the Transfer Schools (related) table. Enforce referential integrity between the two tables.

c. Save the changes and close the Relationships window.

Modify Data in a Form

You will demonstrate changing information in a form.

a. Open the Transfer Students Data Entry form.

b. Change the major for *Cornelius Kavanaugh* to **Elementary Education**. Close the form.

Create a Query

Rey Rivera, a counselor in the center, would like your assistance in helping him find certain information. You will create a query for him and demonstrate how he can change information.

a. Create a new query using Design view. This query will access fields from both the Transfer Schools and Transfer Students tables. From the Transfer Students table, add the FirstName, LastName, Major, Class, and GPA fields. From the Transfer Schools table, add the AdmissionDate, TuitionDue, CreditsEarned, and CreditsTransferred fields.

b. Save the query as **Transfer Credits**.

c. Set the criteria in the AdmissionDate field to **8/1/2015**. Run the query (144 records will display).

d. Enter the TuitionDue for Diana Sullivan as **$1500** and the GPA for Audrey Owen as **3.51**.

e. Save the query.

Create Calculated Fields

Now that you have created the query, you will create a second query for Rey that will calculate the number of credits students lost upon transfer, the tuition payments for which they will be responsible (assuming three payments per semester), and the payment due date.

a. Switch to Design view of the Transfer Credits query. Save the query as **Transfer Credit Calculations**.

b. Remove the criteria from the AdmissionDate field.

c. Create a calculated field in the first empty field cell of the query named **LostCredits** that subtracts CreditsTransferred from CreditsEarned.

d. Create another calculated field named **TuitionPayments** that determines tuition paid in three installments. Using the Pmt function, replace the rate argument with **0.025/3**, the num_periods argument with **3**, and the present_value argument with the student's tuition payment. Use **0** for the future_value and type arguments. Ensure the payment appears as a positive number.

e. Format the TuitionPayments calculated field as **Currency**.

f. Create another calculated field named **DueDate** after the TuitionPayments field. To calculate the due date, add **30** to their AdmissionDate. Run the query and verify that the three calculated fields have valid data.

g. Add a total row to the query. Average the GPA column and sum the LostCredits column. Save and close the query.

Create a Totals Query

Cala Hajjar, the director of the center, needs to summarize information about the transfer students for the 2015–2016 academic year to present to the College's Board of Trustees. You will create a totals query for her to summarize the number of transfer students, average number of credits earned and transferred, and total tuition earned by transfer institution.

a. Create a new query in Design view. Add the Transfer Schools table.

b. Add the AdmittingSchool, StudentID, CreditsEarned, CreditsTransferred, and TuitionDue fields.

c. Sort the query by AdmittingSchool in ascending order.

d. Show the Total row. Group by AdmittingSchool and show the count of StudentID, the average CreditsEarned, the average of CreditsTransferred, and the sum of TuitionDue.

e. Format both average fields as **Standard**.

f. Change the caption for the StudentID field to **NumStudents**, the caption for the CreditsEarned average to **AvgCreditsEarned**, the caption for the CreditsTransferred average to **AvgCredits Transferred**, and the caption for SumOfTuitionDue to **TotalTuition**.

g. Run the query. Resize columns so all data are shown.

h. Save the query as **Transfer Summary**.

i. Close the query.

Create a Form

Hideo Sasaki, the department's administrative assistant, will handle data entry. He has asked you to simplify the way he inputs information into the new table. You will create a form based on the new Transfer Schools table.

a. Create a Split Form using the Transfer Schools table as the source.

b. Change the height of the AdmittingSchool field to reduce extra space.

c. Remove the layout. Shrink each field so it is only as large as it needs to be.

d. Click on record 123455 in the bottom half of the split form. Make sure all fields are still visible. If not, adjust the controls so all values are visible.

e. Move the CreditsTransferred field so it is to the right of the CreditsEarned field on the same row.

f. Change the format of the TuitionDue field so the font size is **18** and the font color is **Red** (last row, second column in the *Standard Colors* section).

g. Change the fill color of the StudentID field to be **Yellow** (last row, fourth column in the *Standard Colors* section).

h. Save the form as **Transfer Schools Form**. Save and close the form.

Create a Report

Cala Hajjar, the director of the center, saw the query you created for Rey. She is hoping you can create a more print-friendly version for her to distribute to the Board of Trustees. You will create a report based on the Transfer Credits Calculations query.

a. Create a report using the Report Wizard. Add the Class, FirstName, LastName, Major, GPA, and LostCredits fields from the Transfer Credit Calculations query. Do not add any grouping or sorting. Ensure the report is in Landscape orientation.

b. Save the report as **Transfer Students Report** and view the report in Layout view.

Format a Report

Now that you have included the fields Cala has asked for, you will work to format the report to make the information more obvious.

a. Apply the **Wisp theme** (third row, first column) to this object only.

b. Group the report by the Class field. Sort the records within each group by LastName then by FirstName, both in ascending order.

c. Change the font size of the Class field to **16**.

d. Adjust the text boxes so the values are completely visible.

e. Switch to Print Preview mode and verify the report is only one page wide (note: it may be a number of pages long).

f. Export the results as a PDF document using the file name **a00c1Transfer_LastFirst**.

g. Save and close the report.

Close and Submit Database

a. Compact and repair the database.

b. Create a backup of the database. Accept the default name for the backup.

c. Close all database objects and exit Access.

d. Submit the database, backup, and PDF based on your instructor's directions.

Access Comprehensive Application Capstone Exercise

In this project, you will add fields to a table and set data validation rules. You will also import a text file into a database, design advanced queries, and create a navigation form. Additionally, you will use SQL to modify a record source and create an embedded macro to automate opening a report.

Database File Setup

a. Start Access. Open the file named *a00c2Drivers*, click the **FILE tab**, click **Save As**, click **Save As**, and then type **a00c2Drivers_LastFirst**. Click **Save**.

Import a Text File into the Database and Modify the Table

a. Create a table in the database by importing the delimited text file named *Insurance_Text.txt*. Use the first row of the file as field names, use **InsuranceID** as the primary key, and then name the table **InsuranceCos_Text**. Accept all other default options.

b. Create a new field in the Agency Info table after *InsPhone* named **Web site** with the **Hyperlink data type**. Save the table. In Datasheet view, add the Web site **http://William_Smith.com** to the William Smith record (1).

c. Create a new field in the Agency Info table after *Web site* named **AgentPhoto** with the **Attachment data type**. Save the table. In Datasheet view for Record 1 (William Smith), add the picture file named *a00c2WmSmith.jpg* to the AgentPhoto field.

d. Set the validation rule of the InsuranceCo field to accept the values **AS**, **NAT**, or **SF** only. Set the validation text to read **Please enter AS, NAT, or SF.** (include the period).

e. Make InsuranceCo a lookup field in the Agency Info table. Set the lookup to get values from the InsuranceID field in the InsuranceCos_Text table. Accept the default label and save the table. In Datasheet view, click in any InsuranceCo cell and click the arrow to view the options. Close the table.

Create Queries to Analyze, Update, and Delete Records

a. Create a new query using Design view. From the Insurance table, add the DriverID, AutoType, TagID, and TagExpiration fields (in that order). Save the query as **Missing Tag Dates**.

b. Switch to Design view of the same query and set the criteria in the TagExpiration field to find null values. Run the query (two records will display). Save and close the query.

c. Change the query type to **Update** and set the criteria to update drivers whose class is *Minor* to **Junior**. Run the query (eight records will update). Save the query as **Driver Class_Update** and close the query. View the updates in the Drivers table and close the table.

d. Create a new query using Design view. From the Drivers table, add the Class field. Save the query as **Driver Class_Delete**.

e. Change the query type to **Delete** and set the criteria to delete drivers whose class is *Special*. Run the query (one record will delete). Save and close the query. View the changes in the Drivers table and close the table.

Create a Query to Prompt for Data

a. Create a new query using Design view. From the Insurance table, add the DriverID, AutoType, AutoYear, and TagID fields (in that order). Save the query as **Auto Year_Parameter**.

b. Set the criteria in the Auto Year field to display the prompt as **Enter the auto year:** and run the query. In the prompt, enter **2007** and click **OK** to view the results (two records). Close the query.

Use the Performance Analyzer

a. Use the Performance Analyzer to analyze the Drivers table. Note the idea to change the data type of the Weight field from Short Text to Long Integer. In the Drivers table, set the data type of the Weight field to **Number (Long Integer)** and save and close the table.

Create a Navigation Form

a. Create a Navigation form based on the Vertical Tabs, Left template. Drag and drop the Drivers form onto the first tab of the form. Drop the Insurance form onto the second tab.

b. Drag and drop the Drivers report onto the third tab of the Navigation form. View the form in Form view, click each of the tabs, and then save the form as **Navigator**. Close the form.

Add an SQL Statement as a Record Source and Create an Embedded Macro

a. Open the Drivers report in Design view. Modify the record source of the report using a SQL statement to select all Drivers records with a Class of **Adult**. Print Preview the report (eight records will display). Save and close the report.

b. Open the Drivers form in Design view, click to add a command button at the intersection of the six-inch mark on the horizontal ruler and the three-inch mark on the vertical ruler.

c. Set the command button to open the report named *Drivers*. Use the default picture as the button. Set the name and the caption of the button to **Open Drivers Report**. Save the form. View the form in Form view and click the command button.

d. Close all database objects, close the database, and then exit Access. Submit the database as directed.

Glossary

Access (Office Fundamentals) Relational database management software that enables you to record and link data, query databases, and create forms and reports. (Access) A database management system included in the Microsoft Office 2013 Professional suite.

Access Database Executable (ACCDE) A file that has had all VBA source code removed, prohibits users from making design and name changes to forms or reports within the database, and prohibits users from creating new forms and reports.

Action query A query that adds, updates, or deletes data in a database.

Aggregate function Performs calculations on an entire column of data and returns a single value. Includes functions such as Sum, Avg, and Count.

AND logical operator Returns only records that meet all criteria.

Anomaly An error or inconsistency within a database that occurs when you add, edit, or delete data.

Append query A query that selects records from one or more tables (the source) and adds them to an existing table (the destination).

Argument A variable, constant, or expression that is needed to produce the output for a function or action.

Ascending A sort that lists text data in alphabetical order or a numeric list in lowest to highest order.

Attachment control A control that enables you to manage attached files in forms and reports.

Attachment field Use an Access attachment to attach multiple files of any format to an individual record; attached files can be launched from Access.

AutoNumber A number data type that is generated by Access and is incremented each time a record is added.

Back Up Database An Access utility that creates a duplicate copy of the database.

Back-end database Contains the tables of the database.

Backstage view A component of Office 2013 that provides a concise collection of commands related to common file activities and provides information on an open file.

Backup A copy of a file or folder on another drive.

Bound control A control that is connected to a field in a table or query.

Calculated control A control containing an expression that generates a calculated result.

Calculated field Produces a value from an expression or function that references one or more existing fields.

CamelCase notation Uses no spaces in multiword field names but uses uppercase letters to distinguish the first letter of each new word.

CAPTCHA A scrambled code used with online forms to prevent mass sign-ups. It helps to ensure that an actual person is requesting the account.

Caption property Used to create a more readable label that appears in the top row in Datasheet view and in forms and reports.

Cascade Delete Related Records An option that directs Access to automatically delete all records in related tables that match the primary key that is deleted from a primary table.

Cascade Update Related Fields An option that directs Access to automatically update all foreign key values in a related table when the primary key value table is modified in a primary table.

Certification authority (CA) A commercial company, such as VeriSign, that issues and validates identities by using digital signatures for a fee.

Charms A toolbar for Windows 8.1.1 made up of five icons (Search, Share, Start, Devices, and Settings) that enables you to search for files and applications, share information with others within an application that is running, return to the Start screen, control devices that are connected to your computer, or modify various settings depending on which application is running when accessing the Setting icon.

Clip art An electronic illustration that can be inserted into an Office project.

Clipboard An Office feature that temporarily holds selections that have been cut or copied and allows you to paste the selections.

Cloud storage A technology used to store files and to work with programs that are stored in a central location on the Internet.

Column heading The field name displayed at the top of a crosstab query.

Combo box control Provides a drop-down menu displaying a list of options from which the user can choose a single value.

Command A button or area within a group that you click to perform tasks.

Compact and Repair An Access utility that reduces the size of the database and can repair a corrupt database.

Comparison operator An operator used to evaluate the relationship between two quantities.

Composite key A primary key that is made of two or more fields.

Constant A value that does not change.

Contextual tab A Ribbon tab that displays when an object, such as a picture or table, is selected. A contextual tab contains groups and commands specific to the selected object.

Controls The text boxes, buttons, boxes, and other tools you use to add, edit, and display the data in a form or report.

Copy To duplicate an item from the original location and place the copy in the Office Clipboard.

Criteria row A row in the Query Design view that determines which records will be selected.

Criterion A number, text phrase, or an expression used to select records.

Crosstab query A query that summarizes a data source into a few key rows and columns.

CSV text file A file that uses a comma to separate one column from the next column, enabling the receiving software to distinguish one set of field values from the next.

Custom Web app A database that can be built, used, and shared with others through the use of a host server (e.g., SharePoint or Office 365).

Cut To remove an item from the original location and place it in the Office Clipboard.

Data macro A macro that executes a series of actions when a table event occurs.

Data redundancy The unnecessary storing of duplicate data in two or more tables.

Data type Determines the type of data that can be entered and the operations that can be performed on that data.

Data validation A set of constraints or rules that help control how data is entered into a field.

Database A collection of data organized as meaningful information that can be accessed, managed, stored, queried, sorted, and reported.

Database Documenter A tool that creates a report that contains detailed information for each selected object.

Database management system (DBMS) A software system that provides the tools needed to create, maintain, and use a database.

Database Splitter Enables you to split a database into two files: a back-end database and a front-end database.

Datasheet view A view that enables you to add, edit, and delete the records of a table.

Date arithmetic The process of adding or subtracting one date from another, or adding or subtracting a constant from a date.

Date formatting Affects the date's display without changing the actual underlying value in the table.

Date function Calculates the current date.

DatePart function An Access function that examines a date and returns a portion of the date.

Default Office settings that remain in effect unless you specify otherwise.

Delete query A query that selects records from a table and then removes them from the table.

Delimiter A special character that surrounds the criterion's value.

Descending A sort that lists text data in reverse alphabetical order or a numeric list in highest to lowest order.

Design view A view that enables you to create tables, add and delete fields, and modify field properties; or to change advanced design settings not seen in Layout view, such as a background image.

Detail section Displays the records in the record source.

Dialog box A window that displays when a program requires interaction with you, such as inputting information, before completing a procedure. This window typically provides access to more precise, but less frequently used, commands.

Dialog Box Launcher An icon in a Ribbon group that you can click to open a related dialog box. It is not found in all groups.

Digital signatures Electronic, encryption-based, secure stamps of authentication that confirm who created the file, that the file is valid, and that no changes have been made to the file after its authentication.

Embedded macro A macro that executes when an event attached to a control or object occurs.

Encryption The process of altering digital information by using an algorithm to make it unreadable to anyone except those who possess the key (or secret code).

Enforce referential integrity A relationship option that ensures that data cannot be entered into a related table unless it first exists in a primary table.

Enhanced ScreenTip A feature that provides a brief summary of a command when you point to the command button.

Event Occurs when a user enters, edits, or deletes data; events also occur when users open, use, or close forms and reports.

Excel A software application used to organize records, financial transactions, and business information in the form of worksheets.

Expression A formula used to calculate new fields from the values in existing fields.

Expression Builder An Access tool that helps you create more complicated expressions.

Field The smallest data element in a table, such as first name, last name, address, or phone number.

Field property A characteristic of a field that determines how a field looks and behaves.

Field row A row in the Query Design view that displays the field name.

Field selector The column heading of a datasheet used to select a column.

File Electronic data such as documents, databases, slide shows, worksheets, digital photographs, music, videos, and Web pages.

File Explorer A component of the Windows operating system that can be used to create and manage folders.

Filter Displays a subset of records based on a specified criterion.

Filter by Form A filtering method that displays records based on multiple criteria.

Filter by Selection A filtering method that displays only records that match selected criteria.

Find An Office feature that locates a word or phrase that you indicate in a document.

Find duplicates query A query that helps you identify repeated values in a table.

Find unmatched query A query that compares records in two related tables, and then displays the records found in one table, but not the other.

First normal form (1NF) Satisfied when a table contains no repeating groups or repeating columns.

Fixed-length text file A file that allocates a certain number of characters for each field.

Folder A directory into which you place data files in order to organize them for easier retrieval.

Font A combination of typeface and type style.

Foreign key A field in one table that is also a primary key of another table.

Form   A database object that is used to add, edit, or delete table data.

Form Footer   A footer that displays one time at the bottom of a form.

Form Header   A header that displays once at the top of each form.

Form tool   Used to create data entry forms for customers, employees, products, and other primary tables.

Form view   A simplified interface primarily used for data entry. Does not allow you to make changes to the layout.

Format Painter   A command that copies the formatting of text from one location to another.

FROM keyword   Specifies the table (or tables) that will be searched in an SQL Select Statement

Front-end database   Contains the queries, forms, and reports of the database.

Function   A predefined computation that simplifies creating a complex calculation and produces a result based on inputs known as arguments.

Functional dependency   When the value of one field is determined by the value of another.

Gallery   A set of selections that displays when you click a More button, or in some cases when you click a command, in a Ribbon group.

Group   A subset of a tab that organizes similar tasks together; to combine two or more objects.

Group Footer   Appears just below the *Detail* section in Design view. Appears once each time the grouping field value changes.

Group Header   Appears just above the *Detail* section in Design view, along with the name of the field by which you are grouping. Appears once each time the grouping field value changes.

Grouping   Allows you to summarize your data by the values of a field.

Homegroup   A Windows 8.1.1 feature that enables you to share resources on a home network.

Hyperlink   A data type that enables you to quickly link to any file on your computer or to any Web page on the Internet.

IIf function   Evaluates an expression and displays one value when the expression is true and another value when the expression is false.

Importing   A process that enables you to copy external data into your database without linking it to its source file.

Index   Reduces the time it takes to run queries and reports.

Indexed property   Setting that enables quick sorting in primary key order and quick retrieval based on the primary key.

Input mask   Enables you to restrict the data being input into a field by specifying the exact format of the data entry.

Input Mask Wizard   Frequently used to generate data restrictions for a field based on responses to a few questions.

IsNull function   Checks whether a field has no value.

Join line   A line used to create a relationship between two tables using a common field.

Key Tip   The letter or number for the associated keyboard shortcut that displays over features on the Ribbon or Quick Access Toolbar.

Label Wizard   Enables you to easily create mailing labels, name tags, and other specialized tags.

Landscape   An orientation for a displayed page or worksheet that is wider than it is tall.

Layout control   Provides guides to help keep controls aligned horizontally and vertically and give your form a uniform appearance.

Library   A collection of files from different locations that is displayed as a single unit.

Linking   A process that enables you to connect to a table without having to import the table data into your database.

Live Preview   An Office feature that provides a preview of the results of a selection when you point to an option in a list or gallery. Using Live Preview, you can experiment with settings before making a final choice.

Lookup field   Provides the user with a finite list of values to choose from in a menu.

Lookup Wizard   Creates the menu of finite values by asking you six questions and using your answers to create the options list.

Macro   A series of actions that can be programmed to automate tasks.

Macro Designer   The user interface that enables you to create and edit macros.

Mailing label report   A specialized report that comes preformatted to coordinate with name-brand labels.

Make table query   A query that selects records from one or more tables and uses them to create a new table.

Margin   The area of blank space that displays to the left, right, top, and bottom of a document or worksheet.

Microsoft Office   A productivity software suite including four primary software components, each one specializing in a particular type of output.

Mini toolbar   The feature that provides access to common formatting commands, displayed when text is selected.

Module   An object that is written using Visual Basic for Applications (VBA) and adds functionality to a database.

Multiple Items form   Displays multiple records in a tabular layout similar to a table's Datasheet view, with more customization options such as the ability to add graphical elements, buttons, and other controls.

Multitable query   Contains two or more tables. It enables you to take advantage of the relationships that have been set in your database.

Navigation bar   Bar located at the bottom of a table, query, or form that is used to move through records.

Navigation Form   A tabbed menu system that ties the objects in the database together so that the database is easy to use.

Navigation Pane   (Office Fundamentals) A section of the File Explorer interface that provides ready access to computer resources, folders, files, and networked peripherals. (Access) An interface element that organizes and lists database objects.

Nesting functions   Using one function within another function.

Non-key field   Any field that is not part of the primary key.

Normal form A rule of normalization that indicates the current state of a table.

Normalization The formal process of deciding which fields should be grouped together into which tables.

NOT logical operator Returns all records except the specified criteria.

Null The term Access uses to describe a blank field.

Number data type A data type that can store only numerical data.

Object A main component that is created and used to make a database function.

One-to-many relationship A relationship established when the primary key value in the primary table can match many of the foreign key values in the related table.

OneDrive An application used to store, access, and share files and folders.

Open Exclusive A mode that guarantees that you are the only one currently using the database.

Operating system Software that directs computer activities such as checking all components, managing system resources, and communicating with application software.

OR logical operator Returns records meeting any of the specified criteria.

ORDER BY keyword Used to sort the records by a certain field in either ascending or descending order in an SQL Select Statement.

Order of operations (order of precedence) Determines the sequence by which operations are calculated in an expression.

Page Footer A footer that appears once at the bottom of each page in a form or report.

Page Header A header that appears once at the top of each page in a form or report.

Parameter query A select query where the user provides the criterion at run time.

Paste To place a cut or copied item in another location.

Performance Analyzer Evaluates a database and then makes recommendations for optimizing the database.

Picture A graphic file that is retrieved from storage media or the Internet and placed in an Office project.

Pmt function A predefined formula in Access that calculates the periodic loan payment.

Portable Document Format (PDF) A file type that was created for exchanging documents independent of software applications and operating system environment.

Portrait An orientation for a displayed page or worksheet that is taller than it is wide.

PowerPoint A software application used to create dynamic presentations to inform groups and persuade audiences.

Primary key The field (or combination of fields) that uniquely identifies each record in a table.

Print Preview Enables you to see exactly what the report will look like when it is printed.

Property sheet Enables you to change settings such as number format, number of decimal places, and caption, among many others.

Query Enables you to ask questions about the data stored in a database and then provides the answers to the questions by providing subsets or summaries of data.

Query Design view Enables you to create queries; the Design view is divided into two parts—the top portion displays the tables and the bottom portion (known as the *query design grid*) displays the fields and the criteria.

Query sort order Determines the order of records in the query's Datasheet view.

Quick Access Toolbar A component of Office 2013, located at the top-left corner of the Office window, that provides handy access to commonly executed tasks such as saving a file and undoing recent actions.

Read-only form A form that enables users to view but not change data.

Record A group of related fields representing one entity, such as data for one person, place, event, or concept.

Record selector A small box at the beginning of a row used to select a record.

Record source The table or query that supplies the records for a form or report.

Referential integrity Rules in a database that are used to preserve relationships between tables when records are changed.

Related tables Tables that are joined in a relationship using a common field.

Relational database management system (RDBMS) A database management system that uses the relational model to manage groups of data (tables) and rules (relationships) between tables.

Relationship A connection between two tables using a common field.

Replace An Office feature that finds text and replaces it with a word or phrase that you indicate.

Report An object that contains professional-looking formatted information from underlying tables or queries.

Report Footer A footer that displays one time at the bottom of a report.

Report Header A header that displays once at the top of each report.

Report tool Used to instantly create a tabular report based on the table or query currently selected.

Report view Enables you to see what a printed report will look like in a continuous page layout.

Report Wizard Asks you questions and uses your answers to generate a customized report.

Ribbon The long bar of tabs, groups, and commands located just beneath the Title bar.

Rich Text Format (RTF) A file format that enables documents created in one software application to be opened with a different software application.

Round function Returns a number rounded to a specific number of decimal places.

Row heading The field names displayed along the left side of a crosstab query.

Run command Used to produce query results (the red exclamation point).

Second normal form (2NF) Satisfied when a table meets 1NF criteria and all non-key fields are functionally dependent on the entire primary key.

Section Part of a form or report that can be manipulated separately from other parts of the form or report.

Section bar Marks the top boundary of a section in a form or report.

SELECT keyword Determines which fields will be included in the results of an SQL Select Statement.

Select query A type of query that displays only the records that match criteria entered in Query Design view.

Short text data type A text field that can store up to 255 characters but has a default field size of 50 characters.

Shortcut menu Provides choices related to the selection or area at which you right-click.

Show row A row in the Query Design view that controls whether the field will be displayed in the query results.

Simply Query Wizard Provides dialog boxes to guide you through the query design process.

SmartArt A diagram that presents information visually to effectively communicate a message.

Snip The output of using the Snipping Tool.

Snipping Tool A Windows 8.1.1 accessory program that provides users the ability to capture an image of all (or part of) their computer's screen.

Sort The process of listing records or text in a specific sequence, such as alphabetically by last name.

Sort row A row in the Query Design view that enables you to sort in ascending or descending order.

Split form Combines two views of the same record source—one section is displayed in a stacked layout, and the other section is displayed in a tabular layout.

Splitter bar Divides a form into two halves.

SQL keyword Defines the purpose and the structure of an SQL statement.

SQL SELECT statement Used to retrieve data from the tables in a database.

Stacked layout Displays fields in a vertical column.

Stand-alone macro A macro that can be used independently of other controls or objects.

Start screen The display that you see after you turn on your computer and respond to any username and password prompts.

Status bar A horizontal bar found at the bottom of the program window that contains information relative to the open file.

Structured Query Language (SQL) The industry-standard language for defining, manipulating, and retrieving the data in a database.

Subfolder A folder that is housed within another folder.

Subform Records displayed that are related to records in a main form.

Syntax The rules that dictate the structure and components required to perform the necessary calculations in an equation or to evaluate expressions.

Tab A component of the Ribbon that is designed to appear much like a tab on a file folder, with the active tab highlighted, that is used to organize groups by function.

Tab order The sequential advancing in a form from one field or control to the next when you press Tab.

Table An object used to store and organize data in a series of records (rows) with each record made up of a number of fields (columns) and is the foundation of every database.

Table Analyzer Analyzes the tables in a database and normalizes them for you.

Table row A row in Query Design view that displays the data source.

Tabular layout Displays data horizontally.

Template A predesigned file that incorporates formatting elements, such as theme and layouts, and may include content that can be modified.

Text file A common file format for exchanging data between two computer systems.

Theme A collection of design choices that includes colors, fonts, and special effects used to give a consistent look to a document, workbook, database form or report, or presentation.

Third Normal Form (3NF) Satisfied when a table meets 2NF criteria and no transitive dependencies exist.

Tile A colorful block on the Start screen that when clicked will launch a program, file, folder, or other Windows 8.1.1 app.

Timestamp A combination of the date and time that is encrypted as part of the digital signature.

Title bar A component of Microsoft Office that identifies the current file name and the application in which you are working and includes control buttons that enable you to minimize, maximize, restore down, or close the application window.

Toggle The action of switching from one setting to another. Several Home tab tasks, such as Bold and Italic, are actually toggle commands.

Total row A table row that displays below the last row of records in an Excel table, or in Datasheet view of a table or query, and displays summary or aggregate statistics, such as a sum or an average.

Transitive dependency Occurs when the value of one non-key field is functionally dependent on the value of another non-key field.

Unbound control A control not tied to a specific field.

Uniform resource locator (URL) The location of a Web site or Web page on the Internet.

Update query An action query that changes the data values in one or more fields for all records that meet specific criteria.

User interface The screen display through which you communicate with the software.

Validation rule Prevents invalid data from being entered into a field.

View The way a file appears onscreen.

WHERE keyword Specifies the criteria that records must match to be included in the results of an SQL Select Statement.

Wildcard A special character that can represent one or more characters in the criterion of a query.

Windows 8.1.1 A Microsoft operating system released in 2012 that can operate on touch-screen devices as well as laptops and desktops because it has been designed to accept multiple methods of input.

Windows 8.1.1 app An application specifically designed to run in the Start screen interface of Windows 8.1.1 that is either already installed and ready to use or can be downloaded from the Windows Store.

Word A word processing software application used to produce all sorts of documents, including memos, newsletters, forms, tables, and brochures.

XML Paper Specification (XPS) A file format developed by Microsoft and designed to display a printed page onscreen identically on any computer platform.

Zoom slider A horizontal bar on the far right side of the status bar that enables you to increase or decrease the size of file contents onscreen.

Index

( ) (parentheses), 213
^ (exponentiation), 213
* (multiplication), 213
/ (division), 213
+ (addition), 213
– (subtraction), 213
= (equal sign), comparison operator, 104, 174, 175, 332–333
> (greater than), 174, 175, 332–333
>= (greater than or equal to), 104, 174, 175, 332–333
< (less than), 174, 175, 332–333
<= (less than or equal to), 104, 174, 175, 332–333
<> (not equal to), 104, 174, 175, 332–333

A

ACCDE (Access Database Executable) files, 551–552
Access 2013. *See also* database(s); form(s); macros; modules; queries; report(s); tables
  application characteristics, 22
  data types, 147
  as DBMS, 84–85
  Excel *versus*, 111–112, 325
  exporting data, 463–475
  functionality, 463
  functions, 225–226
  Help, 28–29
  importing data, 484–495
  interface components, 22–29, 86–88
  objects, 85–88
  as RDBMS, 112–114
  Ribbon, 87
  saving in, 91, 93
accounts, Microsoft, 2–3
add commands, to Quick Access Toolbar, 24
adding database records, 92–93
addition (+), 213
Address bar, 10, 11
advanced controls, 419–423
Advanced Find feature, 53–54
advanced forms, 404–413
advanced functions. *See* Expression Builder
advanced select queries. *See* parameter queries
advanced SQL statements, 596
aggregate functions, 233–239, 377, 378, 380, 420, 423, 463
aggregating data, 377–381
Allow Additions property, 404, 405
Allow Deletions property, 404, 405
Allow Edits property, 404, 405
Allow Zero Length, field property, 150
analysis and design tools, 531–540

Analysis Notes box, 534, 535
AND logical operator, 175–176
anomalies, 520
Append dialog box, 364
append Excel data, to database, 490
append queries
  defined, 358, 363
  running, 365
  select queries before, 364
  SQL keyword, 596
apps (non-Windows 8.1.1 apps). *See also* desktop; Office 2013; Web apps
  closing, 39–40
apps (Windows 8.1.1 apps). *See also* Windows 8.1.1
  defined, 3
Apps for Office, 60
Arguments, 572–573. *See also* functions
  defined, 225
  PMT function, 226
Arial font, 268
Arrange tab
  modify forms, 268–269
  modify reports, 287–288
arrow(s)
  back, 24
  commands and, 50
arrow icons, 486, 490, 540
ascending sort, table data, 102
attach embedded macro, to event, 573–575
attachment(s)
  add or edit, 451–452
  database size and, 450–451
attachment controls, 453–455
Attachment data type, 147
Attachment toolbar, 453, 454, 455
Attachments dialog box, 451–452, 453, 455
automatic compact, databases, 93
AutoNumber, 90, 147, 148
AVERAGE function, 233
Avg function, 378, 420

B

back arrow, 24
Back button, File Explorer, 10, 11
Back Up Database utility, 93, 94
back-end database, 538–540
background image
  in forms, 269
  in reports, 288
Backstage Print view, 38–39
Backstage view
  defined, 23
  tasks, 36–40
  using, 23–24
backups, database

action queries and, 359
  DBAs and, 358
  Performance Analyzer and, 535
  update queries and, 362
backups, defined, 16. *See also* OneDrive
Beep argument, 572, 573
behaviors, controls, 423
Best Fit columns, 150
blank desktop database, 119, 120
blank field (null), 175
blank fields, 311, 358
Blank Form, 258, 259, 264
Blank Report tool, 278, 279
bloated database, 451
blue underline, 63
Bold command, 48
bound controls, 419, 420

C

CA (certification authority), 550
Calculated, data type, 147
calculated controls, 420, 422
calculated fields
  defined, 144–145
  errors, 216
  formatting and saving results, 215–217
  in queries, 212–217
  in Totals query, 238–239
  verifying results, 217
CamelCase notation, 146
caption property, 149, 150
career information, DBAs, 358
Cascade Delete Related Records, 162–163
Cascade Update Related Fields, 162–163
caution
  action queries, 359, 368
  backups, 362
  delete queries, 367
  deleting duplicate records, 382
certification authority (CA), 550
Charms, 2, 3–4
Charms bar, 3–4
charting capabilities, Excel, 467
check boxes, for selecting items, 15
Choose Builder dialog box, 575
Choose my own primary key option, 491, 492, 494
clip art, described, 26
Clipboard, Office, 49–52
Clipboard Dialog Box Launcher, 51–52
Clipboard group commands, 49–52
Close (X) button, 23
closing
  files, 39–40
  non-Windows 8.1.1 apps, 39–40
cloud storage, 2–3. *See also* OneDrive
color(s), fonts, 48